MILESTONES

Real Life, Real Development

Available only through McGraw-Hill CONNECT, *Milestones* is an assessable video-based program that tracks a diverse group of infants and children through major milestones of physical, cognitive, social, and emotional development from infancy through adolescence.

Milestones **of Child Development:** By watching one child over time or comparing various children, *Milestones* provides a unique, experiential learning environment that can only be achieved by watching real human development as it happens.

Milestones **Transitions:** Students meet a series of people, from teenagers to individuals in late adulthood, to hear testimonials and perspectives on experiences and changes that occur throughout the lifespan. Through a series of interviews, students are given the opportunity to think critically while exploring the differences in attitudes on everything from body image to changes in emotion, sexuality, cognitive processes, and death and dying.

Milestones provides the opportunity for students to:

* ❋ hone their observational skills

* ❋ engage with real children developing over time

* ❋ identify concepts and apply theories to real children

* ❋ answer comprehension and application-level questions

 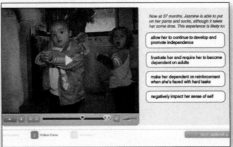 

McGraw-Hill Ryerson

LifeSmart: Exploring Human Development
First Canadian Edition

ISBN-13: 978-1-25-902379-8
ISBN-10: 1-25-902379-6

1 2 3 4 5 6 7 8 9   M   1 9 8 7 6 5 4

Printed and bound in Canada.

Care has been taken to trace ownership of copyright material contained in this text; however, the publisher will welcome any information that enables them to rectify any reference or credit for subsequent editions.

Director Product Management: *Rhondda McNabb*
Senior Product Manager: *Marcia Siekowski*
Marketing Manager: *Margaret Janzen*
Product Developer: *Katherine Goodes*
Senior Product Team Associate: *Marina Sequin*
Supervising Editor: *Stephanie Gay*
Photo/Permissions Research: *Derek Capitaine*
Copy Editor: *Elspeth McFadden*
Proofreader: *Judy Sturrup*
Plant Production Coordinator: *Michelle Saddler*
Manufacturing Production Coordinator: *Lena Keating*
Cover Design: *ArtPlus*
Cover Image: *Thinkstock.com (RF)*
Interior Design: *ArtPlus*
Page Layout: *ArtPlus*
Printer: *Marquis*

Library and Archives Canada Cataloguing in Publication

Fiore, Lisa B., 1970-, author
    LifeSmart : exploring human development / Lisa Fiore, Lesley University,
Ravi Ramkissoonsingh, Niagara College, Laura Hotham, Niagara College.
-- First Canadian edition.

Includes bibliographical references and index.
ISBN 978-1-259-02379-8 (pbk.)

    1. Longevity. 2. Life spans (Biology). 3. Developmental psychology.
I. Ramkissoonsingh, Ravi, author II. Hotham, Laura, author III. Title.
IV. Title: Life smart.

QH528.5.F55 2014   155   C2013-906542-3

LifeSmart

EXPLORING HUMAN DEVELOPMENT

Lisa Fiore, Lesley University

Ravi Ramkissoonsingh, Niagara College

Laura Hotham, Niagara College

McGraw-Hill Education | McGraw-Hill Ryerson

Lisa B. Fiore, Ph.D., is an Associate Professor and Director of Early Childhood Education at Lesley University, in Cambridge, Massachusetts. She primarily teaches graduate students preparing to be early childhood and elementary educators, but also enjoys working with in-service teachers around professional development. Recent interests include the use of documentation to extend and enhance learning environments and the use of rich media in classroom teaching. The mother of two young children, she is reminded daily of the competence and curiosity of young people, and how much grown-ups have to learn about the way things work. She has written several books, the most recent *The Safe Child Handbook* with co-author John Dacey.

Ravi Ramkissoonsingh is a Professor of Psychology at Niagara College in Welland, Ontario. He earned a Bachelor of Arts with High Honours in Psychology, a Master of Arts in Psychology and a Master of Arts in Canadian Studies from Carleton University in Ottawa, Ontario. His graduate research focused on factors that affect jury decision-making and a cross-cultural analysis of UFO and alien encounter narratives. He has taught courses in a variety of areas including abnormal, adolescent, behavioural, developmental, introductory, and social psychology. He has also developed and delivered a popular course in forensic psychology. Ravi was nominated for a Continuing Education Instructor Appreciation Award at Mohawk College. Additionally, he has co-authored an article in the field of Clinical Epidemiology and Biostatistics and is currently pursuing an interest in the intersection between psychology and paranormal phenomena.

Laura Hotham is a Professor of Psychology at Niagara College in Welland, Ontario. She earned a Bachelor of Arts in Psychology from Brock University in St. Catharines, Ontario, as well as a diploma in Nutrition from the Canadian School of Natural Nutrition. Prior to working at Niagara College, Laura spent twelve years working in the Niagara Region as an Advanced Care Paramedic. She teaches psychology and nutrition courses to students enrolled in health-related programs and has developed a course on Psychological Emergencies for post-graduate Police Foundations students.

LifeSmart

BRIEF CONTENTS

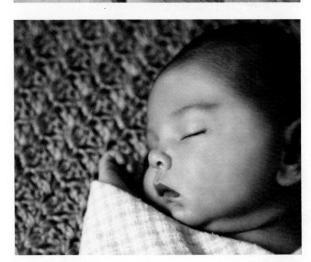

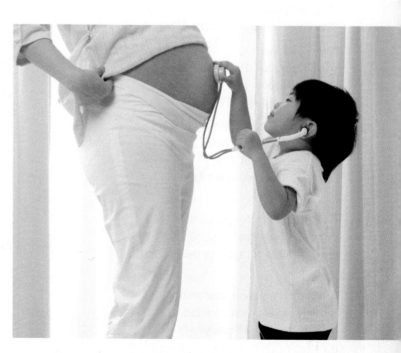

6 Early Childhood

5 Infancy

7 Middle Childhood

8 Adolescence

9 Early Adulthood

10 Middle Adulthood

11   Late Adulthood

12 Dying and Spirituality

Meet LIFESMART with ![McGraw Hill Education] connect®

WE LISTENED TO STUDENTS

Based on extensive student research, we have created a complete learning resource to meet the needs and maximize the workflow of today's college and university students. Students told us they wanted a briefer resource with more visual appeal.

WE ALSO LISTENED TO INSTRUCTORS

We learned about the challenges that they face in their classrooms every day and what their ideal course materials would look like. They told us they needed an engaging solution for their course needs—but without sacrificing quality and content.

WE RESPONDED

LifeSmart blends core content and research with a wealth of real-world examples, career applications, and online interactivities to create a dynamic and engaging learning solution for today's students.

TECH TRENDS show how technology can aid in understanding human development.

PERSPECTIVES ON DIVERSITY discuss human development in the context of race, ethnicity, and cross-cultural issues.

SHORT QUOTATIONS help make the content memorable.

> A great gulf, however, has been opened between man's material advance and his social and moral progress, a gulf in which he may one day be lost if it is not closed or narrowed.
>
> LESTER B. PEARSON

CAREER APPS apply the concepts of human development to real-life careers.

TAKE A STAND asks students to take an informed position on a controversial issue.

FEATURED MEDIA connects popular movies and television shows to topics in the chapter, helping to bring key concepts to life.

CHAPTER REVIEW TEST allows students to check their mastery of core concepts.

LIFESPAN
DEVELOPMENT:

As You READ

After reading this chapter, you should be able to answer the following questions:

LO1 ▶ How would you define and describe lifespan development?

LO2 ▶ What are the different views of lifespan development?

LO3 ▶ What role do biopsychosocial interactions play in lifespan development?

LO4 ▶ What are the major issues in lifespan development?

LO5 ▶ What is the role of research in studying lifespan development?

AN INTRODUCTION

Are you curious?

One of the traits that sets humans apart from other living creatures is the innate desire to find out the answer to the biggest, most commonly asked question since the dawn of time: "Why?" Over the course of a person's life this question takes different forms. For example:

- **Why** is the sky blue?
- **Why** do I need to go to bed so early?
- **Why** can't I find work to inspire me?
- **Why** do I have to pee *again*? (I just went 15 minutes ago!)

If you try to pinpoint which age is the one during which one of the sample "why" questions is most typically asked, you would have a difficult time. A 2-year-old might ask why the sky is blue, as might a graduate student in environmental studies. Similarly, an elderly man might wonder why he has to urinate so frequently, just as a pregnant woman in her mid-20s ponders the same phenomenon. It is precisely this questioning spirit and the desire to search for answers that propels the researcher in all of us to study human development. The material you will read as you work through this book will reveal much new information and some information that you, as a living and breathing individual on Earth, already understand by virtue of being—human being.

The process of following our questions, also called hypotheses, and generalizing our findings to a larger population is the foundation of scientific research. Scientific research is the work on which the field of lifespan development was built, as you will learn in the chapters that follow.

The assumptions and biases that are part of the scientific method may or may not be stated explicitly, either in the original research articles or in the pages of this text. It is for this reason that you should keep the big questions in your mind as you read on. Never be afraid to ask, "Why?" This question is the beginning of a journey that leads you to some answers and, ultimately, more questions.

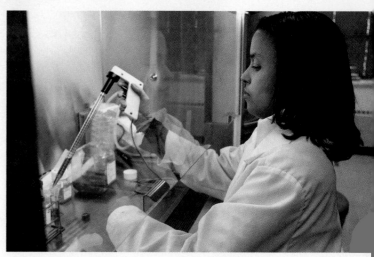

▲ Scientific research is the work that the field of lifespan development is based on.

The highly popular youth fiction series Choose Your Own Adventure remains popular with young readers because the books are designed to let the reader have some control over the outcome of the stories. What a concept—control over our own (or a fictional character's) destiny! This concept of having control over our own lives is one that researchers have investigated for centuries and one that businesses take advantage of as they sell products that promise us that ability. As researchers have studied human development, certain factors have been identified as "risk" factors—things that seem to influence our lives in negative ways. The more risk factors people are faced with in their lives, the harder it will be for them to be happy and successful throughout their lives. Other factors have been identified as protective factors that allow someone to succeed—or even survive—great challenges. The following study underscores the idea that a host of factors, positive and negative, work together in an extremely complex way to influence human development over time.

In 2010, Dr. Malcolm Sears from McMaster University in Hamilton, Ontario, and four other doctors across Canada, developed the Canadian Healthy Infant Longitudinal Development (CHILD) study. To represent the Canadian

From time to time you will be asked to **make a choice.** Your choice may lead to success or disaster! The adventures you take are a result of your choice. You are responsible because you choose! **Remember**—you cannot go back! **Think carefully** before you make a move! One mistake can be your last or it may lead you to fame and fortune!—WARNING!!!

—DISCLAIMER FROM *THE CAVE OF TIME,* THE FIRST BOOK IN THE CHOOSE YOUR OWN ADVENTURE SERIES, BY EDWARD PACKARD (1979)

population, they have recruited over 3500 families from the general population in several cities (including Vancouver, Edmonton, Winnipeg, and Toronto) and two rural areas in Manitoba. The purpose of this study is to learn more about our indoor environment—aspects of our outdoor surroundings that impact our indoor spaces—and how it affects a child's development. The study is specifically looking at increasing risks of developing allergic diseases including food and pet allergies, eczema, allergic rhinitis, and asthma.

Ideally the researchers would like to be able to study the health and environment of every child born in Canada, but since that is not possible, they will gather information from several smaller groups of Canadian families in different provinces and determine which environmental factors potentially affect the health of our children (The Canadian Healthy Infant Longitudinal Development Study, 2010).

> Children are one third of the
> population and **all** of our future.

PANEL FOR THE PROMOTION OF CHILD HEALTH, 1981

In a sense, the families in the McMaster study provide us with a window through which we can view the events that shape the lifespan—the biological, psychological, and environmental interactions that contribute to what we are. These brief glimpses of human development in one study lead us to ask even more questions: What combinations of these forces interact at what levels to produce differences in human development? What are the processes at work that explain what happened? Why?

L01 ▶ Defining Lifespan Development

With these ideas in mind, then, let's first explore the meaning of lifespan development and follow the developmental path of one well-known individual. **Lifespan development** refers to an examination of the biological, cognitive/psychological, and social changes that occur over the course of a human life. As the field of psychology has evolved as a discipline, lifespan development has emerged as one lens through which researchers look for explanations for many phenomena.

Looking closely at one example of lifespan development illustrates how peaks and valleys come into all our lives. Although we all chart an individual course, there remain many similarities in our lives. We walk, we talk, we learn, and we search for satisfying occupations. Yet within this sameness, we all have and choose different experiences that shine a unique light on our journey through the lifespan.

To aid in this analysis of lifespan development, throughout this book we'll explore the notion of **biopsychosocial interactions**, those biological, psychological, and social/environmental forces that act together to shape the path of development.

Such biopsychosocial interaction in turn leads to a consideration of several issues that must be addressed in any scrutiny of lifespan development. Finally, this introductory chapter concludes with an explanation and analysis of relevant research techniques used in studies of human development.

AN EXAMPLE OF DEVELOPMENT THROUGH THE LIFESPAN

If you think about the course of your own life—events you've experienced and those you hope or fear you might experience—you begin to appreciate the complexity of development. Because it's usually difficult to look at ourselves objectively, let's examine the life of one individual—Jordin Tootoo, who has become an important role model for Aboriginal athletes through his success in hockey. His life offers some insight into concepts of lifespan development.

> I want the kids to know that
> **dreams** are always **attainable**
> —if you put your mind to it.

JORDIN TOOTOO

Jordin Tootoo was born in 1983 in Churchill, Manitoba, and today calls Rankin Inlet, Nunavut, his home. One of the most difficult challenges Tootoo was forced to deal with occurred before he was even born. The Canadian government made the decision to relocate Aboriginals to the northern part of Canada. This decision led to unrest and chaos in the North as Aboriginals were forced to learn a new way of life.

By the time Tootoo was growing up and participating in sports, many Aboriginal youth were making poor decisions and getting involved in substance abuse because they were confused and lacked positive role models. Although Tootoo was strong enough to battle through this negative atmosphere, he experienced difficult moments in his life that he had to overcome before he could reach his goals.

One of the most difficult moments in Jordin Tootoo's life was when he lost his brother, Terence, to suicide. Terence was also a talented hockey player and good friend to Jordin.

lifespan development An examination of the biological, cognitive/psychological, and social changes that occur over the course of a human life. This is one perspective in the broader discipline of developmental psychology.

biopsychosocial interactions Biological, psychological, and social/environmental forces that combine to impact human development across the lifespan.

▲ Jordin Tootoo heads home to Nunavut to host the big Kivalliq hockey camp.

One night Terence was caught drinking and driving, and shortly after that he took his own life.

Terence left a note that said, "Do well Jor. Go all the way. Take care of the family. You are the man."

At that point in his life, it would have been easy for Jordin Tootoo to give up, as well. Instead he chose to leave his hometown and continue following his dream. Tootoo is a role model and inspiration for Aboriginal athletes everywhere. He was the first Aboriginal to play in the World Junior Hockey Championships as well as the first Aboriginal to be drafted to the NHL. These two events had a profoundly positive impact on the territory of Nunavut.

> If you don't know where you are going, any road will get you **there**.

LEWIS CARROLL

Aboriginals now view Tootoo as a celebrity. Every summer he runs a hockey camp that is attended by many Aboriginal kids. He also established the Team Tootoo Fund, which is geared toward suicide prevention and youth at risk (Duff, 2013). When you ask Aboriginal kids who their role model is, almost every single one of them will say Jordin Tootoo.

How did this individual who appeared to have the odds stacked against him, become the first Inuk to be drafted into the NHL? Tootoo's parents played a huge role in the success he has obtained. They recognized his talent and made great sacrifices to help their son pursue his dreams. Another important factor

lifespan psychology Study of human development from conception to death.

was Tootoo's own determination to avoid the path that so many around him decided to follow, the path to substance abuse.

Jordin Tootoo is an example of an individual proceeding through his lifespan by remaining faithful to his values, striving to be a good role model for the youth around him, and making the most of the talent he was born with. Considered separately, the components of Tootoo's life may not seem extraordinary and could be the result of choice, luck, or destiny. But as a whole, his biography is a remarkable story of human development.

Thinking About Lifespan Development

Lifespan development studies human development from conception to death. This text presents a *normative* approach to development, studying the typical or average developmental path that people follow, but it also casts a spotlight on individual variations throughout the chapters.

WHY STUDY THE LIFESPAN?

As a discipline, **lifespan psychology** gained momentum when developmental psychologists began to agree that development didn't cease when human beings passed from adolescence to adulthood. A lifespan perspective took psychologists into a wider field. A range of influences, including brain research, analysis of the development of the mind, and research into the ways developmental levels influence individuals' responses to their experiences (Rutter, 2006) prompted the acceptance of development as a lifelong process. Each age or stage (infancy, adolescence, and so on) has its own developmental agenda and contributes to the entire lifespan.

The following are several objectives of studying lifespan development:

- to offer an organized account of development across the lifespan
- to identify the interconnections between earlier and later events
- to account for the mechanisms responsible for lifespan development
- to specify the biological, psychological, and social factors that shape an individual's development

Once these objectives are identified, developmental psychologists attempt to trace the range of individual development, encourage individuals to live their lives as positively as possible, and help them avoid negative outcomes (Baltes, Lindenberger, & Staudinger, 2006).

WHAT IS DEVELOPMENT?

Few readers would argue with the notion that individuals respond to the events of their lives in a manner consistent with their age at that time. Our lives are not static and unchanging, and **development** reflects this underlying assumption of change.

Age alone cannot account for varied responses to life events. Age, as Rutter (2006, p. 314) points out, is an inadequate explanation for behaviour for these reasons:

- Age tells us about biological maturity and little else.
- Different elements of biological growth proceed at different rates.
- Age reflects past experiences that may influence current behaviour.
- Age reflects current social situations.
- Age tells us little about the underlying causal mechanisms.

Two 5-year-olds, Talia and Sora, are sitting on a blanket at a park. Talia pulls a peanut butter and jelly sandwich out of her backpack, and Sora starts to whine, "I'm hungry!" Talia's mom comes over and breaks the sandwich into two pieces, giving each girl one piece. Sora gleefully exclaims, "Now I have a sandwich, too!" and Talia starts to whine, "Now I only have a haaaalf." Age alone doesn't inform us of the psychological mechanism at work here. What seems to happen is that in some contexts, dividing one larger object into two smaller objects does not cause upset, whereas in other situations, the act of dividing implies something negative despite the result of the social act of sharing or mathematical process of making more. You can see that what may appear on the surface to be solely age-related changes is due to factors such as social relationships and cognitive development.

Development indeed implies change, but the two terms are not equal. For the word "change" to be used in a developmental sense, it must possess a systematic, organized structure that contains a successive theme; that is, it should be clear that the changes that occurred at a later time were influenced by earlier changes. Thus the concept of development signifies systematic and successive changes over time (Lerner, 2002). (Keep in mind, though, that even this definition may vary according to the orientation of the psychologists involved—biological, philosophical, and so on.) Our focus will therefore be on *what* changes come about, *whether* they are maintained or lost, and *how* the course of development varies from individual to individual (Rutter & Rutter, 1993). In other words, "Why?" For example, "Why does change occur?" or "Why do individuals change?"

> **development** The process of changing and the changes that occur through the lifespan.

What a distressing **contrast** there is between the radiant intelligence of the **child** and the feeble mentality of the average **adult.**

SIGMUND FREUD

For purposes of research and analysis, the human lifespan is typically divided into developmental stages or periods. It's important to remember that each particular period is part of a greater whole, and these distinct periods will be discussed in detail in this text. The most widely acknowledged sequence of developmental periods includes the following categories: prenatal period, infancy, early childhood, middle childhood, adolescence, early adulthood, middle adulthood, and late adulthood (see Table 1.1). Let's take a look at the varied interpretations that society has embraced regarding lifespan development over hundreds of years.

Changing Views of the Lifespan

◀ L02

If we agree that development indeed implies change, then interpretations of the lifespan over the years should also reflect the notion of change. And, not surprisingly, they do. As the different, evolving images of children, adolescents, and adults are presented in this book, keep in mind that these developmental snapshots were influenced by cultural forces reflecting the dominant ideas and values of a particular era. The power dynamic that exists within a society, culture, or the world cannot be ignored or underestimated.

TABLE 1.1

Developmental Periods of the Lifespan

Period	Characteristics
Prenatal (conception to birth)	Nine months of rapid growth in which organs and systems appear; extreme sensitivity to environmental influences.
Infancy (birth to 2 years)	Continued rapid growth; brain development provides the basis for the emergence of motor, cognitive, and physiological accomplishments.
Early childhood (3 to 6 years)	Physical growth slows somewhat; substantial gains in cognitive and language development; the interplay between socialization and individualization shapes personality and influences adjustment.
Middle childhood (7 to 11 years)	School becomes a major force in development; physical, cognitive, and psychosocial abilities become apparent.
Adolescence (12 to 18 years)	Puberty affects all aspects of development; thought becomes more abstract, academic achievement begins to shape the future; the search for identity continues unabated.
Early adulthood (19 to 34 years)	Higher education or the beginning of work beckons; relationships are a major focus of these years; marriage and children become central concerns of the lifespan.
Middle adulthood (35 to 64 years)	Heightened responsibility; may include care of children and aging parents; growing community involvement; peak period for leadership and influence; a time of physical change (for example, menopause).
Late adulthood (65+)	Retirement; eventual declining health and strength; adjusting to death of loved ones; facing one's own mortality; changing lifestyle to enhance "successful aging"; enjoying greater wisdom.

CHANGING VIEWS OF CHILDHOOD

Although written decades ago, Freud's words strike a familiar chord and highlight a major assumption about lifespan development: along the path from childhood to adulthood something vital changes. But is it the child who changes, or does the way the individual is viewed by society change? Children encapsulate innocence, a joie de vivre that gets diluted as life becomes more complicated and as children either take on increasing responsibilities or have responsibility thrust upon them as demanded by society. The assumption thus creates a challenge in any attempt to understand children: Without understanding a specific context, how can we interpret children's growth, development, and behaviour more generally? How does any society define what a "child" is? Are children seen as miniature adults or as competent, curious youths? What is appropriate for children, and who are the stakeholders in any outcomes?

If historians wish to understand children of the past, they must first discover how adults have viewed the young (Heywood, 2001). The concept of childhood has changed from period to period, place to place, and culture to culture. Viewing children as miniature adults (and treating them that way) is quite different from recognizing the significance of the interactions of heredity and environment in a child's development.

The manner in which societies viewed children has differed throughout history according to culture and prevailing values of the historical period. Greek and Roman scholars believed that ideal human development involved disciplined cultivation of body and mind, and children (mostly male children of wealthy families) were brought up according to specific values and expectations for their life practices. With the gradual spread of Christianity and the belief that humans are inherently evil and need to be shaped to allow optimal moral growth, formal classrooms

FEATUREDMEDIA

Perspectives on Childhood

Bully (2011)—A moving and troubling documentary about the misery some children inflict upon others. Bullying, which has long been tolerated as a fact of life, has now been redefined as a social problem. This movie shows oppressed individuals that they are not alone.

Diary of a Wimpy Kid: Dog Days (2012)—A movie based on a novel from the Diary of a Wimpy Kid series by Jeff Kinney. This movie follows Greg, a middle-school weakling, as he enters what could be the worst summer of his life.

The Odd Life of Timothy Green (2012)—This film is about a magical boy with a special personality who has profound effects on the people in his town.

▲ Children are sometimes treated like miniature adults.

and schools began to appear. The playful, cheerful spirit of children was considered a hindrance to living a moral life. But great changes in the world's technological capabilities, such as the invention of the printing press, and the industrial age and subsequent child labour laws, prompted changing concepts of childhood, and children entered the symbolic world of the written word. Children were slowly becoming objects of concern on a grand scale.

Throughout history, philosophers such as John Locke and Jean-Jacques Rousseau presented challenging, often contradictory, ideas of child rearing. Locke proposed that children were like a *tabula rasa*, or blank slate. Therefore, the role of the parents was to instruct children's minds. Locke believed that by carefully observing children's natural inclinations, parents could use those inclinations to motivate children toward the best paths. Rousseau, on the other hand, believed that children develop naturally and learn behaviours and freedom through the natural course of their everyday being. He did not support verbal learning or forced instruction. Both Locke and Rousseau agreed, however, that childhood should be joyful and celebrated, and that the success of nations depends on it. As the concept of childhood became more accepted and

subject to various interpretations, an important work by the biologist Charles Darwin, titled *Biographical Sketch of an Infant* (1877), heralded a new and innovative analysis of childhood. The book, which consisted of Darwin's careful observations of his infant son's early development, provided a scientific basis for studying children.

When Darwin's book was followed in 1882 by William Preyer's *The Mind of the Child*, a rich, scholarly account of children's competencies based on careful observation, childhood was firmly entrenched as a separate subject deserving of study to answer growing questions about human development. The 19th century yielded remarkable studies of child development, particularly Alfred Binet's study of intelligence and G. Stanley Hall's writings on childhood and adolescence. As the notion of childhood acquired more credence, one of the most powerful interpreters of childhood was Sigmund Freud. In Freud's view, much of adults' behaviour could be linked to experiences in the early years of life. Careful psychoanalysis would reveal these connections and shed light on resulting behaviours. Today, children are viewed as the product of genetic, biological, behavioural, and contextual forces constantly interacting. We see the same level of sophistication applied to the adolescent years.

CHANGING VIEWS OF ADOLESCENCE

Adolescence is recognized as being a very tumultuous time in an individual's life. Perhaps the best way of thinking about adolescence is to consider that it begins in biology and ends in culture (Petersen, 1988).

Technology has transformed the **sexual lives** of adolescents in ways we could never have imagined

LUCIA O'SULLIVAN SPEAKING ON THE TOPIC OF "TWEETING, TEXTING, TEENS AND CHAT: THE INTERNET AND SEX IN THE LIVES OF YOUTH"

As is true for all periods of the lifespan, the physical maturation of human development initiates the process, but social and emotional adolescent experiences strongly shape the nature and direction of behaviour. Lerner and Galambos (1998) summarize the nuances of adolescence when they state that adolescence is that time when a person's biological, cognitive, psychological, and social characteristics are changing from what is considered childlike to what is considered adultlike. A key word is "considered"—considered by *whom*? That is at the heart of the tension that exists for adolescents, who straddle the two distinct realms of childhood and adulthood. What biology deems possible in terms of physical capacity, a teenager may not be ready to accept cognitively and/or emotionally, in terms of responsibility or consequences.

As with childhood, the concept of adolescence has changed remarkably through the years. For centuries adolescents were simply viewed as younger adults who were subject to strict rules and harsh discipline. Not until the industrial revolution in Western societies was the need for better education seen, and with the passage of child labour laws and a demand for universal school attendance came a separation of adolescents from children and adults (Grotevant, 1998). With the advent of the 20th century, adolescence as a separate phase of development was popularized by the writings and teachings of G. Stanley Hall. In his two-volume text *Adolescence* (1904), he suggested a label of adolescence that is still with us today—a time of "storm and stress."

At the beginning of the 21st century, continued speculation and research has changed the picture of adolescence again. Today most psychologists agree that the majority

▲ The increase in technology has significantly changed the period of adolescence.

of adolescents have accepted the values and standards of their parents and the greater society, and that friction between the generations is only slightly higher than that of childhood (Dacey, Kenny, & Margolis, 2002).

One area of particular interest to those currently researching adolescence is the impact of technology on the development of today's teens. Dr. Lucia O'Sullivan, from the University of New Brunswick, studies adolescents and focuses primarily on sexual health, intimate relationships, and the affective and cognitive components of sexual decision-making of young adults and adolescents (University of New Brunswick, 2011).

In spite of numerous risk factors that concern parents and adults in general, most young adults face the challenges of their environment, adjust to the demands made on them, and, with the patience and understanding of the adults in their lives, achieve their goals.

CHANGING VIEWS OF ADULTHOOD

Today we realize that lifespan development involves change throughout the lifespan, in adulthood as well as in the earlier stages. Development is not complete at adulthood

TAKE A **STAND**

Adolescent Abandon

The consumption of drugs and alcohol by teenagers is not just about rebellion or emotional troubles. It's about being one of the cool kids, according to a study led by Jean-Sebastien Fallu at the Université de Montréal. The teenagers involved in this study were well accepted and very sensitive to social codes, and they understood the compromise that it takes to be popular. The findings of this study showed an increase in consumption as the child got older, regardless of their popularity level. However, the more popular a child and his or her friends were, the greater this consumption was (University of Montreal, 2010).

What do you think about the research findings of this study? Do you feel this study accurately describes today's adolescents? Why or why not?

FEATUREDMEDIA

Perspectives on Adolescence

13 Going on 30 (2004)—A 13-year-old girl plays a game on her 13th birthday and wakes up the next day as a 30-year-old woman.

17 Again (2009)—This story is about a man whose life didn't quite turn out how he wanted it to and who wishes he could go back to school and change it. He wakes up one day and is 17 again, and he gets the chance to rewrite his life.

Hairspray (1988, 2007)—Both versions of the film—non-musical and musical—feature "pleasantly plump" teenager Tracy Turnblad, whose dream is to become a dancer on her favourite television program. She experiences some serious dilemmas, ranging from her weight to racial discrimination to bigotry.

(maturity). Rather, development reaches across the entire life course, and developmental changes involve lifelong adaptive processes unique for each phase of the life course, including adulthood. Compared to childhood and adolescence, adulthood is a relatively complex stretch of time, which is increasing in length due to the advances of medical and other technologies.

CHANGING PERSPECTIVES ON AGING

The Canadian Longitudinal Study on Aging (CLSA) is a large national, long-term study that will follow approximately 50,000 men and women between the ages of 45 and 85 for at least 20 years. The study will collect information on the changing biological, medical, psychological, social, lifestyle, and economic aspects of people's lives. These factors will be studied in order to understand how, individually and in combination, they have an impact both in

> Adult development is neither a **footrace** nor a moral **imperative.** It is a road map to help us make sense of where we and where our neighbors might be **located.**
>
> GEORGE VAILLANT (2002)

maintaining health and in the development of disease and disability as people age. The CLSA will be one of the most comprehensive studies of its kind undertaken to date, not only in Canada but around the world (Raina, Kirkland, & Wolfson, 2012).

Another study conducted on aging was the Seattle Longitudinal Study of Adult Intelligence (Schaie, 1994). This study analyzed the cause of an apparent decline in intelligence (as measured by intelligence tests) as people age and came to the following conclusions:

- When *physical health* remains good, cognitive performance suffers only a slight decline. Sight, hearing, and motor coordination play key roles in maintaining the link between health and intellectual performance.

- *Speed of response* is the time taken to perform any task that involves the central nervous system—tasks such as perception, memory, reasoning, and motor movement. It is the basis for efficient cognitive functioning, especially memory. Much of the decline in memory performance in the later years can be attributed to a decline in verbal speed. If the nervous system involvement is slowed, cognitive performance declines because information may be lost during the required cognitive processing (Birren & Fisher, 1992).

- *Attitude*, especially in a testing situation, affects cognitive performance. Test anxiety lowers test scores when older adults find themselves in strange settings. They may fear that their memory will fail them; they may be uncomfortable with the test's problems; they may simply have an expectation of failure because of all they've heard and read about the declining mental abilities of older adults.

These and similar reasons, either singly or in combination, have often led to an underestimation of older people's intelligence. For example, reasoning, problem solving, and wisdom hold up well, and may even improve, with age. Any standardized test of intelligence, or other area, must be challenged as an accurate measure of assessment for a host of reasons, some of which include cultural bias, contextual factors, and validity.

CHART YOUR OWN LIFESPAN

Endeavouring to illustrate how important knowledge of the lifespan is to each of us, Sugarman (1986) has devised a simple exercise that you can do quickly. Using a blank sheet of paper, assume that the left edge of the page represents the beginning of your life and the right edge where you are today. Now draw a line across the page that indicates the peaks and valleys you have experienced so far.

In the sample chart shown in Figure 1.1, the first valley was a financial reversal for the person's parents. The first peak represents happy and productive high school and college years, followed by entry into the work force and then marriage. The deep valley was a serious accident followed by years of recuperation and then the birth of children, the publication of a book, and the death of parents. You can see that it looks like a temperature chart. Try it for yourself.

When you finish, ask yourself these questions:

Are there more peaks than valleys?

Is there a definite shape to my chart?

Would I identify my peaks and valleys as major or minor?

What caused the peaks and valleys?

Could I have done anything to make the peaks higher and the valleys shallower?

What happened during the plateaus?

What's my view of these highs and lows in my life?

You have drawn a picture of your lifespan so far, and the questions that you have just answered are the subject matter of lifespan development.

We end this section as we began it: Different eras have conceived different views of the various developmental periods. Any study of lifespan development must recognize that numerous factors account for observable developmental changes. These differences clearly call for us to appraise the meaning of development more closely.

epigenetic view Stresses the ongoing interaction between heredity and the environment during lifespan development.

culture The customs, values, and traditions inherent in one's environment.

FIGURE 1.1
Milestone Events Across the Lifespan

Financial reversal

School (high school, college)

Marriage, career

Accident

Birth of children, first book

Death of parents

The Importance of Biopsychosocial Interactions

◄L03

This book proposes that lifespan development is the product of biopsychosocial interactions—the influence of genetic, biological, psychological, and social/environmental forces on development. This differs from the **epigenetic view** of development, which focuses on the ongoing interaction between heredity and the environment during development. In the biopsychosocial model, development results from the interaction of biological, psychological, and social/environmental factors and processes (see Figure 1.2).

Biological processes range from the role of genes to adult health concerns, psychological processes include all aspects of cognitive and personality development, and social processes refer to the role of family, school/work, peers, and the media. These processes are so tightly intertwined that it is impossible to determine which plays more of a role in development. In many cases, the processes operate in a bidirectional manner. For example, biological forces affect cognitive forces (skipping breakfast can impact students' performance in schools), and it works in the other direction, too (positive thinking and strong friendships can impact elderly people's health). The goal of lifespan psychology is therefore to probe the multiple and integrated layers (genetic, physical, behavioural, and environmental) that drive human development.

UNDERSTANDING THE ROLE OF CULTURE

It's essential to recognize the contributions that a particular culture makes to the development of individuals and the larger society. **Culture** can be defined as the customs, values, and traditions inherent in one's environment—the features that define values and styles of life (Rutter &

TECH TRENDS

Playing With the Process of Aging

The following sites offer fun (and sometimes shocking!) insights into the aging process:

www.poodwaddle.com/clocks/howoldru—A "How Old R U?" clock that you can use to enter information and find out precisely how old you are today, at this precise moment in time.

www.freebrainagegames.com—You know it is important to exercise your body but what about your brain? Measure your brain age by playing some games.

www.biological-age.com—You know how many years it's been since you were born, but what about your actual body age? Answer this quiz and find out!

FIGURE 1.2

The Biopsychosocial Model

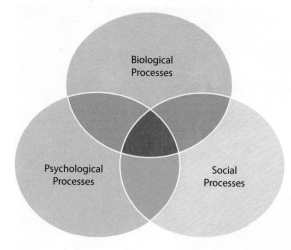

Career Apps

As a developmental psychologist, how might you examine the role that a sense of humour plays in late adolescence?

To help you grasp the significance of culture in development, there are three answers to the question "How well do you understand the cultures of your friends, co-workers, and neighbours?"

1. You may understand at a *superficial* level; that is, you know only the facts that make up a person's cultural history.

2. You may understand at an *intermediate* level; that is, you understand the central behaviours that are at the core of a person's social life. Language usage is a good example here: Does a person's culture tolerate, even encourage, calling out in class? Calling out could be a major problem for teachers not familiar with the acceptable behaviours of this person's culture because it goes against acceptable behaviours in traditional classroom culture.

3. You may understand at a *significant* level; that is, you grasp the values, beliefs, and norms that structure a person's view of the world and how to behave in that world. In other words, you change psychologically as a result of your interactions with a different culture (Casas & Pytluk, 1995).

Nikapota, 2006). Different cultures have different developmental expectations for their children. Asian children, for example, are encouraged to avoid emotional displays, a characteristic that does not necessarily apply to Asian-Canadian children. This example is simply stated, but to truly understand the previous sentence, you must consider the political and social histories of the countries that are implicitly and explicitly named in the generalization, and the emphasis on keeping harmony among a group of individuals as opposed to striving to be the best individual one can be. We also urge you to remember that the equation *biology + psychology + environment = development* plays out differently within the confines of a particular culture.

As you continue studying lifespan development, you therefore need to be aware that different does not mean deficient. Examples of the cultural influence on development are visible in this book in two

▲ Multiple developmental influences affect growth during the lifespan. Think about interactions that occur among biology, psychology, and social factors and how they affect development.

The Impact of Cultural Climate

Toronto is one of the most multicultural communities in the world, which makes the Toronto District School Board (TDSB) one of the largest, most culturally diverse school boards in Canada. According to the TDSB website, there are more than 80 languages represented in their schools with languages from all over the world, such as Urdu, Serbian, Spanish, Swahili, and Cantonese.

At the schools in Toronto, the proportion of "new Canadians" is as high as 80 to 90 percent, depending on the area, with new arrivals being enrolled every day. More than 36 percent of these students come from economically disadvantaged families, whose income is less than 70 percent of the median income (www.tdsb.on.ca).

The TDSB adjusted its curriculum and learning methods to meet the needs of the multicultural diversity in their schools. Principals also try to ensure that there is diversity among their teaching staffs.

To deal with specific issues, they recently started the Inner City Model School initiative, a program designed to reduce the dropout rate and support particularly disadvantaged students and their parents in deprived neighbourhoods (www.tdsb.on.ca).

The classroom is not the only location in which cultures merge. In the business world, people of various cultures and backgrounds work side by side; those designated as minorities may have leadership positions in which members of the dominant culture report to them. As companies become more global and as the number of international markets increases steadily, the workplace is beginning to resemble the classroom as a meeting place of cultures.

One goal in encouraging you to develop a culturally sensitive perspective is to help you reach a level of

significant understanding of people who seem different. If you adopt this perspective, you will come to realize that different people have different world views that decisively influence their thinking. Recognizing how diverse people are in their thinking and behaviour will help you to identify and comprehend variations in people's backgrounds and how they become functioning members of their culture. In this way, you will work, play, and study more congenially with others, thus fostering more positive relations in our society.

ways: through Perspectives on Diversity features and through age-specific examples. The following objectives relating to culture specifically are at the core of the biopsychosocial model:

- to understand the relationship between culture and development
- to identify values and attitudes that promote and sustain healthy development
- to trace the impact of cultural transmission, such as parenting practices and the influence of peers, schools, and media
- to assess current cultural change initiatives that encourage successful development (Harrison, 2000)

CONTRIBUTORS TO BIOPSYCHOSOCIAL INTERACTIONS

If you start to imagine all the factors that contribute to biopsychosocial development, you'll see that it's a daunting task with endless combinations of factors. Multiple developmental influences affect growth during the lifespan. More importantly, we would like you to think about the interactions that occur among biology, psychology, and social factors, and how these interactions affect development. By recognizing the significance of biopsychosocial interactions, you'll be able to understand and remember the material of any given chapter. This perspective also helps to emphasize all of the features that so powerfully influence development through the lifespan.

Issues in Lifespan Development

L04 ▶

In lifespan psychology, as in any field, several issues or themes warrant special attention. The following two issues have been the subject of much controversy and debate, and an awareness of them will increase your understanding of development as you progress through the book.

CONTINUITY VERSUS DISCONTINUITY

In 1980, Orville Brim and Jerome Kagan published *Constancy and Change in Human Development*, which highlighted a long-standing controversy among developmental psychologists. Arguing that humans have a capacity for change across the lifespan, Brim and Kagan brought new life to the question "*How* do these changes occur?" Does each new stage of development contain most of the structures that appeared in an earlier stage (Kagan, 1998)? Do you think you are basically the same person you were when you were 3 years old? 10 years old? 18 years old? Or do you feel quite different? Why? These questions introduce the issue of continuity versus discontinuity. In other words, do developmental changes appear as the result of a slow but steady progression (**continuity**) or as the result of abrupt changes (**discontinuity**)?

To illustrate the distinction between continuity and discontinuity, let's examine the phenomenon known as *attachment* in infancy. Sometime after six months of age, babies begin to show a decided preference for a particular caregiver, usually the mother. This is usually described by noting that the infant has attached to the mother. During any time of stress—anxiety, illness, appearance of strangers—the baby will move to the preferred caregiver. With regard to continuity or discontinuity, does attachment develop slowly as the caregiver and infant interact and exchange subtle and more obvious cues, or does it appear suddenly, as a completely new and different behaviour?

Continuities and discontinuities appear in each of our lives because the term *development* implies change. Puberty, leaving home, marriage, and career all serve to shape psychological functioning. Continuities occur, however, because our initial experiences, our early learning, and our temperaments remain with us. The form of the behaviour may change over the years, but the underlying processes remain the same. For example, the conduct disorders of childhood (such as stealing, fighting, or truancy) may become the violence of adulthood (theft, spousal abuse, child abuse, or murder). Differences or dissimilarities may be evident in types of behaviour, but the underlying processes that cause specific behaviours may be identical, thus arguing for continuity in development (Rutter & Rutter, 1993).

Other behaviours in our lives, however, seem to be quite different from those that preceded them—for example, walking and talking. We also negotiate transitions at appropriate times in our lives, such as leaving home, beginning a career, getting married, and adjusting to the birth of children, and sometimes divorce or the death of a spouse. Some developmental psychologists highlight the role of accidents, wars, famines, disease, and chance encounters in human experience. Lewis therefore believes that the study of developmental change is actually the study of predictable as well as complex, often random, and certainly unpredictable conditions.

Most developmental psychologists now believe that both continuity and discontinuity characterize development. As Lerner notes (2002), any developmental change may be characterized as being either continuous or discontinuous and either stable or unstable. Depending on the particular lens through which behaviour is viewed, the interpretations vary.

> **continuity** Development that is a smooth process, without distinct stages.
>
> **discontinuity** Development that is a series of distinct stages; an individual must accomplish at least one task before progressing to the next stage.

NATURE VERSUS NURTURE

Another enduring issue in developmental psychology has been the question of which exercises a greater influence on development: our inborn tendencies (nature) or our surrounding world (nurture). Again, most developmental psychologists lean toward an interaction between these two forces in shaping development. Such interaction between genes and the environment explains the individual developmental path each of us follows throughout our lifespan. Lerner (2002) has summarized this argument as follows:

1. Nature and nurture are both involved in the production of behaviour.

2. They cannot function in isolation from each other but must interact.

3. The resulting interaction implies that both nature and nurture are completely intertwined.

Perhaps Bjorklund (2005) summarized this issue as well as anyone can when he stated that, for developmental psychologists, there is no nature–nurture controversy because biological factors are inseparable from experiential factors, with the two constantly interacting. It is *how* they interact that produces a particular pattern of development.

These issues help to identify lifespan psychology as a dynamic discipline—one with great theoretical and practical implications. Fascinating though these issues may be, it is crucial to remember the integrated nature of development. With these ideas in mind to use as we interpret developmental data, let's examine the research techniques that developmental psychologists use while seeking to answer questions about the lifespan.

Do Vitamins Increase Life Expectancy?

Much research exists on the benefits of nutrition for overall health. Recent findings by experts argue that taking vitamin supplements has no impact on overall health or mortality and that they can actually increase the risk of early death. Despite this, Canadians spent an estimated $7.84 billion on alternative medicine products and services in the latter half of 2005 and first half of 2006 (Esmail, 2007). Consumers are encouraged to buy dietary supplements to increase some functions and decrease other functions, and physicians, pharmacists, and fitness instructors frequently recommend supplements.

Some evidence supports the use of vitamin supplements to improve health, and common knowledge argues that luck plays a major role in how long we live and how healthy we are throughout our lives. The tension between heredity and environmental factors is well exemplified by the desire to supplement what nature/heredity deals us.

Is our destiny determined by genetics/fate (nature) or is it something we can control with environmental input (nurture)?

L05 ▶ Research in Lifespan Development

After we identify several key developmental issues and theoretical viewpoints, the question becomes "How can we obtain reliable data about these topics so that we may better understand them?" Today there are many approaches to understanding human behaviour, all rooted in a spirit of inquiry, wanting to know "why?" Each has its strengths and weaknesses, and none is completely reliable. Because human beings conduct research, we must accept that humans have conscious or unconscious biases and may make mistakes, and that sometimes pure chance influences the outcomes of an investigation.

Most developmental psychologists employ one of three data collection techniques: (1) descriptive studies, (2) manipulative experiments, and (3) naturalistic experiments. They also use one of four time-variable designs: one-time, one-group studies; longitudinal studies; cross-sectional studies; and a combination of the last two, called sequential studies. Each type of study varies according to the goal of the research and the effect of time on the results.

DATA COLLECTION TECHNIQUES

At the heart of the study of human development is the **scientific method** —an approach to seeking answers through empirical research, data

collection, and testing. When researchers follow the steps of this approach, their work is regarded accordingly in the field as a scientific study. The steps include the following:

1. generating a single research question or a set of guiding questions

2. developing a **hypothesis**—a prediction about something that can be tested and subsequently supported or rejected

3. testing the hypothesis through research to collect data

4. drawing conclusions based on the data and supporting arguments with evidence from the research

When researchers are curious about a particular question, they choose a specific type of study that best suits their investigation. One of the key aspects of any study is systematic, thoughtful observation. Observations can occur in a laboratory or clinical setting as well as in a natural, realistic setting. Careful watching, listening, and recording convey respect for the field and contribute to the effectiveness of the overall study, regardless of which form the study takes. (See Figure 1.3 for a representation of the scientific method.)

Descriptive Studies

In **descriptive studies**, information is gathered on participants without manipulating them in any way. Some studies (called *survey* or *self-report studies*) ask people their opinions about themselves or other people. These studies may involve the use of interviews or questionnaires. An example of this can be seen in research done by Dr. Frances Aboud, a developmental psychologist at McGill University in Montreal, focusing initially on the

scientific method An approach to investigation that includes empirical research, data collection, and testing.

hypothesis A prediction that can be tested through research and subsequently supported or rejected.

descriptive studies Gather information on subjects without manipulating them in any way.

FIGURE 1.3

The Scientific Method

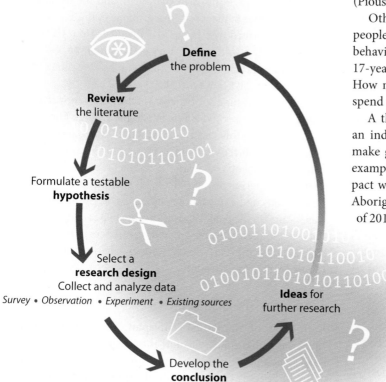

▲ The scientific method allows researchers to evaluate the data they collect objectively and logically. Their findings can suggest ideas for further research.

development of racism in children. Working with her colleague Morton Mendelson, Professor Aboud developed the McGill Friendship Questionnaire. The questionnaire offered insight into how children develop friendships and classify others. Using the questionnaire, her research showed that children often keep an emotional distance from children of other races, but that this distance can be reduced by exposing racist children to children with lower levels of prejudice (Pious, 2010).

Other studies, called *observational studies*, describe people simply by counting the number and the type of behaviour they display. How many 12-year-olds versus 17-year-olds think the government is doing a good job? How much money does the average 40-year-old woman spend per week?

A third type of study, the *case study*, presents data on an individual or individuals in great detail, in order to make generalizations relating to a research question. An example of this approach can be seen when a suicide pact was discovered involving dozens of children, mostly Aboriginals, in a Vancouver community in the early part of 2012. This crisis drew a response from youth and social workers, police and medical officials; together they found that there were gaps in their systems.

The report issued after this event recommended the adoption of a "place-based strategy" to help deal with a high number of children with special needs. Researchers hoped to learn more about adolescent psychology and other factors that could have contributed to this specific situation and could be generalized to a wider population (Drews, 2012).

Another case-study approach involves the study of individual lives from a biographical perspective. For example, Gardner (1997) closely examined the biographies of four eminent individuals: Wolfgang Mozart, Sigmund Freud, Virginia Woolf, and Mahatma Gandhi. From these four cases, he built a new theory about creative innovation.

▼ Case studies of specific individuals can provide valuable information about the general population.

Descriptive studies have a certain appeal because people can generate a lot of data. However, because the sequence of events is not under a researcher's control, causes and effects cannot be determined; that is, just because two variables are associated does not mean that one causes the other.

The assumption that correlation means causation is a common mistake made in interpreting results of research. Correlation refers to the association between factors and can be established through a specific statistical technique. This technique provides a number that represents how strong the association is between any two variables. For instance, height and weight are associated with each other, but not perfectly. The taller people are, the more they tend to weigh, but this is not always true; the correlation between height and weight for a typical sample of people is moderately high. Although there is a definite association, we know that height does not cause weight or vice versa; they are simply correlated. Researchers examine the correlation between variables to find the strength in similar relationships. If the correlation is high, researchers may want to set up experiments to further examine the relationships.

Manipulative Experiments

In an attempt to better learn about the causes of behaviour, psychologists design **manipulative experiments**. In these, the investigators attempt to keep all variables (all the factors that can affect a particular outcome) constant except one, which they carefully manipulate. The variables are known as independent or dependent: *independent variables* are those that the researchers specifically manipulate, while *dependent variables* change as a result of the manipulation, also called the treatment. If differences occur as a result of the experiment, they can be attributed to the variable that was manipulated in the *treatment*. For example, if researchers are curious about the effect of a book on students' learning of a specific subject, they can assign half a class Book A, and the other half Book B (book = independent variable). The whole class could then take a test to determine which book had a greater influence on students' test scores (score = dependent variable).

Though manipulative experiments often can lead us to discover some causes and related effects, they are open to critique. How can we know if the results are reliable? Was the treatment similar to normal conditions? Do subjects see themselves as special because we picked them and thus react a certain way? For these reasons, researchers may turn to naturalistic experiments.

manipulative experiments
The researcher attempts to keep constant all variables (all the factors that can affect a particular outcome) except one, which is carefully manipulated.

naturalistic experiments
The researcher acts solely as an observer and does as little as possible to disturb the environment. "Nature" performs the experiment, and the researcher acts as a recorder of the results.

time-variable designs
A specific amount of time (duration) is allowed for a given study, or there is a specific number of times a measure is used in a given study.

Naturalistic Experiments

In **naturalistic experiments**, the researcher acts solely as an observer and does as little as possible to disturb the environment. "Nature" performs the experiment, and the researcher acts as a recorder of the results. An example of this is research that was performed by a group of individuals from Carleton University in Ottawa, Ontario. They used naturalistic observation to study spectator behaviour at youth hockey games in a large Canadian city (Bowker et al., 2009).

Only with a naturalistic experiment do we have any chance of discovering causes and effects in real-life settings. The main challenges with this technique are that it requires great patience and objectivity, and it is impossible to meet the strict requirements of a true scientific *experiment*. True scientific experiments are deemed such due to certain assumptions and expectations about the scientific process. Depending on the field of study, specific biases and assumptions are more or less present, and researchers must be vigilant about accounting for such biases when reporting the results of their investigations.

TIME-VARIABLE DESIGNS

In studies of the human lifespan, researchers often focus on individuals who fall into a specific age group or else people of different ages for comparison within a study. Several **time-variable designs** afford different

▲ Manipulative experiments can often lead to the discovery of cause and effect. Researchers might, for example, manipulate the diets of rats to see if there is any impact on their size.

▲ By following these three women for several decades, researchers were able to trace their adult behaviours, which have changed since early childhood.

There aren't many pieces of work, especially in film, that have the patience or longevity or the time to honour the drama of ordinary life; and after all, the drama of what we all have to go through—children, jobs, marriage, the things that touch us—is the big drama of life, far more so than the **drama** of movies and television.

MICHAEL APTED

understandings, depending on the intentions of the investigators and their questions.

One-Time, One-Group Studies
As the name implies, **one-time, one-group studies** are those that are carried out only once with one group of participants. It is almost impossible to investigate cause and effect in such studies because a sequence of events or the influence of various factors cannot be known on the basis of a one-time occurrence with one group of people

Longitudinal Studies
Longitudinal studies, which track the same individuals over a period of time, can answer important questions. The study conducted by Dr. Sears and his team, as well as the CLSA, both of which were introduced earlier in this chapter, are examples of longitudinal studies.

Another engaging example of a longitudinal study is the one conducted by filmmaker Michael Apted (2007), represented in the 7 Up documentary series. Apted has been interviewing and filming the same group of British individuals at 7-year intervals since 1964, when they were 7 years old.

one-time, one-group studies Carried out only once with one group of participants.

longitudinal studies The researcher makes several observations of the same individuals at two or more times in their lives. Examples include determining the long-term effects of learning on behaviour, the stability of habits and intelligence, and the factors involved in memory.

cross-sectional studies
Compare groups of indi-
viduals of various ages at
the same time.

sequential (longitudinal/
cross-sectional) studies
Done several times with
the same groups of
individuals.

Every 7 years, he has returned to ask the participants questions about their lives, and the result-ing films capture information about lifespan development that is shown in the personal accounts of each of the individuals and their families. The amazingly complex array of life issues, including chal-lenges, triumphs, and losses, sheds light on developmental patterns and inconsistencies.

The chief advantage of the longitudinal method is that it permits the discovery of lasting habits and of the periods in which they appear. A second advantage is the possibil-ity of tracing those adult behaviours that have changed since early childhood. Longitudinal research, however, has many challenges. It is expensive and often hard to main-tain because of changes in availability of researchers and subjects. Changes in the environment can also distort the results. For example, if a study began in 1960 in the U.S., looking at changes in political attitudes of youths from 10 to 20 years of age, conclusions would likely report that adolescents become more radical as they grow older. But the war in Vietnam would surely have had much to do with this finding. The results of the same study done between 1970 and 1980 would probably not show this trend, and today the data would show something different and unique to this moment in time.

Cross-Sectional Studies

Cross-sectional studies compare groups of individuals of various ages at the same time. For example, if you want to know how creative thinking changes or grows during ado-lescence, you could administer creativity tests to groups of 10-, 12-, 14-, 16-, and 18-year-olds and check on the differ-ences of the average scores of the five groups. Gail Jaquish and Richard Ripple (1981) did this in a cross-sectional study of subjects ranging in age from 18 to 84! (They found that age differences accounted for little variance in creative thinking.)

As with each of the other research designs, challenges exist with this method. Although careful selection can minimize the effects of cultural change, it is possible that the differences you find may be due to differences in age cohort, rather than maturation. Age cohorts are groups of people born at about the same time. Each cohort has had different experiences throughout its history, and this fact, as well as the actual differences in age, can affect the results.

Sequential (Longitudinal/ Cross-Sectional) Studies

A **sequential study** is a cross-sectional study done with the same groups of individuals, several times, over a period of time (such as administering creativity tests to the same five groups of youth, but at three different points in their lives). In this way, the aforementioned prob-lems may be alleviated. Figure 1.4 illustrates a sequential study. Although sequential studies are complicated and expensive, they may be the only type of study capable of answering important questions in the complex and fast-changing times in which we live.

UNDERSTANDING THE RESEARCH ARTICLE

As you continue your reading and work in lifespan devel-opment, you will undoubtedly review articles that shed light on the topic you're studying. Many of these articles present the results of an experiment that reflects the scien-tific method.

The typical research article contains four sections: the *Introduction*, the *Method*, the *Results*, and the *Discussion*. Let's take a look at each of these sections using a well-designed study, "Transmission of Aggression through Imi-tation of Aggressive Models," first published in the *Journal of Abnormal and Social Psychology* (Bandura, Ross & Ross, 1961).

1. **The Introduction** The introduction states the purpose of the article (usually as an attempt to solve a problem) and predicts the outcome of the study (usually in the form of hypotheses). The introduc-tion typically contains a review of the literature. In the introduction to the article by Albert Bandura (a Canadian psychologist born in Mundare, Alberta) and his associates, the researchers state that their intent is to conduct a study to investigate whether social behaviours (e.g., aggression) can be acquired by imitation. They concisely review the pertinent research and suggest a means of evaluating competence.

2. **The Method** The method section informs the reader abut the subjects in the experiment (Who were they? How many? How were they chosen?), it describes any tests that were used, and it summarizes the steps taken to carry out the study. Under controlled conditions, Bandura arranged for 24 boys and girls to watch a male or female model behaving aggressively towards a toy called a Bobo doll. Another 24 children were exposed to a non-aggressive model, and the final 24 children were used as a control group and not exposed to any model at all. The researchers pretested the children for how aggressive they were by observ-ing the children in the nursery and judging their aggressive behaviour on four 5-point rating scales. It was then possible to match the children in each group so that they had similar levels of aggression in their everyday behaviour.

FIGURE 1.4

Sequential (Longitudinal/Cross-Sectional) Study

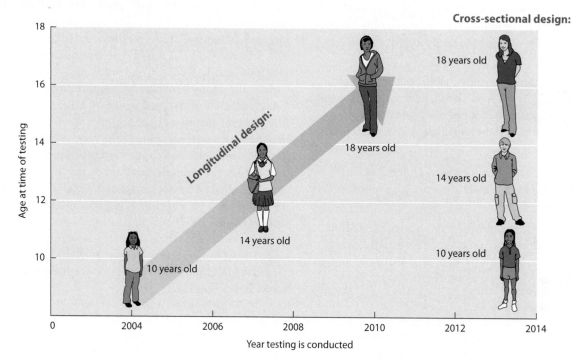

▲ Sequential studies combine both longitudinal and cross-sectional design. The study is performed by testing different groups of individuals of the same age at the same time (cross-sectional design) and then testing those same individuals again at different points in their lives (longitudinal design).

3. **The Results** In the results section, the results are presented, together with the statistics that help us to summarize and interpret the data. Authors typically present their data in several clear tables and show differences between the two groups using appropriate statistics. Bandura's results included the following:

    • Children were more likely to act aggressively when put in aggressive conditions.
    • Boys were more aggressive than girls.
    • Boys were more aggressive when a male model was present.
    • Girls were more physically aggressive with a male model and verbally aggressive with a female model.

4. **Discussion** Finally, the authors of any research article will discuss the importance of what they found (or did not find) and relate their findings to theory and previous research. In the Bandura article, the authors report that the findings support Bandura's Social Learning Theory. Children learn social behaviour such as aggression through the process of observation—through watching the behaviour of another person.

Research articles, while denser than most popular magazine articles, include much information that can be accessed in each of the specific sections. Note the important features of a research article and see how the results could help you better understand people's behaviour at a particular age.

WHEN ARE RESEARCH REFERENCES TOO OLD?

For the rest of your life, you will be reading research—magazine or journal articles, chapters in books, newspaper reports, and so on. When should you decide that a reference is too old to be credible any longer? As with so many aspects of social science, the answer is "it all depends." Guidelines exist, however, so let's try to understand them by looking at several sample references:

1. According to the international 2001–2002 Health Behaviour in School-aged Children study, approximately 15% of Canadian adolescents are overweight and 4% are obese (Hilbrecht & Zuzanek, 2005).

    Decision: Because eating and exercise habits of adolescents are likely to change with the times (depending, among other things, on the economic condition of the country), this statistic is unreliable, because more than ten years have passed since the data were collected.

2. Noise-induced hearing loss is recognized as the second most common cause of irreversible hearing loss in older persons (Surjan, Devald, & Palfalvin, 1973).

   Decision: Here is a study that is over 30 years old, but because there is no known reason to believe that aging factors have changed much over the years, if the study was well designed, we may still accept the results.

3. The major crisis in the first year and a half of human life is the establishment of basic trust (Erikson, 1963).

   Decision: This statement is not a research finding; rather, it represents Erikson's belief as reflected in his psychosocial theory of human development. It is therefore accurate because that is exactly what Erikson said.

code of ethics A guiding set of principles for members of a particular group.

ETHICS

Any research must abide by ethical standards to ensure the safety and integrity of all involved. Before researchers are supported in their work, for example, they must receive approval from the appropriate group that oversees scientific study at their institutions. Within the broader fields of science or psychology, there are disciplines that focus on narrower areas within those fields, and many professions, organizations, and societies articulate a detailed **code of ethics** that guides the work of members of those groups. A code of ethics generally outlines guiding principles that address moral considerations and responsibilities, such as the ethics guidelines developed by the Canadian Psychological Association, which can be found at **http://www.cpa.ca/aboutcpa/committees/ethics/codeofethics/**. Participants in any study must be informed of every aspect of their involvement, must be anonymous unless other terms of confidentiality are discussed, and must be debriefed once their role in the study has concluded.

CONCLUSIONS & SUMMARY

In this chapter, you've been urged to think about lifespan development as a rich, multilayered complex of interactions. The biopsychosocial model of development—the model that forms the structure of this book—was explained. This model can be used to help you grasp and retain the material in the chapters to come. Age groups that constitute the lifespan, and that are the focus of this book, were identified. As a result of reading about the strengths and weaknesses of different research methods, you should be more analytical and critical of the studies that are presented.

Lifespan study can aid us in adjusting to a society in which rapid change seems to be an inevitable process. By acquiring insights into your own development and recognizing the developmental characteristics of people of differing ages, you can hope to have more harmonious relationships with others. How would you define and describe lifespan development?

How would you define and describe lifespan development?

- As psychologists defined childhood and agreed that development does not cease at adolescence but continues into adulthood and old age, lifespan psychology assumed an important place in developmental psychology.
- To understand development is to accept the positive and negative features of change.
- The timing of experiences, as well as the transitions during the lifespan, help us to gain insights into developmental processes.
- Development cannot be explained by age alone.

How have views of lifespan development changed over the years?

- Children today are seen as complex individuals who develop subject to the interaction of many external and internal factors.
- Conflicting interpretations of adolescence (storm and stress, or calm) continue to rage today.
- The adult years are no longer seen as a time devoid of change until decline sets in.
- Intelligence tests performed on the aging population have led to an underestimation of older people's intelligence.

What are the different views of lifespan development?

- A biological interpretation of development emphasizes the powerful impact genes have on development.
- The need for more sophisticated perspectives on development has highlighted the place of reciprocal interactions in development.

What role do biopsychosocial interactions play in lifespan development?

- Biopsychosocial interactions in human development refer to the interactions of biological, psychological, and social/environmental forces.
- Biopsychosocial interactions occur at multiple levels of the developing person, from the genetic to the environmental levels.
- Analyzing development from a biopsychosocial perspective helps to identify the complexities of human development.

What are the major issues in lifespan development?

- If lifespan psychology is to present a complete picture of development, any analysis of lifespan development must address key developmental issues, such as the importance of culture and development.
- Many psychologists believe that development occurs as a steady progression of small accomplishments (continuity); other psychologists believe that development occurs in spurts or stages (discontinuity).
- The controversies over stability versus change and nature versus nurture continue to stimulate debate among developmental psychologists.

What is the role of research in studying lifespan development?

- To explain the various ages and stages of development, we must use the best data available to enrich our insights and to provide a thoughtful perspective on the lifespan.
- Good data demand careful research methods; otherwise, we would be constantly suspicious of our conclusions.
- The most widely used research techniques include descriptive studies, manipulative experiments, and naturalistic experiments.
- Developmental psychologists also use four time-variable designs: one-time, one-group studies; longitudinal studies; cross-sectional studies; and sequential studies.

For REVIEW

1. Consider the biopsychosocial model presented in this chapter. How do you explain its potential value? Now think of an example in your own life, or in the life of someone you know, and describe how biological, psychological, and social factors interacted to produce a particular effect. Do you think the model helped you to explain that person's behaviour?

2. Several issues were presented that thread their way through lifespan studies, such as culture and development and continuity versus discontinuity. Why do you think these are issues? Examine each one separately and defend your reasons for stating that each has strong developmental implications.

3. Throughout the chapter, the important role that the environment or context plays in development was stressed. What do you think of this emphasis? Think about your own life and the influences (both positive and negative) that those around you have had. Cite these personal experiences in your answer.

Chapter REVIEW TEST

1. The CHILD study discussed at the beginning of this chapter is researching children throughout Canada. They are investigating
   a. the effects of vaccinations on child development.
   b. the effects of the environment on child development.
   c. whether Canadian children are the healthiest in the world.
   d. which city in Canada provides the best environment for children.

2. Development is
   a. a lifelong process.
   b. age focused.
   c. topically restricted.
   d. circular in nature.

3. Lifespan psychology assumes that development is
   a. unidimensional.
   b. chronologically explained.
   c. multidimensional.
   d. age limited.

4. Understanding childhood at any historical period depends on what _____ think of children.
   a. peers
   b. scientists
   c. siblings
   d. adults

5. A model that uses the interaction of biological, psychological, and social influences to explain development is the
   a. psychoanalytic model.
   b. cognitive model.
   c. biopsychosocial model.
   d. behavioural model.

6. One of the first outstanding theorists to recognize the importance of the early years was
   a. Skinner.
   b. Freud.
   c. Bandura.
   d. Hebb.

7. When we refer to the values, beliefs, and characteristics of a people, we are referring to
   a. culture.
   b. race.
   c. ethnicity.
   d. customs.

8. Adolescence begins in _____ and ends in _____ .
   a. biology, culture
   b. school, marriage
   c. structures, schema
   d. ego, superego

9. An example of a cross-sectional study is
   a. comparing individuals of various ages at the same time.
   b. continued observations of the same individuals.
   c. careful description by the researcher.
   d. one that requires no manipulation.

10. The typical research article contains four sections. Which item is not included in a research article?
   a. introduction
   b. method
   c. results
   d. author biography

THEORIES OF
DEVELOPMENT:

As You READ

After reading this chapter, you should be able to answer the following questions:

LO1 ▶ How does psychoanalytic theory explain development across the lifespan?

LO2 ▶ What is the relationship between psychosocial crises and lifespan development?

LO3 ▶ How did Piaget explain cognitive development?

LO4 ▶ What impact does culture have on lifespan development?

LO5 ▶ What is the behavioural perspective on development?

LO6 ▶ How does the bioecological model explain development?

LO7 ▶ What is the status of current developmental theory?

INTERPRETING THE LIFESPAN

In this chapter, you'll read about several prominent developmental theories written by people who were curious about different aspects of lifespan development. As you will notice, the theories present one way of interpreting human development, and although no one theory is perfect, the driving force behind all the theories is their usefulness as invitations to consider lifespan development from different angles.

In a society that relies on scientific fact as truth that guides our behaviour, what's the point of studying theories that suggest only "Maybe" and "Perhaps if…" are answers to the "Why?" of lifespan development? The answer is simple: Theories are essential for constructing meaning out of facts. They suggest explanations for phenomena. Good theories

- *help to organize a huge body of information.* Published studies on human development number in the tens of thousands, and the classic theories were written long before technological advances introduced websites, blogs, podcasts, and instant messaging as means of communicating and sharing ideas. The conclusions that research presents would be dizzying unless organized in some meaningful manner. A theory provides a way of examining facts and supplies "hooks" on which we can hang similar types of research findings. In this way, we build a lens through which to view development.

- *help to focus our search for new understandings.* Theories offer guideposts as we search for insights into the mysteries of human development.

- *help to explain how findings may be interpreted.* They offer a detailed guide that leads us to decide which facts are important and what conclusions we can draw.

- *help to identify major disagreements among scholars.* By highlighting these disagreements, theories offer testable ideas that can be confirmed or refuted by research.

When researchers are deciding what to study, they often begin with their emerging hypotheses and work toward formulating a theory. As we saw in Chapter 1, a hypothesis is a tentative explanation for a phenomenon that can be tested through research to see if indeed the explanation holds true in specific situations. For example, a researcher may notice that people in elevators tend to look up, down, or straight ahead rather than make eye contact with fellow riders. The researcher can test this hypothesis by riding in elevators and recording the behaviour of fellow riders. The results of this investigation could lead to further assumptions about behaviour that relate to social and/or psychological ideas. A researcher can develop a theory that people feel awkward about speaking in elevators because they do not wish to appear overly friendly and break social boundaries. **Theory**, then, refers to a belief or idea that develops based on information or

theory A belief or idea that develops based on information or evidence; a proposed explanation for observed phenomena.

evidence. A theory can inform research at the beginning of a study or take shape as the study unfolds. Theories allow people to make predictions about behaviour. A person can predict that when she rides in an elevator, most often people will avoid eye contact. She can test the theory by smiling and blurting a hearty "Hi there!" every time someone gets on to see what, if anything, changes people's behaviour. See what happens when you take your next ride in an elevator!

As you read the theories introduced in this chapter, you will notice the various approaches that theorists bring to their inquiry. Ultimately, the goal of any theory is to provide a framework for the study of human development that furthers scientific vision and leads to the application of that science to public policy and social programs, thereby contributing to the greater good of society.

In this chapter, we explore the ideas of theorists who have guided thinking about lifespan development. A discussion of the present status of developmental theory and several issues related to the direction of developmental theory follows. Finally, you will learn how developmental systems theory and brain research reflect recent thinking regarding new directions in developmental analysis. As you read about these ideas, the overlap between biological,

▲ Theories allow for predictions about human behaviour.

psychological, and social forces will become evident. Is it possible to separate one factor from the others as the most important contributor to lifespan development?

L01 # Psychoanalytic Theories

Mention the word "psychoanalysis" to someone and the following images may spring to her mind: a couch, a therapist sitting in a chair holding pad and pen, the brain, and/or dreams. These images all relate to the ideas of one man who developed an approach to understanding human development that earned him the title "father of modern psychology." In more than 100 years of psychological research, no one has played a larger role than Sigmund Freud. Even his most severe critics admit that his theory on the development of personality is a milestone in the social sciences (Ferris,

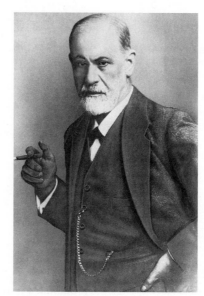

▲ Sigmund Freud

1997). Furthermore, Freud has had arguably the greatest impact of any psychological figure in popular culture. Have you ever described someone as being "anal-retentive" or spoken about one's "libido"? If so, you have been using Freudian terminology without even realizing it! You also may have heard Freudian terms such as "phallic symbol" and "Oedipus complex" used in films or on television. His ideas about the power of the unconscious, called **psychoanalytic theory**—the belief that we possess powerful ideas and impulses of which we're unaware but that exert a strong influence on our behaviour—are a staple in any psychological discussion (Kahn, 2002). Freud's ideas no longer dominate developmental psychology as they did in the early part of the 20th century, due to interpretations by later theorists. However, his insistence on the early years as a vital period in human development remains a powerful concept when considering influences on human development (Crain, 2005).

> The **Freudian theory** is one of the most important foundation stones for an edifice to be built by future generations, the dwelling of a freer and **wiser humanity**.
>
> THOMAS MANN (1939), GERMAN AUTHOR AND CRITIC

FREUD'S THEORY

In Freud's view, development involves moving through five distinct **psychosexual stages**, each one assigned to a specific age range and separate from the others: oral, anal, phallic, latency, and genital (see Figure 2.1). Each stage has a major function based on developmental wants or needs in that period of life and is linked to what Freud calls a pleasure centre. The location of the pleasure centre changes with development, and unless this pleasure centre is satisfied (e.g., during breast-feeding or potty training), a person cannot resolve the inner conflicts relating to her wants or needs. Aspects of her personality remain at that psychosexual stage (Freud's term *fixated*), and she is unable to become a fully mature person (Kahn, 2002). Conflicts arise in each stage, resulting in anxiety. Freud argued that the human personality uses **defence mechanisms** (psychological strategies to cope with anxiety or perceived threats) to deal with these crises. The defence mechanism that has received the most attention is **repression**, in which the individual pushes traumatic and unacceptable thoughts and memories into their unconscious in order to avoid the psychological pain of having to deal with these thoughts and memories at a conscious level. Repression, like other defence mechanisms, provides the person with short-term gain at the expense of long-term pain, as Freud believed that repressed material will eventually contribute to self-destructive behaviour. One of the goals of psychoanalytic treatment is to enable the client to access this repressed material so that they can gain insight into their harmful behaviour.

Freud argued that at different stages of a person's development, personality is influenced by three distinct structures of the mind: the **id**, the **ego**, and the **superego**. They are fueled by the libido, Freud's term for psychic energy, which is similar to the physical energy that drives bodily functions. The characteristics of the three structures of the mind are as follows:

psychoanalytic theory Freud's theory of the development of personality; emphasis on the role of the unconscious.

psychosexual stages Freud's five distinct stages of development in which a pleasure centre must be satisfied in order for the individual to resolve the inner conflicts relating to his or her wants or needs.

defence mechanisms Psychological strategies to cope with anxiety or perceived threats.

repression A defence mechanism in which traumatic and unacceptable thoughts and memories are removed from consciousness and pushed to the unconscious level.

id Freud's structure of mind relating to our basic instincts; strives to secure pleasure.

ego Freud's notion of the central part of our personality; keeps id in check.

superego Freud's concept of our conscience; internal determinant of right and wrong.

FIGURE 2.1
Freudian Psychosexual Stages of Development

1
The Oral Stage

(0 to 1.5 years old)

• The oral cavity (mouth, lips, tongue, gums) is the pleasure centre. Its function is to obtain an appropriate amount of sucking, eating, and biting.

2
The Anal Stage

(1.5 to 3 years old)

• The anus is the pleasure centre. The function here is successful toilet training.

3
The Phallic Stage

(3 to 5 years old)

• The genitals are the pleasure centres in this stage and in the two remaining stages. The major function of this stage is the healthy development of sexual interest, which sometimes involves unconscious sexual desire for the parent of the opposite sex (called the *Oedipus complex* in males and the *Electra complex* in females).

4
The Latency Stage

(5 to 12 years old)

• During this stage, sexual desire becomes dormant. Children tend to put energy into developing physical, intellectual, and social skills, such as sports and schoolwork.

5
The Genital Stage

(12 years old and older)

• At this stage, a surge of sexual hormones occurs in both genders, which brings about a recurrence of the phallic stage. People set about establishing relationships with others outside the immediate family.

The id. This structure, the only one present at birth, contains all the basic instincts, such as the need for food, drink, comfort, and nurturance. The most primitive of the structures, it strives only to secure pleasure.

▲ Several characters in beloved fairy tales exemplify the tension between Freud's mental forces as they encounter situations forcing them to decide between instant gratification and long-term gains.

The superego. The superego is our conscience. Throughout infancy, we gain an increasingly clearer conception of what the world is like. Toward the end of the first year, we begin to internalize parental and societal standards of right and wrong, and we are expected to behave according to these values and beliefs. As a result, the superego often comes into conflict with the id as the latter demands instant gratification of needs while the former emphasizes patience and moral behaviour.

The ego. The ego is the central part of our personality, the (usually) rational part that plans and keeps us in touch with reality, and keeps the id in check. Freud believed that the stronger the ego becomes, the more realistic and usually the more successful a person is likely to be (Lerner, 2002). The desires of the id and the demands of the superego are in constant battle, with the ego struggling to strike compromises between these two powerful forces.

Sometimes a cigar is just a cigar.

SIGMUND FREUD (ATTRIBUTED)

Psychoanalytic theory has undergone many changes since Freud first proposed it, and as the significant role of culture in development has become increasingly apparent, social influences on development have assumed greater importance in psychoanalytic theory (Eagle, 2000; Westin, 2000). These social and cultural influences are precisely what propelled the theory of Erik Erikson, which will be presented in the next section. In spite of the diminished acceptance of Freud's ideas because of the heavy emphasis on sexual instincts, psychoanalytic theory has retained a solid core of support through the years. Recently, neuropsychologist Mark Solm (2004) argued strongly that although Freud's views (focusing on unconscious, invisible influences) took a backseat to brain research and the findings of neuroscientists in the 1980s (focusing on physical, visible biological phenomena), more current research has drawn renewed interest in the concepts of psychoanalysis.

For example, Eric Kandel, a 2000 Nobel Prize winner, called psychoanalysis the most coherent and intellectually satisfying view of the mind. With this statement, Kandel reflected the belief of several modern neuroscientists that some of Freud's conclusions support the research results of current experiments. Cognitive neuroscientists, for example, identify different memory systems as *explicit* or *implicit*, which complements Freud's notion of *conscious* and *unconscious* memory.

As you can imagine, these ideas have not gone unchallenged. J. Allan Hobson, a professor of psychiatry at Harvard Medical School, argued just as forcefully that scientific investigations of Freud's concepts reveal errors in major parts of his theory. For example, most neuroscientists agree that the ego–id struggle does *not* control brain chemistry. To illustrate the wide gulf separating believers from nonbelievers, Hobson (2004) states that psychoanalytic theory is indeed comprehensive, but if it is terribly off the mark, then its comprehensiveness is hardly of any value. Perhaps the "truth" or validity of Freud's theory is less important than its impact on an evolving appreciation of biological, psychological, and social influences. Threads of Freud's theory are tightly woven into the work of other prominent theorists, such as Erikson.

L02▶ ERIKSON'S PSYCHOSOCIAL THEORY

Influenced by Freud, but searching for a different perspective, Erik Erikson developed a **psychosocial theory** of development that emphasizes the impact of social experiences on stages of human development. His seminal work, *Childhood and Society* (1963), is a perceptive and at times poetic description of human life.

Erikson's view of human development flowed from his extensive study of people living in an impressive variety of cultures: Germans, South Asians, the Sioux of South Dakota, the Yuroks of California, and wealthy adolescents in the northeastern United States (Erikson, 1959, 1968). His ideas also stem from intensive studies of historical figures such as Martin Luther (Erikson, 1958) and Mahatma Gandhi (Erikson, 1969). Erikson's theory continues to attract

Career Apps

As a teacher, how might you use fairy tales to help children grapple with their own personal fears or concerns?

considerable attention and thus remains a vital interpretation of human development.

According to Erikson, human life progresses through a series of eight stages (see Table 2.1). Each of these stages is marked by a **life crisis** that must be resolved so that the individual can move on. Erikson used the term *crisis* to signify a time of both increased vulnerability and heightened potential.

psychosocial theory Erikson's stage theory that emphasizes the impact of social experiences throughout human development.

life crisis Erikson's term to describe the main tension that individuals experience and seek to resolve during each of eight life stages.

Let's look at each stage more closely.

1. *Basic trust versus mistrust* (birth to 2 years old). In the first stage, infants develop a sense of basic trust. For Erikson, trust has an unusually broad meaning. To the trusting infant, it is not just that the world is a safe and happy place but that it is an orderly, predictable place. Infants learn about causes and effects. Trust flourishes with warmth, care, and discipline.

2. *Autonomy versus shame and doubt* (2 to 3 years old). When children are about 2 years old, they move into the second stage, characterized by the crisis of autonomy versus shame and doubt. Children begin to feed and dress themselves, and toilet training usually begins during these years. Toilet training is not the only accomplishment of the period; children of this age usually start acquiring self-control.

3. *Initiative versus guilt* (3 to 5 years old). The third crisis, initiative versus guilt, begins when children enter their fourth year. Building on their ability to control themselves, children acquire some influence over others in the family and begin to successfully manipulate their surroundings. They don't merely react, they also initiate. Erikson believed that play is particularly important during these years, to support a child's identity and as a safe way to reduce tension by dealing with problems in a symbolic way (Csikszentmihalyi & Rathunde, 1998).

identity crisis Erikson's term for a situation, usually in adolescence, that causes us to make major decisions about our identity.

4. *Industry versus inferiority* (5 to 12 years old). The fourth stage corresponds closely to the child's elementary school years. The crisis extends beyond imitating ideal models to acquiring necessary information and skills of the culture. Children expand their horizons beyond

▲ Erik Erikson

the family and begin to explore the neighborhood. Children should experience a sense of accomplishment in creating and building; otherwise, they may develop a lasting sense of inferiority.

5. *Identity versus identity confusion* (12 to 18 years old). The main task of the adolescent is to achieve a state of identity. Erikson, who originated the term **identity crisis**, used the word *identity* in a specific way. In addition to thinking of identity as the general picture one has of oneself, Erikson referred to it as a state toward which one strives. In a state of identity, the various aspects of self-image would be aligned.

6. *Intimacy versus isolation* (18 to 25 years old). In the sixth stage, intimacy with others should develop. By intimacy, Erikson means the essential ability to relate one's deepest hopes and fears to another person and to accept in turn another person's need for intimacy.

TABLE 2.1
Erikson's Psychosocial Theory of Development

Age	Stage	Psychosocial Crisis	Psychosocial Strength	Environmental Influence
Birth to 2 years	Infancy	Basic trust vs. mistrust	Hope	Maternal
2–3 years	Early childhood	Autonomy vs. shame and doubt	Willpower	Both parents or adult substitutes
3–5 years	Preschool, nursery school	Initiative vs. guilt	Purpose	Parents, family, friends
5–12 years	Middle childhood	Industry vs. inferiority	Competence	School
12–18 years	Adolescence	Identity vs. identity confusion	Fidelity	Peers
18–25 years	Young adulthood	Intimacy vs. isolation	Love	Partners, spouse/lover, friends
25–65 years	Middle age	Generativity vs. stagnation	Care	Family, society
65 years and older	Old age	Integrity vs. despair	Wisdom	All humans

7. *Generativity versus stagnation* (25 to 65 years old). Generativity means the ability to be useful to self and to society, thus leading to a sense of personal fulfillment. In this stage, individuals strive to make the world a better place for posterity in general and for their own children in particular. Many people become mentors to younger individuals, sharing their knowledge and philosophy of life. When people fail in generativity, they begin to stagnate, to become bored and self-indulgent, unable to contribute to society.

8. *Integrity versus despair* (65 years old and older). To the extent that individuals have been successful in resolving the first seven crises, they achieve a sense of personal integrity. Adults with a sense of integrity accept their lives as having been well spent. They feel a kinship with people of other cultures and of previous and future generations. They have a sense of having helped to create a more dignified life for others. If, however, people look back over their lives and feel they have made the wrong decisions, they see life as lacking integration. Despair is the result of the negative resolution of this crisis. Individuals often hide their terror of death by appearing contemptuous of humanity in general and of those of their own religion or race in particular. The character Ebenezer Scrooge in Charles Dickens's classic novel *A Christmas Carol* is a perfect example of a person experiencing despair, someone who—before being forced to examine his life—cares nothing for those around him.

Erikson's eight stages cover age periods that extend beyond the age-related stages Freud proposed, and many people find Erikson's theory intuitively makes a lot of sense.

▼ Patrick Stewart as Scrooge, who experiences despair when forced to evaluate his life.

CONTRIBUTIONS AND CRITICISM OF PSYCHOANALYTIC THEORIES

Over the years, psychoanalytic theory has contributed much to the study of lifespan development and generated much debate. Some noteworthy contributions include

- an emphasis on the early years of life as critical to human development,
- the influence of the unconscious aspects of the mind on behaviour,
- the idea that personal fears may be confronted in symbolic terms (e.g., fairy tales), and
- that changes occur throughout the entire lifespan.

Criticism includes the following:

- Unconscious thoughts or reconstructed memories may not be reliable sources of influence on development.
- Some aspects of human development are overemphasized, particularly sexual desires.
- Although the roles of family and culture are deemed highly influential, there is a bias toward Western culture as the norm against which all other cultures are evaluated.

Cognitive Theories

Unlike psychoanalytic theories, which stress the unconscious or invisible workings of the mind, cognitive theorists such as Jean Piaget and Lev Vygotsky chose to focus on people's conscious thought processes. Other theorists agree with information-processing theory, which considers actions from a more mechanical standpoint.

PIAGET'S COGNITIVE DEVELOPMENTAL THEORY ◀L03

The Swiss psychologist Jean Piaget's (1896–1980) training as a biologist had a major impact on his thinking about cognitive development. While working in Paris, field-testing questions for a standardized intelligence test, Piaget became fascinated with the thought processes that led children to make incorrect answers in reasoning tests. This caused him to turn his attention to the analysis of children's developing intelligence. Rather than focusing on test scores, Piaget focused on the process by which children actively construct meaning in their environments. Piaget was the first psychologist to systematically study cognitive development and to argue that thought processes influence human behaviour in distinctly different ways throughout the lifespan.

Have you ever been in a restaurant and wondered why a very young infant who accidentally knocks a toy off her highchair tray makes no attempt to find it, whereas a slightly older infant will try to find the toy

▲ Much of Piaget's work developed based on his systematic observations.

or even purposefully drop a toy repeatedly and expect someone to pick it up? This apparently simple behaviour, and many other behaviours like it, fascinated Piaget, who formulated his theory of development based on systematic, close observations of his own children. In the example above, the older infant is exhibiting an understanding of **object permanence**, the realization that objects continue to exist even when they cannot be seen, heard, or touched. In Piaget's theory, object permanence is an important developmental accomplishment of an infant's first 2 years of life. Piaget viewed development as consisting of four distinct, increasingly sophisticated stages of mental representation that individuals pass through on their way to adulthood.

object permanence The realization that objects continue to exist even when they cannot be seen, heard, or touched.

cognitive structures Piaget's term to describe the basic tools of cognitive development.

adaptation A mechanism that consists of the two functional invariants—assimilation and accommodation—in Piaget's theory.

assimilation Piaget's term to describe the manner in which we incorporate data into our cognitive structures.

accommodation Piaget's term to describe the manner by which cognitive structures change.

equilibration Piaget's term to describe the balance between assimilation and accommodation.

schemes Piaget's term for organized patterns of thought and action.

Piaget's Stages

Piaget believed that development occurs as we cultivate increasingly effective **cognitive structures**, mental representations that enable us to organize and adapt to our world. He also believed that individuals form more sophisticated cognitive structures as they pass through four stages: the *sensorimotor stage* (birth to 2 years old); the *preoperational stage* (2 to 7 years old); the *concrete operational stage* (7 to 11 years old); and the *formal operational stage* (11 years old and older). (See Table 2.2.) Piaget believed that cognitive structures begin as responses to concrete phenomena—babies know only what they can touch, taste, or see. Our

ability to use symbols and to think abstractly increases with each stage until we are able to manipulate abstract concepts and consider complex hypothetical alternatives.

Piaget stated that we are able to form cognitive structures because we have inherited a method of intellectual functioning that permits us to respond to our environment. At the heart of this method is the mechanism of **adaptation**.

Piaget believed that adaptation consists of **assimilation** and **accommodation**. When we assimilate something, we incorporate it; we take it in. Think of eating; we take food into the structure of our mouths and change it to fit the shape of our mouths, throats, and digestive tracts. We take objects, concepts, and events into our minds similarly, incorporating this new information to fit our existing mental structures. For example, you are now studying Piaget's views on cognitive development. These ideas are unique and will require effort to understand them. You may attempt to comprehend them by fitting them to the concepts you already know.

Humans also change as a result of accommodation, that is, the adaptation of existing ways of understanding to new information. Just as the food we eat produces biochemical changes, the stimuli we incorporate into our minds produce mental changes. While we change what we take in, we are also changed by it.

Thus, the adaptive process is the heart of Piaget's explanation of learning. As we encounter new information, we try to strike a balance between assimilation and accommodation, a process that is called **equilibration**. By continued interaction with the environment, we correct these mistakes and change our cognitive structures (we have accommodated) into organized patterns of thought and action, which Piaget referred to as **schemes**.

TABLE 2.2

Piaget's Stages of Cognitive Development

Stage	Age	Major Feature
Sensorimotor	Birth to 2 years	Infants' sensory experiences with the environment form patterns that lead to cognitive structures; object permanence develops.
Preoperational	2 to 7 years	Use of symbols; rapid language growth.
Concrete operational	7 to 11 years	Can reason about physical objects.
Formal operational	11+ years	Abstract thinking leads to reasoning with more complex symbols.

Angels All Around Us

The idea of angels—beings that protect us, guide us, or provide for us—has been accepted across cultures for thousands upon thousands of years. Whether the term is most often used to describe earthly creatures or heavenly messengers, there is universal appreciation of (if not blatant belief in) angels among different nationalities, cultures, and ethnicities. It is fascinating that so many believe in angels when this concept defies rational thinking. For example, some young children may believe that the tooth fairy turns teeth into treasure in the form of coins or cash. Some young children may believe that Santa Claus delivers gifts to their homes once a year. Children's thought processes develop to a point where they eventually realize that these "angels" are not real. Yet some adults believe in religious angels who, for example, acted as messengers relating to specific biblical events, record our present-day good or bad actions, or are responsible for earthly elements of wind, fire, and water.

As you read the two examples that follow, think about how the concept of angels incorporates aspects of assimilation and/or accommodation, and how we actively construct meaning in order to make sense of new ideas or experiences.

1. A woman's car won't start and she is parked in an Ottawa parking lot in temperatures of -20 degrees Celsius. Her cell phone battery is drained so she is unable to call for assistance. A man who is also parked in that lot brings over a portable car battery charger and brings her car to life.
2. An earthquake in Haiti devastates the homes and lives of hundreds of thousands of people. Learning of the event and the tragic aftermath through traditional and social media, Canadians donate hundreds of millions of dollars to the relief effort.

Try thinking of Piaget's theory in the following way: Stimuli come from the environment and are filtered through the activities of adaptation and assimilation. For example, you may have had your own idea of what intelligence is, but now you change your structures relating to intelligence because of your new knowledge about Piaget. Your content or behaviour changes because of the changes in your cognitive structures. The following summarizes Piaget's cognitive process:

Environment
filtered through
↓
Assimilation and Accommodation
produce
↓
Cognitive Structures
which combine with behaviour to form
↓
Schemes
(organized patterns of thought and action)

VYGOTSKY'S SOCIOCULTURAL THEORY ◀L04

The work of the Russian psychologist Lev Vygotsky (1896–1934) has attracted considerable attention because of his emphasis on social processes. Born in Russia in 1896, the same year as Piaget, Vygotsky was educated at Moscow University and quickly turned his attention to educational psychology, developmental psychology, and psychopathology. For Vygotsky, the clues to understanding mental development lie in children's social processes. He proposed that development depends on children's interactions with the adults around them.

Tragically, tuberculosis ended Vygotsky's life in 1934. His work today, because of its cultural emphasis, is more popular than it was in his lifetime. In contrast to Piaget, who believed that children function as "little scientists" investigating their own hypotheses as they make sense of the world, Vygotsky turned to social interactions to explain children's cognitive development.

*Through others, we become ***ourselves***.*

LEV VYGOTSKY

Vygotsky identified dual paths of cognitive development—*elementary processes*, which are basically biological, and *psychological processes*, which are essentially sociocultural (Vygotsky, 1978). Children's behaviours emerge from the intertwining of these two paths. For example, brain development provides the mechanism for the appearance of external or visible speech (evidence of a child's thinking), which gradually becomes the internal speech children use to guide their behaviour.

Three fundamental themes run through Vygotsky's work: the unique manner in which he identified and used the concept of development, the social origin of mind, and the role of speech in cognitive development.

1. At the heart of Vygotsky's theory is his belief that elementary biological processes are qualitatively transformed into higher psychological functioning by developmental processes. In other words, such behaviours as speech, thought, and learning are biological at the core, yet are manifested in the context of psychological functions.

2. To understand cognitive development, Vygotsky believed we must examine the social and cultural processes shaping children. Vygotsky argued that any function in a child's cultural development appears twice, on two planes: first, in an interpsychological category (social exchanges with others), and second, within the child as an intrapsychological category (using inner speech to guide behaviour).

   What happens to transform an external activity to an internal activity? For Vygotsky, the answer lies in the phenomenon of internalization—when we observe something (behaviours, customs, rules) and then make it part of our own repertoire over time.

3. Although Vygotsky lacked hard data to explain it, he believed that speech is one of the most powerful tools humans use to progress developmentally. He wrote, "The most significant moment in the course of intellectual development … occurs when speech and practical activity, two previously completely independent lines of development, converge" (Vygotsky, 1978, p. 24). Speech allows us to ask questions, explain our thoughts, feelings, and actions, and connect with other members of family and society.

zone of proximal development (ZPD) Vygotsky's term for a range of ability in a given task, where the higher limit is achieved through interaction with others.

information-processing theory Cognitive theory that uses a computer metaphor to understand how the human mind processes information.

▲ Lev Vygotsky

Vygotsky's concept of the **zone of proximal development (ZPD)** exemplifies the influence of social interaction and connections with others on cognitive development. Vygotsky described a range of ability for a given task, where the bottom of the range represents the actual ability a child might have on a given day, and the top of the range represents the level of ability a child might reach after working with a teacher, mentor, or peer. The social interaction will result in benefits that the child would not have experienced if he or she had worked alone. The ZPD is not limited to children. At any age we may learn a new skill and greatly benefit from support or guidance from a more experienced person.

Researcher Barbara Rogoff has investigated the role of culture in learning, specifically cultural variation in learning processes such as observation. Rogoff's work complements that of Vygotsky, and she shares Vygosky's interest in topics such as collaboration, social interaction, and the influence of mentoring on learning. Her book *Apprenticeship in Thinking* (1991) examines cognitive development in a sociocultural context and is noteworthy because it draws from a variety of her strengths as a contemporary researcher. Rogoff's work is distinctive for drawing from a variety of disciplines, including anthropology, cultural psychology, and research on communication, and contributes to a body of knowledge and solid data about the influence of social and cultural forces.

Table 2.3 summarizes the key differences between Piaget's and Vygotsky's theories.

INFORMATION-PROCESSING THEORY

Distinct from the theories of Piaget and Vygotsky for several reasons, **information-processing theory** contributes another lens through which to consider human thinking. This theory is not attributed to one individual but,

PERSPECTIVES ON **DIVERSITY**

Respect for Culture

Canadian psychologists must be especially sensitive to the influence of culture on behaviour given the multicultural nature of our country. For example, is an individual who claims that he is hearing voices of people who are not physically present showing symptoms of a delusional disorder? From a Western, non-Aboriginal perspective, a psychologist might conclude this to be the case. However, this individual may be part of a culture in which being able to hear disembodied voices is a gift and is seen as evidence that the person is in touch with the spirit world. It is important for Canadian psychologists to take an individual's culture into account before making a diagnosis and prescribing a treatment.

rather, is a broader way of examining cognitive development using the computer as a metaphor. Neither Piaget nor Vygotsky could have imagined computers as we know them today, let alone the important influence that computers would have on psychologists' understandings of cognition. Just as computers perform operations based on their hardware and software, the human brain performs operations based on cognitive structures and thought processes (Bjorkland, 2005).

Information-processing theory is not a stage theory but, rather, a theory of processing capacity. Throughout our lifespan, we develop an increasing capacity for processing information. We are therefore able to perform more complicated tasks as we acquire the knowledge and skills needed

TABLE 2.3

Key Differences Between Theories: Piaget and Vygotsky

	Piaget	Vygotsky
Perspective	Individual child constructs view of world by forming cognitive structures—"the little scientist."	Child's cognitive development progresses by social interactions with others—"social origins of mind."
Basic Psychological Mechanism	Equilibration—child acts to regain equilibrium between external stimuli and the current level of cognitive structures.	Social interaction encourages development through the guidance of skillful adults.
Language	Emerges as cognitive structures develop.	Begins as preintellectual speech and develops into sophisticated form of inner speech; one of the main forces of cognitive development.
Learning	Assimilation and accommodation lead to equilibrium.	Results from the interaction of biological elementary processes and sociocultural interactions.
Problem-Solving	Child independently searches for data needed to change cognitive structures, enabling child to reach solution.	Two aspects of problem-solving—key role of speech to guide "planful" behaviour and joint efforts with others.

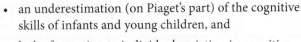

Career Apps

As an early childhood educator in a multicultural country, how might you help children of recent immigrants learn about and adapt to Canadian customs and norms while also respecting the culture of their parents?

classical conditioning
The learning process in which a neutral stimulus produces an involuntary response that is usually elicited by another stimulus.

to do so. For example, a young child may need to pay careful attention as she learns to tie her shoes. With practice and repetition, the child will soon need to pay less attention to the task and is later able to tie her shoes with minimal effort. The same may be said for a teenager learning to drive a car—at first the teen must pay close attention to every hand and foot movement as she coordinates the car's equipment. With practice and experience, the teen will be able to drive with minimal effort, perhaps singing along to favorite tunes on the radio. As you can see, the age of an individual does not matter as much as the specific task. An adult can be an expert or a novice at a task in the same way a child is an expert or novice.

Experts on the subject of information-processing theory, such as D. E. Broadbent (1954) and Robert Siegler (1996), have evolved specific positions on the theory. While Broadbent's work emphasizes the role of selective attention, Siegler's work focuses on the increasing variety of mental processes that we have to draw upon as we age. Consistent with a computer model, information-processing theorists agree that humans perceive, encode, represent, store, and retrieve information. The process repeats itself from situation to situation, and the more strategies we have at our disposal, the quicker and more successfully we are able to think.

CONTRIBUTIONS AND CRITICISM OF COGNITIVE THEORIES

Cognitive theories have contributed to a greater understanding of human development. Some key contributions include:

- a view of people as active participants in constructing knowledge and meaning,
- conscious efforts to understand the world lead to advances in development, and
- viewing biological structures as influenced by social forces, which, in turn, influence our biology.

Some criticisms of cognitive theories include:

- an underestimation (on Piaget's part) of the cognitive skills of infants and young children, and
- lack of attention to individual variation in cognitive development, especially based on cultural and family background.

The Behavioural Approach ◀L05

A strictly behavioural explanation of human development argues that only what can be observed and measured may be scientifically studied. This approach takes us into the world of learning and learning theory. Some of its best-known proponents are Ivan Pavlov (1849–1936) and John Watson (1878–1958) for their work with classical conditioning, B. F. Skinner (1904–1990) for his insights into the role of reinforcement, and Albert Bandura (b. 1925), who called our attention to the power of modelling in development.

PAVLOV'S AND WATSON'S CLASSICAL CONDITIONING

Behavioural theorists argue that development is observable behaviour that can be learned over time. Pavlov had observed that dogs would salivate when they ate food. He also noticed that they would begin to salivate when they heard certain sounds (such as a food cupboard door opening or closing) or saw certain things (such as a person retrieving a food dish) associated with eating. He designed a famous experiment in which the ringing of a bell was paired with food being presented to dogs. Over time, the dogs learned to salivate merely at the ringing of the bell. Pavlov's experiment is noteworthy because he showed that an involuntary response (salivating) could be elicited through a specific learning process. Pavlov called this learning **classical conditioning**.

John Watson shared an interest in classical conditioning but focused on human beings rather than animals. Watson conducted a famous experiment in which he conditioned an infant ("Little Albert") to fear a white rat. Every time Albert played with the rat, a loud noise was made behind him, startling him and causing him to cry. Over time, as play with the rat was paired with the loud noise, Albert began to cry at the mere sight of the rat. Unfortunately, ethical codes of conduct of the sort that exist today were not considered at the time of this experiment. Albert would not have been subjected to repeated upset in a modern

▲ Ivan Pavlov

version of this study, yet the significance of Watson's work must be acknowledged for the attention it brought to human behaviour and the ways in which we are conditioned in our everyday lives.

SKINNER'S OPERANT CONDITIONING

Convinced of the importance of reinforcement, Skinner developed an explanation of learning that stressed the consequences of behaviour—the effects of actions are all-important. Reinforcement, defined as anything that makes a response more likely to happen in the future, has proven to be a powerful tool in the developing, shaping,

▲ B. F. Skinner

and controlling of behaviour in numerous contexts. Prominent in North American psychology for over 60 years, B. F. Skinner inspired and stimulated research and theory.

Skinner preferred the term *reinforcement* to reward and identified two kinds of reinforcement. **Positive reinforcement** refers to any event that, when it occurs after a response, makes that response more likely to happen in the future. **Negative reinforcement** is any event that, when it ceases to occur after a response, makes that response more likely to happen in the future. Note that both types of reinforcement make a response more likely to happen. Giving a child candy for doing the right thing is positive reinforcement. Ceasing to twist your brother's arm when he gives you back your pen is negative reinforcement. The presence or absence of the stimulus causes increase or decrease in behaviour. Thus human development is the result of the continuous flow of learning that comes about from the operant conditioning we receive from the environment every day.

In Skinner's theory, the concept of **operant conditioning** has a large influence on learning. Operant conditioning refers to behaviour or actions that we do voluntarily and how the use of consequences can modify or shape such behaviour. A simple example from everyday life is the notion of a "customer reward program." Many stores, restaurants, and credit cards offer customers points that they can use on future visits or to acquire other items. The more you shop at that store, the more points you acquire. You are rewarded for your purchases, and the likelihood that you will repeat your shopping behaviour is greater with this incentive. Skinner argued that the environment (parents, teachers, peers) reacts to our behaviour and either reinforces or eliminates that behaviour. Consequently, the environment holds the key to understanding behaviour.

Skinner argued that if the environment reinforces a particular behaviour, that action is more likely to occur the next time that the individual is in the same setting. His famous "Skinner box" became renowned for making visible the power of reinforcement on lab rats' behaviours. Skinner devised a box in which rats would receive food pellets when they pushed a certain lever (see Figure 2.2). The rats' behaviour indicated that they learned to push the lever in order to acquire more food.

Skinner also used the terms *punishment* and *extinction* in his discussion of operant conditioning. **Punishment** refers to a decrease in behaviours when an unpleasant response follows the behaviour. **Extinction** is the systematic way in which behaviours are conditioned out of a person's behaviour. In a human scenario, if a teacher repeats a particular question, a student is more likely to give the right answer, because that response was reinforced (the student feels happy and proud). If the response is punished, the response is less likely in the future (the student feels sad and humiliated). If the response is simply ignored, it also becomes less likely in the future (the student learns that her effort is not recognized).

Skinner's ideas about change in human behaviour have been enhanced

positive reinforcement An event that increases the likelihood of a desired response in the future.

negative reinforcement An event that, when it ceases to occur, makes that response more likely to happen in the future.

operant conditioning The use of consequences (reinforcement, punishment) to modify or shape voluntary behaviour or actions.

punishment Process by which an unpleasant response is paired with an undesired behaviour to decrease the likelihood of that behaviour occurring in the future.

extinction The systematic process in which behaviours are de-conditioned or eliminated.

FIGURE 2.2

Skinner Box

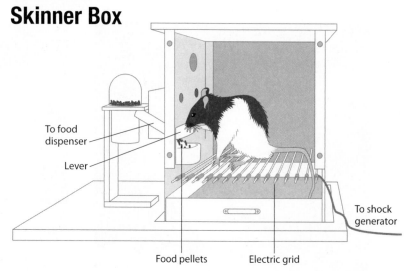

To food dispenser

Lever

Food pellets

Electric grid

To shock generator

modelling Bandura's term for observational learning.

observational learning Bandura's term to explain the information we obtain from observing other people, things, and events.

social (cognitive) learning theory Bandura's explanation for the process whereby the information we glean from observing others influences our behaviour.

self-efficacy A person's belief that she can behave in a certain way to achieve a desired goal.

by the work of Albert Bandura, who expanded the behaviourist view to cover social behaviour.

BANDURA'S SOCIAL COGNITIVE LEARNING

Alberta native Albert Bandura, one of the chief architects of social learning theory, has stressed the potent influence of **modelling** on personality development (Bandura, 1997). He called this **observational learning**. In a famous statement on **social (cognitive) learning theory**, Bandura and Walters (1963) cited evidence to show that learning occurs through observing others, even when the observers do not imitate the model's responses at that time and get no reinforcement. For Bandura, observational learning means that the information we get from observing other people, things, and events influences the way we act (Bjorklund, 2005).

Social learning theory has particular relevance for development. As Bandura noted, children do not always do what adults tell them to do but rather what they see adults do. If Bandura's assumptions are correct, adults can be a potent force in shaping the behaviour of children because of what they do.

The importance of models is seen in Bandura's interpretation of what happens as a result of observing others:

Children may acquire new responses, including socially appropriate behaviours.

Observation of models may strengthen or weaken existing responses.

Observation of a model may cause the reappearance of responses that were seemingly forgotten.

▲ Albert Bandura

If children witness undesirable behaviour that is either rewarded or goes unpunished, undesirable behaviour may result. The reverse is also true.

Bandura, Ross, and Ross (1963) studied the relative effects of live models, films of human aggression, and films of cartoon aggression on preschool children's aggressive behaviour in the classic Bobo doll experiment. The films of human adult models displayed aggression toward an inflated doll; in the filmed cartoon aggression, a cartoon character displayed the same aggression. Later, all the children who observed the aggression were more aggressive than children in the control group. This experiment has serious implications for how modelling can be a powerful force in development. Children are influenced by live models, as well as by behaviours they observe in the media.

Another example of the power of Bandura's ideas is seen in the concept of **self-efficacy**—a person's belief that she can behave in a certain way to achieve a desired goal. Bandura and colleagues (2001) believe that a child's sense of self-efficacy helps him to produce desired

▼ Bandura's Bobo doll study showed that children model aggressive behaviour.

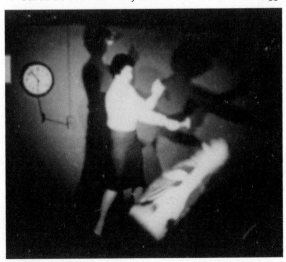

TAKE A **STAND**

Does Playing Violent Video Games Lead to Aggression?

The debate over exposure to violent video games has led to arguments linking the playing of such games to more aggressive behaviour among children and young adults. The school shootings at Columbine High School in Colorado in 1999 and Sandy Hook Elementary School in Connecticut in 2012 have both been linked to the shooters' love of violent video games—first-person shooter games in particular. According to behavioural theory, players of such games would model the behaviour that they see in these games in their real lives. Playing these games may also reinforce feelings of pride and accomplishment in the player as they keep track of how many kills they have accumulated. A groundbreaking study by Anderson and Dill (2000) indeed showed that playing violent video games increased both aggressive thoughts and behaviour in players.

Is it too simplistic to blame violent video games for the aggressive acts that teens and young adults commit? Two of the earliest school shootings in Canada occurred in 1975 at Brampton Centennial Secondary School in Brampton, Ontario, and at St. Pius X High School in Ottawa, Ontario, before such video games existed. Furthermore, while much of the research into this topic shows short-term effects on aggression from playing violent video games, the long-term effects are somewhat less clear and social scientists also acknowledge that those individuals who are already naturally aggressive appear more likely to seek out such games to begin with (known as the selection hypothesis) (Carey, 2013).

However, researchers at Brock University in St. Catharines, Ontario, recently found that there were long-term effects on the aggression of high school students from playing violent video games that could not be explained by the selection hypothesis (Willoughby, Adachi, & Good, 2012).

Undoubtedly, the debate will continue to rage on in both psychology and in society at large about the effects of violent video games on children and young adults. Do you believe that playing violent video games causes aggressive behaviour? Would you let your child play violent video games? Can you think of other factors that may contribute to the aggression of children and young adults?

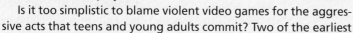

outcomes that might otherwise elude him. Unless children—and adults—believe that their actions will attain desired goals, they have little incentive to act and certainly will not persist in the face of difficulty. Bjorklund (2005) believes that Bandura's ideas testify to the significance of the interaction between a child's cognitive and social worlds.

Because the important role of biology in human development was dismissed, operant conditioning eventually lost its appeal to developmental biologists (Cairns & Cairns, 2006). The idea of a bioecological model of human development became more widely accepted in the mainstream of modern science.

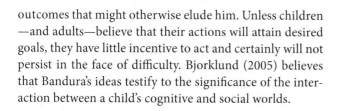

We as a nation need to be reeducated about the necessary and sufficient conditions for making human beings **human**. We need to be reeducated not as parents—but as workers, neighbors, and friends; and as members of the organizations, committees, boards—and, especially, the informal networks that control our social institutions and thereby determine the conditions of life for our families and their **children**.

URI BRONFENBRENNER (1978)

LO6 ▶ A Bioecological Model

Physical, cognitive, and social factors interact in ways that we are only beginning to comprehend. For example, psychologists recognize the importance of **reciprocal interactions** in development. Reciprocal interactions are our responses to others around us, which causes changes in those other people. Their responses to us then change, which in turn produces new changes in us. These don't rely exclusively on either heredity or environment. Rather, the interactions between the two help describe and explain developmental changes that occur from birth, if not sooner.

Thanks to the systems analysis of Uri Bronfenbrenner (1917–2005), we now realize that there are many environments (also called systems) acting on us. Bronfenbrenner's perspective is called the **bioecological model**, defined as the continuity and change in the biopsychosocial characteristics of human beings, both as individuals and as groups. The bioecological model contains four major components. The first component, *proximal processes*, refers to the reciprocal interactions between a person and the environment (often called the *context* of development). Feeding and playing with a child, peer play, and school learning with teachers are all examples of proximal processes. Bronfenbrenner and Morris (1998, 2006) refer to proximal processes as the primary engines of development.

The second component is the *person* involved, especially an individual's temperament or disposition that activates the proximal processes. Third is the person's *context*, those environmental features that either foster or interfere with development. Finally, developmental changes occur over *time*, the fourth component of the bioecological model. Bronfenbrenner realized that most theories represent development in snapshots of developmental periods, so to speak. He recognized that the passing of time greatly influences people throughout their lives as they interact with their surroundings.

Bronfenbrenner visualized the environment as a set of nested systems, each inside the next, as shown in Figure 2.3.

He identified the innermost environmental system as the **microsystem** (for example, the home or school). Next is the **mesosystem**, which refers to the relationship among microsystems. A good example is seen in a child's school achievement. Those

▲ Uri Bronfenbrenner

children who are fortunate enough to be in a family that maintains positive relationships with the school tend to do well in their classwork.

The **exosystem**, Bronfenbrenner's next level, is an environment in which the developing person is not actually present but that nevertheless affects development. One example is a teenager who has a friend whose parents, unlike her own parents, are relaxed about curfews, don't pressure their daughter to complete assignments, and so on. These different parenting practices may eventually cause conflict between the teen and her parents. The **macrosystem**, Bronfenbrenner's final level, is the blueprint of any society, a kind of master plan for human development within

FIGURE 2.3

Bioecological Theory

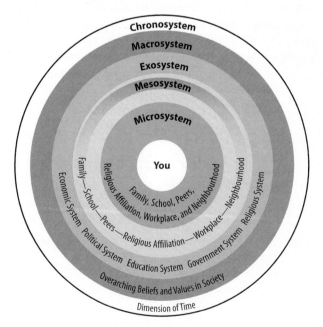

---

reciprocal interactions Our responses to others around us, which causes changes in those other people; their responses to us then change, which in turn produces new changes in us.

bioecological model The continuity and change in the biopsychosocial characteristics of human beings, both as individuals and as groups.

microsystem According to Bronfenbrenner, the innermost environment for the developing individual, such as the home or school.

mesosystem The relationship among different microsystems; for example, between the quality of school that a child attends and the neighbourhood in which they reside.

exosystem Environment in which the developing person is not present but that nevertheless affects development.

macrosystem The blueprint for the cultural experiences of people within any society.

that society. Think for a moment about the experiences of people in the mainland Chinese society differ from the experiences of Canadian citizens.

These systems do not remain isolated from one another but interact over time (sometimes called the *chronosystem*). An example is a child whose father has just lost his job (changes in the exosystem), which then causes the family to move to another location with different friends and schools for the child (changes in the micro- and mesosystems). These examples illustrate how a bioecological analysis emphasizes the role of context in development.

THE IMPORTANCE OF GENES

Supporting the importance of acknowledging complex interactions between systems, Rutter (2002b) has presented a threefold argument stressing that, although genes are at the heart of all psychological traits, it is the interaction of biological, psychological, and social influences that explains behaviour.

1. Given today's remarkable scientific advances, there is little disagreement about the influence of genes. But even from a biological perspective, the real challenge is to discover how genetic influences and brain functions, for example, are altered by experience.

2. Emerging genetic evidence clearly illustrates the significance of *nongenetic* influences. As Rutter notes, even with those traits that are most powerfully influenced by genetic forces, environmental effects are far from trivial.

3. Finally, the same genetic factors may be involved in different types of childhood psychopathology, for example, anxiety and depression.

Developmental Theory: Current Status and Future Directions ◂ L07

A persistent criticism of traditional theorists such as Piaget and Freud is that they were simply too one-dimensional to explain the complexity of development. That is, they focused on only one aspect of development. For example, Piaget focused solely on cognitive development, and Freud spent his lifetime delving into the role of the unconscious in development. But as Lerner (1988) noted, in modern developmental theories, the person is not simply "biologized, psychologized, or sociologized." Such focused viewpoints, however much they help clarify the processes involved in development, present an inadequate portrayal of the richness and vigor of the human lifespan. The nuances of human development cannot be captured by theories limited to one facet of development: motor, cognitive, or language. To address this situation, psychologists have proposed a developmental systems theory, one that encompasses previously hard-won knowledge and searches for explanations in the relationships among the multiple levels that contribute to development (Lewis, 2000). According to this view, to describe and understand the changes that take place over the lifespan, we must pay attention to all the levels at which change can occur and focus on the interactions among these changes.

INTERACTIONS AMONG LEVELS OF DEVELOPMENT

Developmental psychologists currently analyze activity at four levels: genetic, neural, behavioural, and environmental (Gottlieb, 1997; Gottlieb, Wahlsten, & Lickliter, 2006). With close attention paid to the interactions among these levels, the biopsychosocial nature of development is illustrated as new understandings (and new questions) continue to emerge.

Genes produce a particular physical makeup that contributes to a person's behaviour, helping that individual to select a particular environment (peers, activities, and such). One of the world's leading researchers into the importance of genetics in the development of diabetes in Canadian Aboriginal peoples is Dr. Robert Hegele from the Robarts Research Institute in London, Ontario. Hegele and his team have discovered the molecular genetic basis for type 2 diabetes in the Oji-Cree population (Hegele, Cao, Harris, Hanley, & Zinman, 1999). But the environment also acts to influence behaviour, physical status, and even genetic activity. In the case of type 2 diabetes, in addition to genes, the actual foods that people consume (part of the environment) and each individual's eating habits (behaviour) are also factors. In other words, each level interacts with all other levels.

DEVELOPMENTAL SYSTEMS THEORY

It's clear that heredity and environment produce results in a complex, interactive manner that supports the idea of reciprocal interactions. It appears that there are no simple cause-and-effect explanations of development. All humans—children, adolescents, and adults—experience a constant state of reorganization as they move through the life cycle (Lerner, Fisher, & Weinberg, 2000).

Developmental systems theory was popularized by Richard Lerner (1991, 1998, 2002, 2006) and Gilbert Gottlieb (1997). The current version attributed to Gottlieb, Douglas Wahlsten, and Robert Lickliter (2006) argues that all of our characteristics (biological, psychological, and social) function by reciprocal interactions with the environment (a.k.a., context). In this way, developmental systems theory leads to the belief that we *construct* our view of the surrounding world.

Lerner (2002) emphasized that developmental systems theory requires three levels of analysis:

1. Knowledge of the characteristics of those being studied

2. Understanding of a person's context and a justification for why this portion of the context is significant for analysis

3. Conceptualization of the relationship between individual characteristics and the portion of the context

Exchanges between individuals and the multiple levels of their complex contexts propel development (Horowitz, 2000; Lerner & Ashman, 2006). (See Figure 2.4.) The crucial aspect of development is therefore the changing relationship between our own complexity and a multi-layered context. No single level of organization is seen as the primary or the ultimate causal influence on behaviour and development (Dixon & Lerner, 1999). Although developmental systems theory exemplifies current changes in the search for developmental explanations, other ideas continue to emerge.

FIGURE 2.4

Developmental Contextual Model

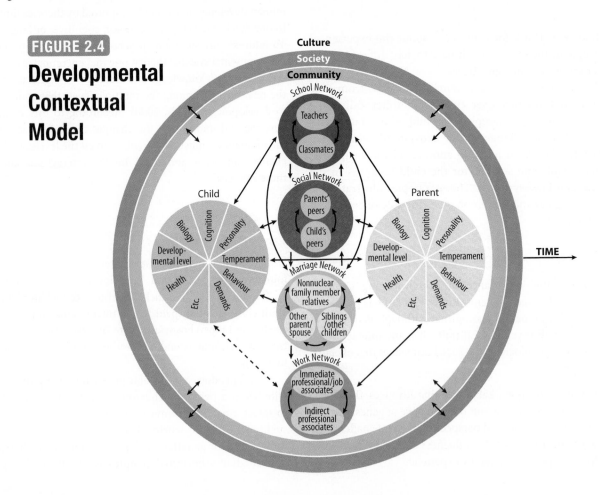

UNIQUE THEORIES OF DEVELOPMENT

While all of the theories discussed so far have a distinct approach to understanding human development, the following theories do not fall into one of the broader theoretical categories but, rather, stand alone as influential in the field. **Life course theory**, proposed by Glen Elder, refers to a sequence of socially defined, age-graded events and roles that individuals enact over time. For example, it is common for a young adult to take on the roles of worker, spouse/partner, and parent, while a middle-aged adult may become a mentor at work and a grandparent. The assumption of these roles can have profound effects on behaviour, such as the young adult becoming more responsible or the middle-aged adult becoming more empathic and nurturing. Life course researchers must

- change from studying children alone to a strategy that focuses on aging over the entire life course;

- rethink how human lives are organized and evolve over time, while searching for patterns of constancy and change;

- relate an individual's life course to an ever-changing society, stressing the developmental changes brought about by this interaction (Elder & Shanahan, 2006).

Evolutionary developmental psychology is an explanation of development that assumes our physiological and psychological systems resulted from evolution by selection. In 1859, Charles Darwin published *On the Origin of Species*, in which he concluded that natural selection is the basic principle of change. Evolutionary theory suggests that psychological mechanisms evolved to bring about specific adaptive functions. It's the study of how our genes are expressed during development and how the context of development influences the expression of genetic action. **Evolutionary developmental psychology** can be defined as the use of principles of Darwinian evolution, particularly natural selection, to explain human development. It involves the physiological and psychological mechanisms that underlie universal development.

Evolutionary developmental psychology has also received support from what has been called the cognitive revolution. Widely and wildly popular with psychologists, studies of cognition provided respectability to explanations of behaviour that were not immediately visible, such as memory and thought processes (Geary & Bjorklund, 2000). Evolutionary psychology brings together revolutionary ideas in science— the cognitive revolution that began in the 1950s and 1960s, which helped us to understand why we have the kind of mind we do, and theories of Darwin, which explained how only the fittest of a species survive. However, as other theories have asserted, environmental factors are important in development, and biology is not our destiny. The work of Harvard professor Steven Pinker, who was born and raised in Montreal and completed his undergraduate degree at McGill University, exemplifies evolutionary developmental psychology, as he considers the development of language in humans to be an adaptive function that evolved through natural selection (Pinker, 1994). However, as we will discuss in later chapters, environment also plays a significant role in language acquisition.

Humanistic psychologist Abraham Maslow's hierarchy of needs (1987), while not a distinctly developmental theory, emphasizes the importance of growing and developing as a person to achieve one's potential. According to Maslow, there are five types of needs: physiological (hunger and sleep), safety (security, protection, stability, and freedom from fear and anxiety), love and belonging (need for family and friends), esteem (positive opinion of self as well as positive opinion of others), and self-actualization (doing all that we think we are capable of doing). (See Figure 2.5.) In Maslow's estimation, only approximately 2% of the world population will ever reach this highest level.

> **life course theory** Theory referring to a sequence of socially defined, age-graded events and roles that individuals enact over time.
>
> **evolutionary developmental psychology** Explanation of development that rests on the assumption that our physiological and psychological systems resulted from evolution by selection.

FIGURE 2.5

Maslow's Hierarchy of Needs

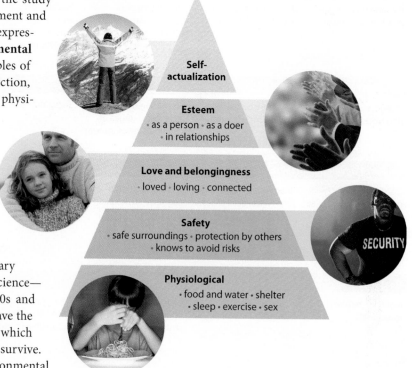

Self-actualization

Esteem
- as a person · as a doer
- in relationships

Love and belongingness
- loved · loving · connected

Safety
- safe surroundings · protection by others
- knows to avoid risks

Physiological
- food and water · shelter
- sleep · exercise · sex

SECURITY

What does Maslow's theory look like in everyday life? Examples of Maslow's theory in action are as follows:

Physiological needs. A child goes to school without eating breakfast in the morning and must summon the energy and focus to accomplish the same tasks as his peers. (How can the child generate the energy and focus required to succeed in the classroom?)

Safety needs. A single parent gets laid off from work and is forced to choose between paying for the heating bill and buying groceries for his family, knowing that whichever choice he makes will lead to severe problems for his loved ones. (How can this dad feel like he's contributing to society and a source of pride to his children?)

Love and belonging needs. A mother moves to a new city and, even though she works part-time and has a loving spouse, feels lonely as she cares for her toddler each day. (How can she find a group of peers to provide support and stimulation as she transitions into her new community?)

Self-esteem needs. A grandfather invites his family on a group vacation to celebrate his 40th wedding anniversary, affording him the chance to function as the patriarch of the group. (How does one express pride and authority among a group of people who have grown over time and have developed different expectations for his role as father and grandfather?)

Self-actualization. A Canadian celebrity decides to leave his mansion in the Rosedale neighbourhood of Toronto and dedicate two years of his life to working with African children who have lost parents to AIDS. (How might he reconcile the creative energy required for his work as an actor and high-profile personality with the realistic demands on his energy, time, and persona in this specific context?)

In an effort to be all we can be, we must consider the needs that must be met on different levels in order for anyone to achieve the ultimate source of satisfaction and generativity. Table 2.4 summarizes the theories of development we have discussed in this chapter.

TABLE 2.4
Comparing Theories of Development

Psychoanalytic	Psychosocial	Cognitive	Cultural	Behavioural	Contextual
Major Figures					
Freud	Erikson	Piaget	Vygotsky	Skinner, Bandura	Lerner
Major Ideas					
Passage through the psychosexual stages	Passage through the psychosocial stages	Development of cognitive structures through stages of cognitive development	Social processes embedded within a culture influence development	Power of operant conditioning; role of modelling in development	Development occurs as an individual's characteristics interact with that person's context
Essential Features					
Id, ego, superego; psychosexual stages	Psychosocial crises; psychosocial stages	Formation of cognitive structures; stages of cognitive development	Social processes	Reinforcement of responses; observational learning (modelling)	Interaction among multiple levels of development
Source of Developmental Problems					
Conflict during development leads to fixation, regression, and personality problems	Inadequate resolution of psychosocial crises	Weak formation of cognitive structures	Environmental support lacking or insufficient	Lack of reinforcement, incorrect pairing of stimuli and responses	Faulty exchanges between the individual and the multiple levels of the context
Goal					
Sexually mature individual	A sense of personal integrity	Satisfactory formation and use of cognitive structures	Recognition and use of social processes to guide development	Acquisition of conditioned acts to fulfill needs	Satisfactory relationships between the individual and a multilayered context

FROM NEURONS TO NEIGHBORHOODS

The study done in 2000 by the National Research Council Institute of Medicine and published in the book *From Neurons to Neighborhoods: The Science of Early Childhood Development*, edited by Jack Shonkoff and Deborah Phillips, has been highly regarded as an attempt to synthesize nearly 50 years of early childhood development research with the goal of improving policies aimed at raising and educating young children. The following 10 statements, taken from the study, synthesize extensive research and investigation, resulting in powerful arguments for the role and responsibility of science and effectively bringing theory into practice.

1. Human development is shaped by a dynamic and continuous interaction between biology and experience.

2. Culture influences every aspect of human development and is reflected in childrearing beliefs and practices designed to promote healthy adaptation.

3. The growth of self-regulation is a cornerstone of early childhood development that cuts across all domains of behaviour.

4. Children are active participants in their own development, reflecting the intrinsic human drive to explore and master their environment.

5. Human relationships, and the effects of relationships on other relationships, are the building blocks of healthy development.

6. The broad range of individual differences among young children often makes it difficult to distinguish normal variations and maturational delays from transient disorders and persistent impairments.

7. The development of children unfolds along individual pathways whose trajectories are characterized by continuities and discontinuities, as well as by a series of significant transitions.

8. Human development is shaped by the ongoing interplay among sources of vulnerability (risk factors) and sources of resilience (protective factors).

9. The timing of early experiences can matter, but more often that not, the developing child remains vulnerable to risks and open to protective influences throughout the early years of life and into adulthood.

10. The course of development can be altered in early childhood by effective interventions that change the balance between risk and protection, thereby shifting the odds in favor of adaptive outcomes.

One of the most important outcomes of this extensive work is that the researchers who conducted the study brought critical issues in human development to light and identified immediate policy efforts that would address critical needs for children. Because young children are often undervalued or ignored in the policy arena, *From Neurons to Neighborhoods* is evidence that society's investment in children will have long-term benefits for all citizens.

Any interpretation of human development is subject to scrutiny and must be considered in the context of history. As you consider the stages of lifespan development in the chapters that follow, the theoretical foundation laid in this chapter will guide you as you pursue your own inquiry and emerging hypotheses. The interactions between biology, psychology, and social forces will continue to emerge as the primary source of development over time.

CONCLUSIONS & SUMMARY

In this chapter, several interpretations of development were introduced to help you understand and integrate development data. While you might not agree with all of the theories or all components of a particular theory, each of the theories can be thought of as "building blocks" toward a more complete understanding of human development.

How does psychoanalytic theory explain development across the lifespan?

- Freud considered the unconscious mind to be the key to understanding human beings.
- Important information in the unconscious mind is kept hidden through an array of defence mechanisms.
- The mind is divided into three constructs—the id, the ego, and the superego—each of which appears at different stages of a child's development.
- Personality development is divided into five psychosexual stages—oral, anal, phallic, latency, and genital—each serving a major function.
- Failure to pass through a stage of development results in fixation, which halts a person from becoming fully mature.

What is the relationship between psychosocial crises and lifespan development?

- Erikson believed that human life progresses through eight "psychosocial" stages, each one marked by a crisis and its resolution.
- Although the ages at which we go through each stage vary, the sequence of stages is fixed. Stages may overlap, however.
- A human being must experience each crisis before proceeding to the next stage. Inadequate resolution of the crisis at any stage hinders development.

How did Piaget explain cognitive development?

- Piaget focused on the development of the cognitive structures of the intellect during childhood and adolescence.
- Organization and adaptation play key roles in the formation of structures.
- Piaget believed that cognitive growth occurred in four discrete stages: sensorimotor, preoperational, concrete operational, and formal operational.

What impact does culture have on lifespan development?

- Lev Vygotsky, a leading commentator on the role of culture in development, emphasized the significance of social processes to bring about satisfactory growth.
- Vygotsky believed that the capacity to learn depends on the abilities of the child's teachers as well as on the child's abilities.
- The difference between the child's ability to learn independently and to learn with help is called the zone of proximal development.

What is the behavioural perspective on development?

- Pavlov, Watson, and Skinner believed that the consequences of behaviour are crucial.
- Skinner's paradigm involves three steps: a stimulus occurs in the environment; a response is made in the presence of that stimulus; and the response is reinforced, punished, or extinguished.
- Bandura has extended Skinner's work to the area of social learning, which he calls observational learning.

How does the bioecological model explain development?

- Physical, cognitive, and social factors interact in ways that we are only beginning to understand.
- Bronfenbrenner postulated that many systems act upon us, including more immediate environments such as our home and school, as well as distant ones such as parenting practices in the community and cultural values and beliefs.
- Rutter's theory demonstrates the importance of genetics as yet another factor that impacts our development through its interaction with psychological and social influences.

What is the current status of developmental theory?

- Interactions among the various levels of development are the focus of current developmental research.
- Lerner's developmental contextualism concentrates on the exchanges between an individual's levels of development and the context to explain developmental processes.

For REVIEW

1. What is your reaction to the statement "The perceived truth of a theory depends on its perceived benefit to society"?

2. Skinner criticized the other theorists discussed in this chapter for believing they can describe what goes on in the human mind. After all, he said, no one has ever looked inside one. What's your position?

3. If, as Erikson argued, identity is a state toward which we strive, how do heredity and the environment work (independently or together) to influence our sense of identity?

Chapter REVIEW TEST

1. Freud believed that development entails moving through psychosexual stages. Difficulty at any stage can cause a person to become
   a. fixated.
   b. operational.
   c. negatively reinforced.
   d. displaced.

2. Bronfenbrenner's theory of development is called the
   a. environmental search model.
   b. generic trace model.
   c. bioecological model.
   d. reinforcement model.

3. The psychosocial crisis of industry versus inferiority must be resolved during
   a. the school years.
   b. early childhood.
   c. adolescence.
   d. adulthood.

4. Piaget's theory of cognitive development focused on the formation and development of
   a. zones of proximal development.
   b. reinforcement schedules.
   c. cognitive structures.
   d. modelling strategies.

5. Although both Piaget and Vygotsky devoted their lives to studying cognitive development, Vygotsky placed greater emphasis on
   a. cognitive structures.
   b. social interactions.
   c. sensitive periods.
   d. observational learning.

6. Skinner carefully analyzed the role of reinforcement in development and distinguished it from
   a. cognitive structures.
   b. reward.
   c. operations.
   d. needs.

7. The great value of observational learning is that a person need not overtly react to learn
   a. mental operations.
   b. new responses.
   c. ego identity.
   d. schedule of reinforcements.

8. Lerner's analysis of development depends on analyzing
   a. multiple levels of development.
   b. schedules of reinforcement.
   c. identity stages.
   d. cognitive stages.

9. The resurgence of interest in biological explanations of development is due to
   a. government subsidies.
   b. the influence of learning theorists.
   c. recent genetic research.
   d. studies of prenatal development.

10. More complex explanations of development depend on the idea of
    a. genes.
    b. reciprocal interactions.
    c. naturalistic research.
    d. stimulus–response experiments.

connect **LEARNSMART** **SMARTBOOK**

For more information on the resources available from McGraw-Hill Ryerson, go to www.mcgrawhill.ca/he/solutions.

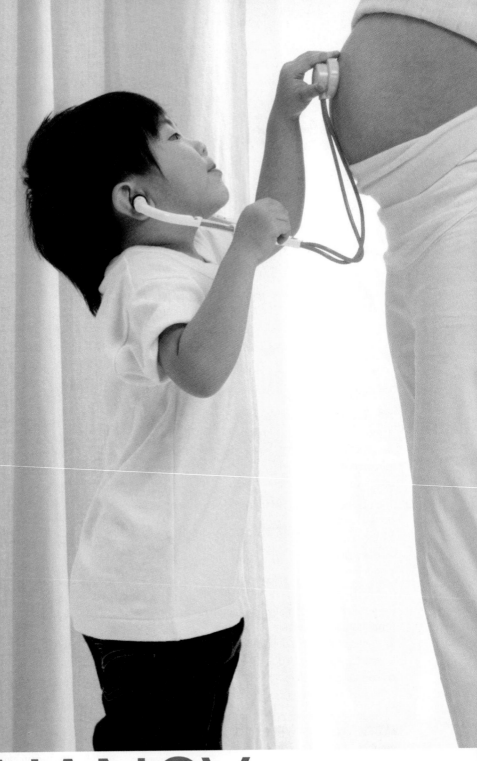

CHAPTER **3**

PREGNANCY
AND PRENATAL
DEVELOPMENT

As You READ

After reading this chapter, you should be able to answer the following questions:

LO1 ▶ How does heredity work, and why doesn't it work well all the time?

LO2 ▶ How does fertilization, both natural and assisted, occur?

LO3 ▶ What are the stages of the prenatal period?

LO4 ▶ What are the major types of prenatal tests?

LO5 ▶ What influences prenatal development, and what precautions can be taken?

The Biological Basis of Development

I t's hard to imagine, but at conception you were but a fertilized egg, or **zygote**—not much bigger than the period at the end of this sentence. From our microscopic beginnings we travel along a developmental path—one that is rooted in biology but affected by psychological and social forces. In this chapter you will learn about our genetic makeup and how heredity and the environment work together (and sometimes at odds) to influence pregnancy and the prenatal environment.

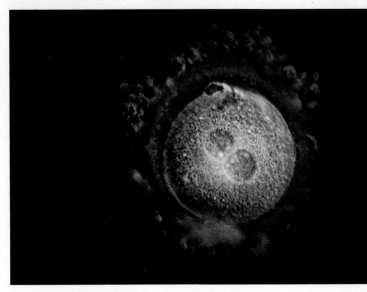

▲ Close-up look at a zygote.

Chromosomes, DNA, and Genes

After the sperm and egg unite, the entire genetic code required to grow into a person made of trillions of cells is activated. Three structures work closely together to coordinate our biological makeup—chromosomes, DNA, and genes. Each of these plays a critical role in the development of a human being. At the centre of each cell in the human body is a nucleus that contains chromosomes. **Chromosomes** are structures in the cell nucleus that are composed of DNA and proteins. They are often described as "threadlike" or "rodlike," or as a clever 7-year-old noted, "tiny versions of *The Very Hungry Caterpillar*"!

Every human cell (excluding egg or sperm cells) has 22 matching chromosome pairs, plus a 23rd pair of sex chromosomes that determine whether a person is male or female. When scientists study

zygote The cell that results when an egg is fertilized by a sperm.

chromosomes Threadlike structures in the cell that come in 23 pairs (46 total) and contain the genetic material DNA. Each parent contributes half of each chromosome pair.

DNA (deoxyribonucleic acid) A molecule with the shape of a double helix that contains genetic information.

gene A segment of DNA that is a unit of hereditary information.

chromosomes, they number the pairs from longest to shortest (1 to 22) plus the last pair of sex chromosomes, for a total of 23 pairs, or 46 total chromosomes. The 23rd pair is made up of two X chromosomes if the person is female (XX), and one X and one Y chromosome if the person is male (XY). Each parent contributes half of each chromosome pair, so an individual's total biological heritage comes from the combination of two parents' chromosomes. Keep in mind that it is the male's X- or Y-carrying sperm that determines the sex of the future zygote—since the female's egg contains only X chromosomes.

The significance of the chromosomes lies in the material they contain. Chromosomes are composed of **DNA (deoxyribonucleic acid)**, which contains crucial genetic information. **Genes** are specific segments of DNA that direct cells to reproduce and combine to build proteins. DNA resembles a long and winding ladder—called a

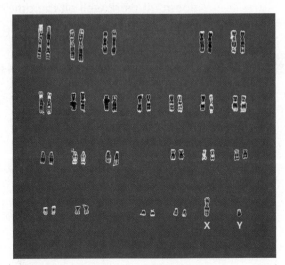

▲ (a) Chromosome structure of males

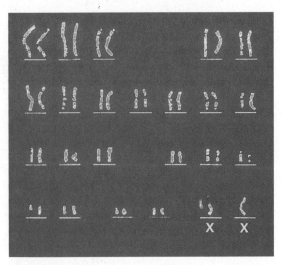

▲ (b) Chromosome structure of females

FIGURE 3.1

Structure of a Cell

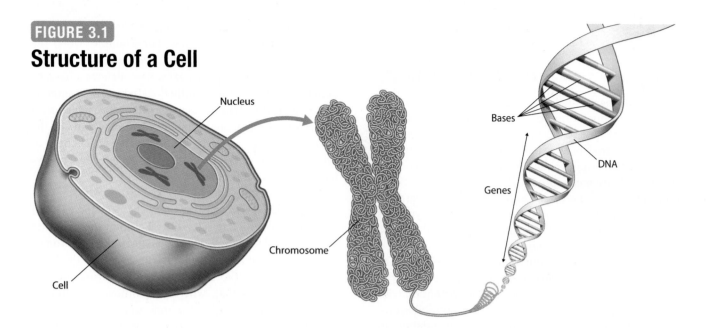

Nucleus

Cell

Chromosome

Bases

DNA

Genes

double helix—and the rungs of the DNA ladder consist of pairs of genes. Each chromosome contains thousands of genes, yet at the most basic level, genes consist of only four building blocks, the chemical bases adenine (A), guanine (G), cytosine (C), and thymine (T). To determine the specific function of any gene, researchers first identify the exact order of the four chemical bases—A G C T—of the gene. (See Figure 3.1.) Estimates are that the entire human **genome** contains about 3 billion letters and is often referred to as the text of a book. Reading this book

▼ Only a small amount of genetic material separates a chimpanzee from a human being.

at the rate of one letter every second, you would spend 11 years finishing it (Shreeve, 2005)!

Every pair of genes ultimately determines the specific traits we inherit, from hair and eye colour to skin shade, the tendency toward baldness, blood type, and so on. Although a single pair of genes determines some traits, other traits require a combination of several pairs of genes in a specific sequence. Our **genotype** (the genetic makeup of an individual that is invisible to the naked eye) is expressed as a **phenotype** (an individual's observable characteristics or traits, such as eye colour and height).

When you look around a room full of people, it may appear that everyone is vastly different from everyone else, but the amount of genetic material shared between human beings is astounding—approximately 99.1% (Gibbons et al., 2004), Therefore, it is only a relatively miniscule amount of genetic material that determines the unique traits that set one person apart from another. Even more surprising are research findings that have determined approximately 98–99% of human DNA to be identical to that of chimpanzees!

The differences between humans, chimpanzees and other mammals, moulds, and bacteria are more than biological. Environmental circumstances affect the way that the genes function and express themselves. For example, some hormones act as a trigger to activate a gene. If hormones are impacted by a person's nutrition or use of medication, this could affect a gene's function. Genes have been shown to affect behaviour in ways that range from food preferences to fussiness. Ultimately, it is the collaboration between multiple factors that results in people being who they are.

> **genome** All of the hereditary information needed to maintain a living organism.
>
> **genotype** A person's genetic makeup that is invisible to the naked eye.
>
> **phenotype** A person's observable characteristics or traits.

MITOSIS AND MEIOSIS

Two processes occur that ensure genes get passed along from one generation to the next—mitosis and meiosis. These processes are two specific kinds of cell division that occur during the human journey from one cell to trillions of cells. Before mitosis and meiosis occur, two important cells—egg and sperm—combine to form the zygote that will ultimately become the new human being. **Mitosis** is the process in which the zygote's nucleus, including the chromosomes, duplicates itself and divides (see Figure 3.2). Much like a zipper unzipping, the strands of DNA split apart lengthwise. Each chromosome half combines with the bases (A, G, C, T) needed to form a new and complete copy of DNA. The two copies of DNA move to opposite sides of the cell, and the cell divides. Two cells are formed, each containing the same DNA as the original cell, with 23 pairs of chromosomes. This process continues as more and more cells are created.

It is during this process that a **mutation** can occur, either through accident or because of environmental influences, such as radiation.

mitosis Cell division in which the number of chromosomes remains the same (46).

mutation A change in DNA, affecting the genes, that occurs during mitosis by accident or because of environmental factors.

meiosis Cell division in which the number of chromosomes is halved to 23.

A mutation refers to some change in DNA that impacts the arrangement of the genes. For example, when the chemical bases A, G, C, and T are pairing up, a mutation can occur that adds an extra base, deletes a base, or exchanges one base for another. As you can imagine, a tiny blip in the DNA sequence can have a ripple effect as strands of DNA duplicate and form new pairs of the DNA zipper. A change in DNA can impact changes in every aspect of a person's life, such as appearance, behaviour, and internal functions.

Meiosis is a different kind of cell division, whereby only the sex cells (sperm cells for men, egg cells for women) duplicate, splitting into cells with 23 chromosomes, rather than 46 (see Figure 3.3). During meiosis, the 46 chromosomes line up in the sex cell nucleus, and then the DNA strands unzip in the same manner as during mitosis. The difference is that, whereas in mitosis the strands of the ladder duplicate and reunite to form new ladder-like DNA structures, in meiosis the strands of the DNA ladders remain halved. As the cell divides, one member of each pair of chromosomes goes into the new cell. As members of each pair of chromosomes are separated, it is pure chance which chromosome in the pair goes into which new cell. This is a critical part of human variation that helps with the survival of our species, because new combinations of genes are created by the exchange

FIGURE 3.2

Mitosis

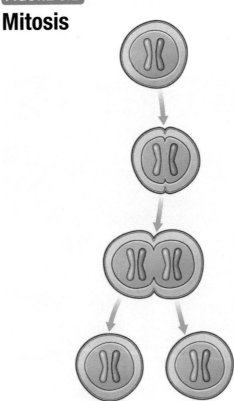

▲ A mitotic division is a cell division in which each new cell receives the same number of chromosomes as a parent cell—46.

of chromosomes during cell division. The division that reduces the number of chromosomes ensures that male and female sex cells can combine in fertilization to result in the necessary number of chromosomes.

L01▶ Hereditary Disorders

As mentioned above, mutations sometimes occur. Such hereditary abnormalities occur at the level of the chromosomes or the genes. Either source of the abnormality affects the entire genetic process.

CHROMOSOMAL DISORDERS

Several human disorders are due to alterations in chromosome number. The cause of chromosomal disorders is often attributed to chance (given that so many cell divisions occur) or to damage to the DNA. Older eggs and sperm have a greater likelihood of containing damaged DNA, which often contributes to disorders such as Down syndrome.

Down syndrome is caused by the presence of an extra copy of chromosome 21, resulting in 47 chromosomes rather than 46. In a large majority of cases, the syndrome results from a failure of the 21st pair of chromosomes to separate during meiosis, so that an individual receives three

FIGURE 3.3
Meiosis

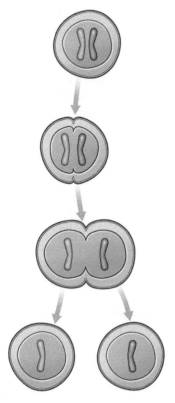

▲ A meiotic division is a cell division in which each new cell receives half of the chromosomes of a parent cell—23.

TECH TRENDS

Heredity at Work

We all know that our genes get passed on from generation to generation, but the "how" that underlies these processes is less commonly understood.

This site lays a solid foundation for all things related to chromosomes:

http://www.dummies.com/how-to/content/genetics-examining-the-basics-of-chromosomes.html

The following two animated videos explain the processes of mitosis and meiosis, respectively, in clear-cut, colourful clips:

http://www.youtube.com/watch?v=VlN7K1-9QB0
http://www.youtube.com/watch?v=D1_-mQS_FZ0

The following video explains the groundbreaking work of the 19th-century scientist Gregor Mendel, which led to our understanding about heredity and the traits we inherit:

http://videos.howstuffworks.com/hsw/10620-genes-and-dna-gregor-mendels-rules-of-heredity-video.htm

of these chromosomes instead of two. An individual with Down syndrome has distinctive facial features, small hands, a large tongue, and possible functional difficulties such as cognitive deficits, heart defects, and an increased risk of leukemia. The incidence of Down syndrome is closely related to the mother's age. Under age 30, the ratio is only 1 in 1200 births; once a woman reaches the age of 45, the incidence increases to 1 in 46 (Gelbart, Griffiths, Lewontin, Miller, 2002).

Research during the past 40 years has led to improvements in life expectancy, overall health, and quality of life for people with Down syndrome. Innovative educational programs, early intervention techniques, and specific therapies have promoted higher-quality functioning and socialization and have helped to reduce stereotypes about the condition.

Other disorders are linked to an abnormal number of the sex chromosomes—the 23rd pair of chromosomes (XX for females, XY for males). In **Klinefelter syndrome**, a male possesses an XXY pattern rather than the normal XY. Those

Down syndrome Chromosomal disorder caused by an extra copy of chromosome 21.

Klinefelter syndrome Chromosomal disorder in males caused by an XXY chromosomal pattern.

FIGURE 3.4

Age-Related Prevalence of Down Syndrome

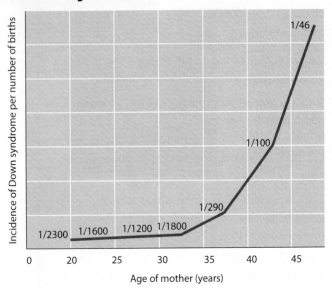

Source: L.S. Penrose and G.F. Smith, *Down's Anomaly*. Little, Brown and Company, 1966. Table 113, Absolute Risks in Different Maternal Age Groups: Incidence per 1,000. p. 270.

▲ Today there are many programs available to support individuals with Down syndrome and help them to reach their full potential.

affected typically have small testes, reduced body hair, possible infertility, and language impairment. Klinefelter syndrome occurs in about 1 in 1000 male births and its effects may be lessened by injections of testosterone (Tsai et al., 2011). In **XYY syndrome**, affected males have an extra Y chromosome, which may cause above-average height and possibly increased aggression (Briken et al., 2006).

In 1970, a condition called **fragile X syndrome** was identified. In this disorder, the end of the X chromosome looks ready to break off. Fragile X syndrome appears in about 1 in 4000 male births and about 1 in 8000 female births. It affects males more severely than females and characteristically leads to learning disabilities and developmental delays in speech and communication skills (Chitayat & Wyatt, 2008).

Females occasionally lack an X chromosome and possess what is called an XO pattern rather than XX. This condition, called **Turner syndrome** affects 1 in every 2000–2500 females born in Canada. It is estimated that there are over 6000 individuals with Turner syndrome in Canada today. It is characterized by small size, webbed neck, and heart abnormalities (Turner Syndrome Society of Canada. (2009).

XYY syndrome Chromosomal disorder in males caused by an extra Y chromosome.

fragile X syndrome Chromosomal disorder caused by an impaired X chromosome.

Turner syndrome Chromosomal disorder in females caused by an XO chromosomal pattern.

Tay-Sachs disease Genetic disorder caused by the lack of an enzyme that breaks down fatty material in the central nervous system.

sickle-cell disease Blood disorder resulting in abnormal hemoglobin.

GENETIC DISORDERS

Some abnormalities are the result of harmful or malfunctioning genes. However, some genetic disorders may go unnoticed in a person's life because other genes compensate (Hartl & Jones, 2005). The presence and functioning of every gene found in the human body has been the subject of much research, speculation, and debate. No one fully understands all of the mysteries that lie in human genes, and why certain combinations result in disorders while other combinations result in healthy functioning, but we're getting closer to gaining a more complete understanding. (See Perspectives on Diversity: The Human Genome Project.)

Tay-Sachs disease, which is caused by a recessive gene, affects Jews of Eastern European origin. Those with Tay-Sachs disease lack an enzyme that breaks down harmful fatty material in the central nervous system (CNS). At birth, the children appear normal, but mental and motor deterioration begin by the age of 6 months, and death usually occurs by the age of 4 or 5. About 1 in 30 Jews of Eastern European origin carries the defective gene. Today there are reliable genetics tests that identify carriers and assess the genetic status of a fetus (Curtis & Barnes, 1998).

Sickle-cell disease, which mainly afflicts people of African descent, is a blood disorder in which red blood cells take on a distorted, sickle shape. Because of this shape, the cells have trouble passing through blood vessels. Cells tend to clump, producing oxygen starvation and severe pain. In the most common form of the disease, the body reacts to eliminate these abnormal cells, causing anemia.

PERSPECTIVES ON **DIVERSITY**

The Human Genome Project

It is obvious that human beings are different in many ways: height, weight, eye colour, skin colour, hair texture, and so on. What is less obvious is how very similar they are.

The goal of the Human Genome Project has been to determine the sequence of the 3 billion bases that make up human DNA and to map the genes of the human genome. The world's human genome scientists have undergone an intensely challenging phase of mapping and sequencing. According to Professor Tsui, who is geneticist-in-chief at Toronto's Hospital for Sick Children and a professor of molecular and medical genetics at the University of Toronto, the truly daunting task is to understand the function and characteristic of each of our genes, their intricate relationships, and how they work in healthy bodies and when disease is present. We also need better technologies to study proteins, tools to handle bioinformatics, and methods to identify the causes of common diseases. Scientists have found that humans have approximately 25,000 genes—many fewer than the estimated 100,000 genes scientists believed were necessary to carry out all the activity humans require. (See Figure 3.5 to see where humans rank against some other species in terms of their number of genes; you may be surprised!)

Because the genes are the result of combinations of approximately 3 billion units of DNA, genes do not program proteins in a one-to-one correspondence, making human genes quite flexible and complex. In fact, we have many more proteins than genes, which supports the notion that genes collaborate with other structures to create proteins.

The implications of the Human Genome Project range from the altruistic to the unethical. In the most ideal sense, the results of this work could mean improved quality of life for humankind and new career opportunities as knowledge grows. On the other hand, some of the major areas of ethical concern are these:

- Who will have access to personal genetic information?
- How will genetic information be used?
- Who oversees the genetic information (ownership and control)?
- Will genetic testing be able to predict human behaviour or potential?
- What are the implications for diversity (physical, cultural, social)?

We know that genes and heredity are only one piece of the human development puzzle. Biopsychosocial interactions result in the life experience of each individual, so learning about human genes can only take us so far in understanding human life.

FIGURE 3.5

Number of Genes —Comparing Several Species

▶ Approximate number of genes in select organisms

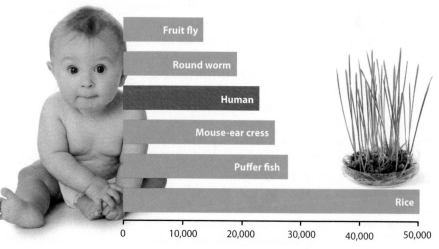

According to the Sickle-Cell Anemia Association of Ontario, sickle-cell anemia affects Black people more than any other racial group. Health Canada states that an exact prevalence of sickle-cell anemia in the Black community in Canada is unknown. It is estimated that approximately 1 in 400 Black babies are born with this disease.

Cystic fibrosis (CF) is an inherited disease in which the lungs, intestines, and pancreas become clogged with thick mucus, causing breathing and digestive problems. It is caused by a mutation in a single gene. In Canada, one person dies from cystic fibrosis each week and 1 in 3600 children have cystic fibrosis (Stephenson, 2010). The CF gene has been identified, however, and this breakthrough has made possible the detection of carriers.

cystic fibrosis (CF) Chromosomal disorder producing a malfunction of the exocrine glands.

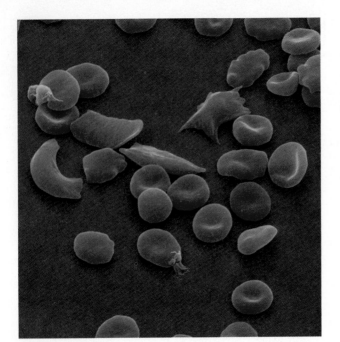
▲ Sickle cells among normal, red blood cells.

Phenylketonuria (PKU), another inherited disease, is also caused by a mutation in a single gene. In phenylketonuria, the enzyme needed to break down the amino acid phenylalanine is lacking. Phenylalanine accumulates and eventually affects the nervous system, causing mental retardation and brain damage. All provinces require infants to be tested at birth. If PKU is present, infants are placed on a diet low in phenylalanine and must remain on the diet for the rest of their lives. This disorder provides an example of the biopsychosocial influence on development. Biology (genes) dictates whether someone is a carrier, but the diet determines whether or not the disorder develops (social).

Another example that shows a biopsychosocial influence is **spina bifida**, which is the failure of the spinal column to close completely. This genetic defect is caused by the interaction of several genes with possible environmental factors. During the formation of the nervous system, if the developing neural tube does not close, spina bifida results (biology). Studies have shown that if women take extra folic acid when they are pregnant, the number of cases of spina bifida decreases (Blackman, 1997).

Duchenne muscular dystrophy is an X-linked disease that affects 1 in 3500 male births in Canada. Affected individuals can have mildly delayed motor milestones, and most are unable to run and jump properly due to muscle weakness (Bushby et al., 2010). According to Muscular Dystrophy Canada, there is a higher incidence of this disease among people of French Canadian descent.

phenylketonuria (PKU) Inherited disease caused by a gene mutation.

spina bifida Genetic disorder resulting in the failure of the spinal column to close completely.

Duchenne muscular dystrophy Genetic disorder resulting in muscular weakness.

ovulation The process in which the egg bursts from the surface of the ovary.

Career Apps

As a genetic counsellor, what questions might arise for you as you advise a couple who wish to have children? They have a family history of Tay-Sachs disease, and one partner has recently been laid off from her job.

Many other diseases also have, or are suspected of having, a strong genetic origin, including diabetes, epilepsy, heart disorders, cancer, arthritis, and some mental illnesses. Some couples wish to learn more about their genetic heritage and the likelihood that their offspring may be at risk for genetic abnormalities. Genetic counsellors gather information from couples using medical tests (such as blood tests) and interviews about family histories and current lifestyle practices to create a profile for each couple. If the outlook is not favourable, some couples prefer to adopt children rather than have children who could be at risk for serious health problems. It is believed that in many cases, genetic, environmental, medical, and lifestyle factors interact to produce problems for children and families.

The Fertilization Process

Although advances in technology continue to develop, the nuts and bolts of making babies haven't changed. What have changed are the opportunities for planning and intervention, which have increased dramatically. Terms like *assisted reproductive technology* and *in vitro fertilization* have become part of the vernacular. In the end, however, it all begins with a sperm and an egg.

MENSTRUAL CYCLE

Beginning at puberty and typically continuing throughout the reproductive years, females experience monthly sexual cycles, involving activity of the brain's hypothalamus, the pituitary gland, ovaries, uterus, vagina, and mammary glands (Moore & Persaud, 2003). The process of **ovulation** triggers a chemical reaction that inhibits the ripening of further eggs. It also prepares the uterine lining for a potential fertilized ovum.

If fertilization does not occur, the prepared uterine lining is shed in menstruation, and the entire process begins again. The monthly cycle during which the egg is released is known as the menstrual cycle. As a woman approaches the end of her reproductive years, these last ova have been present for at least 40 years. This may explain why the children of older women are more susceptible to genetic abnormalities. The eggs have been exposed to environmental hazards (such as radiation) too long to escape damage (Muller et al., 2000).

EGG

Egg cells are produced in a woman's ovaries (see Figure 3.6). Estimates are that about 2 million eggs will be available during a woman's reproductive years, and of these only about 400 will be released (Leifer, 2003). Because only one mature egg is required each month for about 35 years, the number far exceeds the need.

Once the egg is released from the ovary, it passes into one of two **fallopian tubes**, which conduct the egg from the ovary to the uterus. Fertilization occurs in the first part of the fallopian tube. After the union of sperm and egg takes place, it's only a matter of hours (about 24–30) before the single cell begins to divide rapidly. The fertilized egg must now pass through the remainder of the fallopian tube to reach the uterus, a journey of about 3 to 4 days to travel 5 or 6 inches. The fertilized egg attaches itself to the uterine wall during **implantation**.

SPERM

The sole objective of sperm cells is the delivery of DNA to the egg. Sperm are produced in a man's testes and contain half the number of chromosomes (23) found in body cells (46). Sperm remain capable of fertilizing an egg for about 24 to 48 hours after ejaculation (Moore & Persaud, 2003). A normal male ejaculation typically results in anywhere from 100 to 650 million sperm (Campbell & Reece, 2005). Of the more than 200 million sperm that enter the vagina, only about 200 survive the journey to the woman's fallopian tubes, where fertilization occurs.

Multiples

Occasionally, often for reasons unknown, multiple babies are born. The most common type of multiples occurs when a woman's ovaries release two eggs rather than one and both are fertilized by separate sperm. These twins are called **fraternal**, or dizygotic, and their genes are no more

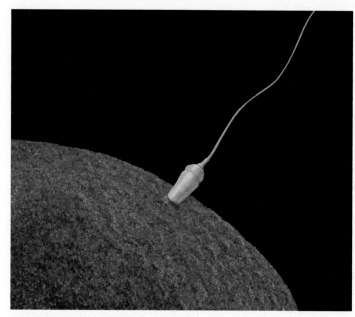

▲ At the moment of fertilization, the sperm measures 5 microns, and the ovum 397 microns. (1 centimetre = 10,000 microns)

alike than those of siblings born of the same parents but at different times. About two thirds of all twins are fraternal.

The increase in the number of twins born in recent decades has been influenced by many factors, such as fertility medications and assistive fertility technologies (Russell et al., 2003). According to the Public Health Agency of Canada, in 2004 there were roughly 120 twin births for every 1000 births in Canada (Canadian Perinatal Health Report, 2008). The rate of fraternal twin births, however, varies considerably from country to country. For example, the rate of fraternal twins is 1 in 500 in Asia, but this rate is 1 in 20 in certain African countries (Moore & Persaud, 2003).

fallopian tube Either of a pair of tubes that join the ovaries to the uterus.

implantation Attachment of the fertilized egg to the uterine wall.

fraternal twins Twins who develop from two eggs fertilized by separate sperm; individuals do not share identical genetic makeup.

FIGURE 3.6

From Ovulation to Implantation

▶ The relationship of ovary, egg, fallopian tube, and uterus

Source: Travers (1982).

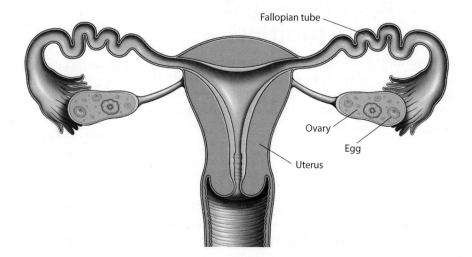

identical twins Twins who develop from a single fertilized egg that divides after conception; individuals share identical genetic makeup.

infertility Inability to achieve pregnancy after 1 year of unprotected intercourse.

sexually transmitted infections (STIs) Infections that may cause infertility.

assisted reproduction technologies (ART) Methods used by an individual to become pregnant through artificial or partially artificial means.

in vitro fertilization (IVF) An ART technique in which fertilization occurs in a petri dish and the resulting embryos are transferred to the woman's uterus.

intrauterine insemination (IUI) An ART technique in which sperm are injected directly into the uterus as part of the fertilization procedure.

gamete intrafallopian transfer (GIFT) An ART technique in which sperm and egg are surgically placed in a fallopian tube with the intent of achieving fertilization.

surrogate mother A woman who carries another woman's fetus.

Less frequently, multiples develop from a single fertilized egg that divides after conception. Two embryos, each in its own amniotic sac, develop within one chorionic sac (fluid-filled sac containing the embryo). This process leads to **identical twins**, known as monozygotic twins, whose genes are identical; that is, they share the same genotype.

Researchers often use twins as a comparison group to explore the influence of genetics on development. Because identical twins share the same genetic material, it is assumed that the environment accounts for any differences between them. In a study that includes both identical twins and other siblings, for example, a researcher can estimate the relative influence of genes and environments on behavioural differences among people. Researchers can focus on topics such as personality, anxiety, or other behaviours to gain insights into the role of genetics on development. The assumption is that if identical twins behave similarly and non-identical siblings behave differently, chances are biology has a major influence on that phenomenon. However, because the environment itself may be influenced by the fact that some children are identical twins (many families emphasize the "sameness" of twins through clothing, furniture, and other household items), it is not accurate to believe that genetic factors alone account for all research findings.

Fertility: Challenges and Opportunities

Although the typical fertilization process is the normal process for most women, there are exceptions. **Infertility** is defined as the inability to conceive a child after 1 year of unprotected sexual intercourse. Many people, attempting to overcome this problem, turn to medical and/or adoption procedures.

CAUSES OF INFERTILITY

In Canada, it is estimated that 1 in 6 couples (16%) experience infertility. The prevalence of infertility has doubled since the 1980s (Bushnik Cook, Yupe, Tough, & Collins, 2012). Low sperm count and inactive sperm are the most common problems for men, and irregular (or lack of) ovulation is cited as problematic for women. Males must deposit a sufficient number of normal sperm near a woman's cervix that can survive the acidic vaginal environment and swim toward the egg (Leifer, 2003). Females must regularly produce normal eggs and possess a uterine environment that will sustain a pregnancy.

Sexually transmitted infections (STIs) may cause infertility or lead to conditions that can result in infertility. Also, a growing number of women are delaying child-bearing. Older women are more likely to become infertile if they have had abdominal surgery or have experienced endometriosis, the growth of endometrial tissue outside the uterus.

If a couple find that they are indeed infertile, their hopes of parenthood may still become a reality, since many assisted reproductive techniques are now available.

ASSISTED REPRODUCTION TECHNOLOGIES

Many forms of **assisted reproduction technologies (ART)** are now available (Gardner et al., 2004; Leifer, 2003; Marrs, Bloch, & Silverman, 1997).

- **In vitro fertilization (IVF).** The best-known type of fertility treatment; fertilization occurs in a petri dish. A woman's eggs are surgically extracted and placed in a solution containing blood serum and nutrients. Treated sperm are added to the solution, where fertilization occurs. The fertilized egg is transferred to a fresh solution, where it remains for 5 to 7 days. The best embryos (typically one or two) are selected for transfer into the woman's uterus, where implantation may occur.

- **Intrauterine insemination (IUI).** Although in vitro fertilization is probably the best-known ART procedure, IUI is by far the most widely used one, often because of favourable health insurance policies: the cost of IUI is sometimes covered by provincial health insurance if the patient meets certain criteria. Potential users of IUI, where sperm is injected into a woman's uterus, have the option of using sperm from the prospective father or donor sperm, depending on the situation.

- **Gamete intrafallopian transfer (GIFT).** Sperm and egg are surgically placed in a fallopian tube with the intent of achieving fertilization in a more natural environment.

- **Sperm and egg donation.** Males and females sometimes donate or sell their sperm and eggs. In Canada, donors do not get paid for donating eggs or sperm. (Gunby, Bissonnette, Librach, & Cowan, 2007).

- **Surrogate mother.** A surrogate mother is a woman who becomes pregnant (usually by IUI or IVF) for the purpose of carrying the fetus to term for another woman.

PERSPECTIVES ON **DIVERSITY**

Worldwide Birth Dearth

A special report in The *Economist* in 2009 reported that in Germany about 25% of women in their 40s have remained childless. The concern, shared by other developed countries around the world, is that as the population ages, it is necessary to have a younger generation to balance the aging population and achieve population stability. In more than 70 countries, including Canada, fertility is currently below replacement level, which is 2.1. The graph in Figure 3.7 shows the fertility rates for Canada from 1871–1996. A study performed in Canada found that roughly half of all the women who were childless in their 40s chose to be that way at a very early age. Today, there are many more choices for women, including whether or not to have children (BBC News, 2010).

Efforts are being made in various countries to entice women to have children, such as offering child-care assistance and financial supports. The reality of raising children today, even from a purely economic standpoint, makes the decision complex. Children can be viewed as a liability rather than an asset, especially when parents are faced with the costs of child care and education, not to mention food, housing, and clothing.

Consider what incentives might work across geographic locations to increase the number of women who would want to have babies—or to encourage women to have more children. Similarly, what ideas might citizens in different countries have about what makes them more or less likely to have children?

More than 3 million babies have been born using IVF and other assisted reproductive technologies since the world's first IVF baby was born in 1978.

ADOPTION

Many people remain childless in spite of several attempts at natural or assisted fertilization, resulting in the pursuit of other channels to welcome a baby or child into their home. **Adoption**, the process of voluntarily taking a child of other parents as one's own, offers a viable option. The poem "Motherbridge of Love" celebrates the bond between a mother and child and offers the perspective of both the adoptive mother and biological mother.

Regardless of race, ethnicity, socioeconomic or marital status, sexual orientation, or religion, people who decide to adopt face stiff competition from other adults. Single parenthood is widely accepted today, and more single women are able to support their children. According to the Adoption Council of Canada, the myth in Canada is that there

FIGURE 3.7

Fertility Rates in Canada

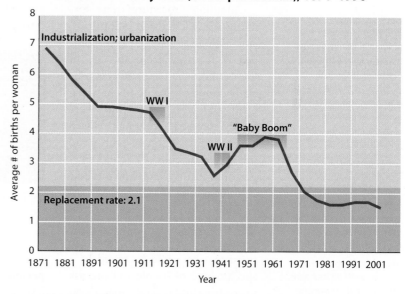

Canadian Fertility Rate (Births per Woman), 1871–1996

Source: "Changing Fertility Patterns: Trends and Implications." Health Canada (2005). Health Policy Research Bulletin, Issue 10, page 8. Reproduced with permission from Minister of Health, 2013.

Once there were two women
who never knew each other.
One you do not know,
the other you call Mother.

"MOTHERBRIDGE OF LOVE" (2007)

are no children to adopt. The truth is, however, that there are thousands of children available for adoption in Canada through the public welfare system, including babies. Although more children are available for adoption than often thought, the waiting period for healthy infants may run into years.

> **adoption** The process of voluntarily taking a child of other parents as one's own.

▲ International adoption has become a popular option for Canadian couples.

Prenatal Development

The prenatal period can be divided into three fairly distinct stages of development: germinal, embryonic, and fetal. Table 3.1 summarizes the milestones of development in these stages.

GERMINAL PERIOD

The **germinal period** extends through the first 2 weeks. The zygote takes the form of a fluid-filled ball of cells called a blastocyst. During the second week, the **blastocyst** becomes firmly implanted in the wall of the uterus. The inner cell layer develops into the embryo itself, and the **placenta**, the **umbilical cord**, and the **amniotic sac** develop from the blastocyst's outer layer of cells. The placenta supplies the embryo with all its needs, carries off all its wastes, and protects it from harm. The placenta has two separate sets of blood vessels, one going to and from the baby through the umbilical cord, the other going to and from the mother through the arteries and veins supplying the placenta.

According to Canada's international adoption statistics for 2010, 1946 children were adopted abroad. The majority of these children came from China (472), Haiti (172), and the U.S. (148) (Adoption Council of Canada, 2011).

Adoption procedures were formerly closed (**closed adoption**), and biological parents were completely removed from the life of their child once the child was officially adopted. The bonds between birth parent(s) and child were legally severed. Although closed adoption was designed with good intentions, it robs the child of a personal history and can increase emotional upset.

Today, however, when a pregnant woman approaches an adoption agency, she has options. She can insist that her child be raised by a specific kind of couple and can ask to see her child several times a year after the adoption. This process is called **open adoption**. Open adoption may help a child to overcome the sense of loss that can accompany adoption (Leon, 2002), but it can also complicate the realities of raising the child. Adoptive parents must accept the idea that their children will want to know more about their biological parents (Brodzinsky & Pinderhughes, 2002).

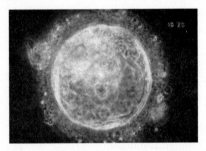

▲ The blastocyst as seen in an ultrasound.

EMBRYONIC PERIOD

Perhaps the most remarkable change in the **embryonic period** (weeks 3–8) is cellular differentiation. Three distinct layers form in the embryo: the ectoderm, which will give rise to skin, hair, nails, teeth, and the nervous system; the mesoderm, which will give rise to muscles, skeleton, and the circulatory and excretory systems; and the endoderm, which will give rise to lungs, liver, and pancreas.

Around the 3rd week, the first signs of the nervous system appear. The mesoderm sends a chemical signal to the ectoderm, and a process called *neural induction* leads to the formation of the neural plate and the rest of the nervous system. A groove forms in the neural plate and begins to fold in on itself, leading to the creation of the neural tube. The top of the tube expands into the brain,

closed adoption Adoption procedure in which the biological parents know nothing about the adopting parents.

open adoption Adoption procedure in which biological parents have considerable input into the adoption process.

germinal period First two weeks following fertilization.

blastocyst The fertilized egg when it reaches the uterus (about 7 days after conception).

placenta Supplies the embryo with all its needs, carries off all its wastes, and protects it from harm.

umbilical cord Contains blood vessels that go to and from the mother through the arteries and veins supplying the placenta.

amniotic sac Fluid-filled uterine sac that surrounds the embryo/fetus.

embryonic period Third through eighth week following fertilization.

TAKE A STAND

A New Ice Age

TABLE 3.1

Milestones in Prenatal Development

Age	Accomplishment
3 weeks	Nervous system begins to form
4 weeks	Heart begins to beat
5 weeks	Head continues rapid growth
8 weeks	Almost all body parts are differentiated
12 weeks	Possible to visually determine baby's sex
	Growth of head slows
	Formation of red blood cells by liver slows
14 weeks	Begins to coordinate limb movements
	Slow eye movements occur
16 weeks	Ultrasound shows clearly defined bone structure
20 weeks	Possible to hear heartbeat with stethoscope
	Baby covered by fine downy hair called lanugo
	Fetal movements called quickening are felt by mother
21 weeks	Rapid eye movements commence
	Substantial weight gain
24 weeks	Fingernails can be seen
28 weeks	Eyes open and close
	Lungs capable of breathing
32 weeks	Skin pink and smooth
	Chubby appearance
38 weeks	Nervous system can carry out some integrative functions
	Reacts to light
	Usually assumes upside-down position as birth approaches

Source: Leifer, 2003; Moore & Persaud, 2003; Olds, London, & Ladewig, 1996.

and the rest will become the spinal cord. The nerve cells at this stage are called *neurons*, and they begin to leave the neural tube and travel to their destination in the developing brain. This process of cell migration typically starts during the 7th prenatal week. The neurons now begin forming 1000 trillion connections in a child's brain, and a pruning process sets in, which is nature's way of ensuring survival of the fittest neurons. From these beginnings, a familiar image of the brain appears. The top of the neural tube leads to the formation of the two cerebral hemispheres and the four lobes of the cerebral cortex.

The heart begins to beat around week 4—the embryo's first detectable movement. During the 5th week, eyes and ears begin to emerge; body buds give clear evidence of becoming arms and legs, and the head is the largest part of the rapidly growing embryo.

During the 6th and 7th weeks, fingers begin to appear on the hands, the outline of toes is seen, and the beginnings of the spinal cord are visible. In this period, the organs are formed—a process called **organogenesis**. After 8 weeks, 95% of the body parts are formed and general body movements are detected.

It's stunning to realize how quickly development occurs. The neuroscientist Marian Diamond (1999) summarizes the rapid growth this way: If fertilization occurred on Monday, by Thursday the embryo would consist of 30 cells clustered together. By Saturday, this cluster of cells (the blastocyst) would have started nestling into the woman's uterine wall. By Tuesday of the following week, the endoderm, mesoderm, and ectoderm would be emerging. Again, remember that all this happens before the woman misses her first period.

> **organogenesis** Process by which organs are formed; occurs around 6th to 7th week of pregnancy.

At the end of the embryonic period, a discernible human being with arms, legs, a beating heart, and a nervous system exists. It receives nourishment and discharges waste through the umbilical cord, which leads to the placenta. The placenta itself never actually joins with the uterus but, instead, exchanges nourishment and waste products through the walls of the blood vessels (Moore & Persaud, 2003). The mother-to-be begins to experience some of the noticeable effects of pregnancy: the need to urinate more frequently, morning sickness, and increasing fullness of breasts.

FEATUREDMEDIA

Humorous Movies about Pregnancy

What to Expect When You're Expecting (2012)—What should soon-to-be mothers and fathers expect when a little one enters their world?

Baby Mama (2008)—What lengths will a successful single businesswoman go to so that she can have the baby she longs for? What are the boundaries between a surrogate mother and the future parent?

Juno (2007)—What does a 16-year-old high school junior do when she finds out she's pregnant after having sex with her best friend?

Knocked Up (2007)—Can a one-night stand turn into a sincere and fulfilling lifelong family commitment?

By the 4th month, the fetus is about 8 to 10 inches in length and weighs about 6 to 8 ounces. The 4th to the 5th month is usually the peak growth period. During this time, the mother begins to feel movement. The fetus now swallows, digests, and discharges urine. Growth is rapid during the 4th month to accommodate an increasing oxygen demand. The fetus produces specialized cells: red blood cells to transport oxygen and white blood cells to combat disease. The fetus is now active—sucking, turning its head, and pushing with hands and feet—and the mother is acutely aware of the life within her.

By the end of the 5th month, the fetus is 10 to 12 inches long, weighs about

FETAL PERIOD

The **fetal period** extends from the beginning of the 3rd month to birth. During this time, the fetus grows rapidly in both height and weight. The sex organs appear, and it is possible to determine the baby's sex. Visible sexual differentiation begins, and the nervous system continues to increase in size and complexity.

fetal period Period that extends from beginning of the 3rd month to birth.

a pound, and sleeps and wakes, even choosing a favourite sleep position. Rapid growth continues in the 6th month, with the fetus gaining another few inches and a pound, but growth typically slows during the 7th month. Viability, the ability to survive if born, is attained.

During fetal testing, the fetal heart rate changes and movement increases, suggesting that the fetus has

▼ Even at the early stages of fetal development, the fetus's anatomical structures are present and visible.

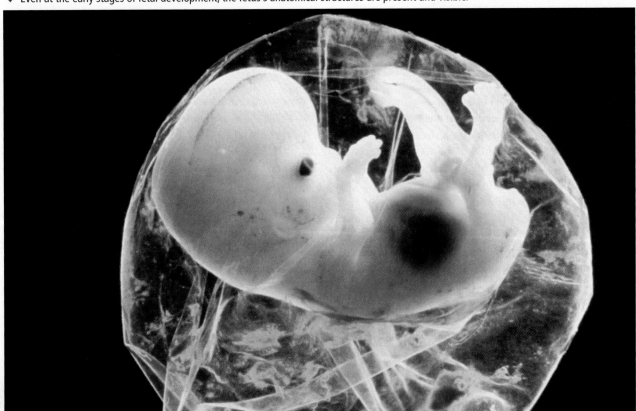

▲ By week 28, a fetus can open and close his or her eyes.

sensed tactile stimulation. Muscular development of the eyes enables the fetus to move its eyes during sleep. From about the 16th week, the fetus is sensitive to any light that penetrates the uterine wall and the amniotic fluid. Toward the end of pregnancy, a bright light pointed at the mother's abdomen causes the fetus to move. The fetus begins to swallow amniotic fluid early in the pregnancy, and researchers have attempted to demonstrate that fetuses can taste and exhibit other sensory functions.

This description of fetal life leads to an inevitable conclusion: Given adequate conditions, the fetus at birth is equipped to deal effectively with the transition from its sheltered environment to the world outside the uterus.

L04 ▶ Prenatal Testing

Some women have a greater chance of developing difficulties during pregnancy or delivering a child with problems. Similar to genetic counselling, the rapidly expanding field of fetal diagnosis not only identifies problems but also offers means of treatment.

ULTRASOUND

Ultrasound is a noninvasive procedure that uses sound waves to produce an image that enables a physician to detect structural abnormalities, to guide other procedures, to confirm fetal viability, and to determine the amount of amniotic fluid (Leifer, 2003). Useful pictures can be obtained as early as 7 weeks. A number of businesses in Canada offer the use of fetal ultrasound machines to make videos of babies in the womb as a keepsake for parents, but Health Canada is recommending that parents not expose their unborn babies to fetal ultrasound for this purpose (Health Canada, 2006, December 7).

> **ultrasound** Use of sound waves and special equipment to produce an image that enables a physician to detect internal structural abnormalities.
>
> **amniocentesis** Fetal testing procedure that involves inserting a needle through the woman's abdomen, piercing the amniotic sac, and withdrawing a sample of amniotic fluid.

AMNIOCENTESIS

Amniocentesis involves inserting a needle through the woman's abdomen, piercing the amniotic sac, and withdrawing a sample of the amniotic fluid. The fluid sample provides information about the child's sex and almost 70 chromosomal abnormalities (Moore & Persaud, 2003). If required, amniocentesis is done after the 15th week of pregnancy.

ALPHA-FETOPROTEIN (AFP) TEST

In fetuses with neural tube problems, AFP (a protein produced by a baby's liver) escapes from the spinal fluid (Jasper, 2000), and then passes into the mother's bloodstream. Babies with spina bifida show a raised level of AFP, which can be detected in the mother's blood. A low level of AFP can indicate Down syndrome. The blood test (done when the mother is 15–17 weeks pregnant) produces false positives, however, which raises the issue of further testing. Pairing the results of the AFP test with an ultrasound provides more accurate information.

▼ An ultrasound allows soon-to-be parents a glimpse of their baby in utero.

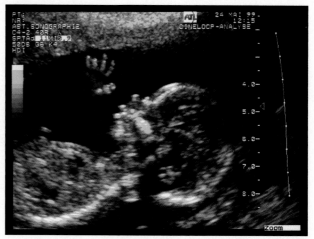

CHORIONIC VILLI SAMPLING (CVS)

The outer layer of the embryo is almost completely covered with chorionic villi, fingerlike projections that reach into the uterine lining. A catheter is inserted through the vagina to the villi, and a small section is suctioned into the tube. **Chorionic villi sampling (CVS)** is an excellent test to determine the fetus's genetic structure and may be done as early as 9 to 10 weeks. Results are available in 3 hours to 7 days, as compared with 2 to 4 weeks for amniocentesis.

L05 ▶
Critical Interactions: Biology and the Environment

At birth an infant has already had 9 months of prenatal living, with all the benefits and harm that can result from biological and environmental influences. The embryonic period can be hazardous for the newly formed organism. During these weeks, embryonic tissue is particularly sensitive to any foreign agents, especially beginning at the 3rd or 4th week of the pregnancy. Estimates are that about 30% of all embryos are aborted at this time without the mother's knowledge and that about 90% of all embryos with chromosomal abnormalities are spontaneously aborted.

Many women currently experience the benefits of the most up-to-date and high-quality prenatal care. Diet, exercise, and rest can be designed to meet the needs of each individual. When women, especially pregnant teenagers, do not receive prenatal care, the rates of prenatal loss, stillbirths, and newborn mortality substantially increase. Health Canada provides information and resources for pregnant women and new mothers to reduce the risk of injury and illness and to promote the healthy development of their infants (**http://www. hc-sc.gc.ca/hl-vs/babies-bebes/index-eng.php**).

NUTRITION AND EXERCISE

Because a fetus depends on its mother for nourishment, most women today are keenly aware of the need to have a proper diet that will help them give birth to a healthy baby. Good nutrition helps women sustain healthy pregnancies. Healthy habits throughout pregnancy attend to both maternal and fetal needs,

and they also carry over after the baby is born. According to Canada's Food Guide, a healthy diet includes the following: at least one dark green and one orange vegetable every day, and vegetables and fruit more often than juice; whole grain products each day; skim, 1%, or 2% milk; meat alternatives such as beans, lentils, and tofu often; at least two servings of fish each week; and a small amount of unsaturated fat each day. A healthy diet is especially necessary during pregnancy, and doctors usually recommend dietary supplements, such as additional protein, iron, calcium, sodium, fibre, folic acid, and vitamins.

Weight gain during pregnancy supports the growth of your baby and the placenta, as well as changes in your body (such as an increased volume of blood and fluid, larger breast size, and some storage of fat). Evidence shows that women who gain the recommended amount of weight during pregnancy have fewer complications, such as Caesarean section, gestational hypertension, and low or high birth weight.

The following guidelines may be useful for you, but keep in mind that weight gain will be different for everybody. Speak with your health-care professional if you are ever concerned that you are gaining too much or too little weight during pregnancy (Lalonde, Schuurmans, & Senikas, 2009).

BMI before pregnancy	Recommended weight gain
Less than 19.8	12.5 to 18 kg (28 to 40 lb)
Between 19.8 and 26	11.5 to 16 kg (25 to 35 lb)
Between 26 and 29	7 to 11.5 kg (15 to 25 lb)
More than 29	At least 6 kg (15 lb)
Twin pregnancies	16 to 20.5 kg (35 to 45 lb)

Maintaining a healthy activity level is also important during pregnancy. The Society of Obstetricians and

▼ Most women today understand the importance of maintaining a healthy diet and getting exercise during their pregnancy.

Gynaecologists of Canada suggests that if you were active at least six months before your pregnancy, you should ask your health-care professional about whether you may continue your sports or workouts safely. You may need to revise your exercise program every trimester to reduce the risk of falls and limit high-impact sports.

EMOTIONS AND SENSE OF SELF

The primary focus for pregnant women involves their new role as a mother, including developing maternal identity and competency. The classic work of Ruth Rubin (1984) attempts to explain the stressful emotional road many pregnant women travel. Rubin believed that women must master four tasks in the transition to motherhood: They must (1) transition from a focus on themselves to a focus on the unborn child, (2) ensure the acceptance of the child by significant persons in the family, (3) establish a bond with the unborn child that grows into a relationship during the milestones of pregnancy, and (4) commit to the realities of "giving of themselves"—the strenuous physical toll pregnancy takes on their bodies and the emotional roller coaster of excitement and anxiety. Rubin believed that mastering these four tasks prepares a woman for the subsequent demands of motherhood.

We could also ask how women *and* men negotiate the change in roles that is about to occur? How will they balance work and parenting, share domestic responsibilities, and come to terms with the profound changes that are about to happen in their lives? Traditional roles—one partner taking care of domestic responsibilities and the other taking care of work outside the home—don't sit well with many contemporary couples. Recognition of the importance of family responsibilities, more flexible work policies, and access to high-quality, affordable child care would help reduce the tension couples experience.

Current advances in technology can provide an endless stream of information to families all around the world, but they also contribute to anxiety when new parents are presented with "expert" opinions—opinions which seldom agree. Often, cultural traditions (what to eat, how to ward off bad luck, etc.) contribute more substantially than current "expert" information to a positive experience with pregnancy and birth.

> Juno: Most Fruitful Yuki?
> What is . . . Oh my god, she's
> a pregnant superhero!

—FROM *JUNO*, WRITTEN BY DIABLO CODY

TECH TRENDS

Instant Information on Pregnancy and Birth

The number of websites dedicated to advice on pregnancy, birth, and child rearing continues to grow as new organizations and individuals share the latest ideas about specific topics. Technology provides a means for people to subscribe to lists or other groups and receive information without seeking it out, once the email address has been entered into the automatic generator of a specific site.

www.todaysparent.com and www.babycenter.ca —These two websites follow a similar format and offer general categories of information as well as subscriptions to age- or pregnancy-stage related emails.

"Are You Smarter Than Your Doctor? Pregnancy Quiz"—This game application for iPhones allows users to learn medical facts and other information relating to pregnancy.

Blogs have also become a popular way for people to share information with others about pregnancy and birth experiences, concerns about parenthood, and more. The challenge is for people to be critical consumers of the information available on all of the blogs and web pages.

CULTURE

Approximately 200,000 immigrants a year from all parts of the globe continue to choose Canada, drawn by its quality of life and its reputation as an open, peaceful, and caring society that welcomes newcomers and values diversity (Canadian Heritage, 2012). Culture plays a major role in the way a woman perceives and prepares for her birthing experience. Each culture has its own attitudes, values, and beliefs surrounding pregnancy and birth. Childbirth educators need to assess and be aware of the cultural, ethical and socioeconomic factors that influence the experience of pregnancy, birth, and parenting (Greene, 2007).

To ensure that a woman's journey through the prenatal months is as safe and satisfying as possible, some basic ideas must be recognized. For example, communication assumes paramount importance—not only language but also such behaviours as body language and tone of voice. How does the woman's family, as members of a particular culture, view the pregnancy? Is it seen as a natural, expected occurrence that doesn't require constant medical care? Does the woman's status change as a result of the pregnancy? Are there cultural dietary considerations that should be addressed? Are there spiritual beliefs that health-care providers should be aware of?

TERATOGENS

In spite of good intentions, all pregnancies expose mother and child to various health risks. **Developmental risk** is a term used to identify children whose well-being is in jeopardy. Such risks involve a range of biopsychosocial conditions. It is clear that the earlier the damage occurs in a child's life, the greater the chance of negative long-term effects.

A major concern relating to developmental risk involves substances that greatly influence the prenatal environment. **Teratogens** are any environmental agents that cause harm to the embryo or fetus. They fall into two classes: infectious diseases and different types of chemical substances (see Table 3.2). Most of these are avoidable risks. For example, in Canada, although it is well known that drinking and smoking during pregnancy are not good for the baby, about 11% of pregnant women continue to smoke cigarettes and 10% of pregnant women report drinking alcohol (Wilson, 2011).

Depending on the age of exposure to particular teratogens, the effects are more or less serious. Medical research has identified specific periods when an embryo's or fetus's critical organs are developing and when the embryo or fetus is therefore susceptible to harm. The harm can range from minor defects to major abnormalities (see Figure 3.8). For example, teratogens can damage the embryo's heart during the first few weeks of development, but the ears are not at such serious risk of damage until several weeks later. Generally speaking, the embryo is at greater risk than the fetus because the

developmental risk Risk to children's well-being involving a range of damaging biopsychosocial conditions.

teratogens Any environmental agents that harm the embryo or fetus.

TABLE 3.2
Teratogens: Their Effects, and Time of Risk

Agent	Possible Effects	Time of Risk During Pregnancy
Infectious Diseases		
HIV/AIDS	Growth failure, low birth weight, developmental delay, death from infection	Before conception, throughout pregnancy, during delivery, during breastfeeding
Rubella	Mental retardation, physical problems, possible death	First 3 months, may have effects during later months
Syphilis	Fetal death, congenital syphilis, prematurity	From 5 months on
CMV	Retardation, deafness, blindness	Uncertain, perhaps 4 to 24 weeks
Herpes simplex	CNS damage, prematurity	Potential risk throughout pregnancy and at birth
Chemical Substances		
Alcohol	Fetal alcohol syndrome (FAS), growth retardation, cognitive deficits	Throughout pregnancy
Aspirin	Bleeding problems	Last month, at birth
Cigarettes	Prematurity, lung problems	After 20 weeks
DES	Cancer of female reproductive system	From 3 to 20 weeks
LSD	Isolated abnormalities	Before conception
Lead	Death, anemia, mental retardation	Throughout pregnancy
Marijuana	Unknown long-term effects, early neurological problems	Throughout pregnancy
Thalidomide	Fetal death, physical and mental abnormalities	The first month
Cocaine	Spontaneous abortion, neurological problems	Throughout pregnancy

groundwork for virtually all body parts is established during the embryonic period.

Some effects of teratogens are not visible to the naked eye, however, and manifest themselves in other ways that may be delayed for months or even years. Some harmful health effects can take a toll on a child's behaviour and psychological well-being. They can impact parent–child relationships, as well as teacher–pupil and peer relationships, for example. The great potential for biopsychosocial consequences of teratogens should not be discounted or taken lightly.

Infectious Diseases

It is estimated that about 15% of all women experience some type of infectious disease during pregnancy. (Arenson & Drake, 2007). The potential risk lies in the type of disease and in the timing of the infection. Some diseases that are potentially harmful to the developing fetus when acquired

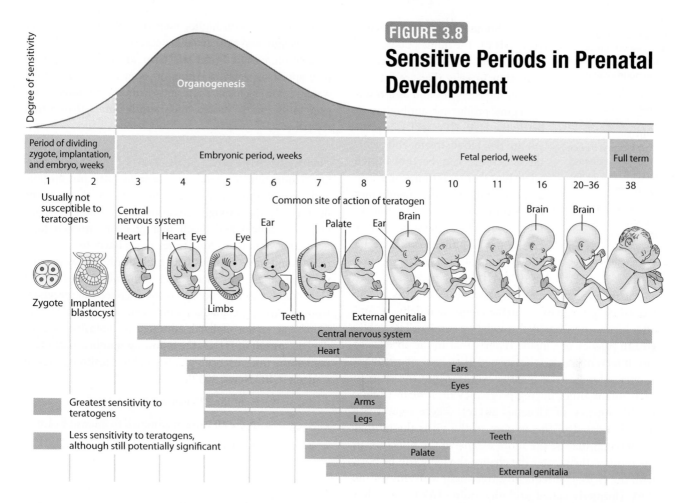

FIGURE 3.8

Sensitive Periods in Prenatal Development

Degree of sensitivity

Organogenesis

Period of dividing zygote, implantation, and embryo, weeks	Embryonic period, weeks	Fetal period, weeks	Full term

| 1 | 2 | 3 | 4 | 5 | 6 | 7 | 8 | 9 | 10 | 11 | 16 | 20–36 | 38 |

Usually not susceptible to teratogens

Central nervous system

Common site of action of teratogen

Heart   Heart   Eye   Eye   Ear   Palate   Ear   Brain   Brain   Brain

Zygote   Implanted blastocyst   Limbs   Teeth   External genitalia

Central nervous system

Heart

Ears

Eyes

Arms

Legs

■ Greatest sensitivity to teratogens

Teeth

Palate

■ Less sensitivity to teratogens, although still potentially significant

External genitalia

either before or during birth are grouped together as the **STORCH diseases** (Blackman, 1997): syphilis, toxoplasmosis, other infections, rubella, cytomegalovirus, and herpes.

SYPHILIS

Syphilis is a sexually transmitted infection that, if untreated, may affect the fetus. It makes no difference whether the mother contracted the disease during pregnancy or many years before. About 25% of infected fetuses die during or after the second trimester, and another 25% die soon after birth. Those who survive may be affected by serious problems such as blindness, mental retardation, and deafness. Because of advances in antibiotic treatments, the incidence of syphilis has steadily decreased, although there has been a recent upsurge due to an increase in numbers of cases among adolescents (Leifer, 2003). In 2008, 1394 cases of syphilis were reported to the Public Health Agency of Canada, corresponding to a rate of 4.2 per 100,000. This is an increase since 1999, when the rate was 0.6 per 100,000 (Public Health Agency of Canada, 2010c).

TOXOPLASMOSIS

Toxoplasmosis is caused by a parasite that is transmitted to humans by many animals, especially cats, or occasionally from raw meat. In fact, pregnant cat owners should avoid contact with kitty litter to avoid contracting toxoplasmosis. Usually harmless in adults, the infection can cause serious problems for the fetus, including spontaneous abortion, premature delivery, and neurological problems such as mental retardation, blindness, and cerebral palsy. Low birth weight, an enlarged liver and spleen, and anemia also characterize the disease. The prevalence of toxoplasmosis is low in most of Canada with the exception of Nunavut and Northern Quebec. In these two areas, the incidences are high due to contaminated water and people consuming raw or undercooked seal meat and water fowl (Messier et al., 2009).

OTHER INFECTIONS

HIV/AIDS

HIV/AIDS is a disease that can be passed from mother to baby during pregnancy, labour, and delivery. **AIDS (acquired immune deficiency syndrome)** is caused

STORCH diseases syphilis, toxoplasmosis, other infections, rubella, cytomegalovirus, herpes; these diseases are especially harmful to the embryo or fetus at certain times during a pregnancy.

syphilis Sexually transmitted disease that, if untreated, may adversely affect the fetus.

toxoplasmosis Infection caused by a parasite; may cause damage to a fetus.

AIDS (acquired immune deficiency syndrome) Disease caused by the HIV virus, which can invade a newborn baby's immune system, thus making it vulnerable to infections and life-threatening illnesses.

by the **human immunodeficiency virus (HIV)**. The human body, once infected with HIV, experiences a reduction in cells that are vital to our immune system and as a result it begins producing antibodies to battle the HIV. HIV, which is present in the bloodstream and genital secretions, can be transmitted when blood or secretions come into contact with mucous membranes (in various parts of the human body) or breaks in the skin (such as cuts or needle punctures). Table 3.3 shows some of the statistics related to HIV/AIDS in Canada.

An infected mother can pass the HIV virus to the fetus during pregnancy, during labour and delivery, and after birth, occasionally through breast milk. The Public Health Agency of Canada reports that in the absence of any intervention, it is estimated that 25% of pregnant women who are HIV positive will transmit the virus to their infant either during pregnancy or at birth (Public Health Agency of Canada, 2011c). These figures are directly related to the amount of the virus the mother is carrying; that is, the more extensive the infection in the mother, the greater the chance the baby will be born with the virus. Consequently, treatment with zidovudine ZDV (formerly called azidothymidine [AZT]) or other drugs early in the pregnancy may help to prevent the transmission of the virus.

The Canadian Medical Association recommends voluntary screening since a positive result can have an impact on many different aspects of a person's life (National Collaborating Centre for Infectious Disease, 2005). When the virus is transmitted, a condition called *AIDS embryopathy* may develop, which causes growth retardation, small head size (microcephaly), flat nose, and widespread, upward-slanted eyes, among other characteristics. AIDS is

also associated with higher rates of preterm disease, low birth weight, and miscarriage. Because AIDS has a shorter incubation period in fetuses than in adults, symptoms may appear as early as 6 months after birth and include weight loss, fever, diarrhea, and chronic infections. Once symptoms appear, babies rarely survive more than 5 to 8 months.

Swine Flu and Other Infections

Other infectious diseases include influenza, chicken pox, and several rare viruses. Recent concern about swine flu (H1N1) has brought attention to the increased risk of severe illness and death that pregnant women face. Pregnant women are four times more likely to be hospitalized and have an unusually high death rate associated with the illness. For this reason, immunizations for both H1N1 and seasonal flu are recommended for pregnant women. Among Canadian women between ages 15 and 50 who were hospitalized, admitted to intensive care, or died as a result of H1N1, the following number were pregnant at the time, according to the Public Health Agency of Canada (CBC News, 2009):

- 45, or 19.1%, of the 235 women hospitalized
- 9, or 15%, of the 60 women admitted to intensive care
- 2, or 40%, of the five women who died

RUBELLA

Rubella (also known as German measles) is an infectious disease generally characterized by a rash, a fever, and swollen lymph nodes. The disease, however, is extremely dangerous to a fetus during the first trimester and can result in serious defects including congenital heart disorder, cataracts, deafness, and/or mental retardation. In 2005, 220 cases of rubella were confirmed in three counties in Ontario (Arsenault, Dontigny, & Martel, 2008). Any woman who had German measles as a child cannot assume that she is immune, so a woman who wishes to become pregnant should take a blood test. If immunity is not found, the woman can receive a vaccination before she becomes pregnant that will protect her and the fetus.

TABLE 3.3
Canadian HIV/AIDS Statistics

Canadian HIV/AIDS Statistics	
People diagnosed with HIV/AIDS in Canada:	65,000
Estimated new HIV infections in Canada each year:	2300–4300 (300–520 in Aboriginal persons)
AIDS deaths in Canada in 2008:	approximately 780
Total number of AIDS deaths in Canada each year:	less than 1000

Source: Public Health Agency of Canada, 2008.

CYTOMEGALOVIRUS (CMV)

Cytomegalovirus (CMV) is a widespread infection that is often unrecognized in pregnant women because the symptoms are mild. It can cause damage to the fetus, ranging from mental retardation to blindness, deafness, and even death. It is the most common cause of congenital infection, affecting 0.2%–2.4% of all infants in Canada (Public Health Agency of Canada, 2010a).

GENITAL HERPES

Genital herpes is a virus that is passed on to the fetus during delivery through the birth canal. The infant develops symptoms during the first week following birth. The eyes and the nervous system are most susceptible to this disease. About one third of infected babies die, and of those who survive, one fourth suffer some form of brain damage. If genital herpes is detected, the baby can be delivered by Caesarean section (through an incision in the mother's abdomen) to prevent exposure to the infection.

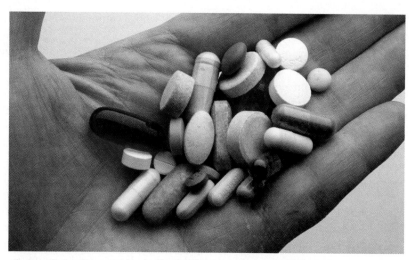

▲ Prescription drugs can have adverse effects on a fetus. Pregnant women need to check with their doctor before taking any over-the-counter drugs.

Prescription and Non-Prescription Drugs

Drugs that are prescribed during pregnancy can have serious effects on the fetus. For example, the acne drug isotretinoin (Accutane) and the psoriasis drug acitretin (Soriatane) are known to cause birth defects, including heart defects, facial deformities such as cleft lip and missing ears, and mental retardation.

The drug **thalidomide**, originally prescribed as a sleeping pill and an anti-nausea medication for pregnant women, produced tragic consequences. In the 1960s, physicians noticed a major increase in children born with either partial or no limbs. In some cases, feet and hands were directly attached to the trunk. Other outcomes were deafness, blindness, and cognitive deficits. In tracing the cause of the outbreak, investigators discovered that the mothers of these children had taken thalidomide early in their pregnancies. As little as a single dose of thalidomide early on in pregnancy was capable of damaging the fetus. This drug is still available today in Canada under the brand name Thalomid. It is used in combination with a chemotherapy drug and a steroid for the treatment of multiple myeloma (Health Canada, 2010).

DES (diethylstilbestrol), a synthetic hormone, is another example of a teratogenic drug. In the late 1940s and 1950s, DES was given to pregnant women to prevent miscarriage. Researchers later found that the daughters of the women who had received this treatment were more susceptible to vaginal and cervical cancer. These daughters also experienced more miscarriages when pregnant than would be expected. Recent suspicions have arisen about the sons of DES women, who seem to have more disorders of their reproductive systems.

Health Canada is currently not recognizing this drug as a potential danger as other countries are, despite the fact that the Motherisk Program at the Toronto Hospital for Sick Children receives an average of 10 to 20 pregnancy exposure reports annually (Andresen, 2006).

We know that prescription and non-prescription drugs pass through the placenta and affect the growing embryo and fetus, and that certain prenatal periods are more susceptible to damage than others, such as the embryonic period. To keep pregnancy as safe as possible, a woman should begin by avoiding any drugs known to cause damage to a fetus, and she should check with her physician before taking over-the-counter medications, dietary supplements, or herbal remedies.

ILLEGAL DRUGS

Most pregnant women who use illegal drugs do not consider the enormous risk they pose to their unborn child. Cocaine, methamphetamine, marijuana, and heroin are well-known illegal drugs that act on the nervous system. People typically use them to alter moods, perceptions, and states of consciousness. Cocaine and methamphetamine are stimulants; they speed up a person's nervous system. Babies born to mothers who used cocaine or methamphetamine during pregnancy may have low birth weight, behavioural problems, and impaired motor development. Marijuana use, which typically causes relaxation and heightened senses in adults, has been less documented in term of the prenatal effects on newborns.

genital herpes Infection that can be contracted by a fetus during delivery; the infant can develop symptoms during the first week following birth.

thalidomide Popular drug prescribed during the early 1960s that was later found to cause a variety of birth defects when taken by women early in their pregnancies.

DES (diethylstilbestrol) A synthetic hormone that was administered to pregnant women in the late 1940s and 1950s supposedly to prevent miscarriage. It was later found that the daughters of the women who had received this treatment were more susceptible to vaginal and cervical cancer.

Some research shows that children whose mothers used marijuana during pregnancy experience problems with memory and depression. Heroin is a highly addictive drug made from morphine (a natural substance extracted from poppy plants). Infants born to mothers who used the drug during pregnancy have many behavioural problems. These babies experience withdrawal symptoms the same as adults—tremors, sleep difficulty, impaired motor control.

SMOKING

Smoking is probably the most common environmental threat to pregnancy. Tobacco use negatively affects everything about the reproduction process: fertility, conception, pregnancy, fetal development, labour, and delivery. Babies of mothers who smoke may have breathing difficulties and low resistance to infection, and they can suffer long-lasting health effects after birth, such as asthma.

fetal alcohol syndrome (FAS) The condition of babies whose mothers drank alcohol during pregnancy; characterized by growth deficiencies, physical abnormalities, and central nervous system dysfunction.

Maternal smoking also produces a condition called intrauterine growth retardation (IUGR). The birth weight of neonates whose mothers smoked during pregnancy is about 7 ounces less than that of babies whose mothers did not smoke. If mothers stop smoking before the 16th week of pregnancy, their babies show a great improvement in their birth weights.

ALCOHOL

When a pregnant woman consumes alcohol, it crosses the placenta to the fetus. Because of this, drinking alcohol can harm the baby's development. Prenatal exposure to alcohol has been linked to so many problems that even moderate drinking is discouraged for pregnant women. Different levels of alcohol affect people differently, so it is hard to come up with safe drinking standards. To date, no safe amount of alcohol consumption during pregnancy has yet been established (Arenson & Drake, 2007).

One of the most severe effects of drinking during pregnancy is **fetal alcohol syndrome (FAS)**, a condition characterized by growth deficiencies, physical abnormalities, and central nervous system dysfunction. FAS is one of the most common known causes of mental disabilities and is the only cause that is entirely preventable. In Canada, it is estimated that 9 in every 1000 infants are born with FAS each year (Health Canada, 2006a). In some Aboriginal communities the rate can be as high as every 1 in 5 (First Nations and Inuit Health, 2005).

CONCLUSIONS & SUMMARY

In this chapter, you have seen how a human being begins a journey through the lifespan. Nature's detailed choreography of prenatal development provides a remarkably complex yet elegant means of ensuring the survival of generations. Once conception occurs, uniting the genetic contribution of mother and father, the developmental process is under way, sheltering the fetus for the first 9 months in the protective cocoon of the womb.

How does heredity work, and why doesn't it work well all the time?

- Heredity and the environment both influence pregnancy and the prenatal environment.
- Every pair of genes determines the specific traits we inherit. Some traits come from a single pair, others from a combination of several pairs.
- Mutations sometimes occur at the level of the chromosomes or the genes.

How does fertilization, both natural and assisted, occur?

- Natural fertilization occurs in the first part of the fallopian tube. The fertilized egg then passes through the remainder of the tube and attaches to the uterine wall.
- One method of assisted fertilization occurs when eggs are surgically removed, fertilized in a petri dish and then transferred into the woman's uterus where implantation occurs.

What are the stages of the prenatal period?

- The germinal period is the time when the fertilized egg passes through the fallopian tube.
- The embryonic period is a time of rapid development and great sensitivity.
- The fetal period is a time of preparation for life outside the womb.
- The senses develop during the prenatal months and are ready to function at birth.

What are the major types of prenatal tests?

- Ultrasound uses sound waves to produce an image of the fetus.
- Amniocentesis involves inserting a needle to pierce the amniotic sac and remove a sample of amniotic fluid.
- Alpha-Fetoprotein (AFP) Test is a blood test performed on the mother to detect neural tube problems.
- Chorionic villi sampling (CVS) involves inserting a catheter into the vagina and suctioning villi off the embryo. This determines the fetus's genetic structure.

What influences prenatal development and what precautions should be taken?

- Developmental risk is a term that applies to those children whose welfare is in jeopardy.
- Teratogens are those agents that cause abnormalities in embryos or fetuses.
- Infectious diseases and chemical agents are the two basic classes of teratogens.
- Today HIV/AIDS is recognized as a potential danger for newborns.
- Maternal nutrition and emotions are important influences during pregnancy.
- Advancing technology has provided diagnostic tools for the detection of many fetal problems.

1. The Human Genome Project could improve the quality of our lives. This work, however, does have some ethical issues. Do you feel it would be fair to predict human behaviour simply because of an individual's genes, without taking their environment into consideration?

2. Why is the discovery of DNA so important in our lives? Can you think of anything you have read or seen in the media that derives from this discovery?

3. What are some ethical considerations regarding frozen embryos? Should frozen embryos be available for adoption? If so, what policies would help regulate the adoption process?

Chapter REVIEW TEST

1. In vitro fertilization takes place
   a. in the fallopian tube.
   b. in the uterus.
   c. outside the woman's body.
   d. in the ovary.

2. Each sex cell carries a total of ___ chromosomes.
   a. 23
   b. 24
   c. 47
   d. 46

3. There is a higher incidence of which genetic disorder in French Canadians?
   a. sickle-cell anemia
   b. Duchenne muscular dystrophy
   c. cystic fibrosis
   d. spina bifida

4. Down syndrome is caused by
   a. the body's failure to break down amino acids.
   b. fragile X syndrome.
   c. a deviation on the 21st pair of chromosomes.
   d. an XO pattern.

5. The Human Genome Project is an endeavour to identify and map
   a. certain substances within cells.
   b. all human genes.
   c. cell divisions.
   d. teratogens.

6. The first 2 weeks following fertilization are called the ___ period.
   a. embryonic
   b. fetal
   c. germinal
   d. pregnancy

7. Which of the following statements is true?
   a. The earlier the damage, the greater the chance of negative long-term effects.
   b. The fetus is safe from all harm while in the womb.
   c. Babies are usually born on the day predicted.
   d. A fetus hears no sound until birth.

8. It is recommended that a woman with a BMI between 19.8 and 26 (before pregnancy) gain
   a. 12.5 to 18 kg.
   b. 11.5 to 16 kg.
   c. 7 to 11.5 kg.
   d. At least 6 kg.

9. _____ is a technique in which a needle is inserted through a pregnant woman's abdomen and into the amniotic sac in order to obtain a fluid sample.
   a. ultrasound
   b. chorionic villi sampling
   c. amniocentesis
   d. non-stress test

10. Mental disability, central nervous system dysfunction, and growth deficiencies can be symptoms of
   a. fetal alcohol syndrome (FAS).
   b. Rh factor.
   c. prematurity.
   d. anoxia.

CHAPTER

4

BIRTH AND THE
NEWBORN CHILD

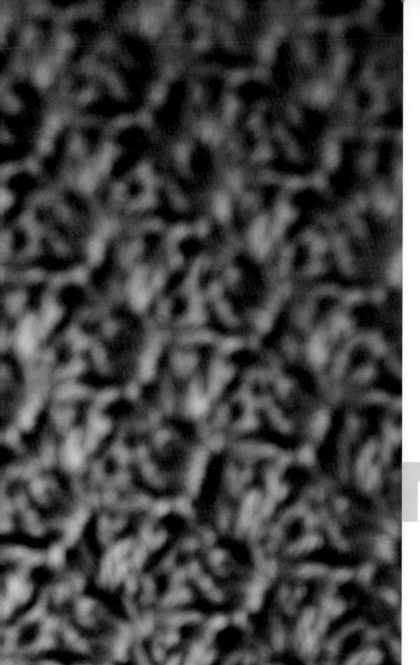

As You READ

After reading this chapter, you should be able to answer the following questions:

LO1 ▶ What is the typical flow of the birth process, and what are some possible difficulties?

LO2 ▶ What are some of the methods of childbirth?

LO3 ▶ What are some challenges that can arise during childbirth, and what are some medical interventions?

LO4 ▶ What are the characteristics of newborns?

LO5 ▶ How do individuals and families adjust after the birth of a child?

The 9-month experience of approximately 370,000 Canadian women each year typically culminates at birth (Statistics Canada, 2012a). No one knows exactly what causes labour to begin or why it begins about 280 days after the first day of the last menstrual period. What we do know is that birth practices over the years have changed remarkably and vary by culture.

Before the 20th century, few babies were born in hospitals. Most women gave birth at home, and medical intervention was not the primary force in childbirth. As concern about safety and sanitation grew, the number of babies born in hospitals increased rapidly, until the middle of the 20th century, when almost 80% were hospital births. Medical advances also meant that women received increasingly heavy medication for pain relief until the realization that these drugs can affect the baby. In the 1960s, an expanding use of childbirth techniques known as natural childbirth helped to minimize reliance on medication. Changes continue to this day, with some women seeking to employ more natural means of treatment and support during all stages of pregnancy and birth while others opt for pain medication that can be safely administered in a hospital setting.

When a person is born, one of the greatest biopsychosocial shifts occurs (Cole, 1999). From the wet, warm prenatal environment, the newborn enters a drier, colder world. The newborn must breathe and eat on its own. For the first time, the newborn encounters other human beings. Parents can suddenly see and touch their child, and the interactions that foster a particular parent–child relationship begin.

L01 ▶ The Birth Process

As women enter the last weeks of pregnancy, wheels are set in motion according to what nature dictates. For example, in most cases the baby will position itself in a head-down position, where the head is resting comfortably in the mother's pelvic region. Mothers-to-be may hear their doctor describe this situation as the dropping or lightening of the baby. Women tend to feel less pressure on their chest and diaphragm, which is a welcome sensation after several weeks of expanding girth.

Many women experience false labour pains as pregnancy progresses, and these pains sometimes occur as early as the second trimester. Experts explain such pains, called **Braxton-Hicks contractions**, as relatively mild and a sort of training for the muscles and mind before real contractions begin. Real labour pains are more intense and more painful than Braxton-Hicks contractions. It's not uncommon for couples to rush to the hospital, anticipating the birth of their child, only to learn that the delivery will likely not occur for several weeks.

Once the birth process truly begins, marked by distinctive signals and events, biopsychosocial factors interact and set the stage for multifaceted lifetime development. For example, the baby may secrete hormones that, in turn, cause the mother's body to secrete hormones that initiate uterine contractions. During labour, the woman's pituitary gland secretes **oxytocin**, a hormone that has been linked to caregiving behaviours and bonding (Feldman, Weller, Zagoory-Sharon, & Levine, 2007). Interestingly, fathers' hormone levels have been shown to change in various ways relating to different aspects of fatherhood and caregiving, so the biopsychosocial effects of birth are not limited to mothers before, during, and after the big event (Berg & Wynne-Edwards, 2001; Storey, Walsh, Quinton, & Wynne-Edwards, 2000).

Braxton-Hicks contractions Relatively mild muscle contractions that occur before real contractions begin.

oxytocin Hormone secreted by the pituitary gland that stimulates uterine contractions; has been linked to bonding between caregivers and infants.

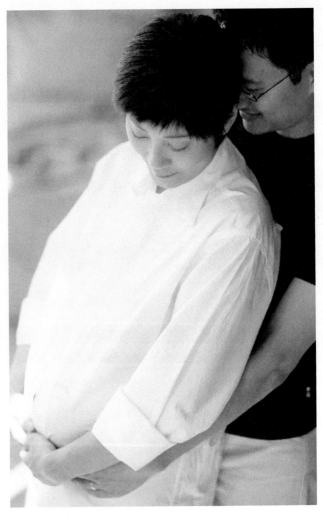

▲ Partners can play a helpful role through the birth process.

Stages in Labour and Delivery

A woman usually becomes aware of the beginning of labour by one or more of these signs:

- *Blood and/or mucus from the vagina.* As the cervix softens before labour, the mucous plug that had sealed the uterus and prevented infection is sometimes expelled with a small amount of blood. This usually means labour will begin within 24 to 48 hours (Arenson & Drake, 2007).

- *Amniotic fluid passing from the ruptured amniotic sac through the vagina.* Commonly known as "water breaking," this occurs before labour much less often than when labour is well under way.

- *Uterine contractions accompanied by significant discomfort.* Although every woman's tolerance of pain varies, there is a marked difference between mild contractions that last about 10 seconds and the stronger, regularly spaced contractions that last longer, occur every few minutes, and thus signal the onset of childbirth.

While the actual amount of time before a baby's arrival is not clear or consistent among women, three clear and distinct stages of labour are certain.

The first stage is called the **dilation** stage. The opening of the mother's cervix must increase in diameter in order for the baby to pass through and enter the world. Dilation is what causes most of the pain associated with labour. In the first stage (the longest of the three stages), the opening of the cervix dilates to about 10 centimetres in diameter. The dilation process and accompanying labour pains may last for several hours; if the birth is a woman's first, the duration is longer than it will be with subsequent deliveries. When labour begins, the duration of each contraction increases to about 60 seconds as labour continues, and the baby's head starts to move into the birth canal (opening of the vagina).

The second stage is the **expulsion** stage. Once the cervix is fully dilated, the baby no longer meets resistance, and the contractions push it along the birth canal. The expulsion phase generally lasts an average of 1.5 hours for first births and about half that time for women who have previously given birth. Most partners, if present, describe the appearance of the head of the baby (called *crowning*) as an amazing experience. Once crowning has occurred, the baby typically emerges in a matter of minutes. If this second stage of labour is prolonged—with no evidence of a problem—surgical intervention typically remains unnecessary.

Many doctors will typically use massage and lubrication in an attempt to widen the vaginal opening, but if the birth canal is still hindering the baby's safe passage, a procedure known as an **episiotomy** may be used to facilitate the birth process. This refers to a surgical cut in the vaginal opening that allows for the baby to pass through the birth canal. Because most episiotomies are easily stitched and quick to heal, they are thought to be a helpful procedure that reduces vaginal tearing and other complications related to a baby's shoulder width or declining heart rate. However, having an episiotomy may cause pain and infection after delivery, and the Society of Obstetricians and Gynaecologists of Canada (2004) does not recommend the use of episiotomy even in assisted vaginal births. The number of episiotomies performed has dropped in the past few decades (Goldberg, Holtz, Hyslop, & Tolosa, 2002), as the use of massage and other techniques has increased women's preference for more natural strategies to widen the vaginal opening.

As the baby's head emerges from the mother's body, different procedures are used to prepare the baby for entry into a dramatically different environment. For example, warm blankets are at the ready to nestle the baby and lessen the shock of transition from the warm uterus to the different temperature and sounds of the birth environment. Parents' preference for method of delivery influences the type of procedures used, and precautions are taken to ensure that the baby's breathing is promoted and risk of infection is limited. By the time the baby has been weighed and measured, has had footprints taken, and has been given an ID bracelet to match the mother's, the mother has moved into the third and final stage of birth.

FEATURED MEDIA

Films About the Birth Process

The Business of Being Born (2008)—Should births be viewed as a natural process or treated as a medical situation? Surprising facts regarding historical and current practices of the childbirth industry are interwoven with actual birth stories.

Junior (1994)—What would happen if men could conceive and deliver babies? What comic pitfalls and realizations could influence the process?

Star Trek (2009)—How does the moment of one baby's birth influence the rest of his life and the lives of infinite beings throughout the galaxy?

dilation The first stage of the birth process, during which the opening of the cervix dilates to about 10 centimetres in diameter.

expulsion Stage 2 of the birth process; the baby passes through the birth canal.

episiotomy A surgical cut made to widen the vaginal opening.

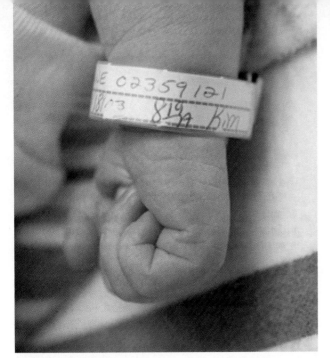

▲ By the time the newborn is given a hospital bracelet, the third stage of birth has begun.

Called the **afterbirth** stage, this final stage is marked by the delivery of the placenta, the remaining umbilical cord, and other membranes. This stage may last only a few minutes or more than an hour. If the spontaneous delivery of the placenta is delayed, a doctor may remove it. The woman's body now acts to terminate any excessive bleeding. Figure 4.1 illustrates the stages of the birth process.

L02 ▶ Methods of Childbirth

A woman's choices for childbirth practices will vary depending on her culture, the society of which she is a part, and her individual temperament. Whereas childbirth was once limited to the home and was a relatively family-centred experience, over the course of many decades delivery has moved to hospitals and other birth facilities for reasons related to hygiene and technology. For example, in the 1960s and 1970s, women whose mothers were sedated during childbirth in the 1930s and 1940s began to choose alternative methods of delivery. Instead of accepting heavy drugs that could potentially harm the baby and dull the mother's sensations during labour, mothers began to seek birth centres and techniques that focused on natural methods.

NATURAL CHILDBIRTH

Many mothers wish to create the most natural, peaceful environment possible during delivery. Methods to reduce mothers' pain and anxiety about delivery have increased in recent years, and many people argue that special tools

afterbirth Stage 3 of the birth process; the placenta and other membranes are discharged.

FIGURE 4.1
The Stages of Birth

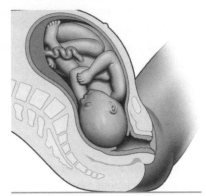

Stage one: Baby positions itself

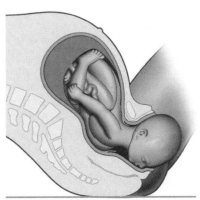

Stage two: Baby begins to emerge

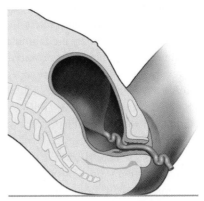

Stage three: Placenta is expelled

Childbirth is more admirable than conquest, more **amazing** than self-defence, and as courageous as either one.

GLORIA STEINEM, *MS.* MAGAZINE (1981)

PERSPECTIVES ON **DIVERSITY**

Cultural Variations of the Birth Process

Although the biological processes involved in labour and birth are similar everywhere, the experience of giving birth varies from culture to culture. Values and expectations determine procedures and identify behaviours, emotions, and reactions to be expected. For example, the Hmong women of Laos may attempt to avoid any internal examination during labour and prefer to give birth in a squatting position. Some Native American women remain upright, and Pueblo women may kneel during the birth process. Vietnamese women attempt to maintain self-control and even keep smiling during labour, while the Ibo of Nigeria consider childbirth as an illness. Japanese women usually will not ask for pain relief. Arabic women are extremely concerned with modesty and try to keep their bodies covered as much as possible. Knowing these cultural variations and preferences leads to more considerate treatment by those supporting the woman during childbirth.

As Rogoff (2003) noted, birth involves cultural practices surrounding labour and delivery (e.g., medications for the mother, different birthing positions, and degree and kind of support). Rogoff explained how a cultural innovation (Caesarean section) saves a child whose head may be too large for the mother's birth canal. Thus, the genes for large heads are preserved and passed on from generation to generation. It's clear that cultural technologies can contribute to nature and that resulting biological changes, in turn, can produce cultural adaptations.

and medications are not needed for women to experience a successful birth experience. Breathing and relaxation techniques are a big part of the process of **natural childbirth**, sometimes called prepared childbirth. Massage, hypnosis, and acupuncture are other options that women explore before and during delivery. The idea is that such techniques will reduce or eliminate the need for pain medication and give the woman more control over and awareness of her body. Other techniques, such as water births (delivering the baby in a tub of warm water), have become more popular as women strive to re-create the environment that the baby has been living in for the past 9 months.

One of the best-known natural childbirth methods is the **Lamaze method**. This method requires that the mother work with a partner before and during the delivery process to learn the techniques they will use during delivery. The partner coaches the mother by timing contractions and providing emotional and physical support.

The use of specific breathing and relaxation exercises is intended to increase a woman's feelings of control during delivery, and to reduce anxiety and pain.

MIDWIVES AND DOULAS

Support during labour and delivery can take many forms. Women have relied on midwives and doulas during the birth process for thousands of years, and many women feel more confident with women trained in these areas than they do with licensed medical doctors. In Canada, a **midwife** is a woman who has been specially trained in delivering babies and spends time with pregnant women before and during delivery.

natural childbirth (or prepared childbirth) Term to describe techniques women use prior to and during the birth process to create the most natural experience possible during delivery.

Lamaze method Natural childbirth method that stresses breathing and relaxation with the support of a partner.

midwife A woman trained in delivering babies; typically a nurse.

▲ This couple is attending a class to help them practise the Lamaze method of childbirth.

A midwife who has met specific requirements for midwife certification is able to call herself a registered midwife. Individuals who are interested in using a midwife should investigate potential midwives to ensure that a particular midwife meets all of the future parents' needs and expectations. Anyone interested in pursuing a career in midwifery should visit the website for the Canadian Association of Midwives at http://www.canadianmidwives.org/.

A **doula** is a woman who provides physical and emotional support for mothers before, during, and after delivery; this support includes providing information as needed to help mothers make educated decisions. *Doula* stems from a Greek word meaning "woman who serves." In order to work as professional doulas, women must be certified by a training organization such as DONA International. Doulas can specialize in birth or postpartum period (the period from delivery to approximately 6 weeks after a woman delivers her baby) practices. Most often, midwives and doulas work together with medical professionals to ensure the safety of the birth while giving the mother as much control over her own delivery as possible.

HOME DELIVERY

Many women who seek the assistance of midwives and doulas often express interest in delivering their babies in the comfort and familiar surroundings of their own home. Interest in home deliveries has risen in the past 30 years, although research indicates that home deliveries carry greater risks for both baby and mother (Pang, Heffelfinger, Huang, Benedetti, & Noell, 2002). Only a very

doula A woman trained as a caregiver to provide ongoing support to pregnant women before, during, and after delivery.

analgesics Mild medications used to alleviate pain; may be used before and during labour.

Career Apps

As a midwife, what strategies could you use to encourage family participation during labour and delivery?

small number of deliveries—less than 1.7% of births in Canada—occur somewhere other than a hospital (Statistics Canada, 2013a). Medical doctors facilitate some home births, but most home births are not attended by physicians. If the mother is in good health and the likelihood of complications is low, home deliveries are generally safe for both mother and baby. However, if there is any doubt as to the well-being of mother or baby, the most appropriate place for delivery to occur is a hospital.

USE OF MEDICATION

Hospitals provide a safe setting for the use of medication, and doctors and nurses help inform decisions that mothers make about which medication is best for them at specific points in the birth process. **Analgesics** are drugs used to alleviate pain and can be administered in small doses to help the mother relax during labour. Analgesics range from over-the-counter brands of acetaminophen, such as Tylenol, to tranquilizers and narcotics, such as Demerol.

▼ This woman is giving birth at home.

Anaesthetics are stronger forms of medication and can be used to control pain in the various stages of labour. For example, a mother may be given local anaesthetics to numb specific areas of the body, such as an epidural block that numbs the body from the waist down. General anaesthetics are not often used today, although women received them for years in the early 20th century. General anaesthetics put mothers to sleep so that they experience little to none of the actual delivery, and the use of these anaesthetics requires longer recovery time.

CAESAREAN SECTION

One situation that requires the use of anaesthetics, local and rarely general, is a procedure called a **Caesarean section**. If the baby cannot come through the birth canal successfully, surgery is performed to deliver the baby through the mother's abdomen. An incision is made in the mother's abdomen and the baby is delivered directly from the uterus. (The term *Caesarean* is derived from the historical figure Julius Caesar, who is believed to have been delivered in the same manner.) Conditions suggesting a Caesarean (also called a C-section) include the mother's health being in danger, fetal distress, the mother's pelvis being too narrow for a vaginal delivery, the baby's position being abnormal, and previous Caesareans (Smith, 2000). Medical reasoning is that a Caesarean section will likely produce a healthier baby than prolonged labour and a difficult birth. However, the procedure also involves certain risks, such as increased chance of infection for the mother, increased anxiety for parents, longer hospital stays, and longer recovery time associated with the surgery.

A Caesarean section is considered major surgery and is not recommended unless necessary. The rate of Caesarean births in Canada has almost doubled since the early 1990s (Kirkey, 2012). In 2010–11, 18.1% of Canadian women who delivered for the first time underwent a Caesarean section while 82.3% of those who had previously had at least one C-section delivered by that method again (Canadian Institute for Health Information, 2012). Some doctors tend to be conservative when they suspect a risky delivery and therefore recommend a C-section. Some doctors may recommend C-sections, largely because of concern about lawsuits related to vaginal deliveries that have increased in recent years. There has also been a growing trend of women who request Caesarean sections because it provides them with some control over factors such as the baby's delivery date, pain, and stress on the babies' and their own bodies. Fortunately, what was once a surgical procedure used most often as an emergency measure has become less likely to cause problems for the mother and baby than in the past.

> **anaesthetics** Stronger medications used during labour to control pain; can numb mother to pain in the various stages of labour.
>
> **Caesarean section** Surgery performed to deliver the baby through the abdomen if the baby cannot come through the birth canal.

▼ This mother and her newborn are bonding after birth.

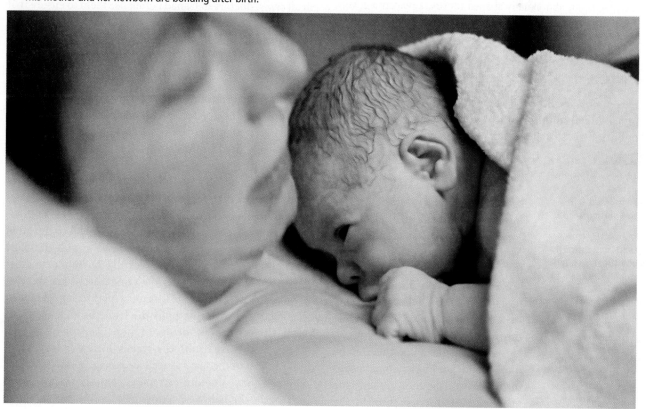

L03 ▶ Complications and Interventions

The birth process, as complex as it may be, usually proceeds with manageable levels of pain for most women. However, complications arise for women across all cultures, geographic locations, and socioeconomic levels. In industrialized societies, particularly in North America, use of medical monitoring and intervention occurs in an extremely high proportion of cases. Advances in medical technologies (such as assisted fertilization) allow for multiple births and high-risk deliveries to occur, but the chance of complications and use of interventions increase. The following are a few of the more common complications that sometimes occur and the interventions that have been designed to avoid or address them.

BREECH BIRTH

During the last month of pregnancy, most babies "turn" or move into a head-down position. Most babies who don't turn during this time are in the **breech birth** position (see Figure 4.2). It's almost as if the baby is sitting in the uterus, head up and feet down. Breech babies must be carefully guided through the birth canal feet first, buttocks first, or in a crosswise position, but most are born healthy.

Breech births cause concern and often require a Caesarean section because a baby's position in the uterus is not conducive to an optimal delivery. Several conditions can contribute to a breech presentation: more than one fetus in the uterus, an abnormally shaped uterus, a placenta covering all or part of the uterine opening, and prematurity.

FETAL MONITORING

When a woman enters the first stage of labour, it is not uncommon for her to be fitted with an electronic device called a **fetal monitor** to register the baby's heartbeat and inform medical staff as to any distress or irregularities the baby may be experiencing. This information will affect decisions about delivery proceedings, such as specific techniques, medications, and instruments that will be needed.

Two kinds of fetal monitors are used in hospitals and birthing centres—external and internal monitors. The most common device is external and worn like a belt across the mother's belly during labour. While this is not an invasive device, it can be somewhat uncomfortable for the mother and can hinder some movement during labour. Another type of monitor is inserted through the

breech birth Birth in which the baby is born feet first, buttocks first, or in a crosswise position (transverse presentation).

fetal monitor Electronic device used to monitor the baby's heartbeat throughout labour.

forceps Metal clamps placed around the baby's head to pull the baby through the birth canal.

vacuum extractor Plastic cup attached to a suction device that pulls the baby through the birth canal.

FIGURE 4.2
Fetus in Breech Presentation

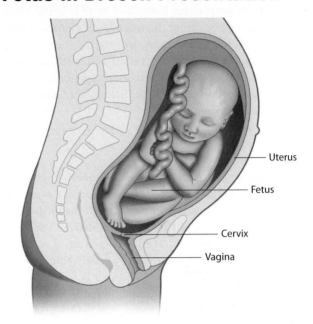

- Uterus
- Fetus
- Cervix
- Vagina

woman's cervix and rests directly on the baby's scalp. This internal monitor is more comfortable for the mother and is also highly sensitive, registering information about the baby as well as the mother's contractions. Both types of monitors are safe, and the medical use of fetal monitoring has resulted in a higher number of safe deliveries in high-risk situations. Even though the use of monitors is not necessary in all cases, doctors in Canada often use them to ensure that they have taken every possible step to facilitate a healthy delivery for mother and newborn.

USE OF INSTRUMENTS

If doctors determine that the baby is in jeopardy, they may opt for the use of special instruments to assist in the delivery of the newborn. Two kinds of instruments are typically used in most cases: forceps and the vacuum extractor. This type of assistance has been practised for centuries when there is sufficient cause for concern over need for a speedier delivery. In Canada, vacuum extractors tend to be the preferred tool (The Society of Obstetricians and Gynaecologists, 2004). **Forceps** are metal clamps that are gently placed around a baby's head to pull the baby through the birth canal. More recently, vacuum extractors have been chosen for much the same purpose as forceps. A **vacuum extractor** consists of a plastic cup attached to a suction device that pulls the baby through the birth canal. Concern about the use of these instruments is warranted, as the use of forceps greatly increases the risk of brain injury to the baby as well as damage to the baby's or mother's body. Vacuum extractors can cause bleeding on or beneath the baby's scalp, or they can create a conelike shape to the baby's head that may last for many months in a small number of cases. However, vacuum extractors are less likely than forceps to injure the mother's body. The baby's scalp is at risk of injury when either instrument is used.

The use of forceps and vacuum extractors has declined in recent years, due to an increased number of Caesarean sections and efforts to reduce risk of brain damage to the baby. As complications arise during the birth process, these instruments do continue to be used by doctors in a small percentage of births. Figure 4.3 compares the use of forceps and the vacuum extractor in delivery.

Forceps vs. Vacuum Extractor in Delivery

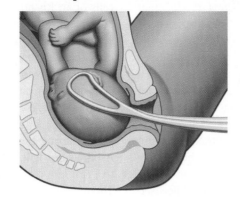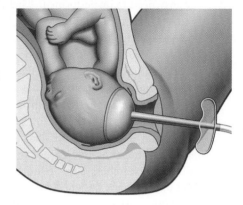

INDUCED LABOUR

One strategy that is used to hasten the delivery of a baby is **induced labour**. Induced labour is initiated by doctors through use of medication and occurs before the mother's own body initiates the birth process. Doctors induce labour when they determine that there is significant risk to either mother or child if a pregnancy continues, such as when a baby is well past the due date and growing bigger than is safe for a mother to deliver, or if there are problems with the placenta and the baby is no longer receiving sufficient nutrition.

Some suggestions for inducing labour without medical intervention are often shared by women who have had babies, and are commonly found in magazines, books, or on the Internet. For example, riding in a car down a bumpy road, being pushed on a park swing, and eating spicy food close to the delivery date are common suggestions. The success of these methods has not been scientifically tested, and yet many women place much confidence in them. The most reliable way to induce labour, however, is for a doctor to break the amniotic sac, which signals the body to go into labour. Coupled with medication, this typically stimulates contractions. For example, oxytocin (Pitocin), a contraction-causing hormone naturally produced by a woman's body during labour, is often given by injection or through an IV to speed up labour.

As a result of induced labour, a woman may experience more intense contractions that occur closer together than with a non-induced labour. This can compromise the baby's oxygen supply and the mother's ability to maintain control using prepared childbirth techniques, such as breathing exercises. The use of medication and instruments becomes greater in these instances. If efforts at an induced labour do not succeed, a Caesarean section will likely be the next course of action. In fact, the rate of Caesarean sections is much higher for induced labours than for natural labours.

OXYGEN DEPRIVATION

If anything interrupts the flow of oxygen to the fetus during birth, brain damage or death can result. **Anoxia** is the term used for lack of sufficient oxygen supply during labour and delivery. It also can be the result of insufficient blood supply from the mother. A substantial need for oxygen exists during birth because pressure on the fetal head can cause some rupturing of the blood vessels in the brain. Failure to receive oxygen can cause brain damage or death. It is difficult to predict whether the damage is permanent (Carlson, 2004).

Complications with the umbilical cord, placenta, or lungs can also cause anoxia. Before a baby is born, if the umbilical cord is squeezed or otherwise impaired, a baby may suffer oxygen deprivation. Immediately after birth, once the umbilical cord is cut, a delay in lung breathing is also dangerous. Inside the womb, if the mother's placenta separates

induced labour Labour initiated by doctors through use of medication and/or by breaking the amniotic sac.

anoxia Insufficient oxygen supply during labour and delivery, which can cause fetal brain damage or death.

▼ A Cool-cap greatly reduces brain injury and risk of death for infants who experience anoxia.

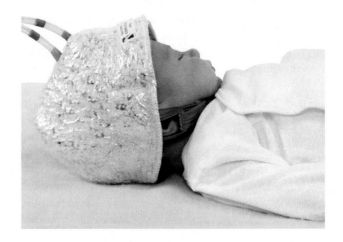

before the baby is born (*placenta abruptio*), or develops in a position that covers the opening of a woman's cervix (*placenta previa*) and therefore detaches, an emergency Caesarean may need to be performed. A baby's lung development is linked to anoxia, either because the baby experienced prenatal damage to the respiratory system or because the baby's lungs are not able to function well enough for him or her to breathe successfully. When an infant's lungs are in a serious condition, the air sacs may collapse and the infant may need to be supported by medical interventions, such as respirators.

If a baby does experience anoxia and subsequent brain injury, additional brain damage can result even hours after delivery. Researchers have found that cooling an infant's head in a specially designed apparatus (Cool-cap) licensed by Health Canada, or placing the infant on a cooling blanket, significantly reduces brain injury and infant death (Shankaran et al., 2005).

Children who have experienced anoxia display impaired cognitive abilities, such as language skills, in early and middle childhood, but these impairments sometimes improve as children age. Milder cases of anoxia tend to result in milder impairment. One condition that results from brain damage before or during labour and delivery, or shortly after birth is **cerebral palsy**, a condition resulting from an inability of the brain to control the body. The disorder is classified into four types: difficult or rigid movement, lack of balance and depth perception, involuntary movements, or a combination of the other types. Over 50,000 people in Canada are diagnosed with cerebral palsy (Ontario Federation for Cerebral Palsy, 2009), and between 1 in 500 and 1 in 1000 newborns are diagnosed annually ("Cerebral palsy", n.d.). About 10% of children diagnosed with cerebral palsy experienced anoxia before or during labour, or after delivery.

THE RH FACTOR

As much as every mother wishes to protect her baby from harm, there are some instances when unintentional damage may occur unless screening measures identify potential risks. In some cases, there is a possible incompatibility between the blood types of mother and baby. This incompatibility is related to the Rh factor. The **Rh factor** is a type of protein located on the surface of red blood cells. If the mother is Rh-negative and the baby is Rh-positive, miscarriage or infant death can result. During birth, some of the baby's blood inevitably enters the mother's bloodstream. The mother then develops antibodies to defend against the Rh factor; she is said to be "sensitized" to the Rh factor. The antibodies created by the mother's body can attack the blood cells of an Rh-positive baby, thereby causing the baby to become anemic. In many cases, a woman's first baby may not experience any harm. During later pregnancies, however, these antibodies may pass into the fetus's blood and start to destroy the red blood cells of an Rh-positive baby.

Routine screening during pregnancy, which involves a simple blood test, can provide medical staff and mothers with critical information. This screening is often suggested during the middle stage of a woman's pregnancy. A blood test will indicate whether the Rh factor is positive (present) or negative (absent) in the mother's blood. The majority of women are Rh-positive. An unsensitized Rh-negative mother can be treated with injections of a blood product called Rh immune globulin (RhIg) to prevent sensitization.

PREMATURE BIRTH AND SMALL-FOR-DATE BABIES

Another complication that sometimes occurs despite a mother's best attempts at a healthy pregnancy is **premature birth**. The average duration of a healthy pregnancy is 40 weeks. Babies who are born early—at or before 37 weeks after conception—are referred to as preterm, or premature, and are often called "preemies." Birth weight has been shown to be the best indicator of a preemie's likelihood of health challenges or successful development. For example, preemies born weighing less than 1.5 kg often struggle with developmental challenges that eventually become impossible to overcome. Even when a preemie succeeds in conquering initial challenges, other problems can persist for decades, such as high susceptibility to illness, impaired motor control, emotional and behavioural issues, and learning disabilities.

The Canadian Institute of Health Information (2006) reports that 13.6% of newborns require care in a neonatal intensive care unit (NICU). These babies once had high mortality rates, but today's sophisticated technology greatly increases their chances of survival (Feldman, Weller, Sirota, & Eidelman, 2002). Mothers who are carrying multiple babies are considered at higher risk for complications, mainly because there is limited space in the uterus, and at some point there simply isn't enough room for the babies to reach full term in a space that typically holds one baby.

Some babies are identified as **small for date** at the time of delivery, or close to the expected due date. In simple terms, this means that a baby has not grown as large as expected for the length of the pregnancy, although the baby may indeed be full term. A small-for-date baby who weighs 2.5 kg is considered at a low birth weight; a weight of 1.5 kg or less is considered very low birth

---

cerebral palsy A condition resulting from an inability of the brain to control the body; result of brain damage before, during, or after delivery.

Rh factor Involves possible incompatibility between the blood types of mother and child. If the mother is Rh-negative and the child Rh-positive, miscarriage or even infant death can result.

premature birth Early birth; occurs at or before 37 weeks after conception and is defined by low birth weight and immaturity.

small for date Term used for babies born or assessed as underweight for the length of the pregnancy.

weight. Canadian pediatricians must take ethnicity of the baby into account when assessing birth weight, however. It is not unusual for babies of South Asian and East Asian immigrants to be up to 250 grams (0.25 kg) lighter compared to babies born to Canadian-born women; this can result in the baby being misidentified as being small-for-date (CBC News, 2012).

Smoking, poor nutrition, and drug use in pregnant mothers have been linked to the incidence of small-for-date babies. Small-for-date babies are typically smaller and weigh less than their peers throughout their lifetimes; they also experience more difficulties than preemies, are at greater risk for infection and brain damage, and are likely to have later childhood learning challenges.

The graph in Figure 4.4 depicts percentages of low-birth-weight babies in major industrialized (G7) countries. As can be seen in this figure, Canada has the lowest rate of low-birth-weight babies among these countries, a result that may be a reflection of the quality and availability of prenatal health care that Canadian women receive. The national rate of low-birth-weight babies has been consistent since the late 1970s, although there has been a slight rise in recent years to 6.2% (Human Resources and Skills Development Canada, 2012a). The rates for most of the provinces and territories do not deviate much from the national rate but, interestingly, the Northwest Territories have a significantly lower rate at 3.7% while Nunavut's rate is considerably higher at 7.6%.

Interventions for premature and small-for-date infants include medical and social procedures and processes. Medical practices involve the use of a specially designed bed called an **isolette**. An isolette provides the newborn with a warm, temperature-controlled environment because the bed is enclosed in clear plastic. Isolettes help newborns who cannot regulate their own body heat; they protect the babies from cool drafts of air that could stimulate infection. Air is filtered for the infant, and physical needs relating to feeding and receiving medication can all be done within the isolette through the use of tubes and an intravenous needle, or IV.

Although premature infants may differ from full-term babies in the early days of their development, most reach developmental levels similar to those of full-term babies, although a little more slowly than usual. (This is not generally true for small-for-date babies, who have developmental challenges throughout their lives.) For example, motor development may develop more slowly for preemies. In a study conducted by Jeng, Yau, Liao, Chen, & Chen (2000), very-low-birth-weight infants began walking a few months later than infants born full term at healthy weights. Depending on the extreme nature of low birth weight, difficulties vary from one preemie to another.

Unfortunately, negative stereotypes exist and impact people's perceptions about preemies and their abilities,

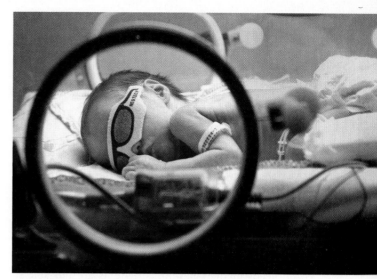

▲ An isolette provides a safe environment for preemies.

temperaments, and overall competence. Preemies are often viewed as vulnerable, fragile, and less competent, even *after* they have caught up with babies who experienced a full-term pregnancy and healthy birth weight. In one study, observers were told that a healthy-looking 9-month-old infant had been premature. These observers subsequently described the baby as "weaker, less physically mature, less sociable, and less cognitively competent" than full-term infants, a tendency called "prematurity stereotyping." Fortunately, studies indicate that by 12 to 18 months, most parents and their preterm babies have established a relationship quite similar to that of full-term infants and their parents (Goldberg & DiVitto, 2002).

isolette Specially designed bed for premature infants that is temperature-controlled and enclosed in clear plastic; often referred to as an incubator.

FIGURE 4.4

Percentages of Low-Birth-Weight Babies in Major Industrialized (G7) Countries

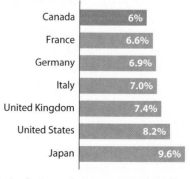

Canada	6%
France	6.6%
Germany	6.9%
Italy	7.0%
United Kingdom	7.4%
United States	8.2%
Japan	9.6%

Source: Organization for Economic Co-operation and Development (OECD), Health at a glance 2011: OECD Indicators. Figure 1.8.1. p. 39 © OECD 2011.

RESILIENCE AND PREMATURITY

The relationships between premature infants and family members are significantly aided when training and support are readily available. Parents who are fairly stable financially and have a strong social network tend to have less stress associated with premature births. They can accommodate the stresses that present themselves with the arrival of preemies. When a premature infant is born into a situation that is already compromised because of factors that may have contributed to the prematurity in the first place (such as poverty, or drug or alcohol abuse), the stress is compounded for all family members. Parents who live in high-stress, low-income environments greatly benefit from long-term interventions, such as from professionals who coach parents in coping with and responding to the needs of their newborns. Parents are not able to hold preemies in the same way they would full-term infants, and preemies do not appear as cute and cuddly as the babies that parents typically imagine in their minds, which impacts how caregivers and preemies bond in the early months after delivery. Many mothers of preemies report feelings of guilt and low self-esteem and admit to feeling like failures (Bugental & Happaney, 2004).

> Once we believe in ourselves,
> we can risk curiosity, wonder,
> **spontaneous** delight,
> or any experience that
> reveals the human spirit.
>
> E.E. CUMMINGS

Whereas it was once considered unwise and unsafe for preemies to be stimulated in their post-uterine environment, it is now known to be beneficial for preemies to receive regular forms of stimulation, whether it is music being played in their rooms, parents showing toys to infants and pointing out characteristics such as colour and texture, or skin-to-skin contact such as massage or a practice called kangaroo care. **Kangaroo care** involves the baby spending some amount of time every day in a vertical position, either on the mother's chest (typically placed between the breasts) or on the father's chest, under clothing so that the baby's skin and caregiver's skin touch for specific periods of time, sometimes several hours at a time.

There are benefits of kangaroo care for both caregiver and infant. The caregiver's body responds to the needs of the infant's body, and it regulates the infant's body temperature more easily than can be

kangaroo care Practice of skin-to-skin contact, positioning baby against caregiver's bare chest.

neonate An infant in the first days and weeks after birth.

▲ Kangaroo care involves a baby spending time in a vertical position, chest to chest with a caregiver, with their skin touching.

done in an isolette. Mother's milk adjusts accordingly, and the baby sleeps more soundly and gains weight more rapidly than when solely in an isolette. Perhaps one of the greatest benefits for caregivers is the confidence they develop with daily experience caring for their newborn. Caregivers are able to gain an appreciation for their new roles as well as their infant's abilities. They also experience the joys of daily gains in physical, cognitive, and social development.

Characteristics of Neonates ◀L04

From the moment of birth until about 1 month, the newborn infant is called a **neonate**. Even as recently as 50 years ago, most people assumed that neonates cannot do much other than lie down, eat, cry, and wait for others to tend to their needs. Today, however, we know that neonates begin to use their abilities to adapt to, and exercise some control over, their environment immediately after birth. Although they are not able to walk or talk, newborn babies display competence that contributes to their survival and elicits attention from others who will provide them with basic care. For example, neonates have the ability to imitate almost immediately after birth. Infants' imitation of tongue movements is well established in babies as young as a few hours (Gopnik, Meltzoff, & Kuhl, 1999; Jones, 1996).

▶ Neonates have the ability to imitate others, beginning shortly after birth.

Courtesy of Dr. Tiffany Field and *Science*. From Field et al., model and infant expressions from "Discrimination and Imitation of Facial Express by Neonates" in *Science*, Fig. 2, Vol. 218, pp. 179–181, October 8, 1982. Reprinted by permission of the American Association for the Advancement of Science

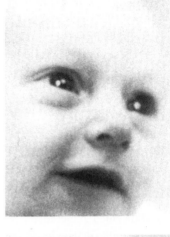

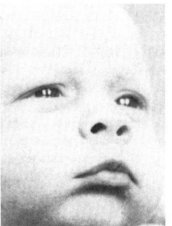

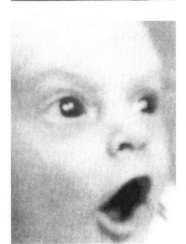

SENSORY COMPETENCE

Neonates are active seekers of stimulation. They want and need people, sounds, and physical contact to stimulate their cognitive development and to give them a feeling of security in their world. While infants spend much of their time trying to gain some control over and regulate bodily functions such as eating, breathing, and heart rate, they will take a break for brief moments and pay close attention to the environment in search of stimulation.

Vision

There is often some misperception about neonates' abilities to see at birth. They are indeed able to see, yet their visual abilities are the least developed of all the sensory abilities at birth. For example, they are nearsighted, meaning that they can see objects that are close to them (less than 30 centimetres from their faces) better than objects that are farther away. If a neonate's attention is drawn to an object (such as a small, red rubber ball held at about 4 centimetres from the face), he or she will track it as the object is moved slowly from side to side.

Neonates do not possess the level of eye-muscle control and eye–brain communication at birth that they will develop rapidly over the next few months. For example, the muscles that control the lenses of the eyes are not strong enough to allow neonates to focus on and discriminate images at different distances. Neonates will focus on objects with consistent sharpness or acuity—more accurately, lack of acuity—across a range of distances. Between 2 and 4 months of age, infants generally react to bright colours; depth perception appears at about 4 to 5 months (Brazelton & Nugent, 1995). The coordination of vision with other senses, such as smell, allows repetitive exposure to certain images to create meaningful preferences for the images, such as a mother's face. As seen in the photographs, infants are able to imitate facial expressions with great accuracy.

Smell

Neonates' ability to distinguish smells is most evident in their reactions to breast milk. Infants show a preference for the scent of human milk—even if it is not their own mother's—over formula in their first days of life (Marlier & Schaal, 2005). Neonates tend to orient themselves toward the smell of their mothers' bodies and have been shown to prefer the smell of their mothers' chests, nipples, and underarms to those of other women.

The powerful draw of a mother's scent likely has survival value, for a baby is more likely to survive if he or she is able to find food and receive care and protection from a strong, able caregiver. Furthermore, preferences for pleasant odors (such as chocolate) over unpleasant odors (such as vinegar) elicit different facial expressions that provide evidence of neonates' specific tastes. Similar facial expressions are elicited when neonates experience different tastes, because taste is closely associated with smell.

Taste

Neonates tend to make certain faces when they taste sweet flavours (relaxed lips) and quite different faces when they taste sour and bitter flavours (open or arched mouth). As with smell preferences, neonates prefer the taste of human milk, which likely has survival value, ensuring that a neonate remains close to the caregiver. As infants' tastes develop over their first year, they acquire a liking for saltier flavours, which likely facilitates their move from a liquid diet to solid foods.

Hearing

Infants can hear at birth and can perceive the direction of sound. In a famous yet simple experiment, Michael Wertheimer (1962) sounded a clicker from different sides of a delivery room only 10 minutes after an infant's birth. The infant not only reacted to the noise but also attempted to turn in the direction of the sound, indicating that babies immediately tune in to their environment. Although neonates have less developed ear–brain communication at birth than in subsequent months, they are sensitive to a variety of sounds.

Neonates pay closer attention to human speech, regardless of specific language, than sounds constructed in a pattern distinctly different from human sounds. They are able to recognize sound patterns, distinguish between two- and three-syllable sounds, and respond to tone of voice that would indicate a specific mood (e.g., happy versus angry tone). When adults speak to neonates in soft, low tones, for example, they are more able to soothe infants. The connection between sound and feelings associated with comfort and care promotes the bond between neonates and their caregivers.

Touch

You have already learned how the simple act of skin-to-skin contact in kangaroo care can benefit preemies. The same is true for all neonates. Sense of touch plays an important role in how infants gain information about the world around them; touch also stimulates their physical, cognitive, and emotional growth. Certain techniques, such as swaddling an infant, developed as cultures around the world recognized the soothing effect that a warm, tightly wrapped blanket has on an infant's behaviour. Infants may learn to respond to swaddling because of the subsequent comfort they feel, or it may be that swaddling and other touch sensations are connected to reflexes that are biologically based, prewired into every human being.

NEONATAL REFLEXES

Unlike the environment, which a baby is born into, a **reflex** is an inborn, automatic response to certain stimuli. Popular examples include the eye blink and the knee jerk. Critical reflexes needed to survive are present at birth (breathing, sucking, swallowing, and elimination) and require no learning to execute. For example, reflexes associated with feeding include sucking and swallowing during the prenatal period and infancy. Infants demonstrate the **rooting reflex** when a nipple or finger is gently placed on their cheek or near their lips. Infants will turn toward the stimulation and attempt to get the nipple or finger into their mouths. The neonate's sucking reflex grows stronger as the infant grows, and eventually the reflex becomes voluntary. Neonates also adjust their breathing accordingly when feeding. Their ability to breathe comfortably while feeding is critical to their survival. They also demonstrate developing breathing control when crying and reacting to new stimuli in their world (Rose, 2005). Breathing patterns are not fully established at birth: it is common for infants to stop breathing for brief periods (lasting 2–5 seconds), a condition called **apnea**.

The **Moro reflex** is also known as the *startle reflex*, because the neonate's physical movements appear as if the infant is startled. The arms and legs flail out and back in toward the chest quickly, and the back arches. This reflex typically occurs when the neonate experiences a sensation like falling or loss of support—if the infant's head or neck is released suddenly or the infant's crib or stroller is bumped into. Absence of the Moro reflex can indicate brain damage or immature development.

Neonates exhibit grasping reflexes of the hands and feet. The **grasping reflex** of the hands is seen when neonates instinctively grasp objects placed in the palms of their hands, whether the object is a human finger, a rattle, or the corner of a blanket. Similarly, the **plantar reflex** is seen when neonates curl their toes toward pressure placed on the balls of their feet. Each of these grasping reflexes diminishes during the first several months of life, and babies develop increasing ability to grasp things voluntarily with their hands (and, at times, with their feet!).

reflex An inborn, automatic response to certain stimuli.

rooting reflex Automatic response in which an infant turns toward a finger or nipple placed gently on the cheek, attempting to get it into his or her mouth.

apnea Brief periods when breathing is suspended.

Moro reflex Infant's automatic response to sudden change in position or unexpected movement; arms and legs flail out and back in toward chest, and back arches.

grasping reflex Automatic response in which an infant's fingers curl toward palm of hand when object or finger is placed in palm.

plantar reflex Automatic response in which an infant's toes curl inward when pressure is placed on balls of feet.

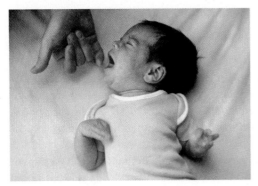

▲ The rooting reflex

▲ The Moro reflex

▲ The grasping reflex

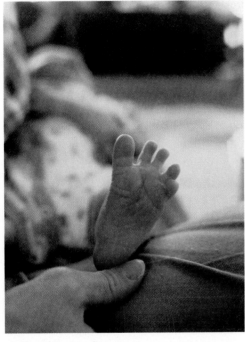

▲ The Babinski reflex

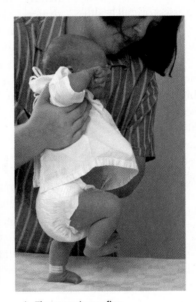

▲ The stepping reflex

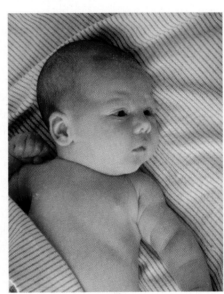

▲ The tonic-neck reflex

Similar, yet slightly different from the plantar grasp, the **Babinski reflex** is demonstrated when the neonate spreads out her toes in response to gentle stroking of the bottom of the foot, from heel to toes. Eventually this reflex changes and the infant curls toes toward the pressure instead of fanning out the toes.

As early as the first days of life, neonates demonstrate movements that appear similar to walking. If infants are held under their arms so that their feet are touching a tabletop or other flat surface, they demonstrate the **stepping reflex**, in which their feet look like they are trying to walk, placing one foot down and then the other. Preemies often step in a "tiptoe" manner, whereas full-term babies step heel to toe, in the manner that humans eventually do walk.

When a neonate is placed on his or her back, and turns his or her head to one side, the **tonic-neck reflex**

is apparent. The infant extends the arm and leg on the side that corresponds to the direction he or she is looking, while flexing the arm and leg on the other side. This reflex, also known as the *fencing reflex*, diminishes in frequency over the first few months of life.

Pediatricians are able to assess a neonate's overall neurological functioning by assessing the various reflexes. Many of these reflexes diminish after a few months and are substituted with other, voluntary actions. Other reflexes disappear altogether. The photos above illustrate neonatal reflexes.

Babinski reflex Automatic response in which an infant's toes spread out in response to stroking the sole of the foot from heel to toes.

stepping reflex Automatic response in which the neonate, held under the arms with feet touching a flat surface, makes stepping movements similar to actual walking.

tonic-neck reflex Automatic response in which an infant extends arm and leg on same side as the direction in which he or she is looking, while flexing other arm and leg.

Glossary (sidebar)

Apgar scale A test to evaluate a newborn's basic life signs administered at 1 minute and 5 minutes after birth.

neurological assessment A neonatal test that identifies any neurological problem, suggests means of monitoring the problem, and offers a prognosis about the problem.

Brazelton Neonatal Behavioural Assessment Scale Device to assess an infant's behaviour; examines both neurological and psychological responses.

postpartum period Period lasting approximately 6 weeks after birth as mother adjusts physically and psychologically.

NEONATAL ASSESSMENT TECHNIQUES

Although all infants are born with these reflexes and abilities, they possess them to varying degrees. For example, some neonates demonstrate weaker reflex action than others, which affects their chances of surviving. Links to neurological functioning also influence doctors' desires to gain accurate information about each neonate. Efforts to develop reliable measures of early behaviour, called *neonatal assessment*, have therefore increased over time. Three basic neonatal tests used to assess overall health of the infant are the Apgar scale, neurological assessment, and behavioural assessment.

The **Apgar scale**, shown in Figure 4.5, is administered twice—1 minute and 5 minutes after birth—to evaluate a newborn's basic life signs. Using five life signs (heart rate, respiratory rate, muscle tone, reflex irritability, and skin colour), an observer evaluates the infant on a 3-point scale. Each life sign receives a 0, 1, or 2, with 0 indicating severe problems and 2 suggesting an absence of major difficulties. A total of 8 or more points indicates a successful transition to life outside the womb (Arenson & Drake, 2007).

Neurological assessment is used for:

- identification of any neurological problem,
- constant monitoring of a neurological problem, and
- prognosis about some neurological problem.

Each of these purposes requires testing the infant's reflexes, which is critical for neurological evaluation and basic for all infant tests. There are different neurological assessment tools specifically designed for newborns, but they all aim to identify potential problems for the neonates.

The **Brazelton Neonatal Behavioural Assessment Scale** has become a significant worldwide tool for infant behavioural assessment. It focuses on a neonate's reflexes, responses to stimuli (e.g., sounds, light, and touch), attention, orientation to face and voice, ability to be soothed, motor coordination, and transitions from one emotional state to another. Brazelton and Nugent (1995) believe that the baby's state of consciousness (sleepy, drowsy, alert, or fussy) is the single most important element in the examination. The assessment is administered when the neonate is 3 days old and again a few days later to strive for accuracy. This assessment is intended to measure various aspects of a neonate's behaviour, so important for survival.

Postpartum Adjustment ◀L05

With so much attention placed on the neonate, it is important to focus some attention on the impact that birth has on the mother and other family members. Immediately after birth and continuing for about 6 weeks, women enter the **postpartum period**, a time of physical and psychological adjustment to pregnancy and birth.

FIGURE 4.5
The Apgar Scale

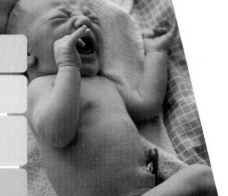

Score	0	1	2
Heart rate	Absent	Slow—less than 100 beats per minute	Fast—100–140 beats per minute
Respiratory rate	No breathing for more than one minute	Irregular and slow	Good breathing with normal crying
Muscle tone	Limp and flaccid	Weak, inactive, but some flexion of extremities	Strong, active motion
Body color	Blue and pale	Body pink, but extremities blue	Entire body pink
Reflex irritability	No response	Grimace	Coughing, sneezing and crying

TAKE A **STAND**

How Much Information Is Too Much?

There is no question that families and medical professionals know more today than they did years ago about neonates' abilities. Technology provides people with access to information before conception, during pregnancy, at the moment of birth, and after. Some people argue that the wealth of available information contributes to a growing anxiety about birth and a neonate's abilities. It is not uncommon for a mother to worry if her newborn does not respond well to sounds at 3 days old—does that mean the child is at risk for future cognitive impairment?

How can people balance the medical benefits of various tests with the emotional effects of anticipation and of processing the information provided as a result of the assessments?

▲ Alanis Morissette is a strong advocate for mothers, raising awareness about postpartum experiences and the need for greater awareness and sensitivity.

DEPRESSION

Hormonal changes after birth, a sense of anticlimax after completing something anticipated for so many months, sheer fatigue, and tension about care of the baby (especially after a first birth) may cause feelings of sadness or a "letdown" in the new mother. Anywhere from 25% to 85% of women have feelings described as "the blues" for a few days postpartum. Such feelings are usually temporary and wane during the first week or two after delivery. However, if these feelings persist longer than 2 or 3 weeks, professional help may be needed. Approximately 17% of Canadian women exhibit **postpartum depression** symptomatology (PPDS) (Lanes, Kuk, & Tamim, 2011). Women with a history of mental illness are at higher risk for experiencing postpartum depression. While it is clearly a difficult experience for the mother, it also seriously impacts her parenting, which has a significant impact on the neonate's development. Figure 4.6 shows the rates of PPDS by province. Note that the rate for the territories (including the Northwest Territories, Nunavut, and the Yukon) is considerably higher than for the rest of the country. Lanes, Kuk, & Tamim (2011) have proposed two explanations for this finding. First, the measurement of PPDS for the territories was taken during the winter months when residents are exposed to very little daylight; lack of daylight can affect mood. Second, there are a higher proportion of Aboriginal people residing in the territories and Aboriginals have been shown to be at an increased risk of depression.

Singer Alanis Morissette has shared her personal experience with postpartum depression, citing feelings of pain and shame. She referred to her baby's arrival as "amazing" but the letdown after delivery rendered her despondent. She successfully came back from her postpartum depression, after "various therapies," and is now a strong advocate for breastfeeding and attachment parenting (Byrne, 2012).

postpartum depression Feelings of sadness and emotional withdrawal that may continue for many weeks or months after delivery.

Methods of treating postpartum depression often involve medication and contact with others, such as a parent support group. Most women respond well to treatment with antidepressant medication. Because patients are leaving hospitals earlier after delivery than in decades past—due to medical advances and the costs of health care—the challenges of motherhood are experienced differently. Mothers are thrust sooner into their new roles and relationships—into the uncertainty attached to navigating uncharted territory.

FIGURE 4.6

Postpartum Depression Symptoms (PPDS) among Canadian Women

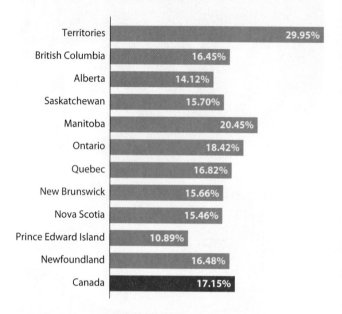

Region	PPDS
Territories	29.95%
British Columbia	16.45%
Alberta	14.12%
Saskatchewan	15.70%
Manitoba	20.45%
Ontario	18.42%
Quebec	16.82%
New Brunswick	15.66%
Nova Scotia	15.46%
Prince Edward Island	10.89%
Newfoundland	16.48%
Canada	17.15%

Source: Lanes, Kuk, & Tamim (2011)

BONDING

Bonding refers to the formation of a close connection, or attachment, between the newborn and caregiver, typically parents. The connection begins as a physical connection but evolves into a psychological and emotional one that is considered crucial for a child's well-being. Hospital practices reflect the importance of bonding, as seen in the increased practice of keeping neonates in their mothers' hospital rooms as much as possible. A mother is more readily able to hold and feed her baby and begin adjusting to her new role. Still under the care of medical professionals who are concerned for the mother's well-being as well as that of the newborn, mothers can opt for some time alone in the room if they wish.

It is important to note that extended time together immediately after birth does not guarantee a healthy and harmonious parent–child relationship in later years, and lack of time together shortly after birth does not mean that bonding will not occur. For instance, adoptive parents and their adopted children experience deep and rewarding bonding equal to that of biological parents and their children. It may be argued that quality, not quantity, of time together more significantly influences the connection.

bonding The formation of a close connection, or attachment, between a newborn and caregiver.

TECH TRENDS

Not Your Mother's Cranial Stimulator

When celebrity mothers, such as Alanis Morissette and Celine Dion, shared their personal experiences with postpartum depression and medical treatment, many people criticized their use of medical intervention for their psychological problems. A new form of treatment that does not rely on medication—the Fisher Wallace Cranial Stimulator—is a safe and effective way to reduce the stress that leads to depression and other psychological problems.

The device consists of a headband, two sponge applicators, and the base unit. The sponges are moistened and held in place with the headband. When the base unit is turned on, it sends mild radio waves to stimulate production of serotonin and dopamine—two neurotransmitters (chemicals in the brain) associated with mood. The effects on brain activity have been argued to be a healthy alternative to prescription medication for postpartum and other kinds of depression.

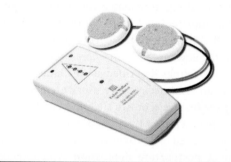

SINGLE-PARENT FAMILIES

The percentage of babies in Canada born to single (never married) mothers is approximately 29% (Statistics Canada, 2012a). The number of births to single mothers has increased only slightly since 2006 and is over 10% less than the rate of births to single mothers in the United States (Martin et al., 2009). The lower rate of teen motherhood that is seen in Canada in comparison to the United States may be due to more liberal attitudes in Canada towards sex education in schools and the availability of contraception for teenagers. Some researchers believe that, as an increasing number of young Canadian women see that there are viable educational and career options for them as they enter their adult years, it makes it less likely that they will have a baby at a young age (Proudfoot, 2010). Aboriginal teens are more than twice as likely to become pregnant compared with other Canadian teens (Luong, 2008). We will discuss teenage pregnancy further in Chapter 8.

There is no question that support is needed to help single mothers, but it is important to note that to identify a mother as unmarried does not necessarily mean that she is alone or without a loving family or other support network. Nonetheless, the fact remains that the majority of births to single mothers occur for women who are in their 20s, at a low income level, and without significant social and financial support. The absence of social and financial support can compound feelings of insecurity for women and can negatively impact a child's development for his or her entire lifetime. Interventions, such as counselling, support groups, and home visits by professional social workers or early-intervention specialists, greatly assist mothers and other family members with the transitions associated with welcoming the neonate into the world.

FAMILY DYNAMICS

In many cases, the birth of a baby creates new expectations for family members. For example, it is common that some of the more stereotypical gender-associated activities fall to the mother. Feeding the neonate is a natural task for mothers, especially if they are nursing their babies. Fathers can feed babies the mother's breast milk in a bottle, which greatly helps the mother with feeding responsibilities. All relationships with partners or spouses require cooperation, negotiation, and distribution of labour; but the birth of a child often brings these issues to the forefront, regardless of any discussion or agreements that occurred before delivery.

The average age of Canadian women giving birth in 2011 was 29.7 years of age (Statistics Canada, 2013b). When couples wait until they are older and more established in their chosen careers to become parents, the transition to parenthood is somewhat easier. Fathers tend to be more comfortable with their parenting role if they feel more secure financially. Also, an older father is more

TAKE A STAND

Maternity and Parental Leave: How much is appropriate?

In Canadian workplaces, a woman who delivers a baby is entitled to paid time off, thanks to the Canada Labour Code, which allows employees to take time off up to 52 workweeks in any 12-month period for the birth or adoption of a child. A birth mother is entitled to no more than 17 weeks of maternity leave while either parent can take or split between them up to 37 weeks of parental leave provided that the total of maternity and parental leave does not exceed 52 weeks. Same-sex couples also have the right to parental leave. **(www.labour.gc.ca/eng/standards_equity/ st/pubs_st/maternity.shtml)**

Canada's maternity and parental leave benefits are much more generous than those of the United States, where mothers are entitled to no more than 12 weeks of maternity leave; however, Canada's benefits are less generous than those of Sweden which has a maximum of 420 days.

How much leave do you believe is appropriate for new parents to receive to take care of their infant? Which factors do you believe governments should be considering in determining how much maternity and parental leave parents are provided?

inclined to pitch in with household responsibilities while a mother is regaining strength and establishing routines. All families in whatever form they take—including adoptive families, families with gay or lesbian parents, blended families, and single-parent families—must make an adjustment when the neonate arrives. As the newborn grows into infancy, the strategies used and lessons learned will shift once again.

CONCLUSIONS & SUMMARY

This chapter provides information about the complex birth process as well as many challenges and interventions that impact the experience for mother, child, family members, and the professionals involved in the process. Today, thanks to technological advances, preemies have a much greater chance of survival and of healthy physical and psychological development. As the neonate transitions into the world, assessments highlight strengths and challenges from the neonate's very first moments, assessments that provide information that serves as a baseline for future development. The family's adjustment to the newborn involves multiple factors, including physical, financial, social, and emotional elements.

What is the typical sequence of the birth process?

- Birth occurs as a series of stages that bring the baby from the uterine environment into his or her new world.
- Complications such as breech presentations, anoxia, and the Rh factor are among the difficulties that can develop during the birth process.

What are some methods of childbirth?

- Childbirth methods are constantly evolving to ease the transition from womb to world. These include breathing techniques, relaxation, and drugs to alleviate pain and anxiety.

What are some challenges that can arise in childbirth?

- Breech birth, the use of instruments during labour, the induction of labour, oxygen deprivation, and incompatibility of blood type between mother and baby are all complications that can arise during childbirth.

What are some characteristics of newborns?

- Neonates exhibit their competence through their sensory abilities and reflexes. Neonatal assessment focuses on neurological functioning and other behaviours to gain information about the neonate's abilities.

How do people adjust after the birth of a newborn?

- Families must adjust to the birth of a new child, which impacts people in different ways, according to expectations and family dynamics. About 17% of women experience symptoms of postpartum depression, which is related to the physical and emotional letdown following delivery. Medical and other interventions are available to help mothers with this condition.

For REVIEW

1. Adults typically interact with newborns quite differently than with older children and adults. Is our behaviour influenced by what we learn about appropriate means of interacting with neonates, or might some of our behaviour be innate?

2. Various forms of neonatal assessment exist to provide information to parents and medical professionals. How many assessments are necessary to gain a clear picture of a neonate's abilities?

3. What is important to know about the postpartum period? What physical and emotional adjustments does a woman make after delivery?

Chapter REVIEW TEST

1. When a baby is positioned inside the mother's uterus in a feet-down orientation, this is known as a _____ position.
   a. topsy-turvy
   b. upside-down
   c. breech
   d. organic

2. False labour pains are marked by a woman experiencing _____ contractions.
   a. Braxton-Hicks
   b. Brazelton
   c. tight
   d. Moro reflex

3. A woman trained as a caregiver to provide ongoing support to pregnant women in all stages of pregnancy and delivery is a certified
   a. pregnancy mentor.
   b. doula.
   c. nurse-practitioner.
   d. Lamaze coach.

4. The frequency of deliveries by _____ has increased over the years, even though it is considered major surgery.
   a. Caesarean section
   b. water birth
   c. induced labour
   d. surrogate delivery

5. A(n) _____ is an electronic device that provides important information about the baby's and mother's conditions during labour.
   a. episiotomy
   b. epidural
   c. spinal block
   d. fetal monitor

6. _____ is the term used to describe a muscle condition caused by brain damage before, during, and after delivery.
   a. Braxton-Hicks
   b. Cerebral palsy
   c. Locus of control
   d. Episiotomy

7. Babies who are born more than 3 weeks before full term and weigh less than 2.5 kg at birth are considered
   a. premature.
   b. slow to warm up.
   c. breech.
   d. complex deliverables.

8. The practice of skin-to-skin contact that is recommended for preemies and their caregivers is known as
   a. swaddling.
   b. attachment.
   c. kangaroo care.
   d. Babinski reflex.

9. The _____ reflex is sometimes called the startle reflex because the neonate flails his or her arms and legs out and back in toward the chest and arches his or her back.
   a. grasping
   b. rooting
   c. plantar
   d. Moro

10. Women who experience lingering feelings of sadness and withdrawal after delivery may suffer from postpartum
    a. anoxia.
    b. hypertension.
    c. depression.
    d. anxiety.

INFANCY

As You READ

After reading this chapter, you should be able to answer the following questions:

LO1 ▶ What are the major physical accomplishments of the infancy period?

LO2 ▶ How do infants acquire information about their world?

LO3 ▶ What are the differences between Piaget's view of cognitive development in infancy and that of information-processing theorists?

LO4 ▶ How do infants acquire their language?

LO5 ▶ What is the role of relationships in psychosocial development?

LO6 ▶ How do children develop and control their emotions?

LO7 ▶ How would you assess the importance of attachment in psychosocial development?

LO8 ▶ How does temperament affect the relationship between parents and their children?

My friend has a **baby**. I'm recording all the noises he makes so later I can ask him what he **meant**.

STEPHEN WRIGHT

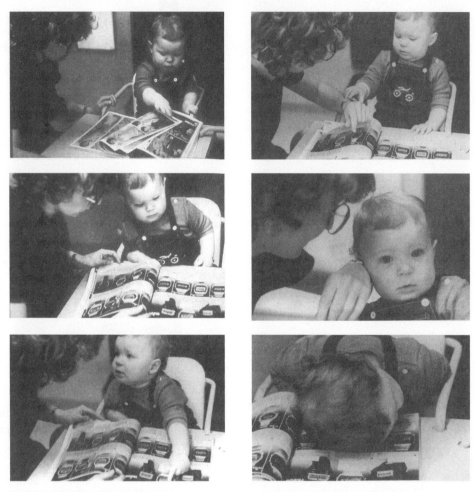

▲ Infants have the ability to master an array of physical, cognitive, and emotional skills at a very young age.

Infants are more than cute and cuddly, drooling and squirming milk guzzlers. Between birth and the age of 2, children master an incredible array of physical, cognitive, and emotional skills and tasks. Because they are so dependant on their caregivers, however, infants are often completely underestimated in their abilities. Theorists in the field of lifespan development have viewed infants along a range of competencies, from small sponges waiting for something to absorb (Skinner), to active constructors of their own world (Piaget). Beliefs about what infants are capable of have powerful impact—on parents' views of their children, on educators' views of how infant/toddler care should be designed, and on policymakers' views of how money and resources should be allocated.

One of the most influential approaches to infant/toddler and preschool education is widely recognized in the work of educators in Reggio Emilia, Italy, who are known for their innovative approach to early education. One principle of the Reggio Emilia philosophy is that even the youngest infants exercise some control over the direction of their learning. One feature that distinguishes the municipal infant/toddler centres and preschools in Reggio Emilia is their systematic use of documentation to inform and extend the learning experiences of the children as well as the educators and families (Edwards, Gandini, & Forman, 1998).

The images of Laura, above, speak to the curiosity and competency of young children and have been recorded, analyzed, and revisited by people around the world. Notice how she and the teacher are looking at a catalogue, at a picture of a watch. The teacher, seeing Laura's interest in the watch, shows Laura her own wristwatch and lets Laura listen to the ticking sound the watch makes. Laura, using the new knowledge she's just acquired, puts her ear to the catalogue to see if the watch in the photo also makes a

 # PERSPECTIVES ON **DIVERSITY**

ticking sound. Not even 1 year old, Laura has taken her new learning, generated a hypothesis (all watches make a ticking sound), and tested her hypothesis (if I listen to the photo of a watch, will it tick?). At the heart of the Reggio Emilia approach, exemplified in these images, is a celebration of relationships—between child and teacher, child and environment, teacher and caregiver(s), and all combinations of these participants in children's learning and development.

This chapter will help you to understand how development in infancy is viewed today. First, infants' physical development is presented, followed by specific domains of infant development: motor, perception, cognitive, language, and social and emotional. Themes relating to biopsychosocial interactions are woven throughout the material, and you'll notice how virtually every aspect of development is affected by multiple influences. Many factors influence the interactions between parent and infant; they also set the stage for interactions that will evolve over a lifetime.

L01 ▶ Physical Development in Infancy

Infancy is a time of rapid physical development. A typical newborn weighs about 3.4 kilograms and is about 50 centimetres long. In the year after birth, an infant's length increases by one half and its weight almost triples.

While infancy is a time of rapid growth and increasing physical ability, it is also a time of extreme vulnerability. The infant morality rate is the number of deaths that occur in the first year of life for 1000 live births. According to Statistics Canada, infant mortality in Canada was 4.9 infant deaths per 1000 live births in 2009, a decrease of more than half from 1979 (10.9 deaths per 1000 live births). Figure 5.1

shows that among G7 countries, in 2009, infant mortality ranged from 2.4 infant deaths per 1000 live births in Japan to 6.4 deaths in the United States. Canada ranked second highest with a 4.9 infant mortality rate. Although infant death in Canada is often due to babies being born too small or too early, there is a link to poor mothers with less education being at a higher risk of early delivery.

DEVELOPMENTAL MILESTONES OF INFANCY

Growing children experience rapid changes in body shape and composition, distribution of tissues, and in motor skills. For example, the infant's head at birth is about a quarter of the body's total length, but in the adult it is about

FIGURE 5.1

Infant Mortality Rates

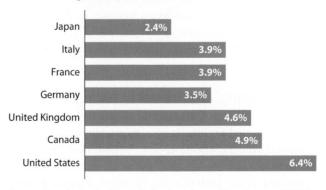

Infant Mortality, G7 countries, 2009 (per 1000 live births)

Source: Organization for Economic Co-operation and Development (OECD) (2013), "Infant mortality," Health: Key Tables from OECD, No. 14. doi: 10.1787/inf-mort-table-2013-1-en

FIGURE 5.2

Changes in Proportions of the Human Body

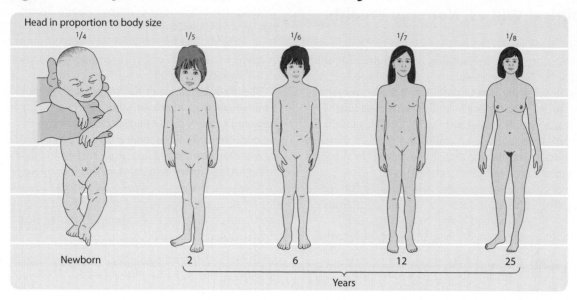

Head in proportion to body size

1/4   1/5   1/6   1/7   1/8

Newborn   2   6   12   25

Years

one seventh of body length. The head becomes noticeably smaller compared to the rest of the body as we develop. (See Figure 5.2.) Total growth represents a complex series of changes that occur in developmental sequence. Underlying this rapidly unfolding and complex process is, of course, proper nutrition.

NUTRITION

Good nutrition is crucial for a healthy baby, and ideally all infants would receive a balance of necessary nutrients. Yet infants' nutritional needs are quite different from adults'. Meeting ideal needs can be difficult because of an infant's small stomach and immature digestive system (Ball & Bindler, 2006). Fortunately, until infants' bodies develop the mechanisms needed to chew, swallow, store, and digest solid food, their nutritional needs can be taken care of through liquid nutrition in the form of breast milk or formula. Just as babies do not choose the families they are born into, they also do not choose whether or not their caregivers follow a healthy diet or whether they are breast- or formula-fed. The decision to breastfeed is one that is often influenced by pressure from family and society.

Breastfeeding versus Bottle-Feeding

Most doctors, nurses, and mothers agree that human milk is the ideal food for infants up to six months (Leifer, 2003), and yet this belief wasn't always the dominant viewpoint. Throughout much of the 20th century, women were discouraged from breastfeeding as some medical experts believed that babies could get better nutrition through formulas. Doctors and family often actively discouraged

breastfeeding, which was frowned upon in public places and banned in some of them.

▼ Although breastfeeding is a natural process, not all women are able to do so, even when they have the desire to.

Breastfeeding has definite advantages over formula-feeding. First is protection against disease. Breastfed babies tend to experience less illness than formula-fed babies. Second, breastfed babies are less at risk for allergic reactions than are formula-fed babies. Other findings from research indicate that breastfed babies have stronger bones, more advanced cognitive development, easier transitions to solid food, and lower risk for obesity than those who are formula-fed.

A joint statement of Health Canada, Canadian Paediatric Society, Dietitians of Canada, and the Breastfeeding Committee for Canada recommends breastfeeding exclusively for the first six months and sustained for up to two years or longer with appropriate complementary feeding (Statistics Canada, 2009). This is important for the nutrition, immunologic protection, and growth and development of infants and toddlers.

According to Statistics Canada, the percentage of women who initiated breastfeeding rose from 81.5% in 2001 to 87.0% in 2005 and has held steady since then (Statistics Canada, 2009). The proportion of mothers who began to breastfeed was above the national average in Alberta (92.4%), British Columbia (97.3%), and Yukon, where all the women who were interviewed in 2009 had begun to breastfeed. The proportion of women who began to breastfeed was below the national average in Newfoundland and Labrador (61.1%), Nova Scotia (76.7%) and Quebec (81.8%).

There are specific situations, however, when a woman should not breastfeed her baby. If a woman is infected with AIDS or another infectious disease, has active tuberculosis, or is currently taking medication that could be harmful to the child, then she should not breastfeed her child.

The availability of formula is an important factor in the decision of feeding an infant. One of the advantages of formula feeding is that others, including fathers, can feed the baby. This is a relief to some mothers who, despite their wishes to breastfeed, are not physically able to. Although breastfeeding is best for babies' health and development, some mothers will need or want to bottle-feed and can be reassured that the nutrition of most formulas is sufficient. Assuming that the formula is appropriate, nutritional problems should not arise.

In the course of one year, infants progress from either breast- or bottle-feeding to eating a variety of solid foods. As infants develop, tremendous brain growth occurs that helps make advances in feeding possible; and the more diverse range of foods, in turn, fuels the brain for more growth. The motor skills needed to pick up small pieces of food, the chewing and swallowing required to consume the food, and the language skills that emerge as a child learns to ask for "more!" are all connected to the brain.

TECH TRENDS

Podcasts for Nursing Mothers

In case mothers aren't multitasking enough, the Breastfeeding Management application for iPhone or iPod Touch (available via iTunes) offers free information about breastfeeding that interested women can access while exercising, driving, working, or nursing! This app was designed to help clinicians identify and treat common breastfeeding problems. It has a link to the LactMed database and news about medications, which most mothers might find interesting but not use as often as other key features—frequently asked questions, and links to highly respected resources, such as the World Health Organization.

Other Canadian resources for new mothers include:

www.themothersprogram.ca

www.babycenter.ca

www.lllc.ca (La Leche League Canada)

BRAIN DEVELOPMENT

Scientists have reexamined their ideas about babies' brains. Rather than an empty vessel waiting to be filled, the baby's brain is actually more active than an adult's brain, taking in large amounts of information in short periods of time. What once had been viewed as a deficit, such as infants' undeveloped language ability or short attention span, is now considered essential to the learning process (Lehrer, 2009). Figure 5.3 illustrates the various areas of the brain.

> **infantile amnesia** The inability to remember events from early in life.

Because babies aren't able to tell us what they're thinking or feeling, and we all experience the phenomenon called **infantile amnesia**—the inability to remember events from early in life—brain researchers rely heavily on tests that provide results they can then compare to results from an adult brain. Any conclusions that researchers make about infant brains are therefore speculative and supported with stronger or weaker data from various techniques:

- *Electroencephalogram (EEG)*. Electrodes are placed on the scalp to (1) measure neuron/nerve activity that registers as electrical signals and (2) identify different behavioural states, such as deep sleep.
- *Computed tomography (CT)*. An advanced version of X-ray techniques, the commonly used CT scan presents three-dimensional pictures of the brain.

FIGURE 5.3

The Human Brain

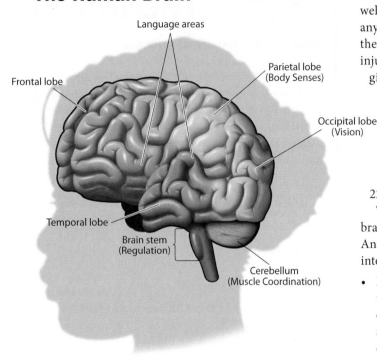

Language areas

Frontal lobe

Parietal lobe
(Body Senses)

Occipital lobe
(Vision)

Temporal lobe

Brain stem
(Regulation)

Cerebellum
(Muscle Coordination)

- *Positron emission tomography (PET)*. PET scans measure the amount of blood flow associated with brain activity. Tiny radioactive elements (about the same amount of radioactivity you would receive from a chest X-ray) are injected into the bloodstream and become tracers that the PET scan can detect.

- *Magnetic resonance imaging (MRI)*. The popular MRI depends on the magnetic quality of blood to measure internal structures.

neurons Nerve cells that transmit information with electrochemical signals.

axons Branchlike ends of neurons that send electrochemical signals between cells.

dendrites Branchlike ends of neurons that receive and conduct the electrochemical signals between the cells.

synapse A small gap between neurons that allows communication between neurons to occur.

myelin Sheath of insulation around axons that facilitates communication between neurons.

EEGs are most often used with infants, because radiation poses a risk to their health and they won't stay still for an MRI. Findings from EEGs have noted bursts of activity that may correspond to bursts in cognitive and language development, and they have also been used as predictors of behaviour problems in toddlers.

During infancy, the baby's brain is about one fourth of its adult weight and contains billions of nerve cells, called **neurons**. Neurons transmit information by electrochemical signals, and at this age connections between neurons increase to as many as 100 to 1000 connections for each of the billions of neurons. The brain grows from

0.23 kg at birth to about 0.68 kg at the end of the first year. By age 5, the brain weighs about 1.36 kg and is adult size (Eliot, 2000). Because infants' neck muscles are not well developed and provide little support for their heads, any violent movement thrusts the brain back and forth in the skull and puts infants at risk for brain trauma. In the injury known as *shaken baby syndrome*, frustrated caregivers shake babies so hard that brain damage occurs, resulting in a baby's loss of control over such vital functions as heart rate, respiration, blood pressure, and temperature. Recent Canadian data on children hospitalized for shaken baby syndrome show that 19% died, 59% had neurological, visual impairment and/or other health effects, and only 22% appeared well at discharge (Health Canada, 2001).

Thanks to research, we know that infants shape their brains through their experience with the outside world. An infant translates information from the outside world into brain action in the following way:

- Electrical nerve impulses travel along neurons (see Figure 5.4), forming connections between **axons** and the **dendrites** of other neurons along their pathways. The axons send the signals from one neuron to another, and dendrites catch and conduct the electrochemical signals between the cells.

- The small gaps between neurons are called **synapses**. Each synapse allows communication between neurons to occur.

- The process is made quicker because of a sheath (coating) on the axons called **myelin**, which is like insulation around the axon and is critical for brain function. Myelination, the formation of a myelin sheath around

▲ Electroencephalograms are often used to help predict behaviour problems in infants.

FIGURE 5.4

Structure of a Typical Neuron

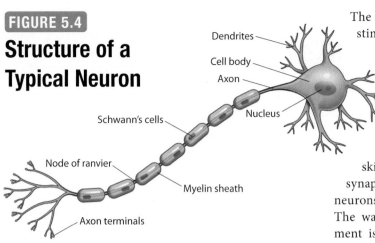

Dendrites
Cell body
Axon
Nucleus
Schwann's cells
Node of ranvier
Myelin sheath
Axon terminals

The infant's brain awaits sensory stimulation and experiences that will guide brain development. As the brain is stimulated, neurons continue to form connections, resulting in an increase in synapses. More synapses, in turn, increase communication systems in the brain that foster development of more complex skills. Neurons that are not stimulated lose their synapses in a pruning process, thereby allowing those neurons to be utilized in other synaptic connections. The warmer and more supportive the baby's environment is, the more connections in the brain the baby makes relating to emotions and relationships. The role of environment on physical and cognitive brain growth underscores the biopsychosocial model of development and implications for life experiences.

> **artificial intelligence**
> Human intelligence simulated by machines; a specific field of computer science.

axons, is rapid during the first 2 years of life and allows for quicker communication among axons by improving the efficiency of the signal transmission.

As infants process information from stimuli, the brain works to form connections that shape learning and development. The brain cells that receive new or familiar information survive; those that don't, die. It's as simple as that. Activity is critical to sustaining brain function in an infant's environment.

Environmental stimulation—parents, teachers, and other people and events—affect all parts of the brain.

MOTOR DEVELOPMENT

Parents are fascinated by their child's motor development: Is he holding up his head? Shouldn't she be crawling by now? When will he walk? Motor development occurs in two directions—from head to feet (cephalocaudal) and from the centre of the body to the arms and legs (proximodistal). In the early years, most growth occurs from

TAKE A **STAND**

Creeping and Crawling, or Just Plain Creepy?

Canadian scientists are developing a robot that mimics the expressions of the human face and tactile processes of the human hand. They feel that this robot will be useful in areas like nursing and could even act as a companion. This project is being led by Emil Petriu, a computer engineer at the University of Ottawa, who has also done work for the Canadian Space Agency (CBC, 2012a).

Petriu believes robots could one day be our companions in a symbiotic relationship. "Our society is becoming more and more disconnected," he said, pointing to a generation that increasingly spends time alone, socializing virtually. The presence of a robot could offer physical companionship without the complications of a human relationship (CBC, 2012).

A Japanese research team based out of Osaka University has also designed a robot, called CB2. This robot can breathe, relate to emotional states, and recognize human touch. While skeptics argue that a robot can never have the same emotional capacity as humans, Japanese cultural beliefs in animism (the belief that things in nature have souls or consciousness) may contribute to wider acceptance of a robo species.

▲ University of Ottawa scientist Emil Petriu is shown with a robot in his lab. Petriu and his colleagues are replacing the robot's mechanical parts with more human-like parts they are designing. (Peter Thornton/University of Ottawa)

Do you think it's possible for **artificial intelligence** (human intelligence simulated by machines) to replicate or replace human capabilities? What boundaries, if any, should be placed on such research?

the head to feet, with brain development leading the way. For example, babies can see things and communicate about them before they can grab them or crawl to them. Likewise, babies can control their midsection and core muscles enough to sit up before they can control their fingers. Although there is a typical progression, as shown in Figure 5.5, there is always variation among individual babies.

Dr. Warren Eaton, a psychology professor at the University of Manitoba and a developmental researcher, is heading up the Infant Developmental Milestones Study. This is an ongoing longitudinal study of more than 550 infants, babies, toddlers, and preschoolers. Looking at children around the world, this study is looking at why children develop at different rates (Eaton, 2012).

Important characteristics of motor control include head and body movement.

▲ Motor development occurs in two different directions.

creeping Movement whereby the infant's abdomen touches the floor and the weight of the head and shoulders rests on the elbows.

crawling Movement on hands and knees; the trunk does not touch the ground.

Head Control

A baby's most obvious initial head movements are from side to side, although a 1-month-old infant can occasionally lift his head when lying face down. Four-month-old infants can hold their heads steady while sitting and will lift their head and shoulders to a 90-degree angle when on their stomachs. By the age of 6 months, most babies can balance their heads quite well.

Creeping and Crawling

Creeping and crawling are two distinct developmental phases. In **creeping**, the infant's abdomen touches the floor, and the elbows support the weight of the head and shoulders. Movement occurs mainly by arm action. The legs usually drag, although some youngsters push with their legs. Most youngsters can creep after age 7 months. **Crawling** is more advanced than creeping, because movement is on hands and knees and the middle of the body does not touch the ground. After age 9 months, most youngsters can crawl.

The typical progression is from movement on the abdomen to quick movements on hands and knees, but

FIGURE 5.5

Milestones in Gross Motor Development

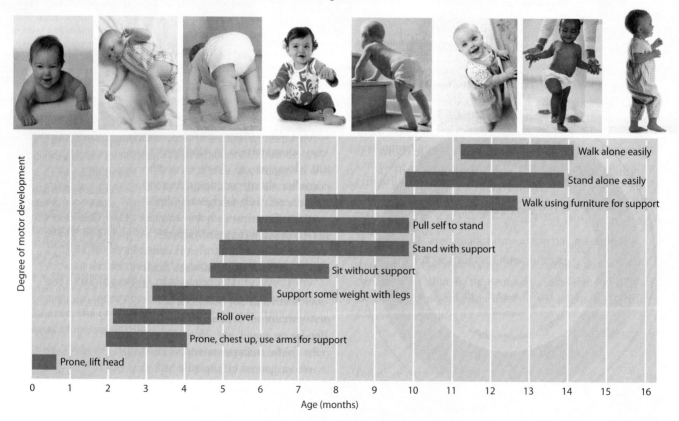

▲ Most youngsters follow the same progression when developing motor skills. They learn to sit, begin to creep, and then master crawling.

the sequence varies. Babies display an amusing array of positions and movements that can only be loosely grouped together.

Standing and Walking

After about age 7 to 9 months, babies, when held, support most of their weight on their legs. Coordination of arm and leg movements enables babies to pull themselves up and gain control of leg movements. First steps are clumsy waddles, with each step down heavy and deliberate. Gradually a smooth, confident step emerges. The world now belongs to the infant.

Once babies begin to walk, their attention darts from one thing to another, thus sharpening their perception. Tremendous energy and mobility, coupled with innate curiosity, drive infants to explore their world. It is an exciting time, but a watchful time for caregivers, who must draw the line between encouraging curiosity and initiative and protecting the child from injury. The task is not easy. It is, however, a tension found in all stages of development between giving reasonable freedom and showing unreasonable restraint. All infants experience bumps and bruises, but some infants enter the world with specific challenges.

Neonatal Problems

Occasionally the typical developmental sequence does not progress smoothly. The most common newborn problems include failure to thrive, sudden infant death syndrome, sleeping disorders, and respiratory distress syndrome.

FAILURE TO THRIVE

Failure to thrive (FTT) is a condition that occurs when an infant does not grow at the expected rate. The weight and height of failure-to-thrive infants are consistently far below average. Such infants are estimated to be in the bottom 3% of height and weight measures.

There are two types of FTT: organic and nonorganic. Organic FTT accounts for 30% of FTT cases, and the problem is usually some gastrointestinal disease and occasionally a problem with the nervous system. Nonorganic FTT, much more difficult to diagnose and treat, lacks a physical cause. Researchers have identified environmental causes such as poverty, neglect, abuse, and ignorance of good parenting practices (Block et al., 2005). The seriousness of this problem is evident from the outlook for FTT infants: Almost half of these infants continue to experience physical, cognitive, and behavioural problems for several years. A follow-up study of FTT children at age 8 (Black, Dubowitz, Krishnakumar, & Starr, 2007) indicated that FTT negatively affected height, math performance, and study habits.

Michel Boivin is Canada Research Chair in Child Development and a professor of psychology at Université Laval in Quebec. He has played a central role in the Quebec Longitudinal Study of Child Development (QLSCD). This is an ongoing study evaluating the influence of family, child care, and the broader social environment on various aspects of well-being. This study is focusing on health, development (motor, social, and cognitive), behaviour, diet, sleep, the family, and the economic environment as they all influence the growth and development of an infant (Institut de la statistique Québec, 2012; Royal Society of Canada, 2013).

SUDDEN INFANT DEATH SYNDROME

One of the most devastating and perplexing problems facing parents and researchers is **sudden infant death syndrome (SIDS)**, a condition in which an infant dies suddenly, usually during the night, without an apparent cause. SIDS is the second leading cause of death in Canada for infants between the ages of one month and one year. One in every 3000 babies die from SIDS

failure to thrive (FTT) Medical term for infants whose weight gain and physical growth fall far below average during the first years of life.

sudden infant death syndrome (SIDS) Unexpected death of an apparently healthy infant, usually between 2 and 4 months of age.

each year in Canada (Canadian Foundation for the Study of Infant Deaths, 2012). The cause of SIDS is still unknown; however, there are a number of studies that address this issue by looking at physiological changes in infancy, variation in genetics, and children who have died from SIDS compared to those who have survived (Mitchell, 2011). Sadly, First Nations communities in Canada face at least a three times higher rate of SIDS among their infants. Although it is unknown why this is the case, the SIDS Canada website offers additional strategies for this high-risk group.

Theories about the cause of SIDS involve impaired brain functioning, which can result in infants being unable to change their positions or turn their heads if their breathing is hindered by clothing, bedding, or spit-up. Environmental factors, such as cigarette smoking and drug abuse during and after pregnancy, increase the risk of SIDS.

A SIDS death is particularly devastating for parents because of the lack of warning. Today, special services have been established to counsel grieving families.

The Public Health Agency of Canada suggests some steps that parents can take to help create a safe environment for their baby and lower the risk of SIDS.

- Provide a smoke-free environment before and after the baby is born.
- Breastfeed.
- Always place the baby on his or her back to sleep at nap time and night time.
- Place the baby on a firm surface with no pillows, comforters, quilts, or bumper pads.
- Place the baby in a crib, cradle, or bassinet next to your bed.

(Public Health Agency, 2012b)

SLEEPING DISORDERS

Although less serious than FTT or SIDS, some infant sleeping problems negatively affect development. Sleep specialist Richard Ferber (2006) explains that parents often have a child between the ages of 5 months and 4 years who does not sleep readily at night and wakes repeatedly. Parents therefore become tired, frustrated, and angry, and the relationship between parents becomes tense. Most often a sleeping disorder has nothing to do with parenting, and nothing is wrong with the child physically or mentally. Yet some sleep problems do exist because of physical or psychological influences, such as a bladder infection or night terrors.

> People who say they sleep like a **baby** usually don't have one.
>
> LEO J. BURKE

Most parents would agree that sleep becomes a precious commodity once babies arrive. Sleep patterns in infants range from about 16 to 17 hours in the first week to 13 hours at age 2, with most deep-sleep periods lasting about 20 minutes. **REM (rapid eye-movement) sleep** refers to a period of deep sleep marked by eye movements and is known to be the time when vivid dreams occur. Infants tend to spend 80% of sleep in REM sleep (compared to 20–25% in adults), and brain activity during REM sleep is similar to that when infants are awake. Perhaps the large amount of REM sleep provides infants with the extra stimulation they need to promote healthy brain development.

As infants grow into toddlerhood and later childhood, the patterns of sleep change, as do patterns of brain development. Figure 5.6 shows sleep patterns from newborn to older adulthood.

Some adults choose to bring their babies into their own beds so that they can get some sleep and so their children can also fall asleep feeling safe and loved in the parents' bed. Parents need to exercise caution when they take children into their own beds (called shared sleeping or co-sleeping). Agreement between parents, safety considerations for the child, and a decision about when to stop co-sleeping must be considered (Ferber, 2006).

RESPIRATORY DISTRESS SYNDROME

Although most common with premature infants, **respiratory distress syndrome (RDS)** may strike full-term infants whose lungs are particularly immature. RDS is caused by the lack of a substance called surfactant that keeps air sacs in the lungs open. When the air sacs close up, the lungs can collapse, causing severe breathing problems. Because most babies do not produce sufficient surfactant until the 35th prenatal week, it is a serious problem for premature infants. Full-term newborns whose mothers are diabetic and babies who have undergone a difficult birth also seem vulnerable to RDS. The good news is that today 90% of these youngsters survive, and early detection and treatment make their outlook excellent.

Perceptual Development ◀L02

If you stop reading for a moment and look around, you'll see some things that you recognize immediately: this book, a lamp, shoes, paper, cellphone, and such. But you may also notice something that seems new or unfamiliar, such as a

FIGURE 5.6
Sleep Patterns across the Lifespan

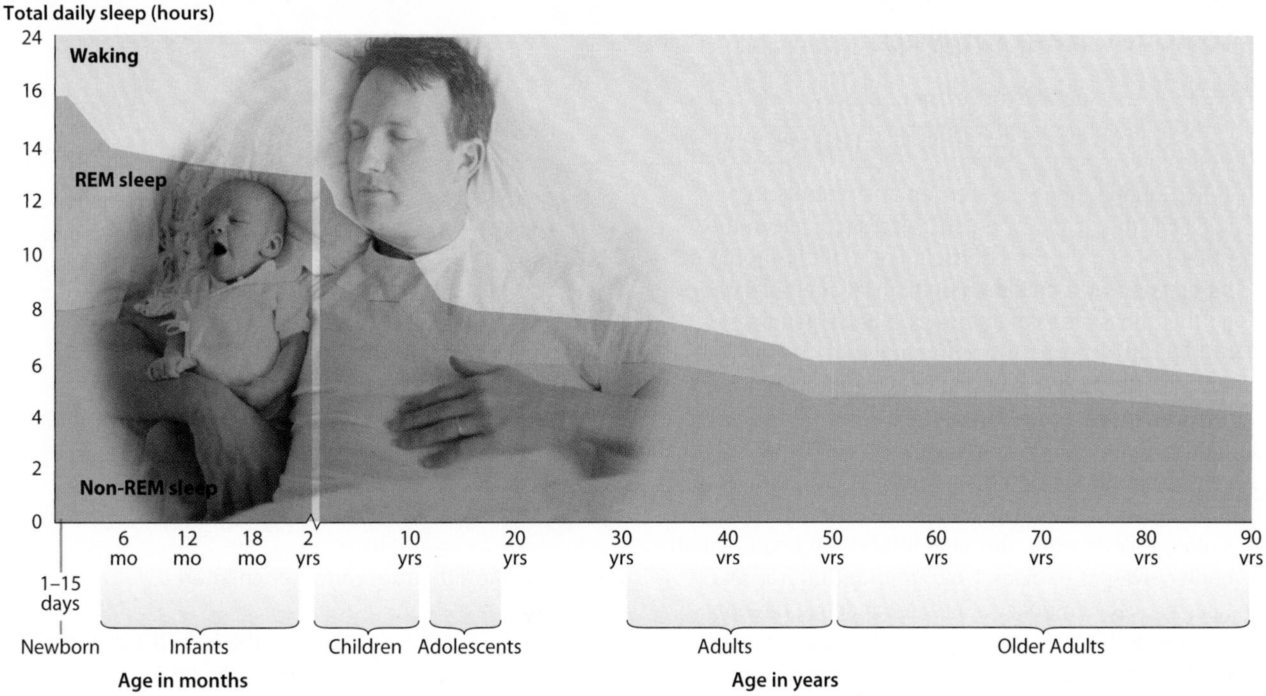

Total daily sleep (hours)

Waking

REM sleep

Non-REM sleep

24 16 14 12 10 8 6 4 2 0

6 mo | 12 mo | 18 mo | 2 yrs | 10 yrs | 20 yrs | 30 yrs | 40 yrs | 50 yrs | 60 yrs | 70 yrs | 80 yrs | 90 yrs

1–15 days

Newborn | Infants | Children | Adolescents | Adults | Older Adults

Age in months | **Age in years**

new student in class or a flyer announcing an upcoming concert. Our ability to recognize the familiar and to realize what we don't know depends on perception.

Perception is defined as the process of obtaining and interpreting information from stimuli. It is the key to our experiences in the world. It is also the basis for growth of thought, regulation of emotions, social interactions, and progress in almost all aspects of development.

Infants are quite clever at obtaining information from stimuli around them. During infancy, the capacity to take in information through the major sensory channels, make sense of the environment, and assign meaning to information improves dramatically (Bornstein, 2002). In the first year of life, infants discern patterns, depth, orientation, location, movement, and colour. During infancy, babies also discover what they can do with objects, which furthers their perceptual development.

Infants are born ready to attend to changes in physical stimulation. Stimuli presented often cause **habituation**, a decrease in an infant's attention. If the stimuli are altered, the infant again pays attention, showing awareness of the difference. For example, if you show an infant an engaging picture, he or she is first fascinated, but then becomes bored; the infant has habituated. If you change the picture, you can regain the infant's attention.

Perception depends on both learning and maturation. An infant's perceptual system undergoes much development following birth, as he or she becomes familiar with objects and events in the world and continues to grow.

Most research on infant perceptual development has emphasized vision and hearing because of their importance and rapid development.

Ontario researchers Daphne Maurer (McMaster University, Hamilton), Catherine Mondloch (Brock University, St. Catharines), and Terri Lewis (The Hospital for Sick Children, Toronto) have done some important research in infant perceptual development. They conducted research on the effects of early visual deprivation on perceptual and cognitive development. They found that during early infancy, visual capabilities are quite limited but that patterned visual input during this period is necessary for the later development of normal vision for some, but not all, aspects of visual perception (Maurer, Mondloch, & Lewis, 2007).

VISUAL PERCEPTION

Infants are born able to see and quickly exhibit a preference for patterns. They tend to show definite preferences based on as much complexity as they can handle (Gibson & Pick, 2000). Robert Fantz's (1965) classic work on visual preferences revealed that children look at different things for different amounts of time. He designed a "looking chamber" so that an experimenter could see which of two images an infant looked at longer. The knowledge about babies' visual preferences is

> **perception** The process of obtaining and interpreting information from stimuli.
>
> **habituation** A decrease in an infant's attention.

PERSPECTIVES ON **DIVERSITY**

A Global Look at the Rush to Toilet Train (or Not)

While sleep issues can drive caregivers crazy and create stress in the household, toilet training is another major source of stress for families.

In Canada, physicians encourage parents to consider the "child-oriented" approach before the toilet training process starts. Toilet training should not be dictated by a child's chronological age but rather by their physiological and psychological readiness to begin the process. Parents should be prepared to devote attention and patience to the task on a daily basis for several months (Clifford & Gorodzinsky, 2000).

Cultural belief systems influence the timing of toilet training. In traditionally Eastern countries such as China, toileting routines with infants are begun much earlier, even as early as 1 month old. Cultural practices typically emphasize interdependence between adult and infant, and an adult is readily available to hold an infant over the toilet. Open-crotch garments facilitate the process. Economic realities also play a role. In a small affluent family that can afford disposable diapers, the need to get children toilet trained is not urgent. A large family with less disposable income

▲ Swedish children's characters, Kiss and Bajs (Pee and Poo).

might be more motivated to get children toilet trained as early as possible.

Despite "expert" opinions on the benefits of toilet training at a certain age, families have been operating for thousands of years with varying toileting practices. Cultural and individual preferences, as well as health conditions, should be the primary considerations for when a baby is ready for the potty.

apparent today—a stroll through the newborn section of any toy store will lead you past many black, white, and red toys; you'll also see many checkerboard, striped, and polka-dotted items. Human faces, which are remarkably complex, also capture babies' attention on mobiles and other items.

DEPTH PERCEPTION

The study of visual development sparks questions about how visual skills help infants to adjust to their environment. In their famous visual cliff experiment, Gibson and Walk (1960) reasoned that infants would use visual stimuli to gauge both depth and distance. The visual cliff consisted of a board dividing a large sheet of heavy glass. A checkerboard pattern was attached to one half of the bottom of the glass, giving the impression of solidity. The investigators then placed a similar sheet on the floor under the other half, creating a sense of depth—the visual cliff. Thirty-six infants from ages 6 to 14 months were tested. After each infant was placed on the centre board, the mother called the child from the shallow side and then the cliff side. Twenty-seven of the youngsters moved onto the shallow side toward the mother. When

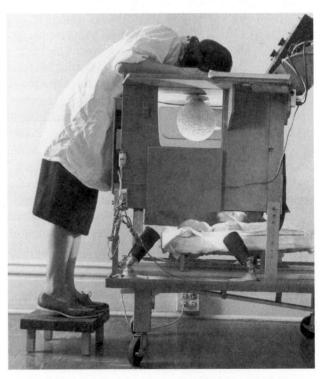

▲ Fantz's "looking chamber" helped to determine which objects infants looked at longer.

◀ The visual cliff experiment suggests that infants can discriminate depth when they begin crawling.

called from the cliff side, only three infants ventured over the depth. The experiment suggests that infants discriminate depth when they begin crawling.

By 2 to 4 months of age, infant perception is fairly sophisticated. Infants perceive figures as organized wholes, react to the relationship among elements rather than single elements, perceive colour, and are fascinated by complex patterns. They scan the environment, pick up information, then encode and process information (Gibson & Pick, 2000).

AUDITORY PERCEPTION

Infants display notable auditory abilities in the uterus and at birth. Hearing and auditory discrimination are well developed since sounds are carried to the fetus through the amniotic fluid as a series of vibrations. Infants display sensitivity to differences in the quality of sounds. For example, some babies may prefer music to other sounds, they can discriminate their mothers' voices from those of other women, and they can locate the direction of a sound.

Infants pay special attention to speechlike sounds (Siegler & Alibali, 2005). Although significant in itself, this perceptual sensitivity underscores the importance of auditory perception in language development. For example, infants are able to differentiate the sounds of their language and tune in to the speech they hear around them (Bjorklund, 2005). It's as if nature has determined that infants must immediately attend to important information in their aural environment.

L03▶ Cognitive Development

The biological basis of cognition—such as genetic influences on behaviour, the role of the brain in processing music, and biological insights into language development—plays a role in human behaviour. The study of cognitive development must therefore examine both the brain's role and the sociocultural basis of cognitive development (Bjorklund, 2005).

PIAGET'S SENSORIMOTOR PERIOD

As you will recall from Chapter 2, the work of Jean Piaget embodies the interaction between biological, psychological, and social factors. Did you ever wonder what infants are thinking? How do their interactions with their environment shape their thinking, which, in turn, shapes the structure of the brain? These are questions that Piaget addressed, and his research made a lasting impression on studies of cognitive development.

Piaget believed that the first few years of life are marked by extraordinary mental growth and influence the entire course of development. It is through the senses that infants begin to make sense of the world. Initially, everything centres on them, and they see the world only from their point of view. **Egocentrism** describes this initial relationship of children to their world. The egocentric child is simply unaware of any other viewpoint.

The remarkable changes of the **sensorimotor period** (about the first 2 years of life) occur within a sequence of six stages that involve **circular reactions**. An infant experiences something through his or her own motor activity, even by pure chance, and tries to repeat the experience. Finally, the infant adds the action to a growing body of knowledge about the world and the way things work.

Stage 1

During the first stage, which Piaget referred to as **simple reflexes**, children do little more than exercise their inborn reflexes. For example, Piaget (1952b) stated that the sucking reflex is hereditary and functions from birth. At first, infants suck anything that touches their lips, then they suck when nothing touches their lips, and then they actively search for the nipple. This involves steady development of the coordination of the eye, mouth, arm, and hand. Through these activities, patterns form in the brain—physically through neuron connections and emotionally

egocentrism Piaget's term for the child's focus on self in early phases of cognitive development.

sensorimotor period The first 2 years of life.

circular reactions Piaget's term for infants' motor activity that is repeated in developing stages.

simple reflexes The first stage of the sensorimotor period, when children do little more than exercise their inborn reflexes.

through memory and learning—that build a foundation for forming cognitive structures.

Stage 2

Piaget referred to stage 2 (from about 1 to 4 months) as the stage of **primary circular reactions**. During stage 2, first habits emerge as infants tend to repeat actions involving their bodies, even if the actions are accidental. For example, they have learned that they are fed when hungry, and they have mastered the sucking reflex so that it can now be done voluntarily, even when nothing is present. Infants seem to have no external goals behind these actions other than the pleasure of self-exploration, but they are learning something about their own bodies.

Stage 3

Secondary circular reactions emerge during the third stage, which extends from about 4 to 8 months. During this stage, infants direct their activities toward objects and events outside themselves. For example, a baby may accidentally swat a mobile with one hand while squirming in the crib, and the mobile makes a jingling sound and moves. The infant will try again to swat the mobile. Secondary circular reactions produce results in the environment, and not, as with the primary circular reactions, on the child's own body.

Stage 4

From about 8 to 12 months of age, infants engage in **coordination of secondary schemes** to form new kinds of behaviour (Piaget & Inhelder, 1969). The baby first decides on a goal, such as finding an object that is hidden under a small blanket. Then the infant attempts to move the blanket to reach the object. In stage 4, the infant coordinates previously learned actions to carry out the desired goal. Infants use multiple senses in the process of coordinating their actions and learning about materials. They often look at and feel items, or shake and listen to items. Here we see the first signs of intentional behaviour.

Stage 5

Tertiary circular reactions appear from 12 to 18 months of age. In the tertiary circular reaction, repetition occurs again, but now with variation. The infant is exploring the world's possibilities. Piaget thought that the infant purposefully attempts to provoke new results instead of merely reproducing activities. Tertiary circular reactions

indicate experimentation and an interest in novelty for its own sake.

Have you ever seen a baby standing in a crib, dropping everything on the floor? Through Piaget's lens you could watch how the baby drops things, from different locations and different heights. Does it sound the same when it hits the floor as when it hits the rug? Is it as loud dropped from here or higher? Each repetition is actually a chance to learn.

Stage 6

During stage 6 (between 18 and 24 months), the last stage of the sensorimotor period, children develop a basic kind of **internalization of schemes**. They begin to use symbols (internalized representation of an event) to think about real events without actually experiencing them. For example, a budding toddler has seen her father using a leaf blower outside their house many times. She picks up a discarded paper-towel tube and moves her arm in a side-to-side motion, making a "Brrrrrrrr" sound, mimicking the sound of the leaf blower.

Progress through the sensorimotor period leads to four major accomplishments:

- Object permanence: Children realize that objects continue to exist even when out of sight. Out of sight does not mean not gone forever. This is significant because it signals that babies have a sense that objects are separate from them.

- Sense of space: Children realize objects in the environment have a spatial relationship.

- Causality: Children realize the relationship between actions and their consequences.

- Time sequences: Children realize that one thing comes after another.

▲ Infants realize that objects continue to exist even when out of their sight.

By the end of the sensorimotor period, children move from purely sensory and motor functioning to symbolic kinds of activity, in which the child takes a real-life event and recreates it according to his or her own ideas. This is seen as children develop their make-believe play and represent happenings from their own world in play settings.

EVALUATION OF PIAGET

Although Piaget left a major legacy, his ideas have not gone unchallenged. Piaget proposed a theory of development as a sequence of distinct stages, each of which entails important changes in the way a child thinks, feels, and behaves. However, acquiring cognitive structures may be gradual rather than abrupt and may not be a matter of all or nothing. For some theorists, a child's level of cognitive development depends more on the nature of the task than on a rigid classification system.

In one of the first important challenges to Piaget, Gelman and Baillargeon (1983) found that children can accomplish specific tasks at earlier ages than Piaget believed. Criticism that Piaget underestimated infants' abilities has led to a closer examination of the times during which children acquire certain cognitive abilities. For example, Piaget believed that infants will retrieve an object that is hidden from them (in stage 4) beginning at about 8 to 12 months. Before this age, if a blanket is thrown over a toy the infant is looking at, the child stops reaching for it as if it doesn't exist. More recent research has argued that infants can see objects as separate from themselves as early as age 3 to 4 months.

Linda Siegel, a psychology professor at the University of British Columbia, wrote a paper called "Amazing new discovery: Piaget was wrong!" This paper mentions a number of inadequacies in Piaget's theory. One important point that is discussed is that the child in the Piagetian world does not understand the principles of logic and physics. Siegel and her colleagues have discovered, however, that with tasks that use appropriate operational definitions, young children can be shown to reason logically (Siegel, 1993).

INFORMATION PROCESSING IN INFANCY

Information-processing theorists propose that cognitive development occurs through the gradual refining of such cognitive processes as attention and memory.

The sequence of information processing is shown in Figure 5.7.

Infants and Attention

Attention strategies enable children to decide what is important, what is needed, or what is dangerous. They also help infants gradually ignore everything else. Infants attend to different stimuli for a variety of reasons: intensity, complexity of the stimuli, visual ability, and novelty. They enjoy human faces, voices, and movements.

The brain is the biological basis of attention; when infants attend to something, a series of brain activities is activated. For example, auditory receptors pick up the sound of the mother's voice, and a structure in the brain stem brings the baby to a higher state of alertness. An inner-brain system now swings into action, involving memory and emotion. Finally, cortical areas interpret what was said and how it was said. Was it directed at something? Was it soothing? Was it pleasant?

In terms of psychology, the following describes what attention means for developing infants:

- *Their attention is selective*—infants can't attend to everything.

- *Their attention involves cognitive processing*—infants don't just passively accept stimuli; they actively process incoming information.

Adults must assume some responsibility for monitoring the sights and sounds that their infants experience to shield them from overly intense stimulation. Many caregivers intuitively read their babies' signals and react appropriately, reflecting sensitive responsiveness to a child's needs.

Infants and Memory

Four important discoveries should frame your thinking about infant memory:

1. The brain as a whole is involved in memory; memories don't reside in one particular location.

2. Memories are retrieved in the same manner as they were formed.

FIGURE 5.7

Information-Processing Model

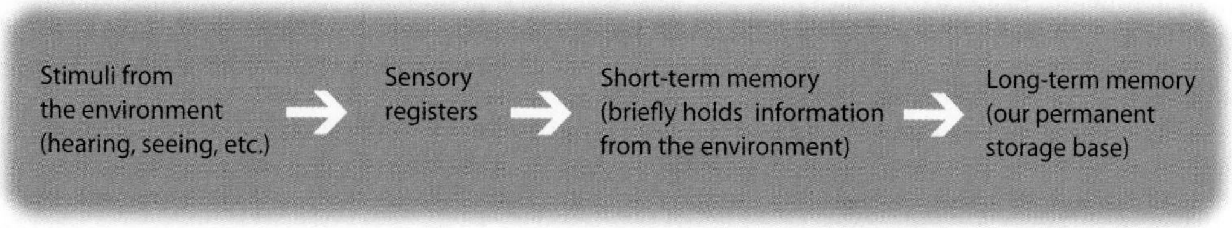

| Stimuli from the environment (hearing, seeing, etc.) | → | Sensory registers | → | Short-term memory (briefly holds information from the environment) | → | Long-term memory (our permanent storage base) |

3. Memories are stored in the brain's synapses, which are the connections between neurons.

4. These synaptic connections can be strengthened through use, and learning can form new synaptic processes.

Obviously, infants must have some ability to remember, or they could never learn about their world. They love to repeat actions that bring them pleasure. Infants demonstrate one type of memory (habituation) after the first few months following birth. By the end of the second year, an infant's memory more closely resembles that of older children, and they can recall sounds that, when strung together, elicit responses from others and a mutual understanding based on a shared language.

> It's my belief we developed language because of our deep inner need to complain.
>
> LILY TOMLIN

L04 ▶ Language Development

One of the most amazing accomplishments in infancy is the beginning of speech. With no formal training—in fact, often exposed to dramatically faulty language models—children learn words and meanings, and how to combine them in a logical, purposeful manner. Because all children acquire their own language in a similar manner, it's important to consider this drive toward language.

Children in all parts of the world go through a process whereby they first emit sounds, then single words, two words, and then complex sentences (see Table 5.1). By the time they are about 5 years old, they have acquired the basics of their language—a huge accomplishment.

The researchers of the McGill Infant Research Group at McGill University, Montreal, are interested in finding out what very young infants understand about the world around them. They are conducting research on speech perception, language and cognition, and communication and children's cognitive social development. (For more information about their research, visit **http://www.psych.mcgill.ca/labs/bebe/english/**.)

THE PACE OF LANGUAGE ACQUISITION

How does this uniquely human achievement occur? First, children learn the rules of their language, which they then apply in a wide variety of situations. Then, by the end of the second year, children learn to apply a label to an object without anyone telling them.

fast mapping Children's use of surrounding context to understand words' meaning.

TECH TRENDS

What Gorilla?

In an experiment on visual cognition, participants were asked to watch a video of people passing a ball to each other. The instructions directed people to count the number of times the people wearing white shirts passed the ball to each other in the video clip. At one point in the video, a person in a gorilla suit strolls right through the action. Yet, after viewing the video, when participants were asked about the gorilla, a remarkable number of people didn't remember seeing the gorilla at all!

This failure to notice the gorilla relates to the roles of attention and memory in our developing cognition. Most babies would notice the gorilla right away but would not succeed at counting the number of basketball tosses. (Not to mention the fact that babies can't count!) Babies have many more neurons than adults, but they are less efficient at using their knowledge to achieve a desired goal. As babies grow, the pruning process refines the number of neurons and overall brain activity.

Go to **www.theinvisiblegorilla.com/gorilla_experiment.html** to view the visual cognition video (Simons, 2007).

Even when children don't understand a word, they acquire information about it from the surrounding context, a phenomenon called **fast mapping** (Bjorklund, 2005).

TABLE 5.1

Language Development During Infancy

Language	Age
Crying	From birth
Cooing	2–5 months
Babbling	5–7 months
Single words	12 months
Two words	18 months
Phrases	2 years

▲ Reading to children at an early age can help them with speech development.

The process of acquiring language goes on at a fast pace until the fundamentals have been acquired, around age 5 for most children. By the time children enter elementary school, they are remarkably sophisticated language users. Then it becomes a matter of expanding and refining language skills, a task that can often define success or failure in a formal education setting.

VYGOTSKY'S STAGES OF LANGUAGE DEVELOPMENT

Psychologist Lev Vygotsky emphasized the role of context in language development. He argued that language begins as preintellectual speech and develops into a sophisticated form of what he called *inner speech*. The use of speech propels cognitive development as we literally talk ourselves through a task. In *Thought and Language* (1962), Vygotsky clearly presented his views about the four stages of language development.

1. The first stage, which he called **preintellectual speech**, refers to such early processes as crying, cooing, babbling, and bodily movements that gradually develop into sophisticated forms of speech and behaviour. Although human beings have an inborn ability to develop language, they must then interact with the environment if language development is to fulfill its potential.

2. Vygotsky referred to the second stage of language development as **naive psychology**, in which children explore the concrete objects in their world. At this stage, children begin to label the objects around them and acquire the grammar of their speech.

3. At about 3 years of age, **egocentric speech** emerges, that form of speech in which children carry on lively conversations, whether or not anyone is present or listening to them.

4. Finally, speech turns inward (**inner speech**) and serves an important function in guiding and planning behaviour. Inner speech often accompanies physical movements, guiding behaviour. What begins as talking aloud to himself or herself eventually turns inward. For difficult tasks, inner speech is used to plan as well as guide behaviour. For example, a child working on a jigsaw puzzle might remind himself or herself to look for the flat-edged pieces so that he or she can form the border to frame the puzzle.

In many cases, children who aren't permitted these vocalizations struggle to accomplish a task. In fact, the more complex the task, the greater is the need for egocentric and inner speech.

preintellectual speech Vygotsky's category for cooing, crying, babbling, and bodily movements that develop into more sophisticated forms of speech.

naive psychology Vygotsky's stage in which children explore objects and label objects as they acquire the grammar of their speech.

egocentric speech The form of speech in which children carry on lively conversations with themselves or others.

inner speech Internal speech that often accompanies physical movements, guiding behaviour.

Career Apps

As a speech therapist, how could you help families recognize children's early sounds as serious attempts at communication?

KEY MILESTONES OF LANGUAGE DEVELOPMENT

During the first 2 months, babies develop sounds associated with breathing, feeding, and crying. **Cooing** (gurgling, vowel-like) appears during the second month. Between 5 and 7 months, babies play with the sounds they can make, and this output begins to take on the sounds of consonants and syllables, the beginning of **babbling**. Babbling probably appears initially because of biological maturation. At 7 or 8 months, sounds like syllables appear—da-da-da, ba-ba-ba, a pattern that continues for the remainder of the first year (Pinker, 1994). This is a phenomenon that occurs in all languages.

First Words

Around their first birthday, babies produce single words, about half of which are for objects (food, clothing, toys). Throughout the world, children's first words express similar meanings. These words refer to people, animals, toys, vehicles, and other objects that fascinate children. Children quickly learn the sounds of their language (**phonology**), the meanings of words (**semantics**), how to construct sentences (**syntax**), and how to communicate (**pragmatics**).

At 18 months, children acquire words at the rate of about 40 per week (Woodward & Markman, 1998). This rapid increase in vocabulary lasts until about 3 years of age and is frequently referred to as the **word spurt**. Vocabulary constantly expands, but estimating the extent of a child's vocabulary is difficult because youngsters know more words than they articulate. Estimates are that a 1-year-old child may use from 2 to 6 words. These first words, or **holophrases**, are usually nouns, adjectives, or self-inventive words and often contain multiple meanings. The single word "ball" may mean not only the ball itself but also "Throw the ball to me." A 2-year-old has a vocabulary ranging from 50 to 250 words. Children at this stage also begin to combine two words (Pinker, 1994). By first grade, children may understand 10,000 words, and by fifth grade they understand about 40,000 words (Woodward & Markman, 1998).

Two-Word Sentences

At about 18 to 24 months of age, children's vocabularies begin to expand rapidly, and a form of communication called **telegraphic speech** appears. Telegraphic speech consists of simple two-word sentences without conjunctions, articles, or (often)

cooing Early language sounds that resemble vowels.

babbling Infants' production of sounds approximating speech between 5 and 7 months.

phonology Sounds of a language.

semantics Meaning of words and sentences.

syntax The way in which words are put together to construct sentences.

pragmatics Ability to communicate with others.

word spurt Rapid increase of vocabulary from 18 months to 3 years.

holophrase One word that can communicate many meanings and ideas.

telegraphic speech Initial multiple-word utterances, usually two or three words.

verbs. For example, the phrase "Mommy milk" might stand for "Mommy, I would like to have a glass of milk."

When the two-word stage appears (any time from 18 to 24 months), children initially struggle to convey tense (past and present) and number (singular and plural). They also experience difficulty with grammar. Children usually employ word order ("me go") for meaning, only gradually mastering inflection (how language handles plurals, tenses, possessives, gender, and so on) as they begin to form three-word sentences. They use nouns and verbs initially ("doggie sleep," "mama kiss").

Children begin to use multiple words to refer to the things that they previously named with single words.

Rather than learning rules of word combination to express new ideas, children learn to use new word forms. Combining words in phrases and sentences suggests that children are learning the structure of their language.

Word order and inflection become increasingly important. During the first stages of language acquisition, word order is paramount. At first, children combine words without concern for inflections, and word order provides clues as to their level of syntactic (grammatical) development. Once 2-word sentences are used, inflection and 3-word sentences soon appear ("Where *ball* go?"). The appearance of inflections seems to follow a pattern: first the plural of nouns, then tense and person of verbs, and then possessives.

The biopsychosocial model of development is evident as various phases of development converge in a child's use of language (see Table 5.2). Motor development is visible when a child runs excitedly toward her mother. Language development is visible when the child lifts her arms upon reaching her mother, saying, "Mommy, UP!" Cognitive development is visible in terms of the attachment the child displays to the mother. The integration of these developmental forces is linked to social and emotional factors that shape the infant's life.

Figure 5.8 shows the regions of the brain that are most closely associated with language acquisition.

L05 ▶ Social and Emotional Development

Think back to the example of Laura at the beginning of this chapter and the importance of relationships in a child's development. Relationships can be considered as patterns of interactions between people over time.

FIGURE 5.8

The Brain and Language

Broca's area   Wernicke's area

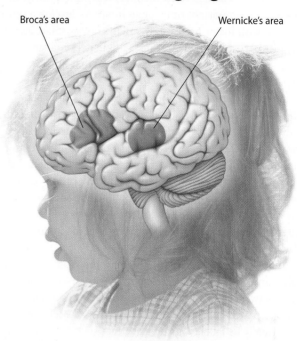

▲ Specific areas of the brain have been identified for their role in language production and comprehension. Debate exists over whether the acquisition of these skills is innate or learned.

A baby's relationships involve many aspects of development, such as playing (physical and social), talking and communicating (language), understanding self and others (cognitive), and attachment (emotional). In other words, a relationship is a good example of the importance of biopsychosocial interactions.

TABLE 5.2

Developmental Characteristics of Infancy

Age (months)	Height (cm)	Weight (kg)	Language Development	Motor Development	Cognitive (Piaget)
3	60.9	5.9–6.3	Cooing	Supports head in prone position	Primary circular reactions
6	66	7.7–8.1	Babbling: single syllable sounds	Sits erect when supported	Secondary circular reactions
9	66	9.1–9.9	Repetition of sounds signals emotions	Stands with support	Coordination of secondary schemes
12	74.9	9.9–10.8	Single words: mama, dada	Walks when held by hand	Same
18	81.2	11.3–11.7	3–50 words	Grasps objects accurately, walks steadily	Tertiary circular reaction
24	86.3	12.2–13.1	50–250 words, 2–3-word sentences	Walks and runs up and down stairs	Representation

CHILDREN'S DEVELOPING RELATIONSHIPS

Erik Erikson characterized the first stage of life (birth to 2 years) as an important time for an infant to develop a sense of trust with his or her caregiver. During this stage, infants begin to trust their environment, if it is predictable and their needs are met. They begin to learn that others can be depended on.

Infants interact with their environments and begin to structure their own relationships according to their individual temperaments. The interactions occurring among family members—parent–parent, parent–child's siblings, sibling–sibling—produce a ripple effect that colours the parent–child relationship. Thus, the nature of the relationships between parents and their children emerges from the temperament and characteristics of each and from the interactions that occur among them (Rubin, Bukowski, & Parker, 2006).

Infants quickly focus on their mothers as sources of relief and satisfaction. Mothers, in turn, rapidly discriminate between their infants' cries: hunger, discomfort, fear. Thus, a pattern of interactions is established. Relationships can usually be labelled using adjectives such as warm, cold, accepting, rejecting, friendly, and hostile. Any relationship may be marked by seemingly contradictory interactions. A mother may have a warm relationship with her child as shown by hugging and kissing, but she may also yell when yelling might be needed to protect the child from harm. To understand the relationship, we must understand the interactions.

THE ROLE OF RECIPROCAL INTERACTIONS

From the moment children are born, they immediately seek stimulation from their environment and instantly interpret and react to how they are being treated—the process called reciprocal interactions. Not only do infants attempt to make sense of their world as they develop cognitively, they also "tune in to" the social and emotional atmosphere surrounding them and immediately begin to shape their relationships with others.

Infants are not merely passive; they also exercise some control over the interactions. Adults respond to infants partly because of the way that infants respond to adults. An infant's staring, cooing, smiling, and kicking can all be used to maintain interactions. Early interactions establish the nature of the relationship between parent and child, giving it a particular tone or style.

Parents bring some preconceived ideas about the role they should play in their relationships with their children. How they exercise their power and how their children react to their suggestions and encouragements, their demands and commands, ultimately determine the success of the relationship. In an ideal world, their ideas, expectations,

TAKE A STAND

Nature or Nurture?

There has been ongoing debate about whether language is a biological, innate ability that all humans possess or whether it is learned through interactions in the environment. Noam Chomsky (1957) argued that humans are born prewired with the ability to acquire the rules of language, detect and re-create sounds, and receive and express meaning. He called this inborn ability a *language acquisition device (LAD)*; and while not situated in a specific region of the brain (such as Broca's area, involved in producing words, or Wernicke's area, involved in comprehension), there is evidence that people in all different parts of the world develop language in the same sequence.

Behaviourists believe that environment and reinforcement are at the heart of language development. They believe that infants exposed to a certain language acquire the language based on the responses that caregivers give them. Currently, people who argue for the influence of environment on language development find that context plays a large role. For instance, a child who grows up exposed to many books and printed materials will be more likely to acquire language skills than a child who does not grow up in a print-rich environment.

Do you think biology or environment plays a bigger role in language development? What examples can you think of to support your argument? What implications does this have on children's early education?

and sense of their roles as parents should mesh perfectly with their child's personality and abilities.

ROLE OF EMOTIONS IN DEVELOPMENT

◄ L06

It's easy to see how a child's life is affected by the impact of attachment and early relationships. Healthy emotional development helps children to define their individuality. During infancy, emotions generate adaptive functions that help to define the meaning of a child's experiences. How can we define emotions? According to pediatrician, psychiatrist, and author Daniel Siegel, "Emotions represent dynamic processes created within the socially influenced, value-appraising processes of the brain" (1999, p. 123). For example, infants' emotions motivate them to either approach or withdraw from situations and to either communicate or not communicate their needs to those around them. When others respond, infants learn about social

▲ Infants learn to respond to their caregiver's emotions.

exchanges, which furthers their social development. These emotional interchanges help to explain why emotions are often referred to as the language of infancy (Emde, 1998).

When we think about various emotions, we must remember that *different* responses may be made to any one emotion. A smile, for example, may signal joy, nervousness, or some other emotion. Also, different theorists may suggest slightly different schedules for the appearance of various emotions, but the basic explanation of *how* they develop is identical. Emotional development occurs as the result of an infant's dispositional tendencies combined with a complex interaction between growing cognitive skills and social interactions (see Table 5.3).

TABLE 5.3

Timetable of Emotional Development

Age	Emotion	Features
Birth–3 months	Pleasure, distress, disgust	A range of emerging emotions from happiness to anger
3–6 months	Delight, wariness, anger	More specific responses to specific stimulation
6–9 months	Fear, anxiety, shyness, pleasure	Emotions slowly becoming differentiated with increasing cognitive development
9–12 months	Stranger anxiety, separation anxiety	Concentrated focus on main caregiver
12–18 months	Elation, security	Feelings of security and well-being encourage exploration of environment
18–24 months	Shame, defiance	Integration of emotional and cognitive features

In the first year of life, infants gradually develop the ability to stop or reduce the duration and intensity of emotional reactions. Two processes seem to be involved—one related to the appearance of emotions and one involving the management of emotions. Any psychological explanation of child development must recognize the importance of emotions as motivators. Emotions can help infants analyze situations and prepare themselves to act.

Appropriate emotions and behaviour are heavily influenced by cultural values. For example, behavioural inhibition is more highly valued in China than in North America, and researchers have found that Chinese infants are more inhibited than Canadian infants (Chen et al., 1998).

ANALYZING EMOTIONAL EXPRESSIONS

One of the first signs of emotion is a baby's smile, which most parents immediately interpret as a sign of happiness. Yet newborns' smiles don't indicate pleasure in the sense that the smiles of older infants do. By the baby's third week, the human female voice elicits a brief, real smile; by the sixth week, the beginnings of the true social smile appear, especially in response to the human face.

Two-month-old infants are often described as "smilers," whereas frequent and socially significant smiles emerge around 3 months (Kagan & Fox, 2006). Babies smile instinctively at faces—real or drawn—and this probably reflects the human tendency to attend to patterns. Infants gradually learn that familiar faces usually mean pleasure, and smiling becomes a key element in securing positive reinforcement from those around the infant.

Finally, infants smile at any high-contrast stimuli and at the human beings around them; and they discover a relationship between their behaviour and events in the external world. When infants smile, they elicit attention from those around them and begin to associate the human face with pleasure. Current research on emotional development reinforces the biopsychosocial basis for this book: Emotional expression appears immediately after birth, acquires meaning, and expands rapidly because of the socially interactive nature of emotional communication. As children grow, the circumstances that elicit their emotions change; that is, the emotional experiences at different ages vary drastically. The happiness that a 6-month-old child shows when tickled by her mother is far different from a 16-year-old's happiness sharing a funny story with a friend. We may label both "happiness," but is the emotion the same?

Emotional development seems to move from the general (positive versus negative emotions) to the specific—general positive states morph into such emotions as joy and interest; general negative states morph into fear, disgust, or anger. These primary emotions emerge during the

Happy	Sad	Angry	Anxious
Guilty	Satisfied	Cautious	Shy
Bored	Surprised	Afraid	Lonely
Curious	Jealous	Puzzled	Hurt

▲ Children and adults recognize the various emotions that they display with each other in everyday interactions.

For example, embarrassment or shame at spilling a cup of water may weaken a child's sense of competence. For emotions such as embarrassment to appear, children must have developed a sense of self.

Attachment ◀L07

How significant is the mother–infant relationship in the first days and weeks after birth? Infants who develop a secure **attachment** to their mothers have the willingness and confidence to seek out future relationships. Attachment figures are secure bases that encourage infants to explore their environments but remain reliable retreats when stress and uncertainty appear. Among the first researchers to stress the significance of relationships in an infant's life were John Bowlby and Mary Salter Ainsworth. Mary Salter Ainsworth obtained her degree in psychology from and later taught at the University of Toronto.

EXAMINING ATTACHMENT

Using concepts from psychology and **ethology**, a field that stresses that behaviour is strongly influenced by biology, John Bowlby formulated his basic premise: A warm, intimate relationship between mother and infant is essential to mental health, because a child's need for its mother's presence is as great as its need for food. A mother's continued absence can generate a sense of loss and feelings of anger. Even though most attachment research tends to focus on mothers' relationships with children, Bowlby stated that an infant's principal attachment figure can be someone other than the biological mother. Further, Bowlby noted that attachment patterns between fathers and children closely resemble those between mothers and their children. This is reminiscent of the work of ethologist Konrad Lorenz (1965), who determined that newborn ducks and geese would follow the first object they saw after hatching. In a now-famous experiment, the first thing these young geese saw after hatching was Lorenz!

attachment Behaviour intended to keep a child (or adult) in close proximity to a significant other.

ethology Scientific field that stresses that behaviour is strongly influenced by biology and is linked to evolution.

first 6 months. Sometime after 18 months of age, secondary emotions appear that are associated with a child's growing cognitive capacity for self-awareness. As early as 2 or 3 years of age, children begin to display complex emotions, such as shame, guilt, and jealousy (Volling, McElwain, & Miller, 2002). These new emotions emerge from a child's increasing cognitive maturity, and they have a strong influence on self-esteem.

▲ Infants learn that familiar faces often mean pleasure and therefore smile instinctively when they see their caregivers.

▲ Konrad Lorenz

Bowlby and his colleagues initiated a series of studies in which children were separated from their parents. A predictable sequence of behaviours was observed: (1) *Protest* begins almost immediately and lasts up to 1 week, with loud crying, extreme restlessness, and rejection of all adult figures; (2) *despair* is typified by a growing hopelessness, with monotonous crying, inactivity, and steady withdrawal; and (3) *detachment* appears when an infant displays renewed interest in its surroundings—but a remote, distant kind of interest. Bowlby described the behaviour of this final phase as apathetic, even if the mother reappeared. Bowlby also believed that although attachment is most obvious in infancy and early childhood, it can be observed throughout the life cycle.

To assess the quality of attachment, Mary Salter Ainsworth (1973, 1979; Ainsworth & Bowlby, 1991), designed an experiment known as the **strange situation**. In her experimental scenario, Ainsworth had a mother and an infant taken to an observation room. The child was placed on the floor and allowed to play with toys. A stranger (female) then entered the room and began to talk to the mother. Observers watched to see how the infant reacted to the stranger and to what extent the child used the mother as a secure base. The mother then left the child alone in the room with the stranger; observers then noted how distressed the child became. The mother returned and the quality of the child's reaction to the mother's return was assessed. Next, the infant was left completely alone, followed by the stranger's entrance and then that of the mother. The behaviour exhibited by children in the strange situation is used to categorize children as follows:

- *Securely attached children*, who use their mothers as a base from which to explore. Separation intensifies their attachment behaviour; they exhibit considerable distress, stop their explorations, and seek contact with their mothers at reunions.
- *Avoidantly attached children*, who rarely cry during separation and avoid their mothers at reunion. The mothers of these babies seem to dislike or are indifferent to physical contact.

- *Ambivalently attached children*, who manifest anxiety before separation and who are intensely distressed by the separation. Yet on reunion, they display ambivalent behaviour toward their mothers; they seek contact but simultaneously seem to resist it.
- *Disorganized/disoriented children*, who show a confused sort of behaviour at reunion. For example, they may look at the mother and then look away, showing little emotion.

strange situation Measure designed to assess the quality of attachment.

Ainsworth reported other studies, conducted in Baltimore, Washington, D.C., Scotland, and Uganda, noting that cultural influences may affect the ways in which different attachment behaviours develop. Nevertheless, geographic location did not affect the existence of attachment behaviours.

ATTACHMENT CHALLENGES

Obstacles to successful attachment exist in many forms, such as child maltreatment and neglect. In a classic study, Harlow and Suomi (1971) studied rhesus monkeys that were caged without real mothers but, instead, with substitute "mothers" constructed out of wire or terry-cloth towels. Harlow and Suomi found that the monkeys placed in cages with the softer surrogate mothers fared better than those

▲ Harlow's rhesus monkeys chose the comfort from surrogate mothers over those that offered food.

temperament Individual differences; unique and stable styles of behaving.

goodness of fit Concept coined by Chess and Thomas (1977) that describes the match between a child's temperament and his/her environment.

monkeys caged with the cold, hard stand-ins. Also, given the choice, they chose softer surrogates over those that offered food. In each case, however, the monkeys exhibited clear effects from being deprived of maternal affection. For example, as the monkeys grew older, they tended to avoid other monkeys and cowered in the corner when confronted or attacked, rocking themselves back and forth.

Later studies produced some encouraging results. When the socially deprived monkeys were placed in cages with younger monkeys, researchers found that deprived monkeys would eventually interact playfully with others.

Clearly, ethical and moral parameters would prevent such a study with children, but there is strong evidence of the impact that neglect and abuse have on children raised in neglectful orphanages and other institutions. Receiving little to no attention, children in such settings display signs of depression and impaired emotional regulation, even if their physical needs are met in terms of minimal food, shelter, and clothing.

Kim Chisholm of St Francis Xavier University in Antigonish, Nova Scotia, examined adopted Romanian orphans and evaluated their degrees of attachment. She found that one-third of orphanage children were securely attached to their adoptive parent, one-third were insecurely attached to their parent (which is not uncommon to find in normative samples of adopted? children) and one-third of orphanage children displayed atypical insecure attachment. Chisholm found that the more extreme discriminate behaviours (i.e., wandering without distress and being willing to go home with a stranger) were associated with insecure attachment (Chisholm, 1998).

Organizations such as the National Children's Alliance (**http://www.nationalchildrensalliance.com**) promote the health and well-being of children and youth in Canada, in ways that are beneficial to the community as well.

L08 ▶ Temperament

Simply put, **temperament** refers to individual differences—our unique and stable styles of behaving. Temperament is a critical personality trait, especially in the first days and weeks after birth, and is persistent. Temperaments provide clues to why infants behave in the ways they do and the manner in which they interact with others.

THE DIMENSIONS OF TEMPERAMENT

Throughout life, a child's family, the social environment, socioeconomic status, and cultural influences contribute to the shaping of a child's temperament. Examining this

FEATURED MEDIA

Baby, You're a Star!

Life as We Know It (2010)—Two single adults become caregivers to an orphaned girl when their mutual best friends die in an accident. Will they be able to put their differences aside in order to carry out their friend's wishes?

Baby Boom (1987)—How does a Type A, fiercely competitive career woman balance work with the needs of an infant she's just inherited?

Monsters, Inc. (2001)—How can an infant scare a big, furry monster that scares children for a living? What happens when assumptions and biases about young children are confronted and found to be inaccurate?

Parenthood (1989)—How does a family juggle issues for all family members and give each person his or her due attention? What biological, social, and economic factors influence the family unit?

Three Men and a Baby (1987)—What are some of the everyday challenges of raising a baby? What happens when three bachelors are thrown into fatherhood mode, and they're not sure which of them (if any) is the biological father?

developmentally interactive process, Thompson (1999) offered these conclusions:

- A child's temperament may or may not mesh well with the demands of the social setting. This **goodness of fit** between temperament and environment has a major impact on personality and adjustment. Yet a child's environment changes dramatically through the years, and these changes have powerful effects on development and adjustment.

- Temperament influences how a child selects and responds to different aspects of the environment. This affects how people respond to the child.

- Temperament impacts how a child perceives and thinks about the environment.

Based in biology, temperament is an evolving feature of behaviour that is influenced by other factors.

CHESS AND THOMAS'S CLASSIFICATION OF TEMPERAMENT

Two child psychiatrists, Stella Chess and Alexander Thomas (1987, 1999), were struck by the behaviours of their own children in the days immediately following birth—differences that could not be attributed solely to the environment. Intrigued, they devised the **New York Longitudinal Study** of 141 children. Chess and Thomas discovered that even with children as young as 2 or 3 months of age, they could identify and categorize three types of temperament:

- *Easy*, characterized by regularity of bodily functions, low or moderate intensity of reactions, and acceptance of, rather than withdrawal from, new situations (40% of the children).

- *Difficult*, characterized by irregularity in bodily functions, intense reactions, and withdrawal from new stimuli (10% of the children).

- *Slow to warm up*, characterized by a low intensity of reactions and a somewhat negative mood (15% of the children).

Note that a significant number of children (35%) could not be classified into any of the categories. If parents recognize similar characteristics in their children—e.g., the need for sleep at a certain time, a unique manner of reacting to strangers or the unknown, the intensity of concentration on a task—they can use their knowledge of such characteristics to build a goodness-of-fit relationship. Table 5.4 summarizes the behaviours

▲ Parents need to recognize the uniqueness of their child's personality and respond appropriately in order to raise more responsive children.

of children in three categories of temperament.

The importance of parents' and children's temperaments in establishing a goodness-of-fit relationship has shown the significance of **sensitive responsiveness**. An example of sensitive responsiveness would be that although most infants like to be held, some dislike physical contact. How does a mother respond to an infant who stiffens and pulls away, especially if her older children liked being held when they were young? Infants instantly tune in to their environment. They give clues to their personalities so that a mother's and father's responses to their child's signals must be appropriate for *that* child; that is, greater parental sensitivity produces more responsive infants.

New York Longitudinal Study Long-term study by Chess and Thomas of the personality characteristics of children.

sensitive responsiveness The ability to recognize the meaning of a child's behaviour.

TABLE 5.4

Categories of Temperament

Behaviours	Easy Children	Difficult Children	Slow-to-Warm-Up Children
Activity level	Varies	Low to moderate	Varies
Approach or withdrawal	Positive approach	Withdrawal	Initial withdrawal
Adaptability	Very adaptable	Slowly adaptable	Adaptable
Quality of mood	Positive	Negative	Slightly negative

CONCLUSIONS & SUMMARY

Our view of an infant today is of an individual with enormous potential, one whose activity and competence are much greater than originally believed. It is as if a newborn enters the world with all systems ready to function and eager for growth. What happens during the first two years has important implications for future development. Setbacks—physical and psychological—will occur, but need not cause permanent damage. Human infants show remarkable resiliency.

What are the major physical accomplishments of the infancy period?

- Newborns display clear signs of their competence: movement, seeing, hearing, interacting.
- Infants' physical and motor abilities influence all aspects of development.
- Motor development follows a well-documented schedule.

How do infants acquire information about their world?

- Infants are capable of acquiring and interpreting information from their immediate surroundings through the major sensory channels; in this way, they make sense of the environment and assign meaning to information.
- During infancy, babies discover what they can do with objects, which furthers their perceptual development.

What are the differences between Piaget's view of cognitive development in infancy and that of information-processing theorists?

- Piaget proposed that development is a sequence of distinct stages.
- Each stage involves important changes in the way a child thinks, feels and behaves.
- Information-processing theorists' major focus is on functions such as attention and memory, not on stages of development.

How do infants acquire their language?

- First they emit sounds, then single words, two word "sentences," and then complex sentences.
- Even when children don't understand a specific word, they acquire information about it from the surrounding context (fast mapping).

What is the role of relationships in psychosocial development?

- Relationships involve almost all aspects of development.
- Infants, as active partners in their development, help to shape their relationships.
- To understand relationships, we must analyze and understand the reciprocal interactions involved.

How do children develop and control their emotions?

- Emotions are developed through social exchanges with others.
- Infants' emotions motivate then either to approach or to withdraw from a situation, depending on their previous experiences in that situation.

How would you assess the importance of attachment in psychosocial development?

- Bowlby and his colleagues, studying the separation of children from their parents, identified attachment as an important part of psychosocial development.
- Ainsworth's strange situation technique is designed to assess the security of an infant's attachment.
- Attachment is a cross-cultural phenomenon that offers clues to psychosocial development.
- Chisholm's research on Romanian orphans explains attachment challenges.

How does temperament affect the relationship between parents and their children?

- Temperament refers to a child's unique way of interacting with the environment.
- An infant's temperament immediately affects interactions with adults.
- To maintain goodness of fit, parents must constantly adapt their parenting style to match the developmental changes in their children.

For REVIEW

1. The shift from considering an infant as nothing more than a passive sponge to seeing infants as amazingly competent carries with it certain responsibilities. What are some rights that babies have, as our youngest citizens, that deserve attention and advocacy efforts? How does the environment impact the rights of infants?

2. Infant mortality rates are considered a key indictor of the overall quality of a country's health-care system. What changes do you feel need to be made to Canada's health-care system in order to lower the number of infant deaths that occur? What are other (lower-ranked) countries doing to decrease the rate of infant mortlity?

3. After reading this chapter on infancy, how do you feel about this stage of life as one in which seeds for the future are planted? Select one phase of development (for example, cognitive development) and show how a stimulating environment can help to lay the foundation for future cognitive growth.

Chapter REVIEW TEST

Answers: 1d, 2a, 3a, 4c, 5b, 6d, 7c, 8 b, 9c, 10a

1. Which of the following is not a reflex?
   a. breathing
   b. sucking
   c. swallowing
   d. laughing

2. Piaget noted that _____ are a critical feature of the sensorimotor stage.
   a. circular reactions
   b. rootings
   c. babblings
   d. habits

3. The famous experiment conducted by the Harlows examined social deprivation in
   a. the school years.
   b. early childhood.
   c. adolescence.
   d. adulthood.

4. Most research on infant perceptual development has emphasized
   a. motor and vision.
   b. motor and hearing.
   c. vision and hearing.
   d. only motor.

5. When infants demonstrate a decrease in attention, this is called
   a. repression.
   b. habituation.
   c. egocentrism.
   d. permanence.

6. What parents see as their _____ affects parent–child relationships.
   a. interactions
   b. socioeconomic status
   c. background
   d. role

7. According to this chapter, children's _____ contribute(s) significantly to their interactions with their environments.
   a. ages
   b. gender
   c. temperaments
   d. culture

8. Chisholm found that children who demonstrated extreme indiscriminate behaviours were associated with
   a. secure attachment.
   b. insecure attachment.
   c. disorganized attachment.
   d. ambivalent attachment.

9. Biologically based individual differences are known as
   a. interactions.
   b. attachments.
   c. temperament.
   d. parental signposts.

10. The author of the strange situation test is
    a. Ainsworth.
    b. Bowlby.
    c. Brazelton.
    d. Kagan.

connect LEARNSMART SMARTBOOK

For more information on the resources available from McGraw-Hill Ryerson, go to www.mcgrawhill.ca/he/solutions.

EARLY
CHILDHOOD

As You READ

After reading this chapter, you should be able to answer the following questions:

LO1 ▶ What are the major physical and motor accomplishments of the early childhood years?

LO2 ▶ How do Piaget's and Vygotsky's views on cognitive development differ from those of information-processing theorists?

LO3 ▶ What types of early childhood education seem most promising?

LO4 ▶ How does children's language acquisition proceed during these years?

LO5 ▶ How do children of this age acquire a sense of self?

LO6 ▶ What role does family play in development during these early childhood years?

LO7 ▶ How do children come to understand the meaning of gender?

LO8 ▶ What is the value of play for children's development and learning?

These are "magic" years because children in their early years are magicians—in the psychological sense. Their earliest conceptions of the world are magical ones; they **believe** that their actions and thoughts can bring about events. Later, they extend this magic system and find human attributes in natural phenomena and see human or **suprahuman** causes for natural events or for ordinary occurrences in their lives.

SELMA FRAIBERG, *THE MAGIC YEARS* (1959), P. IX

In one of the great classics describing early childhood, Selma Fraiberg (1959) immortalized ages 2 to 6 as *The Magic Years*. She describes how children perceive and interpret events through the use of "magical thought," the idea that children believe their thoughts can bring about the events they witness. Wonderful at times, such as when magical thought enables children to see themselves as heroic firefighters saving others, magical thought can also be upsetting, such as when children blame themselves for their parents' divorce. The early childhood years are exciting, rewarding, and challenging—for both children and those who care for them. The goal of this chapter is to help you better understand the magical world of early childhood.

Boundless energy, constant curiosity, and growing mental maturity all characterize children from 2 to 6 years of age. Children's developmental changes combine with feelings of confidence—"I can do it myself!" Cognitively, the preschool years correspond to the second stage in Piaget's theory of development, the preoperational period, when children begin to use symbols such as language to represent objects. During this time, many young children also experience some form of preschool education, which contributes to their cognitive and social growth on many complex, interconnected levels. As children's own mental structures interact with messages and values in their environment, they increasingly make sense of the world. While the demands of this period of life are many, healthy children have the abundant energy required to tackle these challenges.

L01 ▶ Physical and Motor Development

Growth in early childhood proceeds at a slower pace than in infancy, yet is quite complex (see Figure 6.1). Some changes are obvious—during the years 2 to 6, children grow about 30 centimetres and continue to gain weight at the rate of about 2.3 kilograms a year. Boys and girls show about the same rate of growth during these years, and although there is a predictable pattern for growth in most parts of the body, growth varies from child to child. Other changes are not visible, but are critically important—rapid growth in the brain's frontal lobe impacts planning and organizing of thought and actions.

FEATURES OF PHYSICAL DEVELOPMENT

We know that different cells, tissues, and organs grow at different rates. In early childhood, children tend to slim down as their trunks lengthen and body fat declines. While girls tend to be a bit shorter and less heavy than boys, girls' bodies tend to have more fatty tissue than boys' bodies, which have more muscle tissue. As children begin to notice obvious differences in physical appearance and growth, they

▲ More time is spent interacting with peers in early childhood than in infancy.

FIGURE 6.1

World Health Organization Growth Charts for Canada

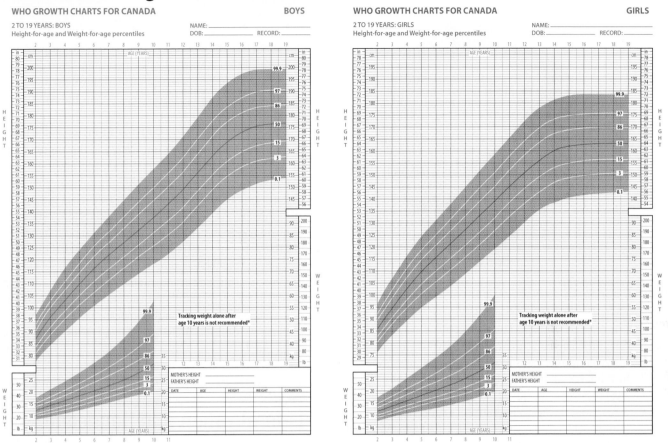

Source: © Dietitians of Canada, 2012. Tracking children's growth. http://www.dietitians.ca/growthcharts

enjoy comparing their body parts to learn about themselves and others. For example, children are happily aware of loose and missing teeth as "baby" teeth fall out to make way for "grown-up" teeth.

▲ Watching SpongeBob SquarePants has been shown to negatively affect children's attention.

BRAIN DEVELOPMENT

As young children compare themselves to others, their brain development allows them to construct new understandings. Although the brain does not grow as much in early childhood as it did during infancy, the number of patterns in specific parts of the brain, such as the frontal lobe, increase tremendously. The patterns that form in the brain promote connections in the form of neural pathways (nerve impulses that travel along axons and connect with dendrites of other neurons along the way) and connections between children and their environment, as an increasing number of cognitive abilities enable them to participate in richer experiences and interactions. Young children are exposed to tremendous amounts of information in their world that they take in through their five senses. The patterns in the specific part of the frontal lobe known as the *prefrontal cortex* (see Figure 6.2) allow young children to organize their attention and actions.

Over time, this organized information helps children plan their activities and use resources efficiently. At times this organization occurs automatically, as brain matter grows to accommodate the increasing number of pathways that are formed and other areas pare down unused brain

FIGURE 6.2

Prefrontal Cortex

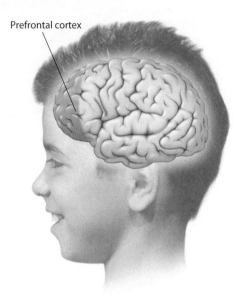

Prefrontal cortex

▲ The prefrontal cortex in relation to the rest of the brain

cells. In Chapter 5, the process by which nerve impulses travel along axons was introduced. Recall that myelin refers to the layer of fat cells that insulate the axons. The presence of myelin speeds up the rate that information travels throughout the nervous system in a process called myelination, which continues throughout childhood. **Myelination** has been shown to influence visible skills, such as hand-eye coordination, as well as skills that are harder to detect, such as a child's ability to focus attention.

The ability to organize information is also impacted by behaviour, such as children's preference in handedness. Although the brain's two hemispheres seem to be almost identical, there are important differences between the two halves of the brain that are linked to specific functions, a concept called *lateralization*. More people around the world are right-handed than left-handed, and for decades parents and teachers forced children to write with their right hand, even when they showed a clear preference for their left hand. The reasons for this include superstitions as well as the reality that much of the world is geared toward right-handedness (consider scissors, musical instruments, and notebook bindings). Today, most adults allow children to pursue the handedness to which they naturally gravitate, and many brain functions have been recognized as being linked to both hemispheres. In fact, a person's ability to utilize both hemispheres of

the brain and coordinate function between them is tied to increased performance in several areas, such as creativity and language processing, production, and recall (see Figure 6.3).

GROWING MOTOR SKILLS

It's easy to take the physical accomplishments of 6-year-olds for granted, but a great deal of neuromuscular development must occur before the motor skills involved in actions such as kicking, cutting, throwing, zipping, and tying shoes become effortless.

These actions fall into two types of motor skills: **gross motor skills** (using the large muscles) and **fine motor skills** (using the small muscles of the hands and fingers). Gross motor skills are visible as young children enjoy a wider variety of movement, from running and dancing to hopping and climbing. As their abilities increase, children are more prone to taking some risks in their physical play; for example, they will climb a structure on the playground that once seemed unconquerable. Fine motor skills, such as picking up objects using finger and thumb (pincer grip), develop greatly during early childhood and are evident in children's play with puzzles and building blocks, as well as in their evolving writing and drawing. Table 6.1 gives examples of gross and fine motor skills at ages 2 to 6 years.

FIGURE 6.3

Lateralization and Handedness

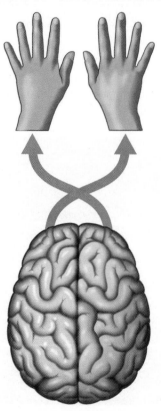

▲ Lateralization links the left side of the brain with right-handedness and the right side of the brain with left-handedness.

myelination Process by which the speed of information travelling through the nervous system increases, due to a fatty layer of cells on nerve cells in the brain.

gross motor skills Large muscle skills resulting from physical development enabling children to perform smooth and coordinated physical acts.

fine motor skills Small muscle skills involving hands and fingers that result from physical development.

TABLE 6.1
The Emergence of Motor Skills

Age	Gross Motor Skills	Fine Motor Skills
2 years	Runs, climbs stairs, jumps from object (both feet)	Throws ball, kicks ball, turns page, begins to scribble
3 years	Hops, climb stairs with alternating feet, jumps from bottom step	Copies circle, opposes thumb to finger, scribbling continues to improve
4 years	Runs well, jumps skillfully, begins to skip, pedals tricycle	Holds pencil, copies square, walks balance beam
5 years	Hops about 50 feet, balances on one foot, can catch large ball, good skipping	Colours within lines, forms letters, dresses and undresses self with help, eats more neatly
6 years	Carries bundles, begins to ride bicycle, jumps rope, can catch tennis ball	Ties shoes, uses scissors, uses knife and fork, washes self with help

The forces described above illustrate the influence of biopsychosocial interactions. It's impossible to argue that physical growth is determined solely by heredity or the environment. The neuroscientist Lise Eliot (2000) summarizes this reality when she notes that while genes direct the formation of the organs of the nervous system, experience ultimately determines the extent of children's brain development. An array of factors combine to explain skills acquired throughout development.

Physical changes, while observable and exciting, are not the only significant changes occurring during early childhood. Young children's cognitive abilities develop with their increasing use of ideas and rapid growth in language. Theories of cognitive development help explain what is happening in the cognitive world of young children.

BIOPSYCHOSOCIAL INFLUENCES ON PHYSICAL DEVELOPMENT

Physical development impacts all aspects of children's lives, but the interplay between biological, psychological, and social forces plays a huge role in developmental outcomes. Some major forces that interact to influence physical development are as follows:

- *Genetic elements.* Genes, which we inherit from our parents, control growth to some degree. The genetic growth plan is created at conception and functions throughout the lifespan.
- *Nutrition.* Active preschoolers need a well-balanced diet. Healthy eating habits established in early childhood last a lifetime.
- *Disease.* Short-term illnesses do not permanently impede growth rate, although if the child's diet is consistently poor, problems can occur. Major disease usually causes a slowing of growth, followed by a catch-up period if the situation improves.
- *Psychological issues.* Stress and anxiety are associated with a predisposition to physical and mental disorders (Rutter & Taylor, 2002), but they certainly impact ordinary experiences, such as transition to school and relationships with new adults. For some children, seemingly simple experiences can feel traumatic.
- *Socioeconomic status.* Children from different socioeconomic backgrounds differ in average body size at all ages. A consistent pattern appears in research studies, indicating that children in more favourable circumstances develop differently than those growing up under less favourable economic conditions, perhaps due to factors including nutrition, sleep, and recreation (Graham, 2005).

All things are connected.
Whatever befalls the earth befalls
the **children** of the earth.

CHIEF SEATTLE, SUQWAMISH AND DUWAMISH

Cognitive Development ◀L02

Piaget's theory of cognitive development is perhaps the best-known theory relating to children's thinking, yet other ideas about children's intellect—such as Vygotsky's consideration of social and cultural influences and information-processing theory—provide additional insights into children's competence in early childhood and the mechanisms that enable them to make sense of the world.

PIAGET'S PREOPERATIONAL PERIOD

During Piaget's **preoperational period**, young children begin to use symbols to represent objects and events in their environment, and the relationships among them. They remember and talk about their memories, and this process signals growing symbolic ability and language acquisition. They gradually acquire the basics of their language, a feat of such magnitude that its secret still eludes scholars.

In early childhood, children become more comfortable with symbols, as seen when they read and understand what they read. They continue to explore and learn about their environment through their play. Yet their mental ability during these years remains limited.

> **preoperational period** Piaget's second stage of cognitive development, extending from about 2 to 7 years.

representation Piaget's term for a child's application of abstract thinking during the preoperational period.

animism Children's preoperational activity in which they consider inanimate objects to possess human thought, feelings, and actions.

deferred imitation Children's preoperational behaviour that continues after they witnessed the original action or event.

symbolic play Children's mental representation of an object or event and reenactment of it in their play; one object may represent a different object in the play scenario.

For Piaget, *preoperational* refers to children who cannot take two things into consideration at the same time (a flower is both red and a tulip), who cannot return to the beginning of a thought sequence (how to reverse the action of 3 + 2 = 5), and who cannot believe that the properties of substances remain the same even if you change their shape or arrangement. These children are at a level of thinking that precedes operational thought (thinking marked by reversible mental actions).

Features of the Preoperational Period

For Piaget, the great accomplishment of the preoperational period is a growing ability to represent, which is how we record or express information. For example, the word "car" is a **representation**, because it stands for the idea of something with wheels that people drive. Playing "house" is also an example of representation, as playmates are assigned to play the roles of parents and children.

Other activities typical of preoperational children reflect their use of internal representation and include the following:

- **Animism** Young children tend to believe that inanimate objects have thoughts and feelings as they do. At the preoperational stage, children attribute actions and abilities to objects and animals. You'll notice that most children's literature features animals as the main characters, which supports this kind of thinking.

▲ These children are engaging in imitative and symbolic play.

TECH TRENDS

Using Video to Illustrate (and Argue!) Children's Strengths

Videatives.com, a website that features hundreds of video clips showing children in ordinary situations, combines the power of the written word with the power of visual images. A "videative" is a written text (narrative) with rich video clips embedded within the text (video). The creators of this innovative site recognize the competence of young children and thoughtfully interpret events captured on video to explain the developmental implications for children's actions, how educators might extend their own practice with young children, and how society at large might come to appreciate what young children know and can do. Viewers can opt to view the clips with or without accompanying narrative. The site features clips of children with a diverse range of abilities, as well as cultural, ethnic, and language differences. Viewers may opt to purchase a subscription to the site, but there are free clips from the most recent issue and from back issues ("Videatives Views Archives") that provide much rich and stimulating material.

- **Deferred imitation** Preoperational children can imitate some action or event they previously witnessed; for example, they walk like an animal they saw at the zoo earlier in the day.
- **Symbolic play** Children enjoy pretending that they are someone or something else. Piaget argued eloquently for recognizing the importance of play in a youngster's life. As children adapt to social and physical worlds that they only slightly understand and appreciate, they must have some outlet that permits them to assimilate reality to themselves. Children find this possible through play, using the tools characteristic of symbolic play.

Limitations of Preoperational Thought

Although we see the steady development of thought during this period, preoperational thought has several limitations. In the period of preoperational thought, children cannot assume the role of another person or recognize that other viewpoints exist, a state called egocentrism. In Piaget's classic experiment, illustrated in Figure 6.4, a child is shown a display of three mountains varying in height and colour. The child stands on one side of the table, looking at the mountains; a doll is then placed at various spots

FIGURE 6.4

Piaget's Mountains Task

FIGURE 6.5

Piaget's Conservation Task

around the mountains. The child is next shown several pictures of the mountains and asked to pick the one that shows what part of the mountains the doll saw. Egocentric children pick the photo that shows the mountains as they saw them.

Another striking feature of preoperational thought is **centration**, the centring of attention on one aspect of an object and the neglecting of any other features. Preoperational children are unable to notice features that would give balance to their reasoning. A good example of this is the process of **classification**. Piaget and Inhelder (1969) provide a fascinating example of the limitations of classification at this age. If there are 8 roses and 4 daisies, preoperational youngsters can differentiate between the roses and the daisies. But when asked if there are more flowers or more roses, preoperational children will generally say there are more roses than flowers. The understanding that subclasses can be part of a larger class does not appear until about age 8.

Another limitation of the period is the lack of **conservation**, the understanding that an object retains certain properties no matter how its form changes. The most popular illustration is to show a young child two identical glasses, each half-filled with water, as shown in Figure 6.5. The child agrees that each glass contains an equal amount. But if you then pour the water from one of the glasses into a taller, thinner glass, the preoperational child now says that the new glass contains more liquid because the water level is now higher. Children consider only the appearance of the liquid and ignore what happened. They also do not perceive the reversibility of the transformation—if they pour the water back into the original glass, the amounts of water will be equal.

Reversibility is a cognitive act in which a child recognizes that she can use stages of reasoning to solve a problem and then proceed in reverse, tracing the steps back to the original question or premise. The preoperational child's

thought is irreversible, and although the child is able to rationalize her thinking and actions, the adults see the contradictions in the child's logic.

Evaluation of Piaget

Piaget's theory has been tested, retested, challenged, and refuted in many respects. Training studies have repeatedly shown that young children possess more cognitive competence than Piaget believed. For example, 4-year-olds can be taught conservation (Bjorklund, 2000). (See the conservation task illustrated in Figure 6.6.) Other theories complement Piaget's theory and fill some of the gaps that critics identify as weaknesses in understanding children's cognitive development.

VYGOTSKY'S THEORY

Recognizing that children do not develop in isolation, Vygotsky stressed the role of social interactions and learning contexts, two areas less emphasized by Piaget but deserving much attention. Both Vygotsky and Piaget believed learning to be an active process—known as **constructivism** in the fields of education and psychology—but Vygotsky's

centration Feature of preoperational thought; the centring of attention on one aspect of an object and the neglecting of any other features.

classification Ability to group objects with some similarities within a larger category.

conservation The understanding that an object retains certain properties even though surface features change.

reversibility A cognitive act in which a child recognizes that he or she can use stages of reasoning to solve a problem and then trace the steps back to the original question or premise.

constructivism The belief that children create, organize, and transform knowledge through active engagement in their environment.

FIGURE 6.6

Conservation Tasks

Type of Conservation	Initial Presentation	Manipulation	Preoperational Child's Answer
Number	Two identical rows of objects are shown to the child, who agrees they have the same number.	One row is lengthened and the child is asked whether one row now has more objects.	Yes, the longer row.
Matter	Two identical balls of clay are shown to the child. The child agrees that they are equal.	The experimenter changes the shape of one of the balls and asks the child whether they still contain equal amounts of clay.	No, the longer one has more.
Length	Two sticks are aligned in front of the child. The child agrees that they are the same length.	The experimenter moves one stick to the right, then asks the child if they are equal in length.	No, the one on the top is longer.

social constructivism The belief that children construct knowledge through social interactions.

scaffolding The systematic use of support to assist a child in his or her performance on a given task.

attention to social influences gave rise to the term **social constructivism**.

One of the social influences that Vygotsky stressed as important to children's learning is instruction, which may be formal, such as teacher–child instruction in the classroom, or informal, such as parent–child interaction at the dinner table. As discussed in Chapter 2, Vygotsky developed the term *zone of proximal development (ZPD)* to refer to the range of ability that a child has when faced with a task. The range includes what a child can do alone and what a child can do with guidance from adults or older children; it reflects the dynamic nature of children's cognitive abilities at a given point in time. With practice or assistance from others, children's zones of proximal development can improve greatly.

The concept of **scaffolding** is linked to the ZPD and refers to the systematic support that a child receives from a parent or teacher to help him get from one point to the next in a given task. For example, a first-grade teacher wouldn't expect a 6-year-old to know how to write a journal entry on the first day of school. By the end of the year, when the child has had direct instruction and practice writing, editing, and "publishing," he will have a well-formed idea of

Career Apps

As an early childhood educator, how might you satisfy the desire of a screaming 3-year-old who wants two cookies at snack time, when his parents explicitly asked you to limit his sugary treats? (Hint: Most cookies break easily.)

what is involved in writing a journal entry. Just as we notice scaffolding on the outside of buildings under construction, children's thinking is supported through smaller, structured tasks on the way to completing a larger task.

INFORMATION-PROCESSING THEORY

In early childhood, children process huge amounts of information. Information-processing theory attempts to explain the ways in which children's thinking develops. Rather than being attributed to one individual theorist, such as Piaget or Vygotsky, information-processing theory provides a broad theory of children's cognitive development that has been interpreted and adapted by different theorists since the 1960s. The underlying belief is that as children develop strategies to notice and process information, they are better able to retain and recall this information (Munakata, 2006).

Attention

Attention involves a lengthy process in which children translate what they know into appropriate actions and then rely on these strategies to gather new information. Selective attention—the ability to focus on specific activities or stimuli—becomes increasingly important as children move through early childhood and become better at concentrating on pertinent information. The selectivity with which children focus their attention on relevant items increases greatly between 3 and 8 years. Researchers have been interested in whether the types of TV programs that children watch affect their ability to pay attention. A study by Lillard and Peterson (2011) found that four-year-old children who had watched nine minutes of the fast-paced television program *SpongeBob SquarePants* had more difficulty subsequently paying attention to and

PERSPECTIVES ON **DIVERSITY**

Aboriginal Head Start on Reserve and the Indian Residential School Program

The Indian Residential School program was a boarding school program funded by the federal government. It began in 1874 and involved 150,000 Aboriginal, Inuit, and Métis children being removed from their homes and forced to live away from their families and their communities (Aboriginal Affairs and Northern Development Canada, 2012). As a result, these children suffered the loss of their cultural heritage. Many experienced sexual and physical abuse at these schools, creating long-lasting effects on them and their communities.

The federal government established Aboriginal Head Start in 1995 to help our nation's Aboriginal, Inuit, and Métis children to be better prepared for their entrance into formal education (Health Canada, 2011). Incidentally, the establishment of Aboriginal Head Start happened 2 years before the final Indian Residential School closed.

An expansion of Aboriginal Head Start, known as Aboriginal Head Start on Reserve (AHSOR), takes the opposite approach to the residential school program by providing early developmental intervention within First Nations communities. AHSOR focuses on six areas of development including education, health promotion, culture and language, nutrition, social support, and parental/family involvement. It is hoped that this program can help to address problems such as violence, crime, poor health, and poverty, which have plagued our First Nations communities for far too long.

completing a problem-solving task than did children who had either watched *Caillou*, a slower-paced Canadian television cartoon, or been drawing for the nine minutes. The researchers believe that the fast pace of some programs, such as *SpongeBob SquarePants*, may over-excite children, thus affecting their ability to concentrate, or may serve as a model for their own behaviour (Beckford, 2011).

Memory

Unlike Piaget's or Vygotsky's theories, information-processing theory assumes that our minds, like computers, have a limited space with which to operate efficiently. It is therefore critical that children (1) develop strategies for attending to relevant information to carry out tasks, (2) remember relevant information using rehearsal and organization strategies, and (3) retrieve information relevant to the task.

During the early childhood years, children begin to develop memory strategies, such as rehearsal, organization, and retrieval. **Rehearsal** (repeating target information) allows children to hold on to information for as long as possible, increasing the possibility of storing the information in long-term memory, memory that can last from a few days to decades. Such strategies also impact short-term memory (up to 30 seconds, or longer with rehearsal), as children actively work on tasks in the immediate, present situation.

Organization (discovering or imposing structure on a set of items to guide behaviour) allows children to group items in chunks and reduce the number of things they are trying to remember. If a child is shown a list of 20 items to remember, organizing the items into 5 categories relating to function would help the child remember the list. Such strategies allow much information processing to occur in the mind's limited space.

Retrieval (obtaining information from memory) takes two forms: recognition and recall. Recognition tasks require a child to correctly distinguish between a stimulus that they have previously encountered and one(s) that they have not. Recall tasks are those that require a child to report the details of a stimulus without being given any cues. Most children find recognition tasks fairly simple, but recall offers a challenge. Older children tend to use spontaneous retrieval cues, such as remembering what colour shirt they were wearing when they ate a certain flavour of ice cream, more often than a preschooler will.

rehearsal Mnemonic strategy that describes a person repeating target information.

organization Memory strategy that entails discovering and imposing an easy-to-remember structure on items to be memorized.

retrieval Memory strategy that enables obtaining information from memory; includes recognition and recall.

▲ Technological advances have changed the ways in which children learn.

asked what other children might think was inside the box. Three-year-old children often answered, "Pencils," whereas 5-year-old children often answered, "Band-Aids." The older children could understand that other children could be fooled as they had been, but the younger children were tied to the reality of what was actually in the box.

Early Childhood Education ◀L03

Early childhood education refers to formal education for children aged from 2 to 5 years of age. As Howard Gardner (2003) noted, two considerations are critical in any early childhood program: assumptions about the minds of children and our views about the kind of society we desire. Are children's minds empty vessels to be filled or are children curious and competent? Are children equal citizens in a community, entitled to rights and privileges like adults, or are they not? Classroom expectations and responsibilities will reflect such beliefs in the environment and materials that children encounter. Early childhood education tends to reflect a rich mixture of ideas from educational philosophy and educational and developmental psychology.

An understanding of the complexities of children's thinking at different developmental levels is important as educators design classroom practices that are appropriate for young children.

THEORY OF MIND

theory of mind Children's understanding of their own thoughts and mental processes.

constructivist approach Learning approach in which children are encouraged to be active participants in constructing knowledge and learn by interacting with their environment.

As children's cognitive processes develop, children become aware of their own thinking and begin to understand that the thinking of others may be different than their own. Known as **theory of mind** (Flavell, 1999), children's understanding of their own thoughts and mental processes develops throughout childhood. Around ages 2 to 3 years, children begin to understand what it means to desire something, and they also realize that the success or failure to obtain something results in related feelings of happiness, sadness, frustration, and so on.

A key development around ages 4 to 5 years is the ability to recognize false beliefs—beliefs that are not true. One study of false beliefs involved a box of Band-Aids (Jenkins & Astington, 1996). Children were asked what was inside the box, but when they opened the box to verify their answers, they found pencils inside. The children were then

CONSTRUCTIVIST APPROACHES TO LEARNING

Early childhood programs based on developmental theory rather than behavioural theory reflect constructivism, an approach to learning influenced by Piaget's and Vygotsky's theories. In the **constructivist approach**, children are encouraged to be active participants in constructing knowledge and learn by interacting with their environment. Early childhood programs integrate content so that one cooking activity can meet provincial standards for

▶ Children learn through play.

math (quantity), science (measuring ingredients, noting changes in temperature), and literacy (reading a recipe). Relationships with others are stressed, including teacher–child, child–child, caregiver–child, and all permutations. The value of social interaction is seen in examples of collaborative activities, such as children working at clusters of desks, rather than sitting at individual desks in rows.

Although Piaget never specified using his developmental theory as part of a constructivist approach to learning, his emphasis on a child's progression through cognitive stages has clear implications for classroom practice. Consider the use of materials, for example: a 3-year-old might not be able to complete a jigsaw puzzle successfully, whereas a 6-year-old can complete a jigsaw puzzle more easily, as well as describe specific strategies he uses to work with puzzles, such as finding all of the straight-edged pieces first. Piaget's theory stresses children's active interactions with their environment, not the rote memorization of facts. Rather than expecting children to memorize names of animals based on seeing pictures of them, providing colourful plastic or wooden animal figures and a farm area to play with (or taking a field trip to a farm) is a more engaging learning strategy, as children create their own meaning from the experiences.

Maria Montessori (1870–1952), an Italian educator, was a vocal proponent of early childhood programs. She believed that developing children pass through different physical and mental growth phases that alternate with periods of transition, suggesting that there are times when a child is especially ready for certain types of learning. These periods—called **sensitive periods**—differ so sharply that Montessori referred to them as a "series of new births."

Another Italian influence in early childhood education comes not from one person, but from an entire community. Recognized in 1991 by *Newsweek* magazine as some of the best preschools in the world, the schools in Reggio Emilia, Italy (also discussed in Chapter 5), embody an approach to early childhood education that has been widely embraced around the world (Edwards, Gandini, & Forman, 1998).

Following the devastation of World War II, community members in Reggio Emilia began the process of rebuilding schools brick by brick. A young teacher named Loris Malaguzzi visited Reggio Emilia and, inspired by what he observed, became the driving force behind what came to be the first infant–toddler centres and preschools of the community. Viewing children as curious and competent citizens with rights and valuable contributions, educators and families in Reggio Emilia value collaboration and support children's developing interests. Experts in art and pedagogy work with classroom teachers on a daily basis to document and extend the learning that occurs in the classrooms. The pictures of Laura at the beginning of Chapter 5 are

▲ Maria Montessori with her students.

a beautiful example of the Reggio Emilia philosophy in action.

In the Reggio Emilia schools, the classroom and school environment are considered another teacher, which means that beauty, nature, and transparency (to foster communication between individuals) are explicitly demonstrated in many ways—from placement of windows in the building to allow ample natural light and views into other classrooms to the array of natural materials from which children create sculptures, collages, and other creations. Many people have the misperception that Reggio Emilia–inspired schools in Canada are for children from wealthy, advantaged families. On the contrary, some of the most inspirational work has been conducted in urban, economically challenged schools, such as the work in Canada's diverse urban communities (see Wein, 2008).

sensitive periods Montessori's term for periods of children's development marked by sensitivity/ readiness to learn.

Aboriginal Head Start Government-supported early childhood program that provides education, health, and parenting education services to First Nations families.

CANADIAN EARLY CHILDHOOD EDUCATION PROGRAMS

Aboriginal Head Start is a national program to increase school readiness among Aboriginal children by providing educational, health, nutrition, social, and other services to First Nations children and their families. In addition to the Aboriginal Head Start on Reserve program, which is discussed in the

▲ Loris Malaguzzi, founder of the Reggio Emilia approach.

FIGURE 6.7

Aboriginal Head Start Data

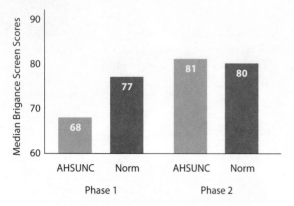

▲ Research has shown that participants in the Aboriginal Head Start in Urban and Northern Communities program catch up to their peers in school readiness within one academic year.

Source: Public Health Agency of Canada (2011a).

Perspectives on Diversity box, there is a program for families who live off-reserve. The Aboriginal Head Start in Urban and Northern Communities (AHSUNC) serves 4640 children between the ages of 0 and 6 each year (Public Health Agency of Canada, 2012a). As Figure 6.7 shows, the AHSUNC program has produced the desired results as students in the program catch up to their peers within one academic year.

Six provinces—British Columbia, New Brunswick, Nova Scotia, Ontario, Prince Edward Island, and Quebec—now offer full-day kindergarten. According to the influential report *Early Years Study 3: Making decisions, taking action*, this should only be the start in ultimately expanding publicly funded preschool education to all children between 2 and 5 years of age (McCain, Mustard, & McCuaig, 2011). The report's authors write that currently 1 in 4 children are underprepared to start kindergarten; these children are less likely to succeed in high school or attend post-secondary school, resulting in personal and occupational difficulties as adults. The authors of the report believe that the time for government to invest in early education to create a stronger future for the entire country is now. The report advocates play-based learning, which prominent Canadian physician Fraser Mustard believes "expands intelligence, stimulates the imagination, encourages creative problem solving, and helps develop confidence, self-esteem, and a positive attitude towards learning" (Council of Ministers of Education,

Canada, n.d.). Play-based learning is central to the full-day kindergarten programs in both Ontario and British Columbia (Hammer, 2011).

Language Development ◂L04

Language acquisition is a key milestone in early childhood development. With no formal training, and often exposed to incorrect language models, children learn sounds, combine sounds into words, and—following a complex sequence of grammatical rules—form sentences. The acquisition of language skills is an accomplishment that is often taken for granted, yet by the time children are ready to enter first grade, most have a vocabulary of about 10,000 words; they use questions, negative statements, and dependent clauses, and they have learned to use language in a variety of social situations. They are relatively sophisticated language users.

LANGUAGE RULES

As children acquire the basics of their language, they learn the guidelines that make language a powerful tool. For example, by the age of 4 or 5, children know that rules exist for combining sounds into words, that individual words have specific meanings, and that there are rules for combining words into meaningful sentences and participating in a dialogue. These rules help children to detect the meaning of a word with which they are unfamiliar. Rules also provide a foundation from which children create their own expressive vocabulary and become more active participants in their environment.

▼ The use of language improves in leaps and bounds during early childhood.

The rules can be summarized as follows:

- Rules of phonology describe a language's sound system—that is, how to put sounds together to form words. Children notice and imitate sounds in rhymes, songs, and names, even creating their own sounds to represent objects and happenings in their world.
- Rules of syntax determine sentence structure and word order. Children realize that word placement changes with a question or statement: when they ask, "Where doggie go?" as opposed to stating "Doggie go home."
- Rules of semantics describe how to interpret the meaning of words. Children gain new vocabulary words at an amazing rate between ages 18 months and 6 years, aiding their understanding of new words in relation to familiar ones.
- Rules of pragmatics describe how language is used in social contexts: in other words, how people converse. Children learn to speak about past, present, and future events accordingly, and they tailor their speech to speak to younger children (and animals!), whom older children recognize might not be as advanced in their own speech.

As we trace the path of language development in the early childhood years, children clearly show an ability for **receptive language** before they produce **expressive language**: They are able to indicate that they understand words before they are able to articulate them themselves.

> Simply by making noises with our mouths, we can reliably cause precise new **combinations** of ideas to arise in each other's minds.
>
> STEVEN PINKER

LANGUAGE IRREGULARITIES

When speech emerges, children tend to use certain language irregularities that are quite normal and to be expected. For example, **overextensions** mark children's beginning words. Assume that a child has learned the name of the house pet, Doggy. Think what that label means: an animal with a head, tail, body, and four legs. Now consider what other animals "fit" this label: cats, horses, donkeys, and cows. Consequently, children may briefly apply "doggy" to all four-legged creatures; they quickly eliminate overextensions, however, as they learn about their world.

Overregularization is a similar phenomenon in which children extend regular grammatical rules to irregular

words. As youngsters begin to use two- and three-word sentences, they struggle to convey more-precise meanings by mastering the grammatical rules of their language. For example, many English verbs add -*ed* to indicate past tense. Youngsters who do not know that the past tense of come is came may say "Daddy comed home" instead of "Daddy came home."

During the early childhood years, children begin to display a growing mastery of meaning. As their vocabulary continues to increase dramatically, they begin to combine words to refine their meaning. Yet they also must learn to suggest the correct meaning for the correct word. For example, saying, "Right!" could indicate correctness or direction. Sometimes children's levels of understanding are more advanced than their language ability, so instead of saying, "That dog licked me!" a young child might say, "I got tongued!" Their meaning is still clear.

As children come to the end of the early childhood period, several language milestones have been achieved. At this point, children

- are skillful at building words, adding suffixes such as -*er*, -*man*, and -*ist* to form nouns (the person who teaches is a *teacher*);
- are comfortable with passive sentences (the glass *was broken* by the rock);
- can pronounce almost all speech sounds accurately;
- have experienced the "language explosion"—vocabulary has grown rapidly; and
- are aware of grammatical correctness.

One of the most noticeable features of children's language development is children's ability to express themselves and communicate ideas and feelings to others. A developing awareness of the self involves a complex interaction between numerous biopsychosocial variables that affect individual children.

The Self Emerges ◀ L05

Young children's cognitive and emotional development paves the way for greater self-awareness in all aspects of development. How do children construct a sense of self—this sense of who they are and what makes them different from everyone else? Children's increasing ability to understand people and happenings in the world provides them with deeper insights into themselves. Children recognize that they are individuals as well as members of a larger group.

receptive language The ability of the child to understand written and spoken language.

expressive language The language children use to express their ideas and needs.

overextension A language irregularity in which children apply a word in a broad manner to objects that do not fit.

overregularization Children's strict application of language rules they have learned.

THE DEVELOPMENT OF SELF

Initially, in describing themselves, most children tend to focus on physical characteristics—hair colour, colour of eyes, presence of freckles, and so on—or on tangible things such as food and toys. As children grow, their sense of self isn't limited to their reflections in a mirror, and they have acquired language to tell us what they think of themselves. Their self-judgments reflect their changing cognitive and social maturity. As representational thinking continues to improve and they compare their performances with those of others, more realistic evaluations begin to appear (Harter, 2006).

Erik Erikson categorized early childhood as the stage when children grapple with initiative versus guilt. They experience a tension between their increasing abilities and their developing conscience. Although they may feel proud and confident with their initiative to tackle various challenges, they also feel the effects of judgment from self and others. Examples of this are when a 5-year-old tries to pour a bowl of Cheerios and the Cheerios spill all over the table, or when a 6-year-old reads aloud from a favourite book and an older sibling corrects his or her pronunciation of words. Interestingly, the opinions of others become increasingly important as children strive to establish their self-understanding.

▲ Authors of the children's book *And Tango Makes Three*, Justin Richardson and Peter Parnell recently welcomed daughter Gemma into their family.

ways. Despite many changes that have occurred in the definition of family over time, the vast majority of individuals live in some type of family, which testifies to the enduring strength of the family as the basic social structure.

L06 ▶ Social Development

When we consider the interplay among many variables affecting human development, we realize that social relationships influence children both directly and indirectly. Children's developing sense of self, combined with the ability to express themselves and appreciate the perspective of others, is very much influenced by their relationships with family and peers.

THE ROLE OF THE FAMILY

Parenting styles, sibling relationships, and other caregivers can impact children in positive and negative

PARENTING STYLES

Parents do many things—select clothes, limit television time, and enforce rules—but they alone can't determine the nature of the relationship with their children. Parents and children construct their relationships together, and no one model fits all. Diana Baumrind's (1967, 1971, 1986, 1991a, 1991b) pioneering work on parenting style identified three kinds of parental behaviour, and later research (Maccoby & Martin, 1983) suggested a fourth style of parenting that impacts children's development and family relationships.

The family generally, and parenting specifically, are today in a greater state of flux, question, and redefinition than perhaps ever before. We are witnessing the emergence of striking **permutations** on the theme of parenting: blended families, lesbian and gay parents, teen versus 50s first-time moms and dads.

MARC BORNSTEIN, *HANDBOOK OF PARENTING* (2002)

The Puzzling Topic of Punishment

No child is perfect, and most parents are concerned about what to do when their children misbehave. Punishment generally takes one of two paths: Something unpleasant is done to a child (scolding or corporal punishment, i.e., spanking), or something pleasant is withdrawn (temporary loss of a video game).

Most child experts, including pediatricians, oppose the use of corporal punishment for many reasons, mostly because it too often leads to child abuse. New research indicates that corporal punishment can lead to lower IQs in children (see Figure 6.8) (Straus & Paschall, 2009). Nonphysical methods, such as positive reinforcement, time-out, or removal of privileges are more desirable. Still, spanking is routinely used by many parents who believe it is the most effective form of punishment.

Conversely, eleven countries—Sweden, Finland, Norway, Austria, Denmark, Cyprus, Latvia, Croatia, Israel, Germany, and Iceland—have abolished physical punishment of children (Trocmé, Durrant, Ensom & Marwah, 2004).

Do you think spanking is a useful form of punishment for children? If so, what are the appropriate boundaries for spanking behaviour? Who should determine whether or not spanking is acceptable—families, doctors, human service agencies, or the courts? In 2004, the Supreme Court of Canada upheld Section 43 of the Criminal Code, which allows for any person in authority to use force in order to correct a child so long as that force is not unreasonable for the circumstances. Do you believe that the Supreme Court made the correct decision in upholding this law?

As most of the countries that have abolished physical punishment of children are in Europe, it would appear that there are different attitudes towards how children should be disciplined between many European cultures and the rest of the world, including Canada. What do you believe are these different attitudes? Would you spank your child? Why or why not?

FIGURE 6.8

Effects of Spanking on Cognitive Activity

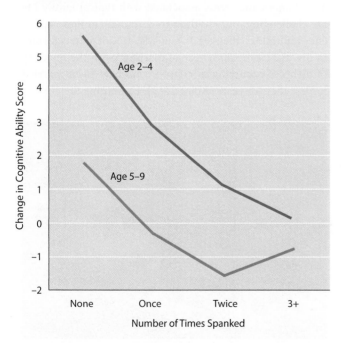

▲ Children who were spanked had a lower cognitive ability 4 years later than those who were not spanked.

- **Authoritarian parenting**
Parents who adopt this style are demanding, and for them immediate obedience is the most desirable trait in a child. When there is any conflict between these parents and their children, no consideration is given to the child's view or communication. It's a simple case of "Do it my way or else!"

- **Authoritative parenting** These parents respond to their children's needs and wishes. Believing in parental control, they attempt to explain the reasons for it to their children. Authoritative parents expect mature behaviour and will enforce rules, but they encourage their children's independence and attempts to reach their potential.

- **Permissive parenting** Parents who adopt this parenting approach take a tolerant, accepting view of their children's behaviour, including both aggressive and sexual urges. They rarely use punishment or make demands of their children. Children make almost all their own decisions.

authoritarian parenting Baumrind's term for parents who are demanding and want immediate obedience as the most desirable trait in a child.

authoritative parenting Baumrind's term for parents who respond to their child's needs and wishes; they believe in parental control and attempt to explain the reasons for it to their child.

permissive parenting Baumrind's term for parents who take a tolerant, accepting view of their child's behaviour and rarely make demands or use punishment.

TABLE 6.2

Parental Behaviours and Children's Characteristics

Parental Behaviours			
Authoritarian	*Authoritative*	*Permissive*	*Uninvolved*
Children's Characteristics			
Withdrawn	Self-assertive	Impulsive	Antisocial
Lack of enthusiasm	Independent	Low self-reliance	Low self-regulation
Shy (girls)	Friendly	Low self-control	Low self-control
Hostile (boys)	Cooperative	Low maturity	Low maturity
Low need	High need	Aggressive	High need
Achievement	Achievement	Low achievement	Low achievement
Low competence	High competence	Lack of responsibility	Low competence

- **Uninvolved/neglectful parenting** These parents tend to be quite detached from their children's lives. They place few demands on their children, but are also unresponsive and communicate little while still tending to their children's basic needs. In the extreme, these parents may reject or neglect their children.

In a longitudinal study from preschool to adolescence, Baumrind (1991c) found that authoritative parenting was associated with positive developmental outcomes. More recent research suggests that in some ethnic groups, authoritarian parenting leads to positive outcomes (Chao, 2001), stressing the role of context in development. It's important to remember that Baumrind's findings don't necessarily indicate a cause-and-effect relationship between the categories and a child's characteristics. A child's temperament also affects how she or he is treated. Table 6.2 lists children's characteristics in response to the four types of parental behaviour.

THE ROLE OF SIBLINGS

Because of their behaviour toward one another, siblings create a unique family environment and play a critical role in socialization. In early childhood, older siblings often act as caregivers for their younger brothers and sisters, providing opportunities for them to learn about the needs of others (Eisenberg, Fabes, & Spinrad, 2006). Older siblings become models for younger children to imitate. Older siblings often ease the way for younger ones by running interference with parents. In this way, bonds are formed that usually last a lifetime, often longer than those between husband and wife or parent and child.

As young children make sense of their world, siblings act as

uninvolved/neglectful parenting Term for parents who are undemanding and emotionally unsupportive of their child.

sibling underworld Familial subsystem, or coalition, of brothers and/ or sisters.

non-threatening sounding boards for one another. New behaviours, new roles, and new ideas can be tested on siblings, and their reactions, whether positive or negative, lack the doomsday quality of many parental judgments. Siblings also form subsystems that are the basis for the formation of powerful coalitions, often called the **sibling underworld**. Older siblings can warn their younger brothers and sisters about parental moods and prohibitions, thus averting problems. An older sibling can also contribute to a sense of inferiority as the younger child struggles to keep up with the older sibling. There are many complex issues related to sibling relationships, including sibling rivalry, birth order, and only children. Some common perceptions about siblings exist, such as that first-borns tend to be more motivated and academically oriented and that only children tend to interact more comfortably with adults and are highly verbal. Many similarities exist between first-borns and between youngest siblings that have attracted attention in research studies. Generalizations about birth order and only children must be considered in light of the specific family context and should not become stereotypes. In general, however, research has shown that birth order has a limited ability to predict behaviour.

CHILDREN OF DIVORCE

The changes and stress associated with typical family life are challenging, but children in divorced families experience multiple challenges. In Canada, 41% of marriages end in divorce by the 30th year of marriage with the majority of divorces occurring in couples who have been married for less than 15 years (Kelly, 2012). Examining the current

▲ Siblings can play a key role in the socialization of young children.

state of children of divorce, Judith Wallerstein and her colleagues note that as a society we have not yet come to terms with a divorce culture (Wallerstein, Lewis, & Blakeslee, 2002). Expectations for relationships have changed: fear of commitment and a hesitancy to trust a companion's intentions and to express intimate feelings have impacted the nature of relationships. These have long-term influences on children's understanding of adults' behaviour and responsibilities.

▲ Witnessing parental conflict can have long-term psychological effects on children.

Because the conflict that leads to divorce begins long before the divorce itself, young children too often witness displays of hostility, anger, and arguments between their parents. Viewing angry adults is emotionally disturbing for children and may lead to childhood and adolescent problems such as aggression and poor psychological adjustment, unless adults also model reconciliation and forgiveness (Friedman & Chase-Lansdale, 2002). Parents' actual separation may not be the major cause of any problem behaviour, because too many other possible factors may have intervened, including exposure to conflict, economic decline, and erratic parenting. As families attempt to adjust to life after divorce, overall quality of life and parent–child relationships play an important role in children's long-term well-being.

Although studies of the age at which children most strongly experience the effects of divorce remain inconclusive, suspicion persists that young children are particularly vulnerable. Unable to understand the reasons for the family upset, they are more adversely affected by the divorce than are older children (Hetherington & Stanley-Hagan, 2002). Their ability to engage in abstract thinking is still limited, and they may think that they are responsible for the divorce. During early childhood, children may demonstrate intense separation anxiety and fear of abandonment by both parents (Hetherington & Stanley-Hagan, 1995; Lamb, Hwang, Ketterlinus, & Fracasso, 1999).

Some researchers have explored whether children are better off living in intact families where parents may be fighting or unhappy, than in divorced families, and the findings vary. Most agree that children from divorced families show poorer adjustment and are more likely to have social and academic problems than children who live in intact families where parents are fighting or unhappy (Conger & Chao, 1996; Hetherington, 2005). Yet one study found that an overwhelming majority of adult children of divorce believed their parents' decision to divorce was the right choice (Ahrons, 2004). Ultimately,

children's temperament and support from outside caregivers have a significant impact on their overall adjustment.

NONPARENTAL CHILD CARE

In their thoughtful analysis of non-parental child care, Michael Lamb and Lieselotte Ahnert (2006) pose two questions intended to help researchers reshape their evaluation of modern child care:

- What type of and how much care do young children receive from adults other than their parents?
- What effects do such care arrangements have on the children's development?

These questions shape the direction of current research and evaluation, because we now realize that it is useless to ask simply whether child care is good or bad for children. Rather, researchers must examine the nature, extent, quality, and age at onset of child care as well as the characteristics of the children from different backgrounds and needs.

Facts about Daycare

When most people hear the term *caregiver*, they tend to think of daycare. **Daycare** typically refers to child care outside the home, as opposed to the more general term *child care*. Considering the fact that some children spend more time each day under the care of a daycare provider than a parent, the influence of daycare is significant because of its impact on children's development. Less than 22% of 0 to 5-year-olds and about 20% of 0 to 12-year-olds have access to regulated daycare in Canada (Childcare Resource and Research Unit, 2013).

The types of child care arrangement vary enormously: One mother may charge another mother several dollars to take care of her child; a relative may care for several family children; businesses may run large operations; some centres may be funded by local or provincial government as an aid to the less affluent; others are run on a for-profit basis. In 2010, the average monthly cost of child care for a 2-year-old in a daycare centre was between $154 (in Quebec) to $850 (in British Columbia), according to the Childcare Resource and Research Unit (2013). The rate in Quebec is an anomaly, though, as all other provinces had a monthly rate of at least $414. Almost everyone agrees that the best centres hire teachers with a background in early childhood education.

daycare Services and care for children provided outside the children's home.

sex Biological maleness or femaleness.

gender Social/psychological aspects of being male or female.

gender identity The conviction that one is either male or female.

Existing research on daycare offers the following conclusions:

- In Canada, while only about 1 in every 5 children under the age of 6 is in regulated daycare, over 70% of mothers of young children are in the labour force, a situation that results in the majority of children being placed in unlicensed daycare. A 2008 study by the United Nations Children's Fund (UNICEF) ranked Canada alongside Ireland in last place among 25 developed nations in early-learning and child-care services (Monsebraaten, 2011).

- Attendance in a daycare facility can aid motor development and seems to be associated with increases in height and weight. However, children in daycare centres contract colds, flu, and ear infections earlier than children who do not attend daycare. They tend to contract fewer illnesses after they begin school.

- Children who attend daycare programs are more independent of their mothers, but their attachment to their mothers is not threatened (Clarke-Stewart & Allhusen, 2005).

- Enrollment in daycare during early childhood does not aid or impede positive relationships with peers (Lamb & Ahnert, 2006).

- Children who attend daycare programs have advanced cognitive and language development (Clarke-Stewart & Allhusen, 2005).

- Non-parental child care may be associated with increased behaviour problems, a result closely linked with the quality of care offered (Lamb & Ahnert, 2006).

- High-quality daycare may have a positive effect on children's intellectual development (Clarke-Stewart & Allhusen, 2005).

Table 6.3 lists the characteristics of high-quality daycare.

TABLE 6.3
Characteristics of High-Quality Daycare

Site Features	Functional Features
Good staff-child ratio	Concern with personal care
Superior staff education	Supervised motor activities
Good staff training	Attention to language
Higher staff wages	Opportunity for creativity
Attractive, safe environment	Social relationships encouraged

FEATUREDMEDIA
Films about Childhood and Gender

Billy Elliot (2000)—How does a boy balance his desire to please his father and follow his own heart to pursue ballet lessons? How can political and emotional issues impact all aspects of a young boy's life?

Boys Don't Cry (1999)—How does a transgender teen find the courage to live life and find love in a society that holds no respect for any visible differences? What protection can society offer teens who find themselves in dangerous situations based on their human needs?

Ma Vie en Rose (My Life in Pink) (1997)—What happens when a French boy's natural inclinations toward stereotypical girl behaviour become more than passing fancy? How does the discomfort of others affect his identity?

Mulan (1998)—What lengths would a Chinese girl go to save her father's life and her family's honour, and to risk severe penalties as a result of ignoring cultural expectations for women? How does the film's conclusion fit with implicit and explicit messages of the rest of the film?

Gender Development ◀L07

Although expectations for gender roles are slowly changing, sharp differences of opinion are still evident. Many parents want their children to follow traditional gender roles (sports for boys, dolls for girls), whereas other parents want to break down what they consider to be rigid gender stereotypes. Young children are influenced by social interactions and come to recognize that qualities they notice in others reflect aspects of themselves. A boy who admires a classmate's ability to catch the ball and play "tough" during kickball may wish he were less afraid of getting hurt during a kickball game so that he could also display such bravery and skill.

Developmental psychologists have urged that the terms *sex* and *gender* be used carefully. Therefore, in this discussion, **sex** refers to biological maleness or femaleness (the sex chromosomes) and **gender** refers to the psychosocial aspects of maleness and femaleness.

Within this framework, we can distinguish among gender identity, gender stereotypes, and gender role.

- **Gender identity** is a conviction about being male or female.

- **Gender stereotypes** reflect rigid beliefs about the characteristics associated with being male or female.
- **Gender role** refers to culturally defined expectations about how females and males should act.

ACQUIRING GENDER IDENTITY

One of the first categories children form is sex related—there is a neat division in their minds between male and female. Children first indicate their ability to label their own sex and the sex of others between 2 and 3 years of age. By 4 years of age, children are aware that sex identity is stable over time. They then come to realize that sex identity remains the same despite any changes in clothing, hairstyle, or activities (Lips, 2007; Ruble, Martin, & Berenbaum, 2006).

Children move from the observable physical differences between the sexes and begin to acquire gender knowledge about the behaviour expected of males and females. Gender-role stereotyping has commenced and attitudes toward gender are being shaped. What do we know about the forces influencing this process?

Role of the Family

Evidence clearly suggests that parents typically treat boy and girl babies differently—even before birth—by the way they decorate the baby's room, the toys they supply, and the type of gender behaviour they encourage (Ruble, Martin, & Berenbaum, 2006). Adults tend to engage in rougher play with boys, give them stereotypical toys (cars and trucks, dinosaurs and soldiers), and speak differently to them than they do to girls. Consistent with social learning theory explanations of gender development, parents often reinforce girls for playing with dolls and boys for playing with trucks, reinforce girls for helping their mothers around the house and boys for being brave. Parents are usually unaware of the extent to which they engage in this type of reinforcement.

Because about 80% of children have siblings and spend considerable time with them, sibling relationships also exercise considerable influence on gender identity. An older brother shows a younger brother how to hold a bat, and a younger sister watches her older sister play with dolls. Although same-sex siblings would seem to exercise a greater influence on gender-typed activities by modelling or reinforcing gender-appropriate behaviour, the influence of other-sex siblings on gender typing is also quite strong.

Role of Peers

When children form friendships and play, activities often foster and maintain sex-typed play. Depending on the environment, when children engage in non-stereotypical play (boys with dolls, girls with a football), peers may make comments and even isolate them ("sissy," "tomboy"). Although these stereotypes have decreased in recent decades, the tendency to sexually compartmentalize behaviour increases with age until most adolescents react to intense demands for conformity to stereotypical gender roles.

During development, youngsters of the same sex tend to play together, a custom called **sex cleavage**. If you think back on your own experiences, remember your friends at this age and recall how imitation, reinforcement, and cognitive development come together to intensify what a boy thinks is masculine and what a girl thinks is feminine.

> **gender stereotypes** Rigid beliefs about characteristics of males and females.
>
> **gender role** Culturally defined expectations about how females and males should act.
>
> **sex cleavage** Youngsters of the same sex tend to play and do things together.

Role of the Schools

Schools are an important socializing agent in gender development. The vast majority of Canadian elementary and kindergarten teachers are female. According to the 2006 census, females comprised 87% of such positions, a number that remained virtually unchanged from 15 years earlier (Service Canada, 2012). The lack of male role models in the early grades has been advanced as a reason for why girls outperform boys on average in school. Professor of Education Jon Bradley of Montreal's McGill University has suggested that the early school years have been made

▲ Children acquire gender stereotypes from exposure to popular media.

more difficult for boys because female teachers emphasize cooperation (a stereotypically feminine trait) in their classrooms over competition (a stereotypically masculine trait) and put too much focus on sitting still in class (Abraham, 2010).

Think about the different programs in your school and how many of them have substantially more of one gender than the other. While there are more male nurses and female engineering students today than there used to be, helping professions and technology programs are still dominated by female and male students respectively. Clearly, students continue to receive messages about which subjects girls and boys are expected to be studying as they proceed through their school years, ultimately impacting career choice in the adult years.

Role of the Media

Another influence on gender development that carries important messages about what is desirable for males and females is the media, especially television. Television has assumed such a powerful place in the socialization of children, it is safe to say that it is almost as significant as family, peers, and school. What is most disturbing is the stereotypical behaviour that it presents as both positive and desirable. The more television children watch, the more stereotypical is their behaviour (Lips, 2007).

With this brief examination of the forces that contribute to gender identity, let's next look at what happens when gender stereotypes are formed.

GENDER STEREOTYPING

As mentioned earlier, gender stereotyping refers to beliefs that we have about characteristics and behaviour associated with males and females. Recent research (Ruble, Martin, & Berenbaum, 2006) suggests that children are aware of gender stereotypes by $2^1/_2$ years of age; knowledge of stereotypical activities for children and adults appears between 3 and 5 years, peaking at about the time of entrance to first grade.

Video and computer games reflect and underscore gender stereotypes. In one year, the 6 best-selling computer games for girls were all Barbie games. Popular boys' games take them into virtual worlds where enemies are defeated, aliens are battled, and race cars break speed records. When the characteristics associated with a label create a negative image, problems arise. Even so-called positive images or stereotyping can be problematic, once people start to treat

play Activity people engage in because they enjoy it for its own sake.

others according to the stereotype. The implications for such stereotyping are large, especially in the classroom context. Although equality between the sexes is widely accepted today, gender stereotyping is still alive and well.

One way that young children can challenge stereotypes and attempt to gain mastery over their observations and ideas is through play. Girls can play the part of "Mommy" but can also be police officers who save the day. Boys can wear a dress and pocketbook in the dramatic play area but still build rockets with Lego bricks. It is not up to children to change the sociopolitical culture in which they live; but play does provide children opportunities to be protagonists in their own physical, cognitive, and social development.

The Importance of Play ◀ L08

One thing that children do effortlessly and without training is to play. **Play** is an activity that children engage in because they enjoy it for its own sake. Some of the benefits of play are that it allows children to explore the environment on their own terms and to take in any meaningful experiences at their own rate and on their own level. Young children also play for the sheer exuberance of it, which enables them to exercise their bodies and improve motor skills. Such uninhibited behaviour also permits children to relieve tension and cope with anxiety. When children play, they learn about themselves, others, and their world; play becomes the medium through which other processes occur.

Play in early childhood may also influence the learning skills and interests of the future. What children learn as "fun" can become the foundation for intrinsic motivation later. For example, a love of board games that involve counting dice or tallying numerical scores can lend itself to a child's desire to solve math problems. What kind of play did you enjoy as a child? How do you think it contributed to who you are today?

KINDS OF PLAY

In their efforts to understand the role of play in a child's life, scholars have presented several types of classification. One of the earliest and most enduring schemes was proposed in 1932 by Mildred Parten, who suggested categories of play that children tend to progress through as they mature:

- *Unoccupied play,* in which children are seen as observers and not actually engaged in any activity

Play may be one of the most **profound** expressions of human nature and one of the greatest innate resources for learning and invention.

MARTHA BRONSON, EARLY CHILDHOOD EDUCATOR AND ADVOCATE

- *Solitary play,* in which children play by themselves and are not involved with others
- *Onlooker play,* in which children watch others and do not become active themselves, but may call out suggestions or questions
- *Parallel play,* in which children play beside, but not with, other children
- *Associative play,* in which children play with others but seem more interested in the social interactions than the activity itself
- *Cooperative play,* in which children play with others and are active participants in the goal of the activity

DEVELOPMENTAL ASPECTS OF PLAY

It is clear that play involves developing social skills and awareness of enjoyment, but children's play also impacts other areas of development. In a significant event held in 1989, the United Nations Convention on the Rights of the Child recognized that all children possess certain rights, including "the right of the child to rest and leisure, to engage in play and recreational activities appropriate to the age of the child and to participate freely in cultural life and the arts" (UNICEF, 1989). Play is not simply a way to pass the time in between learning academic skills but, rather, a means through which critical thinking and other skills develop (Figure 6.9 demonstrates that teachers support play as a strategy in the classroom; administrators, on the other hand, are not always so supportive.)

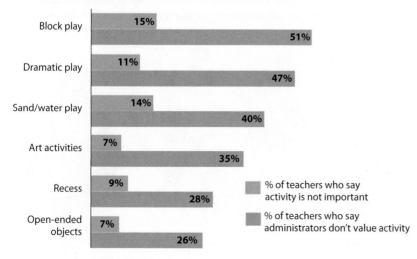

FIGURE 6.9
Perceived Importance of Play

- Block play: 15% / 51%
- Dramatic play: 11% / 47%
- Sand/water play: 14% / 40%
- Art activities: 7% / 35%
- Recess: 9% / 28%
- Open-ended objects: 7% / 26%

% of teachers who say activity is not important

% of teachers who say administrators don't value activity

▲ This graph shows teachers' views versus perceived administration views of the importance of various playful and creative activities.

Source: Alliance for Childhood (2009).

Cognitive Development

Through play, children learn about the objects in their world, what these objects do, what they are made of, and how they work. To use Piaget's terms, children use symbols to represent their ideas and their world, and also learn behavioural skills that will help them in the future.

Vygotsky believed that play contributes significantly to cognitive development because children learn to use objects and actions appropriately and thus further their ability to think symbolically. Vygotsky (1978) also argued that children's imaginary situations provide zones of proximal development that function as mental support systems. Children's levels of play change as they are guided by the suggestions, hints, and ideas offered by peers and adults. As Vygotsky noted, children tend to play at a level above their average age and above their daily behaviour. The safety afforded by imaginary scenarios allows children to pretend to do things that they would not be able to do in reality, as determined by their developmental abilities.

Social Development

Play helps social development during this period, because the involvement of others demands a give-and-take that teaches young children the basics of forming relationships. Social skills demand the same building processes as cognitive skills, and children begin to share symbolic meanings through their use of pretend play.

At 3 years of age, children prefer playmates of their own sex. Girls show a stronger preference than boys do at this age. From 4 to 5 years, it is boys who show a stronger preference for same-sex playmates, although they still play in mixed-sex groups. Gender differentiation from 3 to 5 years becomes ever more apparent. During free-play sessions in preschool and daycare centres, children of the same sex are the close partners, a trend that underscores the prevalence of sex cleavage.

Why are some 5- and 6-year-olds more popular with their classmates than others are? Watching closely, you can often discover the reasons: decreasing egocentrism, recognition of the rights of others, and a willingness to share. These social skills do not simply appear; they are learned, and much of the learning comes through play.

Emotional Development

Play helps children to master the intense, sometimes overpowering, experiences that all children encounter. In their play, they avoid the right-or-wrong, life-and-death

TAKE A **STAND**

Intentional versus Accidental Art

In October 2008, a gallery owner in Melbourne, Australia, was asked to consider showing the abstract paintings of an artist called Aelita Andre. The owner agreed to add them to a group show in his studio, promoting the show and placing ads in art magazines. Only at that point did the owner find out that the artist was not a professional artist but, rather, a 2-year-old—the daughter of artist Michael Andre and photographer Nikka Kalashnikova.

Can a 2-year-old truly create art deemed comparable to the work of professional artists? Is this a practical joke at the expense of the art world or the story of a child prodigy?

feelings that accompany interactions with adults. Children can be creative without worrying about failure and work out their emotional tensions through play. As children transition into later developmental periods of life, the lessons learned in early childhood will accompany them and form the basis for other biopsychosocial interactions.

PLAY MATERIALS

When parents shop for their children's toys, they might ask themselves a basic question: What kind of activities can this toy encourage? Too often, the answer is "nothing good." Today's toys frequently promote violence, involve candy, or depend on electronic technology that turns children into passive observers. As Martha Bronson (1995) noted, the play materials we supply our children are loaded with multiple messages. They cause children to do certain things because of the nature of the toy, and they also convey messages about what parents think is acceptable. For example, some parents would never give a child a toy gun, while others think playing with toy guns is a normal part of growing up.

Play materials are typically grouped into four categories: social and fantasy; exploration and mastery; music, art, and movement; and gross motor play. Social and fantasy play materials include items that encourage the use of imagination and the mental representation of objects and events, as well as a deeper understanding of people and the rules we live by. Play materials in this category are often used in dramatic play, solitary fantasy play, and role play. Exploration and mastery materials such as puzzles, pattern-making games, and sand, water, and string increase children's knowledge about the physical world, encouraging them to devise ways to enrich their comprehension of how things work. Music, art, and movement

aid in the development of artistic expression. Gross-motor play materials, including playground and gym equipment, push-and-pull toys, and sports equipment foster large-muscle development and skills.

Children's Artwork

Children love to draw for the sheer physical act as well as the cognitive stimulation. Their artwork has long attracted the attention of scholars, and culture plays a large role in children's aesthetic development. Young children innately progress from the pincer movements of infancy to random scribbles to skillful creations. Learning to draw is like learning a language: Children acquire increasingly complex and effective drawing rules, which is one of the major achievements of the human mind (Willat, 2005).

▲ Children's artwork can reveal much about their cognitive and emotional lives

PERSPECTIVES ON **DIVERSITY**

Children and Their Drawings

The work of anthropologist Alexander Alland (1983) has focused on cultural differences evident in children's artwork. Studying the drawings of children from Japan, Bali, Taiwan, Ponape, France, and the United States, he argued against theories of specific universal stages of development and proposed that children internalize culturally specific rules that are manifest in their drawings. An example of this influence may be seen in the influence of Manga (a type of comic book) in Japanese culture. These popular books have had an impact on the artwork that children produce. Not only do children re-create the style of Manga in their own work, but they imitate the style of dress and hair as well.

The work of Rhoda Kellogg (1970) focused on universals in children's artwork. Kellogg collected more than 1 million children's drawings and paintings, created by thousands of children, and argued that children's drawing passes through the following four stages:

1. *Placement,* which refers to where on the paper the child places the drawing (2 to 3 years)

2. *Shape,* which refers to diagrams with different shapes (about 3 years)

3. *Design,* which refers to a combination of forms (about 3 to 4 years)

4. *Pictorial,* which refers to representations of humans, animals, buildings, and so on (about 4 to 5 years)

Kellogg concluded that child art contains the aesthetic forms most commonly used in all art.

Children's drawings not only are good clues to their motor coordination but also provide insights into their cognitive and emotional lives. Children who frequently draw violent scenes, featuring bloodshed and dead bodies, might be helped by some conversation about what they are drawing. Such a child might observe much through television and video games that could inspire drawings with violent content, but might also witness real-life violence in his or her home and neighbourhood. These situations demand the attention of adults who can help the child process the scenes he or she has observed and the feelings that result from such images.

Career Apps

As an art therapist, how might you encourage a child to express herself through art when she might not be able to (or want to) articulate her feelings verbally?

CONCLUSIONS & SUMMARY

Although the rate of physical growth slows in early childhood, it continues at a steady pace. Physical and motor skills become more refined. Cognitive development leads to a world of representation in which children are expected to acquire and manipulate symbols. Language gradually becomes a powerful tool for adapting to the environment.

How do Piaget's and Vygotsky's views on cognitive development differ from those of information-processing theorists?

- These years are the time of Piaget's preoperational period and the continued appearance of symbolic abilities.
- Information-processing theorists differ from Piaget and Vygotsky in their belief that the human mind has a limited capacity, which children are able to use more efficiently as they age.
- During the early childhood years, children develop a theory of mind.
- Many current early childhood programs have a constructivist orientation.

What types of early childhood education seem most promising?

- Early childhood programs in Reggio Emilia, Italy, emphasize children's competence and curiosity.
- Aboriginal Head Start is designed to offer educational and developmental services to First Nations children and their families, and positive outcomes are associated with it.
- Full-day kindergarten programs now exist in six Canadian provinces. Play-based learning is central to the programs in Ontario and British Columbia.

How does children's language acquisition proceed during these years?

- Children acquire the basics of their language during these years with little, if any, instruction.

By the end of early childhood, most children enter formal schooling. What role does family play in development during these years?

- The meaning of "family" in our society has changed over time.
- Baumrind's types of parenting clarify the role of parents in children's development.
- Consistent and reasonable discipline is key as children try to gain mastery over themselves and their surroundings.
- Research has demonstrated how divorce affects children.
- Many children attend some form of daycare, and the developmental outcomes of these experiences are still in question.

How do children of this age acquire a sense of self and gender?

- The emergence of the self is very much influenced by interactions with family and peers.
- Various theories have been proposed to explain how children achieve their sense of gender.
- Children initially seem to acquire an understanding of gender before they manifest sex-typed behaviour.

What is the value of play?

- Play affects all aspects of development: physical, cognitive, social, and emotional.
- The nature of a child's play changes over the years, gradually becoming more symbolic.

1. As you can tell from the data presented in this chapter, young children continue their rapid growth, although at a less rapid rate than during infancy. If you were a parent of a child of this age (boy or girl), how much would you encourage him or her to participate in organized, directed physical activities (swimming, dancing, soccer, and so on)? Be sure to give specific reasons for your answer.

2. Given today's expectations for male and female gender roles, do you think children growing up in these times are more or less confused about gender identity? Why?

3. Think back to your own childhood. How would you categorize the parenting style or styles of your parents? Do you think it affected your behaviour? Explain your answer by linking your parents' behaviour to some of your personal characteristics.

Chapter REVIEW TEST

Answers: 1c, 2a, 3c, 4d, 5d, 6b, 7c, 8c, 9d, 10d

1. The process called _____ allows for faster transmission of information through the nervous system.
   a. coordination
   b. lateralization
   c. myelination
   d. insulation

2. When children show a preference for one hand or the other, this illustrates brain
   a. lateralization.
   b. synapses.
   c. dendrites.
   d. initiative.

3. Using the large muscles is referred to as _____ motor skills.
   a. fine
   b. peripheral
   c. gross
   d. anatomical

4. Which of the following behaviours is not associated with the preoperational period?
   a. symbolic play
   b. drawing
   c. language
   d. walking steadily

5. Aboriginal Head Start was initiated in the
   a. 1960s
   b. 1970s
   c. 1980s
   d. 1990s

6. Educators in Reggio Emilia, Italy, consider the _____ to be another teacher in the classroom.
   a. director
   b. environment
   c. parents
   d. siblings

7. About ___ of Canadian marriages end in divorce within 30 years.
   a. 80%
   b. 73%
   c. 41%
   d. 27%

8. The assumptions that we have about characteristics and behaviour associated with "male" and "female" are called
   a. accommodation.
   b. gender practices.
   c. gender stereotypes.
   d. gender equality.

9. True play has no _____ goals.
   a. divergent
   b. coercive
   c. intrinsic
   d. extrinsic

10. Which of the following is not a kind of play, according to Parten?
    a. solitary
    b. parallel
    c. associative
    d. confrontational

MIDDLE
CHILDHOOD

As You READ

After reading this chapter, you should be able to answer the following questions:

LO1 ▶ How would you describe physical and motor development during these years?

LO2 ▶ What are some of the competing views of cognitive development during the middle childhood years?

LO3 ▶ How do children develop thinking and problem-solving strategies?

LO4 ▶ How would you trace children's progress in moral development?

LO5 ▶ How does children's language change during middle childhood?

LO6 ▶ What are the key elements that help children acquire a personally satisfying and competent sense of self?

LO7 ▶ How influential are peers during these years?

LO8 ▶ What are some effects that different schools and teachers have on children during middle childhood?

LO9 ▶ How do children deal with stress in the middle childhood years?

The term middle childhood covers the ages 7 to 11 years. In middle childhood, children display many competencies—physical, cognitive, and emotional—and yet they are still children—physically, cognitively, and emotionally. For example, older children are often able to use computers in ways that adults can't, yet they still might expect a bedtime story at night. They may have pen pals around the world with whom they email or even text each day, yet they don't realize that the ground turkey Mom buys at the grocery store comes from real animals on a working farm. Children's competencies and limitations are greatly influenced by their complex world. As their skills mature, they must also develop a sense of responsibility that equips them to handle increasing independence. Developmental advances that prepare a young person to move from these last years of childhood into adolescence are of great importance for laying foundations that will impact the entire lifespan.

In this chapter, you will learn about many influences on the middle childhood years, affecting many areas of children's lives, including cognitive growth, moral reasoning, and physical and social development. The middle childhood years launch talents that children have been nurturing, and budding skills become full-blown if children are given support and opportunity.

Although older children may seem more mature than in early childhood, they still depend on adults to make decisions that meet their basic needs relating to health, safety, and self-esteem.

L01 ▶ Physical Development

Physical development proceeds at a slower pace during middle childhood than in early childhood (see Figure 7.1). Most children gain about 2 inches in height and 5 to 7 pounds in weight during middle childhood. Children in this age group are extremely active physically and gradually display a steady improvement in motor coordination. Fine motor skills assist them with self-help tasks, such as buttoning, zipping, and using eating utensils. Gross motor skills are visible as children exhibit more jumping and climbing, as well as bike riding and gymnastics abilities, for example. At the end of middle childhood, the body is more proportionate and more like an adult's: The trunk becomes thinner and longer, and the chest becomes broader and flatter. Among the most complex physical changes, however, are those in brain development.

BRAIN DEVELOPMENT

In middle childhood, the brain continues forming stronger connections, and neurons become more myelinated. By age 8 or 9, the brain has reached about the size it will be in

FIGURE 7.1

Growth Curves Chart for Boys and Girls Aged 5–12

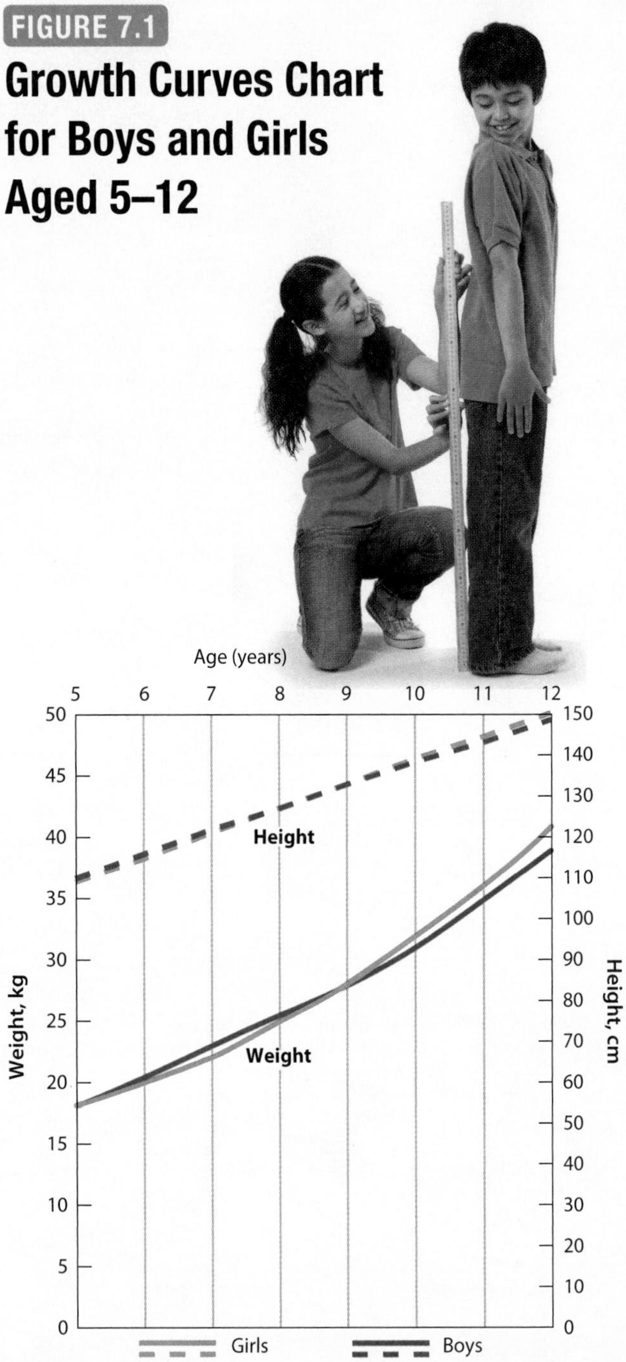

adulthood. Specifically, the frontal lobes experience significant growth, and children are able to engage in increasingly difficult cognitive tasks (see Figure 7.2).

As their abilities increase, children participate in a broader array of experiences, and the number of synapses increases, forming a vast network of pathways and connections. At this age, the brain also refines existing connections by pruning synapses that are unused. The neurons become more selective in their responses to chemical messages, particularly those deemed inessential, based on the child's experiences with people, materials, and surroundings.

FIGURE 7.2

The Human Brain

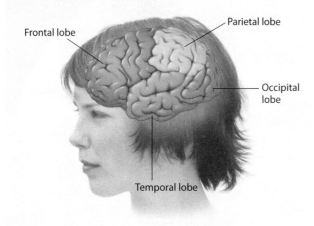

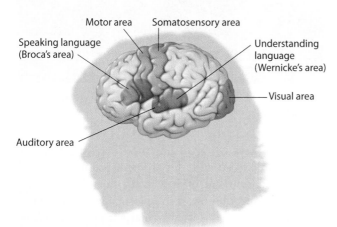

▲ The brain at middle childhood and the regions involved in various aspects of development.

As children learn and experience the world, memory improves, attention sharpens, judgment becomes more mature, and problem-solving progresses. The task of adults who are around children during these amazing years is to provide stimulation that will encourage them to participate in this enticing world, thereby adding new connections and strengthening those already present. In this way, biological and environmental forces work together to shape the developing brain.

HEALTH AND NUTRITION

Generally speaking, middle childhood is a period of healthy development. Risks of infancy and early childhood are in the past, and children possess strength and energy that help promote their current development and prepare them for adolescence.

Among the most common reasons for children missing school are asthma and injuries caused by accidents, such as broken bones. **Asthma** is a lung disorder caused by a person's bronchial tubes (tubes connecting the throat to the lungs) reacting to external conditions by filling with mucus and tightening. Children who suffer from asthma experience symptoms including coughing and wheezing, and sometimes problems breathing. Many external conditions can contribute to asthma, such as cold weather, intense physical activity (such as running), allergies, and stress—all of which are commonly experienced in middle childhood. Doctors have also noted connections to pollution and smoking in a child's home in their research to explain the increase in the number of asthma cases over the past few decades.

> **asthma** Lung disorder resulting in bronchial tubes filling with mucus and tightening.

Injuries caused by accidents are most often related to riding a bike, because the child either was riding the bike or was struck by someone riding a bike. Injuries are also common when children are playing organized team sports. Many parents push their children to excel at sports at an early age, without considering their physical limitations or lack of developmental readiness. The most direct way for adults to protect children from accidental injury is to be mindful of risk factors and to teach children about practices that will form a foundation for long-term health benefits. In middle childhood, modelling by teachers and caregivers is the most effective way to send children strong messages about safety rules and safety gear.

Eating habits are important to a child's long-term health, and school-age children need to eat a well-balanced diet so that they have enough energy to support their learning in school. After-school activities with friends can interfere with plans for healthy, focused mealtimes. However, given children's slower growth rate during middle childhood, less food is needed—it's quality that counts. The lastest version of Canada's Food Guide

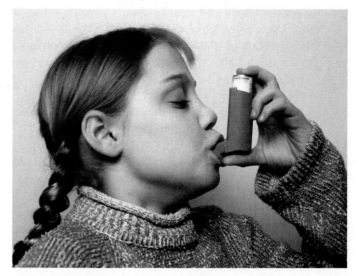

▲ Research shows that an increase in the number of children suffering from asthma may be due to pollution and smoking in the child's home.

(updated in 2007) makes the following recommendations for a healthy diet:

- Eat at least one dark green and one orange vegetable each day. Prepare fruits and vegetables with little or no added fat, sugar, or salt. Limit intake of fruit and vegetable juices as they contain sugar.

- Make at least half of your grain products whole grain each day.

- Drink skim, 1%, or 2% milk each day.

- Select at least two Food Guide Servings of fish each week, and select lean meat and alternatives prepared with little or no added fat or salt.

For the first time, a national food guide has been created that reflects the values, traditions, and food choices of First Nations Inuit and Métis.

In middle childhood, school schedules influence breakfast and lunch meals, and children often make their own decisions about food. Peer and media influences are important elements in children's decisions about what to eat, but the models that children observe at home have the most influence. Some parents raise children on vegetarian or vegan diets, and some children avoid meat because of their love of animals. The child's body is preparing for the growth spurt that occurs in adolescence, so middle childhood is an ideal time to encourage good eating habits, especially outside the home.

OVERWEIGHT

Over recent decades, the incidence of obese children has risen in many countries. In 2004, 26% of Canadian children and adolescents aged 2 to 17 were overweight or obese based on the body mass index. In 12- to 17-year-olds, the combined overweight/obesity proportion more than doubled from 14% to 29% and the **obesity** proportion tripled from 3% to 9% (Statistics Canada, 2006). When a child's **body mass index (BMI)** is greater than the 85th percentile for sex and age, the child is considered obese (Miller et al., 2004). (See Figure 7.3.)

The increase in overweight children is of serious concern for several reasons. The likelihood that an obese child will be obese in adulthood grows as children progress through middle childhood. Being obese also raises the risk of related diseases, such as diabetes, high blood pressure, and heart, respiratory, and bone problems.

The causes of childhood obesity involve biopsychosocial forces, such as heredity, mental health, and environment. Obese children often have obese or overweight parents, and therefore grow up with eating practices that make it

obesity Based on BMI, greater than 85th percentile for sex and age.

body mass index (BMI) Measurement used to compare a person's height and weight to determine a healthy body weight; BMI = weight/height².

▲ Children are more likely to participate in physical activity when their parents accompany them.

likely that they will grow up to be overweight. While heredity might account for a predisposition to obesity, the environment plays a major role. Research has shown a connection between low socioeconomic status (SES) and obesity; this is particularly true among ethnic minority groups. Factors such as having less knowledge about healthy nutrition, choosing cheaper, less-healthy foods, and being less physically active are involved. Successful intervention can be accomplished on several fronts, such as encouraging healthy eating habits and exercise, limiting television and computer time, and helping children become aware of their lifestyle choices.

The Canadian Paediatrics Society recommends that children participate in 90 minutes of physical activity a day with at least 10 minutes involving vigorous activities (Pradinuk, Chanoine, & Goldman, 2011).

Access to health care is another factor that can affect a child's health and well-being. Although the Canada Health Act clearly states that all Canadians must be provided with the same access to health care, a major issue in Canada today is that 4.4 million Canadians aged 12 and older (15.3% of children in that age group) do not have a regular medical doctor. The proportion of

Career Apps

As a nutritionist, how might you recommend healthy eating practices to families on a budget?

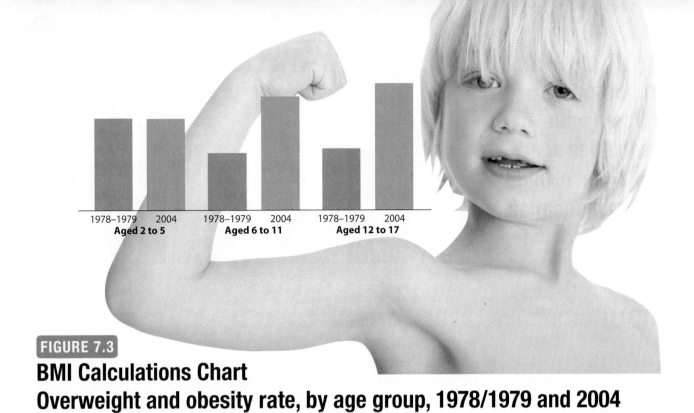

| 1978–1979 | 2004 | 1978–1979 | 2004 | 1978–1979 | 2004 |

Aged 2 to 5　　　**Aged 6 to 11**　　　**Aged 12 to 17**

FIGURE 7.3

BMI Calculations Chart
Overweight and obesity rate, by age group, 1978/1979 and 2004

Source: Statistics Canada, "Overweight and obesity rate, by age group, 1978/79 and 2004," Cat. No. 86-620-MIE2005001. Published by authority of the Minister responsible for Statistics Canada. © Minister of Industry, 2013. All rights reserved. Use of this publication is governed by the Statistics Canada Open License Agreement.

adults and children who were without a regular doctor was lower than the national average in five provinces: Newfoundland and Labrador (8.9%), Nova Scotia (6.5%), New Brunswick (7.5%), Ontario (9.1%), and British Columbia (13.9%). A higher proportion of residents of Quebec (25.5%), Saskatchewan (19.5%), Alberta (20.3%), Yukon (20.6%), Northwest Territories (63.6%)

▲ Childhood obesity rates have increased in Canada over recent decades.

and Nunavut (84.5%) were without a regular doctor, compared to the national level. In the territories, a nurse practitioner is often used as the first point of medical contact, rather than a medical doctor (Statistics Canada, 2011c).

LEARNING DISABILITIES

Children's perceptions of themselves and others include more than visible differences in shape and size. In 2006, 4.6% of Canadian children between the ages of 5 and 14 had been identified as having a **learning disability** (Statistics Canada, 2008a). A learning disability is a neurological disorder that impacts the brain's functioning. Learning disabilities are defined by three components: (1) a minimum IQ level, (2) significant difficulty in a school-related area, and (3) exclusion of only severe emotional disorders, second-language background, sensory issues, or neurological issues (Siegel, 2003). Learning, speech, and chronic conditions were the leading types of learning disabilities for children in this age group (Statistics Canada, 2008). Table 7.1 indicates the percentage of children receiving special education across Canada.

Boys are more often diagnosed with a learning disability than girls, perhaps due to teachers' perceptions of boys and behaviour issues. Most often, children's learning disabilities are recognized in the academic areas of reading and math. Difficulties with attention, specifically being able

learning disability A neurological disorder that impacts the brain's functioning.

TABLE 7.1

Proportion of children with disabilities aged 5 to 14 receiving special education, by province and territory, 2006

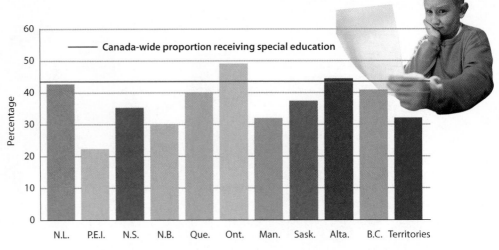

— Canada-wide proportion receiving special education

Percentage (y-axis: 0, 10, 20, 30, 40, 50, 60)

N.L. P.E.I. N.S. N.B. Que. Ont. Man. Sask. Alta. B.C. Territories

Source: Statistics Canada, "Participation and Activity Limitation Survey," Table, "Children with disabilities aged 5 to 14 receiving special education by province and territories," 2006. Published by authority of the Minister responsible for Statistics Canada. © Minister of Industry, 2013. All rights reserved. Use of this publication is governed by the Statistics Canada Open License Agreement.

decode To pronounce words correctly using knowledge of letters and sounds.

attention deficit hyperactivity disorder (ADHD) A disability related to inattention, hyperactivity, and impulsivity.

attention deficit disorder A disability related to inattention and lack of focus.

concrete operational stage Piaget's third stage of cognitive development, between the ages of 7 and 11 years, in which children's thinking is much more flexible than in early childhood.

to focus on relevant information needed to **decode** words or solve a problem, are quite common.

ATTENTION DISORDERS

Attention deficit hyperactivity disorder (ADHD) is one of the more common diagnoses for children who are easily distracted, seem to fidget constantly, and are unable to focus. ADHD is also related to poor impulse control. Children display ADHD differently, and some exhibit lack of attention or focus without hyperactive behaviours, which is called **attention deficit disorder (ADD)**. They may seem focused on what someone is saying, or a lesson a teacher is giving, but their minds are a million miles away. ADHD affects 1 in 20 Canadian children (Feldman and Belanger, 2009).

Although there are no definitive causes of ADHD, heredity, exposure to lead, and biochemical substances (or lack of them) have been suggested. Helping children with ADD/ADHD succeed in the classroom context requires consideration of physical, emotional, and environmental factors, lending support to the power of the biopsychosocial approach to human development. Treatment often includes medication (such as Ritalin), behaviour plans that help children become less easily distracted, nutrition plans that minimize certain foods (e.g., sugars), and appropriate exercise.

L02 ▶ Cognitive Development

Once children begin formal schooling, their growing cognitive abilities help them to meet the increasingly demanding tasks set by the school. Piaget's explanation of cognitive

development in the middle childhood years is one lens through which we can learn about children's thinking and how children construct knowledge.

PIAGET'S CONCRETE OPERATIONAL STAGE

The **concrete operational stage**, the third of four stages of cognitive development in Piaget's theory, occurs between the ages of 7 and 11 years. In this stage, children's thinking is much more flexible than in early childhood. For example, children can reverse their mental actions. They understand that rain turns into snow when temperatures drop below a certain level and that, if the weather turns warmer, the snow will melt into the watery state that it was before it turned

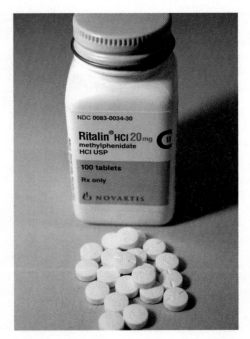

▲ Ritalin is often prescribed to children who have been diagnosed with ADD/ADHD.

TAKE A STAND

The Ritalin Debate

There is continuing debate over whether or not children who have been diagnosed with ADHD or ADD need medication, such as methylphenidate (Ritalin), to be successful in school and in life. Ritalin is a stimulant that works by increasing the activity of the central nervous system. While Ritalin is widely prescribed for ADHD, its value is controversial and its long-term effects on the brain are unknown. The controversy centres on the argument that children who display problematic behaviours are simply overly energetic or otherwise unfocused versus the argument that there is brain-related evidence supporting the success of medication that helps children in ways that behavioural strategies do not. Some parents are hesitant to give their children Ritalin, even when prescribed by medical professionals. In a 2010 report, the *Globe and Mail* documented the meteoric rise in prescriptions for Ritalin and other amphetamine-like drugs for ADHD in Canada (up to 2.9 million in 2009, mostly for children under 17, a 55 percent increase over four years) (Belluz, 2012).

Is prescribing drugs an appropriate response for the child who does not perform well in the modern school environment, or do drugs like Ritalin distract adults from solving important problems in the child's environment?

▲ In middle childhood, children are diagnosed with ADHD more often than other specific learning disabilities.

to snow. Children gradually begin to use logical thought processes and are able to reason accordingly with specific, concrete materials—objects, people, and/or events that they can see and touch.

Cognitive Achievements in the Concrete Operational Stage

Recall Piaget's famous task with two identical glasses of water, one of which is poured into a taller, thinner glass (see Figure 6.5 in Chapter 6). Children in the concrete operational stage see that the amount of water in the two glasses is the same, a characteristic called conservation. They can imagine pouring the water back into the first glass. By reversing their thinking in this manner, they conserve the basic idea: The amount of water remains the same.

Conservation involves Piaget's notion of **decentration**—the child's ability to concentrate on more than one aspect of a problem or to connect the different aspects. This is seen when a child is able to recognize that in order to win at the card game Go Fish, the child needs not only to make pairs with the cards, but also to have the most pairs at the end of the game. Reversibility, the ability to think through steps involved in a problem and then retrace the mental actions, is evident as children learn math concepts, such

as number families (e.g., 3 + 2 = 5; 5 − 2 = 3; 2 + 3 = 5; 5 − 3 = 2). Other notable features of children's thinking in the concrete operational stage include the following:

- Classification—In middle childhood, children demonstrate Piaget's concept of class inclusion—the ability to group objects with some similarities within a larger category (e.g., roses and daisies are all flowers; Red Sox and Yankees are both baseball teams).

- **Seriation**—The ability to order objects along a qualitative dimension, such as increasing or decreasing size or weight, is a characteristic of the concrete operational stage. For example, Piaget asked children to place sticks in order of size. An essential aspect of seriation is **transitivity**, which refers to the ability to understand relationships and combine them mentally to draw new conclusions. An example would be in a seriation task, where stick A is longer than stick B, and stick B is longer than stick C. A child who understands the principle of transitivity would infer that stick A is also longer than stick C.

> **decentration** The ability to focus on several features of an object or task.
>
> **seriation** The ability to order items along a quantitative dimension such as length or weight.
>
> **transitivity** The ability to understand relationships and combine them mentally to draw new conclusions.

Exceptional Children

Although the term "exceptional" can refer to children who are deemed gifted and talented, it more often refers to children with special needs. At one time, children with special needs were either refused admission to public schools or educated in the public school system but at a different location from mainstream students.

In 1982, the *Canadian Charter of Rights and Freedoms* guaranteed equality for persons with mental and physical disabilities and prohibited discrimination based on an individual's handicaps. Although Canadian provinces do have education laws that ensure all students receive appropriate education, definitions of "appropriate education" vary province to province.

Policies have changed over the years as issues arose, and in 1999, the Government of Canada released its disability agenda, called Working Together for Full Citizenship, to address several issues, one being the acute needs of Aboriginal people with disabilities. More recently, the Agreement on Early Childhood Development Initiatives (EDCI) was signed by the federal government and provincial/territorial governments (except Quebec), acknowledging the need for all levels of government to work together to support families and local communities. Starting in 2001–2002, the federal government invested $2.2 billion over a five-year span to fund this initiative (www.ccl-cca.ca).

Individualized education plan (IEP): This document identifies the student's specific learning expectations and outlines how the school will address these expectations through appropriate accommodations,

program modifications, and/or alternative programs as well as specific instructional and assessment strategies.

While best educational practices are designed to benefit all children, there are some children who are at a disadvantage because of several factors, including caregivers' inability to advocate for them, school boards' lack of funding to provide ideal supports, and misperceptions about their abilities due to biases related to culture, language, or poverty.

Some of Piaget's strongest conclusions about cognitive development in middle childhood are (1) that children are cognitively active—not passive recipients—as they construct their mental worlds and (2) that children's thinking can be analyzed based on clear evidence with concrete objects, not simply described based on assumptions about their abilities.

Piaget's ideas have inspired others to develop ideas about how children's thinking develops at this stage. Here are some examples:

- When the nature of the task is changed, researchers have found that children accomplish specific tasks at earlier ages than Piaget thought. For example, reducing the number of objects children must manipulate in a conservation of number task helps younger children more clearly see the relationship between the number of objects in a row and the length of the row of objects, such as coloured plastic bears (often used in children's math games) or seashells.

▲ By middle childhood, children can group objects into categories.

- When given materials and time to practise, young children can be trained to master concrete operational tasks (see Figure 7.4). The very act of attending school increases children's performance on some tasks (classification, transitivity), while life experience and maturity provide enough experience for children to develop other skills (conservation) (Artman & Cahan, 2006).

- Cognitive development may not proceed through four discrete stages.

Although Piaget has left an enduring legacy, other psychologists have devised new ways of explaining children's cognitive abilities. The broad category of *intelligence* is often used to explore what children know and how we know what they know. **Intelligence** refers to a person's problem-solving skills and use of everyday experiences to inform learning. The work of Howard Gardner and Robert Sternberg has been influential in exploring connections between intelligence and educational practice.

FIGURE 7.4
Conservation Tasks

Conservation of	Example	Approximate age
1. Number	Which has more?	6–7 years
2. Liquids	Which has more?	7–8 years
3. Length	Are they the same length?	7–8 years
4. Substance	Are they the same?	7–8 years
5. Area	Which has more room?	7–8 years
6. Weight	Will they weigh the same?	9–10 years
7. Volume	Will they displace the same amount of water?	11–12 years

▲ Different kinds of conservation appear at different ages.

Source: Travers (1982)

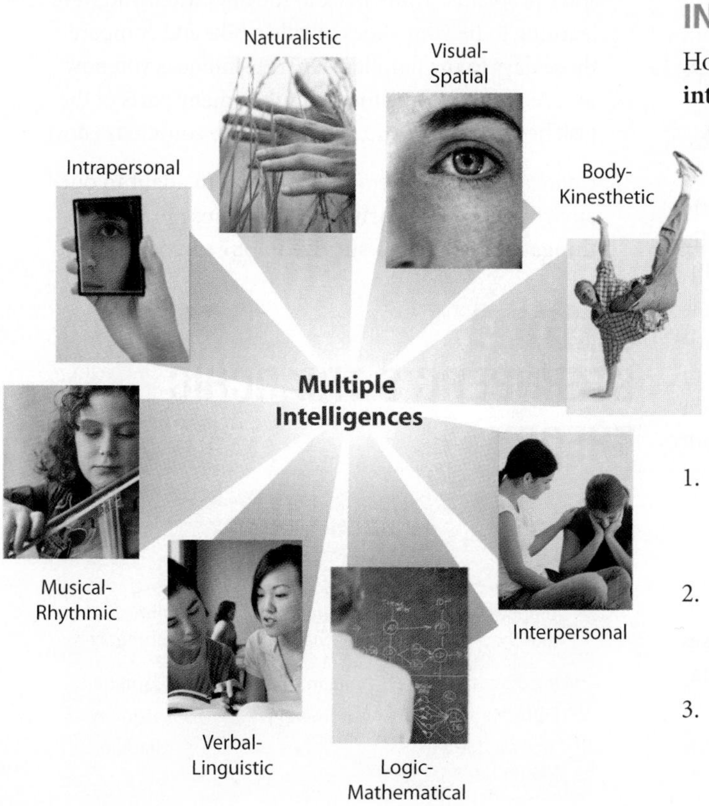

Naturalistic
Visual-Spatial
Intrapersonal
Body-Kinesthetic
Musical-Rhythmic
Interpersonal
Verbal-Linguistic
Logic-Mathematical

Multiple Intelligences

GARDNER AND MULTIPLE INTELLIGENCES

Howard Gardner's **theory of multiple intelligences** challenges the traditional concept of intelligence—either you've got it or you don't—by proposing that everyone has different strengths and areas of growth. Gardner defines intelligence as the ability to solve problems or fashion products that are of consequence in a particular cultural setting or community.

Instead of one general intelligence, Gardner's theory identifies eight equal intelligences:

1. *Linguistic:* The ability to use words and language well to communicate and create. Examples: poet, translator, lawyer, marketing executive.

2. *Musical:* The ability to play an instrument, sing, or otherwise demonstrate sensitivity to rhythm, tone, and melody. Examples: musician, singer, conductor, composer.

3. *Logical-mathematical:* The ability to use and understand objects, numbers, and operations. Examples: accountant, scientist, engineer.

intelligence A person's problem-solving skills and use of everyday experiences to inform learning.

theory of multiple intelligences Gardner's theory that attributes eight types of intelligence to humans.

▲ Author Lucy Maud Montgomery—linguistic

▲ Art of M. C. Escher—spatial

▲ The Dalai Lama—intrapersonal

4. *Spatial:* The ability to think about and represent objects in three dimensions. Examples: artist, architect, cartographer.

5. *Bodily-kinesthetic:* The ability to handle objects and use the body skillfully. Examples: surgeon, dancer, acrobat, electrician.

6. *Interpersonal:* The ability to recognize what is distinctive in others; to interact effectively with others. Examples: teacher, politician, therapist, actor.

7. *Intrapersonal:* The ability to understand our own feelings. Examples: psychologist, author, theologian.

8. *Naturalist:* The ability to discriminate among living things; sensitivity to the natural world. Examples: farmer, landscape architect, environmentalist.

Many teachers and parents have embraced Gardner's theory because it suggests children develop and succeed according to their natural abilities and inclinations. Tension arises when children are assessed using traditional assessments that are typically geared to linguistic and logical-mathematical thinking. Until there is a broadly accepted method of evaluating children's multiple intelligences in a way that translates into the type of data that is used to determine success and funding for school districts, the theory of multiple intelligences may remain something that teachers practise but it may not be reflected in educational policies.

> **triarchic theory of intelligence** Sternberg's theory that intelligence consists of componential, experiential, and contextual parts.

STERNBERG'S TRIARCHIC THEORY

Robert Sternberg's **triarchic theory of intelligence** focuses on three subtheories of intelligence that are part of information-processing theory (see Figure 7.5):

1. *Componential.* These are the information-processing skills that contribute to intelligent behaviour. These skills consist of the ability to plan, monitor, and evaluate problem-solving strategies, and help execute the instructions of the plan to solve problems. For example, consider children planning a field trip to a recycling centre. The children decide on the site to visit, plan the day, monitor the surroundings, and evaluate the planned experience. Then they take part in the execution of the field trip, such as packing a lunch or snack and bringing recyclables from home to deposit at the centre. Finally, with the information they have acquired they conduct research about recycling and the environment prior to and during the visit.

2. *Experiential.* Life experience improves our ability to deal with novel tasks and to use pertinent information to solve problems. Think back to the days when you were learning to tie your shoes or ride a bike and compare those days to the familiar, expert techniques you now use. As tasks become more familiar, many parts of the task become automatic, requiring little conscious effort.

3. *Contextual.* This refers to the ability to adapt to our environment. We learn how to do those practical things that help us to survive in our surroundings,

FIGURE 7.5

STERNBERG'S TRIARCHIC THEORY

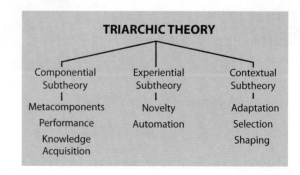

▲ Intelligence involves adapting to our environment when necessary.

such as riding a bus and getting along with others. In other words, intelligence must be viewed in the context in which it occurs. The context of intelligence enables us to adapt to our environment, create and/or shape our environment, and select new environments (Sternberg, 2003).

Sternberg argues that successful intelligence demands active involvement by individuals, as opposed to the inert intelligence measured by tests. It consists of analytical, creative, and practical aspects. Successfully intelligent people capitalize on their intellectual strengths and compensate for and correct their weaknesses.

INTELLIGENCE TESTING

Many formal evaluations of intelligence take the form of standardized tests that define and assess children's thinking in ways that are not necessarily developmentally appropriate or culturally sensitive. When intelligence testing incorporates a child's problem-solving skills as well as his or her everyday experiences, then a more valid indication of the child's intelligence may be formed.

When most people hear the phrase "intelligence tests," they think of paper-and-pencil tests designed in the early 20th century by Alfred Binet. Binet developed a measure of assessing children's intelligence to identify children who were unable to perform well in school. His test resulted in a score that reflected a child's **mental age**—an individual's mental development compared to that of others. The concept of an **intelligence quotient**—commonly known as an IQ—was developed by William Stern several years later. An IQ is calculated by dividing a child's mental age

by chronological age, and then multiplying by 100. An IQ score of 90–109 is considered average intelligence. (Such a method obviously does not work for adults.)

The Binet test has been revised many times and is currently known as the Stanford-Binet test. It measures a person's abilities in four areas—verbal reasoning, quantitative reasoning, abstract/visual reasoning, and short-term memory. Intelligence tests such as the Stanford-Binet are relatively simple to administer and quick to score, but they are widely criticized for not taking into account a child's cultural background, native language, or other individual differences that could render the measure invalid. Furthermore, traditional IQ tests calculate intelligence in an "either you've got it or you don't" general way, rather than viewing intelligence as a multifaceted, complex concept across numerous domains.

Most children score between 70 and 130 on IQ tests. Children who score above 130 are identified as gifted, whereas those who score below 70 are labelled mentally retarded. Gifted children are often identified as having above-average skills in areas outside of academics, such as art, dance, or sports. Children labelled as mentally retarded typically possess limited cognitive abilities, and the disability often has biological roots. For example, as discussed in Chapter 3, Down syndrome is a chromosomal disorder that results in some degree of mental retardation. Brain damage that occurs to a fetus in utero, such as that due to the mother's alcohol or drug consumption, can also result in

mental age Binet's measure of an individual's mental development compared to that of others.

intelligence quotient (IQ) Stern's concept of a child's intelligence, calculated by dividing mental age by chronological age, and multiplying by 100.

impaired cognitive functioning. Delays in cognitive development that occur after birth can sometimes be linked to environmental factors, such as malnutrition, neglect, and lack of stimulation in the home.

L03 ▸ Critical Thinking and Problem-Solving

The skills that children need to adapt to their environments change with the times. Unless adults are able to teach children innovative skills and help them keep up to date with technological advances, they will be unprepared to meet the demands of a changing environment. Children need critical thinking skills and problem-solving strategies that enable them to adapt to change.

Once children have accumulated knowledge, they must plan what to do with it. It's not enough just to obtain knowledge; children need to apply what they have learned, to integrate it with other facts, and to evaluate the process and outcomes. Parents and teachers who are attempting to help children improve their thinking skills should try to stretch and challenge children's thinking abilities by encouraging application, analysis, synthesis, and evaluation. These skills are emphasized in the creative work of thinking skills programs, such as Odyssey of the Mind BC.

Odyssey of the Mind BC is a school-based, international program that promotes problem-solving for students from kindergarten through college. Under the guidance of a coach, teams of five to seven students learn creative thinking and problem-solving skills. Children are encouraged to solve long-term problems that fall into five categories: mechanical/vehicle, technical performance, classics, structure, and humour. Competitions take place throughout British Columbia and globally as well. For more information, go to http://www.odysseybc.ca.

PROBLEM-SOLVING STRATEGIES

Solving a problem occurs when a child has a particular goal in mind that can't be attained immediately. There are four criteria needed for problem-solving to occur: goals, obstacles, strategies, and evaluation (Bjorklund, 2005). Children need to focus their attention on the task at hand in order to recognize what resources are needed to solve the problem and reach a desired *goal*. An assessment of the obstacles that may lie in the path of task completion helps a child accurately gauge realistic expectations for completing the task successfully. Strategies enable a child to solve a problem through various means, and evaluation provides a means for considering how well the child met the set goals. Problem-solving

elaboration An association between two or more pieces of information that are not necessarily related.

moral development Thinking, feeling, and behaving based on rules and customs about how people interact with others.

strategies come in many forms; the collaborative activity used in Odyssey of the Mind BC is one such form.

Memory shows marked improvement in middle childhood. This is largely due to the fact that attention dramatically improves as children learn to shut out distractions and concentrate on the immediate task. Short-term memory span increases as they acquire and use various memory strategies, and older children become more capable of transferring ever-increasing amounts of information to long-term memory by strengthening synaptic connections (Squire & Kandel, 2000).

One memory strategy that children employ is known as **elaboration**, an association between two or more pieces of information that are not necessarily related. This ability helps children engage in a wider range of information processing because they are able to remember more information by organizing it into meaningful units.

OBSTACLES TO SUCCESSFUL PROBLEM-SOLVING

Sometimes, despite their best efforts, children have trouble solving problems. Experts often point to cognitive processing as a factor: If children aren't able to process information from the environment accurately, how can they solve a problem successfully? Sometimes, paying attention to critical stimuli is the key to success, and attention deficits pose a challenge.

Other obstacles to successful problem-solving include challenges relating to a specific academic area or behaviour. Many children develop strategies to compensate for their problems, and they choose the best strategy to fit the situation. For example, a child may realize that he or she can't concentrate on homework when there is background noise, so the child will always choose a quiet spot to do homework. Other strategies, such as relying on others in class to help with classroom activities, do not help students retain information, even though the student may experience short-term success on assignments. Strategies that children develop to succeed on their own and that result in success tend to increase in frequency, and motivation increases as well.

Moral Development ◂ L04

Adults are held to a different standard than children when it comes to right and wrong, because we assume adults know better.

Morality will always be of primary concern to humans, yet the concept is hard to define because its developmental pathways are numerous, complex, and interactive. We want children to be kind, truthful, wise, courageous, and virtuous. We also want them to behave according to an internalized code of conduct that reflects such desirable characteristics. **Moral development**, therefore, entails thinking, feeling, and behaving based on rules and customs about how people interact with others.

as non-negotiable, and by age 10 children felt comfortable modifying rules and creating their own.

While observing the marbles game, Piaget also asked children about fairness and justice, breaking the rules, and punishment. From this information, he devised a theory of moral development:

- Up to about 4 years of age, children are not concerned with morality. Rules are meaningless, so they are unaware of any rule violations.

- Around 4 years, children believe that rules are fixed and unchangeable. Rules come from authority figures and are to be obeyed without question (**heteronomous morality**). Children make judgments about right or wrong based on the consequences of behaviour; for example, it is more serious to break five dishes than one. They also believe that anyone who breaks a rule will be punished immediately (**immanent justice**).

- From around 7 to 11 years of age, children begin to realize that because rules are made by people, they can be changed. At this age, children think punishment for any violation of rules should be linked to the intent of the violator. Older children realize that opinions and feelings of others matter and that what they do might affect someone else. By the end of middle childhood, children clearly include intention in their thinking. For 6-year-olds, stealing is wrong because they might get punished; for the 11-year-old, stealing is wrong because it takes away from someone else (**autonomous morality**).

heteronomous morality Piaget's term for moral development in children aged 4 to 7; they conceive of rules as unchangeable.

immanent justice Piaget's term for a child's belief that broken rules will be punished immediately.

autonomous morality Piaget's term for moral development in children after age 11; actions must be thought of in terms of intentions and consequences.

▲ According to various theorists, as children get older their concept of life's "rules" changes.

Children internalize moral standards, and they also develop an evolving moral capacity that influences how they think about moral issues, how they feel about moral matters, and how they behave in complex situations. This mixture of *cognition* (thinking about what to do), *emotion* (feelings about what to do or what was done), and *behaviour* (what is actually done) is reflected in theories of moral development.

PIAGET'S EXPLANATION

Piaget explained children's moral development from his cognitive perspective. He based his ideas on close observations of children playing a game of marbles. Watching the children, talking to them, and applying his cognitive theory to their actions, he interpreted how children conform to rules. Young children (under 5) played with no specific rules, children aged 5 to 10 played with rules they viewed

KOHLBERG'S THEORY

Piaget's ideas influenced a more elaborate theory devised by Lawrence Kohlberg (see Table 7.2). Kohlberg's theory traces moral development through six stages, each reflecting development of cognitive structures. In middle childhood, children are typically at Kohlberg's preconventional level of morality, where authority dictates whether something is right or wrong, reward and punishment are key, and a child's self-interest heavily influences decisions. As children reach adolescence,

A great gulf, however, has been opened between man's **material** advance and his social and **moral** progress, a gulf in which he may one day be lost if it is not closed or narrowed.

LESTER B. PEARSON

TABLE 7.2
Kohlberg's Stages of Moral Development

Level 1 Preconventional	Level 2 Conventional	Level 3 Postconventional
Stage 1 Children follow rules because adults tell them to do so. Fear of punishment motivates actions.	**Stage 3** People value trust, loyalty, and kindness. This impacts their judgments.	**Stage 5** People realize that there are greater rights and principles that support or are above the law.
Stage 2 Children develop and pursue their own interests. The notions of reciprocity and mutual satisfaction emerge.	**Stage 4** Moral judgments include attention to justice and authority.	**Stage 6** People consider universal human rights and follow their conscience.

they begin to edge into the conventional level of morality, where they consider society's views and expectations before rendering judgment. In the postconventional level of morality, typically reached after adolescence, people consider options and weigh them against their own personal code and the notion of a social contract that exists among humankind.

According to Kohlberg, children must overcome their egocentrism before they can make true moral judgments. Cognitive development is just one of many factors that influence moral thinking. Cultural beliefs, family values, gender, and society also shape children's morality. It's important to note that moral development is not the same as moral behaviour. In a given situation, children may know what is right, yet do things they know are wrong. Research suggests that when children are in a stage of developmental transition, they are less sure how to interpret and act on actual events.

GILLIGAN'S ETHICS OF CARE

A well-known critic of Kohlberg's stages is Carol Gilligan. Noting that most of Kohlberg's research was with males rather than females, Gilligan argued that Kohlberg's theory reflects a gender bias and a focus on justice rather than interpersonal relationships. She stressed the idea that people do not make moral decisions in a vacuum but,

ethics of care
Gilligan's perspective on moral thinking in which people view moral decisions in terms of relationships and responsibilities to others.

instead, make them in light of relationships and concern for others.

Gilligan argued for a different sequence of moral development of girls and women that focuses on the **ethics of care**, a view of people in terms of relationships and responsibilities to others:

- Initially, a girl's moral decisions centre on the self and related concerns: "Will it work for me?"

- Gradually, as her attachment to her parents strengthens and loyalty develops, self-interest is redefined in light of "what I should do." A sense of responsibility for others appears (the traditional view of women as caretakers), and goodness is equated with self-sacrifice and concern for others. Gilligan believes that women consider whether it is possible to be responsible to one's self as well as to others. Women come to realize that recognizing their own needs is not selfish, but honest and fair.

- Finally, women resolve the conflict between concern for self and concern for others because of their maturing ability to view relationships from a broader perspective, including a guiding principle of non-violence.

Neither Gilligan nor Kohlberg argued for the superiority of a male or a female sequence of moral development. Yet the difference in emphasis on justice versus care as the basis of moral development raises interesting questions about how society views men and women, and about expectations for behaviour. Children incorporate these ideas into their growing body of knowledge and desire to gain mastery over their environment.

Language Development ◀ L05

Children's skills across domains are not simultaneous accomplishments. This is true of vocabulary and language skills—reading is built on solid skills and helped by growing cognitive abilities (Bjorklund, 2005; Siegler & Alibali, 2005).

CHANGES IN VOCABULARY

During middle childhood, children communicate constantly with their peers, using language rich with humour and expressions they learn from the media. They are quite sophisticated in their knowledge of language because they use language to express thoughts and emotions and use inflection and intonation. By the end of middle childhood, they understand about 50,000 words and are similar to adults in their language usage.

One of the most obvious examples of children's developmental change is reflected in their use of language in ways that are culturally appropriate. They have internalized pragmatics, the use of language in different social contexts and environments. For example, a child may refer to a friend's mother as "Mrs. Kane" when in the presence of his or her own mother, but when playing at the friend's house, the child may address the friend's mother by using the parent's first name.

THEORIES OF READING ACQUISITION

Theorists are divided over two models of how reading skills are acquired: via a stage model of reading acquisition or via a non-stage model. **Stage theorists** believe children's abilities and tasks change according to specific stages of development, each stage qualitatively different from the preceding stage. **Non-stage theorists** argue that reading should unfold naturally, much as a child's language develops, according to the individual child's own readiness and abilities.

An example of stage theory is seen in the work of a leading reading specialist, Jeanne Chall, who has proposed a stage model leading to reading proficiency (Chall, 1983; Chall, Jacobs, & Baldwin, 1990). The features of middle childhood stages are as follows:

- *Ages 6 to 7 years.* Children learn the relationship between letters and sounds and begin to read simple text. They usually experience direct instruction in letter–sound relations (phonics) and use high-frequency words in their reading. For example, many kindergarten and first-grade classrooms feature a "word wall," where commonly used words are displayed so that children have ample opportunities for recognition.

▲ By the end of middle childhood, children are similar to adults in their use of language.

TAKE A STAND

Could the Internet Actually Decrease Literacy?

According to Canadian author Margaret Atwood, the Internet is "a great literacy driver"; she has stated that even reading from a screen is good for the brain. Some researchers, however, do not agree. A growing number of neuroscientists worry that the "expert reading brain" will soon be as obsolete as the paper and ink it once fed on (Barber, 2011).

This is due to the fact that reading from a screen does not require the deep, focused attention that reading a book does. Decades of research in cognitive science have also shown that one of the key alleged advantages of screen-based learning—the ability to multi-task—is "techno-hype," according to reading expert Keith Stanovich, Canada Research Chair of Applied Cognitive Science at the University of Toronto.

"Distractions such as texting and simultaneous things to do on the screen will ensure that no deep reading takes place." (Barber, 2011)

Do you think reading from the Internet has the same effects on your brain as reading from a book? Do you think it's possible to do several tasks effectively at the same time?

- *Ages 7 to 8 years.* Children demonstrate greater fluency in reading simple stories. They combine improved decoding skills with fast mapping in their reading. Fast mapping is using context to figure out the meaning of words.

- *Ages 9 to 13 years.* Reading is now used as a tool to obtain knowledge.

The two major goals of reading acquisition are efficient word identification and the comprehension of increasingly difficult material. Non-stage theorists describe reading acquisition as continuous development within different reading categories. Reading is viewed as the assembly, coordination, and automatic use of several processes (Paris & Paris, 2006).

Whitehurst and Lonigan (1998) have proposed nine components of successful reading: familiarity with the child's language, knowledge of the conventions of print (left to right, top to bottom), knowledge of letters, linguistic awareness (awareness of phonemes, syllables, and so on), the relationship of sounds to letters, emergent reading (pretending to read), emergent writing

stage theorists Reading theorists who argue that reading occurs in distinct developmental stages.

non-stage theorists Reading theorists who argue that reading develops naturally, as does language.

PERSPECTIVES ON DIVERSITY

Culturally Sensitive Practice

Many schools in Canada work with immigrant families. Teachers of English as a Second Language (TESL) in Canada are dedicated to teaching English to non–English-speaking individuals. These students are those whose primary language in the home is a language other than English. There are four main types of ESL learners:

1. Immigrants—those individuals whose families have chosen to come to Canada.

2. Refugees—those who were forced to leave their homelands for safety reasons.

3. Speakers of a different dialect—those who might have been born into English-speaking families, but whose type of English is different from "school" English. In B.C., for example, this most often describes Aboriginal learners.

4. Canadian-born—children born to non–English-speaking families who learn the language of the home and have minimal (if any) English when they arrive at kindergarten.

Learning a new language is an active, social process that takes many years. There is no set curriculum; rather, ESL is a service that supports content learning so students are engaged in real communication.

---

emergent readers
Children who possess skills, knowledge, and attitudes that are developmental precursors to formal reading.

developing readers
Readers who use letter sounds, words, illustrations, and their own knowledge to predict meaning.

independent readers
Competent, confident readers who use skills to derive meaning and enjoyment from reading.

(pretend writing), print motivation (interest in and attention to "breaking the code"), and a mixture of other cognitive skills. Interestingly, the continuous non-stage theory often translates into practices that break reading experiences into distinct, seemingly unrelated units.

THE ISSUE OF LITERACY

School-age readers are typically classified as emergent, developing, or independent readers. These categories are helpful descriptive tools for teachers and families.

- **Emergent readers** are at the beginning of the reading adventure. They know that books tell interesting stories and that words and pictures aid understanding. The skills, knowledge, and attitudes that are the developmental precursors to formal reading are formed at this stage (Whitehurst & Lonigan, 1998).

- **Developing readers** are becoming true readers. They have established the habit of reading for meaning and use their own experiences to enrich the meaning of stories. They have learned to use letter sounds, words, illustrations, and their own knowledge to predict meaning.

- **Independent readers** are those who read on their own and when they are alone. These children are competent, confident readers who use all their skills to derive as much meaning and enjoyment from their reading as possible.

Literacy can be a stressful topic for parents, educators, and children. Parents may become worried if their child is not reading fluently by the time they expect him or her

to. Likewise, if a child is not reading as well as friends in his age group, he may feel embarrassed. With the strong emphasis on literacy and math skills in schools, teachers and administrators may feel responsible to families as well as to provincial and national authorities for their students' success. According to the Life Literacy Canada website (www.abclifeliteracy.ca), studies show beyond dispute that a child's achievement in school improves with increased parent involvement in education.

Other types of literacy are equally important but receive much less formal attention:

- Technological literacy—ability to understand and work with computers, software, and the Internet

- Visual literacy—ability to decipher, interpret, and express ideas using images, charts, graphs, and video

- Cultural literacy—knowledge and appreciation of the diversity of people and cultures

- Global awareness—understanding and recognition of the interrelations of nations, corporations, and world politics

If children are to be citizens of the world in the 21st century, multiple literacies must be considered and supported in schools.

BILINGUALISM

Canada is a very diverse country both ethnically and linguistically. Data from the 2011 census by Statistics Canada revealed that about 200 languages make up the linguistic portrait of the country (The *Canadian Press*, 2012). An issue arising in schools today is the large number of students who are being labelled as English Language Learners (ELL) despite the fact that they were born in Canada. One of the reasons Canadian-born children need ELL help is that they are exposed to only their mother tongues at home (CBC News, 2011).

According to the Peel District School Board in Ontario, 29% of their elementary students need help with their English. Lee Gunderson, a professor of language and literacy at the University of British Columbia, followed the progress of 5000 immigrant students from 1991–2001. These students came from a variety of ethnic and socio-economic backgrounds. Gunderson found that the students who came from poor refugee families where education was not a priority or tradition seemed to experience more difficulties with learning than those who came from wealthy families with a long history of valuing education (Read & Hansen, 2006).

The major question facing educators is this: What is the most effective way to teach English to non-English speakers while maintaining the richness and cultural values of their own languages? Two approaches are at the heart of the discussion: immersion, which places non–English-speaking students in classrooms where the dominant language is spoken exclusively; and bilingual instruction, which emphasizes learning in a child's native language and English.

Bilingual Education Programs

Today in Quebec, Bill 101 states that only those children of parents who studied in English in Quebec or somewhere else in Canada are allowed to attend an English language school. Any immigrants coming to Quebec who are non-English speaking are forced to attend French language schools. This has caused great controversy since the first bill was passed on this issue in 1969.

Meanwhile, French immersion programs were introduced into Canadian schools in the 1970s to encourage bilingualism across the country. While French immersion programs exist in English language school systems in all ten provinces, the percentage of 15-year-olds enrolled in these programs ranges widely, from 2% in British Columbia to 32% in New Brunswick (see Table 7.3).

Because students in bilingual education programs are taught partly in English and partly in French, they acquire subject matter knowledge simultaneously with French. Bilingual programs also allow students to retain their cultural identities while simultaneously progressing in their school subjects.

With the bilingual technique, three major goals are identified:

1. Continued development of the student's primary language
2. Acquisition of a second language, usually French
3. Instruction in content using both languages

The Changing Sense of Self ◀L06

As children experience physical and cognitive challenges, their developing sense of self is affected.

The developmental pathway of the self reflects a child's growing complexity, the gradual transformation of physical features of self (I have blond hair, brown eyes) into more subtle characterizations (I'm a true friend, I get along well with others). These different shadings of the self continue to develop as cognitive and social awareness sharpen. Both self-concept and self-esteem contribute to a child's understanding of who and what "I" am.

TABLE 7.3

French Immersion Programs in Canada

| | Students Enrolled in French immersion in 2000 | | Girls | |
	Enrolled in French immersion	Enrolled in French immersion and started before grade 4 (early immersion)	Immersion	Non-immersion
Percentage of students				
Newfoundland and Labrador	7	57	64	50
Prince Edward Island	20	59	58	51
Nova Scotia	12	21	58	49
New Brunswick	32	39	61	46
Quebec	22	74	52	48
Ontario	6	57	64	51
Manitoba	6	90	60	48
Saskatchewan	3	87	65	48
Alberta	4	80	59	47
British Columbia	2	55	61	49

Source: Program for International Student Assessment (PISA), 2000. Statistics Canada (2008b).

▲ During middle childhood, children begin to develop a sense of self.

THE DEVELOPING SELF-CONCEPT

Self-concept—a person's evaluation of him- or herself—is not something that a person is born with, and it is not unchanging over the course of the lifespan (Harter, 2006). Rather, the self develops through the years as the result of life experience.

The self can be described as both a *cognitive* and a *social* construction (Harter, 2006). Erikson (1963, 1968) described middle childhood in the life stage he called industry versus inferiority. It is a time when children use their tools and skills and acquire a feeling of satisfaction at the completion of satisfactory work. If children are encouraged to engage in work they find fulfilling, such as building, creating art, cooking, or solving math problems, their feeling of industry increases. Their developing sense of competency leads them to understand the perspective of others, which then influences further development of self.

SELF-ESTEEM AND COMPETENCE

Self-esteem can be described as the sense of worth and value that children place on themselves. During middle childhood, children's developing sense of self helps to shape their personal goals. Any discrepancy between the perceived ideal self and the real self can be a strong motivating force. For example, children begin to compare their achievements with those of others. They come to realize that although they may excel in one area (math, for example), someone else is much stronger in a different area (art). This discrepancy can serve as a motivating force for some children to work harder, whereas others

self-concept A person's evaluation of himself or herself.

self-esteem One's personal sense of worth and value.

competence The ability to do something well.

register the information and accept it without desire for change.

As older children begin to assess their personal strengths and weaknesses, they recognize that they have both desirable and undesirable qualities. Their perceptions of self and self-esteem are tightly woven with their satisfaction with their physical appearance, their need for support from those they love and trust, and a belief in their own competence.

Developmental psychologist Susan Harter has been a longtime student of the concept of self-esteem. Studying 8- to 13-year-old children, Harter and her colleagues developed a Self-Perception Profile for Children (SPPC) that tested five types of **competence**—the ability to do something well—as a measure of self-esteem: scholastic competence, athletic competence, social competence, physical appearance, and behavioural conduct (Harter, 1999).

The results indicated that children don't feel they do equally well in all the five types of competence that Harter identified. Most children feel good about themselves in some types of competence but not so good in others.

In the second phase of her study, Harter explored how what others think about children affects children's self-esteem. Children who received much support from the important people in their lives had a high regard for themselves. Those who obtained little, if any, support from significant others showed the lowest self-esteem. These findings provide important insights into how children acquire their sense of self-esteem.

Harter noted a strong link between what children thought of their physical appearance and their level of self-esteem. Researchers Diane Levin and Jean Kilbourne (2008) argue that children are bombarded by sexualized content in popular culture and technology, and

The capacity for conscious and voluntary **self-regulation** is central to our understanding of what it is to be human. It underlies our assumptions about choice, decision making, and planning. Our conceptions of freedom and **responsibility** depend on it.

MARTHA BRONSON, EARLY CHILDHOOD EDUCATOR AND ADVOCATE

companies aggressively produce and market products to children that sustain images of sex and desirability based on appearance and sexuality. They stress how critical it is for adults to communicate with children about these issues and to build children's confidence and self-concept based on developmentally appropriate, respectful experiences.

Praise and recognition for effort and honest achievements go a long way in building children's self-esteem. Honest critique and thoughtful suggestions for improvement also teach children that they don't need to be perfect. For example, a parent or teacher might say, "You didn't do that well this time, but I know if you practise, you'll do better next time." The discipline and desire required to improve one's self are related to another quality—self-regulation.

SELF-REGULATION

As you may imagine, self-regulation refers to many situations: mastering fear, controlling eating and drinking, monitoring one's responses, and refusing dangerous substances. **Self-regulation** reflects higher-level-thinking—an individual's capacity to initiate, terminate, delay, modify, or redirect thought, emotion, behaviour, or action (Compas et al., 2002). Developing these vital coping skills is a key part of psychosocial development (Dacey & Fiore, 2000).

For children to be successful in work and relationships, they must exercise restraint in deciding what to do, how to do it, what to say, and how to say it. Children's temperaments and perceptions of others impact how they respond to others and how others respond to them. Research in this area has shown that children who display impulsivity at a young age tend to be troubled adolescents, with few friends and great psychological difficulties. Young children who delay gratification can later handle frustration well, are focused and calm in the face of challenges, and are self-reliant and popular adolescents (Peake, Hebl, & Mischel, 2002).

L07 ▶ Social Development

Children in middle childhood bring characteristics they formed within their family surroundings to their interactions with those outside the family. Although parents typically spend less time with children in middle childhood

than in early childhood, due to children's increasing competencies and budding desire for independence, they remain a strong influence in their lives. With this in mind, let's examine the impact of families and peers on development in middle childhood.

> **self-regulation** An individual's ability to initiate, terminate, delay, or modify thought, emotion, behaviour, or action.

THE ROLE OF FAMILY AND FRIENDS

During middle childhood, children focus energies in new directions, such as on school activities and peer relationships. Their cognitive abilities allow them to reason with their parents about rules, chores, discipline, and countless other topics. They tend to practise their self-regulation skills on a

▼ Children often try to emulate the looks and behaviour of their favourite movie/TV stars.

bullying The act of using verbal or physical means to intimidate or embarrass someone else.

daily basis; for example, they choose to complete their homework before watching a favourite television program, and gradually internalize their parents' values and expectations.

Children whose parents divorce or who live in a stepfamily face some additional challenges in their development. They must cope with realities of fewer or shared resources and different levels of attention from their biological parents.

Another focus of research on the role of family in children's social development is lesbian, gay, bisexual, and transgender (LGBT) parenting. Findings indicate that parents' sexual orientation is in no way connected to parenting skills. Dr. Anne-Marie Aubert, a Sociology professor at York University in Toronto, has done extensive research in the areas of divorce and remarriage, poverty, and various aspects of the parent–child relationship. She also wrote a paper on same-sex couples and same-sex parent families that addresses the unwarranted fears that this topic raises. To read her online articles on family issues, go to http://www.yorku.ca/ambert/writings/index.html.

One common function that parents serve is acting as chaperone (and/or chauffeur) for children and their peers. During middle childhood, peer interactions increase dramatically to about 30% of all social interactions. The decreasing amount of adult participation in a variety of settings, including school, activities, and phone and online exchanges, parallels the increase in peer interactions. Getting along with peers is a major step in social development, and research findings are consistent with the conclusion that peer rejection directly impairs children's adjustment. Peers more often direct negative behaviours and verbal harassment toward rejected children (Buhs & Ladd, 2001), which also makes it more likely that rejected children will be excluded from social activities (Dodge et al., 2003).

Aggression becomes more verbal and personally hostile in middle childhood, with friendship assuming a greater role in acceptance or rejection (Rubin, Bukowski, & Parker, 2006). Children who have friends are less likely to be picked on or rejected by others. **Bullying**, the act of

Lisa: Why does she only go after the smart ones?
Nelson: That's like asking the square root of a million. No one will ever know.
Lisa: Someone will—I'm going to crack the bully code.

—*THE SIMPSONS*, EPISODE 264

▲ As children enter middle childhood, they begin to learn to reason with their parents about issues such as rules and privileges, discipline, and household chores.

using verbal or physical means to intimidate or embarrass someone else, is a common challenge in schools and neighbourhoods. The challenge is further complicated by technology, specifically incidents of "cyberbullying"—bullying conducted online or via text messages. Of immediate concern is the danger that a child's zones of safety become violent, scary places. Many schools and communities are making greater efforts to adhere to zero tolerance policies with bullying, and this requires a coordinated effort among adults and children.

The Faculty of Education at York University in Toronto holds annual conferences and presentations addressing the many issues of bullying. Their goal is to bring leading research and practical solutions from the field and help incorporate bullying prevention programs into schools. Bully Free Alberta is a website designed by the Government of Alberta to help with the prevention of bullying. Go to http://www.bullyfreealberta.ca for national websites on the subject.

THE ROLE OF SCHOOLS ◀L08

There are many issues facing schools today, including funding, high-stakes testing, and family involvement in and support of children's education. Common sense dictates that any environment in which children sharpen their intellectual skills, learn how to get along with others, work with a diverse cultural group of peers, and assess their self-concepts in competition with others must have a powerful effect on development. Researchers have looked beyond the academic aspects of school to examine how school influences a child's identity, self-esteem, beliefs, and behaviour.

FEATURED MEDIA

Films about Bullies and Bullying

Cyberbully (2011)—What happens to a teenage girl after she signs up to a social networking site?

Max Keeble's Big Move (2001)—What happens when a victim's attempts at revenge backfire? How can bully and victim come to a healthy understanding of appropriate conduct?

Mean Girls (2004)—How do social cliques operate and what effect can they have on other girls?

My Bodyguard (1980)—How does fear unite unlikely friends? What happens when a boy uses money to ensure his own protection?

Odd Girl Out (2005)—How do a mother and daughter deal with the intimidation of peer pressure and the emotionally brutal social rituals of high school?

The Karate Kid (1984; 2010)—What lengths would a boy from the poor side of town go to in order to defend his honour, win the girl of his dreams, and take home the prized karate title? What lessons about friendship are learned along the way?

Clearly, there are different ways to teach children and to hold teachers and schools accountable for the success that students experience. In middle childhood, teachers play a particularly important role as children grapple with both the desire to succeed and feelings of incompetence. Teachers, like parents, help children cope with academic and social demands, and they transmit a set of values and expectations to the classroom (see Figure 7.6). The classroom context is one of many systems that influence a child's development (see Chapter 2).

As children pass through the elementary grades, they experience steady developmental changes, as well as constantly changing subject matter. Recognizing the developmental pathways that children follow, schools must focus on some critical, timeless themes that help children learn:

1. To develop good relationships

2. To acquire effective thinking skills

3. To be part of the solution, not the problem

4. To look at things differently

5. To be goal-oriented

6. To achieve academic success

7. To recognize the difference between right and wrong

8. To know and accept differences in others

9. To see the true self

10. To bounce back and keep trying

Summarizing 40 years of research on schooling, Eccles and Roeser (1999) reach several conclusions about school's impact on children:

- Although school resources are important, the organizational, social, and instructional processes have the greatest impact on children's development.

- Schools produce their effects at different levels: the school as a whole, the classroom, and interpersonal interactions.

- Children's perceptions of the school are powerful predictors of their adjustment, adaptation, and achievement.

- A school's effects on behaviour are determined by individual, psychological processes.

FIGURE 7.6

Ecological Model of Schooling and Development of Self

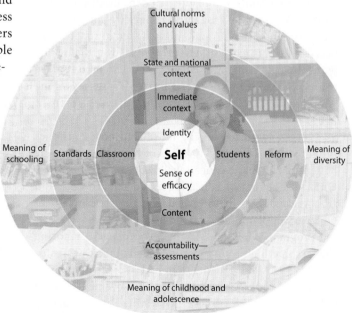

Source: Bronfenbrenner (1986).

▲ During elementary grades, children begin to develop good relationships.

Current Concerns and Controversies

Canada has attempted to ensure accountability between the school boards and schools in the publicly funded system by having provincially mandated tests administered to the students in their classes. Approximately six months later, the results are made available to the public.

The problem with this practice is that school comparisons are made and schools themselves are blamed for poor performances. The truth is that many factors can influence test performance—family stability, parental involvement and expectations for student success in school, early and ongoing home stimulation, student motivation, and absenteeism, as well as student capacity for learning. Since students are not randomly assigned to schools and because schools have little or no control over the majority of the factors mentioned above, any attempt to place the blame for poor test performance on the schools alone is problematic at best and misleading at worst (Simner, 2000).

"The standardized testing movement now consumes millions of dollars and hundreds of hours that could be better spent on basic educational resources" (Moll, 2003). Ontario directors of education asked for a break from this testing when they learned that the government of Ontario was planning to extend its already intensive testing program (Moll, 2003). The government is ignoring the fact that high test scores are usually linked with students from high income families.

An informal movement against excessive testing is occurring around the globe. Teachers in Britain have voted to boycott the tests, parents in Alberta are requesting that their children be exempted from the tests, and some U.S. citizens are even suggesting that all politicians take the test themselves (Moll, 2003).

Expectations and Achievement

Research has demonstrated a powerful relationship between poverty and a child's health, behaviour, and achievement. For example, poor children repeat grades and drop out of high school at a rate that is more than double that of wealthier peers (Duncan & Brooks-Gunn, 2000).

The major difference between growing up as a middle class child from the suburbs and growing up as a poor child from the inner city is opportunity. Many inner city youth don't have the chance to play sports, create art, or access the quality of education that suburban youth do. With few options, many kids turn to criminal activities and gangs (DePape, 2010).

About 15% of Canadian children live in **poverty**. In Canadian schools, students in special education, recent immigrants, some visible minority groups, and Aboriginal youths lag behind national averages of educational achievement (Levin, 2007).

Canada is addressing these equity issues. The high school graduation rate of First Nation students is on the rise. British Columbia is improving outcomes for Aboriginal students in provincial schools, Alberta has its Initiative for School Improvement, and Quebec has a strategy for student success. Ontario has developed strategies to improve literacy and numeracy skills in their schools. Most of these efforts involve working with teachers to improve their ability to support success in diverse student populations (Levin, 2007).

These conditions can be either improved or made worse by the family's belief in education. As Garbarino and Benn noted (1992), parents may not be present in the classroom, but they have a profound influence on the way their children view school and learning. The extent to which the family supports the school's objectives directly affects their child's academic performance. Too often, low parental expectations for their children reflect the parents' own educational experiences.

poverty Living in a household with income less than 50% of the national median.

Career Apps

As a town ombudsperson, how might you advocate for children's rights in the educational system and inform families of available services?

TECH TRENDS

Online Peers and Safety Precautions

The term *social media* is a relatively new term referring to software applications that allow people to communicate and share data. Older children are often more familiar with these forms of communicating than adults, and schools and teachers must keep up with the technology to equip children to use the tools safely and effectively.

Instant messaging (IM): A form of real-time text-based communication between two or more people using personal computers or other devices.

Internet forum (also called a message board): A separate, virtual room where children can talk about topics of interest. Someone starts by thinking of a question or conversation topic and posts it in the forum, and others respond accordingly.

Blogs: Online journals for individuals. Some blogs permit others to leave comments and keep a record of the flow of the conversation.

Wikis: A wiki is a webpage whose content can be edited by visitors. Visitors edit and share thoughts with others online.

Facebook: A social networking website in which users can add friends, send them messages, and post updates to their status and profiles to let friends know what's going on in their lives.

Of most concern to parents is the threat of sexual predators online who may take advantage of a child's desire for independence, friendship, and social acceptance, and who may potentially harm a child. Online bullying (cyberbullying) is another concern. Close supervision and monitoring of children's online activities is vital for adults to ensure that a child's desire to wed social activity and technology results in positive socialization opportunities.

THE ROLE OF TECHNOLOGY

Although today's children are immersed in a media world (movies, television, video games, CDs, DVDs), television is the most widely used medium and undoubtedly has a greater effect on development than do other media (see Figure 7.7).

As previously mentioned in this chapter, children and youth are averaging about 6 hours of screen time per day. Canadian studies suggest:

- School-age children should watch no more than two hours of television per day (less than one hour being ideal) and children should not have televisions in their bedrooms (Canadian Paediatric Society, 2011).

FIGURE 7.7

Children Who Watch Television

Country	Percent
Switzerland	3.0
Norway	3.7
Germany	4.4
Sweden	4.7
France	5.5
Denmark	6.0
Finland	6.1
Italy	9.2
Ireland	11.8
Netherlands	12.6
Canada	14.9
Spain	17.5
United States	21.3

▲ This graph shows the percentage of 9-year-old children who reported watching more than 5 hours of television per weekday in 2005 in 13 countries.

Is TV Making Our Children Obese?

According to SCOPE—Sustainable Childhood Obesity Prevention through Community Engagement—a program piloted in British Columbia, 1 in 4 Canadian children today are overweight or obese. CBC medical contributor Dr. Karl Kabasele said many factors are fuelling child obesity. "The food industry and the processed foods have kind of created this environment where it's so easy to get calories," said Kabasele. "Kids are playing video games, watching TV, not getting out and exercising. So all of these factors are kind of conspiring against kids despite our best efforts" (CBC News, 2012c).

Canadian guidelines suggest that children and youth should be getting at least 90 minutes of physical activity per day—but research shows that they are not. According to the Active Healthy Kids Canada 2010 Report Card, only 12% of children and youth across Canada are meeting this guideline. The amount of time children and youth spend being inactive (e.g., watching TV, playing computer/video games, etc.) is also on the rise. This report showed that children and youth participate in about 6 hours of screen time per day on weekdays and 7 hours of screen time per day on weekends. Children and youth not only need to turn off the TV, they need to find activities that they like to participate in that will increase their overall physical activity levels.

SCOPE hopes to bring families, communities, schools, local businesses, and local governments together to find ways to improve physical activity among children and youth, in these ways:

1. Creating physical activity programs to promote physical activity in children and youth who find accessing and/or participating in physical activity challenging

2. Encouraging active forms of transportation such as walking and biking

3. Limiting screen time and providing opportunities to take part in physical activity alternatives

Do you feel that "active" video games such as the Wii or Xbox Kinect have helped to increase overall activitiy levels in children? Should parents become more strict about how much time their children spend watching TV, playing video games, etc.?

---

stress Anything that upsets a person's equilibrium—psychologically and physiologically.

child abuse Infliction of injury to a child; commonly includes physical, sexual, emotional abuse, neglect or the exposure to domestic violence.

- Excessive screen time has been shown to lead to behavioural difficulties, reduced achievement at school, attention problems, sedentary behaviours and an increased risk of obesity (Rushowy, 2010).

- Most of children's free time should be spent in activities such as playing, reading, exploring, or participating in sports.

2. They can't use their abilities as well as possible.

3. They become discouraged easily and tend to generate feelings of helplessness.

4. Even when successful—academically, emotionally, athletically—children who are stressed don't recognize and accept their progress (Dacey & Fiore, 2000).

Adults can help to provide children with critical emotional security in stressful times and help them develop the coping skills that will serve them well in times of need.

L09 ▶ Stress in Middle Childhood

Stress is defined as anything that upsets a person's equilibrium, psychologically and physiologically. Children today are growing and developing in a climate of stress, which impinges on every part of their lives.

When children are stressed, they encounter four problems:

1. They find it harder than other children to calm themselves in stressful situations.

CHILD ABUSE

Although **child abuse** is an age-old problem, not until the last two decades has it become widely publicized. The Canadian Incidence Study of Reported Child Abuse and Neglect (Public Health Agency, 2003) divided child abuse into five categories: physical abuse, sexual abuse, emotional abuse, neglect, and exposure to domestic violence. Among these types, a review of research conducted between 2000 and 2009 concluded that 4–16% of children are physically abused in

FIGURE 7.8

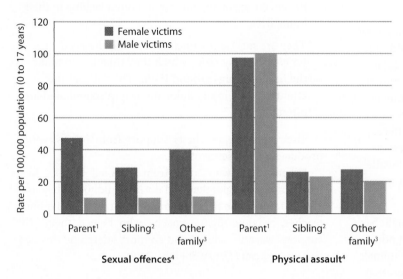

Rate per 100,000 population (0 to 17 years)

Legend: ■ Female victims ■ Male victims

Sexual offences[4]: Parent[1], Sibling[2], Other family[3]

Physical assault[4]: Parent[1], Sibling[2], Other family[3]

◀ Child and youth victims (0 to 17 years) of police-reported sexual offences and physical assault by family members, by sex and accused–victim relationship, Canada, 2009

1. Includes biological, step, adoptive, and foster parents.
2. Includes biological, step, adoptive, and foster brothers and sisters.
3. Includes all other family members related by blood, marriage, or adoption. Examples include spouses (current or former), uncles, aunts, cousins, and grandparents.
4. See Table 2.1 for a list of offences included in each crime category.

Note(s): Excludes incidents where the sex and/or age of the victim was unknown. In 2009, data from the Incident-based Uniform Crime Reporting Survey covered 99% of the population of Canada. Rates are calculated on the basis of 100,000 population. Populations based on July 1 estimates from Statistics Canada, Demography Division.

Sources: Statistics Canada, 2009. Family Violence in Canada: A Statistical Profile Police-reported family violence against children and youth. Published by authority of the Minister responsible for Statistics Canada. © Minister of Industry, 2013. All rights reserved. Use of this publication is governed by the Statistics Canada Open License Agreement.

high-income nations, such as Canada (see Figure 7.8), the United States, the United Kingdom, and Australia. An additional 10% of girls and 5% of boys are victims of sexual abuse (Sharples, 2008).

According to the Department of Justice Canada, the term "child abuse" refers to the violence, mistreatment, or neglect that a child or adolescent may experience while in the care of someone they either trust or depend on, such as a parent, sibling, other relative, caregiver, or guardian. In a diverse population, some parents may not consider certain practices to be abusive. For example, Cambodian families may treat fever with cao gao, a practice of rubbing hot coins over a child's back or chest that leaves a symmetrical pattern of bruises (Wyckoff, 1999).

Children and teens experiencing any kind of abuse or neglect are encouraged to contact Kids Help Phone (1-800-668-6868 or www.kidshelpphone.ca). This is Canada's 24-hour telephone and on-line counselling service for kids and teens. It is a free service, which is available across the country; it is bilingual, confidential, and anonymous.

RESILIENT CHILDREN

Many children can adapt to stress and develop competent social, emotional, and cognitive functioning despite the challenge of powerful stressors (Friedman & Chase-Lansdale, 2002). Resilience is characterized by the ability to recover relatively quickly from setbacks.

Resilient children have endured terrible circumstances and come through; they are not unscathed but they are skilled at fending off feelings of inferiority, helplessness, and isolation (Heller, Larrieu, D'Imperio, & Boris, 1999). What we know about these children points to their ability

to recover from either physiological or psychological trauma and return to a normal developmental path (Cicchetti & Toth, 1998).

What personal characteristics distinguish resilient children? The

resilient children
Children who sustained some type of physiological or psychological trauma yet return to a normal developmental path.

▼ The main characters in the film *Slumdog Millionaire* exhibit resilience despite tremendous challenges..

following features are the results of many years of research (Garmezy & Rutter, 1983, 1985; Werner & Smith, 1992, 2001):

- *They have temperaments that elicit positive responses from those around them.* They are "easy" children: Their eating and sleeping habits are quite regular, they show positive responses when people approach them, they adapt to changes in their environment, and they exhibit a considerable degree of self-regulation. Despite the trauma they have suffered, they are friendly, likable children who possess an inner quality that protects them from their hostile surroundings and enables them to reach out to an adult who could offer support.

- *They have special interests or talents.* Some might be excellent swimmers, dancers, and artists, and others might have a special knack for working with animals or a talent with numbers. Whatever their interest, it serves to absorb them and help shelter them from their environment. These activities seem to provide the encouragement and stability often lacking in their home lives.

- *They are sufficiently intelligent to acquire good problem-solving skills,* which they then use to make the best of things around them. They attract the attention of helpful adults, do well in school, and are often popular.

Their competence elicits support from others, which produces a good sense of self.

When adults who come from troubled families look back on the struggles they had during childhood, they usually mention some person—grandparent, aunt, neighbour, teacher, religious figure, coach—who helped them. The support, warmth, advice, and comfort offered by this person was crucial (Dacey & Fiore, 2000).

CONCLUSIONS & SUMMARY

In middle childhood, children can assimilate and accommodate material they encounter at their developmental level. They are capable of representational thought, but only with concrete objects. They find it difficult to fully comprehend abstract subtleties in reading, social studies, or any subject.

With all of the developmental accomplishments of the previous 6 or 7 years, youngsters want to use their abilities, which means that they sometimes experience failure as well as success, especially in their schoolwork. Now that they are physically active, cognitively capable, and socially receptive, much is expected of these children, especially in school. During these years, children move away from a sheltered home environment into a world of new friends, new challenges, and new problems. Whether the task is adjusting to a new sibling, relating to peers and teachers, or coping with difficulties, children of this age enter a different world. Children deal uniquely with stress, using temperamental qualities and coping skills as best they can.

How would you describe physical and motor development during these years?

- Children consolidate their height and weight gains.
- Children develop considerable coordination in their motor skills.

What are some of the competing views of cognitive development during middle childhood?

- Among the major cognitive achievements of this period are conservation, seriation, classification, numeration, and reversibility.
- Piaget found that at this stage children's thinking is more flexible than in early childhood.
- Gardner and Sternberg have proposed new ways of explaining intelligence.

How do children develop thinking and problem-solving strategies?

- Children learn to focus their attention on the task at hand in order to recognize what resources are needed to solve the problem and reach a desired goal.
- Children today need critical thinking skills to adapt to sophisticated, technological societies.

How would you trace children's progress in moral development?

- Piaget formulated a theory of moral development that is tightly linked to his explanation of cognitive development.
- Kohlberg proposed six levels of moral development that follow a child's progress from about 4 years of age to adulthood.
- Gilligan has challenged the male-oriented basis of Kohlberg's work.

How does children's language change during these years?

- Children's language development during these years shows increasing representation and facility in conversing with others.
- Children develop several strategies to help them with their reading.

What are the key elements in children acquiring a personally satisfying and competent sense of self?

- The link between self-esteem and competence grows stronger.
- The development of self-regulation becomes a key element in a child's success.

How influential are peers during these years?

- During middle childhood, peer interactions increase dramatically to about 30% of all social interactions.

What are some effects of schools and teachers?

- Children encounter considerable change in both curriculum and instructional methods.

How does technology affect children's development?

- Television rivals school for children's time and attention.
- Controversy surrounds the issue of the effects of television violence.
- Television also has potential for encouraging prosocial behaviour.

How do children deal with stress in the middle childhood years?

- Children react differently to stress according to age, gender, and temperament.
- Some children, called resilient, overcome adverse effects of early stressors.

For REVIEW

1. Imagine a 9-year-old boy (Tim), who lives in the suburbs of a large city. He shows signs of becoming a great baseball player, and his father believes that his son could eventually win a university scholarship and go on to become a professional someday. He decides that Tim should not play pickup games with his friends, because he might hurt himself. He also decides that the family should move to a place that is warm all year round so that Tim can play ball all year. How can you relate this scenario to the notion of competence? To family and peer relationships?

2. You are a first-grade teacher and you turn to six-year-old Talia and say, "Talia, Matthew is taller than Sam, who is taller than Ella. Who's the tallest of all?" Talia looks at you quizzically. How would you explain Talia's behaviour in light of Piaget's theory?

3. Research shows that childhood obesity is a serious concern in our society today. What are some of the factors that contribute to this problem? What needs to be done by our schools and our communities to address this issue?

Chapter REVIEW TEST

Answers: 1b, 2d, 3b, 4c, 5b, 6d, 7c, 8a, 9a, 10a

1. Which province has the most students enrolled in French Immersion programs?
   a. British Columbia
   b. New Brunswick
   c. Nova Scotia
   d. Ontario

2. Psychological characteristics of middle childhood include all except
   a. seriation.
   b. conservation.
   c. moral reasoning.
   d. random scribbling.

3. Sternberg's triarchic theory includes metacomponents, knowledge-acquisition components, and _____ components.
   a. gender
   b. performance
   c. age
   d. chromosome

4. Howard Gardner's theory of multiple intelligences includes ____ equal intelligences.
   a. four
   b. five
   c. eight
   d. ten

5. Recognizing what is distinctive in others is an example of which of Gardner's intelligences?
   a. linguistic
   b. interpersonal
   c. logical-mathematical
   d. bodily-kinesthetic

6. One problem with intelligence tests is that the _____ of test takers and test makers may differ.
   a. relationships
   b. circumstances
   c. conditions
   d. values

7. Gilligan's developmental sequence is based on
   a. social justice.
   b. female superiority.
   c. ethics of care.
   d. moral reasoning.

8. Children who have similar levels of competence may have quite different levels of
   a. self-esteem.
   b. friendship.
   c. television viewing.
   d. cognitive development.

9. Friends provide certain resources for children. Which of these is not a resource provided by friends?
   a. membership in the sibling underworld
   b. opportunity for learning skills
   c. chance to compare self with others
   d. chance to belong to a group

10. Among the protective factors for resilient children is
    a. temperament.
    b. interactive error.
    c. geographic mobility.
    d. assimilation.

ADOLESCENCE

As You READ

After reading this chapter, you should be able to answer the following questions:

LO1 ▶ How is adolescence defined?

LO2 ▶ What are the key factors of physical development in adolescence?

LO3 ▶ What are some challenges to physical development in adolescence?

LO4 ▶ How does cognition develop during the adolescent years?

LO5 ▶ What are the leading theories that attempt to explain adolescence?

LO6 ▶ What changes have occurred to Canadian families and their roles in adolescent life in recent years?

LO7 ▶ What is the nature of peer relations during the teen years?

LO8 ▶ How do teens deal with sexual relations?

LO9 ▶ What mental health issues are seen in adolescence?

LO10 ▶ What recent information do we have on adolescent illegal behaviour?

> "Who are you?" said the caterpillar. Alice replied, rather shyly, "I—I
> hardly know, Sir, just at present—at least I know who I was when I got
> up this morning, but I must have changed several times since then."

The musical *Spring Awakening* has become a powerful experience for audiences of all ages. The creators have opened doors for conversations among parents and children about topics they may be nervous to discuss, attempt to ignore, yet yearn to talk about. Research argues that youths are under greater stress than in previous decades (for example, Reisberg, 2000), but *Spring Awakening* testifies to the fact that adolescence has long been a unique and challenging period for young people and their families.

LO1 ▶ What Is Adolescence and When Does It Start?

Frank Wedekind (1864–1918) and Lewis Carroll (1832–1898) both captured elements of adolescence that still ring true today. Adolescence is a time of life marked by transitions. As exemplified in *Spring Awakening* and supported by research, key biological, psychological, and social transitions signal the entry into adolescence.

When did your adolescence begin?

- When you began to menstruate, or when you had your first ejaculation
- When the level of adult hormones rose sharply in your bloodstream
- When you first thought about dating
- When your pubic hair began to grow.
- When you turned 11 years old (girl) or 12 years old (boy)
- When you developed an interest in sex
- When you passed societal initiation rites (e.g., Jewish bar or bat mitzvah; Catholic confirmation)
- When you became really moody
- When you thought about being away from your parents
- When you worried about the way your body looked
- When you could judge actions independent of your own opinions
- When your friends influenced you more than your parents
- When you began to wonder who you really are

▲ *Spring Awakening*, the Broadway musical, is inspired by a piece of work that was considered so dangerous when it was written by German playwright Frank Wedekind over 100 years ago that it was banned from public viewing on the stage. The play, written in 1891, concerns adolescents who are coming to terms with their sexuality and deals with such topics as masturbation, sexual abuse, homosexuality, abortion, rape, and suicide.

FIGURE 8.1

An Average Day in the Life of Some North American Teens

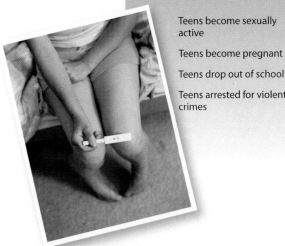

Negative behaviours	Altruistic behaviours
Teens become sexually active	Teens join service club
Teens become pregnant	Teens join Students Against Drunk Driving
Teens drop out of school	Teens volunteer at a homeless shelter
Teens arrested for violent crimes	Teens work a part-time job

▲ Adolescents have been viewed through lenses that reflect altruistic and negative behaviours.

It's possible that there are many adolescence-defining moments, and they don't provide a clear starting point for entry into the rest of life. What is quite clear, however, is the biopsychosocial nature of adolescent experiences. For example, a girl's first menstruation, called **menarche**, can occur at any time from 8 to 16 years of age. A menstruating 8-year-old would not likely be considered an adolescent, but a non-menstruating 16-year-old would likely be considered one. Cognitive factors relating to social values and expectations join with physical realities when considering a girl a child or an adolescent.

In his two-volume set called *Adolescence* (1904), psychologist G. Stanley Hall was the first to offer a specific theory to explain development in the teen years. Based almost entirely on biology, a major aspect of his theory was his speculation that this stage of life is characterized by "storm and stress" because of the amount of change a person experiences in physical, cognitive, and social domains. This stereotype has been perpetuated in the media, but refuted in research and personal accounts. Figure 8.1 illustrates adolescent behaviours that translate into perceptions and stereotypes about teenagers.

Physical Development ◀L02

To better understand physical development in adolescence, let's start with the following questions: What parts of the body are involved? When does puberty start? What are the effects of timing?

Adolescents have many questions about puberty, such as how the organs of our reproductive system function. The musical *Spring Awakening* is a perfect illustration of the degree to which adolescents' healthy biopsychosocial development depends on accurate communication with adults about this topic. Misunderstandings about physical development can impact cognitive and social functions. Figures 8.2 and 8.3 depict the female and male sexual systems.

WHEN DOES PUBERTY START?

The sequence of bodily changes in **puberty** is surprisingly constant. This holds true whether puberty starts early or late, and regardless of the culture in which the child is reared.

Change in hormone levels, called **hormonal balance**, is one of the triggers of puberty, but its beginning is difficult to pinpoint. Measuring skeletal

menarche A girl's first menstruation.

puberty The process of physical changes by which a child's body becomes an adult body capable of reproduction.

hormonal balance Change in hormone levels, one of the triggers of puberty.

Gretchen, my friend, got her **period**. I'm so jealous, God. I hate myself for being so jealous, but I am. I wish you'd help me just a little.

JUDY BLUME, *ARE YOU THERE, GOD? IT'S ME, MARGARET* (1981)

FIGURE 8.2

Female Sexual System

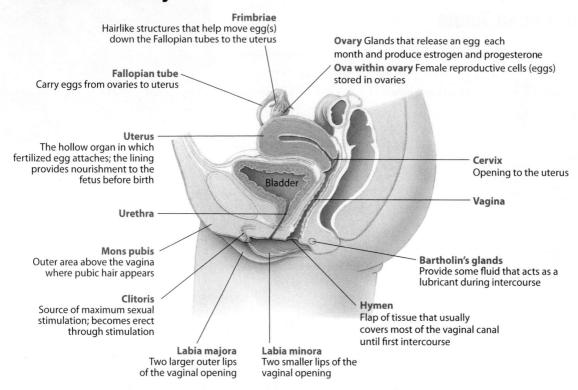

Frimbriae
Hairlike structures that help move egg(s)
down the Fallopian tubes to the uterus

Ovary Glands that release an egg each
month and produce estrogen and progesterone

Ova within ovary Female reproductive cells (eggs)
stored in ovaries

Fallopian tube
Carry eggs from ovaries to uterus

Uterus
The hollow organ in which
fertilized egg attaches; the lining
provides nourishment to the
fetus before birth

Bladder

Cervix
Opening to the uterus

Vagina

Urethra

Mons pubis
Outer area above the vagina
where pubic hair appears

Bartholin's glands
Provide some fluid that acts as a
lubricant during intercourse

Clitoris
Source of maximum sexual
stimulation; becomes erect
through stimulation

Hymen
Flap of tissue that usually
covers most of the vaginal canal
until first intercourse

Labia majora
Two larger outer lips
of the vaginal opening

Labia minora
Two smaller lips of the
vaginal opening

FIGURE 8.3

Male Sexual System

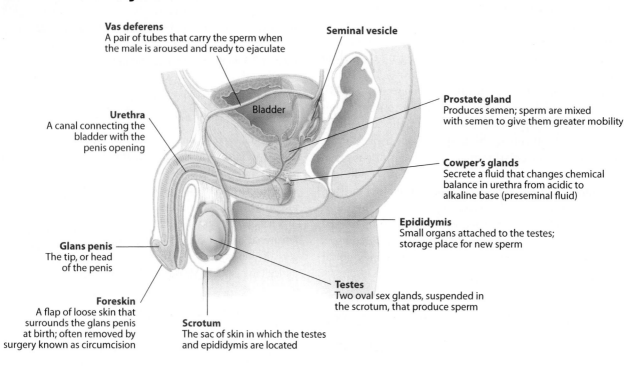

Vas deferens
A pair of tubes that carry the sperm when
the male is aroused and ready to ejaculate

Seminal vesicle

Urethra
A canal connecting the
bladder with the
penis opening

Bladder

Prostate gland
Produces semen; sperm are mixed
with semen to give them greater mobility

Cowper's glands
Secrete a fluid that changes chemical
balance in urethra from acidic to
alkaline base (preseminal fluid)

Epididymis
Small organs attached to the testes;
storage place for new sperm

Glans penis
The tip, or head
of the penis

Foreskin
A flap of loose skin that
surrounds the glans penis
at birth; often removed by
surgery known as circumcision

Scrotum
The sac of skin in which the testes
and epididymis are located

Testes
Two oval sex glands, suspended in
the scrotum, that produce sperm

growth, genital growth, pubic hair, breast development, voice change, or a growth spurt requires recording them over a period of time. Menarche has been suggested as the major turning point for girls, and first ejaculation as the beginning of adolescent puberty for males, but these are not often remembered as events that felt like entry into adulthood. Figure 8.4 illustrates the typical age ranges for events in puberty.

The relatively slow and steady growth patterns of childhood are replaced with a growth spurt in adolescence, as shown in Figure 8.5, and girls tend to grow taller sooner than boys. Adolescent changes in height, soon followed by changes in weight, last for approximately 2 years, and adolescents' eating habits reflect their bodies' energy requirements and demand more fuel. By the time teenagers start high school, girls' and boys' bodies have begun to resemble adults' bodies. Most noticeably, girls develop broader hips and boys develop broader shoulders. The psychological impact

FIGURE 8.4

Typical Age Ranges for Signs of Puberty

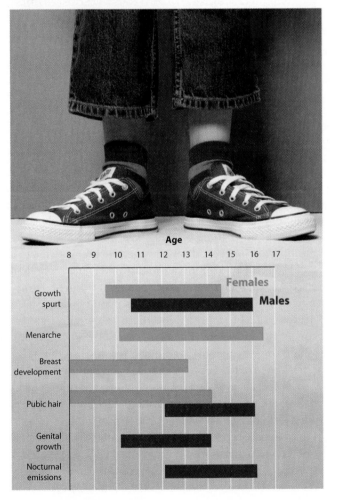

FIGURE 8.5

Adolescent Growth Chart

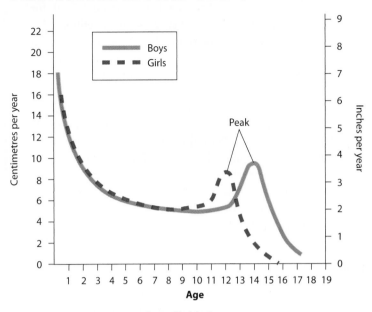

Rate of height increase

of these events, however, can be quite significant. This is especially true with menstruation. When menarche comes early (before 11 years of age), it is more likely to be associated with depression than when it comes later (Beausang & Razor, 2000; Stice, Presenell, & Bearman, 2001). A recent study by Al-Sahab, Ardern, Hamadeh, and Tamim (2012) found that age of menarche in Canadian girls is not associated with substance use (i.e., smoking, heavy alcohol drinking, and drug use) though.

THE SECULAR TREND

In Western countries, the average age of menarche has declined about 3 months per decade over the past 100 years. This phenomenon is called the **secular trend**, which refers to the decreasing age of the onset of puberty. Girls especially are reaching menarche at younger ages. In the mid-19th century, the average age of menarche was 16 to 17. Today, the average age of menarche in Canada is 12.7 (Al-Sahab, Ardern, Hamadeh, & Tamim, 2010).

Ellis and associates (1999) found, however, that factors of family relationships are associated with starting puberty *later*. These include the father's presence in the home, fathers providing more child care, greater supportiveness from both parents, and more affection from both parents for the daughter.

Some boys and girls mature earlier than usual. For boys, this is often associated with self-confidence and popularity, as their increased physical

secular trend The decreasing age of the onset of puberty.

capacity sometimes prepares them to be more skilled at sports and other activities. On the other hand, greater physical ability is sometimes linked with aggression and misbehaviour. Early puberty tends to be more difficult for girls than it is for boys, in that the sexual attention adolescent girls receive is often unwelcome and unwanted. In addition, some researchers have linked childhood obesity with early onset of menarche (Anderson, Dallal, & Must, 2003; Lee et al., 2007).

It is clear that the processes of development and the role of puberty are complicated and occur concurrently (Dorn, Susman, & Ponirakis, 2003). In summary, most humans proceed toward maturity in the same way, but in the last few centuries the timing of the process, especially in females, has changed radically. Although timing is affected mainly by biology, psychological and social forces clearly influence it, too.

L03 ▶ BODY IMAGE AND EATING DISORDERS

At a time when adolescents are preoccupied with their bodies and judging themselves against others, the physical changes of puberty can lead to dissatisfaction with physical appearance. Among Grade 6 to 10 students, 34% of girls and 24% of boys describe themselves as being too fat with the number of girls believing this increasing

anorexia nervosa An eating disorder characterized by low body weight and distorted body image.

FEATUREDMEDIA

Love and Adolescence

High School Musical (2006)—The status quo is challenged when basketball star Troy and science whiz Gabriella break clique barriers and audition for their school play. Musical numbers capture the internal struggles the characters are grappling with as they try on different aspects of their identities and explore friendship, love, and cafeteria politics.

Nick and Norah's Infinite Playlist (2008)—How does a plan to spite less-than-faithful partners turn into the ultimate recipe for romance (not to mention great music)?

Romeo and Juliet (1996)—A modern take on Shakespeare's classic play, set in a modern suburb. The film retains the original dialogue, and presents timeless tensions between teens and their parents.

Twilight (2008), New Moon (2009), Eclipse (2010), and Breaking Dawn, Parts 1 & 2 (2011, 2012)—These films are based on the series of popular romance novels by Stephanie Meyer, which tell the story of teenage Bella and her (much older!) vampire boyfriend Edward. Bella takes many risks to love, and be loved by, Edward.

FIGURE 8.6

Distribution of Early Menarche Rates across the Canadian Provinces (2000/2001)

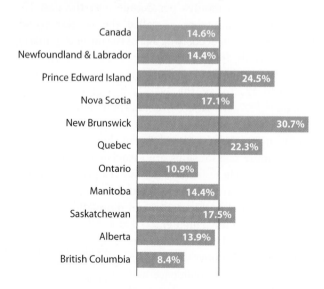

Source: Al-Sahab et al., 2010.

with grade level. However, only 15% of adolescent girls are actually overweight or obese (Public Health Agency of Canada, 2011b). Eating disorders are the third most common chronic condition among adolescents but can develop at other times in life as well. Adolescent girls are hospitalized for these disorders at a rate that is two and a half times the rate for young adult women and more than six times the rate of any other age group (Public Health Agency of Canada, 2011b). The two main types, anorexia nervosa and bulimia nervosa, have in common a deep concern about weight (Jimerson, Pavelski, & Orliss, 2002). While some symptoms are unique to one disorder, there are many parallels between anorexia and bulimia.

Anorexia nervosa is a syndrome of self-starvation, potentially leading to death. It mainly affects adolescent and young adult females, who account for up to 95% of the known cases. Professionals suspect that many males may also be victims (for example, those who must maintain a low weight for sports), but their anorexia is not as obvious and/or publicly discussed (O'Dea & Abraham, 1999). Some key features of

Provincial Differences in Onset of Puberty

Canadian researchers, working with the most recent available data from 2000–2001, have cited significant differences among provinces in the onset of puberty (Al-Sahab et al., 2010). As Figure 8.6 shows, New Brunswick and Prince Edward Island have the highest rates of early menarche while British Columbia and Ontario have the lowest. Al-Sahab et al. (2010) have noted that the provinces with the highest rates have low proportions of foreign-born residents while Ontario and British Columbia have the highest proportion of foreign-born residents.

Further, researchers have cited racial and ethnic differences in the onset of puberty (Chumlea et al., 2003; Obeidallah et al., 2000). The reasons for these differences are not clear, but lifestyle factors such as diet, use of hormone-enhanced products, and exposure to environmental agents could contribute to the differences.

Much more research is required to understand the reasons for the different rates of early menarche from province to province in Canada and how race and ethnicity, among other factors, may contribute to these differences.

▲ The image of femininity has changed over the years. How might this affect teens' perceptions of their bodies?

anorexia nervosa are inability to sustain a healthy weight, fear of any weight gain, and a greatly inaccurate perception of body image (American Psychiatric Association, 2013).

Health professionals have seen an alarming rise in the incidence of anorexia among young women in the past 15 to 20 years. Whether anorexia nervosa has actually increased or whether it is now being more readily recognized has yet to be determined.

Bulimia nervosa is a disorder related to anorexia nervosa and sometimes occurs with it. It is characterized by binge eating followed by purging to prevent weight gain. In addition, the self-evaluation of individuals with bulimia nervosa is excessively influenced by body shape and weight. Bulimia has been observed in women above and below weight, as well as in those who are of average weight, and detailed criteria may be found in the *Diagnostic and Statistical Manual of Mental Disorders*, 5th edition (or DSM-5) (American Psychiatric Association, 2013).

Despite their clinical differences, anorexics and bulimics share some emotional and behavioural traits. The preoccupation with food and the desire to be thin sometimes mask deep psychological issues that lie beneath the surface (Jimerson et al., 2002). A history of abuse—ranging from emotional to sexual—can prompt eating disorders, as can a home environment where children are raised with expectations of perfection.

> **bulimia nervosa** An eating disorder characterized by binge eating followed by purging to prevent weight gain.

Career Apps

As a school nurse, what resources could you share with young men and women to give them an accurate reference relating to body proportions and optimal health?

L04 ▶ Cognitive Development

Adolescence is a complex process of growth and change. Because biological and social changes are often the focus of attention, changes in the young adolescent's ability to think may go unnoticed, yet growth spurts in the parietal and frontal lobes of the brain, as well as subcortical regions, make possible tremendous changes in the quality of a teenager's thinking. During early and middle adolescence, thinking ability reaches Piaget's fourth and last level—the level of abstract thought.

VARIABLES IN COGNITIVE DEVELOPMENT: PIAGET

Recall from Chapter 2 that Jean Piaget proposed that the ability to think develops in four stages: the sensorimotor stage (birth to 2 years old); the preoperational stage (2 to 7 years old); the concrete operational stage (7 to 11 years old); and the formal operational stage (11 years old and up). In the **formal operational stage**, individuals can think abstractly, reason logically, exhibit hypothetical thinking, and combine groups of concrete operations. For example, the adolescent comes to understand democracy by combining concepts such as putting a ballot in a box and hearing that the House of Commons voted to provide funding to help the homeless.

It was Piaget who first noted early adolescents' bent toward democratic values because of this new thinking capacity. This is the age when youths first become committed to the idea that members of a group may change the rules of a game, but once agreed on, all members must follow the new rules. This tendency, Piaget believed, is universal; all teenagers throughout the world commit to this idea.

However, culture and gender also influence cognitive development. Many theorists focus on an ideal developmental progression that reflects their own values and beliefs about maturity. Piaget (1973) acknowledged that his description of the final stage might not apply to all cultures, as evidence showed cultural variation. The influence of context (sociocultural and individual) on development (Rogoff, 1991; Vygotsky, 1978) supports multiple directions for development rather than only one ideal end point. For example, it may be that for some agricultural societies, sophisticated development of the concrete operational stage would be far more useful than development of formal operational thinking. That is, an understanding of the complicated workings of a machine may be concrete, but that does not make that type of thinking inferior to another person's ability to write haiku.

Chavous and associates (2003) studied the effects of culture on cognition, specifically on the academic achievement of African-Americans. They compared Black adolescents on educational beliefs, performance, and level of later attainment (completing high school and college attendance). They found that African-American youths have different interpretations of their racial identities, and these beliefs may lead them down different paths of educational achievement. For instance, some adolescents who were proud of their race but felt as though society viewed their race negatively had the highest rates of post–high school achievement. Perhaps, in this case, they were motivated by their determination to overcome discrimination. Consistent with those findings, Codjoe (2006) found that African-Canadian students who excelled academically were more likely to have knowledge of and pride in their culture and heritage.

Gender also plays a role in defining formal operations. According to Gilligan (1982), most theories of development define the end point of development as being male only and they overlook alternatives that more closely fit the mature female. Gilligan believes that if the definition of maturity changes, so does the entire account of development. Using men as the model of development, researchers see independence and separation as the goals of development. If women are used as the models, the goals of development are relationships with others and interdependence. Gilligan argues that this gender difference also leads to distinctions in development of thinking about morality.

EMOTIONS AND BRAIN DEVELOPMENT

Researchers continue to study how the brain initiates complex emotions such as self-awareness, morality, feelings of free will, and social emotions. Neurons known as **spindle cells** play a large part in how the brain creates emotion (Blakeslee, 2003). These cells are responsible for sending socially relevant signals across the brain. This function, whereby the subcortex filters out all but new and/or really important information, is known as the **reticular activation system (RAS)**. The RAS protects the brain from being overwhelmed by irrelevant data. Despite great similarities among various mammals' brains, only humans and great apes have spindle cells. These cells are not present at the time of birth. Instead, they gradually appear as children develop a concept of moral and social judgments, and then develop more rapidly during adolescence.

Connections between neurons are responsible for communication between the body and the brain. As these connections become more established and complex in adolescence, information is transformed into more

formal operational stage Piaget's fourth stage of cognitive development, featuring abstract thought and scientific thinking.

spindle cells Neurons that play a large role in emotion.

reticular activation system (RAS) Complex subcortical system that protects the brain from being overwhelmed.

sophisticated understandings. Concrete information becomes associated with more intangible emotions along the path. It is through this pathway that the most basic aspects of human nature such as love, sadness, fear, excitement, and anger are processed (Blakeslee, 2003).

In a study conducted by Yurgelun (1998), adults and adolescents were shown photos depicting fear. The adults accurately identified the emotion, but most adolescents incorrectly identified the pictured emotion as anger and worry. After studying brain scans of the teens and adults, Yurgelun found that the amygdala (the part of the brain that is responsible for emotional responses) played a large role in the teens' reactions (see Figure 8.7). In contrast, the prefrontal cortex (the part of the brain that is responsible for reason and thought) played a large role in the adults' responses. Such differences between adolescent and adult brain function may impact why teens' experiences are often described as turbulent (Killgore & Oki, 2001).

ADOLESCENT EGOCENTRISM

Parents often feel frustrated by the attitudes and behaviours of their adolescent children. One explanation is the re-emergence of a pattern of thought that marked early childhood—egocentrism. **Adolescent egocentrism**, a term coined by Elkind (1978), refers to adolescents' tendency to exaggerate the importance, uniqueness, and severity of their social and emotional experiences. Their love is greater than anything others have experienced. Their suffering is more painful and unjust than anyone else's. Developmentally speaking, adolescent egocentrism seems to peak around the age of 13, followed by a gradual and sometimes painful decline as the adolescent comes to find out that he or she is not as unique and as special as once believed. (Elkind & Bowen, 1979).

Elkind sees two parts to this egocentrism. First, teenagers tend to create an **imaginary audience** (Vartanian & Powlishta, 2001). They feel they are on centre stage and that other people are constantly scrutinizing their behaviour and physical appearance. This accounts for some of the mood swings in adolescents. One minute a glance in the mirror launches an elated, confident teenager ready to take on the world, and the next minute a pimple can be cause for staying inside the house all day. In fact, school phobia can become acute during early adolescence because of concerns over physical appearance.

The second component of egocentrism is the **personal fable**. This refers to adolescents' tendency to think of themselves in heroic or mythical terms (Frankenberger, 2000; Vartanian & Powlishta, 2001). The result is that they exaggerate their own abilities and their invincibility. The personal fable sometimes leads to increased risk-taking, such as drug use, dangerous driving, and disregard for the possible consequences of sexual behaviour. Many teenagers simply can't imagine an unhappy ending to their own special story.

INFORMATION PROCESSING

As children transition into adolescence, one of the cognitive changes that is markedly different from that of earlier years is their improved **executive functioning**. Executive functioning includes efforts aimed at allocating attention, cognitive resources that can impact physical and emotional resources, and critical thinking strategies.

adolescent egocentrism Self-centred thinking patterns of childhood that sometimes occur in the teen years.

imaginary audience Adolescents' perception that others are constantly scrutinizing their behaviour and appearance.

personal fable Adolescents' tendency to think of themselves in heroic or mythical terms.

executive functioning Cognitive efforts involving attention and critical thinking.

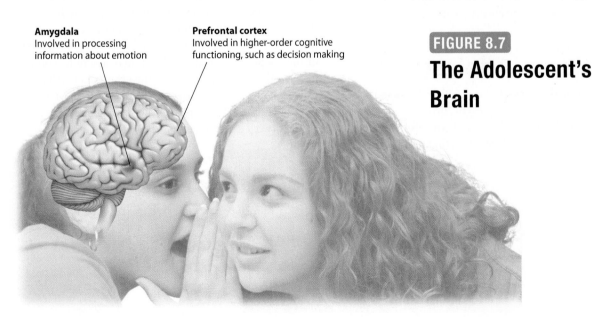

Amygdala
Involved in processing information about emotion

Prefrontal cortex
Involved in higher-order cognitive functioning, such as decision making

FIGURE 8.7

The Adolescent's Brain

convergent thinking
Thinking used when a problem to be solved has one correct answer.

divergent thinking
Thinking used when a problem to be solved has many possible answers.

As teens acquire more strategies for evaluating and solving problems, they can apply these skills to everyday decision-making in various situations (Byrnes, 2005). For example, teens must make decisions about whether or not to experiment with drugs and alcohol, which friends to bring into their close trust, and how to best prepare for college or career.

As with any skills that initially require practice before they become effortless, decision-making skills require practice in real-life situations in order for adolescents, and the adults who care for them, to become confident in their abilities. This holds true for trial-and-error experiences we have at any age, but in adolescence, when teens are poised on the verge of adult recognition and responsibility, decision-making skills come under closer scrutiny and can have larger consequences. For example, a decision to ride in a car with a close friend who has been drinking and now wishes to drive home may result in a life-threatening accident.

CRITICAL THINKING

The role of critical thinking is highlighted in adolescence as teens are able to think about a problem or situation from multiple perspectives. Critical thinking involves two abilities: convergent thinking and divergent thinking.

Convergent thinking is used when we solve a problem by following a series of steps that close in on the correct answer. Only one answer is correct. **Divergent thinking** is just the opposite: This type of thinking is used when a problem to be solved has many possible answers. Divergent thinking can be right or wrong, too, but much more leeway exists for personal opinion than with convergent thinking. Not all divergent thinking is creative, but it is more likely to produce a creative result.

L05 ▶ Identity in Adolescence

The theories of three psychologists, Erik Erikson, James Marcia, and John Hill, represent different views on adolescence and capture the complexities of this developmental period. Considered together, their theories

TECH TRENDS

Games People Play

Sudoku is an example of a game that utilizes convergent thinking—the numbers 1–9 may be placed only in specific squares to complete the game correctly (see http://www.websudoku.com).

In WordTwist, a popular online game featured in Facebook and other sites, players use divergent thinking to list as many words as possible from a mixed-up square of 16 randomly selected letters (see http://www.wordtwist.org). Story-driven games such as "Surviving High School" (http://www.ea.com/surviving-high-school-11-mobile) also encourage divergent thinking, and an infinite number of outcomes are possible, depending on the decisions players make.

provide a perspective on adolescence as a multidimensional period in the lifespan.

ERIKSON'S PSYCHOSOCIAL THEORY

For Erik Erikson (1902–1994), adolescence is the fifth stage of development, that of identity versus identity confusion. The main task is to achieve a state of identity, something toward which one strives, rather than a final, definitive identity. Erikson saw adolescence as a time of intensive exploration and analysis of ways of looking at oneself. He used the term identity crisis (see also Chapter 2) to capture the essence of confusion people feel when they experience discomfort about themselves. For example, a teen who is very smart and competent, but not part of the "popular" crowd at school, may aspire to popularity even though she knows that the group often behaves in ways that go against her personal values. She must grapple with the importance of being true to what she deems correct and what she perceives as being prized and rewarded by others.

Young teenagers today are being forced to make decisions that earlier generations didn't have to make until they were older and more **mature**, and today's teenagers are not getting much support and **guidance**.

DAVID ELKIND

Erikson suggested that identity confusion is likely in a democratic society because so many life choices are available. In a totalitarian society, youths are typically given an identity that they are forced to accept. For example, the paramilitary Hitler Youth of Germany in the 1930s is an example of a mandatory national effort backed by intense propaganda to get all adolescents to identify with prescribed values and attitudes.

Erikson proposed that, in our culture, adolescence is a period of psychosocial moratorium—a "time-out" during which adolescents experiment with a variety of identities, yet experience no responsibility for the consequences. Erikson stated that indecision—and tolerance of it—and idealism are essential in the identity-seeking process. Some youths, however, commit themselves to an identity too early, without adequately considering all choices. As youths search for truth, they are building commitments to people, belief systems, and institutions that help unite their personal values.

MARCIA'S IDENTITY STATUS

Elaborating on Erikson's ideas, James Marcia (Berzonsky & Kuk, 2000; Marcia, 2002) stresses two vital factors in the attainment of a mature identity: crisis and commitment. First, the person must undergo several crises relating to choice, such as deciding whether to hold or to give up one's religious beliefs. Second, the person must commit to these choices. A person may or may not have gone through a crisis of choice and may or may not have made a commitment to choices. Thus, four **identity statuses** are possible (see Table 8.1):

Identity confusion: No crisis has been experienced and no commitments have been made.

Identity foreclosure: No crisis has been experienced, but commitments have been made, usually forced on the person by the parent.

Identity moratorium: A number of crises have been experienced, but no commitments are made.

Identity achievement: Numerous crises have been experienced and resolved, and relatively permanent commitments have been made.

Research indicates that Marcia's identity statuses tend to progress in a linear fashion. The college years, for example, are known to be a time when adolescents make great strides in their identity development. As they are exposed to new information that presents alternate positions on numerous issues, they are forced to experience psychological and social conflicts that contribute to their sense of self and overall identity. Carol Gilligan and others (1982, 1990) have focused on gender differences in identity formation. They have concluded that women are less concerned than men with achieving an independent identity status and more likely to define themselves by their relationships and responsibilities to others.

identity statuses Marcia's categories that depict levels of crisis and commitment that contribute to a sense of identity.

TABLE 8.1

Marcia's Four Identity Statuses

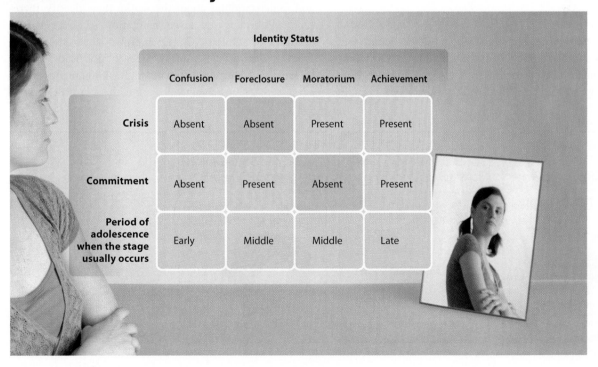

	Identity Status			
	Confusion	Foreclosure	Moratorium	Achievement
Crisis	Absent	Absent	Present	Present
Commitment	Absent	Present	Absent	Present
Period of adolescence when the stage usually occurs	Early	Middle	Middle	Late

HILL'S BIOPSYCHOSOCIAL THEORY

Relationships factor into the theory of psychologist John Hill (1987), whose biopsychosocial theory of adolescence has led to current research on a wide range of adolescent issues (Collins et al., 2001; Keel et al., 2001; Meschke et al., 2000). In Hill's theory, biological factors are central because they are present at birth. However, psychological and social factors begin playing a part immediately after birth. Each factor is embedded in the other two, and the meanings of each are tightly woven. A fourth factor running through the others is time—the aging process from early to late adolescence as well as events during a particular historical period.

Hill's ideas about psychological factors in adolescence are important to note. Hill (1973) discussed "detachment" as a matter of growing "independence in decision making and feelings of confidence in personal goals and standards of behaviour" (p. 37). Hill disagreed with the psychoanalytic view of sexuality—that change in one's sense of a sexual self follows a gradual, continuous pattern. He argued that puberty is brought on by abrupt physiological changes. The social changes involved in acquiring the new self-concept of adolescence force teens to view themselves in a whole new light, potentially influencing intimacy and relationships.

Social Development

As relationships with others assume a prominent position in adolescents' developing identity, the nature of close relationships changes. The changing roles of family and peers are noticeable as teens shift qualities of their intimate relationships from their family to their friends.

L06 ▶ THE ROLE OF FAMILY

Gauthier, Smeeding, and Furstenberg (2004) found that although mothers today spend more time in the workplace than in previous decades, they spend as much time interacting with their children as mothers did decades

ago—perhaps even more. While adolescents' relationships with both parents remain significant, mothers are generally perceived as more supportive than fathers. As adolescents begin to spend less time at home and more time with peers, conflicts with parents can help solidify peer relationships. As they strive for identity and greater independence, adolescents exert greater authority over their lives, but must also accept more responsibility for their choices. Conflict forces adolescents to consider positions with which they may initially disagree. Sometimes, conflicts within the home translate into a difficult environment for adolescents.

Family breakdown is an issue that many adolescents must deal with. Divorce tends to occur most often in families with a newborn, and second most often in families with an adolescent present. The family undergoing divorce clearly contributes additional stress to a developing adolescent. One obvious effect is economic. The increased living expenses that result from the need to pay for two homes most often lead to a significant decrease in the standard of living for the children. Young adolescents may resent being unable to keep up with their peers in terms of material goods (e.g., clothes, computer). Older adolescents are better equipped to cope with this type of additional stress psychologically and financially, because they can enter the workforce.

THE ROLE OF PEERS ◀ L07

Although it is clear that friendships are vital throughout life, there seems to be something special about the role of the peer group during adolescence. Related to the quest for identity, adolescents are attracted to qualities in others that they aspire to themselves. They also take comfort in finding others who share their personal interests, beliefs, and understandings about the world; they identify, therefore, with groups that have a reputation for certain values, attitudes, or activities. Common crowd labels among high school students include "jocks," "geeks," "pot-heads," "popular kids," and "burnouts." Interestingly, although the distinct adolescent groups change over time, these crowds seem to

ZITS © 2008 ZITS Partnership, King Features Syndicate.

exist in some form across all periods in which adolescence has been studied. Brown, Dolcini, and Leventhal (1997) made an important distinction between cliques (subgroups within crowds) and crowds: a **clique** is a group of close friends who share similar interests and activities, whereas a **crowd** is a larger, reputation-based group whose members may or may not spend time with one another.

The formation of peer friendships is an important adolescent achievement that supports an individual's developing sense of self and the desire to form relationships with others.

L08 ▶ Sexual Identity

Sexual identity is linked to other aspects of identity—to an individual's interests, lifestyle and behaviour, and evolving sexual orientation. Whereas some adolescents are comfortable with the physical and emotional sensations that accompany sexuality, others are not. Cognitive and social factors strongly influence how adolescents view their sexuality. Attractions to individuals of the same or opposite sex may be purely physical or emotional, and do not necessarily involve deeper intimacy or love.

Many people identify as **heterosexual**—attracted to members of the opposite sex—but some people experience this attraction to members of the same sex and identify as **homosexual**. Many homosexual adults recall personal struggles with attractions to people of the same sex in childhood and adolescence. Growing sensitivity to the struggles that lesbian, gay, bisexual, and transgender **(LGBT)** youth experience has helped lessen the negative effects of perceived societal norms.

The process of accepting one's sexual orientation is particularly difficult for adolescents who identify as LGBT and face a society that is not necessarily accepting of anything outside traditional expectations for males and females. "Coming out"—proclaiming one's homosexuality to others—is a significant and often painful process for adolescents, whose family and friends may not be supportive. As a result, many LGBT teens often suffer in school, resort to alcohol or drugs to cope with emotional pain, or contemplate or even commit suicide (Russell, 2006).

SEXUAL BEHAVIOUR

Masturbation is the most common sexual outlet in adolescence. Although most people still consider it an embarrassing topic, it has always been a recognized aspect of sexuality. Masturbation is a normal, healthy way for people to discharge their sexual drive, but some teens feel a sense of shame, guilt, and fear about it.

Many adolescents are sexually active, although available data show that sexual activity among Canadian adolescents appears to have declined in the past

▲ Organizations such as Parents, Families, and Friends of Lesbians and Gays (PFLAG) promote the well-being of teens and their families.

15 years, possibly the result of a growing concern about AIDS and other sexually transmitted infections (The Sex Information and Education Council of Canada, 2012). Results of the 2005 Canadian Community Health Survey indicate that the percentage of post-secondary students who have ever been sexually active is about 75% (as cited in Intini, 2007).

When do most Canadians first experience intercourse? The statistics vary, but all research confirms that adolescents are, indeed, sexually active (Gebhardt, Kuyper, & Dusseldorp, 2006; The Sex Information and Education Council of Canada, 2012). In 2009/2010, the Canadian Community Health Survey asked this question of a sample of adolescents: "Have you ever had sexual intercourse?" The results of their survey are featured in Table 8.2 (as cited in The Sex Information and Education Council of Canada, 2012). As shown, the percentage of adolescents who have ever had intercourse has decreased slightly over the last decade and a half, but more than two-thirds have had intercourse before their 20th birthday.

The decision to engage in sexual behaviour with others depends on many factors, and the timing of such decisions varies by culture, gender, and geographic location. Sexual behaviours sometimes contribute to other risk-taking behaviours. For example, risk behaviours such as drug and alcohol abuse and juvenile

clique Group of friends who share similar interests and activities.

crowd Reputation-based group whose members may or may not spend time with one another.

heterosexual Sexual attraction to members of the opposite sex.

homosexual Sexual attraction to members of the same sex.

LGBT An acronym referring to lesbian (female), gay (male), bisexual, and transgender individuals; it can include a Q for queer or questioning (LGBTQ).

TABLE 8.2

Percentage of Canadian Youth Aged 15-17 and 18-19 Reporting Ever Having Sexual Intercourse

Age Group	1996/1997	2003	2005	2009/2010
15-17	32%	30%	29%	30%
18-19	70%	68%	65%	68%

Source: Rotermann, M., 2008, 2012.

delinquency are often associated with intercourse during adolescence (Ngai, Ngai, & Cheung, 2006). Savage and Holcomb (1999) compared the sexual risk-taking behaviours of 9th- through 12th-grade female athletes and their nonathletic counterparts, and found that athletes were less likely to have engaged in risk-taking behaviours as well as less likely to be sexually active; they concluded that participation in sports is positively associated with reduced sexual risk-taking behaviours. Other factors that contribute to adolescents' sexual risk-taking are less parental supervision, a family's low socioeconomic status, and sexually active older siblings (Miller et al., 2002).

Interestingly, Schwartz (2002) found that males and females have considerable levels of sexual exploration before intercourse. Many adolescents do not think they are having sex if their physical acts stop short of actual intercourse.

How to Talk to Teens About Sex (or Anything Else)

Adolescents are more likely to talk to adults who know how to listen—about sex, alcohol, and other important issues. But certain kinds of responses, such as giving too much advice or pretending to have all the answers, have been shown to block the lines of communication.

Effective listening is more than just "not talking." It takes concentration and practice. Following are five communication skills that are useful to anyone who wants to reach adolescents. (These skills can also enhance communication with other adults.)

1. Rephrase the teen's comments to show you understand. This is sometimes called reflective listening. Reflective listening serves these purposes:

   - It assures the teenager that you hear what he or she is saying.

   - It persuades the teen that you correctly understand what is being said (it is sometimes a good idea to ask if your rephrasing is correct).

   - It allows you a chance to reword the teen's statements in ways that are less self-destructive.

TECH TRENDS

"Sexting"

A new trend called sexting refers to people sending sexually explicit messages or images via cellphones or computers. A recent study reports that 65% of 13- to 19-year-olds have sexted (Lipkins, Levy, & Jerabkova, 2009). In Canada, teens can sext one another without fear of prosecution but that is not the case in the United States (Hasinoff, 2012). The act of sending images into the public domain raises serious concerns about safety and privacy. For more information on the topic of sexting among pre-teens and adolescents, see http://www.cbc.ca/doczone/episode/sext-up-kids.html

   - It allows the teen to "rehear" and reconsider what was said.

2. Watch the teen's face and body language. Often a person will assure you that he or she does not feel sad, but a quivering chin or watery eyes will tell you otherwise. When words and body language say two different things, always consider the body language.

3. Give nonverbal support. This may include a smile, a hug, a wink, a pat on the shoulder, eye contact, or holding the person's hand (or wrist).

4. Use the right tone of voice for what you are saying. Remember that your tone communicates as clearly as your words. Make sure your tone does not come across as sarcastic or all-knowing.

5. Use encouraging phrases to show your interest and to keep the conversation going. Helpful phrases such as "Tell me more about that," spoken appropriately during pauses in the conversation, can communicate how much you care.

Remember, if you are judgmental or critical, the teen may decide that you just don't understand. You cannot be a good influence on someone who won't talk to you.

TEENAGE PREGNANCY

Each year, about 30,000 teenage girls in Canada become pregnant. About half of those pregnancies result in live births, with most of the rest resulting in abortion and a smaller number in miscarriages. In 2010, most births to teenagers (92%) were to unmarried mothers (Statistics Canada, 2012a).

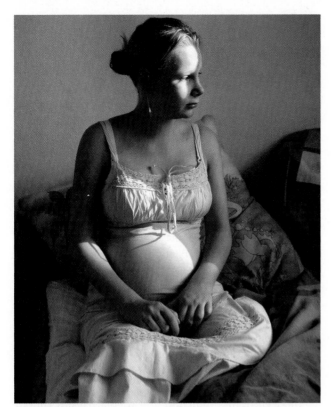

▲ Teen pregnancy in Canada has generally declined over the last four decades.

FIGURE 8.8

Births to Teenage Mothers (by region, per 1,000 female teens)

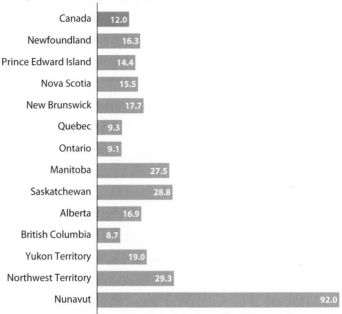

Canada	12.0
Newfoundland	16.3
Prince Edward Island	14.4
Nova Scotia	15.5
New Brunswick	17.7
Quebec	9.3
Ontario	9.1
Manitoba	27.5
Saskatchewan	28.8
Alberta	16.9
British Columbia	8.7
Yukon Territory	19.0
Northwest Territory	29.3
Nunavut	92.0

▲ *Note:* The region is the place of residence of the mother at the time of the birth. The rate of births for teenage mothers is calculated using the population of females aged 14 to 19 years.

Source: Statistics Canada, 2013b, 2013c.

FIGURE 8.9

Trends in Births to Teen Moms

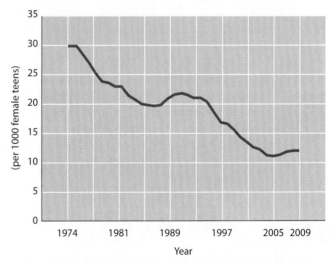

▲ *Note:* The rate of births for teenage mothers is calculated using the population of females aged 14 to 19 years.

Source: HRSDC calculations based on Statistics Canada. For 1974 to 1990: Statistics Canada. Pregnancy outcomes, by age group, Canada, provinces and territories, annual (CANSIM Table 106-9002). Ottawa: Statistics Canada, 2007; and for 1991 to 2009: Statistics Canada. Live births, by age of mother, Canada, provinces and territories, annual (CANSIM Table 102-4503). Ottawa: Statistics Canada, 2012, and Statistics Canada. Estimates of population by age and sex for Canada, provinces and territories, annual (CANSIM Table 051-0001). Ottawa: Statistics Canada, 2012.

There are many reasons that teenage girls get pregnant. Miller and associates (2001) report a series of factors that place some teens at greater risk for pregnancy: poverty, unsafe communities, a single-parent household, a history of sexual abuse, and teenage siblings who are sexually active or are parents. Another reason is the lack of accurate information that teens receive about sex and contraception, as illustrated in the example of Wendla in *Spring Awakening;* Wendla is given insufficient facts about how babies are conceived and born. Without accurate information, adolescents are less likely to make informed decisions or to recognize the consequences of their actions. Some girls desire pregnancy for social or psychological reasons: A pregnancy makes them feel accepted in society as a mother, a caregiver, or, ironically, a responsible adult. Some adolescent girls get pregnant by sheer accident.

Figure 8.8 illustrates the rate of teen pregnancy in Canada. As this figure shows, there are sizable differences among Canadian provinces and territories. Between 2006 and 2010, teen pregnancy rose in several provinces, including Manitoba, New Brunswick, Newfoundland and Labrador, and Nova Scotia although the overall rate did not change significantly during these years. The recent economic decline, which has hit some provinces harder than others, may be a contributing factor to these changes as young women perceive fewer educational and occupational opportunities for which to delay childbearing (Bielski, 2013). Despite this latest blip, the Canadian rate has declined dramatically since the mid-1970s (see Figure 8.9).

Efforts at educating teenagers about pregnancy and contraception have become more widespread, and many families want to have their adolescents informed about the risks involved in sexual activity. Whether sex education deters teens from engaging in sexual activity is not certain, but it is acknowledged to impact teens' choices to use contraception.

SEXUAL ABUSE

When adolescents are abused, it's typically by someone they know and trust. It is often a continuation of abuse that started during childhood. The most common type of serious sexual abuse is incest between father and daughter. This type of relationship may last for several years. The daughter is often manipulated into believing it is all her fault and that, if she says anything to anyone, she'll be a bad person—even be arrested and jailed—or else the father threatens to hurt the mother or a sibling. The outcome is an adolescent at greater risk for running away, having eating disorders, being a sexual victim, and engaging in substance abuse (Connors, 2001; Whitbeck et al., 2001; Yoder et al., 2002).

Adolescents who have been abused tend to discuss their abuse with a friend or with no one. Very seldom do they report it to parents, police, social workers, or other authorities. Research has also found that the effects of abuse may influence a youth's future relationships. Directly following the experience, children may engage in "acting out" behaviours (for example, truancy, running away, sexual promiscuity), but symptoms may persist for years and into adulthood (Deblinger, Mannarino, Cohen, & Steer, 2006; Hussey, Chang, & Kotch, 2006).

Adolescents are not only the victims of sexual abuse; they also are perpetrators of it (Murphy et al., 2001). Male adolescents and adults are most often behind reported abuses (Salter et al., 2003).

Research has led to increased awareness of how to support victims of sexual abuse, including reporting systems, legal definitions, and treatment of victims (Malloy, Lyon, & Quas, 2007). These strategies may help us better understand and intervene so that victims can receive professional attention earlier, reducing the long-term effects of abuse or unwanted pregnancy.

L09 ▶ Mental Health Issues

Several psychologists and psychoanalysts (most notably Freud) have suggested that the distressing, turbulent, unpredictable thoughts deemed normal in adolescence would be considered pathological in an adult. This disruptive state is partly characteristic of the identity stages of confusion and moratorium. Identity confusion is sometimes marked by withdrawal from reality. Researchers propose that true psychopathology (mental illness) is

relatively rare during adolescence. It is impossible to determine the frequency of mental illness, however, because of current disagreements over its definition. Studies do indicate that when adolescents become seriously disturbed and do not receive appropriate treatment right away, their chances of "growing out" of their problems are slim (Dacey, Kenny, & Margolis, 2006; Findling et al., 2001; Woodward, 2001).

The Chief Public Health Officer's Report on the State of Public Health in Canada studied the health and well-being of youth and young adults and issued a report in 2011 (Public Health Agency of Canada, 2011b). Adolescents suffer from a wide range of mental health disorders that affect their typical development and functioning. The most common of these are anxiety disorders (4% of children aged 12 to 19) and depression (2.7% of adolescents) with higher rates of these disorders in off-reserve Aboriginal youth and lower rates among immigrant youth (Public Health Agency of Canada, 2011b). Other disorders adolescents may experience include eating disorders, autism and other pervasive developmental disorders, attention deficit hyperactivity disorder (ADHD), conduct disorders, and substance abuse.

The Centre for Addiction and Mental Health (http://www.camh.ca) is a leader in the care and research of children, adolescents, and adults who suffer from addiction and mental health problems. Among the addictions that are now being studied are gambling and video gaming in adolescents. It is estimated that 2–4% of adolescents have a gambling problem and 12% a problem with video gaming (Centre for Addiction and Mental Health, 2011).

It is unfortunate that many teens are not treated for mental disorders because some parents and doctors believe that the problem the teen is experiencing is just part of adolescence and he or she will grow out of it. Since a number of factors may affect adolescent mental health, such as age, gender, culture, socioeconomic status, and genetics, the diagnosis and treatment of an adolescent's mental health disorder are crucial for the long-term development of the youth. It is especially important for adults to recognize the warning signs of mental health disorders in adolescents so that the adolescents may receive the support they need. Some adolescents may resist help at first for reasons of pride, embarrassment, or sheer will, but most come to appreciate the persistence of caring friends and family.

SUICIDE

Adolescent suicide represents the second leading cause of death among teenagers (Public Health Agency of Canada, 2011b). Approximately five thousand Canadian adolescents and young adults were hospitalized for an attempted suicide in 2005 with females accounting for two-thirds of that number (Public Health Agency of Canada, 2011b).

Adolescent males are three times as likely to complete suicide compared to adolescent females, however, as males tend to use more lethal methods. A number of factors increase the likelihood of a suicide attempt (Shaffer & Pfeffer, 2001). The majority of adolescents who commit suicide suffer from some associated psychiatric disorder. These teens may have poor communication with their parents, have experienced a recent stressful life event, and/or have a history of suicide attempts, substance abuse, abnormal behaviour, or self-destructive behaviour. Teens who attempt and/or achieve suicide are more likely to be friends with peers who have attempted suicide, use drugs, or have psychiatric problems (Ho et al., 2000). LGBT teens and teen survivors of childhood sexual or physical abuse are at higher risk because of factors such as family conflict and harassment at school.

First Nations youth are also at a higher risk for a variety of reasons, including poverty, a sense of hopelessness regarding educational and employment opportunities, and a sense of alienation from the rest of Canadian society. Ross (2011) believes that the legacy of residential schools, discussed in Chapter 6, has a continuing impact on today's First Nations youth as it is their parents, grandparents, and great-grandparents who suffered the indignities that these schools brought. The lasting effects of residential schools include the emotional deficits that resulted from being in such an uncaring environment. These emotional deficits, in turn, have affected how succeeding generations have been parented. First Nations youth have rates of suicide that are more than four times higher than the overall Canadian rate. The rates of suicide and attempted suicide became so high in the tiny northern Ontario First Nation community of Neskantaga (population: 400) in 2013 that a state of emergency had to be declared with the federal government promising additional nursing and counselling staff (CBC News, 2013a). The high rate of addictions in this remote community, especially among youth, along with pressure to meet the demands of the mining industry, are seen as underlying causes of the elevated rates of attempted and completed suicides.

King (2000) suggests the following warning signs for adolescent suicide:

- Depressed mood
- Substance abuse
- Loss of interest in once-pleasurable activities
- Decreased activity and attention levels
- Distractibility
- Withdrawal from others
- Sleep or appetite changes
- Morbid ideation (for example, thinking about death)

- Verbal cues ("I wish I were dead") or written cues (notes, poems)
- Giving possessions away
- A previous suicide attempt
- Low self-esteem or a recent relationship breakup
- Being homosexual
- Coming from an abusive home
- Easy access to a firearm
- Low grades
- Exposure to suicide or suicidal behaviour by another person

SUBSTANCE ABUSE

Table 8.3 highlights some results about substance abuse presented in a study conducted by researchers at the University of Waterloo (Hammond, Ahmed, Yang, Brukhalter, & Leatherdale, 2011). As these data indicate, use of most drugs did not change significantly during these years. However, there was a significant decrease in the use of glue and significant increases in the use of MDMA (ecstasy) and non-medical use of prescription drugs. Another recent study by the Canadian Centre on Substance Abuse (2011) found that both alcohol and cannabis use increase substantially between Grades 7 and 12 and that males and females had similar rates of experimentation. The major gender differences found were that males were more likely to be frequent users of cannabis and were more likely to drive after drinking alcohol than were females. The results of this study suggest that efforts at preventing abuse of alcohol and cannabis should be made no later than the early years of high school before use becomes more widespread.

Recent research points to some alarming evidence that excessive alcohol use during the teen years can impair later brain functioning (Cleveland & Wiebe, 2003). Because teenagers' brains continue to develop throughout adolescence, the toxic effects of alcohol abuse can damage their memories, learning abilities, and language skills. In addition, according to one study, teenagers who begin drinking before 14 are three times more likely to injure themselves while drinking than those who begin drinking after 21. These injuries include falls, burns, unintentional wounds, and automobile accidents (Hingson, Heeren, Jamanka, & Howland, 2000).

Not surprisingly, school context influences the prevalence of smoking and drinking among adolescents (Cleveland & Wiebe, 2003). If a school has many substance-using students, then other students are more likely to imitate the negative actions of their peers. Use of tobacco products such as kreteks (clove cigarettes)

TABLE 8.3

Substance Abuse Trends, 2002–2008

Proportion of "Ever" Drug Use Among Grades 7–9 Students											
	2002 (n=11,757)			2004 (n=16,705)			2006 (n=27,030			2008 (n=24,752)		
	Male	Female	Total	Male	Female	Total	Male	Female	Total	Male	Female	Total
Alcohol	57.1	51.7	54.5	65.6*	60.0*	62.9**	62.2	56.0	59.1*	–	–	–
Tobacco	30.8	32.2	31.5	25.8	26.7	26.2	26.7	24.6	25.7	27.6	23.5	25.6
Cannabis	19.5	16.8	18.2	17.5	16.0	16.7	18.4	15.3	16.9	19.6	14.3	17.0
Any Other drug	12.0	11.2	11.6	12.9	14.1	13.5	13.0	12.3	12.7	13.1	12.7	12.9
Hallucinogens	4.4	3.4	3.9	3.2	3.3	3.3	4.7*	3.0	3.9	5.7	3.8	4.8
Amphetamines	2.1	2.3	2.2	2.2	3.1	2.7	3.2	2.7	3.0	3.7	3.2	3.5
Cocaine	2.0	2.2	2.1	2.1	2.9	2.5	2.6	2.0*	2.3	3.3	2.3	2.8
MDMA	1.3	1.3	1.3	2.0	2.7	2.3	3.4*	2.9	3.2	4.5	4.0	4.2
Heroin	0.8	1.0	0.9	1.0	0.9	0.9	1.6	1.2	1.4*	2.5	1.0	1.8
Glue	6.1	5.6	5.9	7.4	7.6	7.5	6.7	5.8*	6.3	5.0*	4.5**	4.7***
Prescription drugs	3.2	2.7	3.0	3.5	4.3	3.9	3.9	4.8	4.3	6.6***	6.8**	6.7***
Steroids	0.9	0.6	0.7	1.8	0.8	1.3	1.9	0.9	1.4	2.3	0.8	1.6

Asterisks denote difference with previous survey year: ***p<0.001, **p<0.01, *p<0.05, – unrepeatable

Note: Alcohol "ever use" date for 2008 was unrepeatable due to question change

Source: Hammond, et al., 2011.

and bidis (hand-rolled cigarettes primarily made in India) has become popular among high school students. In 2011, the overall prevalence of nicotine use was 12% among Canadian high school students (Health Canada, 2012c), with the rate among Aboriginal youth being more than double that of non-Aboriginal youth (Elton-Marshall, Leatherdale, & Burkholder, 2011) and males outnumbering females (Statistics Canada, 2012f).

STRESS

The relationship between stress and emotional illness is well established. Therefore, it is important to know to what extent adolescents feel that their lives are stressful. The most reliable source for this information is the Higher Education Research Institute at the University of California, Los Angeles (UCLA), which has been studying this question for the past 35 years (Reisberg, 2000). Of the more than 260,000 students interviewed at 462 colleges by the institute in 2000, 30% say they feel "overwhelmed by all I have to do." This is up from 16% in 1985. The concern is almost twice as great among women (39%) than among men (20%). A significant part of this pressure comes from the need to work. The 2012 Canadian University Survey Consortium poll of graduating students showed that 6 in 10 university students are working part-time and encountering the stress of balancing school with work and other demands (as cited in *Maclean's*, 2013).

Adolescents who are not attending college are turning to long hours at work, not always with positive results. Because they are working long hours, they are getting injured more frequently on the job. Over 40% of their occupational fatalities occur when they are engaged in work prohibited by child labour laws (Wright, 2000). There are various federal and provincial regulations in place to restrict the kind of employment that adolescents can and cannot do. Generally, children under the age of 14 cannot be employed, although some provinces, such as Alberta and British Columbia, do allow children as young as 12 to work in certain fields with parental consent (Human Resources and Skills Development Canada, 2011).

Criminal Behaviour ◀L010

The overall crime rate has been dropping for the last four decades, but the one type of violence that has increased slightly is gang violence. The amount of gang violence in Canada is much less than that seen in the U.S., however. Canadian gang membership is only 1% of what is seen south of the border according to results from the 2002 Canadian Police Survey on Youth Gangs, which is the most comprehensive study of this topic (Astwood Strategy Corporation, 2004). Youth gangs in Canada are ethnically diverse with African-Canadian, First Nations, and Caucasian youth being the three most represented groups respectively. Only

Educate or Punish Cyberbullies?

While bullying has long been a problem among children and adolescents, technology has allowed for a new form of this behaviour—cyberbullying—to emerge. Cyberbullying leaves psychological rather than physical scars on victims. It involves the use of technology and the Internet to harm others and includes behaviours such as harassment and stalking. The recent cases of British Columbia teen Amanda Todd and Rehtaeh Parsons of Nova Scotia have brought further attention to this issue and whether cyberbullying should be criminalized or not. Both Todd and Parsons committed suicide as a result of the humiliation they experienced from sexually explicit materials and gossip being posted on social media. In Parsons' case, she was allegedly sexually assaulted by four boys with pictures of the assault being circulated on the internet for 2 years.

As a result of these high profile cases, Prime Minister Stephen Harper's government has promised to close any loopholes in the Criminal Code that would prevent the prosecution of perpetrators of cyberbullying. In addition, the province of Nova Scotia has passed legislation to allow for protection orders against perpetrators of cyberbullying and a fine of up to $5000 or even six months in jail for someone convicted of a first offence (CBC News, 2013b).

Wayne MacKay, a Dalhousie University law professor and chair of Nova Scotia's task force on cyberbullying and a supporter of the new legislation, states that research shows that "you can't simply demonize the bullies and say they should be sent off to some island somewhere and they're a separate species." (CBC News, 2013c). He believes that there needs to be education of both adolescents and their parents to prevent cyberbullying.

What balance of education and punishment do you believe would be most effective in reducing the incidence of cyberbullying among adolescents? How much responsibility should parents of cyberbullies be assigned?

New Brunswick, Newfoundland and Labrador, Prince Edward Island, and the three territories are without gang activity (Astwood Strategy Corporation, 2004). The level of gang violence is thought to be affected by the return from prison sentences of

> **early-onset trajectory**
> Criminal behaviour that begins before puberty.
>
> **late-onset trajectory**
> Criminal behaviour that begins after puberty.

members who may attempt to re-establish their power. To reduce gang violence, many criminologists propose that cities must reinvest in prevention programs, such as Boys and Girls Clubs and youth athletic leagues.

Numerous studies aimed at identifying the causes behind gang popularity have pointed to factors such as financial trouble, family involvement in a gang, drug and alcohol use, and social pressures (Lauber, Marshall, & Myers, 2005). Violence has also been attributed to neglect and lack of physical affection in the home environment (Field, 2002). It should be noted that most youth who join gangs have already been involved in criminal activity (Public Safety Canada, 2007). Fortunately, research shows parenting practices can reduce children's involvement with gangs (Walker-Barnes & Mason, 2004). In addition, programs and interventions help reduce violence and raise awareness in schools and communities (Wright & Fitzpatrick, 2006). Furthermore, the amount of Canadian youth crime should not be overstated, as it has been declining steadily over the past decade. This decline has been happening alongside an increased focus on diversion of youth to informal sanctions such as warnings and referrals to community programs rather than formal charges (Statistics Canada, 2011b).

Increasing attention has been paid to youth violence over the past several years. Specifically, two major paths of youth violence have been identified, known as early-onset and late-onset trajectories. The **early-onset trajectory** refers to children who commit their first violent crime before puberty (about age 13), and the **late-onset trajectory** refers to children whose criminal activity begins after puberty. Early-onset youths generally commit more serious crimes for a longer time than do late-onset individuals, often continuing this pattern into adulthood. However, the majority of youth violence is late onset and stops before adulthood.

Many factors affect how likely a young person is to engage in violent acts. These risk factors are found in family interactions as well as in peer and school influences. During childhood, risk factors include family and individual characteristics, such as poverty, antisocial parents, and aggressive behaviour. During adolescence, however, these risk factors become more peer-oriented, including associations with delinquent friends or gang membership.

As you might expect, researchers are also concerned with finding out which factors might protect young people from becoming perpetrators of violent crime. Again,

▲ Many factors influence an adolescent's likelihood to engage in criminal behaviours.

these factors exist across a number of different areas, such as individual characteristics, family, and peer groups. Examples of these protective factors include an outgoing personality, high IQ, and commitment to achievement in school.

Many are quick to blame the occurrence of youth violence on the changing Canadian family, including working mothers and non-traditional households. Others might say that youth aggression results from increased portrayals of violence in the media, such as on television, in movies, and in song lyrics. Social changes have augmented the number of intervention programs aimed at adolescents. In particular, programs designed to address the complex relationships between teens' problem behaviours have been proven effective.

Resiliency is a characteristic that can be attributed to biopsychosocial factors. Some teens may be born with a temperament that helps them recognize dangerous choices and make wise decisions. Other teens have the support of one person in their lives who buoys their spirits and gives them the strength and guidance their own developmental needs require—emotional support, academic assistance, career advice, or even the most basic needs as outlined in Maslow's hierarchy of needs, discussed in Chapter 2. When a community effort is made to support local teens, it is more likely that adolescence will be less a time of storm and stress, and more a time to lay the groundwork for the next phase of the lifespan—adulthood.

Career Apps

As a social worker at a local Boys and Girls Club, how could you assist teens and their families in developing successful conflict resolution skills?

CONCLUSIONS & SUMMARY

Defining adolescence is a complex task. Any explanation must be biopsychosocial in order to be comprehensive. In terms of biology, there is a marked increase in the flow of sex-related hormones, as well as a maximum growth spurt and the appearance of secondary sex characteristics. Psychologically, the formation of the identity is a prominent process woven throughout adolescence, and cognitive changes such as formal operations, the personal fable, and the imaginary audience occur. The social world of the teen undergoes many changes, including the inauguration of new privileges and new responsibilities.

The good news is that most adolescents develop improved mental abilities that enable them to get a more realistic view of themselves. Evidence suggests that adolescents' cognitive development evolves in stages. Contrary to earlier beliefs, thinking is qualitatively different in childhood, adolescence, and adulthood.

How should we define adolescence?

- The physical changes of adolescence, such as the onset of puberty, are only one marker of the beginning of adolescence.
- Cognitive factors relating to social values and expectations join with physical realities when considering whether one has entered adolescence.
- Hall's interpretation of adolescent development was greatly influenced by his observation that it is a period of storm and stress.

What are the key factors of physical development in adolescence?

- Those who work with adolescents need complete knowledge of the reproductive systems of both sexes.
- The order of physical changes in puberty is largely predictable, but the timing and duration of these changes are not.
- The normal range in pubertal development is very broad and includes early, average, and late maturers.
- Maturity of appearance affects whether adolescents are treated appropriately for their age.
- Early maturing is usually a positive experience for boys but may be negative for girls.
- Late maturing is often difficult for both boys and girls.

What are some challenges to physical development in adolescence?

- Two of the most disruptive problems for adolescents are the eating disorders known as anorexia and bulimia nervosa.
- Adolescent girls develop eating disorders more often than any other group.
- Developmental, cultural, individual, and familial factors are associated with the development of eating disorders.
- Teens are working longer and longer hours, and this has resulted in a serious increase in injuries on the job.

How does cognition develop during the adolescent years?

- Piaget focused on the development of the cognitive structures of the intellect during childhood and adolescence.
- Piaget's highest stage of cognitive development, formal operations, begins to develop in early adolescence.
- Adolescents focus much attention on themselves and tend to believe that everybody is looking at them. This phenomenon is called the imaginary audience.
- Many adolescents also hold beliefs about their own uniqueness and invulnerability. This is known as the personal fable.
- Critical thinking combines both convergent thinking, in which there is only one correct answer to a problem, and divergent thinking, in which there are many possible answers to a problem.
- Effective decision-making, a formal operational process, is a part of critical thinking.

What are the leading theories that attempt to explain adolescence?

- According to Erik Erikson, human life progresses through eight psychosocial stages, each of which is marked by a crisis and its resolution. The fifth stage—identity versus identity confusion—applies to adolescence.
- James Marcia's theory of identity formation includes four possible identity statuses based upon whether the adolescent has experienced a crisis of choice and made a commitment to new choices.
- John Hill's biopsychosocial theory, which includes the factor of time, offers the most inclusive theory of adolescence.

What changes have occurred in Canadian families and their roles in adolescent life in recent years?

- Canadian families have lost many traditional functions; the only remaining one is providing affection for family members.
- A number of effects of divorce pertain in particular ways to adolescents.

What is the nature of peer relations during the teen years?

- Peer groups provide adolescents with a source of social activities and support, as well as an easy entry into opposite-sex friendships.
- The biological, psychological, cognitive, and social changes of adolescence affect the development of a teenager's peer relationships.

How do teens deal with sexual relations?

- Many teenagers are sexually active.
- Homosexuality poses specific challenges for adolescents.
- Masturbation is believed to be a developmental, universal form of human sexual expression.
- Many teens still obtain a great deal of information and misinformation about sex from their peers.

- Effective listening skills are essential for parents who wish to maintain good communication with their adolescents.
- It has been found that teens are at a greater risk of becoming a teenage parent if they live in poverty, unsafe communities, or a single-parent household, or if they have a history of sexual abuse.

What mental health issues are seen in adolescence?

- The idea that those who develop mental illness during adolescence will "grow out of it" is not supported by research. Depression can be an especially dangerous illness at this age.
- Adolescence is not a time of turmoil and distress for most teens. Rates of mental disturbance among teens are very similar to rates of disturbance among adults.

What recent information do we have on adolescent illegal behaviour?

- Drug, alcohol, and tobacco abuse are still a problem among teens, though less so than in previous years.
- There has been growing concern among Canadian police over adolescents' participation in gang violence.

For REVIEW

1. Should children be taught about their bodily functions in school, and should this teaching include information about sexuality? How might you design a program to teach adolescents about potentially awkward, socially charged topics that are based in biology but have extreme social relevance?

2. Describe family life in Canada 50 years from today. What biological, psychological, and social factors are at the core of your ideas, and why?

3. You are the mayor of a medium-sized city. What actions would you take to try to reduce adolescents' high-risk behaviours and promote and sustain healthy alternatives? Whom would you need to involve as partners in your efforts?

Chapter REVIEW TEST

1. What marks the onset of puberty?
   a. menarche for females; first ejaculation for males
   b. the growth spurt for females and males
   c. the beginning of breast development for females; the enlargement of the genitals for males
   d. No single event marks the onset of puberty.

2. The identity status in which numerous crises have been experienced and resolved and relatively permanent commitments have been made is called
   a. identity moratorium.
   b. identity achievement.
   c. foreclosed identity.
   d. confused identity.

3. To think of oneself in heroic or mythical terms is known as
   a. egocentrism.
   b. imaginary audience.
   c. the personal fable.
   d. invincibility.

4. What occurs during Piaget's formal operational stage?
   a. Concrete operations combine to become formal operations.
   b. Preoperations turn into formal operations.
   c. Parts of the sensorimotor stage turn into formal operations.
   d. The preoperational stage and the sensorimotor stage combine to become formal operations.

5. To solve problems that have only one correct answer, we are using _____ thinking.
   a. divergent
   b. convergent
   c. creative
   d. critical

6. The process of declaring one's homosexuality to others is called
   a. identification.
   b. individuation.
   c. coming out.
   d. walkabout.

7. What reason is cited in the text for why there may be a decline in early sexual activity?
   a. concern about AIDS and other sexually transmitted infections
   b. prevailing conservative attitudes
   c. more people devoting time to making money
   d. increasing influence of religion

8. Risk factors that predict teenage pregnancy are
   a. poverty.
   b. growing up in a single-parent household.
   c. both a and b
   d. neither a nor b

9. The youth crime rate in Canada has ___ over the last decade.
   a. increased
   b. stayed the same
   c. fluctuated greatly
   d. decreased

10. Which of the following is the most common mental health problem seen in adolescence?
    a. anxiety disorders
    b. depression
    c. autism
    d. eating disorders

EARLY
ADULTHOOD

As You READ

After reading this chapter, you should be able to answer the following questions:

LO1 ▶ How are Canadian youths being initiated into adulthood today?

LO2 ▶ What are the significant factors affecting physical development in early adulthood?

LO3 ▶ How does cognition change during the early adult years?

LO4 ▶ What are the relationships between sexual identity and gender roles?

LO5 ▶ How do young adults deal with the interpersonal relationships of sexuality and love?

LO6 ▶ What factors affect Canadian marriages and families?

LO7 ▶ What patterns of work typify young adults today?

When does adolescence end and adulthood begin? Is the transition the same around the world? Whereas adolescence is often distinguished by physical changes and capabilities, adulthood is marked more by social and cultural experiences. Many different factors contribute to the transition from adolescence into adulthood, but some may be considered inappropriate by society's standards.

L01 ▶ Initiation into Adulthood

Families and cultural groups have always given meaning to the inevitable passage of time through ritual and ceremony. In modern society, our desire to mark life's transition points is still strong (Cushing, 2012). Throughout the world, adolescents readily engage in transitional activities because they want (or are forced) to be tested, to prove to themselves and society that they have achieved such adult virtues as courage, independence, and self-control. Adolescents should prove that they have attained these traits before being admitted to the "club of maturity"; it is through these activities that an adolescent begins to transition into adulthood.

EMERGING ADULTHOOD IN CANADA

Today, the period between childhood and adulthood, what we know as adolescence, is an entire stage of life. This stage lasts for years, not months. The point when an individual actually becomes an adult is less obvious (Cushing, 2012). The term **emerging adulthood** is commonly used to identify the transition into adulthood. Young adults tend to engage in exploration and experimentation as they attempt to navigate their life paths, often with little structure to guide them.

Traditional initiation rites are not really appropriate for today's Canadian emerging adults. For example, in preindustrial societies, the tribe determined individual status, and success or failure for the tribe determined the prestige of its members. Family background and individual effort usually made little difference. Social scientists call this an **ascribed identity**.

In earlier times in Canada, few children from poor families became merchants, doctors, or lawyers. Today, personal effort and commitment, coupled with family and community support, play a far greater role in an individual's economic and social success. This is called an **achieved identity**. Achieved identity plays a larger role in early adulthood than ascribed identity because of an individual's investment in his or her life course, even though the values of certain cultures continue to dictate roles based on sex and gender.

This is not to say that Canadians have no activities that signal the passage to maturity. We have a number of types of activities, which usually happen at various ages and signal the onset of adulthood in symbolic as well as practical terms (see Table 9.1). Warren Clark, a senior analyst with *Canadian Social Trends*, wrote "Delayed Transitions of Young Adults." In this article, he examines five transitions that many young people make on their way to adulthood: leaving school, leaving their parents' home, having full-time work, entering conjugal relationships, and having children (Clark, 2009).

THE BOOMERANG GENERATION

In recent years, social scientists have found that the transition to adulthood is taking longer to complete. Young people are living with their parents longer, are more highly educated, and attend school for more years than their parents did.

Data from the 2011 census shows that 42% of young Canadian adults between 20 and 29 still live with their parents. Young adults in Canada are either taking a long

emerging adulthood Transition from adolescence to adulthood (approximately ages 18 to 25 years); includes exploration and experimentation.

ascribed identity An individual's sense of self based on the determination of others, not the individual.

achieved identity An individual's sense of self that is based on personal effort and commitment.

Initiation Rites Around the World

There is no one way to cross from childhood into adulthood, and many rituals have existed for thousands of years—attesting to the importance of such acts in societies around the world. Some rites involve physical acts, whereas others are social or introspective. Despite variations, there appears to be a human need to mark the transition into adulthood.

Maasai (Kenya/Tanzania). The Maasai people believe that boys should demonstrate their bravery and skill by hunting lions with spears. In a society that values warrior-like abilities, surviving such a hunting experience demonstrates competence and signals the male's ability to protect the group, ensuring its survival.

Bar/Bat Mitzvah (Israel/worldwide). The Jewish people have been following the tradition of a boy's bar mitzvah for thousands of years and, more recently, a girl's bat mitzvah. In this ceremony, the 13-year-old chants memorized passages of Torah and leads a portion of a religious service, after which he/she is deemed a responsible adult member of the group. In today's society, when life expectancy is much longer than it was thousands of years ago, 13-year-olds are hardly considered adults. When the ceremony originated (over 5000 years ago), however, 13 years may have been one third of a person's life.

Walkabout (Australia). The Aborigines have a tradition of sending their adolescent males into the bush for approximately 6 months, where they are expected to fend for themselves. Upon their return, they are respected for their ability to survive and they can contemplate their roles as members of the group. By surviving themselves, they have proven themselves capable of contributing to the group's survival.

Isolation Period (First Nation Canadians). First Nations young men and women take part in a time of isolation. For a woman, it is called a Berry Fast and is designed to bring awareness to the fact that she is a young woman now. For young men, it occurs when their voice changes and ends after they have killed their first animal.

Ritual Circumcision (Africa). In many African countries, there is a practice of circumcising young men and women as a sign of their eligibility for marriage and adulthood. There has been a growing movement to raise awareness of female genital cutting (FGC), a practice that in some countries is done without the woman's consent and can result in lack of sensation during intercourse and severe mental and physical damage.

TABLE 9.1

North American Rites of Passage

Religious
- Bar/bat mitzvah
- Confirmation
- Baptism

Physical
- Menarche (first menstruation)
- Nocturnal emissions (male "wet dreams")
- First sexual encounter
- Beginning to shave

Educational
- Getting a driver's licence
- Graduating from high school
- Going away to college/university

Social
- Going to the senior prom
- Joining a gang, fraternity, or sorority (hazing)
- Moving away from family and relatives
- Joining the army
- Getting married
- Becoming a parent
- Voting for the first time

Economic
- Getting a chequing account or credit card
- Buying a first car
- Getting a first job
- Buying a first house

start their own households (Rennie, 2012).

Women tend to go through some of these transitions at a younger age than men. Women are more likely to leave home, marry, and have children at a younger age; young men, on the other hand, leave school earlier and have full-time employment at a younger age. It also appears that young adults in general are taking more time to complete the first transition—leaving home—so the transition through the other stages is then prolonged. Since each subsequent transition takes longer to complete, this stretches the process from their late teens to their early 30s.

time to leave their parents' home or they are returning after being away for a while (Rennie, 2012). This is not just a Canadian issue but a global one as well. In North America, these individuals are called Boomerangs for their tendency to keep coming home (if they ever left in the first place). In Italy, they are referred to as Bamboccioni, or big babies; in the U.K., where one in three parents are remortgaging their homes to support adult kids, they are called Yuckies—Young, Unwitting, Costly Kids (CBC News, 2012b).

There are a number of reasons adult children aren't leaving their parents' homes or are returning—a lack of money to support themselves, large students loans that make it difficult to have money for rent or mortgage, inability to find a job after university or college, or divorce. Statistics Canada says young men are more likely than young women to live at home. One possible reason, the agency suggested, could be that women tend to get into relationships earlier than men, so they move out sooner to

Physical Development L02

Physical development provides clear evidence of a person's markedly different appearance and abilities in adulthood, and transcends cultural boundaries. Psychologist Malcolm Knowles (1989) defined the biopsychosocial facets of adulthood as (1) biological—when we reach the age at which we can reproduce, (2) psychological—when we arrive at a self-concept of being responsible for our own lives, and (3) social—when we start to take on adult roles and responsibilities. Let's consider Knowles's first defined area—physical development.

THE PEAK IS REACHED

Early adulthood is the life period during which physical changes slow down after the dramatic changes that occur in adolescence (see Table 9.2).

TABLE 9.2

Physical Development in Early Adulthood

Height
Female: maximum height reached at age 18.
Male: maximum height reached at age 20.

Weight
Female: 14-pound weight gain and increase in body fat.
Male: 15-pound weight gain.

Muscle Structure and Internal Organs
From age 19–26: Internal organs attain greatest physical potential. The young adult is in prime condition as far as speed and strength are concerned.
After age 26: Body slowing process begins. Spinal disks settle, causing decrease in height.

Fatty tissue increases, causing increase in weight. Muscle strength decreases. Reaction times level off and stabilize. Cardiac output declines.

Sensory Function Changes
The process of losing eye lens flexibility begins as early as age 10. This loss results in difficulty focusing on close objects. During early adulthood, women can detect higher-pitched sounds than men.

Nervous System
The brain continues to increase in weight and reaches its maximum potential by the adult years.

> Carpe, carpe diem.
> Seize the day, boys—make
> your lives extraordinary.
>
> JOHN KEATING, *DEAD POETS SOCIETY* (1989)

ORGAN RESERVE

Organ reserve refers to the part of the total capacity of our body's organs that we do not normally need to use. Our bodies are designed to do much more than they are usually called upon to do. Much of our functional capacity is thus held on reserve. As we get older, these extra resources grow smaller. The peak performance capacity of each of our organs, muscles, and bones declines approximately 1% per year after age 30, and it varies from person to person. The most significant decreases in organ reserve occur in the heart, lungs, and kidneys. A 50-year-old man might fish all day with his 25-year-old son and take a long walk with him without becoming exhausted, but he has little chance of winning a footrace against him.

Of course, some individuals regularly try to use the total capacity of their organ reserves. Professional athletes are an example. Here again we see evidence of biopsychosocial interactions: Biology sets the limits, but psychological factors (such as the perseverance to train) and social factors (such as the cheering crowd) determine whether the person can push the limits.

THE EFFECT OF LIFESTYLE ON HEALTH

Young adults are healthier than older adults in just about every way. Good health is clearly related to influences such as genetics, a factor that is beyond a person's control. Increasingly, however, people are realizing that their lifestyle plays an enormous role in their own health.

Diet and Nutrition

Nutrition plays an important role throughout human development. In early adulthood, however, increasing evidence demonstrates the influence of nutrition on two major health concerns, heart disease and cancer. Medical science has established a link between heart disease and **cholesterol**, a natural substance in the blood. Cholesterol, specifically low-density lipoprotein (LDL), has been found to leave deposits on the walls of blood vessels, blocking the flow of blood to the heart and brain. The main culprit in high levels of LDL cholesterol is diets high in fat. Changes to the typical Canadian diet need to be made. The Canada Food Guide recommends reducing fat intake by choosing skim, 1%, or 2% milk, by consuming lean meat and meat alternatives more often, and by

▲ Physical disabilities do not have to limit an individual.

avoiding trans fats (for example, hydrogenated oils used to cook fried chicken and French fries) these dietary adjustments will help lower cholesterol in the body.

Although young adults tend to feel healthy and fit, the nutrition choices they make are not always healthy. Building on the foundation laid in earlier years, young adults who make poor nutrition choices over time compound the results of earlier nutrition, which might lead to later health problems. In the film *Super Size Me*, filmmaker Morgan Spurlock documented the unwelcome effects that a month of eating only at McDonald's had on his biological, psychological, and social well-being. Facts presented in this eye-opening documentary have had a life-changing impact on many who have seen it.

The Canada Food Guide recommends eating at least one dark green and one orange vegetable each day. It also suggests that half of the grain products you consume should be whole grain and that you should make every food serving count wherever you are—at home, at school, at work, or when eating out. Although healthy foods are often not as readily available as fast food options, a little planning can help you to improve your diet. To find a fruit and farm market near you, go

organ reserve
The part of the total capacity of our body's organs that we do not normally need to use.

cholesterol Substance in the blood that can adhere to the walls of the blood vessels, restricting blood flow and causing strokes and heart attacks.

Career Apps

As a registered dietician, how would you work with college students to increase their awareness about healthy eating and overall lifestyle choices?

to www.manta.com where they currently list the location for 933 fruit and vegetable markets located across Canada. There are also food co-op companies that deliver fresh produce right to your door.

Experts argue that our current society has become "obesogenic," meaning that we live in an environment that promotes increased food intake, unhealthy foods, and a sedentary lifestyle (see Figure 9.1). The Public Health Agency of Canada suggests finding an activity you like and getting moving. This will make it easier to maintain a healthy body weight. They also suggest eating balanced meals, choosing foods from the four food groups as outlined in Canada's Food Guide (Public Health Agency of Canada, 2011d). Recent decisions such as the one to eliminate trans fats from many foods, and media attention to the dangers of trans fats in films such as *Food Inc.* (2008), have had a strong influence on the food choices made by young adults, as well as the choices of the aging parents and children that young adults care about.

Physical Fitness

Popular exercise trends in recent years include activities as diverse as Pilates, spinning, Zumba, and boot camp classes. Health benefits are an obvious reason for this enthusiasm for exercise, but among young adults, the social aspects of working out add to the benefits of the physical activity. One of the challenges in early adulthood is finding time for work, exercise, and social activities, so workouts can potentially help balance the busy lives of young adults along with providing real health boosts. Studies have shown that women who increase their physical activity by 2.5 hours a week can add months to their lives (Fitzpatrick, 2003). Moderately intense exercise, such as brisk walking, also reduces the risk of stroke, osteoporosis, some types of cancer, and diabetes.

▲ Young adults often find it difficult to incorporate exercise into their busy schedules.

Many corporations are now providing the time and facilities for employees to build regular exercise into their workday, which is much appreciated by young adults who may have been used to flexible daily schedules in earlier years. Health insurance programs often offer reduced rates to exercise facilities or rebates for membership, looking at the long-term gain of having healthier members of all ages.

FIGURE 9.1

Canadian Obesity Rates, 2011

▶ Obesity rates by province and territory, lighter colours signify lower obesity rates.

Source: Gotay et al., 2013.

Use of Alcohol

Most people consume alcohol to attain the relaxed, uninhibited feeling that alcohol tends to produce. In fact, alcohol dulls the senses. Specifically, it decreases reaction times in the brain and nervous system, and it inhibits the immune system. Heavy drinking is defined as having consumed five or more drinks, per occasion, at least once a month during the past year. This level of alcohol consumption can have serious health and social consequences, especially when combined with other behaviours such as driving while intoxicated. In 2010, males aged 18 to 19 (39.2%) and 20 to 34 (41.1%) were the most likely to report heavy drinking, and females aged 18 to 19 (26.1%) and 20 to 34 (20.2%) were more likely to report heavy drinking than females in all other age groups (see Figure 9.2) (Statistics Canada, 2011a). The statistics show that young adulthood is the time when an individual consumes the most alcohol.

▲ Alcohol can have serious health and social consequences.

Use of Tobacco

Cigarette smoke—a combination of tar, nicotine, carbon monoxide, and various other chemicals—has been proven to cause lung and esophageal cancer, heart disease, and chronic lung disease. It also increases heart rate and blood pressure, constricts blood vessels, and reduces oxygen supply to tissue, thereby straining the heart. However, these sobering facts are not enough to convince many young adults to avoid or quit smoking.

The percentage of the Canadian population that smokes cigarettes has been dropping steadily since anti-smoking efforts began in earnest in the 1970s (CBC News, 2011a). Even though fewer people are smoking today, tobacco still kills about 37,000 Canadians a year (www.lung.ca). People between the ages of 18 and 34—young adults—form the highest proportion of smokers at 28 percent.

Peer pressure from friends is the major reason that young adults smoke. Some see smoking as a way of appearing more mature. Others, especially females, believe that smoking will either help them lose weight or keep them from gaining weight.

To date, more than 300 communities in Canada have by-laws or policies restricting smoking in public places and this number continues to grow. This legislation is usually enacted at local or municipal levels in Canada because the federal government does not have jurisdiction in the majority of these premises (Health Canada, 2012a). Manitoba, Nova Scotia, Newfoundland and Labrador, and Ontario have also prohibited smoking in vehicles with children under 14 years of age (Mullins, 2009).

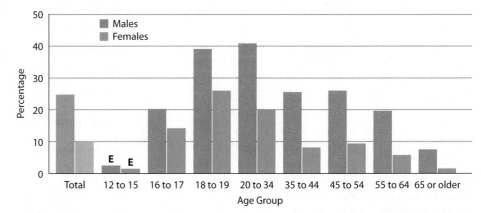
▲ Smoking bylaws in many provinces are making it less enticing for young adults to start or continue smoking.

FIGURE 9.2

Alcohol Use In Canada

▶ Percentage who consumed 5 or more drinks per occasion at least 12 times a year, by age group and sex, household population aged 12 or older, Canada, 2010

E Use with caution (coefficient of variation 16.6% to 33.3%).

Source: Canadian Community Health Survey, 2010; Statistics Canada, 2012. CANSIM 105-0501 and Cat. No. 82-221-X. Published by authority of the Minister responsible for Statistics Canada. © Minister of Industry, 2013. All rights reserved. Use of this publication is governed by the Statistics Canada Open License Agreement.

Chronic Disease

In terms of speed and strength, young adults are in peak condition. A healthy young adult can participate in relatively strenuous activity for years without concern for injury due to age-related restrictions. As the aging process continues, however, the individual will notice a decline in energy and strength. Although early adulthood also marks the beginning of a time when many bodily functions are less efficient, most young adults tend to rate their health as "good" or even better, and tend to report few limitations due to chronic illness.

The Public Health Agency of Canada conducted the Survey on Living with Chronic Diseases in Canada (SLCDC) to provide information on the impact of chronic disease on individuals as well as the effect of managing their health condition. The primary chronic disease for 20-year-olds and over is diabetes.

L03 ▶ Cognitive Development

Young adults' ability to confront challenges is in part due to cognitive changes that occur in early adulthood. In early adulthood, people are able to capitalize on the life experience they've gained prior to and during adolescence, as seen in their ability to focus on a specific area of knowledge and apply information to a specific task. For example, at this time of life, people are able to identify an area of interest or something that they are curious about, and then pursue that topic with formal and informal research. A student curious about Canadian history and Aboriginal people can develop a research plan to answer questions relating to politics and other forces that contributed to socioeconomic inequities.

PIAGET AND EARLY ADULTHOOD

Although both adolescents and adults fall into Piaget's formal operational stage of cognitive development, Piaget argued that young adults generally possess more knowledge than adolescents, especially in specific areas of interest. This is not surprising, given that young adults are older than adolescents and have therefore amassed more everyday life experiences than adolescents. Over the course of cognitive development through the lifespan, some people develop successful strategies for planning and testing ideas, whereas others may never demonstrate that level of thinking and action.

postformal thought
A proposed cognitive development stage after Piaget's formal operations in which people acknowledge the relativistic nature of problems and answers.

Some theorists have argued for another stage of cognitive development, known as **postformal thought**. Postformal thought is more flexible and less absolute than formal operational thought. It takes into account the relativistic

TECH TRENDS

Mindful Living

Many experts in a variety of fields are emphasizing the importance of being in touch with our thoughts and feelings—and the connections between these and our bodies—for healthy living. This is especially important for young adults, who are beginning to take on more responsibilities and become less dependent on others for financial and emotional support. During these years, there is often an increase in stress in the course of everyday life experiences.

Mindfulness is defined as a calm awareness of one's feelings, one's body, and one's consciousness, and is linked to Buddhist and other teachings. The growing profile of Eastern practices such as yoga and tai chi has brought about an interest in meditation as a way to incorporate mindfulness into everyday living.

Among young adults, the growing use of iPods, iPhones, and other portable electronic devices makes a tranquil meditation setting as close as a click away. Popular apps can be found on iTunes and other sites, and include the following:

Mindfulness Meditation: Guided meditations written and spoken by the author of *Meditation for Dummies*, Stephan Bodian.

Meditation Timer: A simple application that provides users with a timer to prepare for meditation, a timer for the actual meditation, and a bell to begin the meditation.

Bubbles: Visuals and sounds of delicate bubbles floating and popping in a relaxing format that lends itself to focusing on thoughts and feelings.

iZen Garden: A daily inspirational quotation; then a tap takes you to a Zen garden of your own design; you choose from stones, shells, sands, rakes, and background sounds.

nature of problems and answers; it acknowledges that the answers to big questions may never be found. In early adulthood, such questions might involve religion, politics, love, and feelings about home and work.

L04 ▶ Gender and Sexuality

Betty Friedan's 1963 book, *The Feminine Mystique*, marked the beginning of a worldwide re-examination of the female gender role and identity. Sparked in part by Friedan's book, the **feminist movement**, defined broadly as a social and political movement that seeks to establish equality for women in all aspects of life, has fostered a new commitment to women's issues and to studies of women themselves. We are still undergoing societal inquiry into the appropriate gender roles of both sexes. As men and women enter early adulthood, confusion about gender roles may compound confusion about their identity. Images in the media and among celebrities present ideas about what is desirable for each sex and their behaviour in society.

First, we need to distinguish between **sexual identity** and gender role. Sexual identity refers to those physical characteristics that are part of our biological inheritance—genetic traits that make us males or females. This relates to how we think of ourselves in terms of sexual and romantic attraction. Gender role, in contrast, is a set of expected behavioural traits associated with men and women in a given social system at any one time—how a person is supposed or not supposed to dress, act, behave, think of him- or herself, and so on. For example, in North American society, it is still more likely that men will be the primary breadwinners in a household, but no known physical cause accounts for this difference. People may accept or reject their sexual identity, their gender role, or both.

ASPECTS OF GENDER ROLE

Some people accept their sexual identity but reject their gender role. Gender role itself has two aspects:

▼ Media plays a significant role in society's views of gender roles.

FEATURED MEDIA

Women's Thinking Portrayed in Films

The Color Purple (1985)—Can the bonds of friendship give women the strength to accept the hands they've been dealt, or to take control of their own lives despite societal obstacles posed by race and gender?

North Country (2005)—How do some women find the strength to stand up for their right to choose any career they want, even if they have to endure harassment from others?

The Sisterhood of the Travelling Pants (2005)—As their life paths lead them in different directions, how can four friends maintain their close connection and still develop their own unique identities in early adulthood?

The Women (2008)—A woman learns that her husband is having an affair. How will her friends help and support her?

- *Gender-role orientation.* Individuals differ in how comfortable they feel about their gender role. Some young adults don't want to characterize themselves according to strict definitions relating to male versus female or heterosexuality versus homosexuality, and prefer to belong to the categories in varying degrees.

- *Gender-role expectations.* Some individuals feel unhappy about their gender role and want society's expectations to change. Even though women commonly have full-time jobs, for example, they are still often expected to be primary caregivers to children and take care of the household. The feminist movement, however, has had a major impact on many of the world's societies in this regard.

Some research indicates that people's gender roles evolve, partly because of relationships with important individuals. Some research suggests that mothers influence the development of their daughters' gender-role attitudes in early life, whereas daughters may influence the development of their mothers' gender-role attitudes as they both mature (Balsam & Fischer, 2006).

> **feminist movement** A social and political movement that seeks to establish equality for women in all aspects of life.

> **sexual identity** How a person thinks of himself or herself in terms of sexual and romantic attraction, linked to genetic traits/physical characteristics of male and female.

Chapter 9 Early Adulthood • 215

TAKE A **STAND**

Gender Differences and Conflict Resolution

Researchers Toussaint and Webb (2005) surveyed 127 individuals, 45 men and 82 women, and found that while women showed higher levels of empathy than men did, empathy was more important for men in terms of forgiveness and resolving conflicts. Such gender differences, however, are not cast in stone. Despite new understandings of the differences in male and female biology, society is clearly guiding the sexes toward less rigid gender roles. As a result, developmental theorists tend to agree on a view of identity that holds men and women are really more similar, especially in our need to interrelate, than we have realized.

Are there gender differences in empathy and forgiveness when men and women engage in conflicts? Do men and women seem different only because we have been taught to think so?

▲ Mother-daughter pair Blythe Danner and Gwyneth Paltrow are one example of women whose relationship influences many aspects of their identity.

EVOLUTIONARY PSYCHOLOGY

Evolutionary psychology presents a more recent theory about gender roles that reflects a biological viewpoint. Proponents of this view hold that our evolutionary history has biologically predisposed men and women to act in certain ways and has constrained us from acting in others (Bjorklund & Pellegrini, 2000; Buss, 2001; Grossman & Kaufman, 2002). Gender-bound behaviours are thought to have evolved over time because they serve a useful purpose.

Over the many centuries of human development, males and females have developed expectations about gender that are linked to biological abilities. For example, many women in early adulthood think about motherhood, which includes the physical act of conceiving and delivering a baby as well as the emotional issues relating to choices about partner, career, and identity. Many males of this age begin to think about their responsibility for protecting and providing for a family, as well as issues relating to partner, career, and identity. For example, current advances in assisted reproduction technologies (as discussed in Chapter 3) have added a new dimension to the previously accepted limits on men and women as determined by biology, affording more flexibility in gender roles and responsibilities.

androgyny Gender-role identification that allows expression of both male and female gender roles.

ANDROGYNY

One gender-role researcher, Sandra Bem (1999), argues that stereotypical gender roles are unhealthy. She has posited that highly masculine males tend to have better psychological adjustment than other males during adolescence, but as adults they tend to become highly anxious and neurotic and often experience low self-acceptance. Highly feminine females suffer in similar ways. Bem believes we would all be much better off if most behaviours were viewed as appropriate to both sexes. **Androgyny** is not merely the midpoint between two poles of masculinity and femininity. Rather, it is a level of gender-role identification that allows expression of both masculine and feminine gender roles.

Identity precedes intimacy for men. . . . For women, intimacy goes with identity, as the female comes to know herself as she is known, through her **relationships** with others.

CAROL GILLIGAN

Androgyny refers to the ability to behave in a way appropriate to a situation, regardless of one's sex. For example, when a male co-worker takes credit for a successful marketing campaign, the traditional female role calls for a woman to look disapproving but to say nothing. The androgynous female would correct the interpretation of the situation and give credit where credit is due. When an unattended baby starts to cry, the traditional male response is to look slightly uncomfortable and find the nearest woman to comfort the baby. The androgynous male would pick up and attempt to soothe the infant. Not surprisingly, Joensson and Carlsson (2000) found that people who were more androgynous

▲ Many young adults today are choosing careers that had traditionally been performed by the opposite sex.

FIGURE 9.3

Global Perspective on the Number of Sex Partners in 2005

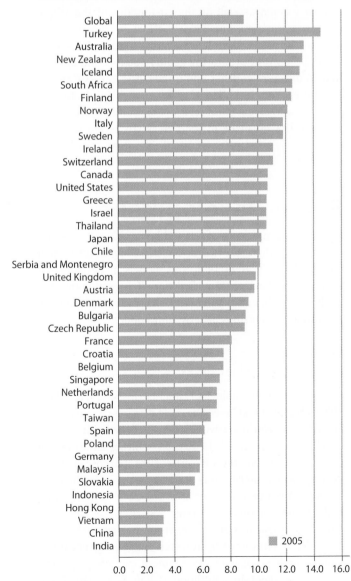

Source: Data from Durex Sexual Wellbeing Global Survey, 2008. www.durex.com/en-ca/sexualwellbeingsurvey

were rated as more creative than people who were either strongly masculine or strongly feminine. Unhindered by restrictive stereotypes, they were able to act according to their instincts.

SEXUAL BEHAVIOUR

In Chapter 8, we noted that in recent years sexual activity among Canadian adolescents appears to have declined. According to a global study performed by the company Durex in 2005, the average number of sexual partners an individual has had is 9. The Canadian average was just above that at 10.7 (see Figure 9.3). The 2002 Canadian Contraception Study found that 35% of unmarried 18- to 34-year-old women who had ever had intercourse were currently using condoms as a method of birth control. Unfortunately, there is very little information about the sexual risk and condom use of the general adult population. This lack of research is a particular concern in the case of adults in their twenties and early thirties because they are likely to be at a higher risk for sexually transmitted infections including human immunodeficiency virus (HIV) (Rotermann and McKay, 2009).

SEXUALLY TRANSMITTED INFECTIONS (STIs)

Although HIV infection rates appear to be relatively low on campuses, rates of other sexually transmitted infections (STIs), such as chlamydia and gonorrhea, are soaring. Chlamydia is the most commonly reported STI in Canada (Public Health Agency of Canada, 2006). This is a bacterial infection that occurs most often among young adults, primarily because the symptoms are virtually invisible. At its worst, chlamydia can cause damage to a woman's reproductive organs and can cause blindness in men and women.

The practice of "pack dating"—going out in groups rather than dating one on one with a romantic partner—may be an attempt, in part, to lessen the risk of contracting an STI. Choosing a sex partner from a small circle of friends allows a person to know the histories and habits of the potential partners, possibly reducing risk. Another explanation for pack dating is that young adults simply don't have time for relationships. Many young adults hold at least one job while carrying a full course load in school, and others are focused on earning grades that will help get them into graduate school or land a desirable job. After graduation, young adults tend to push themselves to achieve career status, a priority that can be consuming in terms of time and energy.

SEXUAL ASSAULT AND SEXUAL HARASSMENT

Women are often the victims of unwanted sexual acts—forcible sex and inappropriate sexual remarks and/or contact. College-age women are four times more likely than women of other ages to be sexually assaulted, which makes this issue especially relevant for young adults (Humphrey & Kahn, 2000).

In 1983, the Criminal Code of Canada was amended to replace the crimes of **sexual assault** and indecent assault with three new sexual assault offences, which focus on the violent rather than sexual nature of the offence. This legislation also clarified that males or females could be the victim of sexual assault (Brennan and Taylor-Butts, 2008).

A form of sexual assault, **date rape** is coercive sexual activity between a victim and an offender who is known or an acquaintance. It is generally considered as criminal a behaviour as a sexual assault perpetrated by a stranger. Victims of date rape often do not perceive the event as sexual assault and hence may be reluctant to report the incident to authorities. Reporting date rape can be emotionally difficult, and victims of date rape are encouraged to get help from support groups for those who have been victims of violence.

Sexual assault is common in areas where alcohol is consumed, such as nightclubs and bars. Mild sexual assaults occur on the dance floors of nightclubs across Canada on a nightly basis.

Whereas sexual assault refers to forced sexual intercourse, **sexual harassment** refers to a broader range of unwelcome sexual advances—repeated requests for sexual favours or other comments, or physical contact—that lead to a very difficult environment for the victim. People tend to associate sexual harassment with the workplace, but it can occur in any setting.

Sexual assault and sexual harassment involve a person exerting power over another person. Men and women of all sexual orientations can be victims of such behaviour, but heterosexual women are the most frequent victims. It is crucial that the environments young adults are in—including home, school, and workplace—support safe, healthy, zero tolerance policies to ensure the comfort and well-being of people in that setting.

The impact of sexual assault—physical and verbal—can have long-term effects on the victim, including substance abuse, depression, and anxiety. Indeed, all lifestyle choices have the potential to affect development, particularly the many facets of cognitive development.

Michael Kaufman is a writer and speaker on violence against women as well as the co-founder of the White Ribbon Campaign, the largest effort in the world of men working to end violence against women. He speaks around the world promoting gender equality and has visited 30 different colleges and universities across Canada. He wrote a booklet called *ManTalk*, which speaks to men about how to create good relationships and ensure dating violence has no place in their lives. To access this free booklet, visit http://www.michaelkaufman.com/books/man-talk/.

Social Development ◀L05

Forming a secure sense of self and being able to relate successfully to others are two of the most important human abilities in early adulthood. The models of development presented by Levinson and Erikson offer insights into the adult personality and the ability to form lasting, mutually rewarding relationships in early adulthood.

LEVINSON'S CONCEPT OF INDIVIDUATION

Developmental psychologist Daniel Levinson (1978, 1990a, 1990b) believed that "even the most disparate lives are governed by the same underlying order—a sequence of eras and developmental periods" (1978, p. 64). During some of these periods, people go through crises. The purpose of these developmental transitions is to cause greater individuation.

Individuation refers to how we develop a separate and special personality, derived less and less from our parents and teachers and more from our own behaviour. This idea is reinforced by research suggesting that problems in earlier stages of development can affect ego and status attainment in adulthood (Chen & Kaplan, 2003; Krettenauer, Ullrich, Hofmann, & Edelstein, 2003). For

sexual assault Refers to all incidents of unwanted sexual activity, including sexual attacks and sexual touching.

date rape Coercive sexual activity between a victim and an offender who is known or an acquaintance.

sexual harassment Any conduct, comment, gesture or contact of a sexual nature that is likely to cause offence or humiliation or that might, on reasonable grounds, be perceived as placing a condition of a sexual nature on employment or on any opportunity for training or promotion.

individuation Refers to our developing a separate and special personality, derived less and less from our parents and teachers and more from our own behaviour.

example, adolescents who struggle in school because of academic or behaviour problems may tend to struggle with self-esteem and achievement in adulthood.

Although Levinson hypothesized more than 10 substages in the course of a man's life, he referred to the relevant phase in early adult development as the **novice phase**. The novice phase of human development extends from age 17 to 33 and includes the early adult transition, entering the adult world, and the age 30 transition. In this phase of life, hopes and dreams are established that motivate decisions related to work and relationships (see Figure 9.4).

Levinson found that age 30 (plus or minus 2 years) is a common time for people to re-examine their feelings about major life tasks. Important decisions are made at this time, such as modifying hopes and dreams, seeking a mentor, changing jobs, and even getting married or divorced. For some, this transitional period proves to be very smooth. In most cases, however, it challenges the very foundations of life itself. Many people, especially men, experience a serious period of self-doubt. Fortunately, most move through the age 30 transition to Levinson's Settling Down phase with a clearer understanding of their strengths and weaknesses and a clearer view of what they wish to make of themselves in middle adulthood.

The fact that Levinson conducted his initial research with only male participants raised questions by many critical thinkers, who argued that the male perspective is not representative of an entire world population.

This prompted Levinson to conduct subsequent research focusing on women's experiences.

MALE AND FEMALE IDENTITIES

Recent research has noted gender differences in identity development (Bergh & Erling, 2005). For the young adult male, identity formation involves establishing himself as an independent, self-sufficient adult who can compete and succeed in the world. For the young adult female, career and self-sufficiency may not be emphasized to the same degree. Gaining the attention and commitment of a man is often viewed as a more important aspect of a woman's identity, and intimacy is the major goal. According to Carol Gilligan and others (1982, 1990), male development is defined by separation and individuation, whereas female development is defined through attachment and relationship. In Gilligan's view, because females believe in the necessity of maintaining relationships within the family, and because this role often involves self-sacrifice, women find it harder to individuate. As a result of their research on the female perspective, Gilligan and others (1982, 1990) have proposed that feminine identity doesn't depend on separation or on the progress of individuation.

novice phase Levinson's phase of human development that captures the early adult transition, entering the adult world, and the age 30 transition.

intimacy Erikson's stage that represents the ability to relate one's deepest hopes and fears to another person and to accept another's need for intimacy in turn.

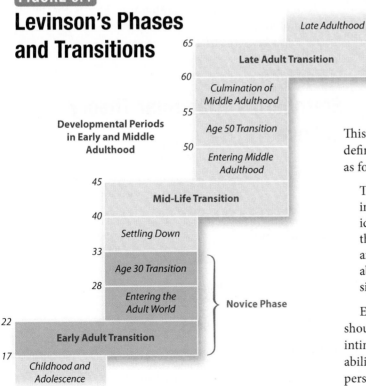

FIGURE 9.4

FIGURE 9.4

Levinson's Phases and Transitions

65 — Late Adulthood
Late Adult Transition
60
Culmination of Middle Adulthood
55
Age 50 Transition
50
Entering Middle Adulthood

Developmental Periods in Early and Middle Adulthood

45
Mid-Life Transition
40
Settling Down
33
Age 30 Transition
28
Entering the Adult World
22
Early Adult Transition
17
Childhood and Adolescence

Novice Phase

ERIKSON'S THEORY: INTIMACY VERSUS ISOLATION

Erikson offered his own views on this time of life, particularly emphasizing young adults' relationships with others and the impact on them of these relationships. In his psychosocial theory of development, the sixth stage is described as one of **intimacy** versus isolation. This stage covers the ages of approximately 18 to 35. In his definition of intimacy, Erikson (1963) described this stage as follows:

> The young adult, emerging from the search for and the insistence on identity, is eager and willing to fuse his identity with others. He is ready for intimacy, that is, the capacity to commit himself to concrete affiliations and partnerships and to develop the ethical strength to abide by such commitments, even though they call for significant sacrifices and compromises. (p. 263)

Erikson pointed out, however, that sexual intercourse should not be assumed to be the most important aspect of intimacy between individuals. By intimacy, he meant the ability to relate one's deepest hopes and fears to another person and to accept another's need for intimacy in turn.

Those who have achieved the stage of intimacy are able to commit themselves to concrete affiliations and partnerships with others and have developed the "ethical strength to abide by such commitments, even though they may call for significant sacrifices and compromises" (Erickson 1963, p. 262).

A tension that people experience related to intimacy is isolation—the readiness people have to isolate or distance themselves from others when feeling threatened by their behaviour. Young adults vacillate between their desires for intimacy and their need for isolation. They need social distance because they are not yet sure of their identity. They are vulnerable to criticism, and because they can't be sure whether the criticisms are true or not, they protect themselves by a "lone wolf" stance.

FRIENDSHIP

Young people seek intimacy in other close relationships that are vital to personal development on many levels. Friendships in early adulthood are especially important as people generally leave the relatively safe environments of home or school to pursue their dreams. Friends provide a source of support, and because they are chosen rather than thrust upon us, as is the case with family, the mutually satisfying benefits of friendships can sustain these relationships for decades.

Although friendships are important throughout the lifespan, more friendships tend to be formed in early adulthood than in other life stages. Because this is also the stage of life when people commonly find their life partners, challenges and balancing acts are required that cause friendships to go through periods of change as friends readjust their relationship when one person finds love with someone outside the friendship bond.

Gender stereotypes exist about friendships, but are not always accurate. For instance, male friendships are characterized as more superficial, focusing on sports, politics, or other external interests, as opposed to the more intimate, deeply emotional sharing that tends to characterize female friendships. Ideas about friendships tend to be rooted in cultural values and expectations, and there is actually much variation among behaviours of same-sex friends. Male–female friendships tend to be less stereotyped, and many people have several close friends of the opposite sex in school or at work. Friendships between sexes may or may not lead to later romance. The popular movie *When Harry Met Sally* (1989) captures the importance of friendships between women and men in numerous pairings.

> Love is better than anger.
> Hope is better than fear.

JACK LAYTON

STERNBERG: LOVE STORIES

One way of looking at love is offered by Robert Sternberg. He suggests (2000) that, throughout early adulthood, everyone develops a personal "love story." He has identified a number of these love stories:

- The travel story ("I believe that beginning a relationship is like starting a journey that promises to be both exciting and challenging.")

- The gardening story ("I believe any relationship that is left unattended will not survive.")

- The horror story ("I find it exciting when I feel my partner to be somewhat frightened of me.")

- The business story ("I believe close relationships are like good partnerships.")

- The pornography story ("It is very important to be able to satisfy all my partner's sexual desires and whims.")

Sternberg argues that, even when couples have similar values and interests, they may still have problems in their love relationship because they are operating from significantly different love stories.

Sternberg also developed a theory about love known as a triangular theory of love. It is represented visually and conceptually by a triangle with three components—passion, intimacy, and commitment. Passion consists of physical and sexual attraction. Intimacy refers to feelings of closeness and sharing with another person. Commitment means that a person is willing to endure challenges and tensions in a relationship because the investment is so rewarding. Sternberg described the forms of love that reflect degrees of passion, intimacy, and commitment (see Figure 9.5). According to Sternberg, consummate love is the fullest form of love an individual can experience and involves all three aspects of the triangular theory of love.

FIGURE 9.5

Sternberg's Triangular Theory of Love

Liking
Intimacy

Romantic Love
Passion + Intimacy

Companionate Love
Intimacy + Commitment

Consummate Love
Intimacy + Passion + Commitment

Infatuation
Passion

Fatuous Love
Passion + Commitment

Empty Love
Commitment

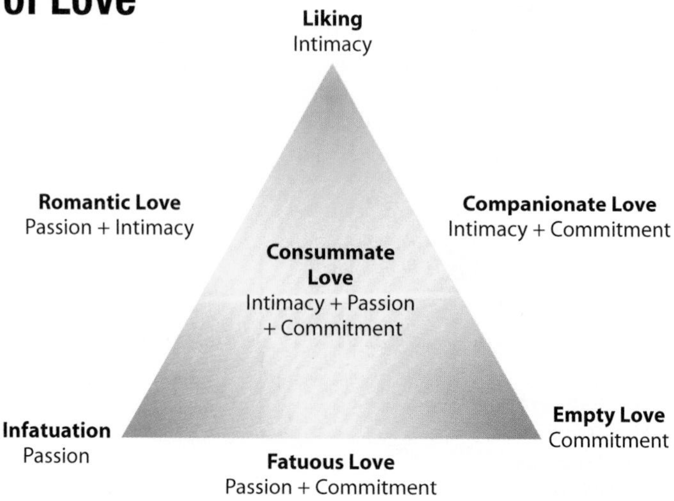

FROMM: VALIDATION

In a classic book on this subject, *The Art of Loving* (1956), Erich Fromm provided a highly respected understanding of the meaning of love. He argued that we must first recognize that we are prisoners in our own bodies. Although we assume that we perceive the world around us in much the same way as others do, we cannot really be sure. We are the only ones who truly know what our own perceptions are, and we cannot be certain they are the same as those of others. In fact, most of us are aware of times when we have misperceived something, such as hearing a phrase differently than everyone else. Thus, we must constantly check on the reality our senses give us.

Fromm argues that as important as these "reality checks" on our physical environment are, checks on our innermost state—our deepest and most important feelings and thoughts—are much more important. To check on the reality of these, we must get the honest reactions of someone we can trust. Such a person tells us, "You're not alone—I feel the same way, too." Even more important, these individuals prove their insight and honesty by sharing with us their own secret thoughts and feelings. In Fromm's words, others give us **validation**.

Validation is essential to our sanity. We are social animals, and we need to know that others approve of us (or, for that matter, when they don't). When someone regularly makes you feel validated, you come to love him or her. This is the essence of what Erikson has called intimacy—the primary focus in the early adulthood period. Intimacy fulfills what Maslow calls the need for self-esteem (see Maslow's hierarchy of needs in Chapter 2, Figure 2.5), so in the process of achieving intimacy and experiencing love, young adults are validating their own identities.

There is, however, great risk in receiving validation. The person who gives it to you is able to do so only because you have revealed your deepest secrets to him or her. This gives the person great power. Because that individual knows you and your imperfections so well, he or she has the ability to hurt you. This is why many break-ups and divorces are so painful. No one knows how to hurt you better than someone with whom you have shared so many intimacies.

L06 ▶ Marriage and the Family

Unlike the early years in the 20th century, when marriage was viewed as the final step in adult development, young adults who choose to marry in the early 21st century view that step as the beginning of their development together and as individuals in a long-term relationship. The goal is not simply to achieve a marriage, but is also to maintain satisfaction in other aspects of their lives.

MARITAL PRACTICES

In Canada in 2008, there were 147,288 marriages, which is 4.4 marriages per 1000 people. This is a historic low for Canada—even lower than that reached during the Great Depression of the 1930s. The average age for women to marry is 29 years and the average age for men is 31 (Human Resources and Skills Development, 2013). Over several decades, the average age for first marriage has been rising (see Figure 9.6). Some people argue that those young adults who marry early (mid-20s or younger) can look forward to a lifetime together. Others take a different stance, arguing that marrying later means that the partners are more mature and financially stable, which lessens the likelihood of divorce or separation. The amount of happiness felt by partners at the time of marriage is no guarantee, however, of the strength or resilience of their love for each other and their union.

> **validation** Fromm's term for the reciprocal sharing of deep secrets and feelings that allows people to feel loved and accepted.
>
> **cohabitation** A living arrangement in which unmarried partners share a residence and personal assets and sometimes have a child.

FIGURE 9.6

Average Age of First Marriage, by Gender in Canada (1921–2008)

Source: For 1921 to 1987: Statistics Canada. Marriage and conjugal life in Canada. Ottawa: Statistics Canada, 1992. (Cat. No. 91-534E); for 1988 to 1999: Statistics Canada, Demography Division; for 2000 to 2004: Statistics Canada. Mean age and median age of males and females, by type of marriage and marital status, Canada, provinces and territories, annual (CANSIM Table 101-1002). Ottawa: Statistics Canada, 2008; and for 2005–2008: Statistics Canada. Canadian Vital Statistics, Marriage Database and Demography Division (population estimates), Ottawa: Statistics Canada, 2011.

> When two people are under the influence of the most violent, most divisive, and most transient of passions, they are required to swear that they will remain in that excited, abnormal, and exhausting condition continuously until **death** do them part.
>
> GEORGE BERNARD SHAW

Increasing numbers of people are choosing to live together without getting married, a practice called **cohabitation**. Cohabitation involves sharing a residence and personal assets, and sometimes having a child, without being married. The proportion of married couples (with or without children) decreased in the 25 years between 1981 and 2001. Common-law parent families represent 15.5% of all families in 2006 (Human Resources and Skills Development, 2013). This includes both heterosexual and homosexual domestic partners.

CHANGING CANADIAN MARRIAGES AND FAMILIES

Statistics Canada defines a family as a married couple (with or without children), a common-law couple (with or without children), or a lone parent family (Statistics Canada, 2012d).

The structure of Canadian families is becoming more diverse. The traditional family of two parents with children is no longer the norm in Canada. In 2006, legally married couples with children made up 34.6% of all families. While the proportion of traditional families has been declining, the proportion of common-law and lone-parent families is increasing. The proportion of married couples (with and without children) decreased in the 25 years between 1981 and 2001, from 83.1% in 1981 to 68.6% in 2006. Common-law and lone-parent families represented 15.5% and 15.9% of all families in 2006. Furthermore, lone-parent families accounted for one out of four Canadian families with children (Human Resources and Skills Development Canada, 2013a).

Parenthood

Becoming a parent is a life-altering event that impacts every facet of a person's life. Many couples choose to delay parenthood until their careers and marriage have achieved a desired level of security. In situations where parenthood is a conscious choice, couples tend to consider having children as a goal for their personal happiness. Despite the stresses that accompany parenting, couples that have realistic expectations for their new roles and responsibilities find the adjustment to parenthood manageable and rewarding.

The birthrate for married women has declined somewhat, but for unmarried women, it has nearly doubled in the past 25 years. This is partly due to the fact that

dramatic changes have occurred in the living arrangements of young adults over that last 30 years. Individuals are less likely to get married and have children; instead they are choosing cohabitation and are having children within a common-law union (Statistics Canada, 2009a).

Divorce

Divorce rates in Canada have been declining for several years. Drops ranged from 4% in British Columbia to 22% in Nova Scotia (Kelly, 2012). According to Statistics Canada, there a number of reasons for divorce to take place:

- Relationship "runs out of steam"/spouses fall out of love
- Communication breakdown
- Unreasonable behaviour
- Infidelity
- Midlife crisis

FEATUREDMEDIA

Films About Relationships

The Break Up (2006)—A cohabiting couple breaks up when the female in the relationship feels unappreciated and perceives her boyfriend as immature. Will they be able to get past their differences and reunite?

Harold and Maude (1971)—What are the limits on age difference in a loving relationship?

Milk (2008) and Monster (2003)—How can personal beliefs about sexual preference and lifestyle choices breed hatred so vicious as to provoke one person to murder another?

Revolutionary Road (2008)—A young couple struggles to come to terms with their personal problems while trying to raise their two children.

Career Apps

As a marriage and family counsellor, how might you help a young adult couple face obstacles in their daily lives that can feel devastating or insurmountable at times?

- Financial issues
- Physical, psychological, or emotional abuse

SAME-SEX RELATIONSHIPS

Defining relationships, whether we're talking about family or marriage, involves a degree of subjectivity that implies judgment, values, and even politics. At the centre of the controversy over homosexuality is same-sex marriage, specifically the question of whether gays and lesbians should be allowed to marry. In Canada, same-sex marriage was legalized in July 2005. From 2006–2011, the number of same-sex married couples nearly tripled, while the number of same-sex common-law couples rose 15% (Statistics Canada, 2012e). Same-sex couples in Canada were more likely to be male than female; female same-sex couples were nearly 5 times more likely to have a child at home than male same-sex couples (Campion-Smith, 2012).

L07 ▶ Patterns of Work

CAREER DEVELOPMENT AND WORK IDENTITY

In early adulthood, people begin to form patterns that affect their future lifestyle; work, in turn, begins to shape a person's identity. For some, years spent in formal education were leading up to the ultimate goal of attaining a job. A person's work situation has direct impact on his or her financial opportunities, peers, leisure time, and living arrangements. An individual can find satisfaction in setting career goals and climbing the career ladder to achieve them. There is also a risk when identity is so tightly woven with career that failure to achieve those career goals may lead to emotional distress or depression. One way to frame the work identity is to separate financial hopes and needs from creative and/or intellectual needs.

Over time, the pace that is set with career and workload impacts later decisions about self and family.

CAREER CHOICES AND CONSIDERATIONS

Knowledge of lifespan development is beneficial, if not required, in many fields. People who possess an

TAKE A **STAND**

And Tango Makes Three

Challenging traditional views of many topics, including love, parenting, and family, this children's story caused quite a stir. It is a story, based on an actual event that occurred at the Central Park Zoo in New York, beginning in 1998, about the relationship between two male penguins that form a couple and eventually raise a baby penguin. The book has won many awards, but has also been banned by organizations that don't agree with the themes presented in the story. The Canadian Library Association reported that this book was challenged again in 2009, making it the only title to appear on the Association's Intellectual Freedom Advisory Committee's annual survey of challenges every year since it began in 2006.

Although same-sex marriages are legal in Canada, this is still a controversial topic for many. What is your reaction to the idea that same-sex parents can create a loving family unit in ways that challenge expectations related to gender roles and sexual behaviour? What argument(s) can you make to support views that are in opposition to your own?

understanding of the physical, cognitive, and social interactions throughout the lifespan will have greater insight into what is developmentally appropriate in a variety of areas. It may seem obvious that teachers and nurses need to possess knowledge about what constitutes typical development (physical, cognitive, and social) at different ages. But other fields, such as business and technology, also benefit from knowledge of lifespan development. For example, the manager of a company who recognizes that his employees need support in their role as parents, due to dual demands of family and career, will seek to provide an environment that reflects care and consideration for families. Similarly, an employee who recognizes the importance of social networking, and the opportunities afforded by technology, will be able to anticipate new opportunities for increasing social interactions between age groups and perhaps carve out a new niche in this rapidly expanding area. Table 9.3 lists a wide range of jobs for those with a background and interest in lifespan development.

The concept of **mentoring**—one individual helping another, often younger, person with work or other tasks—has received considerable attention in recent years

> **mentoring** The act of assisting another, usually younger, person with his or her work or life tasks.

TABLE 9.3

Careers in Lifespan Development/ Helping Professions

Business
Personnel Department Specialist, Human Resources Administrator, Employee Mental Health Coordinator, Department Manager

Communications
Editor, Librarian, Museum Curator, Journalist, Media Officer

Criminal Justice
Correctional Officer, Lawyer, Probation Officer, Police Officer

Education
JK-12 Classroom Teacher, Early Childhood Educator, College/University Professor, Educational Assistant, School Administrator

Elderly Services
Senior Living Manager, Nursing Home Manager, Recreation Advisor

Medicine
Physician, Physician Assistant, Nutritionist/Dietician, Nurse, Registered Practical Nurse, Developmental Disabilities Program Manager, Chiropractor, Communicable Disease Prevention Coordinator, Occupational/Physical Therapist, Acupuncturist, Epidemiologist (epidemics specialist)

Mental Health
Clinical Psychologist, Psychotherapist, Art/Expressive Therapist, Holistic Health Specialist, School Counsellor, Life Coach, Substance Abuse Counselor

Public Service
Social Worker, Homeless Assistance Program Coordinator, Agricultural Agent, Public Health Agent, At-Risk Youth Program Coordinator, Parenting Educator

(Johnson, 2002; Thompson & Kelly-Vance, 2001). A mentor provides the less experienced individual with guidance around life and/or work issues in a way that friends and family cannot. A true mentor relationship offers each person wisdom and mutually rewarding exchange over time. More and more occupations are formally instituting mentor positions, but people can seek out a mentor from any aspect of their lives—hobbies, career, religion, and so on.

dual-career family Family in which both partners work, usually full time.

In Canada, Generation Y or "the echo of the baby boom" are people who were between the ages of 19 and 39 in 2011 (Martel and Menard, 2011). This generation is now entering the work force and companies are finding that mentoring programs designed specifically for this generation are necessary. N-gen is a company that works with other companies to help them get the best out of their employees. They have designed programs that work specifically with mentoring between baby boomers and Generation Y employees. They feel that to get both generations to engage and connect, Baby Boomers must be encouraged to draw on their own experiences when mentoring Generation Ys. In turn, the Generation Ys must focus on their individual learning needs. It is essential to create a successful mentoring relationship based on two-way respect and feedback (Buahene, 2012).

> I know the price of success: dedication, hard work, and an unremitting **devotion** to the things you want to see happen.
>
> FRANK LLOYD WRIGHT

THE DUAL-CAREER FAMILY

The family pattern of the husband who goes off to work to provide for his family and the wife who stays home and manages that family is much less common than it was 50 years ago, although stereotypes remain, as discussed previously. This pattern has been replaced by the family dynamic known as the **dual-career family**, in which both husband and wife work, typically full time. In 2006, 59% of all Canadian women were participating in the paid labour force (see Figure 9.7). Women are choosing and succeeding in careers once considered men's fields, such as finance and medicine. Increased career opportunities for women have led to higher stress levels for some women, while increasing their personal satisfaction (Rosser, 2004; Schmader, Johns, & Barquissau, 2004).

Despite their increased presence in the workforce, most women are still considered responsible for the maintenance of the family. As a result, they often choose jobs that meet family needs and demands and tend to work shorter hours than men do. In addition, women change the nature of their work more often than men do.

Another changing aspect of the Canadian family is the increasingly active role of fathers in the raising of the children. Paternal child care—the father cares for children while the mother works outside the home—is

FIGURE 9.7

Employment Rates of Women and Men, 1976 to 2009

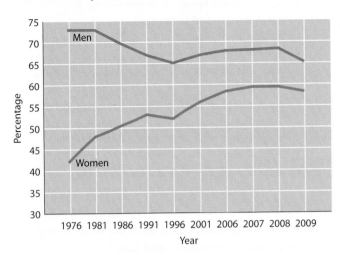

Source: Statistics Canada, 2012g

receiving more attention in the field because of the changing role of fathers and the implications of father involvement for child development, marital relations, and the family's economic situation. Organizations in Canada such as the Father Involvement Research Alliance (FIRA), Father Involvement Initiative–Ontario Network, Involvement Network of BC, Father Involvement Alberta, and the emerging Aboriginal Father Involvement Initiative all recognize that society as a whole, and policies specifically, must be examined to gain an appreciation of what fathers' roles in parenting and child care can and should be.

Paternal child care in Canada occurs most often in families where a mother's salary is high or when the cost of non-maternal child care is comparatively high. The occurrence of paternal child care also strongly depends on factors such as the father's work schedule in a dual-career family, the number of opportunities for the father's employment outside the home, and the extent to which both fathers and mothers identify with traditional gender roles.

ADAM@HOME © 2009 by Universal Uclick. Reprinted with permission. All rights reserved.

CONCLUSIONS & SUMMARY

Youths are initiated into adulthood in preindustrial societies. The transition into adulthood in Canada is much more complex, and clear initiation rites are for the most part absent. In general, this transition involves leaving school, moving out of the parental home, finding employment, and forming a new family unit.

Early adulthood is a period during which many changes are taking place. The peak of physical development is reached, and the decline of certain abilities begins. Lifestyle has a powerful effect on this development, including diet, physical fitness, and use of alcohol, drugs, and tobacco.

The cognitive changes that occur in early adulthood give young adults the ability to confront challenges. These individuals are able to capitalize on the life experience they've gained prior to and during adolescence.

How are Canadian youths being initiated into adulthood today?

- Initiation rites in other cultures offer a formal ceremony marking the transition from child to adult.
- The transition from adolescence to adulthood lasts years, not months.
- Five types of activities signal the passage to maturity in Canada today: religious, physical, social, educational, and economic.

What are the significant factors affecting physical development in early adulthood?

- Young adults experience a peak in energy and strength.
- Lifestyle patterns (exercise, diet) affect current and future health.
- As we do more research, more similarities between male and female development are becoming apparent.
- According to Erikson's theory, early adulthood is defined in terms of intimacy and versus isolation.

How does cognition change during the early adult years?

- Young adults are able to capitalize on the life experience they've gained prior to and during adolescence.
- They are able to focus on a specific area of knowledge and apply information.

What are the relationships between sexual identity and gender roles?

- Sexual identity results from those physical characteristics and behaviours that are part of our biological inheritance.
- Gender role, on the other hand, results partly from genetic makeup and partly from the specific traits in fashion at any one time and in any one culture.
- Views of acceptable gender role behaviours have changed considerably during the past 20 years. Androgyny is now considered an acceptable alternative to masculine and feminine gender roles.
- Pack dating is an important change in the interpersonal relationship patterns among young adults.

How do young adults deal with the interpersonal relationships of sexuality and love?

- Sternberg argues that love involves developing a story.
- Fromm states that people need to have their deepest and most important thoughts and feelings "validated" by others who are significant to them.
- Erikson views early adulthood as a time when individuals experience either intimacy or isolation.

What factors affect Canadian marriages and families?

- An increasing number of people are choosing to cohabit rather than marrying.
- There is much diversity in the structure of Canadian families. The traditional family with two parents and children is no longer the norm.

What patterns of work typify young adults today?

- Women often choose jobs that fit in well with the needs of their family. Women tend to work shorter hours and change the nature of their work more often than men do.
- Economic realities and the feminist movement have given rise to dual-career families, in which both husband and wife work.
- Young adults in Canada are having difficulty finding work after school and are returning to their parents' home for financial reasons.

For REVIEW

1. The trend for young adults today is not to leave their parents' home or to return after being away for a period of time. What factors have contributed to this (other than those listed in the text)? Do you feel society is partly responsible for this trend?

2. The media offer countless advertisements to help a person look younger, feel better, be better. Why are these ads so effective? What do they say about Western society?

3. Levinson found that at age 30 people commonly re-examine their feelings about major life tasks. Why do you think it is at this time in a person's life that they may experience self-doubt?

Chapter REVIEW TEST

Answers: 1a, 2d, 3a, 4b, 5a, 6b, 7a, 8c, 9a, 10a

1. A bar mitzvah or bat mitzvah is an example of a(n) _____ rite of passage.
   a. religious
   b. physical
   c. social
   d. educational

2. The primary chronic disease for Canadians who are 20 years and older is
   a. chronic obstructive pulmonary disease
   b. asthma
   c. arthritis
   d. diabetes

3. Smoking in a vehicle with children 14 years old and younger is restricted in which province?
   a. Manitoba
   b. Alberta
   c. Saskatchewan
   d. British Columbia

4. Which sexually transmitted infection is most commonly reported in Canada?
   a. gonorrhea
   b. chlamydia
   c. venereal warts
   d. syphilis

5. In terms of young adults' dating behaviours, pack dating is
   a. a group of young adults going out together, rather than one on one.
   b. a form of dating that involves cigarettes.
   c. more common in warm climates.
   d. for people who have a habit of dependency in relationships.

6. The role of a ____, according to some theorists, is to provide an individual with guidance during life transitions, assistance with decision making, and a clearer view of what the individual wishes to make of himself or herself.
   a. teacher
   b. mentor
   c. partner
   d. sibling

7. Androgyny refers to
   a. people who are more likely to behave in a way appropriate to a situation, regardless of their sex.
   b. women who have higher-than-average male elements in their personalities.
   c. men who have higher-than-average female elements in their personalities.
   d. the midpoint between the two poles of masculinity and femininity.

8. Researcher Carol Gilligan states that femininity is defined through
   a. work.
   b. personality.
   c. attachment.
   d. separation.

9. Over the last two decades, one reason for the increase in the age of people at first marriage may be higher numbers of women
   a. entering the workforce.
   b. travelling alone.
   c. afraid of divorce.
   d. having children.

10. The person who used the term validation to describe our need, as humans, to feel loved and accepted is
    a. Fromm.
    b. Levinson.
    c. Bem.
    d. Erikson.

CONNECT **LEARNSMART** **SMARTBOOK**

For more information on the resources available from McGraw-Hill Ryerson, go to www.mcgrawhill.ca/he/solutions.

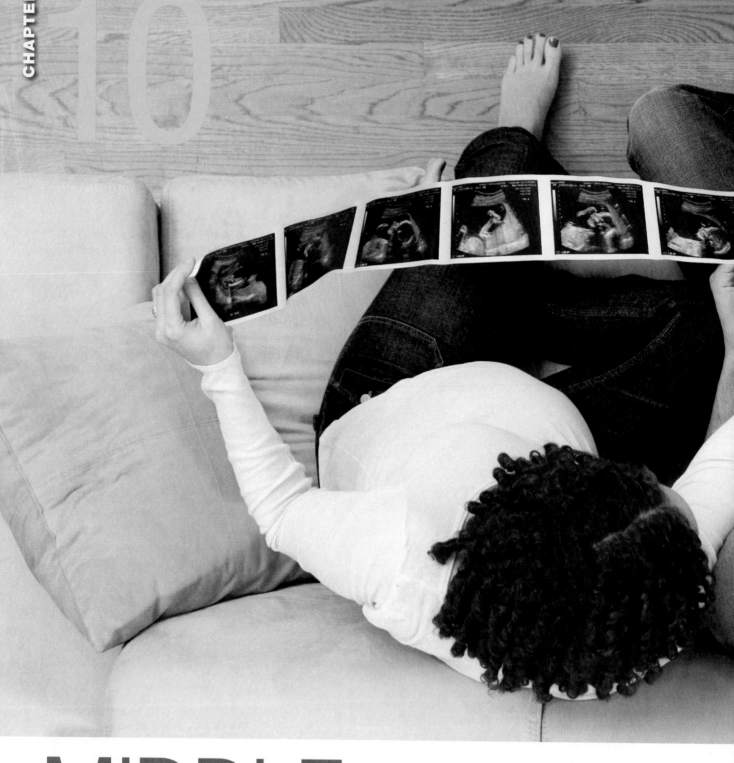

MIDDLE ADULTHOOD

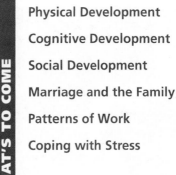

As You READ

After reading this chapter, you should be able to answer the following questions:

LO1 ▶ What kinds of physical changes affect people in middle adulthood?

LO2 ▶ What are the main factors that affect sex and love among middle-aged people?

LO3 ▶ What are the main factors affecting a person's intellectual development in middle adulthood?

LO4 ▶ What happens to relationships in middle adulthood?

LO5 ▶ What happens to personality during the middle adult years? Does it typically change or remain constant?

LO6 ▶ What are the typical patterns of marriage and family relationships during middle adulthood?

LO7 ▶ What are the patterns of work that we most often see in this life stage?

LO8 ▶ How do adults generally deal with the stress caused by the major events and daily hassles of their lives?

I was a veteran before I
was a **teenager**.

MICHAEL JACKSON

The shocking reports of Michael Jackson's death in June 2009 spread with amazing speed and impact around the world. At 50 years of age, Michael was a true superstar, rehearsing for a series of 50 concerts one month away from kickoff. One reason his death came as such a surprise is that people don't associate death with a man considered to be in the prime of life. As the baby boom generation ages, in particular, middle age is becoming much more distinct from old age in public perception.

Middle adulthood is widely accepted to cover the years of 40 to 60. The Japanese use several words for middle age: *sonen*, which refers to the "prime of life"; *hataraki-zakari*, which means the "full bloom of one's working ability"; and *kanroku*, which means "weightiness" or "fullness," which means both bearing a heavy load of authority and being overweight. In Canada, our perception of middle adulthood also takes many forms. While it is a period in which there can be changes due to aging, physical and cognitive abilities do not decline as much as people once thought. Middle adulthood also can be a period in which individuals are just hitting

their stride. In fact, development continues in significant ways. As with all life stages, how we navigate this stage varies considerably from person to person.

Physical Development

"Aged to perfection" is how one T-shirt says it. While physical systems do change with age, decline in middle adulthood is not inevitable and is highly individual. As you will see, biological forces greatly influence physical development, but psychological and social forces are important factors, too.

OVERALL HEALTH

Concerns about health tend to increase in middle adulthood. A person's image of the future becomes increasingly health-related in midlife, because of more firsthand experiences with illnesses and deaths among friends and loved ones than in earlier stages of life. Also beginning in middle adulthood, it is recommended that people get tested for serious conditions that can occur past a certain age. Campaigns about specific threats, such as colon cancer and breast cancer, aim to raise awareness about prevention and therefore reduce incidence and terminal cases of those conditions. These preventive measures

▶ Late Apple Inc.
CEO Steve Jobs

▲ News anchor Lisa LaFlamme, like many in middle adulthood, is in the prime years of her career.

TAKE A **STAND**

force people to become mindful of potential threats to their health, threats of which they had been unaware before.

CARDIOVASCULAR HEALTH

In middle adulthood, changes in the cardiovascular system sometimes result in heart disease, which is typically linked to high blood pressure and high cholesterol levels. A report by the World Health Organization estimated that, in 2005, 30% of all deaths around the world were the result of heart disease (World Health Organization, 2011). Heart disease commonly results from the buildup of fat in the lining of blood vessels, which reduces the flow of blood to the heart and brain. Eating habits from earlier periods in life influence cardiovascular health in middle adulthood, as the blood vessels have experienced years of effects from the two kinds of cholesterol—LDL (low-density lipoprotein) and HDL (high-density lipoprotein). LDL is commonly known as "bad" cholesterol, because it sticks to artery walls when the concentration is too high. Fortunately, HDL can lessen the risk of heart disease, because it counters the threat posed by LDL.

Both high blood pressure and cholesterol levels are affected by diet and exercise. It may be difficult for some

adults to change their lifestyle when in middle adulthood; but doing so can literally save, or at the very least extend, their lives. Researchers have found that middle-aged men and women who had moderate to high levels of physical activity lived 1.3 to 3.7 years longer than those who got little exercise, largely because this kept them from developing heart disease (Franco et al., 2005).

presbyopia The age-related decline in vision in which the individual begins to lose the ability to see objects clearly at close distances.

presbycusis The age-related decline in hearing in which the individual begins to lose the ability to detect certain tones, especially high-pitched ones.

SENSORY ABILITIES—VISION AND HEARING

Everyday experiences depend on one or more of the five physical senses—vision, hearing, smell, taste, and touch. Although the gradual loss of function in the senses is most pronounced in late adulthood, it can become a serious concern in middle age.

In middle adulthood, changes in vision and hearing are most noticeable. Beginning in the early to middle 40s, most individuals will start to experience difficulties with the ability to see clearly at close distances, a condition known as **presbyopia**. This normal aging change continues to progress over time. To compensate for these changes in the eye's focusing ability, people begin to wear reading glasses or bifocals. Another age-related change in vision is that our eyes don't adapt to sudden, intense light or darkness as effectively as they once did. For most people, these changes in visual ability pose a problem only when reading fine print or when lighting is reduced, such as in night driving.

Age-related hearing loss, called **presbycusis**, is very common and begins at around age 40 (see Table 10.1). Individuals begin to lose the ability to detect certain tones, particularly high pitches. To compensate

▲ Middle adulthood can be an active and vibrant time of life.

TABLE 10.1

Hearing Loss

Age group	Total Canadian population	Population with hearing limitations	Hearing limitation rate
		counts	percent
Total–aged 15 and over	25,422,280	1,266,120	5.0
15 to 24	4,147,070	21,810	0.5
25 to 34	3,942,260	27,070	0.7
35 to 44	4,747,620	71,800	1.5
45 to 54	4,912,800	179,020	3.6
55 to 64	3,623,390	231,130	6.4
65 to 74	2,239,630	265,740	11.9
75 and over	1,809,500	469,560	25.9

▲ This table shows the percentage of individuals in different age groups who have experienced hearing loss.

Source: Statistics Canada, 2006.

for these changes, individuals may begin to use hearing aids, which can greatly improve hearing ability. The Centers for Disease Control (2001b) in Atlanta, Georgia, reported that noise-induced hearing loss is the second most reported occupational illness or injury. The use of headphones, such as ear buds with iPods and MP3 players, can impact hearing over time. Small changes in lifestyle early in life, such as listening for no more than about an hour a day and at levels below 60%

of maximum volume, can mean no noise-related hearing loss in middle adulthood.

EFFECTS OF HEALTH HABITS

In middle age, habits that formed in earlier life stages can start to have consequences that affect health and well-being (see Figure 10.1). Binge drinking (more than five drinks in one sitting) is more prevalent among middle-aged adults over 50 than previously thought, with research showing that 22% of individuals between the ages of 50 and 64 had consumed at least five alcoholic beverages in the same day within the past month (Blazer & Wu, 2009). (See Table 10.2 for details.) Binge drinking was associated with the use of tobacco and illicit drugs and, among men, with being separated, divorced, or widowed.

In middle age, as in earlier life stages, being overweight is a matter of concern. The difference is that older individuals often do not have the same time or energy to sustain exercise plans and practices they made in younger years (see Figure 10.2). Obesity in middle age—even without established cardiovascular disease risk factors such as high blood pressure or high cholesterol levels—greatly increases the risk of hospitalization and is linked to generally worse outcomes in many cancers, including breast and prostate cancer (sciencedaily.com, 2009). For some, the influences of heredity and environment result in obesity—about 40% of the people with one obese parent become obese, as compared with only 10% of those whose parents are

▲ Actor Johnny Depp overcame drug and alcohol abuse when he was younger to become one of Hollywood's top leading men in middle adulthood.

FIGURE 10.1

Alcohol Use in Older Adults

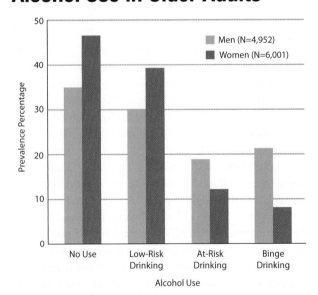

▲ This graph depicts patterns of alcohol use among middle-aged and elderly men and women.

Source: Blazer & Wu, 2009.

not obese (CDC, 2000b). Others become overweight simply because they do not compensate for their lower **basal metabolism rate (BMR)**, the minimum amount of energy an individual tends to use when in a resting state. Therefore, if you continue to consume the same number of calories throughout your life, and do not increase exercise, you will definitely gain weight as you age.

Muscle growth is complete in the average person by age 17; in middle adulthood, there is a common but unnecessary decline in muscular ability. Aerobic activities such as swimming and brisk walking appear to help maintain general health and counter the trend toward middle-adulthood weight gain and muscle loss.

The results of poor health habits can ultimately take a serious toll in the form of illness or death during the middle adult years. Chronic diseases, such as heart or lung disease, are the main causes of death in middle age. Heredity, independent of or combined with choosing to drink alcoholic beverages, smoke cigarettes, overeat, and/or not get enough exercise, increases the likelihood that a chronic condition can contribute to death in this period of life.

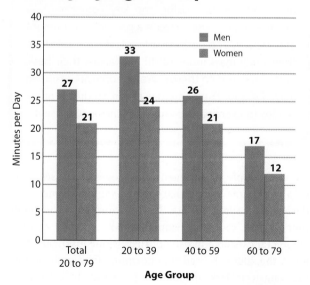

FIGURE 10.2

Average Daily Minutes of Moderate-to-Vigorous Physical Activity by Age Group

Bar chart — Minutes per Day by Age Group

Legend: Men, Women

Age Group	Men	Women
Total 20 to 79	27	21
20 to 39	33	24
40 to 59	26	21
60 to 79	17	12

▲ Only 15% of Canadian adults meet recommended levels of physical activity (at least 150 minutes of moderate-to-vigorous physical activity per week).

Source: Statistics Canada, 2007–2009.

TABLE 10.2

The Face of Binge Drinking

- 20% of men and 6% of women aged 50–64 reported binge drinking within the last month.

- 17% of men and 11% of women reported drinking two or more drinks *a day*.

- Those with *higher* income reported more binge drinking.

- Those who used tobacco and illegal drugs reported more binge drinking.

- Being separated, divorced, or widowed was associated with binge drinking in men.

- Non-medical use of prescription drugs was associated with binge drinking in women.

Many conditions are preventable, however, and lifestyle choices within a person's control can greatly reduce the likelihood that someone in middle age will suffer from a chronic condition. The availability and utilization of health-care resources also plays a role. For example, a recent study (Strumpf, Chai, & Kadilaya, 2010) found that Canadian compliance rates with recommended screenings for breast, colorectal, and prostate cancers were low.

> **basal metabolism rate (BMR)** The minimum amount of energy a person uses when in a resting state.

▲ Poor health habits, such as excessive alcohol use, can take their toll during middle age resulting in chronic health problems.

As men and women go through middle age, physiological changes occur in both males and females, affecting their sexuality in ways that are distinct to this particular time of life. Such changes are often related to hormone levels that influence fertility and reproduction. Changes in sexuality for women and men occur gradually, and while sexual activity declines in middle adulthood, the decline is gradual, as well. According to the 2008 Durex Global Sex Survey, 59% of Canadians engage in sex weekly, which ranks Canada 22nd of 26 countries in that category (see Figure 10.3). Lack of time and energy due to increased demands with work and caring for others—children and aging parents—are likely contributors to the decline in sexual activity during these years.

Changes in sexuality differ between men and women and between any two individuals. Men do not lose their fertility in the same way that a woman's ability to conceive and carry a healthy baby ends, for example, and the timing of a woman's changes varies from person to person and can involve very different experiences and symptoms.

These changes can be summed up in the word **climacteric**, which refers to a relatively abrupt change in the body, brought about by changes in hormonal balances. In women, this is called **menopause**, which typically occurs over several years during a woman's late 40s or early 50s, and refers to the cessation of menstruation. On average, women experience their last periods around age 51, but the transition from regular periods to no periods can span an entire decade.

The main physical change in menopause is that the ovaries cease to produce the hormones estrogen and progesterone. The symptoms related to such reduced hormone production can vary widely among women. Some experience discomfort in the form of stomach aches or queasiness, exhaustion, mood swings, and hot flashes—periods of elevated body temperature that cause a woman to sweat and feel feverish. Lower levels of estrogen can cause less vaginal lubrication, which can make intercourse uncomfortable. Sexual arousal may be somewhat slower, and women may need extra stimulation to attain and sustain orgasm. Some studies have found a reduction of female interest and desire during menopause (Burgess, 2004).

Women do often grapple with some effects of menopause related to hot flashes or other symptoms, and strategies for treating women have been somewhat controversial. **Hormone replacement therapy (HRT)** is a common treatment for the unpleasant side effects of menopause. Supplementing women's reduced supply of estrogen and progesterone seems to help with some symptoms, such as vaginal dryness, hot flashes, and night sweats. In the short term, hormone therapy can reduce a woman's risk of heart disease, colorectal cancer, and osteoporosis (bone loss); but studies in the 2000s showed that hormone therapy increased the long-term risk of blood clots, stroke, breast cancer, and heart disease. Data support the initiation of hormone therapy close to menopause, but the risks increase for older women. The balance of benefits and risks for a woman will be influenced by her personal preferences,

climacteric The midlife change in hormone levels that affects fertility.

menopause Cessation of women's menstruation, typically occurring in the late 40s or early 50s.

hormone replacement therapy (HRT) Menopause treatment whereby women receive hormone supplements.

TECH TRENDS

Using Video to Illustrate (and Argue!) Children's Strengths

One of the main obstacles to maintaining a healthy weight is the lack of time to exercise. Middle-aged adults are often juggling caregiving responsibilities and career, leaving less time . . . period. Thanks to new innovations in the digital age, adults can use computers, phones, or portable media players (such as iPhone or iPod Touch) as well as videogame consoles (Nintendo Wii) to fit exercise into their daily routine without leaving home or the workplace. The following are some examples of technology geared toward a healthier adulthood:

RunKeeper Free—This application for iPhone or iPod Touch tracks all personal statistics for walking or running, and allows people to see a map of their activities on the iPhone and the Web. It's integrated with Facebook and Twitter, so people can connect with friends and motivate each other.

Six Pack App—This comprehensive fitness application for the iPhone or iPod Touch provides a library with pictures and text describing hundreds of exercise techniques.

Wii Fit—This video game system by Nintendo is a best-selling product designed to help keep people fit in four categories: yoga, strength training, aerobics, and balance. Using the key component—a balance board—users create a profile, enter height and weight, and perform a few tests that calculate their body mass index (BMI) and assess their basic balance. Based on these scores, people are assigned a Wii Fit age. The game has about 50 different activities to exercise and entertain those who use it.

FIGURE 10.3

Proportion of Population Having Weekly Sexual Activity by Country

Frequency of having sex varies considerably by country

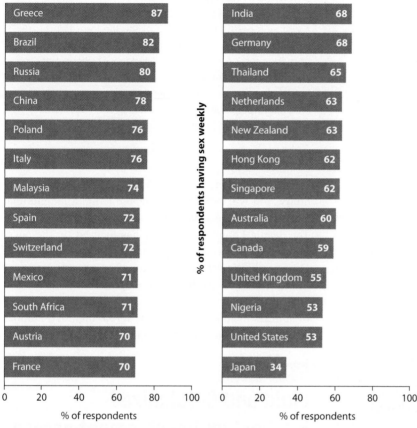

Country	%
Greece	87
Brazil	82
Russia	80
China	78
Poland	76
Italy	76
Malaysia	74
Spain	72
Switzerland	72
Mexico	71
South Africa	71
Austria	70
France	70

% of respondents

Country	%
India	68
Germany	68
Thailand	65
Netherlands	63
New Zealand	63
Hong Kong	62
Singapore	62
Australia	60
Canada	59
United Kingdom	55
Nigeria	53
United States	53
Japan	34

% of respondents

% of respondents having sex weekly

Source: Data from Durex Sexual Wellbeing Global Survey, 2008.www.durex.com/en-ca/SexualWellbeingSurvey/pages/default.aspx.

her risks for specific diseases, and the degree of menopausal symptoms.

One of the big misperceptions about menopause is that it is a very distressing time for women. Most women, however, do not experience a reduction in sexual activity or satisfaction during menopause, and many women are quite relieved to no longer menstruate.

The male climacteric refers to the male change of life, typically related to sexual performance and sperm production. At one time, it was thought that the male hormone balance parallels that of the female, but most men are still able to father children even into old age. Men's sperm count may drop a bit, but not significantly in middle adulthood. Men also experience less of a decline in hormone levels and sexual desire than women. There may be lower levels of testosterone, fewer viable sperm, and changes in the testes and prostate gland (Beutel, Weidner, & Brahler, 2006). There is usually a need for more direct stimulation to the penis to attain and sustain erection, and men have a longer refractory period between ejaculations. Erectile dysfunction (ED) can be a problem impacting middle-aged men. Besides aging, risk factors for ED include conditions such as hypertension and diabetes, and lifestyle habits such as smoking.

Drugs like Viagra and Levitra are used to reduce erectile problems, and have become household names, owing to marketing campaigns. These drugs primarily work by increasing blood flow to the penis (Wright, 2006). Side effects of drug treatment may include headaches, sudden drop in blood pressure, and vision problems. Men who are considering drug treatment for ED should tell their doctors about any medications they are taking for routine health problems. Certain drug combinations can have dangerous effects.

> ### Middle age is the awkward period when Father Time starts catching up with **Mother Nature**.
>
> HAROLD COFFIN, FORMER HUMOUR COLUMNIST FOR THE ASSOCIATED PRESS

"Smoking or nonsmoking? Hormone therapy or nonhormone therapy section?"

Source: www.CartoonStock.com

The Experience of Menopause in Different Cultures

Women in Canada tend to experience hot flashes as the most common symptom of menopause, whereas women in Japan experience hot flashes so infrequently that there is no word in the Japanese language to describe it. Menopausal Japanese women, however, tend to experience symptoms known as "frozen shoulders," which refers to painful, limited shoulder movement. Nigerian women also experience shoulder discomfort during menopause.

Experts have determined that differences in symptoms are related to a woman's diet, as well as genetic and environmental factors. Psychological factors, such as how a woman's aging is perceived in her culture (a place of honour versus a place of loneliness and isolation), impact a woman's personal experience of this life transition.

In Canada, there are cultural differences in awareness of menopause. A recent study (Madden, St. Pierre-Hansen, Kelly, Cromarty, Linkewich, & Payne, 2010) found that First Nations women do not generally discuss menopause and, like the Japanese with hot flashes, may not have a word for it in their language.

L03 ▶ Cognitive Development

Middle adulthood is a time of physical changes. Can we assume that cognitive abilities change too? The question of how our cognitive abilities change has been the focus of much research, which has largely focused on intelligence and creativity.

INTELLIGENCE

No aspect of adult functioning has received more research than intelligence. Most efforts have examined whether intelligence declines with age, and if so, how much and in what ways. Theorist J. L. Horn (1978) described two dimensions of intelligence: fluid and crystallized. **Fluid intelligence** refers to the ability to think and act quickly and solve problems, as well as the ability to use abstract thinking.

Crystallized intelligence refers to accumulated information and verbal skills over time, reflecting the effect of culture and learning. More specifically, crystallized intelligence allows a person to make connections between information and/or objects. As a person develops over time and comes across new information, that person increases the crystallized intelligence that may be accessed in future experiences. Horn hypothesized that while crystallized intelligence does not decline and may even increase with age, fluid intelligence does deteriorate to some degree, since it relies on an efficient nervous system (see Figure 10.4).

fluid intelligence The ability to think and act quickly and solve problems, as well as the ability to use abstract thinking.

crystallized intelligence Accumulated information and verbal skills over time, reflecting the effect of culture and learning; allows a person to make connections between information and/or objects.

NEW VIEWS OF INTELLIGENCE

In a noteworthy attempt to understand the adult range of intellectual abilities, psychologists K. Warner Schaie and Sherry Willis (Schaie, 2005) have been conducting a longitudinal study known as the Seattle Longitudinal Study. You will recall from Chapter 1 that a longitudinal study looks at the same individuals over a period of time. The Seattle Longitudinal Study has focused on the question of individual change versus stability in intelligence: Do our abilities change over time, or are we consistent in our abilities according to intelligence tests? More than 500 participants were initially tested in 1956 on a variety of abilities including vocabulary, verbal memory, number (math calculations), spatial orientation, perceptual speed,

FIGURE 10.4

Fluid and Crystallized Intellectual Development across the Lifespan

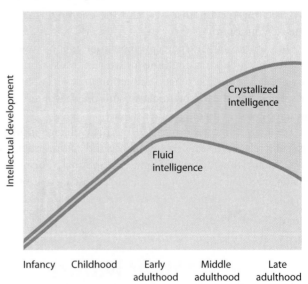

▲ According to Horn, crystallized intelligence increases throughout the lifespan, but fluid intelligence steadily declines from middle adulthood.

> It is a little bit surreal. I never could have anticipated finding myself back playing that same **character** after time had passed. It is sort of surreal and cool.

LAURA LEIGHTON, TELEVISION ACTRESS WHO REPRISED HER ROLE AS SYDNEY ANDREWS ON THE REMAKE OF *MELROSE PLACE*

and inductive reasoning. Schaie and Willis concluded that people reach a peak in many cognitive skills during middle adulthood. Perceptual speed—the ability to compare symbols and objects quickly and accurately—is the one area that declines most noticeably throughout adulthood (see Figure 10.5).

In middle adulthood, measures of intelligence are not as pertinent as they may have been in earlier stages of life, because the information gained from such measures is not as influential during the middle years. Most middle-aged adults are not in school, and are often settled in their careers and family lives; learning new information and developing new skills is not expected in the same way, although it is certainly valued highly. In fact, most commonly used intelligence tests measure only a few of the cognitive abilities that could be considered factors in

TAKE A **STAND**

Socioeconomic Bias and Cognitive Decline

A number of variables have been found to reduce the risk of cognitive decline (Schaie & Elder, 2005):

- The absence of cardiovascular and other chronic diseases
- Living in favourable environmental conditions
- Substantial involvement in activities and stimulating environments, such as travel and extensive reading
- Having a flexible personality style
- Being married to a spouse who has a high cognitive functioning level
- Engaging in activities that require quick perception and thinking
- Being satisfied with one's life accomplishments through midlife

The variables listed above are biopsychosocial in nature and therefore the result of many influences. Using an example from above, how could you argue that socioeconomic status impacts intelligence? For example, which variables become less risky if a person has more money and more options for lifestyle adjustments? Using an example from above, how could you argue that biology trumps environment and determines a person's cognitive path?

FIGURE 10.5

Changes in Intellectual Abilities

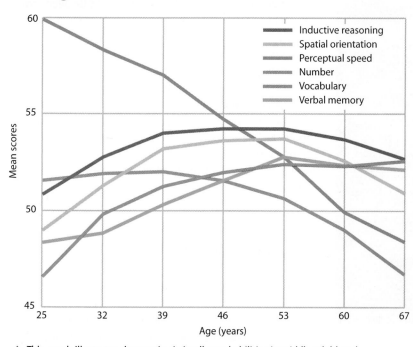

Legend:
- Inductive reasoning
- Spatial orientation
- Perceptual speed
- Number
- Vocabulary
- Verbal memory

Y-axis: Mean scores (45, 50, 55, 60)
X-axis: Age (years) (25, 32, 39, 46, 53, 60, 67)

▲ This graph illustrates changes in six intellectual abilities in middle adulthood.

intelligence, such as memory and perception. Horn believed that intelligence is not the result of one general factor but, rather, a combination of many abilities working in different ways and that different people display intelligence in different ways.

Individuals in middle adulthood may utilize and display several distinct cognitive abilities. For example, the eight types of intelligences in Howard Gardner's (1983) theory of multiple intelligences, presented in Chapter 7, are becoming more widely recognized as a measure of intelligence in middle-aged adults. Although not a formal assessment tool, the recognition of intelligence and ability in specific domains (as proposed by Gardner) is a way to assess intelligence and ability in middle-aged individuals.

analytic intelligence
Sternberg's term to describe a person's ability to break down a problem or situation into the smaller parts of the whole.

creative intelligence
Sternberg's term to describe a person's ability to solve problems in unique ways and to feel comfortable with new or different situations and ideas.

practical intelligence
Sternberg's term to describe "common sense"—a simple, logical understanding of a situation and how to work through a problem.

Robert Sternberg has also challenged traditional views of intelligence tests on the grounds that they measure only crystallized intelligence. He suggests that intelligence isn't as much about quantity as balance—knowing when and how to use analytic, creative, and practical intelligence components. **Analytic intelligence** refers to the ability to break down a problem or situation into the smaller parts of the whole. **Creative intelligence** refers to the ability to solve problems in unique ways and to feel comfortable with new or different situations and ideas. **Practical intelligence** refers to the quality people might call "common sense"—a simple, logical understanding of a situation and how to work through a problem. The abilities Sternberg describes peak in the middle adult years. Because middle-aged adults have a better understanding of their own limits, they can more easily capitalize on their strengths and compensate for their weaknesses.

INFORMATION PROCESSING AND EXPERTISE

As described in previous chapters, our ability to process information is related to cognitive development. Aspects of information-processing theory, such as expertise, speed of

▲ Federal Health Minister Rona Ambrose must be able to perform at a high level of cognitive functioning.

▲ Staying active can result in a rewarding middle adulthood period.

processing, and memory, are especially relevant in middle adulthood. Generally speaking, someone who is new to a task or situation requires more effort, attention, and energy to complete the task than an expert—someone who possesses skills or experience in a specific task or activity.

Over time, as people have more life experiences and acquire more knowledge, they are able to transfer that knowledge into novel situations. This allows people to solve some problems more readily in middle adulthood than at earlier ages because they have more information to draw upon and more resources to refer to when making decisions. Examples can range from knowing how to whip up a delicious dinner when the only food in the refrigerator is eggs and potatoes to knowing what to do when the Canada Revenue Agency calls for an audit.

People experience a gradual decline in the ability to process information quickly, however. This mild decline is noticeable, for example, when a middle-aged adult attempts to retrieve information quickly or participate in an activity that requires him to use quick reflexes, such as retrieving a new name or phone number.

Related to the ability to retrieve information is memory. In the early middle-age years, there is not much difference in memory speed and capacity than in early adulthood. However, as a person approaches late adulthood, a lifetime's accumulated knowledge takes up memory space that can interfere with the acquisition of new knowledge and retrieval of older, previously stored information.

THE ROLE OF CREATIVITY

A key factor in the ability to continue to be productive well into the later years is creativity. Research shows that creativity does not decline with age and that, on the contrary, middle adulthood is one of the peak periods of creativity. As the world changes more and more rapidly, the role of creativity has become an important aspect of cognitive functioning. People live with innovations in all aspects of life (think of iPads, hybrid cars, and robotic surgery), and they need to respond to the challenges new ideas bring.

Creativity studies have found that highly creative adults

- like to do their own planning, make their own decisions, and need the least training and experience in self-guidance;

- do not like to work with others and prefer their own judgment of their work to the judgment of others;

- take a hopeful outlook when presented with complex, difficult tasks;

- have the most ideas when a chance to express individual opinion is presented, even at the risk of incurring ridicule;

- are most likely to stand their ground in the face of criticism;

- are the most resourceful when unusual circumstances arise; and

- are not necessarily the "smartest" or "best" in competitions.

The ideas of creative people are qualitatively different from those of the average person.

▲ Jackson Pollock was famous for making paintings by splattering paint over a large canvas, then cutting out sections he considered to be artistic.

> People underestimate how remarkable it is to create something that no one has ever seen or done before. It's like **discovering** the vaccine for polio.
>
> SHERYL CROW

Classic research has looked at the lives of creative people and their contributions, revealing that the period between 40 and 60 years of age can be a peak period for creative output (Dennis, 1966; Lehman, 1953). (See Figure 10.6.) For example, most scientists and scholars tend to peak in their 40s to 60s, while artists peak in their 40s.

While creativity is easily noticed in famous people, all people have the capacity for creative output in middle adulthood. One of the biggest factors relates to motivation—how much a person cares to create, dares to take risks, and works to learn and refine new ideas and skills.

FIGURE 10.6
Creative Output Through the Years

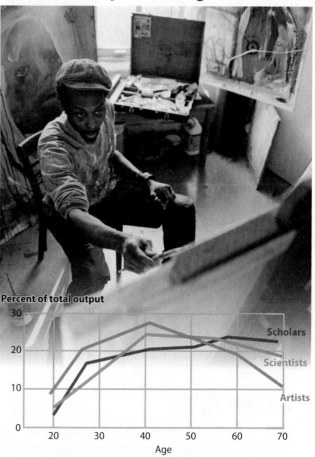

▲ This graph depicts creative activity at different ages.

Source: Dennis, W. (1966). Creative Productivity between 20 and 80 Years, in *Journal of Gerontology*, 21, pp. 1-8.

LEARNING ABILITY

It has been suggested that people in middle adulthood are less motivated to learn than are younger people, but evidence indicates that this is not so. The meaningfulness of a task affects motivation, and the decline in cognitive ability due to aging can often be countered by motivation and new learning experiences. The rate of change and innovation is currently so rapid that learning new skills is a necessity both on the job and off. Routinely required to use computers and related technology at work, people often take classes to gain the technological and other skills needed in order to advance or even maintain their career. With the economic decline in recent years, there has been an increase in the number of middle-aged adults who have been laid off from their jobs and who have subsequently returned to college or university for retraining. These adult students seem at least as motivated to learn as their younger classmates and are appreciated for their valuable contributions to the

midlife transition Levinson's term to describe the period of life that bridges early and middle adulthood, approximately ages 40 to 45.

Career Apps

As a creative arts therapist, how could you use art, music, dance, or drama to encourage self-expression and creativity in middle-aged clients?

classroom environment by their instructors. Middle-aged students are often among the highest achievers in post-secondary classes—further evidence that the ability to learn does not decline at this time of life.

Social Development ◀L04

Individuals experience life events and crises differently, depending on many factors rooted in heredity and the environment, such as temperament or economic realities (e.g., layoffs). Whether or not a person experiences middle adulthood as a period of crisis or opportunity varies greatly.

LEVINSON'S SEASONS OF LIFE

Levinson interviewed groups of men initially, and women later in a separate investigation, and analyzed the findings in relation to how life experiences result in a change in personality.

The Midlife Transition

Middle adulthood corresponds to five of Levinson's stages (see Figure 10.7). Beginning with the settling-down stage, individuals establish a role in society in the central part of their life, in their career or their family life—or both. The final stage applicable to middle adulthood is the culmination of middle adulthood, but between those two periods adults undergo many changes that include a specific transition at age 50. For the purposes of this chapter, Levinson's **midlife transition**—a period that lasts from approximately age 40 to 45—is highlighted. Levinson identified this time as a crucial point in adult development, one that bridges early adulthood and

▲ Changes in technology require middle-aged adults to adapt in order to maintain a high level of performance in their careers.

FIGURE 10.7

Levinson's Middle Adulthood

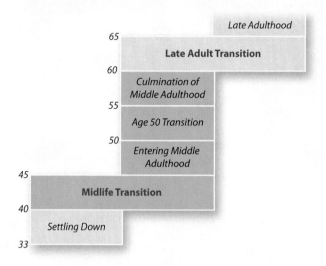

65	Late Adulthood
	Late Adult Transition
60	
	Culmination of Middle Adulthood
55	
	Age 50 Transition
50	
	Entering Middle Adulthood
45	
	Midlife Transition
40	
	Settling Down
33	

middle adulthood. Because people today are expected to live well into their 70s and 80s, the midlife transition does indeed capture the feeling of hitting the middle of one's life, which some encounter as a crisis. Canadian psychologist Elliott Jaques (1917–2003) coined the term "midlife crisis" to describe the phenomenon, often portrayed in television shows and films, of middle-aged adults, usually men, who make dramatic changes to their life upon reaching middle adulthood. These changes can include buying a sports car, changing their physical appearance, or having an affair with someone much younger; they involve an attempt at recapturing their youth. While some middle-aged adults do experience these years as a crisis, this does not appear to be a universal experience and thus Levinson's concept of midlife transition seems more appropriate.

This stage involves three developmental tasks:

- Review, reappraisal, and termination of the early adult period

- Decisions on how middle adulthood should be conducted

- Dealing with the polarities that are the source of division in life at this stage—being young versus being old, being destructive versus being creative, being masculine versus being feminine, and being attached to others versus being separate from others

During the midlife transition, individuals question their past life decisions and accomplishments, and re-evaluate where they are going. The process of the midlife transition can result in a different life structure and goals. According to Levinson, even if individuals do not change their life structures during the midlife transition, they still need to reappraise their lives and come to terms with choices they made earlier in life.

Most people want to feel that their life has made some difference, and they want to leave something behind them that can be remembered. Therefore, it is typical at this time that people become more creative and often work harder than in the past to make a contribution considered worthwhile by those who follow them.

> **generativity** Erikson's term for the ability to be useful to self and to society.
>
> **stagnation** Erikson's term for boredom, self-absorption, and the inability to contribute to society.

Levinson's research revealed that both men and women experience a similar midlife transition. Members of each sex go through an alternating series of structure-building and structure-changing stages. The old division of female homemakers and male providers is outdated today, and members of both sexes experience challenges throughout their lifetimes that affect their development. Individual differences in personality make these experiences unique and compelling in the study of human development.

ERIKSON'S THEORY: GENERATIVITY VERSUS STAGNATION

Erikson described the seventh stage of psychosocial development, covering 25 to 65 years of age, as generativity versus stagnation.

Generativity means the ability to be useful to self and to society, with the goal of being productive and creative. In the generativity stage, one's productivity is aimed at guiding the next generation. The act of being productive is itself rewarding, regardless of recognition or reward.

Although Erikson certainly believed that the procreation of children was an important part of generativity, he did not believe people must become parents in order to achieve generativity. Some people apply this drive to other forms of altruistic concern and creativity, such as socially valued work (Erikson, 1968).

At this stage of adulthood, some people can become bored, self-absorbed, and unable to contribute to society's welfare; they fall prey to **stagnation**. People who have given birth to children may fail to be generative in their parenthood and come to resent the neediness of their offspring.

Research examining generativity has found that adults in midlife may be more psychologically mature and happier than younger people. Sheldon and Kasser (2001) reported that as adults age, their level of psychological maturity influences their level of well-being. Adults in

> Age is an issue of mind over matter: if you don't mind, it **doesn't matter**.
>
> MARK TWAIN

midlife with higher levels of maturity report higher levels of well-being than younger adults. Ackerman, Zuroff, and Moskowitz (2000) found that higher levels of generativity for middle-aged adults are associated with greater feelings of satisfaction with work and life. In addition, differences in the level of generativity for middle-aged adults are associated with the social support they receive from friends and family and their involvement in religious and political activities.

In Erikson's theory, generativity depends on the successful resolution of the six preceding psychosocial crises that define the human life cycle. People who are able to achieve generativity have a chance to reach the highest level of resolution in Erikson's stage theory: integrity.

▲ Generativity can take many forms.

L05 ▶ STABILITY VERSUS CHANGE

You've probably heard someone say, "Oh, he's been like that ever since he was a baby!" Such a comment doesn't sound like a philosophical statement, but think about what it implies: that an individual's personality can remain basically the same throughout the lifespan. Whether this is true or not is a fundamental question asked by adult development researchers. Do human beings really change very much over the course of their lives, or do we all stay pretty much the same? If we assume that people remain the same regardless of what happens to them as their life continues, then the period of early childhood takes on great meaning. Several of the developmental theorists discussed in this book (for example, Freud and Piaget) have focused a lot of their attention on the early years of childhood in the belief that what happens to a person during childhood determines much of what will happen to him or her in the future.

Conversely, theorists such as Erikson and Maslow believe that because people are constantly changing and developing, all life experiences must be considered important. In that case, early childhood becomes a somewhat less significant period in the whole of development, and adolescence and adulthood take on more significance. It also implies that getting children "off on the right foot" is not enough to ensure positive development.

In just the same way, some theorists feel that adults remain basically the same throughout adulthood—that the adult personality remains stable. This is termed *continuity* in adult development. Such researchers look at pieces of the personality (personality traits) as measured by detailed questionnaires. They argue that the answers to such questionnaires assess adult personality. These researchers are known as **trait theorists**. Trait theorists (e.g., McCrae & Costa, 2004; McCrae et al., 2000) might say: "If nothing unusual happens, then the adult personality will stay relatively the same. Normal adult personality development is really the maintenance of personality."

Other theorists consider adults in a consistent process of change and evolution. This stance is referred to as the position of *change* (as opposed to the position of *stability*). These theorists argue that adult personality is quite complicated—more so than a list of personality traits. What is interesting to them is how those traits fit with the whole of the person and how an adult's personality interacts with the world around her or him. These theorists believe that research based on personality traits is too narrow in focus and that we must also look at the stages of change each person goes through. These researchers are known as **stage theorists of personality**. Stage theorists Levinson, Vaillant, and Erikson, looking at the whole of the adult, might say, "The adult personality naturally and normally develops through change. Normal adult personality development is a continual process of growth and change."

> The man who views the world at 50 the same as he did at 20 has **wasted** 30 years of his life.
>
> MUHAMMAD ALI, THREE-TIME WORLD HEAVYWEIGHT CHAMPION

trait theorists Researchers who look at pieces of the personality (personality traits), as measured by detailed questionnaires.

stage theorists of personality Theorists who consider stages of change across the lifespan and how one's personality interacts with the world.

Which theory explains personality development best? Let's start with the position that the adult personality is made up of traits that remain continuously stable, in most cases, throughout adulthood.

CONTINUOUS TRAITS THEORY

An individual trait can be thought of as an individual's tendency to have consistent patterns of thoughts, feelings, and behaviours (McCrae & Costa, 1990). In the **five factor model (FFM) of personality,** McCrae and Costa describe five traits or dimensions of personality: **o**penness to experience, **c**onscientiousness, **e**xtroversion, **a**greeableness, and **n**euroticism, or OCEAN (McCrae & Costa, 2004). Each of these five traits consists of a cluster of qualities (see Figure 10.8). For example, agreeableness includes qualities such as a tendency to be trusting and cooperative rather than suspicious and critical toward others. People vary continuously on the traits, with most people falling in between the extremes.

An extensive body of research has used the five factor model in an effort to understand the influence of personality traits on a wide range of issues. Research has found that the five traits remain stable throughout adulthood even though a person's habits, life events, opinions, and relationships may change over the course of their life.

VAILLANT'S PREDICTIVE POWER

George Vaillant, as a stage theorist, saw adult personality development as continually changing. Vaillant's work focuses on the future, rather than the present, for middle-aged adults in his efforts to understand successful aging. Vaillant has spent the last 35 years as director of the Study of Adult Development at the Harvard University Health Service. As we saw in Chapter 1, Vaillant has overseen longitudinal studies spanning over 70 years, with an emphasis on exploring the components of happiness and successful aging. Vaillant identified seven major factors that predict healthy aging, both physically and psychologically:

- employing mature adaptations
- education
- stable marriage
- not smoking
- not abusing alcohol
- exercise
- healthy weight

Vaillant concluded that in order to reach the age of 80 in a good place, an individual had to have five or six of these factors in place at age 50. Of the men in his study who had only 3 or fewer of these protective factors in place at age 50, none reached the age of 80 in good health. Surprisingly, money and overall income were not related to happiness. When asked what he had learned from the men in the Harvard study, Vaillant responded, "The only thing that really matters in life are your relationships to other people" (Shenk, 2009).

> **five factor model (FFM) of personality** McCrae and Costa's theory that there are five major personality traits, which they believe govern the adult personality.

FRIENDSHIPS

Middle adulthood is typically a time when close friendships become fewer and more precious. The findings of Fung, Cartensen, and Lang (2001) suggest that people begin narrowing their range of social partners long before middle age. In early adulthood, interaction frequency with acquaintances and close friends begins to decline, while it increases with spouses and siblings. It would seem that, at about age 30, individuals choose a select few relationships from which to derive support, self-definition, and a sense of stability. These relationships with a select few become increasingly close and satisfying during middle adulthood. The idea that face-to-face contact is necessary for closeness is no longer true, thanks to technological advances with cellphones, email, social networking, and programs such as Skype, which allow people to communicate instantly despite geographic or other constraints.

Marriage and the Family ◀ L06

Interpersonal relationships in middle adulthood tend to revolve around family. Although individuals may reside under one roof, family members each bring their individual personalities and experiences outside the home into the home environment over a period of many years. What

FIGURE 10.8

The Five Factors of Personality

Openness	**C**onscientiousness	**E**xtroversion	**A**greeableness	**N**euroticism (emotional stability)
• Imaginative or practical	• Organized or disorganized	• Sociable or retiring	• Softhearted or ruthless	• Calm or anxious
• Interested in variety or routine	• Careful or careless	• Fun-loving or sombre	• Trusting or suspicious	• Secure or insecure
• Independent or conforming	• Disciplined or impulsive	• Affectionate or reserved	• Helpful or uncooperative	• Self-satisfied or self-pitying

TAKE A STAND

Celebrate the PFLAG

A national organization that puts family and friends at the heart of its mission is PFLAG—Parents, Families, and Friends of Lesbians and Gays. The group aims to "actively assist in the recognition and growth of gay, lesbian, bisexual, transgender, transsexual, two-spirit, intersex, queer and questioning persons and their families and friends, within their diverse cultures and societies." (http://pflagcanada.ca).

In middle adulthood, many parents choose to support their LGBT children, friends, and others even as issues such as gay marriage and adoption of children by gays and lesbians remain deeply divisive. Supporters and opponents argue over human rights, faith, and basic freedoms.

Who should decide who may marry or adopt children? Do people need to agree on controversial topics in order for society to function? Why or why not? How do controversies over gay marriage and gays and lesbians being allowed to adopt affect people's lives?

---

a parent experienced as a teenager is vastly different from what his 16-year-old experiences today. Likewise, a couple's relationship undergoes significant changes before and after parenting roles and responsibilities emerge, regardless of how much the partners love each other. This means that the complex family relationship involves specific factors that grow and change within a family, just as each individual grows and changes over time.

> The only thing that really matters in life are your relationships to other people.

GEORGE VAILLANT (2008)

MARRIAGE AT MIDDLE AGE

Middle age is often a time when husbands and wives reappraise their marriages. Often, marriages that were challenging in early adulthood grow better with time, as couples learn to communicate and negotiate successfully. A reduction in the stresses relating to money, children, and career achievement can allow couples to rediscover the positive aspects of their relationship. For example, the period after the children leave home can be like a second honeymoon for many couples.

empty nest syndrome The feelings parents may have as a result of their last child leaving home.

emotional divorce Sometimes partners learn to "put up with" each other. The only activities and interests they share are ones that revolve around the children.

After the initial feelings of sadness and loss that result when the last child leaves the home (often called the **empty nest syndrome**), married couples can evaluate the job they have done with their children and focus future plans on their own interests and needs. Because life expectancy is now longer than in years past, the period after children leave home is longer than it used to be, and couples can typically look forward to spending another 30 or more years together.

On the other hand, marital tension is sometimes suppressed while young children live at home. As children leave home to go to college or to start families of their own, these tensions may be more openly expressed. Sometimes partners have learned to "put up with" each other, and the only activities and interests they share are ones that revolve around the children—they have engaged in **emotional divorce**. When the children leave home, the partners realize how far apart they have drifted. Emotional divorce in this situation is often a precursor to legal divorce.

There is an increasing number of Canadians who do not have children. The 2006 Census was the first to show more married couples without children (42.7% of all census families) than with children (41.4%). The gap between these two groups grew over the next five years with the 2011 Census showing 44.5% of couples having no children and only 39.2% with children (Statistics Canada, 2012d). Studies (e.g., Twenge, Campbell, & Foster, 2003) have found that marital satisfaction remains higher in childless couples than in couples who have children. Twenge et al. (2003) believe that this is due to an increase in role conflicts and a decrease in freedom among couples with children.

FIGURE 10.9
Duration of Marriages that Ended in Divorce

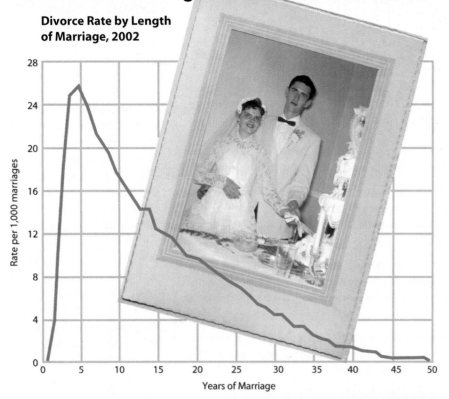

Divorce Rate by Length of Marriage, 2002

Divorce in middle adulthood can have positive and negative aspects, as it does in other life periods. Some of the positive aspects of later divorce are that the adults are typically more financially stable, their children are older and less reliant on them for support, and the partners may have a stronger sense of self that will help them cope with the trauma of divorce and the prospect of living alone. Some negative aspects are that older adults' finances are often more complicated than in early marriage. Spouses may own property together and share investments. Also, if one partner earns substantially more than the other, this can greatly impact the divorce negotiations. Older adults have more-established social networks than younger adults, and friends are sometimes forced to choose their loyalties. The divorcing couple may feel that they have failed at a major part of life and have let down their families.

Canada has also experienced an increase in the number of same-sex marriages in recent years due to the legalization of such marriages in 2005. The highest proportion of same-sex marriages involve those who are in middle adulthood with 27% being between 45 and 54 years of age and 69% between 35 and 64 years of age. Further, 30% of same-sex couples in common-law relationships are in the 45 to 54 age group (Statistics Canada, 2012e). Same-sex couples are as varied as opposite-sex ones in that some have children from previous relationships, some have adopted children together, and others are childless. Future research is needed to investigate the effects of parenthood on marital satisfaction among same-sex couples.

DIVORCE IN MIDDLE ADULTHOOD

Although most divorces take place during the first 5 years of marriage and the number tapers off rapidly after that, the proportion of divorced people in middle adulthood is relatively high, because many who divorced earlier have never remarried. Figure 10.9 shows the duration of marriages that ended in divorce. Additionally, many Canadians become divorced in middle adulthood. The average age of divorce is 44.5 for men and 41.9 for women (Human Resources and Skills Development Canada, 2013a). Figure 10.10 provides additional information about the divorce rate in Canada.

FIGURE 10.10
Divorce Rate by Region

30-year Total Divorce Rate, by Region, 2008
(per 1,000 marriages)

Region	Rate
Canada	407
Newfoundland & Labrador	250
Prince Edward Island	317
Nova Scotia	311
New Brunswick	297
Quebec	474
Ontario	421
Manitoba	315
Saskatchewan	303
Alberta	460
British Columbia	371
Yukon Territory	597
Northwest Territory and Nunavut	351

Note: The total divorce rate represents the proportion of new marriages projected to end in divorce before the thirtieth wedding anniversary, if the divorce rates by marriage duration observed in a given year are repeated in the future.

Source: Statistics Canada. (2011g). Health Statistics Division. Canadian Vital Statistics, Divorce Database and Marriage Database, Ottawa: Statistics Canada.

RELATIONSHIPS WITH AGING PARENTS

Many middle-aged adults enjoy closer relationships with their aging parents at this time. Adult children recognize strengths in their parents that they hadn't noticed before, as they experience some challenges of adulthood that they couldn't appreciate when they were younger. They also tend to see eye to eye on issues they'd clashed over previously, such as politics, religion, and child rearing.

A reality that complicates the lives of many couples in middle adulthood, however, involves relationships with aging parents. Often, the time previously spent caring for young children is filled with concerns and efforts to care for elderly parents. The term **sandwich genera-tion** describes the almost 3 in 10 adults who get squeezed between simultaneously caring for their children and their parents, parents-in-law, or some other elder (Williams, 2004). Many adults, however, avoid the complications of being squeezed because of timing or financial resources that allow them to hire additional help in the care of either the children or the aging parents. Other adults may feel an obligation to care for aging parents due to cultural expectations. This has traditionally been the case in many Asian cultures.

As parents grow older, they sometimes become as dependent on their middle-aged children as those children once were on them. Most people fail to anticipate the costs and emotional strains that the aging of their parents can engender. The most frequently cited problem of middle-aged women is not menopause or aging, but caring for aging parents or parents-in-law (Singleton, 2000). Daughters, often the oldest or the one living the closest with the fewest demands on her, are most likely going to be the primary caregiver of aging parents. Canadian researchers Lori Campbell and Anne Martin-Matthews (2003) have found that a number of factors influence the provision of care by sons. Sons are more likely to provide traditionally male care to their aging parents such as managing money and home mainte-nance and yard work than gender neutral (e.g., trans-portation, assistance with shopping) or traditionally female care (e.g., toileting, preparing meals, feeding), but sons who feel a strong obligation towards car-ing for their parents are more likely to provide the latter two types of care. Caregivers sometimes face a number of issues in bal-ancing work and family, but siblings often recognize the stresses they have, and those without children to care for tend to pick up the slack in caring for aging parents.

In some cases, caring for a family member who is very sick can have negative effects on the psychologi-cal health of the caregiver. For example, Beeson and colleagues (2000) found that caregivers for relatives with Alzheimer's disease were at high risk for feelings of loneliness, because the disease causes the ailing rela-tive to withdraw psychologically and emotionally from any relationship with the caregiver. The loneliness that results from the loss of companionship between the caregiver and the patient has been linked to higher lev-els of depression among caregiving wives, husbands, and daughters. The researchers also found that female caregivers experienced more depression than male care-givers, with caregiving wives experiencing the highest levels of depression. The support of siblings and friends greatly helps reduce the negative effects of caring for elderly parents.

RELATIONSHIPS WITH SIBLINGS

The importance of sibling relationships has long been recognized for its influences on a person's cognitive and social growth. Sibling relationships have the potential to be the most enduring that a person has. People don't usually meet their spouses until young adulthood or at least adolescence. Most parents usually pass away before their children do. Yet most sibling relationships last the lifespan of most adults; they can be very close, somewhat distant, or rife with rivalry.

One would hope that the passage of time and grow-ing maturity would lessen sibling rivalry. Certainly adult

---

sandwich generation Term used to describe adults who are simulta-neously caring for their children and their aging parents, parents-in-law, or some other elder.

FEATUREDMEDIA

Love and Marriage in Middle Adulthood

Kramer vs. Kramer (1979)—How does a newly di-vorced dad learn to take care of himself and his young son, and then ultimately fight to keep him when his ex-wife suddenly demands custody and complicates their new and deep relationship?

War of the Roses (1989)—How low would you stoop to get the onetime love of your life out of your house (and out of your life!) in a divorce bat-tle to end all battles?

Last Chance Harvey (2008)—What happens when two adults, each dealing with their own personal crisis, meet and experience a life-changing week-end together?

The Blind Side (2009)—What inspires a woman to adopt a homeless teen and support him and his dreams of playing football?

---

siblings are faced with more serious tasks than are child-hood siblings. For example, most middle-aged siblings must make mutual decisions concerning the care of their elderly parents and eventually deal with the aftermath of parents' deaths. Changing family patterns raise questions about sibling relationships, as couples more often choose to have fewer or even no children. Children who have few or no siblings to turn to for companionship and psychological support may become adults who consider work and career very important in their lives.

FAMILY VIOLENCE

Family violence is defined as "abusive behaviour that can be physical, sexual, psychological or financial" and "can also take the form of physical or emotional neglect" (Public Health Agency of Canada, 2010b, pg. 1). This kind of violence can be perpetrated on children, parents, and intimate partners. There has been more attention paid to the abuse of aging parents in recent years as an increasing number of middle-aged adults experience the stress of being part of the sandwich generation. A recent study showed that while older adults (those 65 years of age or greater) have lower rates of victimization than any other age group, family violence against seniors increased by 14% between 2004 and 2009 with much of that abuse being perpetrated by grown children (Statistics Canada, 2011e). While intimate partner abuse appears to be a more common problem among younger adults, there

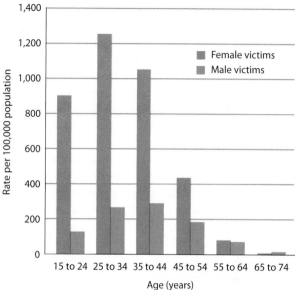

FIGURE 10.11

Dating Violence Victimization by Gender and Age, 2011

Source: Statistics Canada (2013e) catalogue no. 85-002-X: Measuring violence against women: Statistical trends Chart 2.2 p. 56.

are still a substantial number of middle-aged adults who experience such violence. Figure 10.11 shows the level of dating violence experienced by Canadians.

Patterns of Work ◄L07

Work challenges that arise during middle adulthood include working from home, non-traditional work schedules, and caring for ill or aging family members. Whereas employers used to focus most human resources on younger employees, a trend has emerged among employers to acknowledge some concerns of middle-aged employees, such as

- advancing age and death,
- bodily changes related to aging,
- adjusting and attaining career goals, and
- change in family and work relationships.

Businesses have responded to these issues and others with continuing education, workshops, and other forms of professional development. As the demand for new skills grows, training in emerging technologies is common, and employees are sometimes reimbursed if they enroll in degree programs that will make them more valuable contributors in the workplace. A greater appreciation for the contribution of older workers is important. As the labour pool shrinks, the welfare of the older, established workforce becomes more valuable. Employees who feel valued and respected by their

---

ADMIT ONE · 289147 · 289147

FEATURED MEDIA

Adult Sibling Relationshps

Arrested Development (2003–2006)—With Dad in prison, how does one son balance his needs against those of his dysfunctional family?

The Savages (2007)—How do a sister and brother negotiate the responsibilities involved in caring for their infirm father?

Six Feet Under (2001–2005)—What conflicts ensue among family members and love interests as the family struggles to keep their funeral parlour business alive?

You Can Count on Me (2000)—How does a single mother juggle her parenting and romantic relationships when an estranged brother returns to town?

work–family conflict
The phenomenon that occurs when demands of a person's role as a caregiver conflict with demands of his or her role as a worker.

globalization The outsourcing of work to a less expensive labour supply in foreign countries.

downsizing A reduction in a company's workforce to improve its total revenue.

risk factors The stressors that individuals experience, including poverty, chronic illness, and divorce.

employers find their jobs more meaningful and feel more empowered (Gomez & Rosen, 2001; Thompson & Bunderson, 2001).

WORK–FAMILY CONFLICT

Work–family conflict is defined as the phenomenon that occurs when demands of a person's role as a caregiver conflict with or spill over into demands of his or her role as a worker. When this type of role overload or role conflict occurs, it often causes stress for the adult and for the family. The role of family emotional support, the quality of the employee–supervisor relationship, and the personality of the individual all influence feelings of work–family conflict. For example, Bernas and Major (2000) found that higher levels of emotional support from a woman's family were associated with less work–family conflict and decreased reports of stress. Somewhat paradoxically, although a positive employee–supervisor relationship at work often resulted in lower feelings of stress in women studied, it also resulted in the women feeling that their work was spilling over into family life. Men and women often compensate by bringing work home or working from home in order to care for younger family members or aging parents. Women may feel additional conflict because they are still responsible for the majority of the child care within the home.

MID-CAREER CHALLENGES

Considerable attention is now being given to the career challenges people face in middle adulthood. For some, it is a problem of **globalization**, in which much work is outsourced to a less expensive labour supply in foreign countries; for others, **downsizing** is a reality that threatens their lives and livelihood, with layoffs and decreased benefits. Many employers attempt to motivate employees to retire early by promising financial rewards.

By the time a person reaches the age of 40 in a professional or managerial career, it is typically clear whether he or she will make it to the top of the field. If people haven't reached their goals by this time, most adjust their goals or, if possible, begin a new career. Some middle-aged adults take a mentoring attitude toward younger employees.

Middle adulthood is also a time when family expenses, such as university education for children or elder care, can become great. If family income is threatened or insufficient, this obviously can create stress, especially if only one partner is employed. If the non-working spouse decides to get a job, other types of stress can sometimes occur. For other couples, the decision of a non-working spouse to get a job leads to a period of renewed spirit as individuals rise to the challenges and one partner feels a sense of pride in contributing to the welfare of the other partner in a new way.

Coping with Stress ◀L08

The stresses of middle adulthood are unique in one important way: Adults are usually expected to deal with stress entirely on their own. Their children and aging parents (if parents are still living) may not be able to offer significant emotional or financial help. While adults can and should accept help from others, an increasing number of crises call for independent decisions and actions. For example, many families exist in a state of perpetual crisis, facing multiple challenges relating to work, economic status, family safety and support, and health. Researchers have identified these factors as major causes of stress and have created specific strategies to help families reduce stress (Dacey & Fiore, 2006; see also Table 10.3).

RISK AND RESILIENCE

The stressors that individuals experience are called **risk factors**. Risk factors include poverty, chronic illness, parental mental illness and substance abuse, exposure to violence, and family experiences such as divorce and teenage parenthood. Individuals who deal well with stress are said to have resilience. Researchers have been interested in identifying characteristics of resilient individuals that protect them from stress. Three kinds of

TABLE 10.3
Proactive Stress Reduction

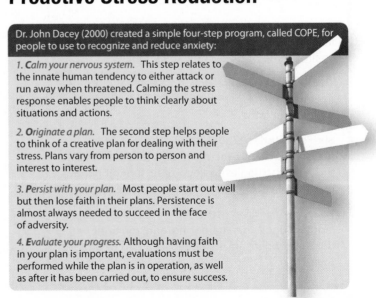

Dr. John Dacey (2000) created a simple four-step program, called COPE, for people to use to recognize and reduce anxiety:

1. Calm your nervous system. This step relates to the innate human tendency to either attack or run away when threatened. Calming the stress response enables people to think clearly about situations and actions.

2. Originate a plan. The second step helps people to think of a creative plan for dealing with their stress. Plans vary from person to person and interest to interest.

3. Persist with your plan. Most people start out well but then lose faith in their plans. Persistence is almost always needed to succeed in the face of adversity.

4. Evaluate your progress. Although having faith in your plan is important, evaluations must be performed while the plan is in operation, as well as after it has been carried out, to ensure success.

PERSPECTIVES ON **DIVERSITY**

Gender and Cultural Differences in Response to Stress

People often assume that men and women experience stress differently. For example, women are described as responding to stress by nurturing offspring and joining social groups to increase resources, while men have been described in terms of the fight-or-flight response (Taylor et al., 2000).

Other researchers have noted cultural differences related to stress, such as the tendency of Asian and African cultures to be communal, work together, and seek support, compared to the view of North American culture as individualistic.

Experts on stress note that while gender differences occur within a specific ecosystem, cultural differences develop between ecosystems (Kashima et al., 1995), so how one individual responds to stress is actually more complex than simply gender or cultural design. For example, the feelings of stress that a Canadian woman experiences, though she may be more socially connected than a man (in terms of concern for offspring and social networks), are also entwined with a sense of self and self-orientation that differs, for example, from that of women in traditional Chinese culture. A Chinese woman may experience stress through the cultural lens of emphasis on the good of the larger group. Political, historical, and evolutionary influences must all be considered when making comparisons about gender and cultural differences.

---

protective factors have been identified: family environments, support networks, and personality characteristics.

We have explored the value of resilience in several of the other stages of development. In middle adulthood, family environments that protect people from stress include individuals who share responsibilities and workload in the home, and financial stability that supports the well-being of the family in terms of physical and emotional needs. Support networks include informal and formal networks, which can range from work colleagues and close friends or family who share concerns and good humour, to Weight Watchers or Alcoholics Anonymous groups that support people with personal challenges. Individual personality characteristics influence the way people experience life stresses and challenges: A person with an easygoing temperament might not be as concerned if she gets laid off from work, whereas another person might immediately begin worrying about her ability to pay the bills, feed her children, and continue on her career path.

While adults do have more control over their lives than younger people, which can reduce stress, adults tend to experience more stress overload—the tendency to manage many activities and circumstances at the same time. When adults are interviewed, however, interpersonal conflict is the most commonly reported cause of stress in middle adulthood.

Seligman and Csikszentmihalyi (2000) propose that **positive psychology**, as a field of psychology and as a profession, can help people identify their strengths and use those strengths to help them succeed and thrive. Recognizing that most of the time people dwell on what has gone wrong in their lives, positive psychology aims to point out the things that individuals and groups do well that contribute to a more positive life and society. For individuals, positive behaviours and traits include courage, the ability to love and forgive others, and wisdom. For groups, these include responsibility and citizenship, nurturance, and a strong work ethic. In middle adulthood, a positive outlook provides people with strength and inspiration to grapple with the biopsychosocial challenges they encounter and prepares them for the next stage of their lives—late adulthood.

> **protective factors** Characteristics of resilient individuals that protect them from stress.
>
> **positive psychology** A branch of psychology that emphasizes the impact of positive psychological traits on individual and group behaviours.

Lisa: Look on the bright side, Dad.
Did you know that the Chinese use the same word
for "crisis" as they do for "opportunity"?
Homer: Yes! Cris-atunity.

THE SIMPSONS, "FEAR OF FLYING" (1994)

CONCLUSIONS & SUMMARY

What kinds of physical changes affect people in middle adulthood?

- Health concerns in middle adulthood include increasing weight and lower basal metabolism rate.
- In the middle period of adulthood, there is a common but often unnecessary decline in muscular ability, due in part to a decrease in exercise.
- Sensory abilities—vision, hearing, smell, and taste—begin to show slight declines in middle adulthood.
- The climacteric, the loss of reproductive ability, occurs at menopause for women but at a much older age for most men.

What are the main factors that affect sexuality among middle-aged people?

- Some minor changes in sexual physiology occur for both sexes, but these need not hamper sexual satisfaction.

What are the main factors affecting a person's intellectual development in middle adulthood?

- Horn suggests that, although fluid intelligence deteriorates with age, crystallized intelligence does not.
- Sternberg suggests three types of intelligence: analytical, creative, and practical.
- Creativity, important in a rapidly changing world, manifests itself at different peak periods throughout adulthood.
- Learning in middle adulthood can be enhanced through motivation, new learning experiences, and changes in education systems.

What happens to relationships in middle adulthood?

- Dealing with change is as serious a challenge in midlife as at any other time.
- Learning new ways to get along with one's spouse, parents, siblings, and children is necessary at this time.
- Erikson's theory placed middle adulthood within the stage labelled "generativity versus stagnation." Generativity means the ability to be useful to ourselves and to society without concern for material reward.

What happens to personality during the adult years? Does it typically change or remain continuous?

- Research by trait theorists such as McCrae and Costa generally supports the notion that human beings remain fairly stable throughout life.
- In contrast, theorists such as Levinson and Erikson argue that human beings are best described as constantly changing and developing throughout life.

- Levinson suggested that most men go through a midlife transition in which they must deal with the polarities between young/old, masculinity/femininity, destruction/creation, and attachment/separation.
- Levinson also suggested that females go through a similar experience to that of males, with some notably different influences, such as the conflict women feel regarding work–family.
- McCrae and Costa defined five major personality traits that they believe govern the adult personality: neuroticism, extroversion, openness to experience, agreeableness, and conscientiousness.
- A deepening of friendships begins in middle age and goes on throughout the rest of life.

What are the typical patterns of marriage and family relationships during middle adulthood?

- Middle age offers a time for marriage reappraisal, which proves positive for most couples.
- Middle age is also a time when most people develop improved relationships with their parents, though in some cases the relationship begins to reverse itself when those parents become dependent on their middle-aged children.
- Sibling relationships have the potential to be the most enduring that a person can have.
- While middle-aged adults are less likely to be involved in violence than other age groups, a substantial number are still victims of intimate partner and dating violence while a smaller number are abusive towards aging parents.

What are the patterns of work that we most often see in this life stage?

- In recent years, a trend has emerged among employers to recognize some of the concerns of middle-aged employees.
- Considerable attention is now being given to the crisis many people undergo in the middle of their careers.
- One major way of dealing with the mid-career crisis is for the middle-aged worker to help younger employees make significant contributions.

How do adults generally deal with the stress caused by the major events and daily hassles in their lives?

- Calming the nervous system, creating a plan to deal with stress, persistence, and evaluating the plan are strategies that help adults cope.
- People who are exposed to many risk factors but develop few behavioural or psychological problems are called resilient.

1. When you look at the physical condition of your parents and grandparents, and their attitudes toward health, do you see evidence of stability or change over time?

2. What are some ways that our society might foster the creative abilities of its adult citizens?

3. Describe an ideal strategy for middle-aged people to take care of their ailing, elderly parents, where everyone feels loved, respected, and valued as a member of the family.

Chapter REVIEW TEST

Answers: 1b, 2d, 3d, 4a, 5b, 6a, 7d, 8d, 9c, 10c

1. Basal metabolism rate refers to
   a. the minimum amount of energy an individual tends to use after exercising.
   b. the minimum amount of energy an individual tends to use when in a resting state.
   c. the maximum amount of energy an individual tends to use after exercising.
   d. the maximum amount of energy an individual tends to use when in a resting state.

2. Middle-aged adults who have five or more drinks of alcohol in one sitting are engaging in the problematic behaviour of
   a. social drinking.
   b. drinking to cope.
   c. addictive drinking.
   d. binge drinking.

3. In the 2008 Durex Global Sex Survey, which asked participants about the frequency of their sexual activity, Canada ranked _____ out of the 26 countries surveyed.
   a. 1st
   b. 10th
   c. 17th
   d. 22nd

4. What is an example of crystallized intelligence?
   a. arithmetical reasoning
   b. letter grouping
   c. recalled paired associates
   d. dominoes

5. A factor in learning ability during middle adulthood is motivation to learn. It is important for researchers to keep in mind that _____ affects an adult's level of motivation.
   a. level of education
   b. meaningfulness of the task
   c. interest
   d. external distraction

6. If a person is experiencing stress related to a crisis in middle adulthood, the first step in a plan to combat related anxiety is
   a. calming the nervous system.
   b. persisting in the face of obstacles.
   c. evaluating a plan.
   d. denying there is a problem.

7. Dave and Meghan have drifted apart over the years but remain married to each other because of their children. Their relationship illustrates the
   a. functional marriage.
   b. practical marriage.
   c. functional divorce.
   d. emotional divorce.

8. What is the most frequently cited problem of middle-aged adult women?
   a. aging
   b. menopause
   c. caring for their children
   d. caring for their aging parents

9. Research suggests that a typical characteristic of a sibling relationship in middle adulthood is
   a. growing distance.
   b. increased animosity.
   c. mutual caring for aging parents.
   d. rivalry over the inheritance.

10. McCrae and Costa argue that, although habits, life events, opinions, and relationships may change over the lifespan, the basic _____ of an individual does not.
    a. value
    b. orientation
    c. personality
    d. coping mechanisms

LATE
ADULTHOOD

Must We Age and Die?

Physiological Theories of Aging

Physical Development

Cognitive Development

Social Development

Patterns of Work

As You READ

After reading this chapter, you should be able to answer the following questions:

LO1 ▶ Must we age and die?

LO2 ▶ What theories have been proposed to explain why we age?

LO3 ▶ What are the key aspects of physical development among the elderly?

LO4 ▶ How is cognitive development affected by old age?

LO5 ▶ How do social relationships develop during late adulthood?

LO6 ▶ What are major factors affecting the older worker?

L01 Must We Age and Die?

Must we all decline as we age, moving inevitably toward death? So far, no person has attained immortality, but not all living things die. Some trees alive today are known to be more than 2,500 years old; they have aged but show no sign of dying. Bacteria apparently are able to live indefinitely, as long as they have the necessary conditions for existence. The fact is, we are not sure why we age, and until we are, we cannot be certain that aging and death are absolutely inevitable. Nor can we overlook those who appear to age well, a process which is often referred to as "successful aging" (Vaillant & Mukamal, 2001; Westerhof et al., 2001). This uncertainty about aging and death contributes to fears about adulthood that are felt by even the very young (Cummings, Knopf, & DeWeaver, 2000).

Vaillant and Mukamal's concept of successful aging contradicts a stereotypical characteristic of old age, that of declining mental ability. Though sometimes difficult to notice because they can be subtle, such assumptions about older people maintain prejudices that result in **ageism**, a discriminatory attitude against older people based on their age (Levy & Banaji, 2002).

Is there some truth to these stereotypes? Does growing old mean doom and gloom for our appearance and abilities, or is there only a relatively slight decline in capacity? Are some negative aspects of aging the result of a self-fulfilling prophecy (people expect to deteriorate, so they stop trying to be fit, and then they do deteriorate)? Could most of us age into capable, happy folks who seem to overcome age and remain vigorous into our nineties and beyond?

> **ageism** Stereotyping or unfair treatment of individuals or groups on the basis of age.
>
> **gerontology** The field of science that deals with issues, problems, and diseases specific to older adults.
>
> **life expectancy** The number of years that a person born in a specific year is expected to live.

In youth we learn, in age we understand.

AUTHOR UNKNOWN

Gerontology is the broad term for the field of science that focuses on these questions and assists older adults with issues and problems that they encounter as they age. Gerontology can include facets of the medical profession, social work, and more. A gerontologist, therefore, is a professional who works with older adults in various capacities.

LIFE EXPECTANCY

The concept of successful aging is not only interesting, it is critical to consider as advances in technology and medicine, among other factors, contribute to a greater number of older people living longer and healthier lives. Human **life expectancy** refers to the number of years that a person born in a specific year is expected to live. In Canada, life expectancy was 81 (80.8) years in 2010. Women in Canada can expect to outlive men by approximately 4 years and this has remained consistent over the past 10 years (Statistics Canada, 2012f). There is little difference among the provinces, but there is a noteable difference between Aboriginal people and the total Canadian population. However, that gap in life expectancy is projected to decrease. In 2017, the life expectancy is projected to be the following:

- Total Canadian population: 79 years for men and 83 years for women
- Inuit population: 64 years for men and 83 years for women

TAKE A **STAND**

Successful Seniors

Ed Whitlock is an 81-year-old Canadian long-distance runner. In 2003, he became the first person over 70 years of age to run a marathon in less than three hours. At age 81, on Sunday September 16, 2012, Whitlock broke the Canadian and unofficial world half-marathon record at the Milton Half-Marathon, running it in 1:30:59 (Ewing, 2012).

What is it that drives individuals like Whitlock to continue pushing themselves physically on a daily basis while others the same age barely have the strength to carry out their daily activities?

PERSPECTIVES ON **DIVERSITY**

The Profile of a Canadian Senior

In 1996, 12% of the population in Canada was over 65. This figure is projected to rise to 18.7% by 2025 (Canadian Encyclopedia). More than one-quarter of all seniors in Canada were born abroad, half of them from Western European countries. This profile will change as younger immigrants from all regions age. The percentage of immigrant seniors born in Asia increased from 5.6% to 19.1% from 1981 to 2001.

Canada's Aboriginal population remains younger than the non-Aboriginal population, but life expectancy is gradually increasing among these people. Seniors are revered in many Aboriginal cultures for their knowledge and experiences, and the integral role that they play in the vitality and well-being of their families, communities, and nations. Aboriginal people turn to elders as key sources of traditional knowledge, wisdom, and cultural continuity (Turcotte & Schellenberg, 2007).

Communities that welcome elderly citizens as vital members of the social group tend to value personal contributions more than financial ones, and these cultures reap the physical and psychological benefits associated with this inclusive stance.

Because of increases in life expectancy, Canada is experiencing a dramatic increase in the numbers of people who live to old age (see Figure 11.1). Experts note that people are living longer, and they are also living more active, healthier lives. This includes exercising and participating in other activities that contribute to overall well-being. There is some concern, however, that the impact of recent economic hardships and related stress may have some effects on senior citizens that is yet to be captured in life expectancy data (Parker-Pope, 2009).

Canada has a higher life expectancy rate than some other countries (e.g., France and Norway) and a lower life expectancy than others (e.g., Japan and Switzerland). Figure 11.2 presents some comparative data. Differences exist because of many interrelated factors, such as quality of and access to medical care, and general health and nutrition.

FIGURE 11.1

Canadian Population 65 and Older

% of the Population 65 or Older

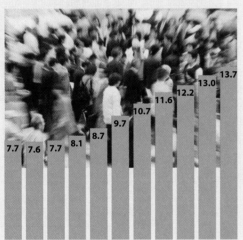

7.7 7.6 7.7 8.1 8.7 9.7 10.7 11.6 12.2 13.0 13.7

1956 1961 1966 1971 1976 1981 1986 1991 1996 2001 2006

Source: Statistics Canada. Censuses of Population, 1956 to 2006. Published by authority of the Minister responsible for Statistics Canada. © Minister of Industry, 2013. All rights reserved. Use of this publication is governed by the Statistics Canada Open License Agreement.

FIGURE 11.2

Life Expectancy Rates Around the World

Life Expectancy, 2009
Grade ■ A ■ B ■ C ■ D

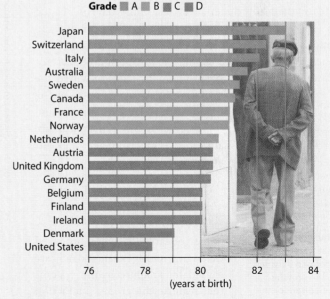

Japan
Switzerland
Italy
Australia
Sweden
Canada
France
Norway
Netherlands
Austria
United Kingdom
Germany
Belgium
Finland
Ireland
Denmark
United States

76   78   80   82   84
(years at birth)

Source: The Conference Board of Canada. Life Expectancy 2009. © Copyright 2013 The Conference Board of Canada.

- Métis and First Nations population: 73–74 years for men and 78–80 years for women

This is an average increase of one to two years from the life expectancy that was recorded for the Aboriginal population in 2001 (Statistics Canada, 2010).

L02 ▶ Physiological Theories of Aging

It is clear that organisms inherit a tendency to live for a certain length of time. The average human lifespan of approximately 70 years is the longest of any mammal. Elephants, horses, and hippopotamuses are known to live as long as 50 years, but most mammals die much sooner.

Some doctors say, "No one ever dies of old age." This is true. People die of some physiological failure, which is more likely to occur as they get older. One likely explanation is that the various life-support systems gradually weaken. Illness and death come about as a cumulative result of various weaknesses. Several different theories have been suggested to account for aging.

AGING BY PROGRAM

According to the **aging by program** theory, we age because aging is programmed into us. It is hard to understand which evolutionary processes, if any, govern longevity. For example, the vast majority of animals die at or before the end of their reproductive period, but human females average 20 to 30 years beyond the end of their reproductive cycles. This may be related to the capacities of the human brain. For example, in times when food is scarce, older people may remember where it was obtained during the last period of scarcity. However, it may be that we humans have outwitted the evolutionary process and, owing to our medical achievements and improvements in lifestyle, are able to live much longer than our ancestors.

aging by program Theory that we age because aging is programmed into us.

homeostatic imbalance Theory that aging is due to a failure in the systems that regulate the proper interaction of the organs.

cross-linkage theory The theory that, when cross-links are formed between peptides, the proteins are altered, often for the worse.

collagen Major connective tissue in the body; provides the elasticity in human skin and blood vessels.

HOMEOSTATIC IMBALANCE

Some researchers have proposed that aging and ultimately death are caused by a failure in the systems that regulate the proper interaction of the organs, rather than by wear and tear on the organs themselves. These homeostatic (feedback) systems are responsible, for example, for the regulation of the sugar and adrenaline levels in the blood. Apparently there is not much difference in the systems of the young and the old when they are in a quiet state. It is when stress is put on the systems (death of a spouse, loss of a job, a frightening experience) that we see the effects of the elderly **homeostatic imbalance**. The older body simply doesn't react as effectively to these stresses. Figure 11.3 shows the progress from homeostasis to failure.

CROSS-LINKAGE THEORY

The proteins that make up a large part of cells are composed of peptides. When cross-links are formed between peptides (a natural process of the body), the proteins are altered, often for the worse. This is known as the **cross-linkage theory**. For example, **collagen** is the major connective tissue in the body; it provides the elasticity in our skin and blood vessels. When its proteins are altered, there is an adverse effect on skin (sagging and wrinkles) and vessels (varicose veins).

FIGURE 11.3
Homeostasis and Health

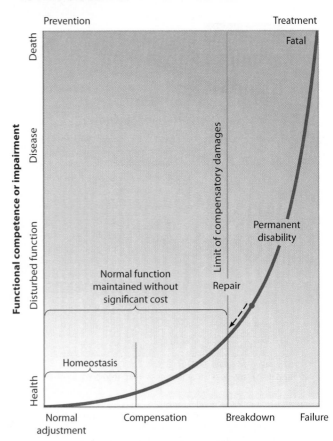

▲ This graph shows the progressive stages of homeostasis from adjustment (health) to failure (death).

Source: Paola S. Timiras. (1972). *Developmental physiology and aging.* Macmillan. Fig. 28.1.

I wish I had a twin, so I could know what I'd look like without plastic **surgery**.

JOAN RIVERS

AUTOIMMUNITY

With increasing age, there is increasing **autoimmunity**—the immune system in the body rejects the body's own tissue. Examples of this are rheumatoid arthritis, diabetes, vascular diseases, and hypertension. It may be that the body's tissues become more and more self-rejecting with age. Figure 11.4 shows several influences on adult mental and physical systems.

Autoimmunity could result from the production of new antigens, substances in the blood that produce antibodies. But sometimes the immune system makes a mistake and attacks the body's own tissue and organs. An antigen may

▲ Monozygotic (identical) twins are more likely to have similar lengths of life than dizygotic (fraternal) twins do.

be a foreign substance, such as a bacterium, or it may originate within the body, such as a toxin. These new antigens may come about for one of two reasons:

> **autoimmunity** Process by which the immune system in the body rejects the body's own tissue.

- Mutations cause the formation of altered RNA or DNA.
- Some cells may be "hidden" in the body during the early part of life. When these cells appear later, the body does not recognize them as its own and forms new antibodies to kill them. This, in turn, may cause organ malfunction.

GENETIC THEORIES OF AGING

Little doubt exists that genes affect how long we live. Kallman and Jarvik's (1959) classic research on identical twins still offers strong evidence of this. These researchers found that monozygotic twins (those who developed from the same fertilized egg) have more similar lengths of life than do dizygotic twins (those who developed from two fertilized eggs).

The *telomere shortening theory* proposes that changes in telomeres—tiny pieces of "junk DNA" at the ends of the chromosomes that make up the genes of all organisms (including humans)—could be a cause of aging. Telomeres protect real DNA during cell division. However, they cannot be copied exactly, so some of the chromosome gets cut off every time a cell divides. As cells continue to divide, the telomeres get shorter until they disappear. At that point, the real DNA copies will be faulty, and the cell ages and dies.

FIGURE 11.4

Influences on Adult Mental and Physical Systems

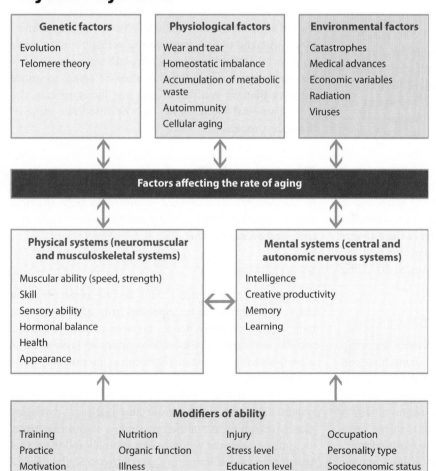

Genetic factors	Physiological factors	Environmental factors
Evolution	Wear and tear	Catastrophes
Telomere theory	Homeostatic imbalance	Medical advances
	Accumulation of metabolic waste	Economic variables
	Autoimmunity	Radiation
	Cellular aging	Viruses

Factors affecting the rate of aging

Physical systems (neuromuscular and musculoskeletal systems)	Mental systems (central and autonomic nervous systems)
Muscular ability (speed, strength)	Intelligence
Skill	Creative productivity
Sensory ability	Memory
Hormonal balance	Learning
Health	
Appearance	

Modifiers of ability

Training	Nutrition	Injury	Occupation
Practice	Organic function	Stress level	Personality type
Motivation	Illness	Education level	Socioeconomic status

▲ Research shows the importance of sensory stimulation for elderly individuals.

CENTENARIANS

There is a distinct group of adults that does not fit neatly into any theory of aging. They are called centenarians—people 100 or older who do not succumb to common causes of death for persons their age. What factors contribute to the survival of these men and women? Research by Smith (1997) suggested that these men and women are not necessarily more robust than the peers they've outlived, yet they are more resistant to cancer and other diseases, such as those of the circulatory system.

Canada's oldest citizen to date is Merle Barwis from Vancouver Island, British Columbia. She turned 112 in December, 2012. She was born in the United States and as a toddler moved north to the Canadian prairies, where her family settled in an area that is known today as the province of Saskatchewan. It is here that Barwis and her husband eventually raised their family before moving to B.C. after retirement. (Boswell, 2012).

OTHER MODIFIERS OF AGING

In addition to physiological and genetic factors that affect the individual's rate of aging, other factors can modify a person's level of ability more directly. Many of these modifiers interact with one another in complex ways. Some of the major modifiers are nutritional status, stress level, educational level, occupation, personality type, and socioeconomic status.

reaction time The time between the presence of a stimulus and the actual muscle activity that indicates a reaction to it.

Although relationships and social networks do not directly affect the survival of elderly people, they are related to their quality of life. Within nursing homes, those who tend to be aggressive and verbally agitated have poor social networks and generally lack intimacy with fellow residents. Because the outcomes of aging are more complex than an analysis of just one factor reveals, the biopsychosocial model is key to a full understanding of the aging process.

Physical Development

In this section, development is presented from multiple angles—reaction time, sensory abilities, other body systems, and overall health.

REACTION TIME

It is assumed that physical skills decline as people grow older. This appears to be especially true of manual dexterity. Although older people are able to perform short, coordinated manual tasks, a long series of tasks such as playing a stringed instrument becomes increasingly difficult for them.

Do physical skills decline because the human nervous system deteriorates? To answer this question, psychologists have completed numerous studies of **reaction time**, the time between the presence of a stimulus and the actual muscle activity that indicates a reaction to it. Studying reaction time is a scientific way of separating the effects of the central nervous system from the ability of the rest of the body to perform manual tasks. Although reaction time appears to decline with age, some researchers have pointed to several reasons for this decline. Most studies show that variables other than sheer neural or motor activities influence most change in physical skills over time. Social factors, such as opportunities for activities with peers, or expectations of family and society in general, can also impact physical behaviours.

People's beliefs and feelings about aging can also affect whether they age successfully; they can lead to a self-fulfilling prophecy. Persistent messages about declining physical abilities may actually lead to physical decline among older people, as people act the way they feel they should act. Older people may begin to believe that they are less capable than their actual performance reveals.

SENSORY ABILITIES

In late adulthood, strong patterns of decline occur in the sensory systems—hearing, vision, and balance (Humes & Floyd, 2005; Wong, 2001). Lack of sensory stimulation is one of many factors that emerges during later phases of life and contributes to the aging process. This comes about in part because elderly people are often less active physically and socially, reducing their exposure to sensory stimulation (such as sports activities) that they may have enjoyed earlier in life.

Although the aging process affects all five senses, decline is most obvious in terms of older people's vision and hearing. As people age, their eyes take longer to adjust when moving from a well-lighted room into darkness. This is a major reason why night driving becomes more challenging for the elderly. Older people also lose their acuity when it comes to depth perception. They are less able to distinguish how near or far objects are: They may have trouble knowing how far they are from the curb when trying to park a car, or how high a step is when they are about to climb a flight of stairs.

Diseases of the eye further complicate the natural aging effects on eyesight. **Macular degeneration** is caused by declines in the retina of the eye, primarily affecting the centre (or focus) of a person's vision. People with macular degeneration may be able to see items with their peripheral vision (around the periphery of the frame of their field of vision), but be unable to see something directly in front of them. The image above demonstrates what a person with macular degeneration experiences every day.

Career Apps

As a music therapist, how could you use percussion instruments with residents of a retirement home to increase their self-esteem?

▲ Individuals with macular degeneration are unable to see something directly in front of them.

Glaucoma is damage to the optic nerve caused by pressure that results from a buildup of fluid in the eye. It is detectable with routine eye exams and can be treated with eye drops; but, if left untreated, glaucoma has the potential to permanently damage a person's vision. **Cataracts**, which are a thickening of the lenses of the eyes, cause blurred, cloudy, or otherwise distorted vision. A routine surgical procedure can remove cataracts and restore optimal vision.

Hearing decline does not typically impact people in a serious way until they are in their 70s. Many hearing problems can be helped by hearing aids (as discussed in Chapter 10). Sometimes, two different hearing aids are recommended so that each ear can experience the extra support needed for optimal hearing at low and high frequencies.

macular degeneration An eye disease that affects the retina, impacting the centre of a person's field of vision.

glaucoma Damage to the optic nerve caused by pressure that results from a buildup of fluid in the eye.

cataracts Thickening of the eye lenses; cause blurred, cloudy vision.

▲ Vision and hearing often decline significantly as an individual ages.

TAKE A **STAND**

Should the Elderly Lose Their Licenses?

The Ontario Provincial Police report that in northeast Ontario, 30% of fatal traffic accidents involve drivers over the age of 55, and they fear this will only get worse as the baby boomers age (CBC News, 2013e). Candrive (the Canadian Driving Research Initiative for Vehicular Safety in the Elderly) is conducting research that aims to improve the safety of older adults and to develop an easy-to-use tool for health care professionals to determine who might be at risk (www.candrive.ca). This is an issue that has to be studied further because for some elderly drivers, having their license denied or revoked represents a significant loss of independence, and it may leave them stranded and without crucial transportation.

There is variation among older drivers' abilities just as there is variation among younger drivers' abilities. At what point should generalizations about older drivers' abilities influence public policy?

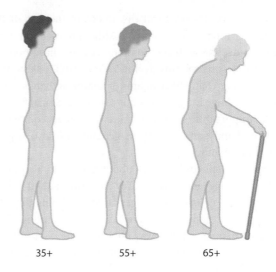

35+   55+   65+

▲ Osteoporosis can have an impact on an individual's height by cause a curve in the spine.

HEALTH ISSUES

Older Canadians are living longer and with fewer disabilities than the generations before them; however, the majority of seniors have at least one chronic disease or condition. In Canada, senior women are more likely than men to have arthritis, cataracts, and back problems. Rates of heart disease, diabetes, cancer, the effects of stroke, and Alzheimer's disease/dementia are higher among senior men (Gilmour & Park, 2006). Our health care system needs to focus more on health promotion and disease prevention than looking for a cure (Edwards & Mawani, 2006).

Osteoporosis

While some changes in the body system mostly affect appearance (yellowing of teeth, thickening fingernails, thinning of hair), a major concern relates to bone density. Bone density is often mistakenly considered only a woman's problem; but men and women alike experience a loss of bone density in late adulthood, with the result that their bones break more easily. **Osteoporosis** is a condition in which the bones are thin and brittle due to calcium loss. Routine bone density screening helps doctors identify patients who would benefit from taking calcium or other nutritional supplements. A more visible indicator of osteoporosis is

osteoporosis A condition in which bones are thin and brittle due to calcium loss.

arthritis Tissue inflammation in and around the joints.

the impact the condition has on a person's height and posture, often seen in a curved spine that resembles a hump, as shown in the accompanying illustration.

Arthritis

Arthritis refers to inflammation that occurs in and around the joints, including fingers as well as knees, elbows, and shoulders; it is characterized by redness, swelling, and possible loss of function in the affected areas. Although arthritis can occur at other stages of life, it is most common in late adulthood.

In late adulthood, concern about general health also includes the incidence of accidents that occur among the elderly population. Clearly, accidents happen randomly throughout the lifespan, but older people face greater consequences as a result of accidents because other body systems are compromised in ways that render them more vulnerable. For instance, misjudging the height of a step on a flight of stairs can cause an elderly person to fall. Decreased bone density results in more frequent fractures, which can result in serious injury. Taking some simple precautions, such as installing safety railings on stairways and in bathrooms, can significantly reduce a number of unnecessary accidents.

Heart Disease, Cancer, And Stroke

After the age of 65, the three causes of death with the highest incidence are heart disease, cancer, and stroke.

HEART DISEASE   Heart disease is linked to hereditary factors, such as race and ethnicity, and also to geographic and educational differences in the general population. Prevention efforts by public health agencies aimed at urban, lower socioeconomic communities strive to reduce the disparities among affected groups. These programs also work to reduce risk factors that contribute to the incidence of heart disease.

CANCER In 2008, cancer was the leading cause of death in every province and territory of Canada, for the first time (Statistics Canada, 2011f). There are sex differences in the incidence of cancer, differences that are caused by behaviour as well as sex hormones. Men have a higher rate of cancers of the stomach and liver. Women have a higher rate of cancers of the gallbladder and thyroid. The incidence of lung cancer is greater in men than in women, but women are catching up.

Prostate cancer is the most common cancer among Canadian men, as reflected in the following statistics (Canadian Cancer Society, 2013):

- An estimated 23,600 men will be diagnosed with prostate cancer in 2013, representing 25% of all new cancer cases in men that year.

- 3900 men will die from prostate cancer in 2013. This represents 10% of that year's cancer deaths in men.

- An average of 65 Canadian men will be diagnosed with prostate cancer, and 11 men will die of it every day.

The Canadian Cancer Society (2012) offers this profile for Canadian women:

- Breast cancer is the most common cancer among Canadian women, representing 26% of newly diagnosed cancers.

- Each year, more than 22,000 women develop breast cancer in Canada; more than 5000 women die of the disease.

- Although the incidence of breast cancer has been declining, the death rate has been declining even more strongly. The death rate peaked in 1986, but has decreased almost 40% since then—decreasing at a rate of 2.2% per year since 1998.

- The death rate from breast cancer is at its lowest since 1950, likely thanks to earlier diagnosis and improved treatments.

STROKE Strokes result from a burst blood vessel or clot in the brain that impedes the flow of blood to some part of the brain. When the affected area of the brain does not receive oxygen for a period of time, damage results in the form of paralysis, speech and vision problems, and memory loss. Some effects of stroke are temporary, yet some are permanent—depending on the type of stroke, the specific part of the brain affected, and the brain injury sustained. Paralysis or weakness in specific parts of the body is commonly experienced short- or long-term.

Strokes are more frequent in men than in women. Reasons for stroke are not clear, but risk factors include obesity and diabetes, which are somewhat avoidable if healthy lifestyle choices are made with regard to exercise and nutrition.

Alzheimer's Disease And Dementia

Much attention has been focused on **Alzheimer's disease** and the elderly. It is the most common form of **dementia**, accounting for 64% of all dementias in Canada (Alzheimer Society of Canada, 2013). A disease of the brain, Alzheimer's disease involves progressive, irreversible loss of neurons. It manifests as impaired memory, judgment, decision-making, orientation to the environment, and language. Alzheimer's disease is a leading cause of dementia, the deterioration of cognitive function over time due to brain infection or disease.

Alzheimer's disease Brain disease involving progressive, irreversible loss of neurons and manifesting as impaired memory, judgment, decision-making, orientation to the environment, and language.

dementia Deterioration of cognitive function over time caused by brain infection or disease.

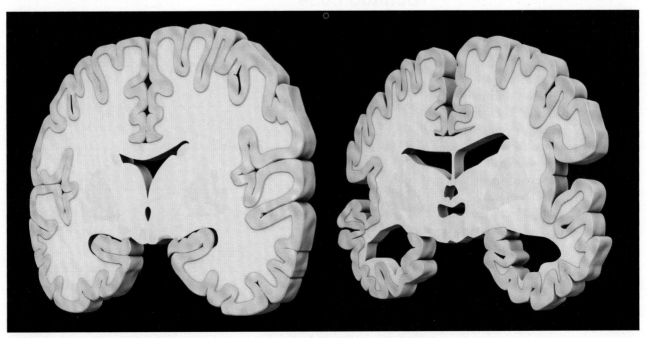

▲ Imaging of a healthy brain (left) compared with a brain affected with Alzheimer's disease (right).

Although researchers may have found a gene that is implicated in the cause of Alzheimer's disease, this does not mean they have found a cure. According to Dr. Christopher Patterson, a professor at McMaster University and Chief of Geriatrics for Hamilton Health Sciences, the understanding of genetic predisposition to dementias and the contribution of other risk factors remains limited. There is still little data to explain the overall risks and benefits of prevention strategies (Patterson et al., 2008). Relatively few of the symptoms of Alzheimer's disease respond to any type of treatment; and when they do, it is only in the earliest stages of the disease. Alzheimer's disease usually progresses over many years. Although Alzheimer's victims are normal in physical appearance, their brains are undergoing severe changes. Brain autopsies unmask severe damage, abnormalities, and death of neurons.

A recent scientific breakthrough by scientists in Alberta provides encouragement for patients suffering with Alzheimer's and their families. Dr. Robert Sutherland from the University of Lethbridge led a five-year project on Alzheimer's disease at the Canadian Centre for Behavioural Neuroscience. In this study, brain cells were destroyed in mice and then they were treated with a naturally occurring growth factor and behavioural memory exercises. The researchers discovered that the memory disorder in the mice was reversed. What they have discovered could become part of a treatment process for a number of memory disorders (CBC News, 2010).

Mental Health

The effects of physical decline can affect older adults' mental health. Men and women in late adulthood are at increased risk for suicide and depression, often because they cannot cope with their own medical problems or the death or declining health of a spouse.

Depression is both under-recognized and undertreated among the elderly. Depressed older adults are at higher risk for poor health and cognitive functioning, for physical disability, and for suicide than non-depressed older adults. (Huang et al., 2000). Figure 11.5 depicts suicide rates for older adults.

Substance Abuse

As older adults struggle with daily health challenges, they frequently require medications to combat symptoms that interfere with the quality of their lives. Drugs commonly used in late adulthood include medication to treat high blood pressure and high cholesterol, sleeping pills, anti-anxiety pills, and antidepressants. There is serious concern about older adults using medications in combinations that can be dangerous, and even lethal, if taken without proper medical supervision. Misuse or abuse of

FIGURE 11.5

Suicide Rates (per 100,000) by Gender, Canada 2004

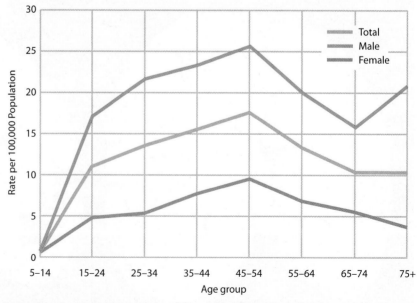

Source: Reproduced with the permission of the publisher, from "Comprehensive mental health action plan 2013–2020: Suicide prevent, country reports". Geneva, World Health Organization, 2004, accessed 15 July 2013.

prescription or over-the-counter medication can cause serious health problems, especially complicated by the consumption of alcohol or other drugs.

The greatest threat to liver health is alcoholism. For adults aged 60 and older, continuous problem drinking and late-onset problem drinking are known to greatly compromise health. Unfortunately, alcohol abuse is often difficult to recognize in elderly adults, who may exhibit conditions related to aging in general. For those taking medications, alcohol may cause adverse reactions or may interfere in the healthy aging process.

Men 65 and older have the highest suicide rate in Canada, and the rate increases among men 90 years and older to 33.1 per 100,000. The Canadian Coalition for Seniors' Mental Health find the following as risk factors for suicide in the elderly: suicide ideation (i.e., thinking about, considering, or planning for suicide), living alone/social isolation, physical handicaps, mental illness, negative life events, loss (of health, relationships, and independence), and depression (Canadian Mental Health Association, 2012).

L04 ▶ Cognitive Development

The effect of aging on mental ability has been the subject of many studies. It has been concluded that some mental deficits do occur with old age. For instance, elderly people take longer to acquire new information, such as learning a different language. Seniors have greater difficulty completing multiple mental tasks at once. In addition, mental illnesses such as dementia or untreated diabetes can greatly limit the mental capacity of older adults.

New research suggests, however, that the effects of aging on the human brain are not all negative (Finch, 2003; Pitkin & Savage, 2004; Söderlund et al., 2003; Toussaint, 2003; Tremblay, Piskosz, & Souza, 2003). Research by Hess and associates (2003) determined that elders make up for most intellectual limitations with better mental abilities in other areas, such as an increased vocabulary and a greater awareness of political and other world events. These researchers concluded that the extreme differences between the intelligence of younger and older adults as found in previous research was due to biases within the studies. It turns out that some aspects of the testing processes greatly affected the results. For example, it is not surprising that elders performed better when they were tested in the morning and on material that was important in their lives.

Other studies show that the brain will make up for much of the cell loss that happens with age by growing new cells and building new connections among those cells. Dr. Molly Wagster, a researcher at the U.S. National Institute on Aging, suggests that there are ways to increase this process of cell growth (Wagster, 2006): Mental exercises, aerobic physical exercise, and good nutrition can lessen the effects of old age on mental competence.

TECH TRENDS

Research Shatters a Long-Standing Belief about Brain Neurons

Scientists have long thought that neurons in the brain are formed only during the fetal period and for a short time after birth. It was assumed that if nerve cells in the brain were damaged or died, the adult human body could not create new ones.

However, that belief has changed dramatically. Researchers have discovered that the human brain does indeed retain the ability to generate neurons throughout life. A study by researchers Peter Eriksson and Fred H. Gage demonstrated that new neurons are generated in the dentate gyrus (a part of the brain that contributes to the formation of new episodic memories) of the adult human brain (Eriksson et al., 1998), and subsequent research has backed this up. Scientists are hoping that it may soon be possible to stimulate intrinsic brain repair mechanisms to replace neurons lost through age, trauma, and disease. Finding ways to stimulate the formation of new neurons may one day lead to novel therapeutic approaches that influence cognitive performance and treat diseases such as Alzheimer's.

TESTS VERSUS OBSERVATIONS

A major question in the science of elderly cognitive development is which is most reliable: results of tests that rate seniors' intelligence or of observations of their actual performance, which are often higher? The answer is not simple. What factors could account for the discrepancy between test scores and actual abilities? Currently there are four hypotheses (Salthouse, 2001):

1. **Differences in type of cognition.** Intelligence tests tend to measure specific aspects of cognitive ability, whereas assessments of real-life activities probably also include non-cognitive capacities, such as personality traits. Thus, some aspects of IQ may decline without causing lowered performance on the job, for example.

2. **Differences in the representativeness of the individuals or observations.** Many examples exist of elderly people who can perform admirably even into their 90s, but do these individuals really represent the average elderly person? Probably not. When we examine the

abilities of successful older persons, we may be studying only the "cream of the crop." Finally, it seems likely that observed competence represents only one type of cognitive ability (balancing the company's books, reading music), whereas intelligence testing involves several (verbal, math, reasoning, and other abilities).

3. **Different standards of evaluation.** Most cognitive tests tend to push individuals to their limits of ability. Assessments of real-life tasks, those with which people are quite familiar (such as reading the newspaper), may require an alternate standard of testing.

4. **Different amounts of experience.** Doing well on an intelligence test requires a person to use traits that are not used every day, such as assembling blocks to re-create certain patterns. The skills assessed in real-life situations are more likely to be those the individual has practised for years. For example, driving ability may remain high if the person continues to drive regularly as he or she ages.

CREATIVITY

The quantity of creative production probably drops in old age, but the quality of production may not. This conclusion is based on studies of actual productivity. What about older individuals' potential for creative production? Might it be that the elderly are capable of great creativity but that factors such as motivation and opportunity prevent them from fulfilling this ability? Might later years be a critical period for creative production?

Dacey (1989b) proposed that there are certain critical periods in life during which creative ability can be cultivated most effectively. The basic premise of this theory is that a person's inherent creativity can blossom best during a period of crisis and change. The six periods shown in Table 11.1 are ages at which most people experience stress owing to life changes.

▲ New and engaging tools like the iPad promote learning and creativity.

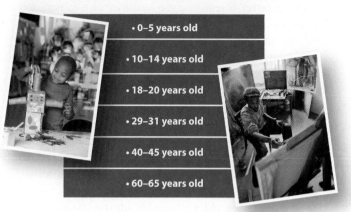

TABLE 11.1
Peak Creative Periods of Life

• 0–5 years old
• 10–14 years old
• 18–20 years old
• 29–31 years old
• 40–45 years old
• 60–65 years old

Source: Dacey & Lennon, 1989.

While some seniors do not cope well with aging and begin withdrawing from society, others take advantage of the change to pursue creative goals that had previously been difficult for them. Obviously a majority of the "young

TECH TRENDS

Easy Reader

New electronic book readers (such as the Kobo reader) offer distinct advantages to the elderly who enjoy reading books but whose eyesight interferes with the pleasures associated with reading. Here are some of the advantages of these products:

• Instant resizing of type for easy visibility in most light conditions.

• Elimination of backlighting used on computers, which is hard on aging eyes. The screen looks like paper.

• A text-to-speech feature in which a voice reads any newspaper, magazine, blog, or book. It even reads material written by the owner, such as poetry and memoirs.

• A free copy of the first chapter of virtually every book so that readers can decide whether they want to buy the book or recognize whether they have already read it.

• Books, both written and audio, are downloaded in minutes, saving a trip to the library or bookstore—perhaps the best feature of all for home- and nursing-home-bound seniors.

old" (the new term for those who are aged 60 to 70) do not suddenly become creative, but a substantial number do. Of the several thousand highly productive people he studied, Lehman (1953, 1962) found more than 100, or almost 5%, whose major productivity began in the years after 60.

WISDOM

The definition of wisdom varies from group to group. Here is a definition that is meaningful to Canada's Aboriginal population:

> The ancient wisdom, the traditions, rituals, languages and cultural values were passed on by Aboriginal Peoples and carried forward. In this process, a primary role was played by the Elders, the Old Ones, the Grandmothers and Grandfathers. As individuals especially knowledgeable and experienced in the culture, they were seen as those most closely in touch with the philosophical teachings of life lived in harmony with the Creator and creation (Royal Commission on Aboriginal Peoples, 1996b).

In academic circles, what is the relationship between intelligence and creativity, and how do they relate to the concept of **wisdom**? Robert Sternberg (1990) has compared the concepts of wisdom, intelligence, and creativity, and identified a relationship among the three concepts and the information-processing model of cognition. Higher levels of expertise and automaticity result in deeper wisdom, higher intelligence, and more creative application of ideas, as evident in the processes older people engage in (such as problem solving) and products created (such as a negotiated settlement). As people develop differing levels of expertise and performance, and automatic versus effortful ability, they are able to exhibit the qualities (see Table 11.2).

Baltes and Staudinger (2000) offer a somewhat different view of the concept of wisdom, defining wisdom as expert knowledge and judgment about important, difficult, and uncertain questions associated with the meaning and conduct of life. They suggest that wisdom is the result of five factors:

1. intelligence, including both fluid and crystallized intelligence;

2. personality traits, such as openness to experience, generativity (see Erikson's theory later in this chapter), and a continuing willingness to meet life's challenges;

3. the personality–intelligence interface, which includes creativity and social intelligence;

4. life experience; and

5. age (by and large, the older the person, the greater the wisdom).

> You shall more command with your years than with your **weapons**.
>
> SHAKESPEARE, *OTHELLO*

MEMORY

Not all aspects of memory decline in late adulthood. As people age, rather than considering them to be at a deficit because of abilities lost, they may be deemed successful by exhibiting strategies to reduce memory loss and adjust to the decline in memory functions. In the field of lifespan development, several kinds of memories have been identified and examined. First, a distinction has been made between memories relating to the future (**prospective memory**) and memories of things from the past or events that occurred in the past (**retrospective memory**).

Examples of prospective memory include remembering to take vitamins or medications each day or to water the plants. Older adults can develop simple strategies such as making lists or posting reminders to do the specific task.

Within the category of retrospective memory, there are two kinds of memories. The first, **explicit memory**, refers to facts and experiences that a person can remember and share. Examples of explicit memory include being able to remember the items you were supposed to bring to your grandchildren's house, or recalling the plot of a book you've read, or remembering a friend's street address. The second kind, **implicit memory**, refers to an automatic or unconscious process

wisdom Superior insight and judgment that can come only from experience.

prospective memory The process of remembering to do something in the future.

retrospective memory Memory of past event or item.

explicit memory Refers to facts and experiences that a person can remember and share.

implicit memory Refers to an unconscious or automatic process of remembering.

TABLE 11.2

Sternberg's Comparison of Wisdom, Intelligence, and Creativity

Aspect	Wisdom	Intelligence	Creativity
Knowledge	Understanding of its presuppositions and meanings as well as its limitations	Recall, analysis, and use	Going beyond what is available
Processes	Understanding of what is automatic and why	Automatization of procedures	Applied to novel tasks
Motivation	Understanding what is known and what it means	To know and use what is known	To go beyond what is known

of remembering, that is, memory primarily involved in motor skills. Examples of implicit memory include tying your shoes, driving a car, or taking a shower. While explicit memory may decline, implicit memory is less affected, partly because our bodies have their own muscle memory that assists us in carrying out the routine tasks.

LANGUAGE

In late adulthood, a decline in memory abilities is often linked to language comprehension—both written and spoken language. Older adults may, for instance, have difficulty comprehending a reading passage or understanding a speaker giving a moderately paced oral presentation or following a television commercial featuring information about a specific product. These challenges are related to tasks involved in information processing.

Adults in this age group may also demonstrate difficulties with their own language production, which is linked to memory. They may have trouble recalling specific vocabulary to express a thought or desire, such as the sensation of knowing that they've used a word before but cannot recall it in the moment of need. Research has found that older adults tend to produce fewer words than they did when they were younger (Hough, 2007).

L05 ▶ Social Development

ERIKSON'S THEORY: INTEGRITY VERSUS DESPAIR

The eighth and last stage of Erikson's theory of psychosocial development, covering the age 65 years and older, is termed integrity versus despair. Erikson believed that the resolution of the first seven stages should lead to the achievement of a sense of personal **integrity**. Older adults who have a sense of integrity feel their lives have been well spent and that they have helped create a better life for others. The decisions and actions they have taken seem to them to fit together—their lives are integrated. They are saddened by the sense that time is running out and that they will not get many more chances to make an impact, but they feel reasonably well satisfied with their achievements.

When people look back over their lives and feel that they have made many wrong decisions or, more commonly, that they have frequently not made any decisions at all, they see life as lacking integrity. They feel **despair**, which is the negative resolution of this last stage. Such individuals are angry that there can never be another chance for their

integrity The resolution of each of the first seven crises in Erikson's theory should lead to the achievement of a sense of personal integrity. Older adults who have a sense of integrity feel their lives have been well spent.

despair The negative resolution of Erikson's last stage; individuals look back over their lives and feel that they have made many wrong decisions, or no decisions at all, and see life as lacking integrity.

FEATURED MEDIA

Rod Serling's Twist on the Twilight Years

Rod Serling created a tremendously successful television series, *The Twilight Zone*, by combining science fiction, suspense, and horror with sometimes poignant subject matter. Famous actors of the time—some still popular today—portrayed characters whose foibles are hauntingly familiar to viewers. The following episodes feature subject matter relating to topics covered in this chapter:

Season 1, Episode 4: "The 16mm Shrine" (1959)—An aging film star lives a life of seclusion in her private screening room.

Season 3, Episode 86: "Kick the Can" (1962)—A retirement-home resident thinks that he has found the secret to youth.

Season 3, Episode 96: "The Trade-Ins" (1962)—An older couple must decide which of them will be made young.

Season 3, Episode 100: "I Sing the Body Electric" (1962)—A robotic grandmother helps a widower raise his children.

Season 5, Episode 131: "A Short Drink from a Certain Fountain" (1963)—An elderly man who has a young wife takes an experimental youth serum.

lives to make sense. They often hide their fear of death by appearing contemptuous of humanity in general and of those of other religions and races in particular.

Erikson (1978) provided a panoramic view of his developmental theory in an analysis of Swedish film director Ingmar Bergman's famous film *Wild Strawberries*. In the movie, an elderly Swedish doctor goes from his hometown to a large city, where he is to be honored for 50 years of service to the medical profession. On the way, he stops by his childhood home and, resting in an old strawberry patch, begins an imaginary journey through his entire life, starting with his earliest memories. Poignantly, the old doctor struggles to make sense out of the events of his life. He is ultimately successful in achieving a sense of integrity. In the ruminations of this old man, Erikson saw clear and specific reflections of the eight stages he proposed; in particular, he saw that this last stage involved a life crisis.

GENDER AND SEXUALITY

You might think that by the time people reach the stage of late adulthood their gender roles and attitudes toward sexuality have become pretty well fixed. In fact, researchers generally agree that this is not the case.

One major concern related to gender roles among the elderly is **role discontinuity**, which refers to an abrupt or disruptive change caused by conflicts among roles in a person's life. A number of gerontologists have noted that people in late adulthood experience a crossover in gender roles, whereby men behave more like women and women behave more like men. Men may take on a more nurturing role, for example, caring for grandchildren or volunteering. Women may become more assertive and independent, taking trips with friends or arguing/advocating for political issues.

The differences between men and women become less important as we age. With the barriers breaking down, older men and women seem to have more in common with each other and thus may be of more comfort to each other as they deal with the disruptive changes of growing old. This is not to say that men and women reverse gender roles. Rather, they move toward androgyny (as discussed in Chapter 9), which means expressing whatever gender role, male or female, is appropriate in a given situation.

Some older individuals feel that talking about gender or sexual matters is embarrassing, because years ago people generally thought it was. Many senior citizens still hesitate to discuss their questions or concerns with professionals (Blank, 2000). Another issue is that society sends men and women the message that they are less sexually attractive as they get older. Elderly adults who have a negative physical self-image might not be as likely to initiate sexual activity as when they were younger. Furthermore, fears about sexual performance that often accompany old age create doubts about their sexual desirability. An extensive Canadian survey on sexuality showed, however, that a large majority of people at age 65 said that sex was important. The majority of those between 65 and 74 considered themselves sexually active (Health Canada, 2006b).

One of the biggest fears in aging males is erectile dysfunction—the inability to attain and sustain an erection. Physical changes, non-supportive partners and peers, and internal fears may be enough to inhibit or terminate sexual activity in males. In many cases a man is capable of having intercourse, but a physical condition such as diabetes impedes it. New types of prosthetic devices can remedy a variety of psychological and physical problems, and drugs such as Viagra have changed the perception of prosthetics as the only solution.

Most sexual issues that women experience are due to hormonal changes. The vaginal walls begin to thin, and intercourse may become painful, with itching and burning sensations. Estrogen pills and hormone creams relieve many of these symptoms. Although women tend to have fewer concerns about sexual performance than men do, they are often worried about losing their attractiveness, which can also have a negative effect on their sex lives.

NEED FOR PROFESSIONAL TRAINING

The Canadian Psychological Association recognizes the need for geropsychology training and is reviewing recommendations to enhance these programs (Konnert, Dobson & Watt, 2009), which include courses in gerontology, developmental and adult psychology, age-related development and decline of cognitive processes, age-related psychological and neurological disorders, social and personality development in aging populations and individuals, and applications to the clinical treatment and care of older adults (Statistics Canada, 2010a).

AGING AND THE FAMILY

Family relationships naturally undergo changes during the aging process. With people living longer, married couples are finding that they have more years together after their children leave home, and they are having longer relationships with generations of their kin (Bengtson, 2001). These relationships remain strong, despite the tremendous diversity in the makeup of families. Most couples go through similar stages in the life cycle. The following are the four basic phases:

1. Child rearing
2. Childlessness before retirement
3. Retirement
4. Widowhood or widowerhood

> **role discontinuity** Abrupt and disruptive change caused by conflicts among a person's various roles in life.

▲ Films like *Something's Gotta Give* present the humour and frustration of relationships in late adulthood.

The duration of each stage in the life cycle and the ages of the family members for each stage vary, of course. Child-bearing patterns have a lot to do with life in the later stages of life. Couples who raise children early in their marriage will have a different lifestyle when their last child leaves home than couples who have babies in their 40s or beyond. The latter may have a dependant child at home when they are ready to retire. This can pose serious economic problems for retirees on fixed incomes, trying to meet the considerable costs of a child's higher education. In addition, with children in the home, saving for retirement is difficult.

As couples spend more years together due to increasing life expectancy, researchers will be interested in seeing whether interactions in a long-term marriage also change or whether they remain stable despite individual development. These data will provide evidence for the debate over whether human development is more stable or unstable—an issue which was discussed in Chapter 10.

Conflict is an inevitable part of any relationship, especially those that last a long time. The relationship between elderly parents and their adult children is no exception. Clarke, Preston, Raksin, and Bengtson (1999) conducted a study of aging parents and their middle-aged children. They were specifically interested in the emergence of common conflict themes. They found six categories of conflict:

- Communication and style of interaction
- Lifestyle choices and habits
- Parenting practices and values
- Religion, ideology, and politics
- Work habits
- Standards of household maintenance

Interesting generational differences were found. For example, older parents more often reported conflicts over habits and lifestyle choices, such as smoking, while their adult children more often reported conflicts in communication and interaction style, such as whether or not to discuss feelings. Regardless of the source of conflict, relationships between older parents and their adult children also provide a tremendous source of strength, which is greatly needed in times of loss.

WIDOWHOOD

Most married women will become widows because, on the average, they marry men who are somewhat older. In Canada, senior widows outnumber senior widowers four to one. Widows accounted for 45% of all women aged 65 and over in 2001. With increased longevity, women will most likely live alone for considerable portions of their lives (Statistics Canada, 2004). Widowhood is a tremendously stressful and life-altering event in the lives of older adults. People who experience the sudden death of a spouse have a more difficult time coping than those who have time to anticipate the death of their spouse (Carr, House, Wortman, Nesse, & Kessler, 2001). However, there is no significant difference between those who experience the sudden death of a spouse and those who anticipated the spouse's passing in terms of their *feelings* about the loss—depression, anger, shock, and grief.

Whether male or female, the surviving spouse faces a number of life changes, from shifting social relationships to the demands of new responsibilities, such as cleaning, cooking, managing household finances, and perhaps even needing to find work. Lee, DeMaris, Bavin, and Sullivan (2001) learned that men and women experience similar levels of depression at the loss of a spouse. However, women are more likely to be the surviving spouse because they outlive men by large margins. Only half of women over 65 are living with a partner. Lee and associates (2001) report that women tend to adapt relatively well to widowhood in the long run.

Social networking online creates additional opportunities for women and men to communicate with each other. Technology has had a major impact on relationships and has changed the boundaries of friendship and intimacy. For example, such free socializing websites as Facebook, Twitter, and Second Life offer opportunities to explore relationships of varying degrees of intimacy. Social media make it possible for people to keep in touch regularly, regardless of age or physical distance. This is especially important for older adults, who may have limits on their physical ability and mobility.

Seniors who choose to remarry enjoy much success if the ingredients of love, companionship, financial security, and consent of offspring are present. In one study, partners in long-standing marriages (between 20 and 29 years) showed lower levels of disease and disability—hypertension, arthritis, and functional limitations, for example—than did their counterparts in marriages of shorter length (Pienta, Hayward, & Jenkins, 2000). However, widows and divorcees tended to report higher levels of these types of health problems than people of any other marital status. It has been found, however, that those marriages in which one spouse suffers a long-term illness do tend to have more problems (Leinonen, Korpisammal, Pulkkinen, & Pukuri, 2001).

ELDERCARE

Elderly people identify their adult children, when they have them, as the primary helpers in their lives. When they have both an adult son and an adult daughter, as mentioned in Chapter 10, tasks often fall into gender-stereotyped categories, with women attending to housework and personal needs, and men handling yard chores, general home repair, and finances (Mosher & Danoff-Burg, 2004).

In the past, responsibility for any eldercare most often fell to unmarried daughters, if there were any. They were expected to do this because it was assumed that the work would be easier for them, as they had no responsibilities for husbands or children. If the elderly person was still employed or had retirement benefits, male and female caregivers would offer less support, regardless of their own employment status.

In 2007, most eldercare (75%) was provided by those between 45 and 64 years of age. That means that 1 in 4 of those providing care to seniors were seniors themselves. Nearly 6 in 10 were women. Caring for senior men can be invisible since many are cared for by their wives, often without the wife reporting it as caregiving. Nearly 70% of care was provided by close family members, although it is not just close family members who provide care. Roughly one-third of all caregivers were friends (14%), extended family (11%), and neighbours (5%) (Cranswick & Dosman, 2008).

The Centre for Studies on Human Stress in Canada has taken an in-depth look at the physical and psychological strain that caregivers can experience. A large number of studies have revealed psychological strains such as poor cognitive function (like memory and attention), depression, anxiety, and stress. Studies have also shown adverse physiological strains—elevated blood pressure, risk for coronary heart disease, elevated stress hormone levels, lower immune functioning, and increased mortality among spousal caregivers. The literature on caregivers clearly indicates that providing care is associated with a multitude of health issues. Society as a whole must get involved in helping caregivers by providing empathy and compassion (Wan, 2010). The Canadian government recognizes that one of the most difficult times for anyone is when a loved one is dying or at risk of death. The government offers compassionate care benefits, which are paid to people who have to be away from work temporarily to provide care or support to a family member who is gravely ill and has a significant risk of death within six months (Service Canada, 2013).

The cultural values of Aboriginal women reflect the respect the Aboriginal community has for the elderly. These values greatly influence how elderly people in geographically isolated communities in Canada are cared for. These values are represented in five themes:

1. the passing on of traditions: There will always be someone to care for the elderly

2. being chosen to care: Not everyone is chosen to take care of the elderly; this role is an honour

3. supporting the circle of healers: The Aboriginal community supports the family of the elderly person

4. (re)establishing the circles of care: As the needs of the elderly change, the typing of caregiving is adapted

TECH TRENDS

Wii: It's Not Just for Kids!

The Wii, a device that allows participants to play sports on any television set, creates excellent opportunities for exercise and socializing. It has become tremendously popular among older adults (Lindberg, 2009). Doctors have witnessed increases in injuries stemming from marathon Wii sessions. In a *New York Times* article on Wii "warriors," one doctor says of an older patient, "I was asking him what happened . . . and he said, 'Well, we bought a Wii system for the grandkids. Next thing I know, my shoulder's killing me'" (Das, 2009). While the benefits of physical activity are significant, anyone starting a new exercise program should always consult a physician. As Dr. Susan Joy says in the same article, "It's good to remember that you're not a kid."

5. accepting or refusing external resources: Caregivers may choose to access the non-Aboriginal community's resources and services, or not (Crosato, Ward-Griffin, & Leipert, 2007).

Race and ethnicity play a role in who should be responsible for caring for the older generation. The ethnic diversity of the aging population in Canada has changed since the main source of immigrants has shifted from Europe to Asia, Africa, and the Middle East. Researchers in this area recognize the importance of understanding the needs of ethnically diverse older adults and their caregivers so appropriate services and supports can be made available to them (Yoshino, 2011).

Most family and close friends still feel that they ought to take care of the elderly in their own homes if possible. Another option for care of the elderly is a retirement or nursing home. If a family does choose long-term care for an elderly parent, how do they choose the right nursing home for that parent? Comfort Life is an organization that provides information on retirement and nursing homes across Canada (www.comfortlife.ca).

THE CHANGING ROLE OF THE GRANDPARENT

Today, many grandparents play a more integral part in the lives of their grandchildren than grandparents did a generation ago.

Increasing numbers of Canadian grandparents are raising their grandchildren, either with the parents or by themselves in what is called a "skip generation" household. In 2001, 57,000 grandparents were raising their grandchildren on their own—a significant increase over the previous decade (Statistics Canada, 2001). Two-thirds of these grandparents were women, and half the children they were raising were 14 or younger (Stepan, 2003). Grandparents who parent their grandchildren keep families together and serve as a safety net to keep children out of the formal foster care system.

Grandparents raising grandchildren have higher rates of fatigue, depression, and other health problems than others their age. They may also suffer through major crises faced by their adult children—incarceration, mental illness, and substance abuse, for example. Some struggle on a limited income to raise their grandchildren through the teen years. Grand-Parenting Again Canada, a volunteer support group for grandparents raising grandchildren reports that up to 85 percent of their members are under severe financial strain, and many rely on food banks (NACA, 2005).

Grandparents are also playing a bigger role as daycare providers for their grandchildren. In order for them to have a positive effect on their grandchildren, it is critical that social and financial supports be made available to ease the challenges associated with such care arrangements and to contribute to grandparents' well-being (Gerard, Landry-Meyer, & Roe, 2006).

RELATIONSHIPS WITH OTHERS

Contrary to the stereotype, getting old need not, and usually does not, mean being lonely. In fact, the elderly, most of whom have a good deal of free time, use their free time to develop their social lives. For example, older adults are the fastest-growing group of Internet users and are accessing technology through various venues (Czaja et al., 2006).

According to the 2001 Census, Aboriginal seniors are more likely than their younger counterparts to live in communities where the majority of people are Aboriginal, such as First Nations reserves or other rural communities. The expression of culture, by participating in cultural activities and using their own language, is presumably easier in areas where most people are culturally similar, as opposed to large urban centres where Aboriginal people often represent a small minority within a larger mosaic of cultures (Turcotte & Schellenberg, 2007).

activity theory Biological maleness or femaleness.

disengagement theory The elderly will remove themselves from many social networks.

What is the optimum pattern of aging in terms of our relationships with other people? For many years, there have been two different positions on this question, known as the activity theory and the disengagement theory.

In three words I can sum up everything I've learned about life: **It goes on**.

According to the **activity theory**, human beings flourish through interaction with other people and through physical activity. People are unhappy when, as they reach the older years, they have fewer contacts with others as a result of death, illness, and societal limitations, such as lack of access to events due to mobility challenges or financial constraints. Those who are able to keep up the level of social activity of their middle years are considered the most successful. Retirement simply means choosing other, hopefully more enjoyable, activities.

Disengagement theory (Cummings & Henry, 1961) contradicts this idea. According to this theory, the idea that activity is better than passivity is a bias of the Western world. This was not always so; the Greeks, for example, valued their warriors and athletes but reserved the highest distinction for such contemplative philosophers as Sophocles, Plato, and Aristotle. Many Eastern cultures also value the isolated thinker or the solitary observer. According to disengagement theory, the most mature adults are likely to gradually disengage themselves from their fellow human beings in preparation for death. They become less interested in their interactions with others and more focused on themselves, on such concerns as their health and finances. They accept the decreasing attention of a society that sees them as losing power.

Does this mean that the tendency toward disengagement is more natural than the tendency toward activity? It is now believed that what has appeared to be disengagement is instead a temporary transition from the highly active role of the middle-aged adult to the more sedate, spiritually oriented role of the elderly person. Most humans truly enjoy social contact, so disengagement from one's fellows may be the result of traumatic experience or a physiological disturbance such as clinical depression. However, activity theory, with its emphasis on social involvement, is also now considered too general. For example, many people may reduce social contacts but keep active with solitary hobbies.

Activity, per se, has not been found to correlate with a personal sense of satisfaction with life. But meaningful activity can enrich a senior's life. Sally Rosen, an 82-year-old Holocaust survivor, speaks at Toronto area schools five to six times a year. She shares with the students her personal experiences about what it was like to be in a concentration camp and reminds them that in 10 to 15 years, survivors like herself will no longer be alive to tell their stories. It will be up to today's children to keep telling them on behalf of themselves.

PERSPECTIVES ON **DIVERSITY**

Gateball in Japan

Gateball, developed in post–World War II Japan, is a team sport combining elements of golf and croquet. It employs strategies that exercise both mind and body. Although the object is to score the most points, a great deal of emphasis is placed on the individual's contributions to the team as opposed to individual achievement.

In addition to exercising both mind and body, gateball provides a social outlet, building relationships around a common interest. Gateball has become immensely popular among "silver agers," as older people are called by the Japanese. In a modern, crowded, industrial country such as Japan, with early retirement and the highest life expectancy in the world, gateball provides a way for seniors to continue their lifelong pattern of group participation in something worthwhile.

Observations of gateball players in action found people who share information, laughter, and a relaxed sense of belonging. When a player who hadn't been there for some time reappeared, he or she was warmly welcomed

back. Exchange of food occurs routinely on the break, and people often encourage others to take some home with them.

In Canada, seniors are often involved in lawn-bowling, curling, fishing, and taking gentle walks. These activities help them to remain healthy as well as connected to other people.

Carstensen (1995, 1996) offered a resolution of the activity–disengagement debate with her **socioemotional selectivity theory**. She suggested that humans use social contact to ensure physical survival, to get information they need, to maintain a sense of self, and to acquire pleasure and comfort. These goals exist throughout life, but the importance of each shifts with age. For the elderly, the need for physical support and the need for information from others become less important, while the need for maintaining a sense of themselves grows. They tend to get this support from relatives and close friends (their "social convoy," as they have been called) more and more, whereas the need for support from casual acquaintances such as co-workers declines.

Furthermore, the challenges faced in later life can be quite different. For example, Lang (2001) found that older adults who are able to maintain their close emotional rela-

Career Apps

As an elder's companion, how would you help an elderly person retain a sense of independence and enjoy activities with others?

tionships and let other, less important relationships go have a greater sense of well-being.

Patterns of Work ◀L06

Only a small percentage of all adults aged 65 and older, about 8.3% (see Figure 11.6), are in the labour force. In the past, many workers were forced to retire. The federal government is improving the quality of life and expanding opportunities for older Canadians by prohibiting federally regulated employers from setting a mandatory retirement age. This will give older workers wishing to work the option of remaining in the workforce (Labour Canada, 2012).

PERFORMANCE

As a greater number of older people live longer and healthier lives, the baby-boom generation (those born between 1946 and 1964) ages, and birth rates decrease, many stereotypes about aging are coming under close scrutiny. The stereotype of an older, less effective workforce is

socioemotional selectivity theory Humans use social contact for four reasons: to ensure physical survival, to gain information, to maintain a sense of self, and to acquire pleasure and comfort.

Chapter 11 Late Adulthood • 271

FIGURE 11.6

Labour Force Participation Rates among Canadian Seniors Aged 65+ (2000–2006)

Participation Rates among Canadian Seniors Aged 65+ 2000–2006

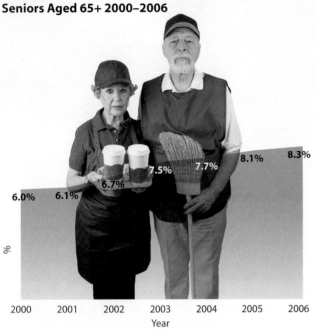

Source: Statistics Canada. Labour Force Historical Review, 2006."

bolstered by research on aging that demonstrates a decline in abilities such as dexterity, speed of response, agility, hearing, and vision. If all these abilities decline, then we might conclude that job performance must decline with age. Yet older workers account for 8% of the total workforce in Canada. People 60 years of age and over have accounted for about a third of all net job gains—about 200,000—since the economic recovery began in mid-2009 (Immen, 2012).

What explanation is there for these results? How does the older worker deal with the mild decline of physical abilities that affects most elderly people? Experience is one answer. There is said to be no substitute for experience, and it is certainly valued by employers. Other reasons cited are that older workers have lower absenteeism, turnover, illness, and accident rates than younger workers; they also tend to have higher job satisfaction and more positive work

values. These qualifications seem to offset any decreases in physical ability that increasing age causes. According to Jan Hein Bax, president of Randstad Canada, a recruitment company, experienced workers find great satisfaction in sharing their knowledge and mentor young people, which will in turn make them more valuable to the organization (Immen, 2012).

RETIREMENT

The path to retirement for older adults can take many different forms. For many people, retirement is a welcome relief from work life. For others, it is just as difficult as being unemployed. Retirement requires changing the habits of a lifetime. For most men and women, late adulthood is the period in which they retire. Even if one spouse has not been active in the labour force, both partners have many adjustments to make because of the spouse's retirement. Most adults are faced with a major adjustment of self-concept at this time in their lives.

The economic downturn of the early 2010s has forced many older workers to reconsider whether they can afford to retire. Five years after the financial crisis and the effect it had on the Canadian economy, 27% of working Canadians expect to retire at age 66. Almost one-third expect to work part-time at age 66, and 26% expect to be working full-time (*Toronto Star*, 2013).

Dychtwald (2005) argues that increased life expectancy and potential for high creativity will usher in a new era of retirement, better termed "rehirement." Seniors with a university degree are more likely to continue working than those with lower level education.

Enjoying retired life seems more likely when individuals plan for it while they are still working. When they do retire, it helps if they participate in physical activities, develop leisure activities or hobbies, and/or engage in volunteer work (Turcotte & Schellenberg, 2007). Retirement is a time to "do good"—retirees can be working at something they really care about rather than just working to pay the bills.

The belief that retired people are an important community resource is growing. Numerous efforts have been made in recent years to tap this powerful resource. Canadian Executive Service Organization (CESO) is one of several Canadian organizations that recruit skilled volunteers (many retired) and place them in development projects here and abroad (www.ceso-saco.com).

Baby boomers are the wealthiest generation in Canadian history. They live in large homes with ample space for their many possessions. They love their garages and their yards. Contrary to popular belief, most Boomers do not intend to downsize anytime soon.

PHIL SOPER, CEO OF ROYAL LEPAGE REAL ESTATE

CONCLUSIONS & SUMMARY

At the beginning of this chapter we asked, "Must we decline as we age?" The answer is that some decline is inevitable, but the picture is much less gloomy than we have been led to believe. The loss of mental and physical abilities is, on the average, relatively slight; some individuals experience only moderate physical loss and no cognitive loss at all. For many older adults, compensatory skills and abilities may replace lost capacities. The same is true for personal and social development.

Must we age and die?

- No person has attained immortality. We are not sure why we age.
- We cannot be certain that aging and death are absolutely inevitable

What theories have been proposed to explain why we age?

- A variety of physiological theories regarding aging and death exist. These include aging by program, homeostatic imbalance, and cross-linkage theories.
- Genetic theories of aging suggest that the program for aging exists in certain harmful genes.
- Major modifiers of ability such as training, nutrition, illness, stress level, and personality type also affect one's rate of aging.

What are key aspects of physical development among the elderly?

- Although reaction time appears to decline with age, some researchers have pointed to several reasons for this decline.
- Variables other than sheer neural or motor activities account for most change in physical skills over time. These include ageism, motivation, depression, anxiety, response strategies, and response style.
- Changes in sensory abilities and the skeletal system are noticeable in late adulthood.
- For both women and men, hormone production slows down during late adulthood.
- In Canada, the most debilitating condition of the elderly is Alzheimer's disease.
- A strong relationship exists between physical and mental health.

How is cognitive development affected by old age?

- A number of factors have been suggested as explaining the difference between tested and observed changes in elderly cognition. These include differences in type of cognition, the representativeness of the individuals or observations, standards of evaluation, and amounts of experience.
- Creativity is evidenced in late adulthood and in some cases may be strongest during this time. Although quantity of creative production probably drops in old age, the quality of creative production and potential for creative production probably do not.
- Wisdom refers to going beyond what is known to an understanding of the implication of things. It is the result of intelligence, personality, the intelligence–personality interaction, life experience, and age.
- For Erikson, the resolution of each of the first seven stages in his theory should lead people to achieve a sense of integrity in the last stage. If not, they experience despair.

How do social relationships develop during late adulthood?

- People in late adulthood tend to experience a crossover in gender roles, with older men becoming more comfortable in the caregiver role and women becoming more assertive.
- In a survey, people at age 65 said sex was important, and those between the ages of 64 and 74 considered themselves sexually active.
- Elderly people identify their adult children, if they have them, as the primary helpers in their lives.
- Aboriginal seniors are more likely to live in communities where the majority of the people are Aboriginal.

What are major factors affecting the older worker?

- Discrimination and stereotypes about older workers underestimate their desire to continue to be involved in the workforce.
- Seniors with a university degree are more likely to continue working than those with a lower level of education.
- For years developmental scientists have held two different positions on what is the optimal pattern of aging: the activity theory of aging (that the elderly simply switch activities as they age) and the disengagement theory (that most elderly people naturally switch from an external to an internal focus). Today, a more accepted explanation of elderly social behaviour is Carstensen's socioemotional selectivity theory.

1. Today in Canada, more and more grandparents are finding themselves in the role of parenting again. Are there organizations in your area to support these individuals? What types of support groups are available to them?

2. Programs in which young people meet regularly with elderly adults seem to have rewards for all involved. By what other means might we better tap the knowledge and creativity of the elderly?

3. Some researchers have said that Erikson's first seven stages describe crises in which action should be taken, yet the eighth and last stage, integrity versus despair, is merely reactive. Did Erikson mean to portray the elderly as sitting in rocking chairs and looking back over their lives? How do you interpret the impact of physical, psychological, and social factors on late adulthood?

Chapter REVIEW TEST

1. Ageism can be defined as
   a. a type of prejudice toward older adults.
   b. an illness that strikes old people after age 75.
   c. physical changes that occur in late adulthood.
   d. the study of human development.

2. In Canada, Alzheimer's disease is
   a. caused largely by bacteria.
   b. suffered most by people whose IQ is in the top third of the population.
   c. easily treated and resolved successfully.
   d. the most common form of dementia that affects the elderly.

3. Dacey proposed that there are certain _____ in life during which creative ability can be cultivated most effectively.
   a. critical periods
   b. ages
   c. educational experiences
   d. work-related experiences

4. A failure in the body's systems to regulate the proper interactions of organs is called
   a. counterpart theory.
   b. homeostatic imbalance.
   c. autoimmunity.
   d. cross-linkage theory.

5. Stress level, educational level, motivation, and personality type are examples of
   a. modifiers of ability.
   b. environmental factors.
   c. genetic factors.
   d. physiological factors.

6. The type of memory that allows us to remember something we need to do in the future is called _____ memory.
   a. episodic
   b. prospective
   c. explicit
   d. implicit

7. Older workers make valued employees for all of the reasons listed except
   a. job skills.
   b. absenteeism.
   c. accident rates.
   d. turnover.

8. The assumptions that we have about characteristics and behaviour associated with "male" and "female" are called
   a. accommodation.
   b. gender practices.
   c. gender stereotypes.
   d. gender equality.

9. A person's decision to retire is largely influenced by the retiree's
   a. education level.
   b. spouse.
   c. boss.
   d. doctor.

10. When adults distance themselves from others in preparation for death and become less interested in their interactions with others, it is referred to as
    a. disengagement.
    b. separation.
    c. personal well-being.
    d. achievement.

DYING AND
SPIRITUALITY

As You READ

After reading this chapter, you should be able to answer the following questions:

LO1 ▶ How is death defined?

LO2 ▶ What is the purpose of grief?

LO3 ▶ What is the meaning of "successful dying"?

LO4 ▶ What are the factors that determine the nature of suicide?

LO5 ▶ How do psychologists define the nature of spirituality?

> To one as young as you, I'm sure it seems incredible, but to Nicolas and Perenelle, it really is like going to bed after a very, very long day. After all, to the well-organized mind, death is but the next great **adventure**.

ALBUS DUMBLEDORE, IN *HARRY POTTER AND THE SORCERER'S STONE*

LO1 ▶ The Meaning of Death

Prior to the 20th century, people were used to seeing death. It was considered a typical part of life. Before the industrial revolution transformed the way people lived in Western societies, one third of all children died within their first year and half died before their 10th birthday. The institution of seemingly simple innovations, such as clean drinking water and organized waste disposal, along with improvements in health care, contributed to a rise in living standards and fall in death rates. Interestingly, over the past 100 years, deaths from some causes (such as tuberculosis, influenza) have declined significantly, while deaths from other causes (for example, cancer) have increased. Figure 12.1 shows the **mortality rates** for the leading causes of death in Canada since 2000.

It remains the case, however, that in modern Western societies, death comes mostly to the elderly. The average life expectancy is at an all-time high of over 81 years (see Figure 12.2). Among G7 countries, Canada is ranked in the middle with Japan having the greatest life expectancy at 83 years and the United States the lowest at 78.5 (Human Resources and Skills Development Canada, 2012b). Canada's universal health care system may be a contributing factor to the country's higher rate of life expectancy compared to the United States.

The life expectancy for First Nations people in Canada has continued to lag behind the overall rate. This situation helps to explain some of the regional differences shown in Figure 12.2. Canada's three territories, Manitoba, and Saskatchewan have lower life expectancy than the rest of the country; they also have a higher proportion of their population comprised of First Nations people. Many of the issues that have been discussed throughout this textbook, including higher rates of poverty, suicide, and mental illness among our First Nations, undoubtedly contribute to these differences.

As death rates fell over the past century, and as death became less a part of life, ironically, the subject of death seemed to become more and more taboo. Avoidance of death, even avoidance of the discussion of death, has become entrenched in the dominant Canadian culture. As a result, social scientists spent little time studying the role of death in life. Fortunately, in recent decades, this has begun to change, and death has become a more approachable subject of both research and public discourse, including media attention. Research and theory from the

mortality rate The number of deaths in a population for a given year; typically, the number of deaths per 100,000 people per year.

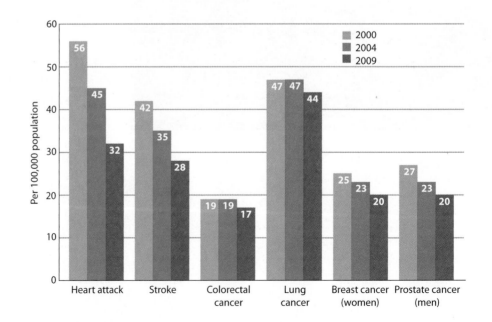

FIGURE 12.1

Death Rates by Cause of Death, 2000–2009 (per 100,000 population)

Source: Statistics Canada, 2012g.

FIGURE 12.2
Average Life Expectancy by Region

Region	
Canada	81.1
Newfoundland	78.9
Prince Edward Island	80.2
Nova Scotia	80.1
New Brunswick	80.2
Quebec	81.2
Ontario	81.5
Manitoba	79.5
Saskatchewan	79.6
Alberta	80.7
British Columbia	81.7
Yukon Territory Northwest Territory Nunavut	75.1

Source: Statistics Canada, 2008c; Statistics Canada, 2008d; Statistics Canada, 2012h

social and physical sciences tend to focus on three major concerns: What is death? How do we deal with the death of others? How do we deal with our own death?

WHAT IS DEATH?

Establishing when people are truly and finally dead has been a medical, and therefore social, problem for centuries. Fear of being prematurely buried alive has been one of humankind's oldest fears. The fear was so strong in the 19th century that in 1882 a patent was granted for a life signal called "Fearnaught," a warning device that could be activated if someone was buried alive inside a coffin (see Figure 12.3). It is no coincidence that Edgar Allen Poe, one of the greatest writers of all time, known for his spine-tingling tales of horror and misfortune, wrote a story titled *The Premature Burial* (1850).

Professionals no longer have any serious problem determining whether a person is dead. Of more concern is determining exactly when death occurs. Because all of the body's systems do not cease at once upon death, disagreements sometimes exist over which system is most significant in judging whether a person is dead.

FOUR TYPES OF DEATH

Today, four types of death are recognized: clinical death, brain death, biological or cellular death, and social death.

Clinical Death

In one sense, the individual is dead when his or her breathing and heartbeat have stopped, which is termed **clinical death.** Actually, clinical death is the least useful to the medical profession and to society at large because it can be unreliable and temporary. Owing to the success of **cardiopulmonary resuscitation (CPR),** many individuals, whose lungs and heart would have ceased to function decades ago before the technique was put into practice, have been saved. In other cases, spontaneous restarting of the heart and lungs has occurred after failure. New CPR findings suggest that mouth-to-mouth breathing may not be necessary to sustain a person's life until emergency aid arrives. Pushing on a person's chest approximately 100 times per minute seems to do the trick, according to several recent studies; and pushing to the beat of the Bee Gee's 1977 song "Staying Alive" gives the approximate number of compressions/minute (Harman, 2008).

Brain Death

Death of the brain occurs when it fails to receive a sufficient supply of oxygen for a period of time (usually 8 to 10 minutes) and all electrical activity has stopped. The cessation of brain function occurs in stages, involving the cortex, the midbrain, and the lower brain stem.

clinical death The individual is dead when his or her respiration and heartbeat have stopped.

cardiopulmonary resuscitation (CPR) Technique for reviving an individual's lungs and heart that have ceased to function.

FIGURE 12.3
"Fearnaught" Device

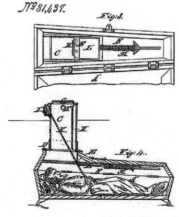

Patented Aug. 25, 1868.

▲ Fear of being buried alive motivated the invention of this casket device. A rope placed in the hands of the coffin occupant could be pulled to ring the bell above ground.

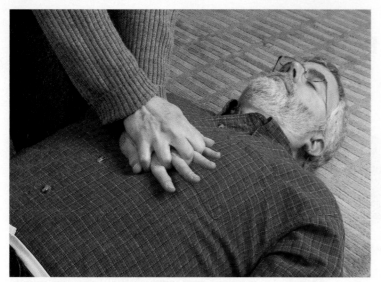

▲ Pushing on a person's chest 100 times per minute may be sufficient to save his or her life.

When the cortex and midbrain cease functioning, **brain death** has occurred, and the person enters an irreversible coma. Consciousness and alertness will never be regained (Sullivan, Seem, & Chabelewski, 1999). It is the loss of these skills and associated abilities that we equate with being human, that is commonly linked with the concept of brain death.

One indication of death is a flat **electroencephalogram (EEG)** for a specified period of time. However, the body can remain alive in this condition for a long time, because the nervous system functions, such as breathing and heartbeat, are governed by the brain stem. When the brain stem ceases functioning, the person is dead.

Biological Death

Biological death follows clinical death and brain death, and cells start dying from lack of oxygen. **Biological death** occurs when it is no longer possible to discern an electrical charge in the tissues of the heart and lungs, thus signalling the permanent end of all life functions. If clinical death is responded to quickly enough, it is possible to prevent biological death, although all tissues and organs would sustain injury from lack of blood supply.

Social Death

Researcher David Sudnow (1967) was the first to suggest the concept of **social death**, the point at which an individual is treated as dead although the person is still biologically alive. He cites cases in which body preparation (for instance, closing the eyes) was started while the patient was still alive, to save time and complete necessary tasks efficiently.

THE LEGAL DEFINITION OF DEATH

The various definitions pertaining to death can be quite confusing. In the legal profession, where language is of utmost importance and words are examined and interpreted on a case-by-case basis, death is regarded as a status, not a process. Proof of death is required for such status to be acknowledged as fact, meaning that there is no room for competing definitions or ambiguity. In an attempt to narrow the definition of death, the Law Reform Commission of Canada suggested

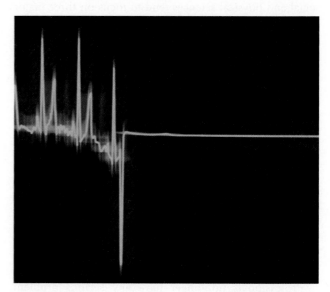

▲ A flat EEG that occurs for a period of time is one indication of brain death.

brain death Occurs when the brain fails to receive a sufficient supply of oxygen for a short period of time (usually 8 to 10 minutes).

Electroencephalogram (EEG) Recording of the electrical activity produced by the firing of neurons in the brain.

biological death Occurs when it is no longer possible to discern an electrical charge in the tissues of the heart and lungs.

social death Point at which a patient is treated essentially as a corpse, although perhaps still "clinically" or "biologically" alive.

According to most studies, people's number one fear is public speaking.
Number two is death. Does that sound right?
This means to the average person, if you go to a funeral,
you're better off in the casket than doing the **eulogy**.

JERRY SEINFELD

TAKE A **STAND**

Whose Right to Decide?

Advances in medical technology have made it possible to prolong a person's time living, but is this desirable? Many people would prefer to die than to live in a painful or unconscious state, placing emotional and physical demands on loved ones.

Children, who are dependent on adults to care for them in a safe and consistent manner, are not typically consulted as to their wishes for medical treatment. A court case that received national attention focused on Tracy Latimer, a 12-year-old girl whose father, Robert, wished to cease the constant pain she was in as a result of numerous mental and physical disabilities stemming from her cerebral palsy. Tracy suffered from seizures, was unable to walk or talk, and faced the prospect of further surgery and the accompanying pain. Robert Latimer was charged with first degree murder after placing Tracy in his truck and exposing her to exhaust fumes which caused her death by carbon monoxide poisoning. Although Robert Latimer claimed that his taking of Tracy's life was an act of mercy, the courts ruled otherwise as he was convicted of second degree murder and sentenced to 10 years in prison after his case proceeded to the Supreme Court of Canada in 2001. He was granted full parole in 2010.

Do you believe that parents like Robert Latimer should have the right to end their child's life, if they believe that their child has a poor quality of life due to a severe illness and if the child is unable to communicate his or her own wishes? In your opinion, what should be the role of the courts in these matters?

the following criteria for **legal death** in 1979: "A person is dead when an irreversible cessation of all that person's brain functions has occurred (which) can be determined by the prolonged absence of spontaneous circulatory and respiratory functions" (as cited in British Columbia Civil Liberties Association, n.d.).

Although people may disagree on the exact nature of death itself, passionate debates have helped inform the field of lifespan development about how people deal, and how they should deal, with the death of their loved ones.

LIFESPAN PERSPECTIVES ON DEATH

Although most people associate dying with late adulthood, we know that death can occur at any point throughout the lifespan—birth through old age. The causes of death can be as varied as the interpretations that people have once death is pending or after it has occurred.

A person's age and corresponding level of cognitive development influence that person's perspective of death and dying. For example, infants are certainly attached to their parents and loved ones, but not in the same way as toddlers, for whom attachment is a major focus of their cognitive and social development. If a child is sick or dying, she might fear that her caregivers will leave her. Hospitalization often requires caregivers to be absent at least some of the time, while children rest or receive treatment, and medical professionals—no matter how kind or well intentioned—are no substitute for close family. If a child's parent or close relative is dying, the child will likely fear abandonment in a similar sense, with very real concerns about "who will take care of me?" Older children often mourn the loss of a pet quite deeply, and their grief is not to be underestimated. Young children typically do not yet have the ability to think abstractly about death, spirituality, or the afterlife, so close contact and reassurance is helpful to their preoperational or concrete operational levels of understanding.

Adolescents, whose thinking is in the formal operational stage of cognitive development and who can think abstractly and reason logically, may still feel confused about death and dying, for they can imagine any number of possibilities to account for their own death or loss of a loved one. Teens, who feel they are invincible to some degree and experience adolescent egocentrism, might not worry about death as younger children do. However, young adults who have served in the military, or who have friends or family who have served, have a quite different view of death. They may feel that some kind of cosmic order is not functioning fairly if someone dies before old age.

> **legal death** A legal pronouncement by a qualified person that a patient should be considered dead under the law.

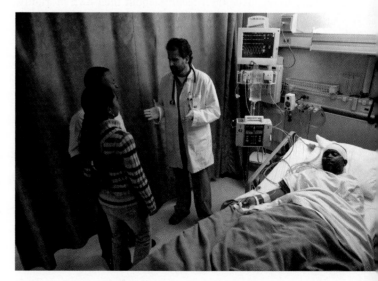

▲ Medical professionals must be sensitive to the needs of the patient's loved ones.

Victims Left Behind

While in Canada the decrease in deaths from AIDS is significant, the same cannot be said for other parts of the world. All too often, children are the ultimate victims who are left behind when a parent (or parents) dies from complications of AIDS. Estimates are that AIDS has orphaned 15 million children around the world, with even more children being "lost" because their communities are unable to care for them. Statistics show that 11.6 million of these "lost" children live in sub-Saharan Africa.

In 2009, in an effort to bring global awareness to the crisis affecting millions of children, an international group (FXB International) proclaimed May 7th to be World AIDS Orphans Day. Founder and president of FXB International, Albina du Boisrouvray, stated, "This day gives a visibility, a voice to a dropped generation, dropped because it does not vote and does not buy and does not count in the global game. Alone we can do nothing, together we can do everything" (FXB International, 2009).

A rational outlook on death and dying develops during adulthood, as people now care for others—children and/or aging parents—and wish to ensure that their loved ones will receive care as long as possible. Risky behaviours are, therefore, not as common as they were during the adolescent years. Death is something that people tend to want to avoid as much as possible so that they may see all tasks through to completion with regard to family and career. Adults have a different perspective on death as they begin to see fewer years of living ahead, compared to the number of years behind them.

Once adults reach the stage of late adulthood, they have likely experienced loss of family and friends. Older adults tend to reconcile their feelings about their own mortality, and often loosen previously rigid ideas about individual differences between people of all races, social classes, religions, genders, or sexual orientations. A general sense of acceptance tends to replace resistance to those who are "different," as the imminent journey into the unknown (death) is something that all people will experience together, regardless of race, social class, or other distinctions. Those who are aware of the state of their own health are often compelled to get all of their business concerning finances and personal property in order so that their death does not cause undue stress on loved ones after their passing.

grief An emotional response to the loss of another; includes feelings of anxiety, despair, sadness, and loneliness.

The Role of Grief ◀L02

Grief is an emotional response to the loss of another person; it includes feelings of anxiety, despair, sadness, and loneliness. Most psychologists who have examined the role of grief have concluded that it is an essential aspect of a healthy encounter with the crisis of death. Grief has a great deal in common with fear, and most grieving people really are afraid, if only unconsciously. They are frightened by the strength of their feelings, and they often fear that they are losing their sanity. Grieving people often feel that they cannot go on, that they are losing

No one ever told me that grief felt so like fear. I am not afraid, but the sensation is like being afraid. The same fluttering in the stomach, the same restlessness, the yawning. . . . There is a sort of **invisible** blanket between the world and me. I find it hard to take in what anyone says. Or perhaps, hard to want to take it in."

C. S. LEWIS

control, and that their loss is so great that their own lives are in danger. Children may exhibit grief differently than adults by "acting-out" or being non-compliant, due to disruptions in their daily routines after the death of a loved one (Willis, 2002).

Grief not only follows death; when there is advance warning that a loved one will die, grief frequently precedes death. Known as **anticipatory grief**, it has four phases: depression, a heightened concern for the ill person, a rehearsal of death, and finally an attempt to adjust to what is likely to occur after the death. Indeed, the grieving process can seem to have a yo-yo effect—a person feels less conscious grief one minute and terrible despair the next.

Numerous factors are involved in how a person processes grief, including personality, perception, religion, and family dynamics (Dunne, 2004). The fact that people experience grief differently reflects personal, as well as cultural, beliefs and practices (Haas, 2003).

UNRESOLVED GRIEF

The process of grieving, painful as it is, is resolved by most individuals. In some cases, however, morbid grief reactions occur that prevent the successful conclusion of this life crisis. Three types of morbid grief reactions are delayed grief, distorted grief, and complicated grief.

Delayed Grief

In some cases, the intense reaction of the first stage is delayed for days, months, and in some cases years. In cases of **delayed grief**, a seemingly unrelated incident may bring to the surface an intense grieving that the individual does not even recognize as grief. Take, for example, the case of a 42-year-old man who underwent therapy to deal with a mysterious depression. During conversation he disclosed that when he was 22, his 42-year-old mother committed suicide. Apparently, the occurrence of his own 42nd birthday brought to the surface many feelings that he had managed to repress.

Distorted Grief

In most cases, **distorted grief** reactions are normal grief symptoms carried to an extreme degree. They include adopting the behaviour traits of the deceased, such as aspects of the deceased's fatal illness, or other **psychosomatic** ailments—physical illness or symptoms caused by mental factors such as stress. One example is a young man whose mother died of lung cancer. At the end of her life, she often had painful coughing fits and sometimes coughed up blood. Some weeks after she died, her son began experiencing pain in his chest and started coughing. Upon examination, he was found to be in perfect health, and his chest X-ray appeared normal. His doctor decided that the only explanation of the symptoms was the young man's grief over the loss of his mother.

▲ Grief is a healthy reaction to the death of a loved one.

The ultimate distorted reaction is depression so deep that it causes the physical deterioration—even death—of the surviving loved one. This is especially likely to happen to widowers (Asch-Goodkin & Kaplan, 2006).

Complicated Grief

With **complicated grief**, the grieving process is prolonged and intensified. Complicated grief can last a long time, whereas distorted grief is not characterized by length of time. Frequently, people suffer from impaired physical and/or mental health caused by complicated grief. The difference between complicated grief and distorted grief is that while people who experience distorted grief reactions may adopt the symptoms of the deceased, people who experience complicated grief can bring about an illness that may be quite different than what the deceased experienced. Extensive therapy helps people experience normal and healthy grief and move on with their lives.

Experts on the grieving process believe that open confrontation of the loss of a loved one is essential to accepting the reality of a world in which the deceased is no longer present. Attempts to repress or avoid thoughts about the loss are only going to push them into the subconscious, where they will continue to cause problems until they are dragged out and fully accepted. Dealing with grief is difficult and can exact a cost. For example, the mortality rate among people who

anticipatory grief Grief that is experienced before the death of a person.

delayed grief Grief that is postponed for an inordinate time.

distorted grief Normal grief carried to an extreme degree; adoption of deceased person's ailments.

psychosomatic Physical illness or symptom brought about by mental factors.

complicated grief Prolonged and intensified grief; may take weeks or months to pass.

Cultural Variations in the Mourning Process

Grieving is a feeling about the death of a loved one; **mourning** is the action taken as a result. For example, some people mistakenly believe that the Japanese don't grieve because in their society, highly emotional displays of mourning are not shared in public. On the other hand, keening (loud lamentations) is an expected mourning behaviour in some Irish cultures, as well as among indigenous peoples in Asia, Africa, and Australia. How do geography and social custom affect the mourning process? There is strong evidence to support biopsychosocial influences on the process of mourning.

In terms of biology, the universal responses to sadness, fear, or despair, such as crying or fainting, occur across cultures. People in all cultures experience other physical symptoms, such as headaches, stomach aches, or sleep disturbances, after a death that is significant to them. In any culture, the deceased person need not be a biological relative to evoke the biological response. For instance, media images showed people around Canada crying at the passing of New Democratic Party leader Jack Layton in 2011.

Psychological factors, such as love, perception of loss, and sadness, can spark physical and social reactions to the event (e.g., crying or wearing black). Culture influences the manifestations of how people perceive loss and the mourning practices that follow (e.g., a boisterous wake versus one that is sombre). Similarly, society as a whole shapes acceptable grieving and mourning practices, and sends messages about what is considered normal and what is considered extreme (such as waiting a certain period of time before dating/remarrying or refusing to wash a deceased loved one's clothes). Those who experience

a death, whether of a family member, a celebrity, or a stranger in the obituary column of a newspaper, may experience feelings that are similar, but those feelings may manifest themselves quite differently because of cognitive and cultural factors.

mourning Actions taken as a result of grieving.

are grieving is seven times higher than it is for a matched sample of non-grieving people. The most recent edition of the *Diagnostic and Statistical Manual of Mental Disorders* (DSM-5) has created some controversy by removing what was known as the "bereavement exclusion" which allowed individuals two months of grieving before they could qualify for a diagnosis of major depressive disorder (MDD). There is concern among some mental health professionals that this change only serves to pathologize the grieving process, while others believe that grieving can predispose a person to MDD which then needs to be recognized and treated (Stetka & Correll, 2013).

THE ROLE OF THE FUNERAL

Research has indicated that the rituals surrounding funerals have therapeutic benefits that facilitate the grieving process. One of the most difficult aspects of dealing with the death of a loved one, though, is deciding how the funeral (if there is to be one) is to be conducted. Funerals have historically been an important part of Canadian life, whether the elaborate burial rituals practised by Aboriginal peoples, the simple funerals of the English and French settlers, or the diverse practices of the numerous ethnic groups that have immigrated to Canada.

Once the intimate responsibility of each family, care for the dead in Canada has been transferred to a paid service industry. The need for this new service was brought about

TECH TRENDS

Online Healing

Many people suffering from grief and the anger that often accompanies it believe that their only option is to "wait it out" and "just get through it." In fact, grief sufferers have a number of options available online that afford people as much or as little communication with others as they want. Options range from websites with information about grief and anger—such as facts and frequently asked questions—to discussion groups and chat rooms where people can meet and exchange thoughts and feelings. Here is a representative sample of online resources:

Website—The Grief Recovery Method (http://www.griefrecoverymethod.com/index.htm) is a comprehensive site providing answers to common questions, as well as opportunities to communicate with others, news, and other information.

Discussion/Support Group—Webhealing.com (http://www.webhealing.com), established by Tom Golden in 1995, was the first interactive website on the Internet. It offers discussion forums as well as general information.

Podcast—"Healing the Grieving Heart" is a free podcast subscription available through iTunes. Created by a marriage and family therapist and adjunct faculty member at Columbia University, the content is geared toward parents of children who have died and their grieving siblings.

▲ The HBO series *Six Feet Under* presented the humourous and poignant sides of life and the commercial aspects associated with death.

families, they also potentially prevent the family from confronting the realities that death entails. This emotional buffer is reinforced by some funeral businesses. For example, during the 1950s and 1960s, funeral homes came under severe criticism for their high costs and their low levels of sensitivity to the needs of the surviving family members.

FEATURED MEDIA

Films About Death and Personal Connections to a Higher Power

The Bucket List (2007)—What would you do if you learned you have terminal cancer and still have a long list of things you want to do before you die?

Defending Your Life (1991)—Could you move ahead to the next phase (in the afterlife), or would you return to Earth (reincarnated) to make up for things you didn't do well, or to your fullest capacity, the first time around?

Ordinary People (1981)—How does grieving, or the inability to grieve, affect a family—even years after the death of a family member?

Heaven Can Wait (1978)—How hard would you fight to live again if you found out that your death was an administrative accident by the powers that be?

by changes in society during the first part of the 20th century. The more mobile, urbanized workforce had less family support and less time to devote to the task of caring for the dead. In a relatively short time, funeral homes and funeral directors became the accepted form of care for one's dead relatives.

This commercialization of care for the dead has had mixed results. Although the services that external agents provide take some of the burden away from grieving

Career Apps

As a grief counsellor, how would you assist an adult son deal with the sudden loss of his parents due to an accident?

L03 ▶ Dealing Successfully with Your Own Death

The acceptance of death is quite painful to many people, who often choose to deny it, and yet concern over death can occur in every stage of human development. At the root of most anxiety is people's belief that they will die if the thing that they most fear comes to pass. For example, a woman who fears flying may truly believe at the deepest level that she will die if she rides in an airplane.

Psychiatrist Elisabeth Kübler-Ross is the most famous student of the process of death and dying. Kübler-Ross discovered that, far from wanting to avoid the topic of death, many dying patients have a strong urge to discuss it. She interviewed hundreds of terminally ill people in the 1960s and, on the basis of these interviews, developed a five-stage theory describing the emotions underlying the process of dying (see Table 12.1). The stages in her theory are flexible, in that people can move through them quickly, slowly, or not at all. Some fluctuation occurs between the stages, but by and large people tend to move through them in this order:

1. *Denial.* In the first stage, a person denies that death is going to happen. This often happens when a terminal diagnosis is first given, but eventually the person must interact with others to consider the practical and logistical matters that need to be addressed.

2. *Anger.* Once a person can no longer deny the fact that death is a reality, he or she often experiences anger and resentment. A dying person may feel robbed of time on earth, regret over goals unattained, or bitterness that it is him or her and not another person who will meet this end.

3. *Bargaining.* In the third stage of dying, a person comes to hope that the death can be avoided or delayed in exchange for other thoughts or behaviours. Promises are sometimes made to oneself, others, or God in hopes of making a narrow escape a reality.

4. *Depression.* In the fourth stage of dying, the dying person begins to accept the inevitable conclusion. The dying person may attempt to create distance from others, to disconnect from relationships in preparation for death, and to help loved ones disconnect. Kübler-Ross deemed this behaviour appropriate, as the person needs to confront the reality of dying.

5. *Acceptance.* In the final stage of dying, a person comes to a state of peace and resolution, and no longer attempts to resist the end of life. Any pain or suffering is no longer viewed as a burden but, rather, part of the natural cycle of life. A feeling of greater connectedness to a higher power is common.

One criticism of Kübler-Ross's stage theory is that no scientific evidence confirms that her sequence of stages is typical or universal. Another criticism is that her theory overlooks the effects of personality, ethnic factors, or religious factors. For example, people in cultures such as some Aboriginal and Asian ethnic groups view death as just another stage of existence and do not dread it.

Whether or not you choose to accept Kübler-Ross's model, the biological, psychological, and social aspects of the process of dying are obviously very complex. Knowledge gained through careful research can help answer questions that emerge as a result of examining the model, but her theory, like all good theories, continues to provide us with constructs that help guide research.

TABLE 12.1

Kübler-Ross's Stages of Dying

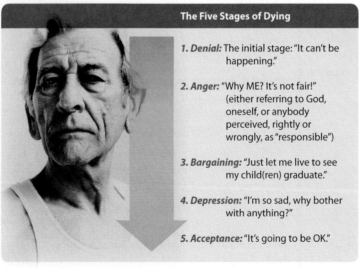

The Five Stages of Dying

1. Denial: The initial stage: "It can't be happening."

2. Anger: "Why ME? It's not fair!" (either referring to God, oneself, or anybody perceived, rightly or wrongly, as "responsible")

3. Bargaining: "Just let me live to see my child(ren) graduate."

4. Depression: "I'm so sad, why bother with anything?"

5. Acceptance: "It's going to be OK."

Source: From *Life Span Development*, 11th edition by John W. Santrock. Copyright © 2008. The McGraw-Hill Companies, Inc. Reprinted with permission.

PERSPECTIVES ON **DIVERSITY**

The Funeral in Other Times and Countries

Looking at the funeral practices of former cultures shows us not only how they buried the dead but also something about their values.

Ancient Egypt. Egyptians believed in life eternal, and thus the body of the dead person was embalmed, or treated with preservatives, in order to prevent decomposition. The body was placed in a tomb, the elegance of which was determined by family wealth and prestige.

Ancient Greece. Within a day after death the body was washed, anointed, dressed in white, and laid out for 1 to 7 days, depending on the social prestige of the deceased. The ancient Greeks prepared their tombs and arranged for subsequent care while they were still alive. About 1000 B.C.E., the Greeks began to cremate their dead. Although cremation never overtook burial in "popularity," the Greeks came to believe in the power of the flame to free the soul.

The Roman Empire. For reasons of sanitation, burial within the walls of Rome was prohibited; consequently, great roads outside the city were lined with elaborate tombs erected for the well-to-do. For the poor, there was no such magnificence; for slaves and foreigners, there was a common burial pit outside the city walls.

Anglo-Saxon England. The body of the deceased was placed in a hearse for the funeral procession, which included priests, friends, relatives, and strangers who

deemed it their duty to join the party. Mass was sung for the dead, the body was laid in the grave (generally without a coffin), the mortuary fee was paid from the estate of the deceased, and alms in the form of money, food, or clothing were given to the poor.

Colonial New England. Neighbours or a nurse washed and laid out the body. The local woodworker built the coffin. In special cases, metal decorations imported from England were used on the coffin. Funeral services consisted of prayers and sermons said over the cloth-covered coffin. Sermons often were printed (with skull and crossbones prominently displayed) and distributed to mourners.

Many researchers agree with the themes presented by Kübler-Ross, but suggest that they do not occur in set stages for all people. Rather, these studies find that the themes are intermingled, with some people ending on a positive note and others ending with feelings of anger or depression.

Death and dying are complicated and important topics that have an important place in the study of life. Over the course of the lifespan, humans have options to cope with death in various ways that are influenced by biological, psychological, and social factors.

DEATH WITH DIGNITY

Physician-Assisted Suicide

No doubt most people would rather not suffer serious physical pain when they die, and many would prefer to avoid the emotional pain that often attends death. Until recently, however, it was the rare occasion when a person would have any choice. Today, debates have formed around

two alternatives, both of them forms of **euthanasia** ("good death" in Greek), the act of ending a life in a painless manner to relieve or prevent suffering.

Passive euthanasia refers to refraining from continuing efforts to sustain someone's life—turning off life-support systems or withdrawing medicine or food, for example. These methods can be covered by a **living will**, which is a legal document that describes a person's wishes for specific life-prolonging treatments (some provinces refer to these as *health care directives*). They can also be determined by the patient's **health-care power of attorney**, a legal document giving someone authority to make health care decisions for a person who is incapacitated.

euthanasia The ending of a life, usually in a person with a terminal illness, to prevent a prolonged and painful death.

passive euthanasia Refraining from continuing efforts to sustain someone's life.

living will Legal document that describes specific life-prolonging medical treatments.

health-care power of attorney Legal document giving someone else authority to make health-care decisions for you if you are incapacitated.

active euthanasia
Intentionally ending a person's life.

physician-assisted suicide (PAS) Active euthanasia whereby doctors give patients death-inducing drugs.

Active euthanasia means intentionally ending a life, either through directly killing the person or by **physician-assisted suicide (PAS)**, which occurs when a doctor gives a patient death-inducing drugs. It is against the law almost everywhere for the physician to give the patient a death-inducing drug, and Dr. Jack Kevorkian was an American doctor (1928-2011) who gained notoriety for doing precisely that. He served 8 years of a 10- to 25-year prison sentence for second-degree murder before being paroled in 2007 due to good behaviour and his own failing health.

In the Netherlands, doctors administer lethal drugs to patients who request them, but with strict legal guidelines. South of our border, a law was passed in Oregon in 1997 (upheld in 2006 by the U.S. Supreme Court) called the Death with Dignity Act. This law allows doctors to prescribe lethal medications to patients who request them, but the patients must administer the medications themselves (Oregon.gov, 2007).

Active euthanasia is illegal in Canada, but there continues to be a lot of debate over the appropriateness of physician-assisted suicide (Bernat, 2001). Those who support it claim a number of advantages for the option: The time of death is up to the patient, it can be used by those for whom the hospice or hospital is inappropriate, and death is painless if the patient is given a high enough dose of morphine. (See the Take a Stand box for more discussion about this topic.)

Canadian Susan Griffiths, who was suffering from a degenerative neurological disorder, travelled to Switzerland in April, 2013, to take advantage of that country's assisted-suicide law (CBC News, 2013). In Switzerland, someone other than a physician can assist with the suicide, but the patient must be the one who administers the lethal medication (Smith, 2013).

Over 66% of Canadians die in hospitals (Statistics Canada, 2012i), and many of those deaths involve some aspect of medical life-support technology, such as breathing, feeding, and waste-elimination equipment. It is essential, therefore, that those who do not want to be maintained on life-support systems if they become terminal put their wishes in writing according to their province's laws. Open communication with your doctor

Career Apps

As a registered practical nurse (RPN), what would you do if a close colleague asked you for help ending her pain and suffering by administering potentially lethal drugs to her?

TAKE A **STAND**

Whose Right to Decide?

Legal attention has been brought to the subject of whether a person has the right to enlist the help of another person, such as a physician, to end his or her life.

Section 241 of the Canadian Criminal Code states that "Every one who a) counsels a person to commit suicide, or b) aids or abets a person to commit suicide, whether suicide ensues or not, is guilty of an indictable offence and liable to imprisonment for a term not exceeding fourteen years" (Criminal Code, 1985, p. 268).

Nadia Kajouji was a first-year Carleton University student who was suffering from depression during her first months away from her Brampton, Ontario home. She took her own life in March of 2008 when she jumped from a bridge and was later found to have drowned in Ottawa's Rideau River. She had been communicating over the Internet with a nurse from the United States who was encouraging her to take her own life. He was later charged and convicted in his home state of Minnesota for assisting in the suicides of Kajouji and also of a British man. Canadian police made the decision not to charge him under Section 241.

Sue Rodriguez was a British Columbia resident who contracted amyotrophic lateral sclerosis (ALS) in 1991 at the age of 40. ALS results in the progressive loss of muscle functioning and eventually leads to death. Rodriguez believed that her quality of life would eventually be compromised by this disease and wished to have a physician end her suffering before that point was reached. As having a physician assist in her suicide would have contravened Section 241(b), she challenged the law on constitutional grounds. She lost her case at the Supreme Court of Canada in 1993 but had an anonymous physician assist in ending her life a few months later.

Section 241 is designed to address situations such as the Kajouji case, but does this law provide justice in cases like Rodriguez's? Do you believe that Section 241 of the Criminal Code should be amended to allow for an individual to end his or her life with the help of another person such as a physician? Do you believe that allowing for assisted suicide could result in abuses of the law, thus making it more likely that incidents such as the Kajouji case could occur?

is also essential (von Gunten, Ferris, & Emanuel, 2000). This type of decision-making before the end of one's life seems to be increasing and is practised in many European countries (van der Heide et al., 2003). In England and Wales, for example, living wills are called *advance decisions*, while in Ireland they are known as *advance health-care directives*.

An increasing number of cases illustrate the ethical problems involved with maintaining lives with the support of technical equipment, in the absence of these legal documents. One such case was that of Terri Schiavo. Schiavo collapsed in her home in 1990. Her collapse was due to heart failure that may have been associated with bulimia. Her husband Michael, as her legal guardian, battled against her blood relatives to allow her to be taken off the life-support mechanisms and allowed to die peacefully, as he claimed she would have wanted. In 2005, the courts determined that Terri Schiavo was in a vegetative state from which she could never return, and therefore her feeding tube was removed. She died 15 days later. A number of medical professionals, philosophers, and theorists have debated the issue of life support, arguing whether maintaining life under these conditions is wrong.

▲ Media coverage closely followed the Terri Schiavo case.

The Hospice: "A Better Way Of Dying"

In 1978, *Time* magazine brought attention to the **hospice**, a program providing comfort and supportive services to those near the end of life and to their families. The *Time* article suggested that hospice care provides patients "a better way of dying." At that time, hospices were still considered a new form of care, although the concept of hospice care dates back many centuries.

The first Canadian hospice opened in Winnipeg, Manitoba, in 1974. Hospices became a more mainstream part of the Canadian medical establishment by the mid-1980s when health care systems began to define patients as acute, chronic, geriatric, or **palliative**. This categorization

implied different treatment for each of these groups (Canadian Hospice Palliative Care Association, 2013). Since then, the Canadian Hospice Palliative Care Association has been formed to help promulgate this movement. It is comprised of groups and individuals who have organized hospice programs that focus on often-neglected areas of care, such as pain management, psychological counselling for patients and their families, and recognition of terminal illness. Currently, hospice programs in Canada provide primarily home-based care, with much of that care provided by relatives. Only 16% to 30% of Canadians who die have access to or receive hospice palliative care (Canadian Institute for Health Information, 2007) although 90% can benefit from such care (Carstairs, 2010). For those who do not have access to hospice care or simply require further information, the Canadian Virtual Hospice is available at http://www.virtualhospice.ca.

hospice A program providing comfort and supportive services to those near the end of life and to their families.

palliative A type of care that is focused primarily on the relief of pain and control of symptoms.

The hospice is a relatively new philosophy of patient care in Canada. Hospice care is different from other types of care because it provides

- a team approach to caring for the individual,
- attention to the spiritual and psychological needs of patients and their families,
- pain and symptom control (i.e., palliative care),
- services in the home or hospice setting, and
- family conferences and bereavement care.

The collaborative nature of hospice care is one of the major factors that distinguishes such care from hospital treatments. Hospice teams include doctors, nurses, social workers, and spiritual supports. Families are consulted to ensure that decisions are made with as much input as possible from all concerned parties.

Because there is an emphasis on quality of life for the patient and family, as opposed to impending death, control of pain and symptoms are goals of hospice care. A patient is typically treated for pain with over-the-counter pain medications such as ibuprofen, aspirin, or acetaminophen. For terminally ill patients, pain levels often increase to the point where these medications no longer help. At that point, the physician will prescribe narcotic medications alone or in combination with other medications. The main objective of medication is to relieve symptoms that interfere with one's quality of life. A major goal of the hospice is to keep the person's mind as clear as possible at all times. A person whose mind is clear can think more cogently about the dying process and explore the feelings associated with death and the meaning of dying (Dobratz, 2003).

L04 ▶ Suicide: The Rejection of Life

There are times that people feel that their personal pain outweighs their ability to cope with the pain. Such thinking occurs in different people for different reasons, at different times of life, regardless of socioeconomic class, religion, race, or gender (see Table 12.2).

Although suicide ranks as the second leading cause of death among people 15 to 24 years of age, middle-aged adults (40 to 59) have the highest rates (Navaneelan, 2012). The levels of stress (e.g., personal, financial, and occupational) that those in middle adulthood experience may account for this. For those over 60, poor health is often a cause of suicide because it is linked to depression. Figure 12.4 shows the suicide rates by age group and sex.

THE INFLUENCE OF BIOLOGICAL SEX

At all ages, there are major sex differences in suicide. Females are hospitalized at one and a half times the rate of men for attempted suicide (Langlois & Morrison, 2002). However, males are about three times more likely to die of suicide attempts than are females, owing to the methods used, the lethality of the attempt, and the person's present state of mental health (Navaneelan, 2012). Suicide attempts for men and women may be influenced by factors such as alcohol and drug use, unemployment, divorce, and death of a spouse or other close friend or relative.

No single factor is in itself a clear cause of suicide, and no one warning sign can be a clear indicator of intent. Several factors or warning signs, however, are cause for concern. Anyone talking about committing suicide should

FEATUREDMEDIA

Films About Suicide

Harold and Maude (1971)—After a chance meeting at a funeral, how does a life-changing relationship between a teenage boy and a 79-year-old woman blossom?

Scent of a Woman (1992)—How does a young man handle the challenge of caring for a cranky ex-colonel who has his own agenda—to end his life?

The Hours (2002)—How are three different women, from three different generations, affected by the same novel?

Leaving Las Vegas (1995)—When a man who thinks he's lost everything goes to Las Vegas to drink himself to death, can new love save him? Or is he determined to end his life?

be taken seriously and a mental health professional should be consulted, even when you feel sure the person is only seeking attention or sympathy.

Health care professionals can play an important role in suicide prevention, providing support and information that highlight alternatives to choosing to end one's life. Examining the practical role of community support in relation to death sheds light on the way we handle the reality of death, which is a fundamental part of the lifespan.

TABLE 12.2
Fact Sheet on Suicide

Suicide Rates in Canada
• Every year approximately 3700 people in Canada commit suicide—a national rate of 11 in 100,000 people.
• Suicide rates are 5 to 7 times higher for Aboriginal youth than for non-Aboriginal youth. However, rates vary widely among Aboriginal communities, and factors such as language and culture retention are seen as important factors in preventing suicide.
• Suicide rates for Inuit youth are among the highest in the world at 11 times the national average.
• Boys and men commit suicide at a rate three to four times greater than do girls and women.
• Many of these deaths could be prevented by early recognition of the signs of suicidal thinking and appropriate intervention, and early identification and effective treatment of mental illness.

Source: Fact Sheet - Suicide Prevention. http://www.cihr-irsc.gc.ca/e/44716.html. Canadian Institutes of Health Research, 2012. Reproduced with the permission of the Minister of Public Works and Government Services Canada, 2013.

FIGURE 12.4
Suicide Rates by Age Group and Sex

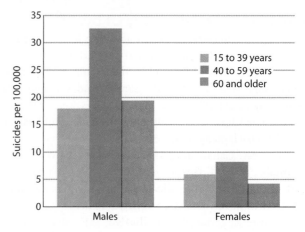

Source: Statistics Canada, 2013c.

L05 ▶ Spirituality

Spirituality refers to issues affecting the spirit or soul. It may involve the attempt to better understand the reasons for living through striving to know the intentions of a higher power.

While spirituality is not the same as religion, there is a clear spiritual element to organized religion, which often involves reflective practice, gathering in a specific place, and considering the self in relation to other people and places. Religion also specifies an accepted body of teachings that defines answers to spiritual questions. Interestingly, Canadians are becoming increasingly irreligious according to the 2011 National Household Survey. Almost a quarter of Canadians (23.9%) report no religious affiliation (Statistics Canada, 2013), so it may be the case that many do not believe in the notion of a spirit or soul.

For those who are spiritual, a basic goal may involve trying to discern life's purpose. People engage in spiritual practices by, for example, examining historical trends and biological changes (such as the study of written texts or scientific advances) to debate the forces underlying human existence. In any case, spirituality includes all of their efforts to gain insight into the forces of life. For many, it is the only justification for moral and ethical behaviour. Those who do not consider themselves to be spiritual may be more concerned with creating purpose in life rather than attempting to discern it. Moral and ethical behaviour for these individuals may be rooted in personal codes of conduct rather than in spirituality or religion.

Spirituality, for many, appears to develop with age. A number of theories have been offered as to how and why this is so, including those of Viennese psychoanalysts Viktor Frankl and Carl Jung and American sociobiologist Edward O. Wilson.

FRANKL'S THEORY OF SPIRITUALITY

Viktor Frankl (1967) described human life as developing in three interdependent stages, according to the primary dimension of each stage:

1. *The somatic (physical) dimension.* All people are motivated by the struggle to keep themselves alive and to help the species survive. This intention is motivated entirely by instincts. It exists at birth and continues throughout life.

2. *The psychological dimension.* Personality begins to form at birth and develops as a result of instincts, drives, capacities, and interactions with the environment. The psychological dimension and the somatic dimension are highly developed by the time a person reaches early adulthood.

3. *The noetic dimension.* The noetic dimension has roots in childhood but primarily develops in late adolescence and beyond. It is spiritual in the sense that it involves the individual's search for the meaning of life.

Frankl believed that development in the physical and psychological dimensions results from the total sum of the influences bearing upon an individual. The developmental nature of the theory is recognizable here, as individuals acquire more skills and understanding throughout their lives, based on interactions with others and the environment. The noetic, however, is greater than the sum of its parts. This means that we as adults are responsible for inventing (or reinventing) ourselves! Whatever weaknesses or challenges we may have been given through biology or our environment, they need not govern our lives; we can and should try to overcome them.

A recent Canadian study by Damianakis and Marziali (2012) found that spiritual beliefs helped older adults in group therapy cope with the recent loss of a spouse by allowing them to honour the life that they had with their mate while at the same time developing a new sense of purpose moving forward. Frankl would be proud!

JUNG'S THEORY OF SPIRITUALITY

Carl Jung, a student of Freud, agreed to a large extent with Freud's description of development in the first half of human life. But he felt that Freud's ideas were inadequate to describe development during the second half of life, middle adulthood and beyond.

The First Half of Life

In Jung's view, the personality develops toward individuation, or the process of coming to know, giving expression to, and harmonizing the various components of the psyche. Most people are well individuated by the middle of life, at approximately age 35; that is, we have become distinct individuals and are most different from one another at this age (see Figure 12.5).

FIGURE 12.5

Jung's Theory, Differentiation by Age

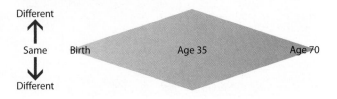

I find hope in the darkest of days, and focus in the **brightest**. I do not judge the universe.

DALAI LAMA

The Second Half of Life

The goal of human development in the second half of life is just the opposite. Somewhere around midlife, people begin turning inward, turning attention to the development of the inner self, marking the beginning of true adult spirituality. The goals of this introspection are to discover a meaning and purpose in life, determine which values and activities you are willing to invest energy and creativity in, and prepare for the final stage of life—death.

By nourishing qualities of yourself that are less developed (such as typically gender-stereotyped characteristics like sensitivity or assertiveness), you come to recognize the spiritual and supernatural aspects of existence.

WILSON'S THEORY OF SPIRITUALITY

In contrast to the self-determination of spirituality seen in Frankl's and Jung's psychological points of view, sociobiology sees spirituality as determined almost entirely by instinct—that is, as a function of genes and heredity. Harvard sociobiologist Edward O. Wilson, the leading spokesperson for the sociobiological point of view, argued that religion and spirituality are inseparable and that together they grant essential benefits to believers.

In Wilson's view, religion is one of the few uniquely human behaviours. He argued that all societies, from hunter–gatherer bands to socialist republics, have religious practices with roots that go back at least as far as the Neanderthal period. According to Wilson, humans have a need to develop simple rules for handling complex problems. Furthermore, religious learning is almost entirely unconscious—most religious tenets are taught and deeply internalized early in life.

The sociobiological explanation of spirituality, then, is that through religious practice, the survival of practitioners is enhanced. Those who practise religion are more likely to stay alive (or at least they were in the past) than those who do not practise religion. The potential

for self-sacrifice can be strengthened in this manner because the willingness of individuals to relinquish rewards or even surrender their own lives will favour group survival. The first responders who died trying to save lives in the 9/11 attacks are an excellent example.

Wilson saw science as taking the place of theology today, because science has explained natural forces more effectively than theology. In fact, he asserted that science has explained theology itself. Although he saw theology as being phased out, he argued that the demise of religion is not at all likely. As long as religions make people more likely to survive and propagate themselves, Wilson suggested, they will continue to enjoy popularity.

If I Had My Life to Live Over

The following question was asked of 122 retired people:

> If you could live your life over again, what would you do differently?

Most people responded that the pursuit of education would be the area they would most like to choose if given another chance. This emphasis among retirees may be because they feel their lack of education led to missed or limited opportunities. People indicated that they would have spent more time doing a variety of things, but they said that they would have spent less time worrying about work.

These feelings are summed up in this poem, attributed to Nadine Stair, an 85-year-old poet:

If I had my life to live over,
I'd dare to make more mistakes next time.
I'd relax. I would limber up.
I would be sillier than I have on this trip.
I would be crazier. I would be less hygienic.
I would take more chances, I would take more trips.
I would climb more mountains, swim more rivers, and watch more sunsets.

I would burn more gasoline. I would eat more ice cream and less beans.
I would have more actual troubles and fewer imaginary ones.
You see, I am one of those people who lives
Prophylactically and sensibly and sanely,
Hour after hour, day after day.
Oh, I have had my moments
And if I had it to do over again, I'd have more of them.
In fact, I'd try to have nothing else.
Just moments, one after another.
Instead of living so many years ahead each day.
I have been one of those people who never go anywhere
Without a thermometer, a hot water bottle, a gargle, a raincoat, and a parachute.
If I had to do it over again, I would go places and do things.
I'd travel lighter than I have.
If I had my life to live over, I would start barefooted
Earlier in the spring and stay that way later in the fall.
I would play hooky more. I wouldn't make such good grades except by accident.
I would ride on merry-go-rounds.
I'd pick more daisies!

As you have reached the end of this book, consider all that you have read. Knowing what you now know about lifespan development, about the biopsychosocial forces that influence us across the lifespan, how has this affected the way you view your own development? What predictions do you make regarding your adult years based on what you now know about the importance of early childhood and family dynamics?

The study of the lifespan allows us to make some educated guesses about the "why" beneath all of human development. Hopefully your curiosity has been piqued and you found ideas that challenged as well as validated your opinions. Best wishes as you continue your own life's journey!

CONCLUSIONS & SUMMARY

The goal of living a good life has many meanings and takes different forms. The same may be said for achieving a successful death. The stages of death and grief reflect the values of a society and culture, and our interpretation and responses to death and spirituality, in turn, contribute in some small way to achieving a good life.

How is death defined?

- Today, four types of death are recognized: clinical death, brain death, biological death, and social death.
- In modern Western societies, death comes mostly to the old. Unfortunately, this is not true in many other areas of the world.

What is the purpose of grief?

- Grief both follows and can precede the death of a loved one.
- In some cases, morbid grief reactions occur that prevent the successful conclusion of the crisis of a loved one's death. These are known as delayed grief, distorted grief, and complicated grief.
- Most experts who have examined the role of grief have concluded that it is a healthy aspect of the crisis of death.

- Funerals have always been an important part of Canadian life. Research has indicated that the rituals surrounding funerals have therapeutic benefits that facilitate the grieving process.
- Kübler-Ross has offered five stages of dying: denial, anger, bargaining, depression, and acceptance.

What is the meaning of "successful dying"?

- The hospice movement has provided people with more control over their own death, making it easier to accept.
- Communicating your wishes in the case of incapacitation in the form of a living will or health-care power of attorney can alleviate much pain for the individual and his or her loved ones.
- Assisted suicide remains a topic of great debate in Canada.

What are the factors that determine the nature of suicide?

- There are major gender differences in suicide, with men being more likely to die from suicide attempts than women.

How do psychologists define the nature of spirituality?

- In recent decades, Canadians have become increasingly irreligious.
- Theories of spirituality have been presented by Frankl, Jung, and Wilson.

For REVIEW

1. It has been suggested that people in Western society typically avoid, or are generally uncomfortable, talking and thinking about death. If so, what factors contribute to this attitude?

2. Are there some old people—those who have lost their spouse and friends or those who are terminally ill—who should be allowed to take their own lives? If so, how should these people be supported?

3. What are some ways that you find a spiritual connection in the world, to a higher power or within yourself?

Chapter REVIEW TEST

1. The three steps involved in brain death include the cortex stopping, the midbrain failing, and function ceasing in the
   a. pituitary glands.
   b. stomach.
   c. brain stem.
   d. optic nerve.

2. The phases of anticipatory grief are
   a. depression, a heightened concern for the ill person, a rehearsal of death, and an attempt to adjust to the consequences that are likely to occur after the death.
   b. depression and rehearsal of death.
   c. a heightened concern for the ill person, a rehearsal of death, and an attempt to adjust to the consequences that are likely to occur after the death.
   d. depression, a heightened concern for the ill person, and a rehearsal of death.

3. Kübler-Ross formulated a theory of dying which is comprised of_____ stages.
   a. 3
   b. 5
   c. 7
   d. 9

4. A young man, whose father died from lung cancer, is displaying grief known as distorted grief. He has
   a. experienced grieving stages that are prolonged and intensified to an abnormal degree.
   b. developed some of the same symptoms his father had, which his doctor determined were entirely psychosomatic.
   c. created a shrine in memory of his father.
   d. experienced anticipatory grief.

5. Active euthanasia is ____ in Canada.
   a. legal
   b. not covered by the law
   c. illegal
   d. None of the answers is correct.

6. Care for terminally ill people is known as
   a. visiting nurses.
   b. hospice care.
   c. behavioural medicine.
   d. home health care.

7. Whether life is worth living and why it is worth living are the major premises of
   a. spirituality.
   b. religion.
   c. separation anxiety.
   d. None of the answers is correct.

8. In what stage of Frankl's theory of spirituality are people motivated by the struggle to keep themselves alive and to help the species survive?
   a. somatic dimension
   b. psychological dimension
   c. noetic dimension
   d. None of the answers is correct.

9. According to Jung, by the age of 35, most people are well
   a. established.
   b. prepared for life's work.
   c. individuated.
   d. on their way to developing a wholeness of personality.

10. In response to the question "If you could live your life over again, what would you do differently?" the most common answer given by respondents was
    a. pursue more education.
    b. have more children.
    c. spend more time working.
    d. have more sexual partners.

A

Aboriginal Head Start   Government-supported early childhood program that provides education, health, and parenting education services to First Nations families.

accommodation   Piaget's term to describe the manner by which cognitive structures change.

achieved identity   An individual's sense of self that is based on personal effort and commitment.

active euthanasia   Intentionally ending a person's life.

activity theory   Humans flourish/thrive through interactions with others and physical activity, and suffer in the absence of such stimulation.

adaptation   A mechanism that consists of the two functional invariants—assimilation and accommodation—in Piaget's theory.

adolescent egocentrism   Self-centred thinking patterns of childhood that sometimes occur in the teen years.

adoption   The process of voluntarily taking a child of other parents as one's own.

afterbirth   Stage 3 of the birth process; the placenta and other membranes are discharged.

ageism   Stereotyping or unfair treatment of individuals or groups on the basis of their age.

aging by program   Theory that we age because aging is programmed into us.

AIDS (acquired immune deficiency syndrome)   Disease caused by the HIV virus, which can invade a newborn baby's immune system, thus making it vulnerable to infections and life-threatening illnesses.

Alzheimer's disease   Brain disease involving progressive, irreversible loss of neurons and manifesting as impaired memory, judgment, decision-making, orientation to the environment, and language.

amniocentesis   Fetal testing procedure that involves inserting a needle through the woman's abdomen, piercing the amniotic sac, and withdrawing a sample of amniotic fluid.

amniotic sac   Fluid-filled uterine sac that surrounds the embryo/fetus.

analgesics   Mild medications used to alleviate pain; may be used before and during labour.

analytic intelligence   Sternberg's term to describe a person's ability to break down a problem or situation into the smaller parts of the whole.

androgyny   Gender-role identification that allows expression of both male and female gender roles.

anaesthetics   Stronger medications used during labour to control pain; can numb mother to pain in the various stages of labour.

animism   Children's preoperational activity in which they consider inanimate objects to possess human thought, feelings, and actions.

anorexia nervosa   An eating disorder characterized by low body weight and distorted body image.

anoxia   Insufficient oxygen supply during labour and delivery, which can cause fetal brain damage or death.

anticipatory grief   Grief that is experienced before the death of a person.

Apgar scale   A test to evaluate a newborn's basic life signs administered at 1 minute and 5 minutes after birth.

apnea   Brief periods when breathing is suspended.

arthritis   Tissue inflammation in and around the joints.

artificial intelligence   Human intelligence simulated by machines; a specific field of computer science.

ascribed identity   An individual's sense of self based on the determination of others, not the individual.

assimilation   Piaget's term to describe the manner in which we incorporate data into our cognitive structures.

assisted reproduction technologies (ART)   Methods used by an individual to become pregnant through artificial or partially artificial means.

asthma   Lung disorder resulting in bronchial tubes filling with mucus and tightening.

attachment   Behaviour intended to keep a child (or adult) in close proximity to a significant other.

attention deficit disorder   A disability related to inattention and lack of focus.

attention deficit hyperactivity disorder (ADHD)   A disability related to inattention, hyperactivity, and impulsivity.

authoritarian parenting   Baumrind's term for parents who are demanding and want immediate obedience as the most desirable trait in a child.

authoritative parenting   Baumrind's term for parents who respond to their child's needs and wishes; they believe in parental control and attempt to explain the reasons for it to their child.

autoimmunity   Process by which the immune system in the body rejects the body's own tissue.

autonomous morality   Piaget's term for moral development in children after age 11; actions must be thought of in terms of intentions and consequences.

axons   Branchlike ends of neurons that send electrochemical signals between cells.

B

babbling   Infants' production of sounds approximating speech between 5 and 7 months.

Babinski reflex   Automatic response in which an infant's toes spread out in response to stroking the sole of the foot from heel to toes.

basal metabolism rate (BMR)   The minimum amount of energy a person uses when in a resting state.

bioecological model   The continuity and change in the biopsychosocial characteristics of human beings, both as individuals and as groups.

biological death   Occurs when it is no longer possible to discern an electrical charge in the tissues of the heart and lungs.

biopsychosocial interactions   Biological, psychological, and social/environmental forces that combine to impact human development across the lifespan.

blastocyst   The fertilized egg when it reaches the uterus (about 7 days after conception).

body mass index (BMI)   Measurement used to compare a person's height and weight to determine a healthy body weight; BMI = weight/height².

bonding   The formation of a close connection between a newborn and caregiver.

brain death   Occurs when the brain fails to receive a sufficient supply of oxygen for a short period of time (usually 8 to 10 minutes).

Braxton-Hicks contractions   Relatively mild muscle contractions that occur before real contractions begin.

Brazelton Neonatal Behavioural Assessment Scale   Device to assess an infant's behaviour; examines both neurological and psychological responses.

breech birth   Birth in which the baby is born feet first, buttocks first, or in a crosswise position (transverse presentation).

bulimia nervosa   An eating disorder characterized by binge eating followed by purging to prevent weight gain.

bullying   The act of using verbal or physical means to intimidate or embarrass someone else.

C

cardiopulmonary resuscitation (CPR)   Technique for reviving an individual's lungs and heart that have ceased to function.

cataracts   Thickening of the eye lenses; causes blurred, cloudy vision.

centration   Feature of preoperational thought; the centring of attention on one aspect of an object and the neglecting of any other features.

cerebral palsy   A condition resulting from an inability of the brain to control the body; result of brain damage before, during, or after delivery.

Caesarean section   Surgery performed to deliver the baby through the abdomen if the baby cannot come through the birth canal.

child abuse   Infliction of injury to a child; commonly includes physical, sexual, and emotional abuse, or neglect.

cholesterol   Substance in the blood that can adhere to the walls of the blood vessels, restricting blood flow and causing strokes and heart attacks.

chorionic villi sampling (CVS)   A prenatal test that examines a small section of the embryo's outer layer.

chromosomes   Threadlike structures in the cell that come in 23 pairs (46 total) and contain the genetic material DNA. Each parent contributes half of each chromosome pair.

circular reactions   Piaget's term for infants' motor activity that is repeated in developing stages.

classical conditioning   The learning process in which a neutral stimulus produces an involuntary response that is usually elicited by another stimulus.

classification   Ability to group objects with some similarities within a larger category.

climacteric   The midlife change in hormone levels that affects fertility.

clinical death   The individual is dead when his or her respiration and heartbeat have stopped.

clique   Group of friends who share similar interests and activities.

closed adoption   Adoption procedure in which the biological parents know nothing about the adopting parents.

code of ethics   A guiding set of principles for members of a particular group.

cognitive structures   Piaget's term to describe the basic tools of cognitive development.

cohabitation   A living arrangement in which unmarried partners share a residence and personal assets and sometimes have a child.

collagen   Major connective tissue in the body; provides the elasticity in human skin and blood vessels.

competence   The ability to do something well.

complicated grief   Prolonged and intensified grief; may take weeks or months to pass.

concrete operational stage   Piaget's third stage of cognitive development, between the ages of 7 and 11 years, in which children's thinking is much more flexible than in early childhood.

conservation   The understanding that an object retains certain properties even though surface features change.

constructivism   The belief that children create, organize, and transform knowledge through active engagement in their environment.

constructivist approach   Learning approach in which children are encouraged to be active participants in constructing knowledge and learn by interacting with their environment.

continuity   Development that is a smooth process, without distinct stages.

convergent thinking   Thinking used when a problem to be solved has one correct answer.

cooing   Early language sounds that resemble vowels.

coordination of secondary schemes   Piaget's term for when infants combine secondary schemes to obtain a goal.

crawling   Movement on hands and knees; the trunk does not touch the ground.

creative intelligence   Sternberg's term to describe a person's ability to solve problems in unique ways and to feel comfortable with new or different situations and ideas.

creeping   Movement whereby the infant's abdomen touches the floor and the weight of the head and shoulders rests on the elbows.

cross-linkage theory The theory that, when cross-links are formed between peptides, the proteins are altered, often for the worse.

cross-sectional studies Compare groups of individuals of various ages at the same time.

crowd Reputation-based group whose members may or may not spend time with one another.

crystallized intelligence Accumulated information and verbal skills over time, reflecting the effect of culture and learning; allows a person to make connections between information and/ or objects.

culture The customs, values, and traditions inherent in one's environment.

cystic fibrosis (CF) Chromosomal disorder producing a malfunction of the exocrine glands.

cytomegalovirus (CMV) A widespread infection, often unrecognized in pregnant women, that can cause severe fetal damage.

D

date rape Coercive sexual activity between a victim and an offender who is known or an acquaintance.

daycare Services and care for children provided outside the children's home.

decentration The ability to focus on several features of an object or task.

decode To pronounce words correctly using knowledge of letters and sounds.

defence mechanisms Psychological strategies to cope with anxiety or perceived threats.

deferred imitation Children's preoperational behaviour that continues after they witnessed the original action or event.

delayed grief Grief that is postponed for an inordinate time.

dementia Deterioration of cognitive function over time caused by brain infection or disease.

dendrites Branchlike ends of neurons that receive and conduct the electrochemical signals between the cells.

descriptive studies Studies that gather information on subjects without manipulating them in any way.

DES (diethylstilbestrol) A synthetic hormone that was administered to pregnant women in the late 1940s and 1950s supposedly to prevent miscarriage. It was later found that the daughters of the women who had received this treatment were more susceptible to vaginal and cervical cancer.

despair The negative resolution of Erikson's last stage; individuals look back over their lives and feel that they have made many wrong decisions, or no decisions at all, and see life as lacking integrity.

developing readers Readers who use letter sounds, words, illustrations, and their own knowledge to predict meaning.

development The process of changing and the changes that occur through the lifespan.

developmental risk Risk to children's well-being involving a range of damaging biopsychosocial conditions.

developmental systems theory Set of beliefs leading to the conclusion that we construct our own views of the world.

dilation The first stage of the birth process, during which the opening of the cervix dilates to about 10 centimetres in diameter.

discontinuity Development that is a series of distinct stages; an individual must accomplish at least one task before progressing to the next stage.

disengagement theory The elderly will remove themselves from many social networks.

distorted grief Normal grief carried to an extreme degree; adoption of deceased person's ailments.

divergent thinking Thinking used when a problem to be solved has many possible answers.

DNA (deoxyribonucleic acid) A molecule with the shape of a double helix that contains genetic information.

doula A woman trained as a caregiver to provide ongoing support to pregnant women before, during, and after delivery.

downsizing A reduction in a company's workforce to improve its total revenue.

Down syndrome Chromosomal disorder caused by an extra copy of chromosome 21.

dual-career family Family in which both partners work, usually full time.

Duchenne muscular dystrophy Genetic disorder resulting in muscular weakness.

E

early-onset trajectory Criminal behaviour that begins before puberty.

ego Freud's notion of the central part of our personality; keeps id in check.

egocentric speech The form of speech in which children carry on lively conversations with themselves or others.

egocentrism Piaget's term for the child's focus on self in early phases of cognitive development.

elaboration An association between two or more pieces of information that are not necessarily related.

Electroencephalogram (EEG) Recording of the electrical activity produced by the firing of neurons in the brain.

embryonic period Third through eighth week following fertilization.

emergent readers Children who possess skills, knowledge, and attitudes that are developmental precursors to formal reading.

emerging adulthood Transition from adolescence to adulthood (approximately ages 18 to 25 years); includes exploration and experimentation.

emotional divorce Sometimes partners learn to "put up with" each other. The only activities and interests they share are ones that revolve around the children.

empty nest syndrome The feelings parents may have as a result of their last child leaving home.

epigenetic view Stresses the ongoing interaction between heredity and the environment during lifespan development.

episiotomy A surgical cut made to widen the vaginal opening.

equilibration Piaget's term to describe the balance between assimilation and accommodation.

ethics of care Gilligan's perspective on moral thinking in which people view moral decisions in terms of relationships and responsibilities to others.

ethology Scientific field that stresses that behaviour is strongly influenced by biology and is linked to evolution.

euthanasia The ending of a life, usually in a person with a terminal illness, to prevent a prolonged and painful death.

evolutionary developmental psychology Explanation of development that rests on the assumption that our physiological and psychological systems resulted from evolution by natural selection.

executive functioning Cognitive efforts involving attention and critical thinking.

exosystem Environment in which the developing person is not present but that nevertheless affects development.

explicit memory Refers to facts and experiences that a person can remember and share.

expressive language The language children use to express their ideas and needs.

expulsion Stage 2 of the birth process; the baby passes through the birth canal.

extinction The systematic process in which behaviours are de-conditioned or eliminated.

F

failure to thrive (FTT) Medical term for infants whose weight gain and physical growth fall far below average during the first years of life.

fallopian tube Either of a pair of tubes that join the ovaries to the uterus.

fast mapping Children's use of surrounding context to understand words' meaning.

feminist movement A social and political movement that seeks to establish equality for women in all aspects of life.

fetal alcohol syndrome (FAS) The condition of babies whose mothers drank alcohol during pregnancy; characterized by growth deficiencies, physical abnormalities, and central nervous system dysfunction.

fetal monitor Electronic device used to monitor the baby's heartbeat throughout labour.

fetal period Period that extends from beginning of the 3rd month to birth.

fine motor skills Small muscle skills involving hands and fingers that result from physical development.

five factor model (FFM) of personality McCrae and Costa's theory that there are five major personality traits, which they believe govern the adult personality.

fluid intelligence The ability to think and act quickly and solve problems, as well as the ability to use abstract thinking.

forceps Metal clamps placed around the baby's head to pull the baby through the birth canal.

formal operational stage Piaget's fourth stage of cognitive development, featuring abstract thought and scientific thinking.

fragile X syndrome Chromosomal disorder caused by an impaired X chromosome.

fraternal twins Twins who develop from two eggs fertilized by separate sperm; individuals do not share identical genetic makeup.

G

gamete intrafallopian transfer (GIFT) An ART technique in which sperm and egg are surgically placed in a fallopian tube with the intent of achieving fertilization.

gender Social/psychological aspects of being male or female.

gender identity The conviction that one is either male or female.

gender role Culturally defined expectations about how females and males should act.

gender stereotypes Rigid beliefs about characteristics of males and females.

gene A segment of DNA that is a unit of hereditary information.

generativity Erikson's term for the ability to be useful to self and to society.

genital herpes Infection that can be contracted by a fetus during delivery; the infant can develop symptoms during the first week following birth.

genome All of the hereditary information needed to maintain a living organism.

genotype A person's genetic makeup that is invisible to the naked eye.

germinal period First two weeks following fertilization.

gerontology The field of science that deals with issues, problems, and diseases specific to older adults.

glaucoma Damage to the optic nerve caused by pressure that results from a buildup of fluid in the eye.

globalization The outsourcing of work to a less expensive labour supply in foreign countries.

goodness of fit Concept coined by Chess and Thomas that describes the match between a child's temperament and his/her environment.

grasping reflex Automatic response in which an infant's fingers curl toward palm of hand when object or finger is placed in palm.

grief An emotional response to the loss of another; includes feelings of anxiety, despair, sadness, and loneliness.

gross motor skills Large muscle skills resulting from physical development enabling children to perform smooth and coordinated physical acts.

H

habituation   A decrease in an infant's attention.

health-care power of attorney   Legal document giving someone else authority to make health-care decisions for you if you are incapacitated.

heteronomous morality   Piaget's term for moral development in children aged 4 to 7; they conceive of rules as unchangeable.

heterosexual   Sexual attraction to members of the opposite sex.

HIV (human immunodeficiency virus)   Virus that attacks T cells of the human immune system.

holophrase   One word that can communicate many meanings and ideas.

homeostatic imbalance   Theory that aging is due to a failure in the systems that regulate the proper interaction of the organs.

homosexual   Sexual attraction to members of the same sex.

hormonal balance   Change in hormone levels, one of the triggers of puberty.

hormone replacement therapy (HRT)   Menopause treatment whereby women receive hormone supplements.

hospice   A program providing comfort and supportive services to those near the end of life and to their families.

humanitarian   Efforts dedicated to improving the lives of human beings.

hypothesis   A prediction that can be tested through research and subsequently supported or rejected.

I

id   Freud's structure of mind relating to our basic instincts; strives to secure pleasure.

identical twins   Twins who develop from a single fertilized egg that divides after conception; individuals share identical genetic makeup.

identity crisis   Erikson's term for a situation, usually in adolescence, that causes us to make major decisions about our identity.

identity statuses   Marcia's categories that depict levels of crisis and commitment that contribute to a sense of identity.

imaginary audience   Adolescents' perception that others are constantly scrutinizing their behaviour and appearance.

immanent justice   Piaget's term for a child's belief that broken rules will be punished immediately.

implantation   Attachment of the fertilized egg to the uterine wall.

implicit memory   Refers to an unconscious or automatic process of remembering.

inclusion   A child with special needs is educated in the regular classroom.

independent readers   Competent, confident readers who use skills to derive meaning and enjoyment from reading.

individuation   Refers to our developing a separate and special personality, derived less and less from our parents and teachers and more from our own behaviour.

induced labour   Labour initiated by doctors through use of medication and/or by breaking the amniotic sac.

infantile amnesia   The inability to remember events from early in life.

infertility   Inability to achieve pregnancy after 1 year of unprotected intercourse.

information-processing theory   Cognitive theory that uses a computer metaphor to understand how the human mind processes information.

inner speech   Internal speech that often accompanies physical movements, guiding behaviour.

inquiry   Investigating, questioning, following a hunch to see what happens.

integrity   The resolution of each of the first seven crises in Erikson's theory should lead to the achievement of a sense of personal integrity. Older adults who have a sense of integrity feel their lives have been well spent.

intelligence   A person's problem-solving skills and use of everyday experiences to inform learning.

intelligence quotient (IQ)   Stern's concept of a child's intelligence, calculated by dividing mental age by chronological age, and multiplying by 100.

internalization of schemes   Children's use of symbols to think about real events without actually experiencing them.

intimacy   Erikson's stage that represents the ability to relate one's deepest hopes and fears to another person and to accept another's need for intimacy in turn.

intrauterine insemination (IUI)   An ART technique in which sperm are injected directly into the uterus as part of the fertilization procedure.

in vitro fertilization (IVF)   An ART technique in which fertilization occurs in a petri dish and the resulting embryos are transferred to the woman's uterus.

isolette   Specially designed bed for premature infants that is temperature-controlled and enclosed in clear plastic; often referred to as an incubator.

K

kangaroo care   Practice of skin-to-skin contact, positioning baby against caregiver's bare chest.

Klinefelter syndrome   Chromosomal disorder in males caused by an XXY chromosomal pattern.

L

Lamaze method   Natural childbirth method that stresses breathing and relaxation with the support of a partner.

late-onset trajectory   Criminal behaviour that begins after puberty.

learning disability   A neurological disorder that impacts the brain's functioning.

legal death   A legal pronouncement by a qualified person that a patient should be considered dead under the law.

LGBT   An acronym referring to lesbian (female), gay (male), bisexual, and transgender individuals; it can include a Q for queer or questioning (LGBTQ).

life course theory   Theory referring to a sequence of socially defined, age-graded events and roles that individuals enact over time.

life crisis   Erikson's term to describe the main tension that individuals experience and seek to resolve during each of eight life stages.

life expectancy   The number of years that a person born in a specific year is expected to live.

lifespan development   An examination of the biological, cognitive/psychological, and social changes that occur over the course of a human life. This is one perspective in the broader discipline of developmental psychology.

lifespan psychology   Study of human development from conception to death.

living will   Legal document that describes specific life-prolonging medical treatments.

longitudinal studies   The researcher makes several observations of the same individuals at two or more times in their lives. Examples include determining the long-term effects of learning on behaviour, the stability of habits and intelligence, and the factors involved in memory.

M

macrosystem   The blueprint for the cultural experiences of people within any society.

macular degeneration   An eye disease that affects the retina, impacting the centre of a person's field of vision.

manipulative experiments   Experiments in which the researcher attempts to keep constant all variables (all the factors that can affect a particular outcome) except one, which is carefully manipulated.

meiosis   Cell division in which the number of chromosomes is halved to 23.

menarche   A girl's first menstruation.

menopause   Cessation of women's menstruation, typically occurring in the late 40s or early 50s.

mental age   Binet's measure of an individual's mental development compared to that of others.

mentoring   The act of assisting another, usually younger, person with his or her work or life tasks.

mesosystem   According to Bronfenbrenner, the relationship among different microsystems; for example, between the quality of school which a child attends and the neighbourhood in which they reside.

microsystem   According to Bronfenbrenner, the innermost environment for the developing individual such as the home or school.

midlife transition   Levinson's term to describe the period of life that bridges early and middle adulthood, approximately ages 40 to 45.

midwife   A woman trained in delivering babies; typically a nurse.

mitosis   Cell division in which the number of chromosomes remains the same (46).

modelling   Bandura's term for observational learning.

moral development   Thinking, feeling, and behaving based on rules and customs about how people interact with others.

Moro reflex   Infant's automatic response to sudden change in position or unexpected movement; arms and legs flail out and back in toward chest, and back arches.

mortality rate   The number of deaths in a population for a given year; typically, the number of deaths per 100,000 people per year.

mourning   Actions taken as a result of grieving.

mutation   A change in DNA, affecting the genes, that occurs during mitosis by accident or because of environmental factors.

myelin   Sheath of insulation around axons that facilitates communication between neurons.

myelination   Process by which speed of information travelling through nervous system increases, due to a fatty layer of cells on nerve cells in the brain.

N

naive psychology   Vygotsky's stage in which children explore objects and label objects as they acquire the grammar of their speech.

natural childbirth (or prepared childbirth)   Term to describe techniques women use prior to and during the birth process to create the most natural experience possible during delivery.

naturalistic experiments   Experiments in which the researcher acts solely as an observer and does as little as possible to disturb the environment. "Nature" performs the experiment, and the researcher acts as a recorder of the results.

negative reinforcement   An event that, when it ceases to occur, makes that response more likely to happen in the future.

neonate   An infant in the first days and weeks after birth.

neurological assessment   A neonatal test that identifies any neurological problem, suggests means of monitoring the problem, and offers a prognosis about the problem.

neurons   Nerve cells that transmit information with electrochemical signals.

New York Longitudinal Study   Long-term study by Chess and Thomas of the personality characteristics of children.

non-stage theorists   Reading theorists who argue that reading develops naturally, as does language.

novice phase   Levinson's phase of human development that captures the early adult transition, entering the adult world, and the age 30 transition.

O

obesity   Based on BMI, greater than 85th percentile for sex and age.

object permanence   The realization that objects continue to exist even when they cannot be seen, heard, or touched.

observational learning   Bandura's term to explain the information we obtain from observing other people, things, and events.

one-time, one-group studies   Carried out only once with one group of participants.

open adoption   Adoption procedure in which biological parents have considerable input into the adoption process.

operant conditioning   The use of consequences (reinforcement, punishment) to modify or shape voluntary behaviour or actions.

organization   Memory strategy that entails discovering and imposing an easy-to-remember structure on items to be memorized.

organogenesis   Process by which organs are formed; occurs around 6 to 7 weeks of pregnancy.

organ reserve   The part of the total capacity of our body's organs that we do not normally need to use.

osteoporosis   A condition in which bones are thin and brittle due to calcium loss.

overextension   A language irregularity in which children apply a word in a broad manner to objects that do not fit.

overregularization   Children's strict application of language rules they have learned.

ovulation   The process in which the egg bursts from the surface of the ovary.

oxytocin   Hormone secreted by the pituitary gland that stimulates uterine contractions; has been linked to bonding between caregivers and infants.

P

palliative   A type of care that is focused primarily on the relief of pain and control of symptoms.

passive euthanasia   Refraining from continuing efforts to sustain someone's life.

perception   The process of obtaining and interpreting information from stimuli.

permissive parenting   Baumrind's term for parents who take a tolerant, accepting view of their child's behaviour and rarely make demands or use punishment.

personal fable   Adolescents' tendency to think of themselves in heroic or mythical terms.

phenotype   A person's observable characteristics or traits.

phenylketonuria (PKU)   Inherited disease caused by a gene mutation.

phonology   Sounds of a language.

physician-assisted suicide (PAS)   Active euthanasia whereby doctors give patients death-inducing drugs.

placenta   Supplies the embryo with all its needs, carries off all its wastes, and protects it from harm.

plantar reflex   Automatic response in which an infant's toes curl inward when pressure is placed on balls of feet.

play   Activity people engage in because they enjoy it for its own sake.

positive psychology   A branch of psychology that emphasizes the impact of positive psychological traits on individual and group behaviours.

positive reinforcement   An event that increases the likelihood of a desired response in the future.

postformal thought   A proposed cognitive development stage after Piaget's formal operations in which people acknowledge the relativistic nature of problems and answers.

postpartum depression   Feelings of sadness and emotional withdrawal that may continue for many weeks or months after delivery.

postpartum period   Period lasting approximately 6 weeks after birth as mother adjusts physically and psychologically.

poverty   Living in a household with income less than 50% of the national median.

practical intelligence   Sternberg's term to describe "common sense"—a simple, logical understanding of a situation and how to work through a problem.

pragmatics   Ability to communicate with others.

preintellectual speech   Vygotsky's category for cooing, crying, babbling, and bodily movements that develop into more sophisticated forms of speech.

premature birth   Early birth; occurs at or before 37 weeks after conception and is defined by low birth weight and immaturity.

preoperational period   Piaget's second stage of cognitive development, extending from about 2 to 7 years.

presbycusis   The age-related decline in hearing in which the individual begins to lose the ability to detect certain tones, especially high-pitched ones.

presbyopia   The age-related decline in vision in which the individual begins to lose the ability to see objects clearly at close distances.

primary circular reactions   Infants' actions that are focused on their own bodies and reflexes.

prospective memory   The process of remembering to do something in the future.

protective factors   Characteristics of resilient individuals that protect them from stress.

psychoanalytic theory   Freud's theory of the development of personality; emphasis on the role of the unconscious.

psychosexual stages   Freud's five distinct stages of development in which a pleasure centre must be satisfied in order for the individual to resolve the inner conflicts relating to his or her wants or needs.

psychosocial theory   Erikson's stage theory that emphasizes the impact of social experiences throughout human development.

psychosomatic Physical illness or symptom brought about by mental factors.

puberty The process of physical changes by which a child's body becomes an adult body capable of reproduction.

punishment Process by which an unpleasant response is paired with an undesired behaviour to decrease the likelihood of that behaviour occurring in the future.

R

reaction time The time between the presence of a stimulus and the actual muscle activity that indicates a reaction to it.

receptive language The ability of the child to understand written and spoken language.

reciprocal interactions Our responses to others around us, which causes changes in those other people; their responses to us then change, which in turn produces new changes in us.

reflex An inborn, automatic response to certain stimuli.

rehearsal Mnemonic strategy that describes a person repeating target information.

reinforcement Anything that increases the likelihood a response will occur in the future.

REM (rapid eye-movement) sleep A period of deep sleep marked by eye movements; when vivid dreams occur.

representation Piaget's term for a child's application of abstract thinking during the preoperational period.

repression A defence mechanism in which traumatic and unacceptable thoughts and memories are removed from consciousness and pushed to the unconscious level.

resilient children Children who sustained some type of physiological or psychological trauma yet return to a normal developmental path.

respiratory distress syndrome (RDS) Problem common with premature babies; caused by lack of a substance called surfactant, which keeps air sacs in the lungs open.

reticular activation system (RAS) Complex subcortical system that protects the brain from being overwhelmed.

retrieval Memory strategy that enables obtaining information from memory; includes recognition and recall.

retrospective memory Memory of past event or item.

reversibility A cognitive act in which a child recognizes that he or she can use stages of reasoning to solve a problem and then trace the steps back to the original question or premise.

Rh factor Involves possible incompatibility between the blood types of mother and child. If the mother is Rh-negative and the child Rh-positive, miscarriage or even infant death can result.

risk factors The stressors that individuals experience, including poverty, chronic illness, and divorce.

role discontinuity Abrupt and disruptive change caused by conflicts among a person's various roles in life.

rooting reflex Automatic response in which an infant turns toward a finger or nipple placed gently on the cheek, attempting to get it into his or her mouth.

rubella (also known as German measles) An infectious disease that can cause serious birth defects, if a woman contracts the disease during pregnancy; extremely dangerous to a fetus during the first trimester.

S

sandwich generation Term used to describe adults who are simultaneously caring for their children and their aging parents, parents-in-law, or some other elder.

scaffolding The systematic use of support to assist a child in his or her performance on a given task.

schemes Piaget's term for organized patterns of thought and action.

scientific method An approach to investigation that includes empirical research, data collection, and testing.

secondary circular reactions Piaget's term for infants' activities that are directed toward objects and events outside themselves.

secular trend The decreasing age of the onset of puberty.

self-concept A person's evaluation of himself or herself.

self-efficacy A person's belief that he or she can behave in a certain way to achieve a desired goal.

self-esteem One's personal sense of worth and value.

self-regulation An individual's ability to initiate, terminate, delay, or modify thought, emotion, behaviour, or action.

semantics Meaning of words and sentences.

sensitive periods Montessori's term for periods of children's development marked by sensitivity/readiness to learn.

sensitive responsiveness The ability to recognize the meaning of a child's behaviour.

sensorimotor period The first 2 years of life.

sequential (longitudinal/cross-sectional) studies Done several times with the same groups of individuals.

seriation The ability to order items along a quantitative dimension such as length or weight.

sex Biological maleness or femaleness.

sex cleavage Youngsters of the same sex tend to play and do things together.

sexual assault Refers to all incidents of unwanted sexual activity, including sexual attacks and sexual touching.

sexual harassment Any conduct, comment, gesture or contact of a sexual nature that is likely to cause offence or humiliation or that might, on reasonable grounds, be perceived as placing a condition of a sexual nature on employment or on any opportunity for training or promotion.

sexual identity How a person thinks of himself or herself in terms of sexual and romantic attraction, linked to genetic traits/physical characteristics of male and female.

sexually transmitted infections (STIs) Infections that may cause infertility.

sibling underworld Familial subsystem, or coalition, of brothers and/or sisters.

sickle-cell disease Blood disorder resulting in abnormal hemoglobin.

simple reflexes The first stage of the sensorimotor period, when children do little more than exercise their inborn reflexes.

small for date Term used for babies born or assessed as underweight for the length of the pregnancy.

social (cognitive) learning theory Bandura's explanation for the process whereby the information we glean from observing others influences our behaviour.

social constructivism The belief that children construct knowledge through social interactions.

social death Point at which a patient is treated essentially as a corpse, although perhaps still "clinically" or "biologically" alive.

socioemotional selectivity theory Humans use social contact for four reasons: to ensure physical survival, to gain information, to maintain a sense of self, and to acquire pleasure and comfort.

spina bifida Genetic disorder resulting in the failure of the spinal column to close completely.

spindle cells Neurons that play a large role in emotion.

stage theorists Reading theorists who argue that reading occurs in distinct developmental stages

stage theorists of personality Theorists who consider stages of change across the lifespan and how one's personality interacts with the world.

stagnation Erikson's term for boredom, self-absorption, and the inability to contribute to society.

stepping reflex Automatic response in which the neonate, held under the arms with feet touching a flat surface, makes stepping movements similar to actual walking.

STORCH diseases Syphilis, toxoplasmosis, other infections, rubella, cytomegalovirus, herpes; these diseases are especially harmful to the embryo or fetus at certain times during a pregnancy.

strange situation Measure designed to assess the quality of attachment.

stress Anything that upsets a person's equilibrium—psychologically and physiologically.

sudden infant death syndrome (SIDS) Unexpected death of an apparently healthy infant, usually between 2 and 4 months of age.

superego Freud's concept of our conscience; internal determinant of right and wrong.

surrogate mother A woman who carries another woman's fetus.

symbolic play Children's mental representation of an object or event and reenactment of it in their play; one object may represent a different object in the play scenario.

synapse A small gap between neurons that allows communication between neurons to occur.

syntax The way in which words are put together to construct sentences.

syphilis Sexually transmitted disease that, if untreated, may adversely affect the fetus.

T

Tay-Sachs disease Genetic disorder caused by the lack of an enzyme that breaks down fatty material in the central nervous system.

telegraphic speech Initial multiple-word utterances, usually two or three words.

temperament Individual differences; unique and stable styles of behaving.

teratogens Any environmental agents that harm the embryo or fetus.

tertiary circular reaction Piaget's term for repetition with variation; the infant is exploring the world's possibilities.

thalidomide Popular drug prescribed during the early 1960s that was later found to cause a variety of birth defects when taken by women early in their pregnancies.

theory A belief or idea that develops based on information or evidence; a proposed explanation for observed phenomena.

theory of mind Children's understanding of their own thoughts and mental processes.

theory of multiple intelligences Gardner's theory that attributes eight types of intelligence to humans.

time-variable designs A specific amount of time (duration) is allowed for a given study, or there is a specific number of times a measure is used in a given study.

tonic-neck reflex Automatic response in which an infant extends arm and leg on same side as the direction in which he or she is looking, while flexing other arm and leg.

toxoplasmosis Infection caused by a parasite; may cause damage to a fetus.

trait theorists Researchers who look at pieces of the personality (personality traits), as measured by detailed questionnaires.

transitivity The ability to understand relationships and combine them mentally to draw new conclusions.

triarchic theory of intelligence Sternberg's theory that intelligence consists of componential, experiential, and contextual parts.

Turner syndrome Chromosomal disorder in females caused by an XO chromosomal pattern.

U

ultrasound Use of sound waves and special equipment to produce an image that enables a physician to detect internal structural abnormalities.

umbilical cord Contains blood vessels that go to and from the mother through the arteries and veins supplying the placenta.

uninvolved/neglectful parenting Term for parents who are undemanding and emotionally unsupportive of their child.

V

vacuum extractor Plastic cup attached to a suction device that pulls the baby through the birth canal.

validation Fromm's term for the reciprocal sharing of deep secrets and feelings that allows people to feel loved and accepted.

W

wisdom Superior insight and judgment that can come only from experience.

word spurt Rapid increase of vocabulary from 18 months to 3 years.

work–family conflict The phenomenon that occurs when demands of a person's role as a caregiver conflict with demands of his or her role as a worker.

X

XYY syndrome Chromosomal disorder in males caused by an extra Y chromosome.

Z

zone of proximal development Vygotsky's term for a range of ability in a given task, where the higher limit is achieved through interaction with others.

zygote The cell that results when an egg is fertilized by a sperm.

A

Aboriginal Affairs and Northern Development Canada (2012). Indian residential schools: Key milestones. Retrieved from http://www.aadnc-aandc.gc.ca/eng/1332939430258/1332939552554

Abraham, C. (2010, October 18). Failing boys: Part 2 of 6—The endangered male teacher. *Globe and Mail*. Retrieved from http://www.theglobeandmail.com/news/national/time-to-lead/part-2-the-endangered-male-teacher/article4330079/

Ackerman, S., Zuroff, D., & Moskowitz, D. (2000). Generativity in midlife and young adults: Links to agency, communion, and subjective well-being. *International Journal of Aging & Human Development, 50*, 17–41.

Active Healthy Kids Canada. (2011). Don't let this be the most physical activity our kids get after school. The Active Healthy Kids Canada 2011 Report Card on Physical Activity for Children and Youth. Toronto: Active Healthy Kids Canada.

Adoption Council of Canada. (2011, December 4). Canadians go abroad to adopt 1946 children in 2010. Retrieved from http://www.adoption.ca/adoption-news?news_id=56

Ahrons, C. (2004). *We're still family*. New York: HarperCollins.

Ainsworth, M. (1973). The development of infant–mother attachment. In B. Caldwell & H. Riccuti (Eds.), *Review of child development research*. Chicago: University of Chicago Press.

Ainsworth, M. (1979). Infant–mother attachment. *American Psychologist, 34*, 932–937.

Ainsworth, M., & Bowlby, J. (1991). An ethological approach to personality. *American Psychologist, 46*, 333–341.

Alland, A. (1983). *Playing with form: Children draw in six cultures*. New York: Columbia University Press.

Alliance for Childhood. (2009). Crisis in the kindergarten: Why children need to play in school. Retrieved from http://allianceforchildhood.org/sites/allianceforchildhood.org/files/file/ kindergarten_report.pdf

Al-Sahab, B., Ardern, C.I., Hamadeh, M.J., & Tamim, H. (2010). Age at menarche in Canada: Results from the National Longitudinal Survey of Children and Youth. *BMC Public Health, 10*, 736.

Al-Sahab, B., Ardern, CI., Hamadeh, M.J., & Tamim, H. (2012). Age at menarche and current substance use among Canadian adolescent girls: Results of a cross-sectional study. *BMC Public Health, 12*, 195

Alzheimer Society of Canada. (2013). What is Alzheimer's disease. Retrieved from http://www.alzheimer.ca/en/About-dementia/Alzheimer-s-disease/What-is-Alzheimer-s-disease

American Alliance for Health, Physical Education, Recreation, and Dance. (2007). Accepting overweight. *Journal of Physical Education, Recreation, and Dance, 78*(1), 3.

American Psychiatric Association. (2013). *Diagnostic and statistical manual of mental disorders: DSM-V*. Washington, DC: American Psychiatric Association.

Anderson, C. A., & Dill, K.E. (2000). Video games and aggressive thoughts, feelings, and behavior in the laboratory and in life. *Journal of Personality and Social Psychology, 78*(4), 772–790.

Anderson., S. E., Dallal, G. E., & Must, A. (2003). Relative weight and race influence average age at menarche: Results from two nationally representative surveys of U.S. girls studied 25 years apart. *Pediatrics, 111*(4), 844–850.

Andresen, M. (2006, June 6). Accutane registry compulsory in U.S., but not Canada. *Canadian Medical Association Journal*. Vol. 174, no.12 doi: 10.1503/cmaj.0605

Arenson, J., & Drake, P. (2007). *Maternal and newborn health*. Sudbury, MA: Jones and Bartlett.

Arsenault, M., Dontigny, L., & Martel, M. (2008). Clinical Practice Guidelines: Rubella in pregnancy. *Journal of Obstetrics and Gynaecology Canada, 203*: 152–153.

Asch-Goodkin, J., & Kaplan, D. (2006). When a spouse is hospitalized (bereavement effect in spouse death). *Patient Care for the Nurse Practitioner*.

Astwood Strategy Corporation (2004). Results of the 2002 Canadian police survey on youth gangs. Retrieved from http://www.astwood.ca/assets/gangs_e.pdf

B

Bakalar, N. (2005, November 22). Premature births increase along with C-sections. *New York Times*. Retrieved from http://www.nytimes.com/2005/11/22/health/22birth.html?_r=1

Ball, J., & Bindler, R. (2006). *Child health nursing: Partnering with children and families*. Upper Saddle River, NJ: Prentice Hall.

Balsam, R. H., & Fischer, R. S. (2006). Mothers and daughters II. *Psychoanalytic Inquiry, 26*(1). New York: Routledge.

Baltes, P., Lindenberger, U., & Staudinger, U. (2006). Lifespan theory in developmental psychology. In W. Damon & R. Lerner (Series Eds.) & R. Lerner (Vol. Ed.), *Handbook of child psychology: Vol. 1. Theoretical models of human development*. New York: Wiley.

Baltes, P. B., & Staudinger, U. M. (2000). Wisdom: A meta-heuristic (pragmatic) to orchestrate mind and virtue toward excellence. *American Psychologist, 55*(1), 122–136.

Bandura, A. (1997). *Self-efficacy: The exercise of control*. New York: Freeman.

Bandura, A., Barbaranelli, C., Caprara, G., & Pastorelli, C. (2001). Self-efficacy beliefs as shapers of children's aspirations and career trajectories. *Child Development, 72*(1), 187–206.

Bandura, A., Ross, D., & Ross, S. (1963). Imitation of film-mediated aggressive models. *Journal of Abnormal and Social Psychology, 66*, 3–11.

Bandura, A., Ross, D., & Ross, S. (1961). Transmission of aggression throough imitation of aggressive models. *Journal of Abnormal and Social Psychology, 63*, 575–82.

Bandura, A., & Walters, R. (1963). *Social learning and personality development*. New York: Holt, Rinehart & Winston.

Barber, J. (2011, December 12). Books vs. screens: Which should your children be reading? *Globe and Mail*. Retrieved from http://www.theglobeandmail.com/arts/books-and-media/books-vs-screens-which-should-your-kids-be-reading/article4180783/

Baumrind, D. (1967). Child-care practices anteceding three patterns of preschool behavior. *Genetic Psychology Monographs, 75*, 43–88.

Baumrind, D. (1971). Current patterns of parental authority. *Developmental Psychology Monographs, 4*, 1–103.

Baumrind, D. (1986). *Familial antecedents of social competence in middle childhood*. Unpublished manuscript.

Baumrind, D. (1991a). The influence of parenting style on adolescent competence and substance use. Special issue: The work of John P. Hill: I. Theoretical, instructional, and policy contributions. *Journal of Early Adolescence, 11*(1), 56–95.

Baumrind, D. (1991b). To nurture nature. *Behavioral and Brain Sciences*, XIV, 386.

Baumrind, D. (1991c). Parenting styles and adolescent development. In R. Lerner, A. Peterson, & J. Brooks-Gunn (Eds.), *The encyclopedia of adolescence*. New York: Garland.

BBC News. (2010, July 29). The women who choose not to be mothers. Retrieved from http://www.bbc.co.uk/news/magazine-10786279

Beausang, C. C., & Razor, A. G. (2000). Young Western women's experiences of menarche and menstruation. *Health Care for Women International, 21*, 517–528.

Beckford, M. (2011). SpongeBob SquarePants bad for concentration. Retrieved from http://www.telegraph.co.uk/education-news/8755839/SpongeBob-SquarePants-bad-for-concentration.html

Beeson, R., Horton-Deutsch, S., Farran, C., & Neundorfer, M. (2000). Loneliness and depression in caregivers of persons with Alzheimer's disease or related disorders. *Issues in Mental Health Nursing, 21*, 779–806.

Belluz, J. (2012, Feb. 2). Psychotropes and children: Are we ruining a generation? *Maclean's*. Retrieved from http://www2.macleans.ca/2012/02/02/psychotropes-and-children-ruining-a-generation/

Bem, S. (1999). *An unconventional family*. New Haven, CT: Yale University Press.

Bem, S. (2001). Exotic becomes erotic: Integrating biological and experiential antecedents of sexual orientation. In A. D'Augelli & C. Patterson (Eds.), *Lesbian, gay, and bisexual identities and youth: Psychological perspectives*. (pp. 52–68). London: Oxford University Press.

Bengtson, V. (2001). Beyond the nuclear family: The increasing importance of multigenerational bonds. *Journal of Marriage and the Family, 63*, 1–16.

Berg, S. J., & Wynne-Edwards, K. (2001). Changes in testosterone, cortisol, and estradiol levels in men becoming fathers. *Mayo Clinic Proceedings, 76*, 582–592.

Bergh, S., & Erling, A. (2005). Adolescent identity formation: A Swedish study of identity status using the EOM-EIS-II. *Adolescence, 40*(158), 377–397.

Bernas, K. H., & Major, D. A. (2000). Contributors to stress resistance: Testing a model of women's work–family conflict. *Psychology of Women Quarterly, 24*, 170–178.

Bernat, J. (2001). Ethical and legal issues in palliative care. *Neurologic Clinics, 19*, 969–987.

Berzonsky, M., & Kuk, L. (2000). Identity status, identity processing style and transition to university. *Journal of Adolescent Research, 15*(1), 81–98.

Beutel, M. E., Weidner, W., & Brahler, E. (2006). Epidemiology of sexual dysfunction in the male population. *Andrologia, 38*(4), 115–121.

Bianchi, S., Robinson, J., & Milkie, M. (2006). *Changing rhythms of American family life* (Rose Series in Sociology). New York: Sage.

Bielski, Z. (2013). Why teen pregnancy is on the rise again in Canada (and spiking in these provinces). *Globe and Mail*. Retrieved from http://www.theglobeandmail.com/life/health-and-fitness/health/why-teen-pregnancy-is-on-the-rise-again-in-canada-and-spiking-in-these-provinces/article7927983/

Birren, J., & Fisher, L. (1992). Aging and slowing of behavior. In J. J. Berman & T. B. Sonderegger (Eds.), *Psychology and aging: Nebraska Symposium on Motivation 1991*. Lincoln: University of Nebraska.

Bjorklund, D. (2000). *Children's thinking: Developmental function and individual differences*. Belmont, CA: Wadsworth.

Bjorklund, D. (2005). Children's thinking. Belmont, CA: Wadsworth.

Bjorklund, D. F., & Pellegrini, A. D. (2000). *The origins of human nature*. New York: Oxford University Press.

Black, M., Dubowitz, H., Krishnakumar, A., & Starr, R. (2007). Early intervention and recovery among children with failure to thrive: Follow-up at age 8. *Pediatrics, 120*(1), 59–69.

Blackman, J. (1997). *Medical aspects of developmental disabilities in children birth to three*. Gaithersburg, MD: Aspen.

Blakeslee, S. (2003, December 9). Humanity? Maybe it's in the wiring. *New York Times*, D1.

Blank, J. (2000). *Still doing it: Women and men over sixty write about their sexuality*. New York: Down There Press.

Blazer, D. G., & Wu, L. (2009). The epidemiology of at-risk and binge drinking among middle-aged and elderly community adults: National Survey on Drug Use and Health. *American Journal of Psychiatry*. Retrieved from http://ajp.psychiatryonline.org/article.aspx?articleID=101223

Block, R., Krebs, N., the Committee on Child Abuse and Neglect, and the Committee on Nutrition. (2005). Failure to thrive as a manifestation of child neglect. *Pediatrics, 116*(5), 1234–1237.

Bornstein, M. (2002). Parenting infants. In M. Bornstein (Ed.) *Handbook of parenting: Vol. 1*. Mahwah, NJ: Erlbaum.

Bornstein, M. (Ed.). (2002). *Handbook of parenting* (2nd ed.). Mahwah, NJ: Erlbaum.

Boswell, R. (2012, December 19). Canada's oldest known citizen prepares to turn 112 on Vancouver Island. *Vancouver Sun*. Postmedia News.

Bowker, A., Boekhoven, B., Nolan, A., Bauhaus, S., Glover, P., Powell, T., and Taylor, S. (2009). Naturalistic observations in spectator behaviour at youth hockey games. *Sport Psychologist, 23*, 301–316. Carleton University: Ottawa, Canada.

Brazelton, T., & Nugent, K. (1995). *Neonatal behavioral assessment scale*. London: MacKeith Press.

Brennan, S., & Taylor-Butts, A. (2008). Sexual assault in Canada. Canadian Centre for Justice Statistics. Statistics Canada.

Briken, P., Habermann, N., Berner, W., & Hill, A. (2006). XYY chromosome abnormality in sexual homicide perpetrators. *American Journal of Medical Genetics B: Neuropsychiatry and Genetics, 141*, 198–200.

Brim, O., & J. Kagan (1980). *Constancy and change in human development*. Cambridge, MA: Harvard University Press.

British Columbia Civil Liberties Association (n.d.). The Canadian Law Reform Commission's definition of death. Retrieved May 18, 2013 from http://bccla.org/our_work/the-canadian-law-reform-commissions-definition-of-death/

Broadbent, D. E. (1954). The role of auditory localization in attention and memory span. *Journal of Experimental Psychology, 47*, 191–196.

Brodzinsky, D., & Pinderhughes, E. (2002). Parenting and child development in adoptive families. In M. Bornstein (Ed.), *Handbook of parenting* (2nd ed.). Mahwah, NJ: Erlbaum.

Bronfenbrenner, U. (1978). *The ecology of human development*. Cambridge, MA: Harvard University Press.

Bronfenbrenner, U. (1986). Ecology of the family as a context for human development: Research perspectives. *Developmental Psychology, 22*, 723–742.

Bronfenbrenner, U., & Morris, P. (1998). The ecology of developmental processes. In R. M. Lerner (Ed.), Handbook of child psychology: Vol. 1. *Theoretical models of human development.* New York: Wiley.

Bronfenbrenner, U., & Morris, P. (2006). The ecology of developmental processes. In W. Damon & R. Lerner (Eds.), *Handbook of child psychology*, (6th ed., pp. 793–829). New York: Wiley.

Bronson, M. (1995). *The right stuff for children birth to 8.* Washington, DC: National Association for the Education of Young People.

Brown, B., Dolcini, M., & Leventhal, A. (1997). Transformations in peer relationships at adolescence: Implications for health-related behavior. In J. Schulenberg & J. L. Maggs (Eds.), *Health risks and developmental transitions during adolescence* (pp. 161–189). New York: Cambridge University Press.

Buahene, A. (2012, October 25). Connecting Gen Ys with baby boomers through formal mentoring N-gen. Retrieved from http://www.ngenperformance.com/blog/gen-y/connecting-gen-ys-with-baby-boomers-through-formal-mentoring

Bugental, D. B., & Happaney, K. (2004). Predicting infant maltreatment in low-income families: The interactive effects of maternal attributions and child status at birth. *Developmental Psychology, 40*(2), 234–243.

Buhs, E., & Ladd, G. (2001). Peer rejections as an antecedent of young children's school adjustment: An examination of mediating processes. *Developmental Psychology, 37*(4), 550–560.

Burgess, E. O. (2004). Sexuality in midlife and later life couples. In J. H. Harvey & A. Wetzel (Eds.), *The handbook of sexuality in close relationships.* Mahwah, NJ: Erlbaum.

Bushby, K., Finkel, R., Birnkrant, D., Case, L., Clemens, P., Cripe, L., . . . Constantin, C. (2010). Diagnosis and management of Duchenne muscular dystrophy, part 1: Diagnosis and pharmacological and psychosocial management. *Lancet Neurol, 9:* 77–93.

Bushnik, T., Cook, J. L., Yupe, S., Tough, S., & Collins, J. (2012). Estimating the prevalence of infertility in Canada. Human Reproduction. Published online January 17. doi: 10.1093/humrep/der465

Buss, D. (2001). Cognitive biases and emotional wisdom in the evolution of conflict between the sexes. *Current Directions in Psychological Science, 10*, 219–223.

Byrne, S. (2012, Aug 24). Alanis Morissette opens up about suffering from postpartum depression. Retrieved from http://ca.omg.yahoo.com/blogs/celebrity-broods/alanis-morissette-opens-suffering-postpartum-depression-151852171.html

Byrnes, J. P. (2005). The development of regulated decision making. In J. E. Jacobs & P. A. Klaczynski (Eds.), *The development of judgment and decision making in children and adolescents.* Mahwah, NJ: Erlbaum.

C

Cahan, S., Greenbaum, C., Artman, L., Deluya, N., & Gappel-Gilon, Y. (2006). The differential effects of age and first-grade schooling on the development of infralogical and logico-mathematical concrete operations. *Cognitive Development, 23*(2), 258–277.

Cairns, R., & Cairns, B. (2006). The making of developmental psychology. In W. Damon & R. Lerner (Series Eds.) & R. Lerner (Vol. Ed.), *Handbook of child psychology: Vol. 1. Theoretical models of human development.* New York: Wiley.

Campbell, L.D., & Martin-Matthews, A. (2003). The gendered nature of men's filial care. *The Journals of Gerontology, 58B*(6), S350-S358.

Campbell, N., & Reece, J. (2005). *Biology.* New York: Pearson/Cummings.

Campion-Smith, B. (2012, Wednesday, September 19). 2011 Census: Canada sees a jump in same-sex marriages. *Star.* Retrieved from http://www.thestar.com/news/canada/2012/09/19/2011_census_canada_sees_a_jump_in_samesex_marriages.html

Canadian Cancer Society. (2012). Media backgrounder: Canadian cancer statistics 2012. Retrieved from http://www.cancer.ca/en/about-us/for-media/media-releases/national/2012/media-backgrounder-canadian-cancer-statistics-2012/?region=qc

Canadian Cancer Society. (2013). Prostate cancer statistics. Retrieved from http://www.cancer.ca/en/cancer-information/cancer-type/prostate/statistics/?region=on#ixzz2cniRkaVM

Canadian Centre on Substance Abuse. (2011). Cross-Canada report on student alcohol and drug use. Retrieved from http://www.ccsa.ca/2011%20CCSA%20Documents/2011_CCSA_Student_Alcohol_and_Drug_Use_en.pdf

Canadian Coalition for Seniors Mental Health. (2006). National guidelines for seniors' mental health: The assessment of suicide risk and prevention of suicide.

Canadian Encyclopedia. (2012). Aging. Retrieved from http://www.thecanadianencyclopedia.com/articles/aging

Canadian Foundation for the Study of Infant Deaths. (2012). Sudden infant death syndrome and aboriginals. Retrieved from http://www.sidscanada.org/reducetherisk/aboriginals.html

Canadian Healthy Infant Longitudinal Development Study (2010, May). Retrieved from http://www.canadianchildstudy.ca/index/html

Canadian Heritage. (2012, December). Canada's commitment to cultural diversity. Cultural diversity: A Canadian perspective. Retrieved from http://www.pch.gc.ca/eng/1332871836953/1332872826975

Canadian Hospice Palliative Care Association (2013). The Canadian Hospice Palliative Care Association … A history. Retrieved May 22, 2013 from http://www.chpca.net/about-us/history.aspx

Canadian Institute for Health Information (2006). Giving birth in Canada: The costs. Retrieved from https://secure.cihi.ca/free_products/Costs_Report_06_Eng.pdf

Canadian Institute for Health Information. (2007). Health care use at the end of life in western Canada. Retrieved from https://secure.cihi.ca/free_products/end_of_life_report_aug07_e.pdf

Canadian Institute for Health Information. (2012). Highlights of 2010-2011: Selected indicators describing the birthing process in Canada. Retrieved from https://secure.cihi.ca/free_products/Childbirth_Highlights_2010-11_EN.pdf

Canadian Mental Health Association. (2012). Centre for Suicide Prevention resource toolkit. Retrieved from http://suicideinfo.ca/LinkClick.aspx?fileticket=cmFwRL4DMJw%3D&tabid=563

Canadian Paediatric Society. (2011). Impact of media use on children and youth. Psychosocial Paediatrics Committee. 2003, reaffirmed February 2011.

Canadian Press. (2012, Oct. 24). Bilingualism growing, but not in French and English. Retrieved from http://www.cbc.ca/news/canada/story/2012/10/24/census-language.html

Canadian Psychological Association. (2000). *Canadian code of ethics for psychologists* (3rd ed.). Ottawa, Ontario.

Canadians For Health Research. (2012). Dr. Shoo Lee: Leading the vanguard in neonatal care. Retrieved from http://www.chrcrm.org/en/rotm/dr-shoo-lee

Carey, B. (2013, February 12). Shooting in the dark. *New York Times.* Retrieved from http://www.nytimes.com/2013/02/12/science/studying-the-effects-of-playing-violent-video-games.html?_r=0

Carlson, B. (2004). *Human embryology and developmental biology.* Philadelphia: Mosby.

Carr, D., House, J., Wortman, C., Nesse, R., & Kessler, R. (2001). Psychological adjustment to sudden and anticipated spousal loss among older widowed persons. *Journal of Gerontology, 56B*, S237–S248.

Carstairs, S. (2010). Raising the bar: A roadmap for the future of palliative care in Canada. Retrieved from http://www.chpca.net/media/7859/Raising_the_Bar_June_2010.pdf

Carstensen, L. L. (1995). Evidence for a lifespan theory of socioemotional selectivity. *Current Directions in Psychological Science, 4*(5), 151–156.

Carstensen, L. L., Edelstein, B. A., & Dornbrand, L. (1996). *The practical handbook of clinical gerontology.* Thousand Oaks, CA: Sage.

Casas, J., & Pytluk, S. (1995). Hispanic identity development: Implications for research and practice. In J. Ponterotto, J. Casas, L. Suzuki, & C. Alexander (Eds.), *Handbook of multicultural counseling.* Thousand Oaks, CA: Sage.

Caufield, T. (2005). Policy conflicts: Gene patents and health care in Canada. *Community Genetics, 8*:223–227.

CBC News. (2009, July 29). Swine-flu risks made pregnant women a priority: CDC. Retrieved from http://www.cbc.ca/news/health/story/2009/07/29/swine-flu-pregnant864.html

CBC News. (2009, November 4). Canada ranked 25th in world infant mortality. Retrieved from http://www.cbc.ca/news/health/story/2009/11/04/infant-mortality-canada.html

CBC News. (2010, July 31). Alberta scientists see Alzheimer's breakthrough. Retrieved from http://www.cbc.ca/news/canada/calgary/alberta-scientists-see-alzheimer-s-breakthrough-1.895313

CBC News. (2011, March 8). 30% of Canadian students need ESL: Peel Board. Even those born in Canada often need some ESL instruction. Retrieved from http://www.cbc.ca/news/canada/toronto/story/2011/03/08/english-language-numbers-peel.html

CBC News. (2011a, July 29). By the numbers: The decline of smoking in Canada. Retrieved from http://www.cbc.ca/news/canada/story/2011/07/29/f-smoking-statistics.html

CBC News. (2011b). Breast cancer screening guide says skip exams. Retrieved from http://www.cbc.ca/news/health/story/2011/11/21/breast-cancer-screening.html

CBC News. (2012). Immigrant babies often wrongly deemed underweight. Retrieved from http://www.cbc.ca/news/health/story/2012/02/14/birth-weight-curves-ethnic.html

CBC News. (2012a, January 20). Life-like robot being built in Ottawa lab: Scientist believes humans, robots can have symbiotic relationship. Retrieved from http://www.cbc.ca/news/technology/life-like-robot-being-built-in-ottawa-lab-1.1146647

CBC News. (2012b, November 17). Generation boomerang. Retrieved from http://www.cbc.ca/doczone/episode/generation-boomerang.html

CBC News. (2012c). 31% of Canadian kids are overweight or obese. Retrieved from http://www.cbc.ca/news/health/story/2012/09/20/child-obesity-statscan.html

CBC News. (2013a). Suicides prompt First Nation to declare state of emergency. Retrieved from http://www.cbc.ca/news/canada/thunder-bay/story/2013/04/18/tby-neskantaga-first-nation-state-of-emergency-suicide.html

CBC News. (2013b). N.S. cyberbullying investigative unit a 1st in Canada. Retrieved from http://www.cbc.ca/news/canada/nova-scotia/story/2013/04/25/ns-rehtaeh-cyberbullying-unit.html

CBC News. (2013c). Cyberbullying bill positive but could use tweaks: Prof. Retrieved from http://www.cbc.ca/news/canada/nova-scotia/story/2013/04/26/ns-mackay-cyber-safety-act.html

CBC News. (2013d). Winnipeg's Susan Griffiths dies by assisted suicide in Zurich. Retrieved from http://www.cbc.ca/news/canada/manitoba/story/2013/04/24/mb-susan-griffiths-assisted-suicide-final-blog.html

CBC News. (2013e). Bad-driving snitch line targeting seniors prompts police apology. Retrieved from http://www.cbc.ca/news/canada/thunder-bay/story/2013/02/22/sby-senior-driving-tip-line-reaction.html

Centers for Disease Control and Prevention (CDC). (2000a). *Sexually transmitted diseases sourcebook.* Atlanta: Author.

Centers for Disease Control and Prevention (CDC). (2000b). *State-specific prevalence of obesity among adults—United States, 2005.* Sept. 2006/55(36), 985–988.

Centers for Disease Control and Prevention (CDC). (2001a). *Women and smoking.* Atlanta: Author.

Centers for Disease Control and Prevention (CDC). (2001b). *Work-related hearing loss.* Retrieved from http://www.cdc.gov/niosh/docs/2001-103/

Centers for Disease Control and Prevention (CDC). (2006b). *Suicide in the U.S.: Statistics and prevention.* Retrieved from http://www.cdc.gov/ncipc/wisqars

Centers for Disease Control and Prevention (CDC). (2009a). *Provisional cases of infrequently reported notifiable diseases—United States. Morbidity and Mortality Weekly Report, 55*(19), 538.

Centre for Addiction and Mental Health. (2011). *Ontario Student Drug Use and Health Survey: The Mental Health and Well-Being of Ontario Students, 1991–2011.* Retrieved from http://www.camh.ca/en/research/news_and_publications/ontario-student-drug-use-and-health-survey/Documents/2011%20OSDUHS%20Docs/2011OSDUHS_Highlights_MentalHealthReport.pdf

Canada.com. (n.d.). Cerebral palsy. Retrieved from http://body-andhealth.canada.com/channel_condition_info_details.asp?disease_id=146&channel_id=9&relation_id=10860

Chall, J. (1983). *Stages of reading development.* New York: McGraw-Hill.

Chall, J., Jacobs, V., & Baldwin, L. (1990). *The reading crisis: Why poor children fall behind.* Cambridge, MA: Harvard University Press.

Chao, R. (2001). Extending research on the consequences of parenting style for Chinese Americans and European Americans. *Child Development, 72*, 1832–1843.

Chavous, T., Bernat, D., Schmeelk-Cone, K., Caldwell, C., Kohn-Wood, L., & Zimmerman, M. (2003, July/August). Racial identity and academic attainment among African American adolescents. *Child Development, 74*(4), 1076–1090.

Chen, X., Hastings, P. D., Rubin, K.H., Chen, H., Cen, G., & Stewart, S. L. (1998). Child-rearing attitudes and behavioural inhibition in Chinese and Canadian toddlers: A cross-cultural study. *Developmental Psychology, 34*, 677–686.

Chen, Z., & Kaplan, H. (2003). School failure in early adolescence and status attainment in middle adulthood: A longitudinal study. *Sociology of Education, 76*, 110–118.

Chess, S., & Thomas, A. (1977). Temperamental individuality from childhood to adolescence. *Journal of Child Psychiatry, 16*, 218–226.

Chess, S., & Thomas, A. (1987). *Know your child.* New York: Basic Books.

Chess, S., & Thomas, A. (1999). *Goodness of fit.* Philadelphia: Brunner/Mazel.

Childcare Resource and Research Unit (2013). *The state of early childhood education and care in Canada: 2010: Trends and analysis.* Toronto, Ontario: Childcare Resource and Research Unit.

Chisholm, K. (1998). A three year follow-up of attachment and indiscrimate friendliness in children adopted from Romanian orphanages. *Child Development, 69*(4), 1092–1106.

Chitayat, D., & Wyatt, P. R. (2008). Fragile X testing in obstetrics and gynaecology in Canada. *Journal of Obstetrics and Gynaecology Canada*, 216.

Chomsky, N. (1957). *Syntactic structure.* The Hague: Mouton.

Chumlea, A. C., Schubert, C. M., Roche, A. F., Kulin, H. F., Lee, P. A., Himes, J. H., et al. (2003). Age at menarche and racial comparisons in U.S. girls. *Pediatrics, 111*(1), 110–113.

Cicchetti, D., & Toth, S. (1998). Perspectives on research and practice in developmental psychopathology. In W. Damon (Series Ed.) & I. Sigel & K. Renninger (Vol. Eds.), *Handbook of child psychology: Vol. 4. Child psychology in practice.* New York: Wiley.

Clark, W. (2009). Delayed transitions of young adults. Canadian Social Trends. Statistics Canada. Retrieved from http://www.statcan.gc.ca/pub/11-008-x/2007004/10311-eng.htm

Clarke, E., Preston, M., Raksin, J., & Bengtson, V. (1999). Types of conflicts and tensions between older parents and adult children. *The Gerontologist, 39*(3), 261–270.

Clarke-Stewart, K., & Allhusen, V. (2005). *What we know about child care.* Cambridge, MA: Harvard University Press.

Cleveland, H., & Wiebe, R. (2003, January/February). The moderation of adolescent-to-peer similarity in tobacco and alcohol use by school levels of substance use. *Child Development, 74*(1), 279–291.

Clifford, T., & Gorodzinsky, F. (2000). Toilet training: Anticipatory guidance with a child-oriented approach. Canadian Paediatric Society, *Paediatric Child Health, 5* (6): 333–5. Reaffirmed Jan 30, 2012.

Codjoe, H. (2006). The role of an affirmed black cultural identity and heritage in the academic achievement of African-Canadian students. *Intercultural Education, 17*(1), 33–54.

Colditz, G. A., & Stein, C. (2005). Smoking cessation, weight gain, and lung function (risk of smoking cessation). *The Lancet, 365*(9471), 1600–1602.

Cole, M. (1996). *Cultural psychology.* Cambridge, MA: Harvard University Press.

Cole, M. (1999). Culture in development. In M. Bornstein & M. Lamb (Eds.), *Developmental psychology: An advanced textbook.* Mahwah, NJ: Erlbaum.

Collins, J. (2011, June 19). Toddlers and tiaras: Sexualizing children: 5 tips to protect your child. *Total Life Counselling.*

Collins, W. A., Maccoby, E. E., Steinberg, L., Hetherington, E. M., & Bornstein, M. H. (2001). Toward nature WITH nurture. *American Psychologist, 56*, 171–173.

Compas, B., Benson, M., Boyer, M., Hocks, T., & Konik, B. (2002). Problem-solving and problem-solving therapies. In M. Rutter and E. Taylor (Eds.). *Child and adolescent psychiatry.* London: Blackwell.

Conference Board of Canada. (2012). Life expectancy. Retrieved from http://www.conferenceboard.ca/hcp/details/health/life-expectancy.aspx

Conger, R., & Chao, W. (1996). Adolescent depressed mood. In R. L. Simons (Ed.), *Understanding differences between divorced and intact families: Stress, interaction, and child outcome.* (pp. 157–175). Thousand Oaks, CA: Sage.

Connors, M. (2001). Relationship of sexual abuse to body image and eating problems. In J. K. Thompson & L. Smolak (Eds.), *Body image, eating disorders, and obesity in youth: Assessment, prevention, and treatment* (pp. 149–167). Washington, DC: American Psychological Association.

Cook-Deegan, R (2008). Gene patents, in bioethics briefing book. Garrison, NY: The Hastings Center. Retrieved from http//:www.thehastingscenter.org

Council of Ministers of Education, Canada (n.d.). CMEC statement on play-based learning. Retrieved from http://www.cmec.ca/Publications/Lists/Publications/Attachments/282/play-based-learning_statement_EN.pdf

Crain, W. (2005). *Theories of development.* Upper Saddle River, NJ: Pearson/Prentice Hall.

Cranswick, K. & Dosman, D. (2008). Eldercare: What we know today. Canadian Social Trends. Statistics Canada. Catalogue no. 11-008-X. Retrieved from http://www.statcan.gc.ca/pub/11-008-x/2008002/article/10689-eng.pdf

Crawford, M., & Unger, R. (2000). Introduction to a feminist psychology of women. In M. Crawford and R. Unger (Eds.), *Women and gender: A feminist psychology* (pp. 2–32). Boston: McGraw-Hill.

Crosato, K. E., Ward-Griffin, C. & Leipert, B. (2007). Aboriginal women caregivers of the elderly in geographically isolated communities. *Rural and Remote Health 7*:796. Online. Retrieved from http://www.rrh.org.au/publishedarticles/article_print_796.pdf

Criminal Code, R.S. c. C-46 (1985). Retrieved from http://laws-lois.justice.gc.ca/PDF/C-46.pdf

Csikszentmihalyi, M., & Rathunde, K. (1998). In R. M. Lerner (Ed.), *Handbook of child psychology: Vol. 1. Theoretical models of human development.* New York: Wiley.

Cummings, E., & Henry, W. (1961). Growing old. New York: Basic Books.

Cummings, S. M., Knopf, N. P., & DeWeaver, K. L. (2000). Knowledge of and attitudes toward aging among non-elders: Gender and race differences. *Journal of Women & Aging, 12*, 77–87.

Curran, J. (2006). Deliberate self-harm in the over 60s. *Mental Health Practice, 10*(1), 29–30.

Cushing, P. (2012, Fall). Ties that bind: Revisiting rites of passage in modern families. *Transition: For Families about Families, 42* (3). The Vanier Institute of the Family.

Czaja, S. J., Charness, N., Fisk, A. D., Hertzog, C., Nair, S. N., Rogers, W. A., & Sharit, J. (2006). Factors predicting the use of technology: Findings from the Center for Research and Education on Aging and Technology (CREATE). *Psychology and Aging, 21*, 333–352.

D

Dacey, J. S. (1989a). Discriminating characteristics of the families of highly creative adolescents. *Journal of Creative Behavior, 24*(4), 263–271.

Dacey, J. S. (1989b). *Fundamentals of creative thinking.* Lexington, MA: D. C. Heath/Lexington Books.

Dacey, J. S., & Fiore, L. (2000). *Your anxious child.* San Francisco: Jossey-Bass.

Dacey, J. S., & Fiore, L. B. (2006). *The safe child handbook: How to protect your family and cope with anxiety in a threat-filled world.* San Francisco: Jossey-Bass.

Dacey, J. S., Kenny, M., & Margolis, D. (2002). *Adolescent development*, Houston: Thompson.

Dacey, J. S., Kenny, M., & Margolis, D. (2006). *Adolescent development.* Belmont, CA: Cengage Learning.

Damianakis, T., & Marziali, E. (2012). Older adults' response to the loss of a spouse: The function of spirituality in understanding the grieving process. *Aging & Mental Health, 16*(1), 57–66. doi:10.1080/13607863.2011.609531

Das, A. (2009, April 21). More Wii warriors are playing hurt. *New York Times.* Retrieved from http://www.nytimes.com/2009/04/21/health/21wii.html

Data360.org. (2005). Percentage of people reporting having had unprotected sex without knowing partners' history. Retrieved from http://www.data360.org/dsg.aspx?Data_Set_Group_Id=1101

Darwin, C. (1877). Biographical sketch of an infant. *Mind, 2,* 285–294.

Deblinger, E., Mannarino, A. P., Cohen, J. A., & Steer, R. A. (2006). A follow-up study of a multisite, randomized, controlled trial for children with sexual abuse-related PTSD symptoms. *Journal of the American Academy of Child and Adolescent Psychiatry, 45*(12), 1474–1485.

Dennis, W. (1966). Creative productivity. *Journal of Gerontology, 21,* 1–8.

DePape, B. (2010). Un-equal access to opportunity between suburban and inner-city youth. Retrieved from http://www.policyalternatives.ca/publications/commentary/un-equal-access-opportunity-between-suburban-and-inner-city-youth

Department of Justice Canada. (2005, November). Child abuse fact sheet. Retrieved from http://publications.gc.ca/collections/Collection/J2-295-2002E.pdf

Diamond, M. (1999). *Magic trees of the mind.* New York: Penguin.

Dieticians of Canada (2012). *Tracking children's growth.* Retrieved from http://www.dietitians.ca/Dietitians-Views/Children-and-Teens/Tracking-Childrens-Growth.aspx

Dixon, R., & Lerner, R. (1999). History and systems in developmental psychology. In M. Bornstein & M. Lamb (Eds.), *Developmental psychology: An advanced textbook.* Mahwah, NJ: Erlbaum.

Dobratz, M. C. (2003). The self-transacting dying: Patterns of social-psychological adaptation in home hospice patients. *Journal of Death & Dying, 46,* 151–163.

Dodge, K., Lansford, J., Burks, V., Bates, J., Pettit, G., Fontaine, R., & Price, J. (2003). Peer rejection and social information-processing factors in the development of aggressive behavior problems in children. *Child Development, 74*(2), 374–393.

Dorn, L. D., Susman, E. J., & Ponirakis, A. (2003). Pubertal timing and adolescent adjustment and behavior: Conclusions vary by rater. *Journal of Youth and Adolescence, 32*(3), 157–167.

Drews, K. (2012, November 23). B.C. community group wants action over "suicide pact." *Canadian Press.* Retrieved from http://www2.macleans.ca/2012/11/23/b-c-community-group-wants-action-over-suicide-pact-incidents-of-self-harm/

Duncan, G., & Brooks-Gunn, J. (2000). Family poverty, welfare reform, and child development. *Child Development, 71*(1), 188–196.

Duff, B. (2013, Feb 21) Tootoo takes brother's death to heart. *Windsor Star.*

Dunn, K. M., Croft, P. R., & Hackett, G. I. (2000). Satisfaction in the sex life of a general population sample. *Journal of Sex and Marital Therapy, 26,* 141–151.

Dunne, K. (2004). Grief and its manifestations (Bereavement). *Nursing Standard, 18*(45), 45–54.

Dychtwald, K. (2005). Ageless aging: The next era of retirement. *The Futurist, 39*(4), 16–22.

E

Eagle, M. (2000). Psychoanalytic theory: History of the field. In A. Kazdin (Ed.), *Encyclopedia of psychology.* Washington, DC: American Psychological Association.

Eastman, P. (2000, January). Scientists piecing Alzheimer's puzzle. *AARP Bulletin, 41*(1), 18–19.

Eaton, W. (2012). The developmental milestones study. University of Manitoba, Department of Psychology. Retrieved from http://home.cc.umanitoba.ca/~eaton/infant-developmental-milestones.htm

Eccles, J., & Roeser, R. (1999). School and community influences on human development. In M. Bornstein & M. Lamb (Eds.), *Developmental psychology: An advanced textbook.* Mahwah, NJ: Erlbaum.

Edwards, C. P., Gandini, L., & Forman, G. E. (Eds.) (1998). *The hundred languages of children: The Reggio Emilia approach—Advanced reflections* (2nd ed.). Greenwich, CT: Ablex.

Edwards, P., & Mawani, A. (2006, September). Healthy aging in Canada: A new vision, a vital investment from evidence to action. A background paper prepared for the Federal, Provincial and Territorial Committee of Officials (Seniors).

Eisenberg, N., Fabes, R., & Spinrad, T. (2006). Prosocial behavior. In W. Damon & R. Lerner (Series Eds.) & N. Eisenberg (Vol. Ed.), *Handbook of child psychology: Vol. 3. Social, emotional, and personality development.* New York: Wiley.

Eisenberg, N., Martin, C., & Fabes, R. (1996). Gender development and gender effects. In D. Berliner & R. Calfee (Eds.), *Handbook of educational psychology.* New York: Macmillan.

Elder, G., & Shanahan, M. (2006). The life course and human development. In W. Damon & R. Lerner (Series Eds.) & R. Lerner (Vol. Ed.), *Handbook of child psychology: Vol. 1. Theoretical models of human development.* New York: Wiley.

Eliot, L. (2000). *What's going on in there?* New York: Bantam.

Elkind, D. (1978). *The child's reality: Three developmental themes.* Hillsdale, NJ: Erlbaum.

Elkind, D., & Bowen, R. (1979). Imaginary audience behavior in children and adolescents. *Developmental Psychology, 15,* 38–44.

Ellis, B. J., McFadyen-Ketchum, S., Dodge, K. A., Pettit, G. S., & Bates, J. E. (1999). Quality of early family relationships and individual differences in the timing of pubertal maturation in girls: A longitudinal test of an evolutionary model. *Journal of Personality & Social Psychology, 77*(2), 387–401.

Elton-Marshall, T., Leatherdale, S.T., & Burkholder, R. (2011). Tobacco, alcohol and illicit drug use among Aboriginal youth living off-reserve: Results from the Youth Smoking Survey. *Canadian Medical Association Journal, 183*(8), E480–E486.

Emde, R. (1998). Early emotional development: New modes of thinking for research and intervention. In J. Warhol & S. Shelov (Eds.), *New perspectives in early emotional development.* New York: Johnson & Johnson Pediatric Institute.

Erikson, E. (1958). *Young man Luther: A study in psychoanalysis and history.* New York: Norton.

Erikson, E. (1959). Growth and crises of the healthy personality. *Psychological Issues, 1,* 40–52.

Erikson, E. (1963). *Childhood and society* (2nd ed.). New York: Norton.

Erikson, E. (1968). *Identity: Youth and crisis.* New York: Norton.

Erikson, E. (1969). *Gandhi's truth: On the origins of militant nonviolence.* New York: Norton.

Erikson, E. (1978). *Adulthood.* New York: Norton.

Eriksson, P. S., Perfilieva, E., Bjork-Eriksson, T., Alborn, A., Nordborg, C., Peterson, D. A., & Gage, F. H. (1998). Neurogenesis in the adult human hippocampus. *Nature Medicine, 4*(11), 1313–1317.

Esmail, N. (2007, July/August). Complementary and alternative medicine in Canada: Trends in use and public attitudes, 1997–2006. Public Policy Sources, no. 87. Vancouver: The Fraser Institute. Retrieved from http://www.fraserinstitute.org/research-news/research/display.aspx?id=12941

European Society of Human Reproduction and Embryology (2009). Babies born after freeze-thawing embryos do just as well regardless of whether they were created via ICSI or standard IVF. Retrieved from http://www.sciencedaily.com/releases/2009/06/090629081802.htm

Ewing, L. (2012, Oct. 11). Ed Whitlock, 81, running for the record books in the Toronto Waterfront Marathon. *Canadian Press.* Retrieved from http://www.thestar.com/sports/2012/10/11/ed_whitlock_81_running_for_the_record_books_at_toronto_waterfront_marathon.html

F

Fantz, R. L. (1965). Visual perception from birth as shown by pattern selectivity. In H. E. Whipple (Ed.), *New issues in infant development. Annals of New York Academy of Science, 118,* 793–814.

Febo, M., Numan, M., & Ferris, C. F. (2005). Functional magnetic resonance imaging shows oxytocin activates brain regions associated with mother–pup bonding during suckling. *Journal of Neuroscience, 25*(10), 11637–11644.

Feldman, M., & Belanger, S. (2009). Extended-release medications for children and adolescents with attention-deficit hyperactivity disorder. Canadian Paediatric Society. *Paediatric Child Health, 14*(19), 593–597.

Feldman, R., Weller, A., Sirota, L., & Eidelman, A. (2002). Skin-to-skin contact (kangaroo care) promotes self-regulation in premature infants: Sleep-wake cyclicity, arousal modulation, and sustained exploration. *Developmental Psychology, 38*(2), 194–207.

Feldman, R., Weller, A., Zagoory-Sharon, O., & Levine, A. (2007, November). Evidence for a neuroendocrinological foundation of human affiliation: Plasma oxytocin levels across pregnancy and the postpartum period predict mother–infant bonding. *Psychological Science, 18*(11): 965–970.

Ferber, R. (2006). *Solve your child's sleep problems.* New York: Simon & Schuster.

Ferris, P. (1997). *Dr. Freud: A life.* Washington, DC: Counterpoint.

Field, T. (2002). Violence and touch deprivation in adolescents. *Adolescence, 37,* 735–745.

Finch, C. (2003). Neurons, glia, and plasticity in normal brain aging. *Neurobiology of Aging, 24* (Suppl. 1), S123–S127.

Findling, R.L., Schulz, S.C., Kashani, J.H., & Harlan, E. (2000). *Psychotic disorders in children and adolescents.* Thousand Oaks, CA: Sage Publications.

First Nations and Inuit Health. (2005, 8 Mar). Fetal alcohol syndrome/fetal effects. Retrieved from Health Canada Website: http://www.hc-sc.gc.ca/fniah-spnia/famil/preg-gros/intro-eng.php

Fitzpatrick, M. (2003). Women on the treadmill (doctoring the risk society). *The Lancet, 361*(9361), 976.

Flavell, J. (1999). Cognitive development: Children's knowledge about the mind. In J. Spence, J. Darley, & D. Foss (Eds.), *Annual Review of Psychology.* Palo Alto, CA: Annual Reviews.

Florence, M. (2011). *Jordin Tootoo.* Toronto, ON: James Lorimer and Company.

Fraiberg, S. (1959). *The magic years.* New York: Charles Scribner's Sons.

Franco, O. H., de Laet, C., Peeters, A., Jonker, J., Mackenbach, J., & Nusselder, W. (2005). Effects of physical activity on life expectancy with cardiovascular disease. *Archives of Internal Medicine, 165,* 2355–2360.

Frankenberger, K. (2000). Adolescent egocentrism: A comparison among adolescents and adults. *Journal of Adolescence, 23,* 343–354.

Frankl, V. (1967). *Psychotherapy and existentialism.* New York: Simon & Schuster.

Friedan, B. (1963). *The feminine mystique.* New York: Norton.

Friedman, R., & Chase-Lansdale, P. L. (2002). Chronic adversities. In M. Rutter and E. Taylor (Eds.), *Child and adolescent psychiatry.* London: Blackwell.

Fromm, E. (1968 [1956]). *The art of loving.* New York: Harper & Row.

Fung, H., Cartensen, L., & Lang, F. (2001). Age-related patterns in social networks among European Americans and African Americans: Implications for socioemotional selectivity across the life span. *International Journal of Aging & Human Development, 52,* 185–206.

FXB International. (2009). Your voice is their future, 8th World AIDS Orphans Day. Retrieved from http://www.fxb.org/updates/your-voice-is-their-future-8th-world-aids-orphans-day/

G

Garbarino, J., & Bedard, C. (2001). *Parents under siege.* New York: The Free Press.

Garbarino, J., & Benn, J. (1992). The ecology of childbearing and childrearing. In J. Garbarino (Ed.), *Children and families in the social environment.* New York: Aldine.

Gardner, D., Weissman, A., Howles, C., & Shoham, Z. (2004). *Textbook of assisted reproductive techniques.* Oxford, England: Taylor & Francis.

Gardner, H. (1983). *Frames of mind: The theory of multiple intelligences.* New York: Basic Books.

Gardner, H. (1997). *Extraordinary minds.* New York: Basic Books.

Garmezy, N., & Rutter, M. (1983). *Stress, coping, and development.* New York: McGraw-Hill.

Garmezy, N., & Rutter, M. (1985). Acute reactions to stress. In M. Rutter & E. A. Taylor (Eds.), *Child and adolescent psychiatry.* Oxford, England: Wiley–Blackwell.

Gauthier, A. H., Smeeding, T. M., & Furstenberg Jr., F. F. (2004). Are parents investing less time in children? Trends in selected industrialized countries. *Population & Development Review, 30*(4), 647–671.

Geary, D., & Bjorklund, D. (2000). Evolutionary developmental psychology. *Child Development, 71*(1), 57–65.

Gebhardt, W. A., Kuyper, L., & Dusseldorp, E. (2006). Condom use at first intercourse with a new partner in female adolescents and young adults: The role of cognitive planning and motives for having sex. *Archives of Sexual Behavior, 35*(2), 217–224.

Gelbart, W.M., Griffiths, A.J., Lewontin, R.C., & Miller, J.H. (2002). *Modern genetic analysis and integrating genes and genomes* (2nd ed.). New York: W.H Freeman and Company.

Gelman, R., & Baillargeon, R. (1983). A review of some Piagetian concepts. In P. Mussen (Ed.), *Handbook of child psychology: Vol. 3.* New York: Wiley.

Gendell, M. (2008, January). Older workers: Increasing their labor force participation and hours of work. *Monthly Labor Review,* 41–54.

Gerard, J. M., Landry-Meyer, L., & Roe, J. G. (2006). Grandparents raising grandchildren: The role of social sup-port in coping with caregiving challenges. (Author abstract). *International Journal of Aging & Human Development, 62*(4), 359–384.

Gibbons, R., Dugaiczyk, L. J., Girke, T., Duistermars, B., Zielinski, R., & Dugaiczyk, A. (2004). Distinguishing humans from great apes with AluYb8 repeats. *Journal of Molecular Biology, 339,* 721–729.

Gibson, E., & Pick, A. (2000). *An ecological approach to perceptual learning and development.* New York: Oxford Press.

Gibson, E., & Walk, R. (1960). The visual cliff. *Scientific American, 202,* 64–71.

Gilligan, C. (1982). *In a different voice.* Cambridge, MA: Harvard University Press.

Gilligan, C., Lyons, N., & Hanmer, T. (1990). *Making connections: The relational worlds of adolescent girls at Emma Willard School.* Cambridge, MA: Harvard University Press.

Gilmour, H, & Park, J. (2006). Dependency, chronic conditions and pain in seniors. Health Reports Supplement, 8:33-45. Statistics Canada, Catalogue 82-003.

Goldberg, J., Holtz, D., Hyslop, T., & Tolosa, J. (2002). Has the use of routine episiotomy decreased? Examination of episiotomy rates from 1983 to 2000. *Obstetrics and Gynecology, 99*(3), 395–400.

Goldberg, S., & DiVitto, B. (2002). Parenting children born pre-term. In M. Bornstein (Ed.), *Handbook of parenting* (2nd ed.). Mahwah, NJ: Erlbaum.

Gomez, C., & Rosen, B. (2001). The leader–member exchange as a link between managerial trust and employee empowerment. *Group and Organization Management, 26*(1), 53–69.

Gopnik, A., Meltzoff, A. N., & Kuhl, P. K. (1999). *The scientist in the crib: Minds, brains, and how children learn.* New York: HarperCollins.

Gotay, C.C., Katzmarzyk, P.T., Janssen, I., Dawson, M.Y., Aminoltejari, K., & Bartley, N.L. (2013). Updating the Canadian obesity maps: An epidemic in progress. *Canadian Journal of Public Health, 104*(1). e64–e68. Figure 1. Retrieved from http://journal.cpha.ca/index.php/cjph/article/view/3513

Gottlieb, G. (1997). *Synthesizing nature–nurture.* Mahwah, NJ: Erlbaum.

Gottlieb, G., Wahlsten, D., & Lickliter, R. (2006).The significance of biology for human development: A developmental psychobiological systems View. In W. Damon & R. Lerner (Series Eds.) & R. Lerner (Vol. Ed.), *Handbook of child psychology: Vol. 1. Theoretical models of human development.* New York: Wiley.

Government of Canada. (n.d.). Eliminating the mandatory retirement age. Retrieved from http://actionplan.gc.ca/en/initiative/eliminating-mandatory-retirement-age

Graham, E. I. (2005). Economic, racial, and cultural influences on the growth and maturation of children. *Pediatrics in Review, 26,* 290–294.

Greene, M. (2007, Spring). Strategies for incorporating cultural competence into childbirth education curriculum. *The Journal of Perinatal Education. 16* (2): 33–37.

Grossman, J., & Kaufman, J. (2002). Evolutionary psychology: Promise and perils. In R. J. Sternberg, & J. C. Kaufman (Eds.), *The evolution of intelligence.* (pp. 9–25). Mahwah, NJ: Erlbaum.

Grotevant, H. (1998). Adolescent development in family contexts. In W. Damon (Series Ed.) & N. Eisenberg (Vol. Ed.), *Handbook of child psychology: Vol. 3. Social, emotional, and personality development.* New York: Wiley.

Gunby, J., Bissonnette, F., Librach, C., & Cowan, L. (2007). Assisted reproductive technologies (ART) in Canada: 2004 results from the Canadian ART Register. *Fertility and Sterility, 88*(2):275–282.

Guttmacher Institute. (2008, April 16). Teen pregnancy rates declined to historic low in 2004—Improved contraceptive use a key factor. Retrieved from http://www.guttmacher.org/pubs/fb_ATSRH.html

H

Haas, F. (2003). Bereavement care: Seeing the body. *Nursing Standards,* 17, 33–37.

Haliburn, J. (2000). Reasons for adolescent suicide attempts. *Journal of the American Academy of Child & Adolescent Psychiatry, 39*(1), 13–14.

Hall, G. S. (1904). *Adolescence.* (2 vols.) New York: Appleton-Century-Crofts.

Hammer, K. (2011, June 13). EQ over IQ: How play-based learning can lead to more success-ful kids. *Globe and Mail.* Retrieved from http://www.theglobeandmail.com/news/toronto/kindergarten/eq-over-iq-how-play-based-learning-can-lead-to-more-successful-kids/article558491/

Hammond, D., Ahmed, R., Yang, W.S., Brukhalter, R., & Leatherdale, S. (2011). Illicit substance use among Canadian youth: Trends between 2002 and 2008. *Canadian Journal of Public Health, 102*(1), 7–12.

Harlow, H. F., & Suomi, S. J. (1971). Social recovery by isolation-reared monkeys. *Proceedings of the National Academy of Science of the United States of America, 68*(7), 1534–1538.

Harman, W. (2008). CPR on the *Today Show:* In case you missed it. Retrieved from http://redcrosschat.org/2008/10/20/cpr-on-the-today-show-in-case-you-missed-it/

Harrison, L. (2000). Why culture matters. In L. Harrison & S. Huntington (Eds.), *Culture matters.* New York: Basic Books.

Harter, S. (1999). *The construction of the self.* New York: Guilford Press.

Harter, S. (2006). The self. In W. Damon & R. Lerner (Series Eds.) & N. Eisenberg (Vol. Ed.), *Handbook of child psychology: Vol. 3. Social, emotional, and personality development.* New York: Wiley.

Hartl, D., & Jones, E. (2005). *Genetics: Analysis of genes and ge-nomes.* Boston: Jones and Bartlett.

Harton, H. C., & Lyons, P. C. (2003). Gender, empathy, and the choice of the psychology major. *Teaching of Psychology, 30*(1), 19–24.

Harvey, E. (1999). Short-term and long-term effects of early paren-tal employment on children of the National Longitudinal Survey of Youth. *Developmental Psychology, 35*(2), 445–459.

Hasinoff, A. A. (2012). Sexting: Should teens have the right to sext? Retrieved from http://www.academia.edu/1308372/Should_teens_have_the_right_to_sext

Health Canada. (2000). Certain circumstances: Issues in equity and responsiveness in access to health care in Canada. Retrieved from http://www.hc-sc.gc.ca/hcs-sss/alt_formats/hpb-dgps/pdf/pubs/2001-certain-equit-acces_e.pdf

Health Canada. (2001). Joint statement on shaken baby syndrome. Minister of Public Works and Government Services, Ottawa. Retrieved from http://www.cpha.ca/uploads/policy/sbs_e.pdf

Health Canada. (2005). Changing fertility patterns: Trends and implications. Health Policy Research Bulletin, issue #10, 8. Retrieved from http://www.hc-sc.gc.ca/sr-sr/pubs/hpr-rpms/bull/2005-10-chang-fertilit/index-eng.php

Health Canada. (2006a, Dec 7). It's your health—fetal alcohol spectrum disorder. Retrieved from http://www.hc-sc.gc.ca/hl-vs/iyh-vsv/diseases-maladies/fasd-etcaf-eng.php

Health Canada. (2006b). It's your health—seniors and aging—sexu-al activity. Retrieved from http://www.hc-sc.gc.ca/hl-vs/iyh-vsv/life-vie/seniors-aines-eng.php

Health Canada. (2010). Fact-sheet-thalomid. Authorization for sale in Canada. Retrieved from http://www.hc-sc.gc.ca/dhp-mps/prodpharma/activit/fs-fi/thalidomide_fs_fd-eng.php

Health Canada. (2011). Aboriginal Head Start on Reserve. Retrieved from http://www.hc-sc.gc.ca/fniah-spnia/famil/develop/ahsor-papa_intro-eng.php

Health Canada. (2011). Eating Well with Canada's Food Guide. Retrieved from http://www.hc-sc.gc.ca/fn-an/alt_formats/hpfb-dgpsa/pdf/food-guide-aliment/print_eatwell_bienmang-eng.pdf

Health Canada. (2012a). Health concerns: Smokefree public places: You can get there. Retrieved from http://www.hc-sc.gc.ca/hc-ps/pubs/tobac-tabac/sfpp-fslp/index-eng.php

Health Canada. (2012b). Healthy living. Healthy babies. Retrieved from http://www.hc-sc.gc.ca/hl-vs/babies-bebes/index-eng.php

Health Canada. (2012c). Canadian tobacco use monitoring survey (CTUMS) 2011. Retrieved from http://www.hc-sc.gc.ca/hc-ps/tobac-tabac/research-recherche/stat/ctums-esutc_2011-eng.php

Hegele, R.A., Cao, H., Harris, S.B., Hanley, A.J.G., & Zinman, B. (1999). The hepatic nuclear factor-1α G319S variant is associated with early-onset type 2 diabetes in Canadian Oji-Cree. *The Journal of Endocrinology and Metabolism, 84*(3), 1077–1082.

Heller, S., Larrieu, J., D'Imperio, R., & Boris, N. (1999). Research on resilience to child maltreatment: Empirical considerations. *Child Abuse & Neglect, 23*(4), 321–338.

Heron, M. P., Hoyert, D. L., Murphy, S. L., Xu, J. Q., Kochanek, K. D., & Tejada-Vera, B. (2009). Deaths: Final data for 2006. *National Vital Statistics Reports, 57*(14). Hyattsville, MD: National Center for Health Statistics.

Hess, T., Auman, C., Colcombe, S., Rahhal, T.A., & Tamara, A. (2003). The impact of stereotype threat on age differences in memory performance. *Journals of Gerontology Series B–Psychological Sciences and Social Sciences, 58*(1), 3–11.

Hetherington, E. M. (2005). Divorce and the adjustment of children. *Pediatrics in Review, 26*, 163–169.

Hetherington, M., & Stanley-Hagan, M. (1995). Parenting in divorced and remarried families. In M. H. Bornstein (Ed.), *Children and parenting: Vol. 4*. Hillsdale, NJ: Erlbaum.

Hetherington, M., & Stanley-Hagan, M. (2002. Parenting in divorced and remarried families. In M. Bornstein (Ed.), *Handbook of parenting* (2nd ed.). Mahwah, NJ: Erlbaum.

Heywood, C. (2001). A history of childhood. Malden, MA: Blackwell.

Hilbrecht, M. & Zuzanek, J. (2005). The relationship of adolescent obesity to time use, eating habits, leisure and well-being. Retrieved from http://lin.ca/sites/default/files/attachments/CCLR11-60.pdf

Hildebrandt, A. (2010, Nov 26). Canadian aid to Haiti gets mixed results. Retrieved from http://www.cbc.ca/news/world/canadian-aid-to-haiti-gets-mixed-results-1.936533

Hill, J. P. (1973). *Some perspectives on adolescence in American society*. Position paper prepared for the Office of Child Development, U.S. Department of Health, Education, and Welfare.

Hill, J. P. (1987). *Central changes during adolescence*. In W. Damon (Ed.), New directions in child psychology. San Francisco: Jossey-Bass.

Hingson, R. W., Heeren, T., Jamanka, A., & Howland, J. (2000). Age of drinking onset and unintentional injury involvement after drinking. *Journal of the American Medical Association, 284*(12), 1527–1533.

Ho, T., Leung, P., Hung, S., Lee, C., & Tang, C. (2000). The mental health of the peers of suicide completers and attempters. *Journal of Child Psychology and Psychiatry, 41*, 301–308.

Hobson, J. A. (2004). Freud returns? Like a bad dream. Scientific American, 290(5), 89.

Horn, J. L. (1978). Human ability systems. In P. B. Baltes (Ed.), *Life-span development and behavior: Vol. 1*. New York: Academic Press.

Horowitz, F. D. (2000). Child development and the PITS: Simple questions, complex answers, and developmental theory. *Child Development, 71*(1), 1–10.

Hough, M. S. (2007). Adult age differences in word fluency for common and goal-directed categories. *Advances in Speech Language Pathology, 9*(2), 154–161.

Huang, B., Cornoni-Huntley, J., Hays, J., Huntley, R., Galanos, A., & Blazer, D. (2000). Impact of depressive symptoms on hospitalization risk in community-dwelling older persons. *Journal of American Geriatric Society, 48*, 1279–1284.

Human Development Report. (2009). *Overcoming barriers: Human mobility and development*. Retrieved from http://hdr.undp.org/en/media/HDR_2009_EN_Complete.pdf

Human Resources and Skills Development Canada (2011). Minimum age for employment in Canada. Retrieved from http://www.hrsdc.gc.ca/eng/labour/labour_law/pdf/minage.pdf

Human Resources and Skills Development Canada (2012a). Indicators of well-being in Canada: Health—low birth weight. Retrieved January 14, 2013, from http://www4.hrsdc.gc.ca/.3ndic.1t.4r@-eng.jsp?iid=4

Human Resources and Skills Development Canada (2012b). Indicators of well-being in Canada: Life expectancy at birth. Retrieved May 18, 2012, from http://www4.hrsdc.gc.ca/.3ndic.1t.4r@-eng.jsp?iid=3

Human Resources and Skills Development. (2013). Indicators of well-being in Canada. Family life–Marriage. Retrieved from: http://www4.hrsdc.gc.ca/.3ndic.1t.4r@-eng.jsp?iid=78

Human Resources and Skills Development Canada (2013a). Indicators of well-being in Canada: Family life–Divorce. Retrieved May 8, 2013, from http://www4.hrsdc.gc.ca/.3ndic.1t.4r@-eng.jsp?iid=76

Humes, L. E., & Floyd, S. S. (2005). Measures of working memory, sequence learning, and speech recognition in the elderly. *Journal of Speech, Language, and Hearing Research, 48*(1), 224–236.

Humphrey, S., & Kahn, A. (2000). Fraternities, athletic teams and rape: Importance of identification with a risky group. *Journal of Interpersonal Violence, 15*(12), 1313–1322.

Hussey, J. M., Chang, J. J., & Kotch, J. B. (2006). Child maltreatment in the United States: Prevalence, risk factors, and adolescent health consequences. *Pediatrics, 118*(3), 933–943.

I

Immen, W. (2012, April 12). On the job: Is 75 the new 65? *Globe and Mail*. Retrieved from http://www.theglobeandmail.com/report-on-business/careers/career-advice/is-75-the-new-65/article4099969/

Institut de la Statistique Québec. (2012). À propos de l'étude longitudinale du développement des enfants du Québec (ÉLDEQ)—Phase 1 (1998-2002). Retrieved from http://www.jesuisjeserai.stat.gouv.qc.ca/etude_phase1.htm

Intini, J. (2007, March 23). When it comes to love, sex hurts. *Maclean's*. Retrieved from http://www.macleans.ca/education/postsecondary/article.jsp?content=20070323_161000_7800

J

Jaquish, G. A., & Ripple, R. E. (1981). Cognitive creative abilities and self-esteem across the adult life-span. *Human Development, 24*(2), 110–119.

Jasper, M. (2000). Antepartum fetal assessment. In S. Mattson & J. Smith (Eds.), *Core curriculum for maternal–newborn nursing*. Philadelphia: Saunders.

Jeng, S. F., Yau, K. I. T., Liao, H. F., Chen, L. C., & Chen, P. S. (2000). Prognostic factors for walking attainment in very low-birth weight preterm infants. *Early Human Development, 59*(3), 159–173.

Jenkins, J., & Astington, J. (1996) Cognitive factors and family structure associated with theory of mind development in young children. *Developmental Psychology, 32*, 70–78.

Jimerson, S., Pavelski, R., & Orliss, M. (2002). Helping children with eating disorders: Quintessential research on etiology, prevention, assessment, and treatment. In J. Sandoval (Ed.), *Handbook of crisis counseling, interven-tion, and prevention in the schools* (2nd ed., pp. 393–415). Mahwah, NJ: Erlbaum.

Joensson, P., & Carlsson, I. (2000). Androgyny and creativity: A study of the relationship between a balanced sex-role and creative functioning. *Scandinavian Journal of Psychology, 41*, 269–274.

Johnson, B. (2002). The intentional mentor: Strategies and guidelines for the practice of mentoring. *Professional Psychology: Research & Practice, 33*, 88–96.

Jones, J. (2009). *Who adopts? Characteristics of women and men who have adopted children* (NCHS Data Brief No. 12). Washington, DC: NCHS.

Jones, S. (1996). Imitation or exploration: Young infants' matching of adults' oral gestures. *Child Development, 67*, 1952–1969.

K

Kagan, J. (1998). Biology and the child. In W. Damon (Series Ed.) & N. Eisenberg (Volume Ed.), *Handbook of child psychology: Vol. 3. Social, emotional, and personality development.* New York: Wiley.

Kagan, J., & Fox, N. (2006). Biology, culture, and temperamental biases. In N. Eisenberg (Ed.), *Handbook of child psychology: Vol. 3. Social, emotional, and personality development.* New York: Wiley.

Kahn, M. (2002). *Basic Freud.* New York: Basic Books.

Kallman, F., & Jarvik, L. (1959). Individual differences in constitution and genetic background. In J. Birren (Ed.), *Handbook of aging and the individual.* Chicago: University of Chicago Press.

Kashima, Y., Kim, U., Gelfand, M. J., Yamaguchi, S., Sang-Chin, C. & Yuki, M. (1995). Culture, gender, and self: A perspective from individualism–collectivism research. *Journal of Personality and Social Psychology, 69*(5), 925–937.

Keel, P., et al. (2001). Vulnerability to eating disorders in childhood and adolescence. In R. E. Ingram & J. M. Price (Eds.), *Vulnerability to psychopathology: Risk across the lifespan.* (pp. 389–411). New York: Guilford Press.

Kellogg, R. (1970). *Analyzing children's art.* Palo Alto, CA: National Press Books.

Kelly, M. (2012, March 28). Divorce cases in civil court, 2010/2011. Component of Statistics Canada. Catologue no. 85-002-X, Juristat.

Killgore, W., & Oki, M. (2001). Sex-specific developmental changes in amygdala responses to affective faces. *Neuroreport: For Rapid Communication of Neuroscience Research, 12*, 427–433.

Kirkey, S. (2012, August 9). Natural births, not C-sections, trigger brain-protecting proteins in babies: Study. Postmedia News, Retrieved from http://www.canada.com/health/Natural+births +sections+trigger+brain+protecting+proteins+babies+Study/ 7060053/story.html

King, K. (2000, February). Common teen suicide myths undermine prevention programs. *American Academy of Pediatrics News.* Elk Grove Village, IL: American Association of Pediatricians.

Knowles, M. (1989). *The adult learner: A neglected species.* Houston: Gulf.

Kohut, A. (2007). Rising environmental concern in 47-nation survey: Global unease with major world powers. *The Pew Global Attitudes Project.* Washington, DC: Pew Research Center. Retrieved from http://pewglobal.org/reports/pdf/256.pdf

Konnert, C., Dobson, K., & Watt, A. (2009, November). Geropsychology training in Canada: A survey of doctoral and internship programs. *Canadian Psychology, 50* (4), 255–260.

Kramer, A., & Willis, S. (2004). Enhancing the cognitive vitality of older adults. In J. Lerner & A. Alberts (Eds.), *Current directions in developmental psychology.* (pp. 160–166). New Jersey: Prentice Hall.

Krettenauer, T., Ullrich, M., Hofmann, V., & Edelstein, W. (2003). Behavioral problems in childhood and adolescence as predictors of ego-level attainment in early adulthood. *Merrill-Palmer Quarterly, 49*, 125–138.

Kübler-Ross, E. (1969). *On death and dying.* Routledge.

L

Labouvie-Vief, G. (2006). Emerging structures of adult thought. In J. J. Arnett & J. L. Tanner (Eds.), *Emerging adults in America.* Washington, DC: American Psychological Association.

Lalonde, A., Schuurmans, N., & Senikas, V. (2009). *Healthy beginnings: Giving your baby the best start from preconception to birth* (4th ed.) Mississauga, ON: John Wiley and Sons Canada.

Lamb, M., & Ahnert, L. (2006). Nonparental child care: Context, concepts, correlates, and consequences. In W. Damon & R. Lerner (Series Eds.) & K. A. Renninger & I. Sigel (Vol. Eds.), *Handbook of child psychology: Vol. 4. Child psychology in practice.* New York: Wiley.

Lamb, M., Hwang, C., Ketterlinus, R., & Fracasso, M. (1999). Parent–child relationships. In M. Bornstein & M. Lamb (Eds.), *Developmental psychology: An advanced textbook.* Mahwah, NJ: Erlbaum.

Lanes, A., Kuk, J. L., & Tamim, H. (2011, May 11). Prevalence and characteristics of postpartum depression symptomatology among Canadian women: A cross-sectional study. *BMC Public Health, 11*, 302.

Lang, F. (2001). Regulation of social relationships in later adulthood. *Journal of Gerontology, 56B*, P321–P326.

Langlois, S., & Morrison, P. (2002). Suicide deaths and suicide attempts. *Health Reports, 13*(2), 9.

Lanman, S. (2009, November). *Fed officials cut forecasts for unemployment rate (Update 1).* Retrieved from http://www.bloomberg. com/apps/news?pid=newsarchive&sid=aFbDgcAh3l9I

Lauber, M., Marshall, M., & Meyers, J. (2005). Gangs. In S. Lee (Ed.), *Encyclopedia of school psychology.* (pp. 220–221). Thousand Oaks, CA: Sage Publications, Inc.

Lee, G., DeMaris, A., Bavin, S., & Sullivan, R. (2001). Gender differences in the depressive effect of widowhood in later life. *Journal of Gerontology, 56B*, S56–S61.

Lee, J. M., Appugliese, D., Kaciroti, N., Corwyn, R. F., Bradley, R. H., & Lumeng, J. C. (2007). Weight status in young girls and the onset of puberty. *Pediatrics, 119*(3), 593–595.

Lehman, H. C. (1953). *Age and achievement.* Princeton, NJ: Princeton University Press.

Lehman, H. C. (1962). The creative production rates of present versus past generations of scientists. *Journal of Gerontology, 17*, 409–417.

Lehrer, J. (2009, April 26) Inside the baby mind. *Boston Globe*, p. C1.

Leifer, G. (2003). *Introduction to maternity and pediatric nursing.* St. Louis: Saunders.

Leinonen, E., Korpisammal, L., Pulkkinen, L., & Pukuri, T. (2001). The comparison of burden between caregiving spouses of depressive and demented patients. *International Journal of Geriatric Psychiatry, 16*, 387–393.

Leon, I. (2002). Adoption losses: Naturally occurring or socially constructed? *Child Development, 73*(2), 652–653.

Leonard, D. (2010). The case for $320,000 kindergarten teachers. *New York Times.*

Lerner, J., & Ashman, O. (2006). Culture and lifespan development. In K. Theis & J. Travers (Eds.), *Handbook of human development for health care professionals.* Sudbury, MA: Jones and Bartlett.

Lerner, R. (1991). Changing organism—context relations as the basic process of development: A developmental contextual perspective. *Developmental Psychology, 27*(1), 27–32.

Lerner, R. (2002). *Concepts and theories of human development* (3rd ed.). Mahwah, NJ: Erlbaum.

Lerner, R., Fisher, C., & Weinberg, R. (2000). Toward a science for and of the people: Promoting civil society through the application of developmental science. *Child Development, 71*(1), 11–20.

Lerner, R., & Galambos, N. (1998). Adolescent development: Challenges and opportunities for research, programs, and policies. In J. Spence, J. Darley, & D. Foss (Eds.), *Annual Review of Psychology*. Palo Alto, CA: Annual Reviews.

Lerner, R. M. (Ed.). (1998). Theoretical models of human development. *Handbook of child psychology: Vol. 1* (5th ed.). New York: Wiley.

Lerner, R. M. (2006). Editor's introduction: Developmental science, developmental systems, and contemporary theories. In R. M. Learner (Ed.). Theoretical models of human development. *Handbook of Child Psychology: Vol. 1* (6th ed.) Editors-in-chief: W. Damon & R. M. Lerner. Hoboken, NJ: Wiley.

Levin, B. (2007, September). In Canada: Schools, poverty and the achievement gap. *Phi Delta Kappan, 89* (01), 75–76.

Levin, D., & Kilbourne, J. (2008). *So sexy so soon: The new sexualized childhood and what parents can do to protect their kids*. New York: Random House.

Levinson, D. (1978). *Seasons of a man's life*. New York: Knopf.

Levinson, D. (1990a). *Seasons of a woman's life*. Presented at the 98th annual convention of the American Psychological Association, Boston.

Levinson, D. (1990b). A theory of life structure development in adulthood. In C. N. Alexander & E. J. Langer (Eds.), *Higher states of human development*. (pp. 35–54). New York: Oxford University Press.

Levy, B. R., & Banaji, M. R. (2002). Implicit ageism. In T. D. Nelson (Ed.), *Ageism: Stereotypes and prejudice against older persons*. (pp. 49–75). Cambridge, MA: MIT Press.

Lewis, M. (1997). *Altering fate: Why the past does not predict the future*. New York: Guilford Press.

Lewis, M. (2000). The promise of dynamic systems approaches for an integrated account of human development. *Child Development, 71*(1), 36–43.

Lillard, A.S. & Peterson, J. (2011) The immediate impact of different types of television on young children's executive function. *Pediatrics, 128*(4), 644–649.

Lindberg, D. (2009, October 22). Seniors use the Wii game and go hi-tech for exercise. Retrieved from http://www.examiner.com/article/seniors-use-the-wii-game-and-go-hi-tech-for-exercise

Lipkins, S., Levy, J. M., & Jerabkova, B. (2009). *Sexting . . .is it all about power?* Retrieved from http://www.realpsychology.com/content/tools-life/sextingis-it-all-about-power

Lips, H. M. (2007). Gender and possible selves. *New Directions for Adult and Continuing Education, 114*, 51–59.

Ljungquist, B., Berg, S., Lanke, J., McClearn, G. E., & Pedersen, N. L. (1998). The effect of genetic factors for longevity: A comparison of identical and fraternal twins in the Swedish Twin Registry. *Journals of Gerontology Series A—Biological Sciences and Medical Sciences, 53A*, 441–446.

Lorenz, K. Z. (1965). *Evolution and the modification of behavior*. Chicago: University of Chicago Press.

Luong, M. (2008). Life after teenage motherhood. *Perspectives on Labour and Income*. Vol. 9, no. 5. May. Statistics Canada Catalogue no. 75-001-XIE.

M

Maccoby, E. E., & Martin, J. A. (1983). Socialization in the context of the family. In E. M. Hetherington (Ed.), *Handbook of child psychology: Vol. 4. Socialization, personality, and social development*. New York: Wiley.

Macera, M. H., & Cohen, S. H. (2006). Psychology as a profession: An effective career exploration and orientation course for undergraduate psychology majors. *Career Development Quarterly, 54*(4), 367–371.

Maclean's (2013), Infographic: How Canadian university students are paying their bills. Retrieved from http://www2.macleans.ca/2013/01/22/infographic-how-canadian-university-students-are-paying-their-bills/

Madden, S., St. Pierre-Hansen, N., Kelly, L., Cromarty, H., Linkewich, B., & Payne, L. (2010). First Nations women's knowledge of menopause. *Canadian Family Physician 56*(9), e331-e337.

Malloy, L. C., Lyon, T. D., & Quas, J. A. (2007). Filial dependency and recantation of child sexual abuse allegations. *Journal of the American Academy of Child and Adolescent Psychiatry, 46*(2), 162–171.

Mann, T. (1939, June 21). *New York Times*.

Marcus, L. (2002). *Ways of telling: Conversations on the art of the picture*. New York: Dutton Books.

Margolis, D. (2005). Gender. In K. Thies & J. Travers (Eds.). *Handbook of human development for health care professionals*. Sudbury, MA: Jones and Bartlett.

Marlier, L., & Schaal, B. (2005). Human newborns prefer human milk: Conspecific milk odor is attractive without postnatal exposure. *Child Development, 76*, 155–168.

Marrs, R., Bloch, L., & Silverman, K. (1997). *Dr. Richard Marrs' fertility book*. New York: Delacorte.

Martel, L., & Menard, F-P. (2011). Generations in Canada. Statistics Canada. Retrieved from http://www12.statcan.gc.ca/census-recensement/2011/as-sa/98-311-x/98-311-x2011003_2-eng.cfm

Martin, J. A., Hamilton, B. E., Sutton, P. D., Ventura, S. J., Menacker, F., Kirmeyer, S., & Mathews, T. J. (2009). Births: Final data for 2006. *National Vital Statistics Reports, 57*(7).

Maslow, A. (1987). *Motivation and personality*. (Revised by R. Frager, J. Fadiman, C. McReynolds, & R. Cox.) New York: Harper & Row.

McCain, M.N., Mustard, J.F., & McCuaig, K. (2011). *Early years study 3: Making decisions, taking action*. Retrieved from http://earlyyearsstudy.ca/en/

Maurer, D., Mondloch, C. J., & Lewis, T. L. (2007). Effects of early visual deprivation on perceptual and cognitive development. Progress in Brain Research, vol. 164, 87.

McCool, J. P., Cameron, L. D., & Petrie, K. J. (2001). Adolescent perceptions of smoking imagery in film. *Social Science and Medicine, 52*(10), 1577–1587.

McCrae, R., & Costa, P. T., Jr. (1990). *Personality in adulthood*. New York: Guilford Press.

McCrae, R., & Costa, P. T., Jr. (2004, February). A contemplated revision of the NEO Five-Factor Inventory. *Personality and Individual Differences, 36*(3), 587–596.

McCrae, R., Costa, P. T., Ostendorf, F., Angleitner, A., Hrebíčková, M., & Avia, M. D., et al. (2000). Nature over nurture: Temperament, personality, and lifespan development. *Journal of Personality and Social Psychology, 78*(1), 173–186.

Meschke, L., & others. (2000). Demographic, biological, psychological, and social predictors of the timing of first intercourse. *Journal of Research on Adolescence, 10*, 315–338.

Messier, V., Levesque, B., Proulx, J. F., Rochette, L., Libman, M. D., Ward, B. J., et al. (2009). Seroprevalence of Toxoplasma gondii among Nunavik Inuit (Canada). *Zoonoses Public Health, 56* (4): 188–97.

Miller, B. C., Benson, B., & Galbraith, K. A. (2001). Family relationships and adolescent pregnancy risk: A research synthesis. *Developmental Review, 21*(1), 1–38.

Miller, J., Rosenbloom, A., & Silverstein, J. (2004). Childhood obesity. *Journal of Clinical Endocrinology & Metabolism, 89*(9), 4211–4218.

Miller, K. E., Barnes, G. M., Melnick, M., Sabo, D. F., & Farrell, M. P. (2002). Gender and racial/ethnic differences in predicting adolescent sexual risk: Athletic participation versus exercise. *Journal of Health and Social Behavior, 43,* 436–450.

Mitchell, I. (2011). Sudden infant death: A global problem, local action. Report to Public Health Agency of Canada (PHAC). University of Calgary.

Moll, M. (2003, May 23). Where are the school tests taking us? *Toronto Star.* Retrieved from http://www.maritamoll.ca/webmom/content/torstaroped.htm

Monsebraaten, L. (2011, February 4). Five years on, children still wait for quality care. *Toronto Star.* Retrieved from http://www.thestar.com/life/parent/2011/02/04/five_years_on_children_still_wait_for_quality_care.html

Moore, K., & Persaud, T. (2003). *Before we are born: Essentials of embryology and birth defects.* Philadelphia: Saunders.

Moran, B. (2000). Maternal infections. In S. Mattson & J. Smith (Eds.), *Core curriculum for maternal–newborn nursing.* Philadelphia: Saunders.

Morris, K., (2006). Genital mutilation and alternative practices. *The Lancet, 368,* 64–67.

Mosher , C.E., & Danoff-Burg, S. (2004). Effects of gender and employment status on support provided to caregivers. *Sex Roles: A Journal of Research, 51,* 589–596.

Mosher, W. D., Chandra, A., & Jones, J. (2005). Sexual behavior and selected health measures: Men and women 15–44 years of age, United States, 2002. *Advance Data for Vital and Health Statistics, 362,* 1–56.

Muller, F., Rebiff, M., Taillander, A., Qury, J. F., & Mornet, E. (2000). Parental origin of the extra chromosome in prenatally diagnosed fetal trisomy. *Human Genetics, 106,* 340–344.

Mullins, K. J. (2009, January 20). Smoking ban starts Wednesday for Ontario cars that carry children. *Digital Journal.* Retrieved from http://www.digitaljournal.com/article/265625

Munakata, Y. (2006). Information processing approaches to development. In W. Damon & R. Lerner (Series Eds.) & R. Lerner (Vol. Ed.), *Handbook of child psychology: Vol. 1. Theoretical models of human development.* New York: Wiley.

Murphy, D. (2012, December 7). Jordin Tootoo heads home to host big Kivalliq hockey camp. Nunatsiaq online.   Nunavet, December 7, 2012. Retrieved from http://www.nunatsiaqonline.ca/stories/article/65674jordin_tootoo_heads_home_to_host_big_kivalliq_hockey_camp/

Murphy, W. D., Haynes, M.R., DiLillo, D. & Steere, E. (2001). An exploration of factors related to deviant sexual arousal among juvenile sex offenders. *Sexual Abuse: Journal of Research & Treatment, 13,* 91–103.

N

National Advisory Council on Aging (NACA). (2005). Grandparenting in the twenty-first century—The times they are a changin'. *Expression, 18,* 3. Retrieved from http://www.ohpe.ca/node/6892

National Center for Education Statistics. (2003). *Fast facts.* Retrieved from http://nces.ed.gov/fastfacts/display.asp?id-59

National Collaborating Centre for Infectious Disease. (2008, June). Evidence review. Winnipeg, MB: NCCID.

National Institute of Health. (n.d.). Child and Adolescent Mental Health Government Guide. Retrieved from http://www.nimh.nih.gov/

Navaneelan, T. (2012). Suicide rates: An overview. Statistics Canada Catalogue no. 82-624-X. Retrieved from http://www.statcan.gc.ca/pub/82-624-x/2012001/article/11696-eng.htm

Ngai, S. S., Ngai, N., & Cheung, C. (2006). Environmental influences on risk taking among Hong Kong young dance partygoers. *Adolescence, 41*(164), 739–753.

O

O'Dea, J. A., & Abraham, S. (1999). Onset of disordered eating attitudes and behaviors in early adolescence: Interplay of pubertal status, gender, weight, and age. *Adolescence, 34*(136), 671–679.

Obeidallah, D. A., Brennan, R. T., Brooks-Gunn, J., Kindlon, D., & Earls, F. (2000). Socioeconomic status, race, and girls' pubertal maturation: Results form the Project on Human Development in Chicago Neighborhoods. *Journal of Research on Adolescence, 10*(4), 443–464.

Olds, S., London, M., & Ladewig, P. (1996). *Maternal–newborn nursing.* Reading, MA: Addison-Wesley.

Ontario Federation for Cerebral Palsy. (2009). Living with CP. Retrieved from http://www.ofcp.ca/living_cp.php#03

Oregon.gov. (2007). Death With Dignity Act. Retrieved from http://Oregon.gov/DHS/ph/pas/oars.html

Organization for Economic Co-operation and Development. (2011). Health at a glance: OECD indicators [cited October 2012].

Organization for Economic Co-operation and Development. (2012). Indicators of well-being in Canada: Family life–infant mortality. Retrieved July 23, 2013, from http://www4.hrsdc.gc.ca/.3ndic.1t.4r@-eng.jsp?iid=2#M_1

P

Pang, J. W. Y., Heffelfinger, J. D., Huang, G. J., Benedetti, T. J., & Noell, S. (2002). Outcomes of planned home births in Washington State: 1989–1996. *Obstetrics & Gynecology, 100*(2), 253–259.

Paris, S., & Paris, A. (2006). Assessment of early reading. In W. Damon & R. Lerner (Series Eds.) & K. Renninger & I. Sigel (Vol. Eds.), *Handbook of child psychology: Vol. 4. Child psychology in practice.* New York: Wiley.

Parker-Pope, T. (2009). *Well.* Retrieved from http://well.blogs.nytimes.com/2009/08/19/us-life-expectancy-at-all-time-high/

Parliamentary Standing Committee on Health. (2001). *Assisting reproduction: Building families.* Research Branch of the Library of Parliament.

Parten, M. (1932). Social participation among preschool children. *Journal of Abnormal Psychology, 27* 243–269.

Patterson, C., Feightner, J., Garcia, A., Hsiung, G-Y., MacKnight, C. & Sadovnick, A. (2008, February 26). Diagnosis and treatment of dementia: 1. Risk assessment and primary prevention of Alzheimer disease. CMAJ, vol. 178, no. 5, 548–556. Retrieved from http://www.cmaj.ca/content/178/5/548.abstract

Peake, P., Hebl, M., & Mischel, W. (2002). Strategic attention deployment for delay of gratification in working and waiting situations. *Developmental Psychology, 38*(2), 313–326.

Pennisi, E. (2005). Why do humans have so few genes? *Science, 309,* 80. http://www.sciencemag.org/cgi/reprint/309/5731/80

Petersen, A. (1988). Adolescent development. *Annual Review of Psychology, 39,* 583–607. Palo Alto, CA: Annual Reviews.

Piaget, J. (1952a). *The origins of intelligence.* New York; Norton.

Piaget, J. (1952b). *The origins of intelligence in children.* New York: International Universities Press.

Piaget, J. (1973). *The child and reality.* New York: Viking.

Piaget, J., & Inhelder, B. (1969). *The psychology of the child*. New York: Basic Books.

Pienta, A. M., Hayward, M. D., & Jenkins, K. R. (2000). Health consequences of marriage for the retirement years. *Journal of Family Issues, 21*(5), 559–586.

Pinker, S. (1994). *The language instinct*. New York: Morrow.

Pious, S. (2010). Frances Aboud. Retrieved from http://aboud.socialpsychology.org

Pitkin, S., & Savage, L. (2004). Age-related vulnerability to diencephalic amnesia produced by thiamine deficiency: The role of time of insult. *Behavioural Brain Research, 148*(1–2), 93–105.

Pradinuk, M., Chanoine, J., Goldman, R. (2011, July). Obesity and physical activity in children. *Canadian Family Physician, 57* (7), 779–782.

Proudfoot, S. (2010). Canadian teen pregnancy rate dropping faster than U.S., Sweden, England. *Canwest News Service*. Retrieved from http://www.canada.com/health/Canadian+teen+pregnancy+rate+dropping+faster+that+Sweden+England/3077442/story.html

Public Health Agency of Canada. (2003). Canadian incidence study of reported child abuse and neglect-2003. Major Findings. Retrieved from http://www.phac-aspc.gc.ca/cm-vee/csca-ecve/

Public Health Agency of Canada. (2006, May). Canadian communicable disease report. 2004 Canadian sexually transmitted infections surveillance report. Retrieved from http://www.phac-aspc.gc.ca/publicat/ccdr-rmtc/07vol33/33s1/

Public Health Agency of Canada. (2008). *Canadian Perinatal Health Report, 2008 Edition*. Ottawa: Public Health Agency of Canada.

Public Health Agency of Canada. (2009). Summary: Estimates of HIV prevalence and incidence in Canada, 2008. Surveillance and Risk Assessment Division. Centre for Communicable Diseases and Infection Control. Retrieved from http://www.phac-aspc.gc.ca/aids-sida/publication/epi/2010/7-eng.php

Public Health Agency of Canada. (2010a). Cytomegalovirus. Pathogen safety data sheet—infectious substances. Retrieved from http://www.phac-aspc.gc.ca/lab-bio/res/psds-ftss/cytomegalovirus-eng.php

Public Health Agency of Canada. (2010b). Family violence initiative performance report for April 2004 to March 2008. Retrieved from http://www.phac-aspc.gc.ca/ncfv-cnivf/sources/fv/fv-perf-rprt-2008/assets/pdf/fvi-perf-rprt-eng.pdf

Public Health Agency of Canada. (2010c). Report on sexually transmitted infections in Canada: 2008. Retrieved from http://www.phac-aspc.gc.ca/std-mts/report/sti-its2008/

Public Health Agency of Canada (2011a). Aboriginal Head Start in urban and northern communities (AHSUNC): A national analysis of the program's geographic reach. Internal document. Ottawa: Public Health Agency of Canada.

Public Health Agency of Canada (2011b). The Chief Public Health Officer's report on the state of public health in Canada, 2011. Retrieved from http://www.phac-aspc.gc.ca/cphorsphc-respcacsp/2011/cphorsphc-respcacsp-06-eng.php

Public Health Agency of Canada. (2011c). Chapter 7: Perinatal HIV transmission in Canada.

Public Health Agency of Canada. (2011d). Healthy living can prevent disease. Retrieved from http://phac-aspc.gc.ca/cd-mc/healthy_living-vie_saine-eng.php

Public Health Agency of Canada (2012a). Evaluation of the Aboriginal Head Start in Urban and Northern Communities Program at the Public Health Agency of Canada. Retrieved from http://www.phac-aspc.gc.ca/about_apropos/evaluation/reports-rapports/2011-2012/ahsunc-papacun/find-const-eng.php

Public Health Agency of Canada. (2012b). Safe sleep for your baby brochure. Retrieved from http://www.phac-aspc.gc.ca/hp-ps/dca-dea/stages-etapes/childhood-enfance_0-2/sids/ssb_brochure-eng.php

Public Safety Canada (2007). Youth gangs in Canada: What do we know? Retrieved from http://www.publicsafety.gc.ca/prg/cp/bldngevd/_fl/2007-YG-1_e.pdf

R

Raina, P., Kirkland, S., & Wolfson, C. (2012, Fall). CLSA Connection. Canadian Longitudinal Study on Aging. No. 6. Retrieved from http://www.clsa-elcv.ca/files/docs/newsletter_english.pdf

Ravitch, D. (2010). *The death and life of the great American school system: How testing and choice are undermining education*. New York: Basic Books.

Read, N., & Hansen, D. A. (2006, August, 25). ESL students fall behind. Retrieved from http://www.canada.com/vancouversun/news/story.html?id=36af16c1-ff5b-4399-97af-7413169b64d7

Reisberg, L. (2000, January 28). Student stress is rising, especially among women. *The Chronicle of Higher Education*, A521.

Rennie, S. (2012, September 19). Boomerang kids mean empty nests not quite so empty: Census. *Canadian Press*. Retrieved from http://www.theglobeandmail.com/news/politics/boomerang-kids-mean-empty-nests-not-quite-so-empty-census/article4553426/

Rogoff, B. (1991). Apprenticeship in thinking: Cognitive development in social context. New York: Oxford University Press.

Rogoff, B. (2003). *The cultural nature of human development*. New York: Oxford University Press.

Rose, S. (2005). *The future of the brain*. New York: Oxford University Press.

Ross, R. (2011). From uncomfortably numb to feeling alive: Overcoming the legacy of residential schools. Cross-Currents: *The Journal of Addiction and Mental Health, 15*(2), 12–13.

Rosser, S. V. (2004). Using POWRE to ADVANCE: Institutional barriers identified by women scientists and engineers. *NWSA Journal, 16*(1), 50–79.

Rotermann, M. (2008). Trends in teen sexual behaviour and condom use. *Health Reports, 19*(3), 1–5.

Rotermann, M. (2012). Sexual behaviour and condom use of 15- to 24-year-olds in 2003 and 2009/2010. *Health Reports, 23*(1), 1–5

Rotermann, M., & McKay, A. (2009). Condom use at last sexual intercourse among unmarried, not living common-law 20-to-34-year-old Canadian young adults. *The Canadian Journal of Human Sexuality, 18* (3).

Royal Commission on Aboriginal Peoples. (1996b). *Gathering strength*. Vol. 4. Ottawa.

Royal Society of Canada. (2013). Speakers list: Michel Boivin. Retrieved from https://rsc-src.ca/en/events/annual-symposium/speakers

Rubin, K., Bukowski, W., & Parker, J. (2006). Peer interactions, relationships, and groups. In W. Damon & R. Lerner (Series Eds.) & N. Eisenberg (Vol. Ed.), *Handbook of child psychology: Vol. 3. Social, emotional, and personality development*. New York: John Wiley.

Rubin, R. (1984). *Maternal identity and maternal experience*. New York: Springer.

Ruble, D., & Martin, C. (1998). Gender development. In W. Damon (Series Ed.) & N. Eisenberg (Vol. Ed.), *Handbook of child psychology: Vol. 3. Child psychology in practice*. New York: Wiley.

Ruble, D., Martin, C., & Berenbaum, S. (2006). Gender development. In W. Damon & R. Lerner (Series Eds.) & N. Eisenberg (Vol. Ed.), *Handbook of child psychology: Vol. 3. Social, emotional, and personality development.* New York: Wiley.

Rushowy, K. (2010, May 3). Watching TV hinders kids' math achievement, study finds. Retrieved from http://www.thestar.com/life/parent/2010/05/03/watching_tv_hinders_kids_math_achievement_study_finds.html

Russell, R. B., Petrini, J. R., Damus, K., Mattison, D. R., & Schwarz, R. H. (2003). The changing epidemiology of multiple births in the United States. *Obstetrics and Gynecology, 1001,* 129–135.

Russell, S. T. (2006). Substance use and abuse and mental health among sexual-minority youths: Evidence from add health. In A. M. Omoto & H. S. Kurtzman (Eds.), *Sexual orientation and mental health: Examining identity and development in lesbian, gay, and bisexual people* (pp. 13–35). Washington, DC: American Psychological Association.

Rutter, M. (2002a). Development and psychopathology. In M. Rutter and E. Taylor (Eds.). *Child and adolescent psychiatry.* London: Blackwell.

Rutter, M. (2002b). Nature, nurture and development: From evangelism through science toward policy and practice. *Child Development, 73*(1), 1–21.

Rutter, M. (2006). *Genes and behavior.* Oxford, England: Blackwell.

Rutter, M., & Nikapota, A. (2006). Culture, ethnicity, society, and psychopathology. In M. Rutter and E. Taylor (Eds.), *Child and adolescent psychiatry.* London: Blackwell.

Rutter, M., & Rutter, M. (1993). *Developing minds.* New York: Basic Books

Rutter, M., & Taylor, E. (Eds.). (2002). *Child and adolescent psychiatry.* London: Blackwell.

S

Salter, D., McMillan, D., Richards, M., Talbot, T. Hodges, J., Bentovim, A., Hastings, R., Stevenson, J., & Skuse, D. (2003). Development of sexually abusive behavior in sexually victimized males: A longitudinal study. *The Lancet, 361*(9356), 471.

Salthouse, T. A. (2001). Structural models of the relations between age and measures of cognitive functioning. *Intelligence, 29,* 93–115.

SAMHSA, Office of Applied Studies. (2008). *National Survey on Drug Use and Health.* Retrieved from http://www.oas.samhsa.gov/NSDUH/2K8NSDUH/tabs/Sect2peTabs17to21.pdf

Sanders, C. M. (1989). *Grief: The mourning after: Dealing with adult bereavement.* New York: Wiley.

Savage, M. P., & Holcomb, D. R. (1999). Adolescent female athletes' sexual risk-taking behaviors. *Journal of Youth and Adolescence, 28,* 595–602.

Schaie, K. W. (1994). The course of adult intellectual development. *American Psychologist, 49*(4), 304–313.

Schaie, K. W. (2005). *Developmental influences on adult intellectual development: The Seattle Longitudinal Study.* New York: Oxford University Press.

Schaie, K. W., & Elder, G. (2005). *Historical influences on lives and aging.* New York: Springer.

Schmader, T., Johns, M., & Barquissau, M. (2004). The cost of accepting gender differences: The role of stereotype endorsement in women's experience in the math domain. *Sex Roles, 50*(11–12) 835–850.

Schwartz, I. (2002). Sexual activity prior to coital interaction: A comparison between males and females. *Archives of Sexual Behavior, 28,* 63–69.

sciencedaily.com. (2009, January). More weight means longer hospital stays. Retrieved from http://www.sciencedaily.com/videos/2009/0108-more_weight_equals_longer_hospital_stays.htm

Selfhout, M. H. W., Delsing, M. J. M. H., ter Bogt, T. F. M., & Meeus, W. H. J. (2008). Heavy metal and hip-hop style preferences and externalizing problem behaviors: A two-wave longitudinal study. *Youth and Society, 39*(4), 435–452.

Seligman, M. E. P., & Csikszentmihalyi, M. (2000). Positive psychology: An introduction. *American Psychologist, 55*(1), 5–14.

Seppa, N. (1996, August). Rwanda starts its long healing process. *APA Monitor,* p. 14.

Service Canada (2012). Elementary and kindergarten teachers. Retrieved from http://www.servicecanada.gc.ca/eng/qc/job_futures/statistics/4142.shtml

Service Canada. (2013). Employment insurance compassionate care benefits. Retrieved from http://www.servicecanada.gc.ca/eng/ei/types/compassionate_care.shtml#Definition

The Sex Information and Education Council of Canada (2012). Statistics related to trends in the sexual behaviours of Canadian teenagers. Retrieved from http://sexualityandu.ca/uploads/files/CTR_TeenageStatistics_JULYAUG2012-EN.pdf

Shaffer, D., & Pfeffer, C. (2001). Practice parameter for assessment and treatment of children and adolescents with suicidal behavior. *Journal of the American Academy of Child and Adolescent Psychiatry, 40,* S24–S51.

Shankaran, S., Laptook, A. R., Ehrenkranz, R. A., Tyson, J. E., McDonald, S. A. & Donovan, E. F. (2005). Whole-body hypothermia for neonates with hypoxic-ischemic encephalopathy. *New England Journal of Medicine, 353,* 1574–1584.

Sharples, T. (2008). Study: Most child abuse goes unreported. *Time.* Retrieved from http://www.time.com/time/health/article/0,8599,1863650,00.html

Sheldon, K., & Kasser, T. (2001). Getting older, getting better? Personal striving and psychological maturity across the life span. *Developmental Psychology, 37,* 491–501.

Shenk, J. W. (2009, June). What makes us happy? *The Atlantic.* Retrieved from http://www.theatlantic.com/magazine/archive/2009/06/what-makes-us-happy/307439/?single_page=true

Shonkoff, J. P., & Phillips, D. A. (Eds.). (2000). *From neurons to neighborhoods: The science of early childhood development.* Washington, DC: National Academy Press.

Shreeve, J. (2005). *The genome war: How Craig Venter tried to capture the code of life and save the world.* New York: Ballantine Books.

Siegel, D. J. (1999). *The developing mind: How relationships and the brain interact to shape who we are.* New York: Guilford Press.

Siegel, L. S. (2003). Learning disabilities. In I. B. Weiner (Ed.), *Handbook of psychology* (Vol. VI). New York: Wiley.

Siegel, L. S. (1993, July). Amazing new discovery: Piaget was wrong. *Canadian Psychology* 34.3:239–245.

Siegler, R. (1996). *Emerging minds: The process of change in children's thinking.* New York: Oxford University Press.

Siegler, R., & Alibali, M. (2005). *Children's thinking.* Upper Saddle River, NJ: Prentice Hall.

Siegler, R. S. (1996). *Emerging minds: The process of change in children's thinking.* New York: Oxford University Press.

Siegler, R. S., DeLoache, J., & Eisenberg, N. (2006). *How children develop* (2nd ed.). New York: Worth.

Simner, M. (2000). A joint position statement by the Canadian psychological association and the Canadian association of school psychologists on the Canadian press coverage of the province-wide achievement test results. Canadian Psychological Association, Ottawa.

Simons, D. J. (2007). Inattentional blindness. *Scholarpedia, 2,* 3244. Retrieved from http://www.scholarpedia.org/article/Inattentional_blindness

Singleton, J. (2000, Summer). Women caring for elderly family members: Shaping non-traditional work and family initiatives. *Journal of Comparative Family Studies, 31*(3), 367–375.

Sleek, S. (1997). Weisel emphasizes need to thank elderly. *APA Monitor, 28* (10), 23.

Smith, D.W.E. (1997). Centenarians: Human longevity outliers. *The Gerontologist, 37*(2), 200–207.

Smith, K. (2000). Normal childbirth. In S. Mattson & J. Smith (Eds.), *Core curriculum for maternal–newborn nursing.* Philadelphia: Saunders.

Smith, W. J. (2013). Medicinal murder. *First Things: A Monthly Journal of Religion & Public Life*, (233), 39–44.

Smylie, J. & Adomako, P. (2009). Indigenous children's health report: Health assessment in action. Retrieved from http://www.stmichaelshospital.com/crich/wp-content/uploads/ichr_report-web.pdf

Society of Obstetricians and Gynaecologists of Canada (2004). Guidelines for operative vaginal birth. *Journal of Obstetrics and Gynaecology Canada, 148,* 747–753.

Society of Obstetricians and Gynaecologists of Canada. (2011, May 4). Healthy eating, exercise and weight gain before and during pregnancy. Retrieved from http://www.sogc.org/health/healthy-eating_e.asp

Söderlund, H., Nyberg, L., Adolfsson, R., Nilsson, L., & Launer, L. J. (2003). High prevalence of white matter hyperintensities in normal aging: Relation to blood pressure and cognition. *Cortex, 39*(4–5), 1093–1105.

Solm, M. (2004). Freud returns. *Scientific American, 290*(5), 82–89.

Squire, L., & Kandel, E. (2000). *Memory: From mind to molecule.* New York: Scientific American Press.

Statistics Canada. (2001). General social survey. Retrieved from http://www.statcan.gc.ca/pub/89f0115x/89f0115x2001001-eng.pdf

Statistics Canada. (2004, July, 22). Study: Economic consequences of widowhood. The Daily. Retrieved from http://www.statcan.gc.ca/daily-quotidien/040722/dq040722b-eng.htm

Statistics Canada. (2006). Childhood obesity: A troubling situation. Retrieved from http://www41.statcan.ca/2006/2966/ceb2966_004-eng.htm

Statistics Canada. (2006a). Labour force historical review: Rates among Canadian seniors aged 65+. Retrieved from http://www.ccsd.ca/factsheets/labour_market/rates/index.htm

Statistics Canada. (2008a). Proportion of children with disabilities aged 5 to 14 receiving special education, by province and territories, 2006. Retrieved from http://www.statcan.gc.ca/pub/89-628-x/2008004/c-g/5201195-eng.htm

Statistics Canada. (2008b). French immersion 30 years later. Retrieved from http://www.statcan.gc.ca/pub/81-004-x/200406/6923-eng.htm

Statistics Canada. (2008c). Life expectancy, abridged life table, at birth and at age 65, by sex, Canada, provinces and territories (Comparable Indicators), annual (years) (CANSIM Table 102-0025). Ottawa: Statistics Canada.

Statistics Canada. (2008d). Life expectancy, abridged life table, at birth and at age 65, by sex, Canada, provinces and territories, annual (years) (CANSIM Table 102-0511). Ottawa: Statistics Canada.

Statistics Canada. (2009). Breastfeeding. Retrieved from http://www.statcan.gc.ca/pub/82-625x/2010002/article/11269-eng.htm

Statistics Canada. (2009a). Delayed transitions of young adults. Retrieved from http://www.statcan.gc.ca/pub/11-008-x/2007004/10311-eng.htm

Statistics Canada. (2009b). Hearing limitation rates by age, 2006. Retrieved from http://www.statcan.gc.ca/pub/89-628-x/2009012/tab/tab1-eng.htm

Statistics Canada. (2010). Classification of instructional programs (CIP), Canada, 2000. Retrieved from http://www.statcan.gc.ca/pub/12-590-x/12-590-x2005001-eng.pdf

Statistics Canada. (2010a). Life expectancy. Catalogue no. 89-645-X. Retrieved from http://www.statcan.gc.ca/pub/89-645-x/2010001/life-expectancy-esperance-vie-eng.htm

Statistics Canada. (2011a). Heavy drinking, 2010. 82-625-X. Retrieved from http://www.statcan.gc.ca/pub/82-625-X/2011001/article/11462-eng.htm

Statistics Canada. (2011b). Police-reported crime statistics in Canada, 2010. Retrieved from http://www.statcan.gc.ca/pub/85-002-x/2011001/article/11523-eng.htm#a6

Statistics Canada. (2011c). Access to a regular medical doctor, 2011. Retrieved from http://www.statcan.gc.ca/pub/82-625-x/2012001/article/11656-eng.htm

Statistics Canada. (2011d). Physical activity results of Canadian adults, 2007 to 2009. Retrieved from http://www.statcan.gc.ca/pub/82-625-x/2011001/article/11552-eng.htm

Statistics Canada. (2011e). Family violence in Canada: A statistical profile. Retrieved from http://www.statcan.gc.ca/pub/85-224-x/85-224-x2010000-eng.pdf

Statistics Canada. (2011f, November). Leading causes of death. The Daily. Retrieved from http://www.statcan.gc.ca/daily-quotidien/111101/dq111101b-eng.htm

Statistics Canada. (2011g). Canadian vital statistics, divorce database and marriage database. Health Statistics Division. Ottawa: Statistics Canada.

Statistics Canada. (2012a). Births and stillbirths, 2010. The Daily, September 27, 2012. Retrieved from http://www.statcan.gc.ca/daily-quotidien/120927/dq120927h-eng.htm

Statistics Canada. (2012b). Overweight and obesity rate, by age group, 1978/1979 and 2004. Retrieved from http://www41.statcan.ca/2006/2966/htm/ceb2966_004_7-eng.htm

Statistics Canada. (2012c). Victims (0 to 17 years) of police-reported sexual offences and physical assault by family members, by sex and accused-victim relationship, Canada, 1009. Retrieved from http://www.statcan.gc.ca/pub/85-224-x/2010000/ct006-eng.htm

Statistics Canada. (2012d). Portrait of families and living arrangements in Canada. Retrieved from http://www12.statcan.gc.ca/census-recensement/2011/as-sa/98-312-x/98-312-x2011001-eng.pdf

Statistics Canada. (2012e). Conjugal status and opposite/same-sex status, sex and age groups for persons living in couples in private households of Canada, provinces, territories and census metropolitan areas, 2011 Census. Retrieved from http://www12.statcan.gc.ca/census-recensement/2011/dp-pd/tbt-tt/Rp-eng.cfm?LANG=E&APATH=3&DETAIL=0&DIM=0&FL=A&FREE=0&GC=0&GID=0&GK=0&GRP=1&PID=102574&PRID=0&PTYPE=101955&S=0&SHOWALL=0&SUB=0&Temporal=2011&THEME=89&VID=0&VNAMEE=&VNAMEF=

Statistics Canada. (2012f). Life expectancy at birth, by sex, by province. Catalogue no. 84-537-XIE. Retrieved from http://www.statcan.gc.ca/tables-tableaux/sum-som/l01/cst01/health26-eng.htm

Statistics Canada. (2012g). Deaths and mortality rate, 2000–1009, by selected causes and sex, Canada, provinces and territories (CANSIM Table 102-0552). Ottawa: Statistics Canada.

Statistics Canada. (2012h). Life expectancy, at birth and at age 65, by sex, Canada, provinces and territories, annual (years) (CANSIM Table 102-0512). Ottawa: Statistics Canada.

Statistics Canada. (2012i). Deaths, 2009. Retrieved from http://www.statcan.gc.ca/pub/84f0211x/84f0211x2009000-eng.pdf

Statistics Canada. (2012j). Smoking, 2011. Retrieved from http://www.statcan.gc.ca/pub/82-625-x/2012001/article/11668-eng.htm

Statistics Canada. (2012k). Paid work. Retrieved from http://www.statcan.gc.ca/pub/89-503-x/2010001/article/11387-eng.htm#a17

Statistics Canada. (2012l). Census family. No. 98-301-XWE. Retrieved from http://www12.statcan.gc.ca/census-recensement/2011/ref/dict/fam004-eng.cfm

Statistics Canada. (2012m). Infant mortality, by sex and birth weight, Canada, provinces and territories, annual (CANSIM Table 102-0504). Ottawa: Statistics Canada.

Statistics Canada. (2012n, September 19). 2011 Census of population: Families, households, marital status, structural type of dwelling, collectives. Retrieved from http://www.statcan.gc.ca/daily-quotidien/120919/dq120919a-eng.pdf

Statistics Canada. (2013). 2011 National Household Survey: Immigration, place of birth, citizenship, ethnic origin, visible minorities, language and religion. The Daily, May 8, 2013. Retrieved from http://www.statcan.gc.ca/daily-quotidien/130508/dq130508b-eng.pdf

Statistics Canada. (2013a, March 19). Births and fetal deaths (stillbirths), by place of birth (hospital and non-hospital), Canada, provinces and territories. (CANSIM Table 102-4516). Retrieved from www5.statcan.gc.ca/cansim

Statistics Canada. (2013b). Live births, by age of mother, Canada, provinces and territories. (CANSIM Table 102-4503). Retrieved from http://www5.statcan.gc.ca/cansim/a05?lang=eng&id=1024503&paSer=&pattern=102-4503&stByVal=1&csid=

Statistics Canada. (2013c). Estimates of population, by age group and sex for July 1, Canada, provinces and territories. (CANSIM Table 051-0001). Ottawa: Statistics Canada.

Statistics Canada. (2013d). Canadian Health Measures Survey, 2007 to 2009. © Minister of Industry. Retrieved from http://www.statcan.gc.ca/pub/82-625-x/2011001/article/11552-eng.htm

Statistics Canada. (2013e). Measuring violence against women: Statistical trends. Retrieved from http://www.statcan.gc.ca/pub/85-002-x/2013001/article/11766-eng.htm

Stepan, C. (2003, December 11). Seniors are becoming moms and dads again. Hamilton Spectator.

Stephenson, A. (2010). Canadian CF patient data registry report. Retrieved from http://www.cysticfibrosis.ca/assets/files/pdf/cpdr_reporte.pdf

Sternberg, R. (1990). Metaphors of mind: Conceptions of the nature of intelligence. New York: Cambridge University Press.

Sternberg, R. (2000). What's your love story? Psychology Today, 32(4), 52–59.

Sternberg, R. (2003). Cognitive psychology. Belmont, CA: Wadsworth/Thompson.

Sterns, H. L., & Miklos, S. M. (1995). The aging worker in a changing environment: Organizational and individual issues. Journal of Vocational Behavior, 47(2), 248–268.

Stetka , B. S., & Correll, C. U. (2013). A guide to DSM-5: Removal of the bereavement exclusion from MDD. Retrieved May 26, 2013 from http://www.medscape.com/viewarticle/803884_10

Stice, E., Presenell, K., & Bearman, S. (2001). Relation of early menarche to depression, eating disorders, substance abuse, and comorbid psychopathology among adolescent girls. Developmental Psychology, 37, 608–619.

Storey, A. E., Walsh, C. J., Quinton, R. L., & Wynne-Edwards, K. E. (2000). Hormonal correlates of paternal responsiveness in new and expectant fathers. Evolution and Human Behavior, 21, 79–95.

Straus, M. A., & Paschall, M. J. (2009). Corporal punishment by mothers and development of children's cognitive ability: A longitudinal study of two nationally representative age cohorts. Journal of Aggression, Maltreatment, & Trauma, 18(5), 459–483.

Strumpf, E.C., Chai, Z., & Kadiyala, S. (2010). Adherence to cancer screening guidelines across Canadian provinces: An observational study. BMC Cancer, 10(304).

Substance Abuse and Mental Health Services Administration (AMHSA). (2008). Results from the 2008 National Survey on Drug Use and Health: National Findings. Rockville, MD: Department of Health and Human Services.

Sudnow, D. (1967). Passing on. Englewood Cliffs, NJ: Prentice Hall.

Sugarman, L. (1986). Lifespan development: Concepts, theories and interventions. New York: Methuen.

Sullivan, J., Seem, D. L., & Chabalewski, F. (1999). Determining brain death. Critical Care Nurse, 19(2), 37–46.

Surjan, L., Devald, J., & Palfalvi, L. (1973). Epidemiology of hearing loss. Audiology, 12, 396–410.

T

Tamiras, P. S. (1972). Developmental physiology and aging. Fig. 28.1. MacMillan.

Taylor, S. E., Kelin, L. C., Lewis, B. P., Guenewald, T. L., Gurung, R. A., & Updegraff, J. A. (2000). Biobehavioral responses to stress in females: Tend-and-befriend, not fight-or-flight. Psychological Review, 107, 411–429.

Thompson, J. A., & Bunderson, J. S. (2001). Work–nonwork conflict and the phenomenology of time. Work and Occupations, 28(1), 17–39.

Thompson, L., & Kelly-Vance, L. (2001). The impact of mentoring on academic achievement of at-risk youth. Children & Youth Services Review, 23, 227–242.

Thompson, R. (1999). The individual child: Temperament, emotion, self, and personality. In M. Bornstein & M. Lamb (Eds.), Developmental psychology: An advanced textbook. Mahwah, NJ: Erlbaum.

Toronto District School Board. (2008). Comprehensive commitment to integration through education. Retrieved from http://www.bertelsmann-stiftung.de/bst/en/media/xcms_bst_dms_25449_25450_2.pdf

Toronto Star. (2013, March 10). Retirement becoming a distant proposition for many Canadians. Retrieved from http://www.thestar.com/business/personal_finance/retirement/2012/02/20/retirement_becoming_a_distant_

Toussaint, L., & Webb, J. R. (2005). Gender differences in the relationship between empathy and forgiveness. The Journal of Social Psychology, 145(6), 673–686.

Toussaint, O. (2003). Normal brain aging: A commentary. Neurobiology of Aging, 24 (Suppl. 1), S129–S130.

Travers, J. F. (1982). The growing child. Glenview, IL: Scott Foresman and Co.

Tremblay, K., Piskosz, M., & Souza, P. (2003). Effects of age and age-related hearing loss on the neural representa-tion of speech cues. Clinical Neurophysiology, 114(7), 1332–1343.

Trocmé, N., Durrant, J., Ensom, R., & Marwah, I. (2004). Physical abuse of children in the context of punishment. The Centres of Excellence for Children's Well-Being Information Sheet #8E. Toronto, ON: Faculty of Social Work, University of Toronto.

Tsai, A. C-H., et al. (2011). Klinefelter syndrome (XXY) section of Genetics and dysmorphology. In W. W. Hay et al (Eds.), *Current Diagnosis and Treatment: Pediatrics* (20th ed.). (p. 1039). New York: McGraw-Hill Medical.

Tsang, A., Fuller-Thomson, E., & Lai, D. (2012, November). Sexuality and health among Chinese seniors in Canada. *Journal of International Migration and Integration.* 13(4), p. 525–540.

Turcotte, M. & Schellenberg, G. (2007). A portrait of seniors in Canada. Statistics Canada. Catalogue no. 89-519-XWE.

Turner Syndrome Society of Canada. (2009). How common is Turner Syndrome? Retrieved from http://www.turner syndrome.ca/turnerssyndrome.html

Twenge, J.M., Campbell, W.K., & Foster, C.A. (2003). Parenthood and marital satisfaction: A meta-analytic review. *Journal of Marriage and Family, 65*(3), 574–583.

Twigg, J., & Atkin, K. (1994). *Careers perceived: Policy and practice in informal care.* Buckingham, England: Open University Press.

U

Unger, R., & Crawford, M. (2000). *Women and gender: A feminist psychology* (3rd ed.). New York: McGraw-Hill.

UNICEF. (1989). United Nations Convention on the Rights of the Child. Retrieved from http://www.unicef.org.uk/Documents/Publication-pdfs/UNCRC_PRESS200910web.pdf

University of Montreal. (2010, September 28). The price and popularity: Drug and alcohol consumption. *ScienceNewsline.* Retrieved from http://www.sciencenewsline.com/articles/2010092812000070.html

V

Valliant, G. (2002). *Aging well.* Boston: Little, Brown.

Vaillant, G., & Mukamal, K. (2001, June). Successful aging. *American Journal of Psychiatry, 158*(6), 839–847.

Van der Heide, A., Deliens, L., Faisst, K., Nilstun, T., Norup, M., & Paci, E., et al. (2003). End-of-life decision-making in six European countries: Descriptive study. *The Lancet, 362*(9381), 345–350.

Vartanian, L., & Powlishta, K. (2001). Demand characteristics and self-report measures of imaginary audience sensitivity: Implications for interpreting age differences in adolescent egocentrism. *Journal of Genetic Psychology, 162,* 187–200.

Ventura, S. J. (2009). *Changing patterns of nonmarital childbearing in the United States* (NCHS Data Brief No. 18). Hyattsville, MD: National Center for Health Statistics.

Volling, B., McElwain, N., & Miller, A. (2002). Emotion regulation in context: The jealousy complex between young siblings and its relations with child and family characteristics. *Child Development, 73*(2), 581–600.

Von Eye, A., & Schuster, C. (2000). The odds of resilience. *Child Development, 71*(3), 563–566.

von Gunten, C., Ferris, F., & Emanuel, L. (2000). Ensuring competency in end-of-life care: Communication and relational skills. *Journal of the American Medical Association, 284,* 3051–3057.

Vygotsky, L. S. (1962). *Thought and language.* Cambridge, MA: MIT Press.

Vygotsky, L. S. (1978). *Mind in society.* Cambridge, MA: Harvard University Press.

W

Wagster, M. V. (Interviewee). (2006). Aging: Preventive maintenance for the brain [Interview transcript]. Retrieved from *Washington Post* website: http://www.washingtonpost.com/wp-dyn/content/article/2006/02/20/AR2006022001001.html

Walker-Barnes, C. J., & Mason, C. A. (2004). Delinquency and substance use among gang-involved youth: The moderating role of parenting practices. *American Journal of Community Psychology, 34*(3–4), 235–251.

Wallerstein, J., Lewis, J., & Blakeslee, S. (2002). *The unexpected legacy of divorce.* New York: Hyperion.

Wan, N. (2010, March). The stress and stigma of caregiving. *Mammoth Magazine, 10.* The Centre for Studies on Stress.

Wawatay News online. (2005, April 7). Elders share rites of passage. Volume 32, #7. Retrieved from http://wawataynews.ca/node/466

Weeks, L. (2010, June 9). *In your Facebook: Social sites are everywhere.* Retrieved from http://www.npr.org/2011/07/22/127527648/in-your-facebook-social-sites-are-everywhere

Wein, C.A. (Ed.). (2008). *Emergent curriculum in the primary classroom: Interpreting the Reggio Emilia approach in schools.* New York: Teachers College Press.

Werner, E. (1995). Resilience in development. *Currents Directions in Psychological Science, 4,* 81–85.

Werner, E. (2001). *Journeys from childhood to midlife: Risk, resilience, and recovery.* New York: Cornell University Press.

Werner, E., & Smith, R. (1992). *Overcoming the odds: High-risk children from birth to adulthood.* Ithaca, NY: Cornell University Press.

Wertheimer, M. (1962). Psychomotor coordination of auditory-visual space at birth. *Science, 134,* 213–216.

Westerhof, G., et al. (2001, November). Beyond life satisfaction: Lay conceptions of well-being among middle-aged and elderly adults. *Social Indicators Research, 56*(2), 179–203.

Westin, D. Psychoanalytic theories. (2000). In A. Kazdin (Ed.), *Encyclopedia of psychology.* Washington, DC: American Psychological Association.

Whitbeck, L., et al. (2001). Deviant behavior and victimization among homeless and runaway adolescents. *Journal of Interpersonal Violence, 16,* 1175–1204.

Whitehurst, G., & Lonigan, C. (1998). Child development and emergent literacy. *Child Development, 69,* 848–872.

Willat, J. (2005). *Making sense of children's drawings.* Mahwah, NJ: Erlbaum.

Williams, C. (2004). The sandwich generation. *Statistics Canada Perspectives on Labour and Income 5*(9), Retrieved from http://www.statcan.gc.ca/pub/75-001-x/75-001-x2004109-eng.pdf

Willis, C. A. (2002). The grieving process in children: Strategies for understanding, education, and reconciling children's perceptions of death. *Early Childhood Education Journal, 29*(4), 221.

Willoughby, T., Adachi, P.J., & Good, M. (2012). A longitudinal study of the association between violent video game play and aggression among adolescents. *Developmental Psychology, 48*(4), 1044–57.

Wilson, R. D. (2011). Genetic Considerations for a Woman's Preconception Evaluation. *Journal of Obstetrics and Gynaecology Canada, 253.*

Wong, T. Y. (2001). Effect of increasing age on cataract surgery outcomes in very elderly patients. *British Medical Journal, 322*(7294), 1104.

Woodward, A., & Markman, E. (1998). Early word learning. In D. Kuhn & R. Siegler (Eds.), *Handbook of child psychology: Vol. 2.* New York: Wiley.

Woodward, L. (2001). Life course outcomes of young people with anxiety disorders in adolescence. *Journal of the American Academy of Child & Adolescent Psychiatry, 40*, 1086–1093.

World Health Organization. (2011, January). Cardiovascular diseases (CVDs). Retrieved from www.who.int/mediacentre/factsheets/fs317/en/

World Health Organization. (n.d.). Suicide rates (per 100,000), by gender and age, Canada. Retrieved from http://www.who.int/mental_health/media/cana.pdf

Wright, D. R., & Fitzpatrick, K. M. (2006). Violence and minority youth: The effects of risk and asset factors on fighting among African American children and adolescents. *Adolescence, 41*(162), 251–263.

Wright, P. J. (2006). PDE5 inhibitors compared. *Journal of Men's Health and Gender, 3*(4), 410.

Wright, V. (1999). Sleeping in adult beds risky for kids under 2. *AAP News, 15*(11), 32.

Wright, V. (2000, February). Knowledge, counseling can help prevent job injuries among teens. Elk Grove Village, IL: American Association of Pediatrics News.

Wyckoff, A. (1999). Physicians should not shy away from confronting parents: Consider religious, ethnic customs when diagnosing child abuse. *AAP News*, 13(5), 18–19.

Y

Yoder, K., et al. (2002). Event history analysis of antecedents to running away from home and being on the street. *American Behavioral Scientist. Special Issue: Advancing the Research Agenda on Homelessness: Politics and Realities, 45*, 51–65.

Yoshino, S. (2011). Ethnic variations in care of older adults in Canada. University of Alberta. Canadian Research Date Centre Network. Retrieved from http://www.rdc-cdr.ca/ethnic-variations-care-older-adults-canada

Yurgelun, Todd D. (1998, November/December). Brain abnormalities in chronic schizophrenia. *Psychology Today*, 56–59.

Z

Zigler, E., & Finn-Stevenson, M. (1999). Applied developmental psychology. In M. Bornstein & M. Lamb (Eds.), *Developmental psychology: An advanced textbook*. Mahwah, NJ: Erlbaum.

1908; *Relativity*, 1953, Lithograph by M.C. Escher. © Topham / The Image Works; Christian Hartmann / Reuters / Corbis; **163:** Bob Daemmrich / The Image Works; **165:** © Cameron / Corbis; **166:** (top) Amos Morgan / Getty Images; (bottom) iStockphoto. com / Catherine Lane. **167:** Courtesy of Lisa Fiore; **170:** Maya Barnes Johansen / The Image Works; **171:** Eric Charbonneau / Getty Images; **172:** JGI / Tom Grill / Blend Images / Corbis; **173:** © BananaStock / PunchStock; **174:** IT Stock / PunchStock; **175:** RubberBall Productions; **177:** Celador Films / The Kobal Collection

Chapter 8

Opener: Digital Vision / Getty Images; **184:** Bryan Bedder / Getty Images; **185:** (left) Image Source / jupiterImages; (right) © Brand X Pictures / PunchStock; **187:** Leonard McLane / Getty Images; **189:** Don Arnold / Getty Images; **191:** © Brand X Pictures / PunchStock; **193:** © PhotoAlto / PunchStock; **194:** ZITS © 2008 ZITS Partnership, King Features Syndicate; **195:** James A. Finley /AP Images; **197:** K. Doepner / SV-Bilderdienst / The Image Works; **198:** © PhotoAlto / PictureQuest; **202:** BananaStock / PunchStock

Chapter 9

Opener: Roberto Westbrook / Getty Images; **208:** WWD / Conde Nast / Corbis; **209:** (top) Hugh Sitton / Corbis; (bottom) Richard T. Norwitz / Corbis; **210:** (top) © iStockphoto.com / Redmal; (bottom) RubberBall Productions; **211:** Wally McNamee / Corbis; **212:** Dan Galic / Alamy; **213:** (top) InkkStudios / iStockphoto. com; (bottom) Charles Sykes / AP Images; **215:** Robb D. Cohen / Retna Ltd. / Corbis; **216:** Mike Coppola / Getty Images; **217:** Natalie Fobes / Corbis; **224:** (top to bottom) © Darrin Klimek / Getty Images; © Andersen Ross / Getty Images; © Image Source; **225:** ADAM@HOME © 2009 by Universal Uclick. Reprinted with permission. All rights reserved.

Chapter 10

Opener: Andersen Ross / Getty Images; **230:** (top to bottom) Lee Celano / Getty Images; © Qi Heng / XinHua / Xinhua Press / Corbis; Jim Wilkes / GetStock.com; **231:** Ryan McVay / Getty Images; **232:** (top) © PhotoAlto / Alix Minde; (bottom) Photoshot / Everett Collection (UFT_149389_0002); **233:** (top) iStockphoto. com / Daniel R. Burch; (bottom) © Esbin-Anderson / The Image Works; **235:** www.cartoonstock.com; **238:** (top) John Kelly / Getty Images; (bottom) CHRIS WATTIE / Reuters / Landov; **239:** (left) Martha Holmes / Time & Life Pictures / Getty; (right) Getty Images; **240:** Digital Vision / Getty Images; **242:** © The Star-Ledger / Ben Solomon / The Image Works; **243:** The McGraw-Hill Companies, Inc. / Jill Braaten, photographer; **245:** iStockphoto.com / Bitter

Chapter 11

Opener: Ronnie Kaufman / Lasrry Hirshowitz / Blend Images; **254:** Nathan Denette / The Canadian Press; **255:** (left to right) Ken Usami / Getty Images; iStockphoto.com / Justin Sneddon; **257:** Alvis Upitis / Getty Images; **258:** © St Petersburg Times / Melissa Lyttle / The Image Works; **259:** (top) Cordelia Molloy / Photo Researchers, Inc.; (bottom) Jonah Light / Getty Images; **261:** Pasieka / Photo Researchers, Inc.; **264:** (top, left to right) Ariel Skelly / Getty Images; Getty Images; (bottom) Bloomberg via Getty Images; **267:** Columbia Tri-Star / The Kobal Collection /

Marshak, Bob; **271:** TWPhoto / Corbis; **272:** © iStockphoto.com / Lisa F. Young

Chapter 12

Opener: Lisa Stirling / Getty Images; **279:** (top) Image Source / Getty Images; (bottom) Lund-Diephuis / Getty Images; **280:** (top) The McGraw-Hill Companies, Inc. / Chris Hammond, photographer; (bottom) Alfred Pasieka / Photo Researchers, Inc.; **281:** © Rubberball / Corbis; **282:** © Karen Kasmauski / Science Faction / Corbis; **283:** © Karen Kazmauski / Science Faction / Corbis; **284:** Mohammed Abed / AFP / Getty Images; **285:** HBO / The Kobal Collection; **286:** © Erin Paul Donovan / Alamy; **287:** © Erin Paul Donovan / Alamy; **289:** Tim Boyles / Getty Images; **292:** Photo by Gary Kramer, USDA Natural Resources Conservation Service

Text Credits
Chapter 1

Table 1.1: From *Human Development Across the Lifespan*, 7th edition, by John Dacey, John Travers, and Lisa Fiore. Copyright © 2009 The McGraw-Hill Companies, Inc. Reprinted with permission. **Take a Stand:** University of Montreal (2010, September 28). The price of popularity: Drug and alcohol consumption. ScienceDaily. **Fig. 1.1:** From *Human Development Across the Lifespan*, 7th edition by John Dacey, John Travers, and Lisa Fiore. Copyright © 2009 The McGraw-Hill Companies, Inc. Reprinted with permission; **Fig. 1.2:** From *Life Span Development*, 11th edition, by John W. Santrock. Copyright © 2008 The McGraw-Hill Companies; **Fig. 1.3:** From *SOC*, 1st edition by Jon Witt. Copyright © 2009 The McGraw-Hill Companies, Inc. Reprinted by permission; **Fig. 1.4:** From *Human Development Across the Lifespan*, 7th edition by John Dacey, John Travers, and Lisa Fiore. Copyright © 2009 The McGraw-Hill Companies, Inc. Reprinted with permission.

Chapter 2

Table 2.1: Adapted from *Childhood and Society* by Erik H. Erikson. Copyright © 1950, 1963 by W.W. Norton & Company, Inc. renewed © 1978, 1991 by Erik H. Erikson. Reprinted with permission. **Fig. 2.3:** From *The Child: Development in the Social Context* by Claire B. Kopp. Copyright © 1982. Printed and electronically reproduced by permission of Pearson Education, Inc. Upper Saddle River, New Jersey. **Fig. 2.4:** From "Changing organism—context relations as the basic process of development: A developmental perspective" by Richard M. Lerner in *Developmental Psychology*, Vol. 27, pp. 27–32. Copyright © 1991 American Psychological Association. **Table 2.4:** From *Human Development Across the Lifespan*, 7th edition, by John Dacey, John Travers, and Lisa Fiore. Copyright © 2009 The McGraw-Hill Companies, Inc. Reprinted with permission.

Chapter 3

Fig. 3.2: From *Human Development Across the Lifespan*, 7th edition, by John Dacey, John Travers, and Lisa Fiore. Copyright © 2009 The McGraw-Hill Companies, Inc. Reprinted with permission. **Fig 3.3:** From *Human Development Across the Lifespan*, 7th edition, by John Dacey, John Travers, and Lisa Fiore. Copyright © 2009 The McGraw-Hill Companies, Inc. Reprinted with permission.

Reports 23(1), pp. 1-5. Table 1, p. 2; **Fig. 8.8:** HRSDC calculations based on Statistics Canada. Live births, by age of mother, Canada, provinces and territories, annual (CANSIM Table 102-4503); Ottawa: Statistics Canada, 2012, and Statistics Canada. Estimates of Population by Age and Sex for Canada, Provinces and Territories, annual (CANSIM Table 051-0001); Ottawa: Statistics Canada, 2012; **Fig. 8.9:** HRSDC calculations based on Statistics Canada. For 1974 to 1990: Statistics Canada. Pregnancy outcomes, by age group, Canada, provinces and territories, annual (CANSIM Table 106-9002). Ottawa: Statistics Canada, 2007; and for 1991 to 2009: Statistics Canada. Live births, by age of mother, Canada, provinces and territories, annual (CANSIM Table 102-4503). Ottawa: Statistics Canada, 2012, and Statistics Canada. Estimates of Population by Age and Sex for Canada, Provinces and Territories, annual (CANSIM Table 051-0001). Ottawa: Statistics Canada, 2012; **Table 8.3:** Source: Hammond, D., et al., "Illicit Substance Use Among Canadian Youth: Trends Between 2002 and 2008", *Canadian Journal of Public Health* (2011) 102(1): 7-12. Table 2: Proportion of 'Ever' Drug Use Among Grades 7-9 Students. p. 8. © Canadian Public Health Association, 2011. All rights reserved.

Chapter 9

Fig. 9.1: www.med.ubc.ca, Gotay, Carolyn C., et al., "Updating the Canadian Obesity Maps: An Epidemic in Progress". *Canadian Journal of Public Health* (2013) 104(1). e64-e68. Figure 1. **Fig. 9.2:** Canadian Community Health Survey, 2010; Statistics Canada, 2012. CANSIM 105-0501 and Cat. No. 82-221-X. Published by authority of the Minister responsible for Statistics Canada. © Minister of Industry, 2013. All rights reserved. Use of this publication is governed by the Statistics Canada Open License Agreement. **Fig. 9.3:** Data from Durex Sexual Wellbeing Global Survey, 2008. www.durex.com/en-ca/sexualwellbeingsurvey. **Fig. 9.6:** For 1921 to 1987: Statistics Canada. Marriage and conjugal life in Canada. Ottawa: Statistics Canada, 1992. (Cat. No. 91-534E); for 1988 to 1999: Statistics Canada, Demography Division; for 2000 to 2004: Statistics Canada. Mean age and median age of males and females, by type of marriage and marital status, Canada, provinces and territories, annual (CANSIM Table 101-1002). Ottawa: Statistics Canada, 2008; and for 2005-2008: Statistics Canada. Canadian Vital Statistics, Marriage Database and Demography Division (population estimates), Ottawa: Statistics Canada, 2011.**Table 9.7:** Statistics Canada, Labour Force Survey. Published by authority of the Minister responsible for Statistics Canada. © Minister of Industry, 2013. All rights reserved. Use of this publication is governed by the Statistics Canada Open License Agreement.

Chapter 10

Table 10.1: Statistics Canada, 2006. Cat. No. 89-628-X. Published by authority of the Minister responsible for Statistics Canada. © Minister of Industry, 2013. All rights reserved. Use of this publication is governed by the Statistics Canada Open License Agreement; **Fig. 10.1:** Patterns of Alcohol Use by Sex in Middle-Aged and Elderly Adults in "The Epidemiology of At-Risk and Binge Drinking Among Middle-Aged and Elderly Community Adults: National Survey on Drug Use and Health" by Dan G. Blazer and Li-Tzy Wu, *American Journal of Psychiatry*, October 2009; 166: 1162–1169, Fig. 1, p. 2. Copyright © 2009 American Psychiatric Association. Reprinted with permission; **Fig. 10.2:** Statistics Canada, Canadian Health Measures Survey, 2007 to 2009. Published by authority of the Minister responsible for Statistics Canada. © Minister of Industry, 2013. All rights reserved. Use of this publication is governed by the Statistics

Canada Open License Agreement; **Fig. 10.3:** Data from Durex Sexual Wellbeing Global Survey, 2008. http://www.durex.com/en-CA/SexualWellbeingSurvey/pages/default.aspx; **Fig. 10.4:** From *Life Span Development*, 11th edition, by John W. Santrock. Copyright © 2008. The McGraw-Hill Companies, Inc. Reprinted with permission; **Fig. 10.5:** From *Life Span Development*, 11th edition, by John W. Santrock. Copyright © 2008. The McGraw-Hill Companies, Inc. Reprinted with permission. **Fig. 10.6:** Dennis, W. (1966). Creative Productivity between 20 and 80 Years, in *Journal of Gerontology*, 21, pp. 1–8. **Fig. 10.9:** Statistics Canada, 2002. Published by authority of the Minister responsible for Statistics Canada. © Minister of Industry, 2013. All rights reserved. Use of this publication is governed by the Statistics Canada Open License Agreement. **Fig. 10.10:** Statistics Canada, Health Statistics Division. Canadian Vital Statistics, Divorce Database and Marriage Database, Ottawa: Statistics Canada, 2011; **Fig. 10.11:** Statistics Canada, 2011. "Measuring violence against women: Statistical trends." Cat. No. 85-002-X, Chart 2.2 p. 56.

Chapter 11

Fig. 11.1: Statistics Canada. Censuses of Population, 1956 to 2006. Published by authority of the Minister responsible for Statistics Canada. © Minister of Industry, 2013. All rights reserved. Use of this publication is governed by the Statistics Canada Open License Agreement. **Fig. 11.2:** The Conference Board of Canada. Life Expectancy 2009. © Copyright 2013, The Conference Board of Canada. **Fig. 11.3:** Paola S. Timiras, Developmental Physiology and Aging 1972. Macmillan. Fig. 28.1.; **Fig. 11.4:** From *Human Development Across the Lifespan*, 7th edition, by John Dacey, John Travers, and Lisa Fiore. Copyright © 2009 The McGraw-Hill Companies, Inc. Reprinted with permission. **Fig. 11.5:** Reproduced with the permission of the publisher, from "Comprehensive mental health action plan 2013–2020: Suicide prevent, country reports." Geneva, World Health Organization, 2004, accessed 15 July 2013. **Table 11.1:** Dacey & Lennon, 1989. **Fig. 11.6:** Statistics Canada. Labour Force Historical Review, 2006.

Chapter 12

Fig. 12.1: Statistics Canada. Deaths and mortality rate, 2000–2009, by selected causes and sex, Canada, provinces and territories (CANSIM Table 102-0552). Ottawa: Statistics Canada, 2012. Published by authority of the Minister responsible for Statistics Canada. © Minister of Industry, 2013. All rights reserved. Use of this publication is governed by the Statistics Canada Open License Agreement. **Fig. 12.2:** For 1979 to 1990, Statistics Canada. Life expectancy, abridged life table, at birth and at age 65, by sex, Canada, provinces and territories (Comparable Indicators), annual (years) (CANSIM Table 102-0025). Ottawa: Statistics Canada, 2008; for 1991 to 1993, Statistics Canada. Life expectancy, abridged life table, at birth and at age 65, by sex, Canada, provinces and territories, annual (years) (CANSIM Table 102-0511). Ottawa: Statistics Canada, 2008; and for 1994 to 2009, Statistics Canada. Life expectancy, at birth and at age 65, by sex, Canada, **Table 12.1:** From *Life Span Development*, 11th edition, by John W. Santrock. Copyright © 2008. The McGraw-Hill Companies, Inc. Reprinted with permission. **Table 12.2:** Fact Sheet—Suicide Prevention. http://www.cihr-irsc.gc.ca/e/44716.html. Canadian Institutes of Health Research, 2012. Reproduced with the permission of the Minister of Public Works and Government Services Canada, 2013. **Fig. 12.4:** Statistics Canada, Canadian Vital Statistics Death Database; Statistics Canada, CANSIM, table 051-0001—Estimates of population, by age group and sex for July 1, Canada, provinces and territories.

Edwards, C.P., 100, 137
Edwards, P., 260
EEG (electroencephalogram), 103, 280
Efron, Zac, 208
Egg cells, 59, 63
Egg donation, 60
Ego, 29–30
Egocentric speech, 115
Egocentrism, 111, 132–133, 191
Ehrenkranz, R.A., 86
Eidelman, A., 86
Eisenberg, N., 142
Elaboration, 164
Elder, G., 45, 237
Eldercare, 268–269
Elderly. see also Aging; Later adulthood
  driving by, 260
Electroencephalogram (EEG), 103, 280
Electronic book readers, 264
Elementary processes, 36
Eliot, L., 104, 131
Elkind, D., 191, 192
ELL (English Language Learners), 168
Ellis, B.J., 187
Elton-Marshall, T., 200
Emanuel, L., 289
Embryonic period, 62–64
Emde, R., 119
Emergent readers, 168
Emerging adulthood, 201
Emotional development, and play, 147–148
Emotional divorce, 244
Emotions
  during adolescence, 190–191
  expressions, 119–120
  in infancy, 117–120
  during pregnancy, 67
  timetable of emotional development, 119t
Empathy, 216
Employment. see Careers; Work
Employment rates, 225f
Empty nest syndrome, 244
English as a Second Language (ESL), 168
English Language Learners (ELL), 168
Ensom, R., 141
Environment
  bioecological model, 42
  and biology, 66–68
  developmental systems theory, 44
  goodness of fit, 122
Environment factors in infant brain development, 105
Epidural blocks, 83
Epigenetic view, 12
Episiotomy, 79
Equilibration, 34
Erectile dysfunction (ED), 235, 267
Erikson, Erik, 22, 30, 31–33, 118, 140, 170, 192–193, 219–220, 241–242, 266
Eriksson, Peter, 263

Erin Brockovich (film), 240
Erling, A., 219
Escher, M.C., 162
ESL (English as a Second Language), 168
Ethics, 22, 57
Ethics of care, 166
Ethnicity
  and birth weight, 87
  and caring for the aging, 269
  and heart disease, 260
Ethology, 120
European Society for Human Reproduction and Embryology, 63
Euthanasia, 287
Evening (film), 262
Evolutionary developmental psychology, 45
Evolutionary psychology, 216
Ewing, L., 254
Exceptional children, 160
Executive functioning, 191
Exercise
  in early adulthood, 212
  in middle adulthood, 233f
  and pregnancy, 66–67
Exosystem, 42
Experiential (triarchic theory of intelligence), 162
Explicit memory, 31, 265
Expressions, 119–120
Expressive language, 139
Expulsion stage of labour, 79
External fetal monitors, 84
Extinction, 39

Fabes, R., 142
Facebook, 175, 268
Fact sheet on suicide, 290t
Failure to thrive (FTT), 107
Faisst, K., 289
Fallopian tubes, 59
False beliefs study, 136
Families. see also Parenting/parents
  and aging, 267–268
  defined, 222
  dual-career, 224–225
  in early adulthood, 222–223
  in later adulthood, 267–268
  in middle adulthood, 243, 246–247
  neonates, and family dynamics, 95
  and onset of puberty, 187
  paternal child care, 224–225
  role in adolescence, 194
  role in gender identity, 145
  role of, in social development, 140, 171–172
  single-parent families, 94–95
  work-family conflict, 248
Family violence, 247
Fantz, Robert, 109
Farran, C., 246
Farrell, M.P., 196
FAS (fetal alcohol syndrome), 68t, 72
Fast mapping, 114
Fatherhood, 78
Father Involvement Alberta, 225

Father Involvement Initiative–Ontario Network, 225
Father Involvement Research Alliance (FIRA), 225
Fearnaught device, 279
Feightner, J., 262
Feldman, M., 158
Feldman, R., 78, 86
Female genital cutting (FGC), 209
Females. see also Gender differences; Women
  and aging parents, 246
  alcohol consumption in older adults, 232f
  chromosome structure of, 52
  dating violence victimization by gender and age, 247f
  employment rates, 225f
  growth of, 128–129, 154f
  identity development, 219
  midlife sexuality, 234–235
  and puberty, 185, 187
  sexual system, 186f
  and stress, 249
  and suicide, 290
  suicide rates by gender, 262f
Feminine Mystique, The (Friedan), 215
Feminist movement, 215
Fencing reflex, 91
Ferber, Richard, 108
Ferris, F., 289
Ferris, P., 29
Fertility, 60–62
Fertilization process, 58–59
Fetal alcohol syndrome (FAS), 72
Fetal monitors, 84
Fetal period, 64–65
Field, T., 201
Films
  on adolescence, 31
  on adult sibling relationships, 247
  on Alzheimer's disease, 262
  on bullies and bullying, 173
  childbirth, 79
  on childhood, 144
  childhood, perspectives on, 9
  on death and personal connection to a higher power, 285
  on gender, 144
  on infancy, 122
  lives of creative people, 240
  love and adolescence, 188
  on love and marriage in middle adulthood, 246
  on pregnancy, 64
  psychoanalysis, 31
  on relationships, 222, 262
  on suicide, 290
  women's thinking portrayed in, 215
Finch, C., 263
Findling, R., 198
Fine motor skills
  early childhood, 130–131t
  middle childhood, 154
Finkel, R., 58
Fiore, L., 171, 176, 178
First Nations. see also Aboriginal peoples

Aboriginal Head Start on Reserve (AHSOR), 135
  high school graduates, 174
  initiation rites of, 209
  life expectancy for, 278
  sudden infant death syndrome (SIDS), 107–108
  and suicide, 199
  women and menopause, 236
First Nations and Inuit Health, 72
First words, 116
Fischer, R.S., 215
Fish, A.D., 270
Fisher, C., 44
Fisher, L., 11
Fisher Wallace Cranial Stimulator, 94
Fitzpatrick, K.M., 201, 212
Five factor model (FFM) of personality, 243
Fixated stage, 29
Flavell, J., 136
Floyd, S.S., 259
Fluid intelligence, 236
Fontaine, R., 172
Food Inc. (film), 212
Forceps, 84–85
Formal operational stage, 34, 190
Forman, G.E., 100, 137
Formula feeding, 102–103
Foster, C.A., 244
Fox, N., 119
Fracasso, M., 143
Fragile X syndrome, 56
Fraiberg, Selma, 128
Franco, O.H., 231
Frankenberger, K., 191
Frankl, Viktor, 291
Fraternal twins, 59
French immersion programs, 169t
Freud, Sigmund, 7, 9, 17, 29–31, 43, 242
Friedan, Betty, 215
Friedman, R., 143, 177
Friendship. see also Peers
  in early adulthood, 220
  in middle adulthood, 243
  role of, in social development, 171–172
Fromm, Erich, 221
From Neurons to Neighborhoods: The Science of Early Childhood Development (Shonkoff and Phillips), 47
Frozen embryos, 63
Frozen shoulders, 236
Funerals, 284–285, 287
Fung, H., 243
Furstenberg, F.F., Jr., 194
FXB International, 282

G7 countries
  infant mortality rates, 101f
  low-birth-weight babies, 87
Gage, Fred H., 263
Galambos, N., 10
Galanos, A., 262
Galbraith, K.A., 197
Gamete intrafallopian transfer (GIFT), 60

Osteoporosis, 260
O'Sullivan, Lucia, 9, 10
Othello (Shakespeare), 265
Overextensions, 139
Overregularization, 139
Overweight. *see also* Weight
  adolescent girls, 188
  children, 156–157
Ovulation, 58, 59f
Ovulation to implantation, 59f
Oxygen deprivation, 85–86
Oxytocin, 78, 85

Paci, E., 289
Packard, Edward, 4
Pack dating, 218
Palfalvi, L., 22
Palliative, 289
Pang, J.W.Y., 82
Parallel play, 147
Parental leave, 95
Parenthood (film), 122
Parenting/parents. *see also* Families
  aging, 246
  bonding with newborn, 94
  changing role, 222
  eldercare, 268–269
  and gangs, 201
  grandparents, changing role of, 269–270
  listening to adolescents, 196
  parenting styles, 140–142
  reciprocal interactions, 118
  relationships with aging parents, 246
  role in gender identity, 145
  single-parent families, 94–95
Parents, Families, and Friends of Lesbians and Gays (PFLAG), 244
Paris, A., 167
Paris, S., 167
Park, J., 260
Parker, J., 118, 172
Parker-Pope, T., 255
Parliamentary Standing Committee on Health, 54
Parnell, Peter, 140
Parsons, Rehtaeh, 201
Parten, Mildred, 146
Paschall, M.J., 141
Passive euthanasia, 287
Patents, gene, 54
Paternal child care, 224–225
Patterns of work, 223–225, 247–248, 271–272
Patterson, Christopher, 262
Pavelski, R., 188, 189
Pavlov, Ivan, 38
Payne, L., 236
Peake, P., 171
Pearson, Lester B., 165
Peel District School Board, 169
Peers. *see also* Friendship
  role in adolescence, 194–195
  role in gender identity, 145
Peeters, A., 231
Pellegrini, A.D., 216
Perception, 108–111, 109

Perfilieva, E., 263
Performance (work), 272
Permissive parenting, 141–142t
Persaud, T., 58, 59, 65
Personal fable, 191
Personality, 243, 243f
PET (positron emission tomography), 104
Petersen, A., 9
Peterson, D.A., 263
Peterson, J., 134
Petrini, J.R., 59
Petriu, Emil, 105
Pettit, G., 172
Pettit, G.S., 187
Pfeffer, C., 199
PFLAG (Parents, Families, and Friends of Lesbians and Gays), 244
Phallic stage, 30f
Phenotype, 53
Phenylketonuria (PKU), 58
Phillips, Deborah, 47
Phonology, 116, 139
Physical activity by age group, average daily, 233f
Physical assault, 176–177
Physical development
  during adolescence, 185–190
  in early adulthood, 210–214
  in early childhood, 128–131
  in infancy, 101–107
  in later adulthood, 258–263
  in middle adulthood, 230–235
  in middle childhood, 154–158
Physical fitness
  early adulthood, 212
  in middle adulthood, 233f
  and pregnancy, 66–67
Physician-assisted suicide (PAS), 287–288
Physiological needs (Maslow's hierarchy of needs), 45–46
Physiological theories of aging, 256–258
Piaget, Jean, 33–35, 43, 100, 111–113, 112, 133, 242
  and early adulthood, 214
  evaluation of, 113, 133
  on moral development, 165
Piaget's conservation task, 133, 159
Piaget's mountains task, 132–133f
Piaget's stages of cognitive development
  concrete operational stage, 158–161
  described, 34–35
  formal operational stage, 34, 190
  preoperational period, 131–133
  sensorimotor, 111–113
Pick, A., 109, 111
Pienta, A.M., 268
Pierre-Hansen, St., N., 236
Pinderhughes, E., 62
Pinker, S., 45, 116, 139
Pious, S., 17
Piskosz, M., 263
Pitkin, S., 263
PKU (phenylketonuria), 58

Place-based strategy, 17
Placenta, 62
Placenta abruptio, 86
Placenta previa, 86
Plantar reflex, 90
Play
  defined, 146
  developmental aspects of, 147–148
  and early childhood, 146–148
  kinds of, 146–147
  materials for, 148
  perceived importance of, 147f
  symbolic play, 132
Podcasts
  for grieving, 285
  for nursing mothers, 103
Poe, Edgar Allen, 279
Pollack (film), 240
Pollock, Jackson, 239
Ponirakis, A., 188
Positive psychology, 249
Positive reinforcement, 39, 141
Positron emission tomography (PET), 104
Postformal thought, 214
Postpartum depression symptomatology (PPDS), 93–94f
Postpartum period, 92
Poverty, 174
Powell, T., 18
Powlishta, K., 191
PPDS (postpartum depression symptomatology), 93–94f
Practical intelligence, 238
Pradinuk, M., 156
Pragmatics, 116, 139
Preemies, 86
Prefrontal cortex, 129–130f, 191
Pregnancy
  blogs, 67
  chemical substances, 68t
  and culture, 67–68
  emotions and sense of self, 67
  fertilization process, 58–59
  films about, 64
  infectious diseases, 68–71
  nutrition and exercise, 66–67
  prenatal development, 62–65
  prenatal testing, 65–66
  prescription and non-prescription drugs, 71–72
  teenage, 196–198
  teratogens, 68, 68t
  websites on, 67
Preintellectual speech, 115
Premature babies, and resilience, 88
Premature births, 86–87
Premature Burial, The (Poe), 279
Prenatal development, 62–65, 63t, 66–67, 69f
Prenatal period, characteristics of, 8t
Prenatal testing, 65–66
Preoperational stage, 34, 131–133
Presbycusis, 231
Presbyopia, 231
Preschool education, 100–101
Prescription drugs, 71–72
Presenell, K., 187

Preston, M., 268
Preyer, William, 9
Price, J., 172
Primary circular reactions, 112
Proactive stress reduction, 248t
Problem-solving
  during adolescence, 191–192
  in middle childhood, 164
Proportions, changes in human body, 102f
Prospective memory, 265
Prostate cancer, 232, 261
Protective factors, of stress, 249
Protest, 121
Proudfoot, S., 95
Proulx, J.F., 69
Proximal processes, 42
Psychoanalysis, 9, 29–31
Psychoanalytic theories, 29
  contributions and criticism, 33, 43
  Freud's theory, 29–31
Psychological dimension of spirituality theory, 291
Psychological issues, in early childhood, 131
Psychological processes, 36
Psychosexual stages, 29, 30f
Psychosocial theory
  compared with other theories, 46t
  defined, 31
  Erikson's eight stages, 32–33, 43, 192–193, 266
  generativity *vs.* stagnation, 241–242
  integrity *vs.* despair, 33, 266
Psychosomatic, 283
Puberty
  defined, 185
  provincial differences in onset of, 189
  and secular trend, 187–188
  typical age ranges for signs of, 187f
Public Health Agency of Canada, 59, 69, 70, 108, 138, 176, 188, 198, 212, 214, 217, 247
Public Safety Canada, 201
Pukuri, T., 268
Pulkkinen, L., 268
Punishment, 39, 141
Pytluk, S., 13

Quas, J.A., 198
Quebec Longitudinal Study of Child Development (QLSCD), 107
Question, "why," 4, 16, 28
Quinton, R.L., 78
Qury, J.F., 58

Race, and caring for the aging, 269
Rahhal, T.A., 263
Raksin, J., 268
Rape, 218
Rapid eye-movement (REM) sleep, 108
Razor, A.G., 187
Reaction time, 258–259
Read, N., 169
Readers, types of, 168
Reading acquisition, 167–168

Rebiff, M., 58
Receptive language, 139
Reciprocal interactions, 42, 118
Reece, J., 59
Reflexes, 90–91, 111–112
Reflexes, of neonates, 90–91
Reggio Emilia, 100–101, 137
Rehearsal, 135
Rehirement, 272
Reinforcement, 39
Reisberg, L., 184
Relationships
   with aging parents, 246
   films about, 222
   of infants, 118
   in later adulthood, 270–271
   same-sex, 223
   with siblings, 246–247
REM (rapid eye-movement) sleep, 108
Rennie, S., 210
Representation, 132
Repression, 29
Research
   cross-sectional studies, 20
   data collection techniques, 16–18
   descriptive studies, 16–18
   longitudinal studies, 19–20
   manipulative experiments, 18
   naturalistic experiments, 18
   one-time, one-group studies, 19
   references, 21–22
   research article, 20–21
   scientific method, 16, 17f
   sequential (longitudinal/cross-sectional) studies, 20, 21f
   time-variable designs, 18–20
Resiliency
   in adolescents, 202
   in children, 177–178
   in middle adulthood, 248–249
Respiratory distress syndrome (RDS), 108
Results section, 20
Reticular activation system (RAS), 190
Retirement, 272
Retrieval, 135
Retrospective memory, 265
Reversibility, 133
Revolutionary Road (film), 222
Rh factor, 86
Richards, M., 198
Richardson, Justin, 140
Right-handedness, 130
Ripple, Richard, 20
Risk factors
   of stress, 248
   of suicide, 263
   teratogens, 68t
   violent acts, 201–202
Risk-taking behaviours, adolescent, 196
Ritalin, 158–159
Rites of passage, 208–210
Ritual circumcision (initiation rite), 209
Rivers, Joan, 257
Robots, 105

Roche, A.F., 189
Rochette, L., 69
Rodriguez, Sue, 288
Roe, J.G., 270
Roeser, R., 173
Rogers, W.A., 270
Rogoff, Barbara, 36, 81, 190
Role discontinuity, 267
Roman Empire, and funerals, 287
Romeo and Juliet (film), 188
Rooting reflex, 90
Rose, S., 90
Rosen, B., 248
Rosen, Sally, 270
Rosenbloom, A., 156
Ross, D., 20, 40, 199
Ross, S., 20, 40
Rosser, S.V., 224
Rotermann, M., 217
Rousseau, Jean-Jacques, 9
Rubella, 68t, 70
Rubin, K., 118, 172
Rubin, K.H., 119
Rubin, Ruth, 67
Ruble, D., 145, 146
RunKeeper Free, 234
Rushowy, K., 176
Russell, R.B., 59, 195
Rutter, M., 6, 7, 12, 15, 43, 131, 178

Sabo, D.F., 196
Sadovnick, A., 262
Safety needs (Maslow's hierarchy of needs), 45–46
Safety with online communication, 175
Salter, D., 198
Salthouse, T.A., 263
Same-sex relationships, 223, 245
   see also Lesbian, gay, bisexual, and transgender (LGBT)
Sandwich generation, 246
Sang-Chin, Choi, 249
Savage, L., 263
Savage, M.P., 196
Savages, The (film), 247
Scaffolding, 134
Scent of a Woman (film), 290
Schaal, B., 89
Schaie, K.W., 11, 236, 237
Schellenberg, G., 255, 270, 272
Schemes, 34, 35
Schiavo, Terri, 289
Schmader, T., 224
Schmeelk-Cone, K., 190
Schools. see also Education
   role in gender identity, 145
   role in social development, 172–174
Schubert, C.M., 189
Schwartz, I., 196
Schwarz, R.H., 59
Sciencedaily.com, 232
Scientific method, 16, 17f
Scientific research, foundation of, 4
SCOPE (Sustainable Childhood Obesity Prevention through Community Engagement), 176
Sears, Malcolm, 4

Seattle Longitudinal Study of Adult Intelligence, 11, 236
Secondary circular reactions, 112
Secular trend, 187–188
Securely attached children, 121
Seem, D.L., 280
Seinfeld, Jerry, 280
Self, development of
   early childhood, 139–140
   and ecological model of schooling, 173f
   middle childhood, 169–171
Self-actualization needs (Maslow's hierarchy of needs), 45–46
Self-concept, 170
Self-efficacy, 40
Self-esteem, 170–171
Self-esteem needs (Maslow's hierarchy of needs), 45–46, 221
Self-regulation, 171
Self-report studies, 16
Seligman, M.E.P., 249
Semantics, 116, 139
Seniors. see Later adulthood
Sense of self during pregnancy, 67
Senses
   in later adulthood, 259
   in middle adulthood, 231–232
   of neonates, 89–90
Sensitive periods, 137
Sensitive periods in prenatal development, 69f
Sensitive responsiveness, 123
Sensorimotor period, 111
Sensorimotor stage (Piaget), 34, 111–113
Sequential (longitudinal/cross-sectional) studies, 20, 21f
Seriation, 159
Series of new births, 137
Serling, Rod, 266
Service Canada, 145, 269
Sex, 144
Sex chromosomes, 52
Sex cleavage, 145
Sex Information and Education Council of Canada, 195
Sexting, 196
Sexual abuse, 198
Sexual activity by country, 235f
Sexual assault, 218
Sexual behaviour
   during adolescence, 195–196
   in early adulthood, 217
   number of sex partners, 217f
Sexual harassment, 218
Sexual identity, 195–198, 215
Sexual intercourse, and adolescents, 195–196
Sexuality
   early adulthood, 216–218
   in later adulthood, 267
   in middle adulthood, 234–235
Sexually transmitted infections (STIs), 60, 217–218
Sexual offences, 176–177
Sexual predators online, 175
Sexual system of females, and males, 186f

Shaffer, D., 199
Shaken baby syndrome, 104
Shakespeare, William, 265
Shanahan, M., 45
Shankaran, S., 86
Shared sleeping, 108
Sharit, J., 270
Sharples, T., 177
Shaw, George Bernard, 222
Sheldon, K., 241
Shenk, J.W., 243
Shoham, Z., 60
Shonkoff, Jack, 47
Siblings
   films about, 247
   and middle adulthood, 246–247
   role of, in early childhood, 142
Sibling underworld, 142
Sickle-cell disease, 56–57
SIDS (sudden infant death syndrome), 107–108
Siegel, Daniel, 118
Siegel, Linda, 113
Siegel, L.S., 157
Siegler, Robert, 38, 111, 166
Silverman, K., 60
Silverstein, J., 156
Simner, M., 174
Simons, D.J., 114
Simple reflexes, 111–112
Simpsons, The, 172, 249
Single-parent families, 94–95
Singleton, J., 246
Sirota, L., 86
Sisterhood of the Travelling Pants, The (film), 215
Six Feet Under (TV show), 247, 285
Six Pack App, 234
Skinner, B.F., 39, 100
Skinner Box, 39f
Skip generation, 270
Skuse, D., 198
Sleeping disorders in infancy, 108
Sleep patterns across the lifespan, 109f
Slow to warm up temperament, 123
Slumdog Millionaire (film), 177
Small for date babies, 86–87
Smeeding, T.M., 194
Smell, of neonates, 89
Smiling, in infancy, 119–120
Smith, D.W.E., 258
Smith, K., 83
Smith, R., 178
Smith, W.J., 288
Smoking, 68t, 72, 107–108, 213
Smylie, Janet, 101
Social constructivism, 134
Social death, 280
Social development
   during adolescence, 194–195
   in early adulthood, 218–221
   in early childhood, 140–144
   in infancy, 117–120
   in later adulthood, 266–271
   in middle adulthood, 240–243
   in middle childhood, 171–176
   and play, 147
Social (cognitive) learning theory, 40–41

Ullrich, M., 218
Ultrasound, 65
Umbilical cord, 62
Unconscious memory, 31
UNICEF (United Nations Children's Fund), 144, 147
Uninvolved/neglectful parenting, 142
United Nations Children's Fund (UNICEF), 144
University of Montreal, 10
University of New Brunswick, 10
Unoccupied play, 146
Unresolved grief, 283–284
Updegraff, J.A., 249

Vacuum extractor, 84–85
Vaillant, George, 11, 242, 243, 244, 254
Validation, 221
Van der Heide, A., 289
Variables, 18
Vartanian, L., 191
Ventura, S.J., 94
Viagra, 235, 267
Videatives, 132
Video games
  and aggression, 41
  and gender stereotyping, 146
  Wii Fit, 234
Violence
  dating violence victimization by gender and age, 247f
  family, 247
  and gangs, 200–201
  and spanking, 141
  video games and aggression, 41
  and youth, 201–202
Vision
  in later adulthood, 259
  in middle adulthood, 231–232
  of neonates, 89
Visual cliff experiment, 110–111
Visual cognition experiment, 114
Visual literacy, 168
Visual perception, 109–110
Vitamin supplements, 16
Vocabulary, in middle childhood,

166–167
Volling, B., 120
Von Gunten, C., 289
Vygotsky, Lev, 33, 35–36, 115, 133–134, 147, 190

Wagster, Molly, 263
Wahlsten, Douglas, 43, 44
Walk, R., 110
Walkabout (initiation rite), 209
Walker-Barnes, C.J., 201
Walking, infants, 107
WALL-E (film), 116
Wallerstein, Judith, 143
Walsh, C.J., 78
Wan, N., 269
Ward, B.J., 69
Ward-Griffin, C., 269
Warning signs for adolescent suicide, 199
War of the Roses (film), 246
Water births, 81
Water breaking, 79
Watson, John, 38–39
Watt, A., 267
Webb, J.R., 216
Webhealing.com, 285
Websites
  on aging, 12
  birth, 67
  chromosomes, 55
  on grief, 285
  Life Literacy Canada, 168
  for new mothers, 103
  on pregnancy, 67
  and social networking, 268
Wedekind, Frank, 184
Weidner, W., 235
Weight. see also Overweight
  early adulthood, 210t
  of infant, 117t
  of newborn, 101
Wein, C.A., 137
Weinberg, R., 44
Weissman, A., 60
Weller, A., 78, 86
Werner, E., 178

Wernicke's area, 117f
Westerhof, G., 254
Westin, D., 30
What to Expect When You're Expecting (film), 64
When Harry Met Sally (film), 220
Whitbeck, L., 198
Whitehurst, G., 167, 168
White Ribbon Campaign, 218
Whitlock, Ed, 254
"Why" question, 4, 16, 28
Widowhood, 268
Wiebe, R., 199
Wii (Nintendo), 234, 269
Wikis, 175
Wild Strawberries (film), 266
Willat, J., 148
Williams, C., 246
Willis, C.A., 283
Willis, Sherry, 236, 237
Wilson, Edward O., 292–293
Wilson, R.D., 68
Wilson's theory of spirituality, 292–293
Wisdom, 265
Women. see also Females
  Aboriginal cultural values for the elderly, 269
  climacteric, 234–235
  eldercare, 268–269
  and feminist movement, 215
  and infertility, 60
  in the labour force, 224–225
  life expectancy of, 254–256
  mammograms, 231
  and menopause, 234, 236
  postpartum depression symptomatology (PPDS), 93–94f
  sexual assault and harassment of, 218
  women's thinking portrayed in films, 215
Women, The (film), 215
Wong, T.Y., 259
Woodward, A., 116, 198
Woolf, Virginia, 17
Word order, 117

Word spurt, 116
WordTwist, 192
Work
  dual-career families, 224–225
  labour force participation rates among seniors, 272f
  patterns of, 223–225, 247–248, 271–272
  and work-family conflict, 248
Work identity, 223
Working Together for Full Citizenship, 160
World AIDS Orphans Day, 282
World Health Organization, 103, 231
Wortman, C., 268
Wright, D.R., 201
Wright, Frank Lloyd, 224
Wright, P.J., 235
Wright, Stephen, 100
Wright, V., 200
Wu, L., 232
Wyckoff, A., 177
Wynne-Edwards, K., 78

X chromosome, 52, 56
XYY syndrome, 56

Yamaguchi, S., 249
Yang, W.S., 199
Yau, K.I.T., 87
Yoder, K., 198
Yoshino, S., 269
You Can Count on Me (film), 247
Yuki, M., 249
Yupe, S., 60
Yurgelun, Todd D., 191

Zagoory-Sharon, O., 78
Zidovudine (ZDV), 70
Zielinski, R., 53
Zimmerman, M., 190
Zone of proximal development (ZPD), 36, 134
Zuroff, D., 242
Zuzanek, J., 21
Zygote, 52